The Anatomy of a
High-Performance Microprocessor
A Systems Perspective

Bruce Shriver
Bennett Smith

IEEE
COMPUTER
SOCIETY

IEEE Computer Society Press
Los Alamitos, California

Washington • Brussels • Tokyo

Library of Congress Cataloging-in-Publication Data

Shriver, Bruce D., 1940–
    The anatomy of a high-performance microprocessor: a systems perspective /
Bruce Shriver, Bennett Smith
        p.   cm.
    Includes index.
    ISBN 0-8186-8400-3
    1. Microprocessors. 2. High performance computing.
 3. Computer architecture.I. Smith, Bennett. II. Title.
QA76.5.S499 1998
004.16—dc21

                                                        98-17345
                                                            CIP

IEEE Computer Society Press Order Number BP08400
Library of Congress Number 98-17345
ISBN 0-8186-8400-3

Additional copies may be ordered from:

IEEE Computer Society Press
Customer Service Center
10662 Los Vaqueros Circle
P.O. Box 3014
Los Alamitos, CA 90720-1314
Tel: +1-714-821-8380
Fax: +1-714-821-4641
Email: cs.books@computer.org

IEEE Service Center
445 Hoes Lane
P.O. Box 1331
Piscataway, NJ 08855-1331
Tel: +1-732-981-1393
Fax: +1-732-981-9667
mis.custserv@computer.org

IEEE Computer Society
13, Avenue de l'Aquilon
B-1200 Brussels
BELGIUM
Tel: +32-2-770-2198
Fax: +32-2-770-8505
euro.ofc@computer.org

IEEE Computer Society
Ooshima Building
2-19-1 Minami-Aoyama
Minato-ku, Tokyo 107
JAPAN
Tel: +81-3-3408-3118
Fax: +81-3-3408-3553
tokyo.ofc@computer.org

Publisher: Matt Loeb
Project Editor: Cheryl Baltes
Advertising/Promotions: Tom Fink
Production Editor: Lisa O'Conner
Printed in the United States of America

To my wife, Beverly, without whose patience, understanding, and encouragement this book would never have been written. Bruce Shriver

To my father, Walstein Smith, Jr., and my wife's father, Wallace Williams, both of whom were an inspiration for doing the best with what one has. Bennett Smith

Preface

This book presents a detailed description of the microarchitecture of a high-performance microprocessor and discusses the platform and systems issues related to designing and implementing microprocessor-based systems. We believe it is unique in its content and its approach. This is easily seen when contrasting it with other computer architecture books. We chose our particular content and approach for three important reasons:

1. *to appeal to three diverse audiences*—practitioners in the field, ranging from microarchitects to platform designers and implementers; university faculty and students in Computer Science, Computer Engineering, and Electrical Engineering Departments, as well as those in other technical and science disciplines; and technical and project management.

2. *to give an integrated treatment of microarchitecture, platform, and systems issues.* There are substantial sections of the book dealing with topics that surround the design, implementation, and use of a commercially deployed microprocessor. These issues are often ignored or only treated lightly in contemporary computer architecture books. For example, motherboard, chipset and BIOS[i] issues, design and implementation implications for desktop, entertainment, and mobile platforms, and a number of the VLSI and fabrication process challenges—all of which are fundamentally important today—are discussed in this book.

3. *to provide a valuable reference book.* There is a wealth of material on the CD-ROM that accompanies this book. It ranges from the complete text of tutorial and survey articles from professional society periodicals and conference proceedings to important industry standards and specifications. This and the other material on the CD-ROM, which will be described later, will prove a

---

[i] The BIOS, Basic Input/Output System, is low-level software for providing fundamental I/O service routines callable by other system software and low-level applications. After a system has been successfully powered up, the BIOS is always resident in memory.

valuable addition to your personal library. In the university context, the material on the CD-ROM can provide fertile ground for both assignments and projects. If the book is used by the practitioner or technical manager, this material can be used as a basis for self-study.

One of the themes discussed in several chapters is to examine how the ultimate uses of a microprocessor impact its design and implementation. In doing so, fundamental guidelines emerge that transcend the design, implementation, and use of a specific microprocessor. Thus, this book is worthy of study by those involved in computer architecture and computer systems-related research, development, implementation, or use.

STUDYING REAL MACHINES

Much can be learned from studying the design and implementation of real machines. Consider the following quote from Harold Stone's book[ii]:

"One of the disappointing aspects of the existing literature in high-performance systems is that relatively few machines have been thoroughly documented in the published literature. Thornton's [1970] analysis of the CDC-6600 is a notable exception, and there are a few others, such as Organick [1972] on the Multics system and Organick [1973] on the Burroughs' B5700 and B6700 machines.

High-speed implementations have grown far more complex since these books appeared, and there are many opportunities to increase that complexity to achieve greater performance by steadily increasing the average number of instructions completed per clock cycle. The literature of the 1970s and 1980s does not adequately reflect the actual state of the art in machine design, because in this field many advances are realized in physical machines and in the hands of users before the research and academic community have the opportunity to study them."

Our book, in part, helps fill this gap. We use AMD's K6 3D microprocessor as the "case study" basis for discussing microarchitectural, platform, and systems issues. Each of our three target audiences can benefit from this approach:

1. *practitioners* can benefit from this book because of its detailed description of how a contemporary high-performance microprocessor works and of how to incorporate one into a number of different platforms.

2. *university faculty and students* can benefit from its treatment of

---

[ii]   Harold S. Stone, *High-Performance Computer Architecture*, 3rd Edition, Addison-Wesley Publishing Company, 1993.

important technology issues (e.g., VLSI design and fabrication process-related issues) and the in-depth discussion of the system and platform issues involved in using microprocessors (e.g., bus structures, core logic chipset, and BIOS-related issues). Such technology, system, and platform issues are often lacking in contemporary texts on computer architecture.

3. *technical and product managers* can benefit from this book by understanding the evolving nature of microprocessors in general and what skill base is required to integrate them in various system platforms (e.g., 3D graphics platforms).

The book is divided into six main chapters:

1. an overview of issues that arise in the design and implementation of microprocessors and microprocessor-based systems.

2. a microarchitecture case study.

3. the K6 3D microarchitecture.

4. technology components of platform architectures.

5. platform memory technology.

6. platform optimization techniques and directions.

In general, each chapter starts with an overview meant for all three audiences. The discussion then proceeds into detail meant for both the practitioner and the university audiences. Various sections of the each chapter that we believe might be of specific interest to each of the audiences are identified in the chapter *road maps* which are introduced at the beginning of each chapter. The road maps help the reader pick out sections to read in-depth as well as sections to bypass. The six chapters fall roughly into two sections. The first section deals with microarchitecture and the second section deals with platform and systems issues. We will now examine each of these sections.

INTRODUCTORY NOTIONS: THE TOOLS OF THE TRADE

The basic underlying engineering approach to designing, implementing, testing, and fabricating processors—and integrating them into various platforms and systems—has not changed substantially since the computer industry began to take form in the mid-1960s. Computer architects, computer engineers, and platform designers employ now, as they did then, a variety of tools:

1. iterative design techniques based on performance and cost analyses and trade-offs. The trade-offs occur along a number of dimensions ranging from the complexity, engineering resource requirements, and impact on the software a particular solution

has, to the amount of area, power, and pins it requires.

2. simulators, emulators, prototyping systems, and models and related analysis tools used, first, to verify behavioral and functional specifications, compatibility requirements, and adherence to standards, and, second, to explore and analyze alternative solutions, such as impact of the static or dynamic binding of a specific aspect of the processor. Trace-driven detailed performance models have become an increasingly important component of tools in this category.

3. measurement tools to collect data gathered from the simulators, emulators, prototype systems or models to determine what systems actually do when executing either real or synthetic programs, (e.g., data from address and instruction traces that yields information about the frequency of occurrence of branches and other types of instructions, address modes, exception conditions, and interrupts).

4. formal analysis methods that attempt to predict one or more aspects of a specific system component or of overall system behavior such as performance, critical speed paths, latency, hit-rates and line-sizes, bandwidth requirements, or availability.

The disciplines of computer architecture and platform design both involve balancing a large collection of highly dependent trade-offs.

Indeed, the discipline of computer architecture is one of balancing a large collection of often highly dependent trade-offs. The same statement is equally true of platform design and implementation. What has changed in the intervening years are the tools, the design solutions, and the underlying semiconductor manufacturing process. The dramatic densities achieved by advances in the semiconductor manufacturing process continue seemingly unabated, as do their impact. Additionally, the range and quality of tools that computer architects, computer engineers, and platform designers have at their disposal for undertaking the above tasks have also improved substantially.

One can credibly argue that without the improvements in the tools, the industry could not have taken advantage of the advances in semiconductor technology. Moreover, the range of solutions to resolve architectural performance problems and provide increased functionality has also increased significantly—both in the form of enhancements or modifications of older solutions as well as the development of entirely new approaches. This observation is true not only because of the options created by advances in technology but also because of the options that emerge based on what we learn by studying existing processors and platforms. As with most disciplines, we advance by learning from and building upon past results.

TECHNOLOGY AND APPLICATIONS

The reason processor and system platform architectures continue to rapidly evolve stems from the dual impact of technology and applications:

technology pull, application push

1. *technology pull*—the relentlessly increasing density of circuits that can be included on a chip and the concurrent reductions in the costs of the chips forces us to continually rethink how they can be exploited to achieve significant increases in functionality and performance at substantially reduced price points; other important aspects of this pull that are important are the ways in which the circuits can be grouped, how the chips are packaged, and their power and cooling requirements.

2. *application push*—the rapid growth of the diverse ways in which computer systems are used; for example,

    a. accessing and manipulating streams of rich, multimedia data such as full-motion video and high-resolution, highly textured graphics.

    b. relying on integrated, high-speed communications to local networks, the Internet, and multiple, geographically dispersed intranets.

    c. exploiting the evolution of highly interactive human-machine interfaces such as virtual reality and real-time, speaker-independent speech input.

    d. providing the central functions for a wide variety of consumer electronics devices (e.g., cameras, VCRs, high-fidelity and home entertainment systems, set-top boxes, security systems, cellular phones, pagers, and other wireless devices, and home appliances, as well as in automobiles, boats, trains, airplanes, geo-positioning systems, and production lines in factories) has placed different requirements on the underlying processor architecture, core logic chipset, bus and memory architectures, motherboard functionality, and overall platform.

It is worth noting in passing that there have also been rather dramatic shifts in the way processors and platforms are marketed and distributed. These shifts have had a profound impact on the products and services supplied and on the growth of the computer industry. However, they are not the topic of this book.

ARCHITECTURE, MICROARCHITECTURE, AND PLATFORM AND SYSTEM LITERATURE

There are many fine textbooks, periodicals, and conference proceedings that deal with various aspects of designing, implementing, and testing high-performance processors and microprocessors. However, this base of literature typically does not deal with the platform and systems related issues such as core logic chipset and BIOS design, bus and memory architectures, motherboard functionality, and overall platform packaging that are associated with integrating processors into various types of systems.

SUGGESTED READINGS

Technology Pull and Application Push

A reading of the articles in the September 1997 issue of *Computer* magazine (Vol. 30, No.9) will readily verify that the field is ripe with discussion on various approaches to address both the *technology pull* and the *application push*. A partial listing of these articles is:

1. D. Matzke, *Will Physical Scalability Sabotage Performance Gains?*, pp. 37-39.
2. J. A. Fisher, *Walk-Time Techniques: Catalyst for Architectural Change*, pp. 40-42.
3. K. Diefendorff and P.K. Dubey, *How Multimedia Workloads Will Change Processor Design*, pp. 43-45.
4. Y. N. Patt, S.J. Patel, M. Evers, D.H. Friendly and J. Stark, *One Billion Transistors, One Uniprocessor, One Chip*, pp.51-57
5. M.H. Lipasti and J.P. Shen, *Superspeculative Microarchitecture for Beyond* AD 2000, pp. 59-66.
6. J. E. Smith, and S. Vajapeyam, *Trace Processors: Moving to Fourth-Generation Microarchitectures*, pp. 68-74.
7. L. Hammond, B.A. Nayfeh and K. Olukotun, *A Single-Chip Multiprocessor*, pp. 79-85.

 You can find the full text versions of articles 3, 4 and 5 on the companion CD-ROM.

Moreover, this same literature base does not treat fabrication related issues and how they impact what can and what cannot be included in the architecture, microarchitecture, platform, or system. For example, when producing a microprocessor, the microarchitectural design team and implementation team might have to work closely with those doing the floorplanning of the chip in order to know the ultimate size of specific resources on the chip, (e.g., the on-chip caches or associated TLBs). Such restrictions will have a great deal to do with the ability to reach a specific price/performance point and might steer the design group to choose other processor features (a larger prefetch buffer, for example) in an attempt to compensate for the restrictions. Few existing books deal with the numerous steps involved in taking a high-level design and translating it into silicon.

Architecture and Microarchitecture

Computer architecture and microprocessor books typically deal with processors at various levels of abstraction—the instruction set architecture level, the microarchitecture level, the logical design level, and the actual microprocessor chip itself. These levels are differentiated from one another in this book as follows:

DEFINITION
Architecture
Architecture refers to the instruction set, resources, and features of a processor that are visible to software programs running on the processor. The architecture determines what software the processor can directly execute and essentially forms a specification for the microarchitecture.

The term *architecture* as defined here is often called the instruction set architecture.

instruction set architecture

DEFINITION
Microarchitecture
Microarchitecture refers to the set of resources and methods used to realize the architecture specification. The term typically includes the way in which these resources are organized as well as the design techniques used in the processor to reach the target cost and performance goals. The microarchitecture essentially forms a specification for the logical implementation.

Sometimes in the computer architecture literature the *architecture* is called the "virtual machine" and the *microarchitecture* is called "host machine." This definition of microarchitecture leads us to a definition for the *logical design or logical implementation* level.

virtual machine
host machine

DEFINITION
Logical Design or Logical Implementation
Logical design or logical implementation refers to the actual logic and circuit designs used to realize the microarchitecture specifications. These designs essentially form a specification for the microprocessor chip itself.

And finally, this brings us to the physical implementation of the *microprocessor chip* itself,

DEFINITION
Microprocessor Chip
The microprocessor chip is the physical implementation of the logical design in a given semiconductor process technology.

Many contemporary architecture and microprocessor textbooks deal with a set of core issues in designing computers, such as:

1. the structure and control of basic building blocks (combinational logic, sequential logic, adders, shifters, decoders, multiplexers, etc.).

2. basic control mechanisms (finite state machines, field programmable gate arrays, microcode, state machines, etc.).

3. instruction set design (register and memory addressing, highly/minimally encoded opcodes, compiler issues, operating system issues, architecture state, etc.).

4. parallelism, synchronization, and consistency issues (pipelining, hazards, multiple functional units, instruction level parallelism, task switching, multi-computer and multi-processor support, etc.).

5. cache and memory design (cache organizations and protocols, memory hierarchies, burst and pipeline accesses, virtual memory, coherency, etc.).

6. input/output systems (interrupt, handlers, masking, channels, device controllers, etc.).

7. interconnection and network technology (buses, crossbars, switches, routers, hubs, etc.)

Introductory texts in the field deal with the more fundamental of these issues while the more advanced texts assume the fundamentals as background. Many of the books aid the reader in understanding specific issues by using examples of real architectures to demonstrate a particular solution to a given problem and discussing the implications of the specific solution. Almost none, except for the Thornton book and the two Organick books cited above, deal with a specific commercially successful architecture in depth, giving the reader a reasonably thorough understanding of how it works. The Golze text presents a thorough treatment of a non-commercially available microprocessor but is, nonetheless, instructive.

SUGGESTED READINGS

Books and Articles on Computer Architecture and Microprocessors

Some contemporary books of interest are:

1. Harold S. Stone, *High-Performance Computer Architecture*, 3rd Edition, Addison-Wesley, 1993.
2. Michael J. Flynn, *Computer Architecture: Pipelined and Parallel Processor Design*, Jones and Bartlett, 1995.
3. David A. Patterson, and John L. Hennessy, *Computer Architecture: A Quantitative Approach*, 2nd Edition, Morgan Kaufmann, 1996.

Additionally, the proceedings of the Annual International Symposium on Computer Architecture (ISCA) are extremely important in the evolution of the field. The following three books are important because of the collection (and analysis) of early processor designs which they contain. In our opinion, every student of computer architecture should examine them:

1. Daniel P. Siewiorek, C. Gordon Bell, and Allen Newell, *Computer Structures: Principles and Examples*, McGraw-Hill, 1982.
2. C. Gordon Bell, and Allen Newell, *Computer Structures: Readings and Examples*, McGraw-Hill, 1971.
3. Peter M. Kogge, *The Architecture of Pipelined Computers*, McGraw-Hill, 1981.

Other informative historical books, because of their in-depth treatment of interesting and important computers, are:

1. J. E. Thornton, *Design of a Computer: The Control Data 6600*, Foresman Press, 1970.
2. E. I. Organick, *The Multics System: An Examination of Its Structure*, MIT Press, 1972.
3. E. I. Organick, *Computer System Organization: the B5700/B6700 Series*, Academic Press, 1973.

A recent book, presenting a comprehensive treatment of the design and implementation of the University of Braunschweig's TOOBSIE microprocessor can be found in Ulrich Golze, *VLSI Chip Design with the Hardware Description Language Verilog: An Introduction Based on a Large RISC Processor Design*, Springer-Verlag, 1996.

PC Platforms and Systems

We integrate microprocessors and a number of other components to form *platforms* that address the needs of specific market segments, such as those required in the desktop, workstation, or laptop markets.

DEFINITION
Platform
A platform consists of a number of key components and interconnections on a motherboard and typically includes a high-performance peripheral bus and ports, main memory, an I/O module, a processor module and appropriate BIOS code. The processor module typically includes the processor, processor local bus, optional external cache, and a controller for the peripheral bus and the main memory. The I/O module includes bus controllers and ports for standardized and optional peripherals.

Systems are built from platforms.

DEFINITION
System
A system consists of a platform extended with a number of essential and optional peripherals, an operating system, device drivers including BIOS extensions, other configuration and power management software, and a basic set of applications software. Examples are a Microsoft Windows 95 desktop system and a Unix-based workstation system.

Platform and systems literature exist in an environment similar to that of architecture and microarchitecture: namely, there are many excellent existing information resources for platform and system design, including developer documentation, system architecture books, design guides, industry standards, conference proceedings, seminars, and workshops. Examples of these sources are shown in the *Suggested Readings* inset on the next page. While invaluable and recommended, these information sources do have shortcomings.

Conferences and seminars are relatively expensive, have limited geographic and calendar availability, and are essentially only accessible to a limited number of people. Currently available books, while generally affordable and easy to obtain, do not lend themselves to easy study by the computer engineer or computer scientist who are new to platform and system design. The system architecture books are in-depth reference materials on narrow facets of platform architecture and are suitable for advanced self-study by those already well versed in PC platforms. System design guides and standards documents conversely are comprehensive in breadth, but have little depth, being essentially platform product specifications targeted for veteran platform designers.

Examples of Platform and Systems-Related Resources

Several Annual Conferences and Seminars are valuable, but have limited accessibility:

1. Microsoft's Windows Hardware Engineering Conference or WinHEC.
2. Micro Design Resources' Microprocessor Forum.

The following books are targeted at practitioners and have extensive details on narrow facets of system architecture:

1. Tom Shanley & Don Anderson, *PCI System Architecture,* Addison-Wesley, 3rd Edition, 1995.
2. Richard F. Ferraro, *Programmer's Guide to the EGA, VGA, and Super VGA Cards*, Addison-Wesley, 1994.

The next book is a systematic and all encompassing system specification for PC Platforms; it is broad, but has little depth:

1. *PC98 System Design Guide*, Microsoft Press, 1997.

The following WEB-sites include developer documentation, however the material tends to be disjoint and loosely organized collections of diverse documents:

1. http://www.microsoft.com/hwdev/
2. http://developer.intel.com/

(A note about URLs: URL links change frequently, especially at the lower levels of directory structures. If the links provided become invalid, try looking for the same topic at a higher level in the Web-site's directory hierarchy.)

PC Technical Reference guides that survey the entire PC platform are valuable for their breadth, but they are primarily targeted at PC "enthusiasts" and not practitioners. The following book is one of the best of this genre:

1. Winn L Rosch, *Hardware Bible*, Premiere Edition, SAMS, 1996.

Moreover, there are a number of PC-systems readings of historical interest that we can recommend to you:

1. "Perspective" Section articles from *Understanding x86 Microprocessors*, Ziff-Davis Press, 1987.
2. Lewis C. Eggebrecht, *Interfacing to the IBM Personal Computer*, Howard W. Sams & Co., 1986.
3. Edward Solari, *ISA & EISA Theory and Operation*, Annabooks, 1993.

Our book, in part, provides a needed survey and overview of the key concepts and essential standards of PC platform and systems. We hope you achieve a level of understanding and insight that will enable you to quickly make effective use of the other information resources such as those above and those referred to in later chapters.

Developer documentation generally takes the form of product support literature and is disjointed and scattered, rather than being organized in a compact collection facilitating the study of platform and system design. We make use of an extensive set of references through the systems-based chapters. The following inset gives some examples showing the breadth of content and sources of platform and systems-related literature.

Given this summary of the architecture and microarchitecture and the platform and systems-related literature, we now proceed to the roles of this book.

THE DUAL ROLES OF THE CHAPTERS THAT LIE AHEAD

Our book is not meant to replace any of the contemporary books in a course on computer architecture, computer engineering, or computer systems. Rather, it is intended to both complement and extend them by:

1. providing an in-depth look at the microarchitecture of a specific contemporary high-performance, high-volume microprocessor, AMD's K6 3D that employs many of the techniques discussed in conventional texts. Thus the book presents a detailed and coherent context to study and understand these techniques and their impact on the overall design of a microprocessor.

2. addressing the platform and systems issues identified above and examining the impact of these issues in designing different types of platforms—e.g., desktop systems, mobile systems, and entertainment systems.

Thus, our book is to be used in conjunction with a contemporary book on computer architecture or as a second book by those who have already taken a course in computer architecture. As mentioned earlier, the book is divided into two complementary sections; the first section describes the microarchitecture of the K6 3D microprocessor and the second deals with the platform and systems issues. We examine both of these roles—providing a detailed and coherent context for studying microarchitecture issues and providing a detailed and coherent treatment for studying platform and systems issues—sequentially in the following discussion.

PROVIDING A CONTEXT FOR STUDYING MICROARCHITECTURE ISSUES

When used to provide a detailed and coherent context for studying microprocessors, an instructor can:

1. assign specific sections of this book as additional reading material corresponding to specific topic coverage in the course's textbook.

2. direct specific questions, as appropriate, at the end of the chapters in a conventional architecture text to the microarchitecture presented in this book.

3. frame entirely new questions related to design approaches

represented in the K6 3D's microarchitecture (e.g., evaluating a particular feature by modeling it or examining the implications of substituting a different design solution).

4. combine these approaches.

Assuming a prerequisite or concurrent course in computer architecture, this book can be used as a reference book or as a text in a graduate seminar course as a basis for studying and discussing issues in high-performance computing and instruction level parallelism. Whether used in conjunction with a text or as a reference volume, we believe that you will extend the range of solutions available to you in your own microprocessor-based projects.

PROVIDING A CONTEXT FOR STUDYING PLATFORM AND SYSTEMS ISSUES

When used to provide a detailed and coherent treatment for studying platform- and systems-related issues, an instructor can:

1. assign specific sections of this book as additional reading material corresponding to specific topic coverage in the course's textbook.

2. develop individual or team projects to design and simulate one or more platform components (e.g., the Rambus memory channel and interface, which is discussed in detail in Chapter 5).

3. develop individual or team projects that center around the simulation, analysis, and prototyping of small platforms and systems using the platform- and systems-related chapters as appropriate background.

4. combine these approaches.

Again, assuming a prerequisite or concurrent course in computer architecture, the book can be used as a reference book or text in the study of platforms and systems by the practitioner or student who wants to understand the design and implementation of microprocessor-based systems. Indeed, the book could be used as a text in an undergraduate or graduate project or seminar course as a basis for studying system implementations. This will become clearer when we expand on our approach to discussing these issues later in this chapter.

What must be done, of course, in a book that attempts to give the reader a substantive understanding of a specific microarchitecture and to systematically treat related platform and systems issues is to achieve the sometimes difficult balance of giving *enough* detail, but not *too much* detail.

On the microarchitecture side of the ledger, we try to achieve this balance by limiting our detailed discussions to three main aspects of the

THE AMOUNT OF DETAIL AND THE TASK AT HAND

K6 3D, namely, its out-of-order, speculative scheduler, its operation commit unit, and its register renaming scheme. To do this, we must burrow down into its microarchitecture to see how instructions are predecoded and then decoded, how multiple internal operations result from this decoding process, how these operations go through a substantial expansion process before they are loaded into its centralized scheduler, how its pipelines are controlled and what type of work they do at each stage, how the decoding of instructions and the execution of the resulting operations are decoupled from one another, and how and when predicted branches are ultimately resolved. Because explaining some of these concepts requires knowing a bit about the internal operation set of the microarchitecture and the internal representation of operations within the scheduler, we must present some detail of both.

On the platform and systems side of the ledger, our goals for the platform and systems chapters are complementary, but not without tension. We strive to maintain a balance between general applicability and commercial relevance. The PC platform is by far the most significant class of high-performance microprocessor-based system in terms of unit and dollar volume. Furthermore, it exerts tremendous influence in the design of PC-platform-compatible processors, such as the K6 3D. Thus, we have elected to complement the microarchitecture material by (a) providing insights into the PC-based systems environment in which high-performance microprocessors are currently designed, and (b) establishing a broadly applicable framework for microprocessor-based system design.

The PC-based systems environment is dominated by Microsoft Windows-based PC systems. Therefore, we explore this environment by providing a guide to the hardware architecture of PC platforms that support Windows. We examine how they are organized and optimized. This is done against a backdrop of examining the directions in which the PC industry is moving. The examples used throughout the systems-related chapters of the book are based on a PC platform targeted for desktop consumer 3D graphics applications. As 3D graphics continues to evolve, it presents a seemingly ever-growing demand on the bandwidth of the platform's buses, peripherals, and subsystems. However, in presenting this material, we must again deal with the issue of *too much* versus *not enough* detail.

DETAIL AND SIMULATION

In the end, our criteria for *enough* detail was based on what we believe you need to know to help translate the passive words in this text into an active (and concrete) learning experience. We have given you enough detail to allow you to simulate important portions of the microarchitecture and platform components. You can gain a much greater understanding of how these chunks of a design actually work by doing simulations.

There are many important issues to consider when simulating something—issues arise for which there are no immediate answers and you have to make assumptions in order to get on with the work at hand. The knowledge gained from such an undertaking is important in understanding the cost and performance trade-offs involved in taking an abstract design of a microarchitecture and producing a working chip from it and, given the chip, the complexities of producing a platform from it. To aid you on this learning excursion, we have given "register transfer level"-like descriptions of key elements of the microarchitecture in Chapter 2. These descriptions provide a basis for the simulations which we are encouraging you to undertake. There are copies of VHDL and Verilog simulators and an interactive HDL simulation environment for both of these languages on the CD-ROM which accompanies this book for readers who do not have access to either type of simulator. In any case, you can hand translate the descriptions into the appropriate input form for whatever simulation system you want to use. It is quite obvious that we believe in the old axiom of the Dewey school of education, "Learn by doing."

We hope that our explanations turn out to facilitate your understanding and enjoyment of this material, and that we don't turn out to be like the authors that Don Norman comments on in the adjacent side panel, who would make this a difficult and uninteresting task.

We will start our journey into this text by examining the overall process of designing and implementing a microprocessor. We begin our journey into the platform and systems-related issues by giving a hardware overview of the design and implementation of a consumer-market 3D graphics PC platform. Both of these journey's begin in Chapter 1.

This concludes our introductory remarks regarding the technical content of the book. In closing, we briefly discuss the text insets, the companion CD-ROM, and give acknowledgments to those who helped us with this project.

"But These Are Complicated Topics. *One standard excuse of obscurantist authors is that the material in question is complex and technical, sometimes very abstract and refined. The fact that the writing is difficult to follow is unavoidable. The argument then gets turned around: The inability of readers like me to follow such complex thoughts reflects upon me, the reader, not upon the writing. If I really cared, I would do the work required to understand. And, if I still can't, well, I should just face up to the fact that my mind isn't sufficiently powerful. Complex ideas require complex writing, and then complex powerful minds to deal with them. Simple writing is for simple ideas, simple minds. Is there any case to be made for this? It sounds to me suspiciously like those folks who told me that if I made errors using the Unix computer system, why then I had no business using it. Clearly those who are incompetent to use something or to understand a text have no business trying to do so. Isn't this a great defense? You can cover up any kind of inelegant design or writing this way. Wonderful."* Donald Norman, *Turn Signals are the Facial Expressions of Automobiles*, Addison-Wesley, 1992, pp.178-179.

TEXT INSETS

From time-to-time, *text insets* appear in the body of the text and are labeled as either *Design Notes, Comparative Analysis, Historical Comments, Industry Standards, Pseudo-RTL Descriptions,* or *Suggested Readings*. The *Design Notes* sections are meant to specifically identify for the reader interesting, novel, or new design approaches that are implemented in the K6 3D. The *Comparative Analysis* sections show how the K6 3D distinguishes itself from other microprocessors and what the differences amount to in terms of cost, performance, or fabrication- and production-related issues. The *Historical Comments* sections reestablish our connections to the first several decades of processor design, lest we think everything in microarchitecture and instruction level parallelism is newly developed. As is true with many areas of computer science and engineering, some results are often "re-discovered." The *Industry Standards* sections call your attention to specific industry standards and platform or system specifications that are important to the specific topic under discussion. The *Suggested Readings* sections, often appear with *Historical Comments*, suggest information sources that can prove valuable to both students and practitioners alike. The *Pseudo-RTL Description* sections, briefly introduced in Chapter 1 and treated extensively in Chapter 3, form the basis of simulations that we encourage you to perform.

DESCRIPTION, CONTENT AND USE OF THE CD-ROM

The complete text of the book, including all figures and tables, are on the companion CD-ROM and can be viewed using Adobe's Acrobat Reader. There are a substantial number of hyperlinks throughout the CD-ROM version of the book. For example, all entries in the Table of Contents, List of Figures, List of Tables, and the Glossary/Index[iii] are hyperlinked into the appropriate section of the book. All cross-references are hyperlinked and the *entire* book has been indexed so that arbitrary, free text, multiple-term Boolean queries can be used to identify sections of interest using the Adobe Acrobat Search Plug-In. Moreover, may of the key figures in the text are hyperlinked, i.e., clicking on an element within the figure will take you to the text that deals with that element.

In reality, the CD-ROM provided with this book provides you with multiple books, not just one. A wide variety of items are included on it, such as complete data books, articles from journals and conference proceedings, manuscripts of important historical interest, industry standards, increasingly significant industry platform and system specifications, VHDL and Verilog simulators and a number of video and audio clips. The following icons are used in the text to identify relevant material on the CD-ROM that is related to the particular topic under discussion.

 The "article" icon indicates that there is a copy of an article on the CD-ROM that appeared in either a periodical or conference proceedings sponsored by a professional society, such as the IEEE Computer Society.

[iii] Following the example in Stone's book, cited above, an extensive glossary appears within the book's index.

The "rubber stamp" icon with the word "STANDARD" indicates there is a copy on the CD-ROM of either (a) an IEEE Standard or (b) an industry document that has already emerged (or which we believe will emerge) as a "de facto" industry standard.

 The "rubber stamp" icon with the word "REPORT" on it is used to identify all other technical articles and documents (i.e., those which do not appear in a professional society periodical or conference proceedings) on the CD-ROM. Some examples are: white papers; product data sheets; articles that appeared in industry newsletters; government or university reports; and industry developed specifications.

 Additionally, there are several "video clips" on the CD-ROM. In these videos, various technical questions are presented to key members of the K6 3D design and implementations team.

 There are also a number of "audio clips" on the CD-ROM that give overviews of specific technical topics. While some are directed at summarizing topics in the text, others expand on material given less detailed treatment.

 There are a number of simulations on the CD-ROM that are identified by the "simulation screen" icon. We encourage the reader to run these simulations while studying the sections of the text in which they appear.

 There are copies of a number of technical presentations on the CD-ROM covering important topics (e.g., the evolution of high-performance instruction set architectures, speculative execution, Socket 7, and Rambus technology). Technical presentations are identified by the "overhead projection" icon.

Adobe FrameMaker 5.5.2 and Adobe Acrobat 3.01 were used to produce this book in PostScript form for the printed version and in PDF form for the CD-ROM version. This allows you to use license-free readers/viewers (e.g., Adobe's Acrobat Reader and Apple's QuickTime viewer) as the vehicles for accessing material on the CD-ROM. See the CD-ROM User's Guide for relevant information on using the companion CD-ROM.

WEB-SITE

Readers can submit questions, comments, detected errors, and suggestions at the Web-site that is associated with the book and its companion CD-ROM. They can receive a list of verified errata and corrections and a variety of other information related to the book at this Web-site. The URL for the site is:

http://computer.org/books/anatomy.htm

Whenever additional material is made available, in any of the categories discussed earlier in the section titled, "Description, Content and Use of the CD-ROM," it will be made available at this Web-site. Examples of such material are: articles, reports, standards, suggested readings, and links to additional technical material; audio clips; book extensions, if and when they become available; exercises and problems posted by readers of the book, along with solutions when available; simulations of the various chunks of logic described by the pseudo-RTL descriptions of the architectural elements; and additional technical presentations as they become available and pointers to technical presentations

ACKNOWLEDGMENTS

We give our sincerest thanks to Atiq Raza, Chief Technology Officer and Executive Vice President of AMD, who has been supportive of this project from its very inception; without his encouragement and support, it undoubtedly would not have been undertaken or completed. We would like to thank Harold Stone, NEC Research Laboratory, not only for his encouragement to proceed with this project after he had reviewed some early material regarding its content and form, but also for the numerous and substantive comments he made on the draft manuscript in an effort to improve its overall quality.

Similarly, we would like to thank Greg Favor, the chief architect of the K6 3D, and Amos Ben-Meir, the chief designer of the K6 3D, who gave substantial amounts of their time to not only describing the processor to us, but reviewing what we had written about it. We thank Bill Siegle, AMD's Chief Scientist, and Keith Schakel, Warren Stapleton, and Anu Mitra, members of AMD's technical staff, who were involved in this information transfer and review process.

We thank the IEEE CS Press reviewers, Tore Larsen, University of Tromso (Norway), Ed Gallizzi, Eckerd College, and Ron Hoelzeman, University of Pittsburgh, for their technical reviews of the draft version of this manuscript. They made numerous recommendations to improve the technical content and presentation of the material. We also thank Yale Patt, University of Michigan, who reviewed and commented on very early versions of material that eventually found its way into Chapters 1 and 2.

There are technical contributions in Chapter 1 by Mario Barbacci, Carnegie-Mellon University, and by the Eckert-Mauchly Award Winners Robert Tomasulo, retired, Yale Patt, University of Michigan, Michael Flynn, Stanford University, Daniel Siewiorek, Carnegie-Mellon University, Harvey Cragon, University of Texas, Austin, and John Cocke, retired. Furthermore, Don Draper of AMD played an important role in the writing of the sections on gate and circuit-level simulation, netlists and physical layout, and mask generation, wafer fabrication, and packaging in Chapter 1. We thank each of them for these contributions.

Special thanks are due to Ricky See and Keith Schakel, both of AMD, for helping with the pseudo-RTL descriptions found in Chapters 2 and 3, to Jeff Trull of AMD for discussions and the diagrams related to the scan chains in Chapters 2 and 3, and to Mike Yamamura of AMD for help with the die photographs and the floorplan diagrams in Chapter 1.

We would like to thank Louise Burnham, the copy-editor, and, additionally, Beverly Shriver, Eva Mae Connell, and Mary Lou Wenger for their efforts in improving the readability of the manuscript. We acknowledge the efforts of Elaine Rose and Crystal Jacobson, both of AMD, and Joanne Winningham for their help with the myriad administrative issues related to the publication of a book and CD-ROM. We owe special thanks to Lisa O'Conner of the IEEE Computer Society not only for all of her work scanning and converting a substantial number of the articles that appear on the CD-ROM so they could be electronically searched by the reader, but also for shepherding this project through the production process. We thank Tom Fink, IEEE Computer Society, for his work on the book's Web-site. We also thank Joseph Daigle of Studio Productions for his work on the book jacket, book cover, CD-ROM packaging, and CD-ROM label.

With respect to acquiring many of the technical articles and other platform- and system-related material on the CD-ROM and in the body of the book, we must acknowledge:

> Matt Loeb of the IEEE Computer Society for helping acquire permission to reprint material from the IEEE and the IEEE Computer Society (and, importantly, for his unfailing and enthusiastic support of this project).

> Judith Gorman of the IEEE for helping us with the permission associated with the IEEE Standards and to Susan Tatiner and Greg Kohn, both of the IEEE, for producing the associated PDF files.

> Satinder Singh, Jeff Ferris, Ned Finkle, Jerry Isaac, David Kyle, Levi Murray, and Jim Reilly, all of AMD, for helping us with K6-related documents and other special requests.

> Gene Hoffnagel of IBM for helping us obtain permission to reprint the articles from the *IBM Journal of Research and Development*.

> J.A.N. Lee of Virginia Tech for helping us locate a copy of the 1945 von Neumann article and to Michael Godfrey of Stanford University for providing us with a postscript version of it.

> Bill Aspray at the Computing Research Association for

helping us locate a copy of the Burks, Goldsine, and von Neumann article.

Dennis Allison of Stanford University and Linley Gwennap of MicroDesign Resources for their help in obtaining permission to reprint articles from the *Microprocessor Report*.

Additionally, we need to thank AMD, AMP, IBM, Molex, Rambus, SLDRAM and Standard Microsystems Corporation for allowing us to include numerous tables, figures, and/or other material in the hard-copy version of the book or on the CD-ROM.

The design and layout of both the book and the CD-ROM were collaborative efforts led by Bruce Shriver and involved Bennett Smith, Dennis Hays (Dennis Hays Information Design), Matthew Shriver (Fish & Neave), Lynn Edwards (Bookmark Media, in the early phases of the project), and feedback from Michael Elliott (IEEE Computer Society), and several reviewers. A number of graphics components were designed specifically for this book. Among them are the icons used in the hard copy of the book, the icons used on the CD-ROM, the CD-ROM packaging graphics, and the book jacket and CD-ROM images. We owe our thanks to the creative talents of Matthew Shriver who did all of these graphics and contributed to the project in additional ways. We also thank Alexander Bovone (composer) for the audio accompaniment to Matthew's animation on the CD-ROM.

Donna Mitchell of SynaptiCAD Inc., Elliot Mednick of Wellspring Solutions, Inc., and Dave Pellerin of Accolade Design Automation, Inc. gave their time, energy, and effort to not only make sure we had the most recent versions of their simulation systems and documentation but also to ensure that we had tutorials on their use.

We should acknowledge Marshall Eisen and Dan Geller of StoryLine Productions and Sandra Wheatly and Scott Allen of AMD for their help with filming, editing, and administrative issues related to the production if the video clips. Lastly, David Slone of Townsend, Townsend, & Crew, Bob Flynn, Ahmed Aslam, and Titus Chi of Polytechnic University, Mark Podlipec of Bay Networks, and Brent Hailpern and Hank Warren of IBM T. J. Watson Research Center all helped with the testing of the CD-ROM for cross-platform compatibility.

Enjoy,

Bruce Shriver, Ossining, New York
Bennett Smith, Palo Alto, California
1998

Contents

4 Technology Components of Platform Architecture   315

5 Platform Memory Technology   427

6 Platform Optimization Techniques and Directions 463

References to Authors and Other Individuals 515

References to Suggested Readings 519

Copyright and Legal Notices 521

Glossary/Index 525

List of Figures

3 The K6 3D Microarchitecture   183

4 Technology Components of Platform Architecture   315

5 Platform Memory Technology 427

6 Platform Optimization Techniques and Directions 463

List of Tables

3 The K6 3D Microarchitecture   183

4 Technology Components of Platform Architecture   315

Chapter 1
Microprocessors, Platforms, and Systems

T his chapter examines the process of designing and implementing a microprocessor and then examines issues that arise in the process of designing and implementing a 3D graphics PC platform. Toward the end of the chapter, several Eckert-Mauchly award winners share their insights regarding important references in the field of computer architecture. Although this chapter is written for each of the books intended[1] audiences, there are some subsections that have details that will be of more interest and use to practitioners and those in universities. The following *road map* for this chapter identifies these sections.

ROAD MAP OF CHAPTER 1

Section	Audience
The following are more detailed subsections: Model at the Gate and Circuit Levels Gate and Circuit Level Simulation and Hardware Emulation Generate Netlists and Physical Layout Mask Generation, Wafer Fabrication, and Packaging	Practitioners, University Professors, and Students

What makes microprocessors especially difficult to design and implement are their complex nature, large size as measured in the number of electronic devices required in their implementation and the number of highly dependent trade-offs that must be made to achieve given size, yield, voltage, power, temperature, price, and performance points. The situation

DESIGNING AND IMPLEMENTING A MICROPROCESSOR

---

[1] See the Preface

is complicated by the fact that the performance of the microprocessor *should not* be looked at independently of how it is integrated into a platform and a system. Issues such as the performance characteristics (bandwidth, latency, clock rate, etc.) of the core logic chipset, the memory architecture, the number and types of buses and their characteristics, and the I/O device support integrated onto the motherboard must be considered in a number of the design trade-offs. It makes little sense to have the fastest microprocessor in the world integrated into a system with an inappropriate bus or memory architecture or I/O support.

hardware-software co-design

This implies that the core logic chipset, bus, memory architecture, and motherboard design teams must work intimately with the microprocessor design team. Each of these system elements is also significantly impacted by the rate of increases in clock speed and circuit density as well as important changes in packaging technology. Instead of advocating *hardware-software co-design*, we advocate *hardware-system co-design*. The "hardware" component of hardware-software co-design often refers only to processor design. Even when used in this restricted context, the hardware-software co-design process has substantive advantages when contrasted with the approach used just a few years ago of designing a processor without on-going, detailed interactions with software teams, such as compiler writers and operating systems implementers, that ultimately leads to the co-evolution, testing, and integration of the processor and the software.

ARTICLE ON CD-ROM

 An insightful article that clearly shows the dependent nature of processor and compiler design is, "Compiler Technology for Future Microprocessors," by Wen-Mei Hwu, Richard E. Hank, Daniel M. Lavery, Grant E. Haab, John C. Gyllenhaal, and David I. August, *Proceedings of the IEEE*, December 1995.

hardware-system co-design

We use the term *hardware-system co-design* to extend these notions to include on-going, detailed interactions with the teams involved in the design of the core logic chipset, the BIOS, the bus and memory architectures, the motherboard and any special device controller chips that will be integrated on the motherboard, (e.g., graphics controller chip, a high-speed FAX-data-voice modem chip, or a high-performance network controller chip). The second half of this book deals with many of these issues. In the first half, we focus on the microarchitecture of the microprocessor.

WHAT NEEDS TO BE DONE?

How do you go about implementing a microprocessor? What needs to be done can be stated quite simply: We need to take the high-level instruction set architecture representation or model of the microprocessor's architecture and transform it into a correctly working, high-performance silicon chip that will have a long, failure-free life. Doing that is, of course, not so simple.

We use the terms "representation" and "model" interchangeably in this discussion.

Models play an integral role in the *transformation* process. Models are used to explore and analyze alternative design solutions and to verify behavioral (functional) specifications, compatibility requirements, and adherence to standards. A model—a representation of the microprocessor expressed in some language—is typically implemented in a simulator, emulator, or a combination of both. The model can represent the microprocessor at the architecture, microarchitecture, logical implementation, or chip level, or it can span one or more of these levels. While computer architects typically tend to deal with issues at the architecture and microarchitecture levels, digital design engineers tend to be more directly involved with issues at the logical implementation and chip levels. As a result, these two groups often approach the modeling and simulations issues from different perspectives and often with a different set of terminology and tools. For example, some digital system designers might refer to the levels of abstraction shown in Table 1.1 when discussing the modeling and simulation of digital systems:

Table 1.1 LEVELS OF ABSTRACTION COMPARISON

Digital Design Engineer's Level	Examples of Modeled Entity	Approximate Equivalence to Computer Architect's Level
system level	pipelines, instruction decoders, and TLBs	microarchitecture
register transfer level (RTL)	registers, buses, multiplexers, and combinational logic	microarchitecture and logical implementation
gate level or logic level	library cells of AND, OR, etc. gates	logical implementation
transistor level	transistors in various process technologies	chip
layout level	geometries, transistor placements	chip

These levels of abstractions (sometimes also called stages) are shown in more detail in Figure 1.1. The differences between the terminology and tools each group employs are lessening because:

1. the size and complexity of the microprocessors and the impact of the implementation-related issues on the cost/performance of the overall system require these groups to work closer together, with the result that the boundaries between some of the adjacent stages in the design process are becoming increasingly blurred.

2. the decreasing cost of high-performance computer platforms has precipitated a movement of electronic design automation tools from specialized workstations to more widely available desktop platforms resulting in an increase in the power and scope of these tools.

Let us now take a look at the design and implementation process represented in Figure 1.1 in more detail.

CONSTRAINTS

We assume that the instruction set architecture to be implemented has been previously defined. Thus the design and implementation process does not start with the design of the instruction set architecture but with the design of the microarchitecture, (i.e., the set of resources and methods used to implement the instruction set architecture). Recall from the earlier definition of the term microarchitecture that it includes the way in which these resources are organized as well as the design techniques used to reach the target cost and performance goals. Presumably, the instruction set architecture has been designed with an intimate knowledge of what the programs implemented actually do, (e.g., knowing what systems resources are used and how frequently, and knowing what memory bandwidth various classes of algorithms require). Knowing what programs do is absolutely essential to identifying what resources and instructions are required in the architecture.

The detailed analysis of performance data and the subsequent use of that analysis in the design process is the cornerstone of many, if not most, architectural design decisions.

It cannot be emphasized strongly enough the importance of understanding what the processor is doing when it executes specific benchmarks or workloads. This assumes that the benchmarks and workloads are truly representative of how the system will be used. This assumption, however, is one that is difficult to meet. Not only must suitable workloads be created, but representative traces from those workloads must also be developed. Using bad trace data in good performance models has been the cause of more than one processor's performance deficiencies. Moreover, deciding on what workloads are representative of current (or future) target markets can be extremely difficult.

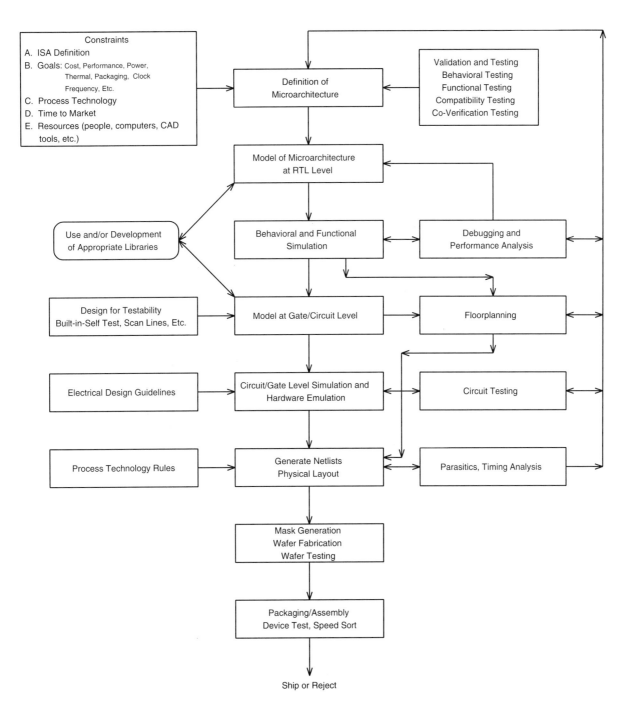

Figure 1.1 DESIGN PROCESS

Even given these difficulties with developing good performance models and good trace data, it is safe to say that the detailed analysis of performance data and the subsequent use of that analysis is the cornerstone of many, if not most, central architectural design decisions. Some examples are data from address traces that yields information about such things as the frequency of occurrence of conditional branches, address modes, exception conditions, and interrupts.

The design of specific workloads and benchmarks is an art in itself.

The workloads and benchmarks and subsequent analysis may be targeted at a specific component of the processor (e.g., the integer unit or the floating-point unit), a group of components (e.g., the chunks of logic involved in the fetching, predicating, and decoding of instructions), the entire processor itself, or the processor interconnected with one or more of its external system components (e.g., the chipset or off-chip cache). The design of specific workloads and benchmarks is an art in itself as often millions of instruction executions are needed to gain some understanding of the specific behavior you are attempting to study. Both the architect and the digital systems engineer need to know where the bottlenecks are in their respective models of the microprocessor in order to remove these bottlenecks.

Clearly, one of the most important constraints placed on the microarchitecture design team is the definition of the instruction set architecture that they need to support. For the K6 3D microarchitecture, it is the widely used x86 instruction set architecture. Indeed, one view of the K6 3D is that it is a high-performance CISC-on-RISC microprocessor. The CISC-component is the x86 instruction set architecture, while the underlying RISC-component is known as the Enhanced RISC86 microarchitecture. The most important implication of this constraint is that the K6 must be fully x86 binary code compatible, including code using the x86 MMX multimedia instruction set extensions. We will learn later that the K6 3D also provides an additional set of AMD-developed instruction set extensions called the AMD-3D instructions which support high-performance 3D graphics, audio, and physics-based modeling and simulation processing.

VIDEO ON CD-ROM

Amos Ben-Meir, Principal Designer of the K6 3D, addresses two questions of interest in this video clip: "What is needed to design state-of-the art microprocessors?" and "What were the design methods that enabled the K6 3D to be implemented in such a short period of time?"

Other constraints, both from a platform and performance point of view have to do with systems-related issues. Among the design goals for the K6 3D processor were explicit objectives for it to be Socket 7 compatible and for it to fit within the electrical, power and thermal specifications, and the EMI envelope of the Intel Pentium processor. If it were successful in meeting these objectives, it could readily integrate into industry-standard Pentium-compatible motherboards, chipsets, power supplies, and thermal designs.

COMPARATIVE ANALYSIS

Socket 7 Compatible

Socket 7 compatible means that the system bus interface is compatible with the industry-standard 64-bit Pentium P55C bus protocol and motherboard socket. One of the most important differences between the K6 and Intel's Pentium Pro and Pentium II processors is the way in which the microprocessor chips connect to the rest of the system and the system bus interface.

The K6, like the Intel Pentium and the Intel Pentium MMX (P55C), are "Socket 7 compatible" as defined above. However the Intel Pentium Pro and the Intel Pentium II (Klamath) use a different bus interface or protocol (called the P6 bus interface) and each uses a different physical motherboard connector. The Intel Pentium Pro uses a dual-cavity PGA packaging technology. The Intel Pentium II uses Intel's Single Edge Cartridge (SEC) technology and its Slot 1 and Slot 2 connectors. These issues and their design implications (e.g., the way in which the L2-Cache is interfaced to the system and the performance issues involved) are discussed in Chapter 4 and Chapter 6.

The analysis of the instruction set architecture is based on knowledge of typical application and system software, typical coding practice, behavior or nature of code generated by various compilers, and analysis of instruction and data reference traces of actual software. On this last point, which is one of the most significant inputs to the microarchitecture development process, the following elements are key:

1. the capability to capture traces of the execution of any and all code, (e.g., privileged OS code, device driver code, and application code).

2. the capability to use long traces—ten million to one billion instructions long.

3. the need to have an accurate and detailed trace-driven performance model of the design that can output a wide variety of performance-related statistics and that can be readily changed to explore alternative design options.

TESTING

During the design process, we undertake different types of testing—functional (i.e., behavioral) testing, structural testing, compatibility testing, and performance testing. There are basically three different levels of testing that need to be considered for each of these types. The testing of:

1. the design (i.e., verifying the design realizes the instruction set architecture without any errors).

2. the logical implementation (i.e., verifying the logical implementation realizes the design without any errors).

3. the chip (i.e., verifying the physical device realizes the logical implementation without any errors).

Functional (Behavioral) Testing

Functional (behavioral) testing is a method for verifying design correctness via simulation. A "block" or "component" representing a set of functions or system behavior is modeled. A simulator is constructed for the model. An input stimulus is applied to the block's inputs and the block's outputs are compared with the expected outputs. Trace buffers are used to chronicle the behavior of the block, permitting examination of the behavior for an arbitrary period of time prior to matching results. Such computer modeling of the design is begun at an early stage in the design process to verify design concepts in a top-down fashion. Functional testing is continued as more detail is added to the design and changes are made.

Initially the simulations are strictly at a highly abstract behavioral level and are performed on large blocks that model major functional areas of the design. As design implementation progresses, the original blocks are usually hierarchically decomposed into sub-blocks. The model is managed to track the design hierarchy and thus becomes more detailed over time. Testing is generally performed first on each new sub-block and then interactions between blocks are confirmed.

DEFINITION
Test Vector
Test vectors are the collection of values of input stimulus and expected output results for each sequential stage of simulation. The test vectors are intended to cover all inputs and outputs (pins entering or leaving) each block being tested. Test vectors for larger blocks don't need to include I/Os of smaller blocks that do not appear at the boundary of the larger block.

The development of test vectors is time-consuming and may be naively omitted from project scheduling or its extent may be underestimated. Writing the vectors generally requires a detailed knowledge of the blocks being tested. Often the logic designer of the blocks must write the vectors or at least define an initial template for others to follow. Insuring comprehensive testing coverage for large complex blocks is a specialized field, because exhaustive testing of all possible combinations of inputs may not be practical. Once confidence in the test vectors is obtained, vectors may be used in gate-level or other lower-level simulations, to verify bottom-up design correctness.

Functional simulators are generally restricted to behavioral modeling. When the gate-level design of a block is synthesized or manually designed, it too can be modeled using a gate-level simulation. Gate-level simulators generally can handle the simulation of sub-blocks that have behavioral descriptions. Thus some blocks may be at a gate-level, while others are still using a behavioral model. Often the focus is on verifying the gate-level design of a particular block, and blocks providing stimulus to or sampling outputs from the block of interest need only be behaviorally modeled.

Design for Testability

A digital circuit is an implementation of the specification of a desired function, (i.e., it exhibits a desired behavior). A microprocessor is a collection of hundreds of thousands of such circuits. Given the complexity of the resulting microprocessor chips, the testing of them must be integral in their design from the onset. Incorporating testing technology into a design from its inception is often referred to as "design for testability" or DFT. Using DFT techniques invariably reduces costs and design time.

There have been a number of important DFT advances made at the logical implementation and chip level, such as boundary scan testing, full operational scan of internal state elements (e.g., flip-flops), built-in self-test (BIST), test vector generation, signature analysis, and observers. A number of these approaches required additional circuitry to be included in the design, solely for the testing function, reducing the amount of the total gates on the chip that are available to implement the microprocessor. Thus, another trade-off emerges regarding the distribution of gates between functionality and testing and the benefits from the use of DFT techniques.

A substantive treatment of testing—dealing with issues such as fault modeling, fault manifestation,[2] fault detection (controllability and

---

[2] For example, at the chip level one needs to conjecture how fabrication faults such as holes in insulating layers, bridging connections in metal layers, missed contacts, and poor control of etching will be manifested so that it is possible to test for them.

observability), test design, test data (collection and generation), and test coverage—is well beyond the scope of this book. Particularly since each of these topics needs to be discussed in the context of testing the design, the implementation, and the chip. However, a number of fundamental ideas are presented so the reader has an appreciation of the issues involved.

Suggested Readings

Design for Testability

1. H. P. G. Vranken, M. F. Willeman, and R. C. van Wuijswinkel, "Design for Testability in Hardware-Software Systems," *IEEE Design & Test of Computers*, Vol. 13, No. 3, Fall 1996, pp. 79-87.

2. K. P. Parker, *The Boundary Scan Handbook*, Kluwer Academic Publishers, 1992.

3. IEEE Standard 1149.1-1990, *Test Access Port and Boundary Scan Architecture*, January 1992 and the associated standard, 1149.1b, *Boundary Scan Description Language (BSDL)*, 1991.

4. M. Tegethoff, "IEEE Standard 1149.1: Where Are We? Where From Here?" *IEEE Design & Test of Computers*, Vol. 12, No. 2, Summer 1995, pp. 53-59.

5. B. T. Murray and J. P. Hayes, "Testing ICs: Getting to the Core of the Problem," Computer, November 1996.

6. V. D. Agrawal and C. R. Kime and K. K. Saluja, "A Tutorial on Built-in Self-Test, Part 1: Principles," *IEEE Design & Test of Computers*, Vol. 10., No. 1, May 1993, pp. 73-82.

7. V. D. Agrawal and C.R. Kime and K. K. Saluja, "A Tutorial on Built-in Self-Test, Part 2: Applications," *IEEE Design & Test of Computers*, Vol. 10., No. 2, June 1993, pp. 69-77.

 You can find the full text versions of *Part 1* and *Part 2* of the Agrawal, Kime, and Saluja tutorial as well as the Murray and Hayes article, on the companion CD-ROM.

Compatibility Testing

The difficulty of achieving x86 architectural compatibility is generally underestimated. The business issues surrounding compatibility are generally equally underestimated. We will see that these business issues contribute directly to the technical difficulties in achieving compatibility.

From a business perspective, x86 compatibility is an absolute requirement. First of all, if it is perceived that the affected microprocessors are flawed merchandise, there is the real possibility of being held liable to recall or field-replace the flawed units. Equally important however, is that consumers simply will not accept a microprocessor if there is a lack of confidence that the microprocessor will not successfully run popular or legacy software. This latter problem is aggravated by the fact that the programmers of such software may have relied on unintended and undocumented behaviors, which historically have been prevalent in x86 microprocessors.

Undocumented or imprecisely documented behaviors are at the center of the difficulty in achieving compatibility. The user and programming manuals for x86 microprocessors have historically not compared with documents like the *IBM/370 Principles of Operation* manuals. The x86 manuals have generally been little more than abstractions that approximate the exact behavior of the microprocessor. Such x86 manuals cannot be considered as formal reference documents, written and edited with extreme care, and thereby suitable for design purposes.

Generally speaking, the first vendor to implement a commercially successful microprocessor will de facto determine its behavior for all implementations to follow. Even if part of that initial behavior includes unintended and undocumented artifacts, the earliest implementation defines the compatibility requirements for all other vendors. The first vendor does not need to reverse engineer the behavior, at least not until a subsequent generation's implementation. Even then, this vendor has knowledge of the exact logic underlying the original implementation, and can use that to retroactively deduce the precise behavior. The second implementer to market the instruction set architecture of the microprocessor does not have these luxuries.

Designers take great risks when making extensions to instruction sets. If the extensions are not useful, they will increase the cost of the processor without returning benefit. If the extensions are useful, but implemented inefficiently, they leave room for competitors to make improvements. The x86 architecture has had a number of extensions over its history. An early extension was the introduction of the 80286 instruction set, which extended the addressable memory from 1-MByte to 16-MBytes. This extension was not very successful. It failed to support compatibility with the underlying 8086 architecture in a way that could be used efficiently in practice. Some commercial software used the larger memory model, but two key operating systems at the time, Microsoft's Windows and IBM's OS/2, were unable to produce widely accepted versions using these extensions. Subsequent instruction set extensions embodied in the 80386 architecture provided an efficient 8086 emulation mode, and that enabled new operating systems to run 80386 and legacy 8086 code with equal efficiency.

One of the lessons to be learned from these examples is that instruction set extensions should be done in concert with the development of both the operating systems and important software applications that will use them. This suggests that computer architects and software designers should sit down together to determine what the extensions should do and how they should be implemented (see *hardware-software co-design* and *hardware-system co-design* on page 2). From a competitive point of view, this means that some proprietary information has to be shared across the

Compatibility must not only deal with "official" or "publicly" documented features, but must also deal with "unofficial" and "undocumented" features and with behaviors in obscure cases.

industry with some partners while kept secret from companies in the business of designing competitive microprocessors.

The ideal strategy is to publicly announce the instruction set extensions and the operating systems and applications software use of the extensions at the same time. In reality, the software announcements usually always follow the availability of the instruction set extensions, often by as much as a year. As an example, the x86 MMX instruction set extensions were announced in the spring of 1997. By early 1998, very little MMX software had been released, although a large number of the potential developers who could make use of the extensions had committed to use them in their applications. So, it looks promising that these extensions will indeed succeed.

On the other hand, the 80286 instruction set extensions were never truly successful. Yet they were used by enough software to force 80286 compatibility to a component of x86 designs through the 1990s and possibly beyond. Virtually all 80286 applications that were running in the late 1990s had long ago been converted to the 80386 memory model. But the possibility that some still exist for the 80286 memory model creates what amounts to a tax on the x86 architecture to support software that, in all probability, is no longer in use. Given this background into some of the problems involved in extending an instruction set, let us return to the issues regarding compatibility testing.

compatibility test suites

Because the published x86 documentation is not adequate for compatible design, design houses for x86 processors must make a large investment in time to develop extensive compatibility test suites. These suites are used to compare their parts against the de facto standard Intel x86 microprocessors. The compatibility suites exercise the functionality of individual instructions and inter-instruction interactions. Many tests are written that create result arrays in memory. Comparison of the result arrays for the microprocessor with the device under test, is more efficient than tests that require comparison of register values. Subsequent to such tests, compatibility testing includes extensive trials of major applications and operating systems. Comprehensive system tests are also performed using a wide range of peripherals. After much internal testing, outside compatibility laboratories are employed to give independent certification, and hence added credibility that the microprocessor is indeed compatible.

Clearly part of the difficulty in compatibility testing stems from x86 architectural complexity, particularly in the context of high-performance implementations, which act to further complicate compatibility testing. Some x86 architectural complexity issues are well known. These include the existence of complex instructions with variable-length instructions, non uniform instruction decoding, many address modes and inherently multiple cycle operations; a segmented addressing model, requiring continual effective and linear address calculations; precise interrupts; and IEEE compatible floating-point.

The foregoing well-known complexity issues are just the beginning. Beyond these are many more problems. Historically, x86 programmers have exploited the use of self-modifying code. Compatibility requires close monitoring for store-into-instruction stream events and extensive design efforts to ensure instruction cache coherency, which must extend over multiple levels of cache hierarchy, deep into the branch prediction, prefetch, and instruction decode logic. The x86 has multiple operating modes, including real-mode, virtual 86 mode, segmentation without paging, and segmentation with paging. Paging involves a 2-level translation with a TLB and also introduces additional user and supervisor-like protection features. Beyond addressing issues, segmentation has extensive protection model features, including the use of selectors and segment descriptors, call-gate transitions between protection levels, task-gate transitions between tasks, protected stack operations, and virtualized I/O. Miscellaneous x86 complexity that complicates compatibility testing stems from the existence of a "System Management" mode for facilitating system power management, instruction prefix operations, non uniform register operations (8-bit, 16-bit, and 32-bit operations), and the implicit instruction use of dedicated registers.

Because the K6 3D executes x86 instructions directly, a significant compatibility effort was undertaken from the very beginning of the project to ensure its x86 binary code compatibility. Its verification included all of the steps above plus validation for several major operating systems environments. Some of the validation steps were simplified because of tools and experience in building three earlier generations of x86 processors, but no steps were omitted..

VIDEO ON THE COMPANION CD-ROM

There is a video interview on the CD-ROM with Warren Stapleton, Leader of Model Development and Verification of the K6 3D and Anu Mitra, Verification Manager of the K6 3D in which they discuss the design process employed and the extensive role verification played in the project from its inception.

DEFINING A PROCESSOR'S INSTRUCTION SET ARCHITECTURE

The genesis of a processor's instruction set architecture is often quite informal in nature—ranging from discussions where diagrams are drawn on backs of envelopes to talking one or two people into writing a report or a white paper discussing what might be done.

Historical Comment and Suggested Reading

The von Neumann Machine

Two of the most significant papers in the history of computer architecture are related to what is called the *"von Neumann machine."* They are:

1. John von Neumann, "The First Draft of a Report on the EDVAC," Moore School of Electrical Engineering, University of Pennsylvania, June 30, 1945, republished in the *IEEE Annals of the History of Computing*, 1993.

2. Arthur W. Burks, Herman H. Goldstine, and John von Neumann, "Preliminary Discussion of the Logical Design of an Electronic Computing Instrument," report prepared for U.S. Army Ordnance Dept., 1946, reprinted in *Datamation*, Vol. 8, No. 9, pp. 24-31, September 1962 (Part I) and *Datamation*, Vol. 8, No. 10, pp. 36-41, October, 1962 (Part II).

An interesting augmentation to the von Neumann paper cited above can be found in:

3. M. D. Godfrey and D. F. Henry, "The Computer as von Neumann Planned It," *IEEE Annals of the History of Computing*, 1993.

An historical account of RISC technology within IBM, a good deal of which is relevant to topics discussed in this book, can be found in:

4. John Cocke and V. Markstein, "The Evolution of RISC Technology at IBM," *IBM Journal of Research and Development*, January 1990.

 Complete full-text versions of *each* of the above important, historical articles can be found on the companion CD-ROM. We encourage you to read each of them.

These modest beginnings often lead to forming a small group of people to undertake both analytical studies and simulations to explore the feasibility of some of the newer concepts inherent in the design, to define some aspects of the instruction set architecture with a bit more rigor, to examine the implications of a number of the design constraints. If the results of these efforts are promising, a project to design and implement the processor is typically launched, consistent with available resources. It should come as no surprise that a microarchitecture also evolves in a similar way to an instruction set architecture.

There are a wide variety of factors that influence the nature of the processor's instruction set and the candidate microarchitectures for implementing the resultant instruction set architecture.

Some of the higher-level issues are:

1. target applications and operating systems.
2. target platform context—e.g., desktop, portable, or server.
3. target cost/performance level.
4. need to support legacy 16-bit and 32-bit code.

Some of the lower-level issues are:

1. target die size and cost.
2. target platform/system environment—e.g., external caches, bus speeds, and I/O speeds.

Suggested Readings

Instruction Set Design

Consider what Michael Flynn on pp. 2-3 in *Computer Architecture, Pipelined and Parallel Processor Design*, Jones and Bartlett, 1995 has to say about instruction set design:

"There are always trade-offs in instruction set design. A well-designed instruction set allows variability in implementation technology and is less sensitive to technology changes. As time goes by, even a well-designed set must undergo changes—additions to accommodate new functionality and perhaps a de-emphasis of older features. Thus, at any moment, a successful architecture includes an instruction set consisting of:

- *A core of frequently used instructions.*
- *Some features extending or correcting limitations in the original design.*
- *Some instructions no longer expected to be used (either superseded or "out-of-vogue"), which remain for reasons of compatibility."*

Also, consider Harold Stone's related comments on p. 9 in *High Performance Computer Architecture*, 3rd Edition, Addison Wesley, 1993:

"… The architect should measure the quality of the architecture across a number of applications that characterize how an architecture is to be used. The effectiveness may vary considerably from application to application, and such measurements should reveal where the architecture is truly beneficial to the user and where other approaches are superior.

A computer architecture might well have some minor but costly inherent flaws that escape the scrutiny of its designer. A different designer who can build essentially the same architecture with those flaws repaired can produce a more effective, and therefore more competitive, machine. Architects cannot hide inefficiency by arguing that hardware costs nothing."

Some typical design decisions that need to be made are:

1. will the design focus on employing multiple parallel pipelines or fewer, deeper pipelines—i.e., a maximum superscalar versus a maximum frequency approach.
2. how many instruction decodes/clock.
3. how many functional units and how deeply will they be pipelined.
4. how will functions be apportioned or assigned to each pipeline stage.
5. what type of caching.

The models employed by the hardware/system co-design teams need to be flexible enough and detailed enough to allow alternatives to this wide range of design issues to be evaluated.

MODEL OF THE MICROPROCESSOR AT THE RTL LEVEL

There has been a rich history of the use of both formal and informal textual and graphical representations of computer architecture. In the following extended Historical Comment, Dr. Mario Barbacci of CMU shares some of that history with us.

HISTORICAL COMMENT

The Evolution of Architecture Description Languages
by
Dr. Mario Barbacci
CMU

Designers and students of computer architectures have always made use of graphical and textual conventions to describe computer architectures. Early notations varied in their degree of formality and descriptive power and were not in widespread use (for reasons that will become apparent later). A significant event in the evolution of architecture description languages took place in 1964 with the publication of a formal description of the recently announced IBM SYSTEM/360 [5]. This description provided a definition for a computer architecture namely, the behavior and the state visible to the programmer:

> "*This paper presents a precise formal description of a complete computer system, the IBM SYSTEM/360. The description is functional: it describes the behavior of the machine as seen by the programmer, irrespective of any particular physical implementation, and expressly specifies the state of every register or facility accessible to the programmer for every moment of system operation at which this information is actually available.*"

continued on next page...

HISTORICAL COMMENT (CONT.)

The Evolution of Architecture Description Languages

The description of SYSTEM/360 consisted of a set of programs in APL [7] organized in two sections, the central processing system (nine programs) and the input/output (five programs). The programs were complemented with auxiliary tables that provided, for example, definitions of variables and locations (line numbers) in the programs where the variables are read or written. The legendary terseness of the language makes a study of the description a slow process at best, and the process is not helped by the naming conventions (e.g., "For brevity, single characters are used for all variables except for those which occur infrequently, such as the panel switches occurring in CP, the control panel program.") Nevertheless, this is a milestone in the evolution of Architecture Description Languages and must read for any serious student of the subject.

As integrated circuits increased in density during the 1960's, new computers began to proliferate and it was possible, for the first time, to collect, study, and classify these artifacts, just like one could study plants or animals or rocks. The publication of [3] was the first attempt to organize computer structures into levels, represented with uniform notations:

"The structures that we call computer systems continue to grow in complexity, in size, and in diversity. This book is linked firmly to the nature of this growth. The book is about the upper levels of computer structure: about instruction sets, which define a computer system at the programming level; and about organizations of processors, memories, switches, input-output devices, controllers, and communication links, which provide the ultimate functioning system. These levels are just emerging into well-defined system levels, with developed symbolic techniques of analysis and synthesis and accumulated engineering know-how, all expressed in a crystallized representation."

The book provided a large collection of detailed examples illustrating actual computers. The authors felt that a sufficiently large number of computers had been designed over the previous 25 years that it was possible to systematize the space of computer designs, to provide a framework for the study of computers as a class of artifacts and not as isolated, independent inventions.

The framework consisted of a hierarchy of levels of descriptions complemented by two notations, one for instruction sets, called ISP, and the other for configurations of major components, called PMS.

According to [3] a digital system can be described at many different levels of detail in order to depict structural or behavioral aspects. Thus a system can be described at the gate level as a network of logic gates and flip-flops whose behavior is specified by timing diagrams, Boolean equations, or truth tables. While a complete digital computer could be described at this level, the amount of information to be conveyed would be too extensive for a human designer to comprehend, and higher levels are introduced to abstract details: Combinatorial and Sequential Register Transfer levels.

The existence of digital components capable of interpreting instructions stored in memory (i.e., instruction set processors) motivated Bell and Newell to introduce the programming level of description.

continued on next page...

HISTORICAL COMMENT (CONT.)

The Evolution of Architecture Description Languages

At the programming level, the basic components are the interpretation cycle, the machine instructions, and operations (all of which are defined as register transfer level operations). The programming level arises from the need to describe the behavior rather than the structure of processors—in particular the behavior as seen by the programmers of the machine (i.e., the goal of Falkoff et al, in the SYSTEM/360 description)

The system levels correspond closely to the technology available for analysis and synthesis of computer systems. During the 1940's and 1950's computer architectures were simple, often linked to one unique implementation, and the need for a description language were satisfied by logic diagrams and Boolean equations. The situation changed with the introduction of SYSTEM/360 because it consisted of a large family of implementation of the same instruction set—the architecture had to be abstracted from the implementation, thus the need for a different notation. In 1971, Bell and Newell characterized the situation thus,

"Each of these levels exists in fact, precisely to the extent that a technology has become well developed. Thus both the circuit level and the lower half of the logic level (combinatorial and sequential circuits) are highly polished technologies. They are what one learns today, if one wants to become a computer engineer. Textbooks exist, courses are taught, and there is a flourishing, cumulative technical literature. As we progress up the systems levels, matters become progressively worse. The register-transfer level is not yet well established, although there is considerable current activity and the next few years may see its universal establishment."

No such consensus was apparent at the programming or system levels although the increased complexity of computer systems was increasing the importance of these higher levels.

One decade later technology advances had led to an explosion in the number of computer types, with a large number of instruction sets and data types, as reflected in a revised and expanded version of [3]. By the time [8] was published, the programming level of description was firmly established and the leading notation, ISPS, a formally defined programming language, based on the original ISP notation had been used in a variety of analysis and synthesis applications. In ISPS [1] a processor is described by declarations of carriers and procedures specifying the behavior of the system:

1. information carriers - registers and memories used to store programs, data, and other state information.

2. instruction set - procedures describing the behavior of the processor instructions.

3. addressing modes - procedures describing the operand and instruction fetch and store operations.

4. interpretation cycle - typically, the main procedure of an ISP description. It defines the fetch, decode, and execute sequence of a digital processor.

continued on the next page....

The Evolution of Architecture Description Languages

The PMS notation remained a graphical language for describing uniprocessor structures but never evolved to the point of being formalized and implemented as a serious design tool.

The story was very different at the lower levels of detail, where a number of notations known collectively as "Hardware Description Languages" continued to be developed and used. Hardware Description Languages (HDL) are notations and languages that facilitate the documentation, design, simulation, and manufacturing of digital computer systems [2]. Most of these languages (see suggested reading material) were used mostly in research and academic environments, as input notations for experimental simulation, analysis, or synthesis tools. In the industrial world, however, additional requirements had to be considered, namely the need to create, modify and support many design and manufacturing details across manufacturers and throughout the product's lifecycle.

To address these requirements, several industry-supported efforts have led to standard formats to represent product data in a standard format. Two of these efforts were the Very High Speed Integrated Circuits Hardware Description Languages (VHDL) [6] and the Electronic Design Interchange Format (EDIF). VHDL and EDIF became standards in 1987 (IEEE Standard, 1076 and EIA RS44 respectively) [4].

In VHDL each hardware entity has an interface and a body or architecture. The interface descriptions consist of input and output ports and various attributes associated with the interface, such as pin names, timing constraints, etc. The body describes the function or the structure of the design. The body may be written as an algorithm or as a combination of algorithms and real hardware representations (e.g., gates, arithmetic-logic units) or made up totally as a structure of real hardware representations.

EDIF provides a hierarchical syntax for data necessary for chip and printed circuit board fabrication. Note that EDIF is a format, not a language. EDIF's primary application is as a means of transferring design data from the design environment to the fabrication environment. The format provides for libraries, cells, views, interfaces, and information on the content within each cell. Test data, mask layout data, physical layout data, connectivity data, and simulation data can be represented in EDIF.

These various standards attempt to answer the needs of the various product life-cycle activities. However, the development of these standards have not been coordinated, and users still need a thorough understanding of the objectives and uses of each standard. The technology of HDLs has not matured to the point that a standard language or format can satisfy the wide diversity of product description requirements, at least for the foreseeable future.

By the early 80's, the dimensions of an emerging level, the network level, were noticed. It had the character of a different level because the performance of a network was far more dependent on operating systems, network topology, protocols, bandwidth, than on the instruction sets of individual processors.

At the time of this writing, 15 years after [8], an explosion on the number of network types, protocols, and communications has taken place. Millions of personal computer users connected to intranets and the Internet have created an enormous demand for new technology. The technology is changing so rapidly that it will be a while before "the level" begins to settle down and "the notation" emerges.

continued on the next page...

HISTORICAL COMMENT (CONT.)

References: The Evolution of Architecture Description Languages

1. [Barbacci 81] Mario R. Barbacci, "Instruction Set Processor Specifications (ISPS): The Notation and its Applications," *IEEE Transactions on Computers*, C-30, 1, (January), 1981.

2. [Barbacci 93] Mario R. Barbacci, Ron Waxman, "Hardware Description Languages," in *Encyclopedia of Computer Science*, 3rd Edition, Anthony Ralston and Edwin D. Reilly (Eds.), Van Nostrand Reinhold, 1993.

3. [Bell and Newell 71] C. Gordon Bell and Allen Newell, *Computer Structures: Readings and Examples*, McGraw-Hill Book Company, 1971.

4. [EDF 87] *EIA/EDIF/IS-44 Specification, Electronic Design Interchange Format*, Version 2.0.0, May 1987.

5. [Falkoff 1964] A.D. Falkoff, K.E. Iverson, E.H. Sussenguth, "A formal description of SYSTEM/360," *IBM Systems Journal*, Vol. 3, No. 3, 1964.

6. [IEEE 87] IEEE, "VHDL Language Reference Manual," Standard 1076, December 1987.

7. [Iverson 62] Kenneth E. Iverson, *A Programming Language*, Wiley, 1962.

8. [Siewiorek 82], Siewiorek, Daniel P., Bell, C. Gordon and Newell, Allen, *Computer Structures: Principles and Examples*, McGraw-Hill, 1982.

Additional Readings: The Evolution of Architecture Description Languages

1. Mario Barbacci, "A Comparison of Register Transfer Languages for Describing Computers and Digital Systems," *IEEE Transactions on Computers*, Vol C-24, No. 2, February 1975, pp. 137-150.

2. Robert Piloty, Mario Barbacci, Dominique Borrione, Donald Dietmeyer, Fredrick Hill, Pat Skelly, "CONLAN Report," *Lecture Notes in Computer Science*, 151, Springer-Verlag.

3. Yaohan Chu (Guest Editor), special issue on Computer Hardware Description Languages, *Computer*, Vol. 7 No. 12, December 1974, pp. 18-22.

4. Stephen Y.S. Su (Guest Editor), special issue on Computer Hardware Description Languages, *Computer*, Vol. 10 No. 6, June 1977, pp. 10-13.

5. Mario Barbacci and Takao Uehara (Guest Editors), special issue on Computer Hardware Description languages, *Computer*, Vol. 18 No. 2, February 1985, pp. 6-8.

6. Allen Dewey (Guest Editor), "VHDL and Next-Generation Design Automation," Guest Editor's Introduction to *IEEE Design and Test of Computers*, Vol. 9, No. 2, June 1992, special issue on VHDL.

7. "Three Decades of HDLs," Collections of short notes by various authors: Part 1, "CDL Through TI-HDL," *IEEE Design and Test of Computers*, Vol. 9, No. 2, June 1992; Part 2, "CONLAN through Verilog," *IEEE Design and Test of Computers*, Vol. 9, No. 3, September 1992.

Among the important issues to consider when modeling a microprocessor are: what the model will be used for, the type of model required and its representation, the ease of use of the model, and cost. The specific level of abstraction is selected consistent with the goals of the modeling effort. It is not only important to decide how the logic and circuit designs of the actual microprocessor are going to be represented but also how the "simulation environment" within which the microprocessor will be "exercised" will itself be designed and implemented. This is the part of the system that generates stimulus for the model and checks that it is behaving properly. For a microprocessor, the simulation environment must be able to display and check the state of various conditions within the processor and it must accommodate such things as distributing clock signals and modeling of the main memory and system bus architecture and protocols. A software simulator may be coupled to various hardware emulators to form a hardware/software co-simulation environment.

Modeling is a compromise between accuracy (the level of representation, the details described, and the precision with which they are described) and speed. An accurate model of a microprocessor at the physical level would have to model physical device characteristics. A simulation of such a model would be so slow that it would be completely useless for functional compatibility tests. Moreover, there needs to be a tool that can be used to conveniently describe a microprocessor's complex behavior and structure. Specialized high-level programming languages have evolved to meet this need.

Suggested Readings

Full-Custom and Semi-Custom Design

From page 3 of the book by Ulrich Golze, (with Peter Blinzer, Elmar Cochlovius, Michael Schafers, and Klaus-Peter Wachsmann), *VLSI Chip Design with the Hardware Description Language VERILOG*, Springer, 1996, which was mentioned earlier, we have:

"In full-custom design, all details of the circuit had now to be designed, the transistors had to be dimensioned and composed to meaningful geometrical layouts which were afterward verified by an analog simulator. A layout is a true-to-scale template for the structures to be produced, however strongly enlarged. ... Around the middle of the 1980s, semi-custom design style became the workhorse of VLSI design. With the user interface again moving upward, the semi-custom design employs optimized library cells, typically logic gates, adders, etc., composes them to logic wiring diagrams (gate netlists, schematics) and simulates them logically. The transformation into a geometric layout is achieved by efficient placement and layout programs. The designer, in general, is not involved with single transistors, he often does not even know the internal structure of the library cells used."

There is substantial debate in the industry about the adequacy of current hardware description languages to handle system-level designs, behavioral and logic synthesis, simulation, and formal verification. See for example, "DAC 97 Panel: Next-Generation HDLs," by L. Lavango and N. Collins, IEEE Design & Test of Computers, July-September, 1997, Vol. 13, No. 3, p. 7.

Programming languages, extended to include notions of time, parallelism and synchronization, and architectural and hardware data structure extensions, have emerged to dominate in semi-custom design. Such languages are called hardware description languages or HDLs. A model, which is the definition of the microprocessor implemented as a program in the HDL, can be simulated by compiling and executing it. Since the program can be written to describe the microprocessor at any level of abstraction, the simulation will be of the microprocessor at that particular level.

GOLDEN REPRESENTATION

The HDL description becomes the "*golden representation*" of the microprocessor. Changes are made to the golden representation, and all other representations must change to match the golden representation. The flow of change is one way, starting with the golden representation. When this representation becomes detailed enough, it can be transformed by a process called *logic synthesis* to be input to the layout and placement stage of the design process.

Independent descriptions of the microprocessor can be made for each level of abstraction. Beginning with its behavioral description and employing step-wise refinement to model more and more of the underlying structure, one could extend the description down to the gate level. These lower-level design representations must be "cross-verified" against the *golden representation* to ensure they are functionally equivalent. Cross-verification is necessary mainly when the lower-level representations are generated in part or totally by hand. If they are completely machine-generated, cross-verification is less necessary unless the software tools that generate the lower-level representations are suspect.

ARTICLES ON CD-ROM

 A full text version of "Introduction to High-Level Synthesis," by Daniel D. Gajski and Loganath Ramachandran, *IEEE Design & Test of Computers*, Winter 1994 can be found on the companion CD-ROM. Two related articles, "Specification and Design of Embedded Hardware-Software Systems," by Daniel D. Gajski and Frank Vahid, *IEEE Design & Test of Computers*, Spring 1995 and "Introduction to the Scheduling Problem," by Robert A. Walker and Samit Chaudhuri, *IEEE Design & Test*, Summer, 1995 are also on the CD-ROM.

A growing number of digital system designs are currently represented in one of two popular hardware description languages, Verilog or VHDL.

Selecting one over the other is seen by some as mostly a matter of religion. However there are some concrete reasons why one might be better suited to a particular design than the other. If Verilog was to be compared to C, then it might be reasonable to say that VHDL is like C++. VHDL is a much more complex language that allows practically all aspects of its definition to be redefined. In most cases VHDL is used with standard packages that define the operators to work in the most logical and expected fashion. A typical complaint is that VHDL is difficult to learn and is a verbose language. Some authors state that one advantage of VHDL is that its simulation semantics are reasonably well defined; thus, most vendors' simulators for VHDL behave exactly the same. However, we caution that the same can be said about Verilog simulators noting that they are based on a de facto definition as evidenced by the Verilog simulator of Cadence Design Systems, Inc. VHDL is the accepted HDL used for military applications and also is often used for describing extensible libraries. On the other hand, Verilog has gained widespread acceptance because it is easy to learn and many consider it more practical. Many engineers say they were able to use Verilog in just a few days. The Verilog language looks familiar because it is like a combination of Pascal and C mixed together with additional constructs to represent hardware design and simulation semantics.

BEHAVIORAL (FUNCTIONAL) SIMULATION

Unfortunately, hardware designs, like software designs, usually have some errors (bugs). For a complex design like a microprocessor, there are likely to be thousands of bugs that have to be identified and fixed throughout the design process. Obviously any speedup in the process of identifying bugs will shorten the entire design cycle. Simulators typically provide mechanisms for displaying selected design variables, either every cycle or when they change value. This information can be used by other tools that allow the data to be displayed in a more convenient and meaningful manner as either waveforms or state dumps. There are two basic styles of writing simulators to study the behavior of a particular model—cycle-based and event-driven. Cycle-based simulation corresponds to examining model variables "every cycle" whereas event-driven simulation corresponds to examining model variables "when they change."

One of the problems with describing and simulating hardware is that hardware can execute a number of things in parallel. However, these items are resolved at different stages of execution in a simulator. For example, a 3-input AND gate may have only two inputs ready when the simulator has reached the stage of executing the model that represents the AND gate. This means that the evaluation of the AND gate will not produce the final result and will have to be evaluated again once the 3rd input is ready.

cycle-based simulation

Using C++ as an HDL

The K6 family of microprocessors requires a rather large systems-based simulation environment. The team decided that contemporary hardware description languages were not good for the general purpose programming that would be required. They chose to model the microarchitecture using C++ and to then take advantage of this general purpose programming language to represent the entire model (i.e., the design plus the simulation environment). There were a number of advantages to using C++:

1. *object-oriented nature*: The object-oriented nature of the C++ programming language allowed the team to define an elegant way to represent the logic of the design, and was flexible enough to generate complex models of expected behavior.

2. *ability to override operators*: One main advantage that HDLs have over programming languages is their ability to manipulate individual bits of data. To overcome this limitation the operator() function was overridden to represent bit and part selection.

3. *expressiveness*: It was possible to write equations in the form of "signal1(3,2) = signal2(1,0)" or "signal1 = signal 2 & signal 3" which are just as convenient as using one of the hardware description languages.

4. *speed*: The K6 3D simulator needed to be very fast. This was another key reason for choosing a compiled language. Minimizing the amount of time to debug a problem, making a modification, recompiling, and verifying that the problem is indeed fixed was key to the success of the project.

5. *debugging aids*: design assertions and instrumentation code were easily included in the simulator.

6. *execution in desktop PCs*: ability to run simulations of large systems on desktop PCs and workstations with relatively modest amounts of main memory as well as on servers.

7. *quick development loop*: relatively fast simulate-debug-change-compile loop compared to typical HDL environments.

For a discussion of related issues related to the use of "traditional" programming languages as HDLs, see the article, "Using a Programming Language for Digital System Design," by R. K. Gupta and S. Y. Liao, *IEEE Design & Test of Computers*, April-June 1997 on the book's companion CD-ROM.

In this video clip, Amos Ben-Meir, Principal Designer of the K6 3D, addresses the question, "Was software simulation used in the verification of the K6 3D?" and Warren Stapleton, the K6 3D's Leader of Model Development and Verification, addresses the question, "Why did the K6 3D team choose to use its own proprietary modeling and simulation tools?"

Given the importance simulation plays in the design and implementation of microprocessors, we have included three simulators on the CD-ROM. In Chapter 3, we give pseudo-RTL descriptions that describe various chunks of microarchitecture logic and recommend the reader simulated them on these simulators.

In *cycle-based* simulation many things (e.g., register loads and signal transitions) can occur in parallel. These actions are "flattened and re-ordered" in order to create the effect of all events occurring in their proper order. Cycle-based simulation eliminates the need to re-evaluate sections of code due to having unresolved terms. Again, this is done by flattening and reordering so that everything computes and resolves in one pass through the simulator. In a cycle-based simulation, there are inputs defined and expected outputs derived for every cycle. Cycle-based simulators have difficulty in dealing with multiple clock domains and generally cannot deal with delay simulation at all.

Event-driven simulators take the approach of re-evaluating models every time there is an event on one of the inputs or variables of the model. It is easier to handle multiple clocking domains with this type of simulator, as well as delay simulation. The disadvantage is that this type of simulator is generally slower than cycle-based simulators. *event-driven*

Cycle-accurate model refers to a model describing the behavior of a functional unit down to the cycle level. This means that the functional unit's behavior is modeled accurately enough so that the model's pins behave identically to the "real thing" on a cycle-by-cycle basis. This allows generating test vectors from the model so that the "real thing" can be verified with these. An example of a model that may not be cycle-accurate is a performance model. A performance model may only approximate the cycle behavior since its purpose is to gauge the performance of the functional unit within some range of accuracy. *cycle-accurate*

As mentioned earlier, one of the most important uses of simulators is to verify the behavior of and to debug the system being modeled.

HISTORICAL COMMENT
Verification Technology
From P. Shepherd, *Integrated Circuit Design, Fabrication, and Test*, McGraw-Hill, 1996, pp. 120-121, we learn: *"Before software tools were developed, the verification of a particular circuit design could only be achieved by constructing a prototype circuit. While the design could use standard digital and analogue techniques to design the circuit on paper, it was almost impossible to determine whether the circuit would perform as expected to in practice. …. When built, the circuit would be thoroughly tested and design modifications made on the basis of these tests. The next version of the process was then constructed and the process repeated. Such a technique was very time-consuming and expensive. …. Redesign and rework of the mask set added further delay and expense to the product development."*

Debugging a design usually differs significantly from debugging a program. When writing programs, source level debug tools that allow the code to be single stepped while examining individual variables are key to boosting debug productivity. Although this capability is available in some simulator environments it is not used that often. A good environment for debugging a design should provide fast access to all of the key signal values, in a logically formatted display, after each cycle has completed. Also, many simulators keep a history of selected variables so that one can step backwards in time from an erroneous state to determine the events that forced the system into that state. Keeping in mind the simplicity of most hardware description languages, the bugs are more likely to be conceptual in nature rather than simple coding errors.

MODEL AT THE GATE AND CIRCUIT LEVELS

Gate-level models are models that describe the function of a particular block or chip at the gate level. A gate is generally a basic building block of the design that implements a simple Boolean function. The gates are then connected together to create a more complex functional unit. Circuit-level models are typically models that go one level below the gates (i.e., to the transistor level).

GATE AND CIRCUIT LEVEL SIMULATION AND HARDWARE EMULATION

The simulation models for the basic gates are generally part of a gate library that contains multiple representations of these gates (in chip design, this is typically layout, timing models, ATPG models, transistor level netlist/schematic and simulation models). When doing gate-level simulation, the functional unit being simulated must already have a netlist with a gate implementation. This netlist can then be simulated with one of the multiple commercial simulators or proprietary in-house simulators.

When doing functional simulation with circuit-level models (transistor-level models), there is usually an abstraction phase where the transistors are translated into gates and then these gates are simulated. This is done to improve the speed of transistor level simulations. There are simulators that are able to simulate at the transistor level, treating the transistor as a 3-node switch and computing the values on each node. This is typically very slow and requires much compute time. In addition, many transistor topologies that have analog behavior do not lend themselves well to switch-level simulation—i.e., it is difficult for the simulator to resolve what the circuit is doing. These analog sections typically require creation of simple RTL or gate models to describe their logic behavior.

ARTICLES ON CD-ROM

 Full text versions of two articles that deal with the topics discussed in this subsection: see "Circuit Techniques in a 266-MHz MMX-Enabled Processor," by Donald A. Draper, Matt Crowley, John Holst, Greg Favor, Albrecht Schoy, Jeff Trull, Amos Ben-Meir, Rajesh Khanna, Dennie Wendell, Ravi Krishna, Joe Nolan, Dhiraj Mallick, Hamid Partovi, Mark Roberts, Mark Johnson, and Thomas Lee, *IEEE Journal of Solid-State Circuits*, November 1997 and "An x86 Microprocessor with Multimedia Extensions," by Donald A. Draper, Matthew P. Crowley, John Holst, Greg Favor, Albrecht Schoy, Amos Ben-Meir, Jeff Trull, Raj Khanna, Dennie Wendell, Ravi Krishna, Joe Nolan, Hamid Partovi, Mark Johnson, Tom Lee, Dhiraj Mallick, Gene Frydel, Anderson Vuong, Stanley Yu, Reading Maley, and Bruce Kaufmann 1997 *ISSCC Digest of Technical Papers*. You can find the full text versions of both of the above articles on the companion CD-ROM.

DEFINITIONS

Co-simulation and Co-verification

Co-simulation and co-verification are terms generally used to describe a situation where two different types of models (gates and RTL for example) are simulated together. Both models receive identical stimulus, then their outputs are compared on every cycle to guarantee that the two models behave identically. The goal of this type of simulation is to prove functional equivalence between two representations of a design.

Hardware emulation is the process of taking a functional unit netlist or a full-chip netlist and building it in some form of real hardware, such as FPGAs and memories. Then that hardware can be plugged into a real system for testing (though at fairly low frequencies, 100's of KHz or a few number of MHz). The hardware can also be used as a very fast simulator provided there is an environment that allows passing stimulus to the emulator and receiving the outputs from the emulator and then comparing the outputs with expected results to check for correctness.

hardware emulation

One of the goals of emulation is to provide a way to run the design in a real-world environment. Usually this means being able to plug the emulator into the actual socket that the chip will plug into and using the complete final product as if it had a real chip installed. This goal can be achieved in several different ways. One approach is simply to build an extremely fast simulator using parallel processors to get the required speed. The more traditional approach is to use a large number of interconnected FPGAs (Field Programmable Gate Arrays) and program them with a version of the gate-level netlist of the design.

DESIGN NOTE

Using Emulation in the Design and Testing of the
K6 Family of Microprocessors

Hardware emulation was one of the keys to the success of the K6 project. The team programmed interconnected FPGAs with a version of the gate-level netlist of the design. They used the commercially available Quickturn emulation system to do this. What made the K6 emulation unique was that the team was able to get the gate-level design working quite some time before the initial fabrication of the chip. Prior to committing the design to manufacturing they were able to initialize and run all of the available x86 operating systems and run a significant number of standard applications, thus proving their design and its compatibility very early in the design cycle.

In addition to finding a handful of obscure bugs that probably would not have been found with conventional simulation, they were able to verify the built-in engineering debug features of the chip that would have required too many cycles to verify with the C++ model.

There were also some intangible benefits of emulation: The emulation lab provided experience for a multi-disciplined team that included BIOS developers, system experts, and chip designers. This experience was valuable when silicon returned from the fabrication facility. When the team booted the Windows 95 Operating System for the first time in the emulation laboratory the event gave an additional boost to the morale of the entire development team, which helped them get through the last few months before chip tapeout.

GENERATE NETLISTS AND PHYSICAL LAYOUT

The gates described at the behavioral level are selected from a library of cells which have been created for optimal realization of the logical functions in a particular process. These cells consist of nands, nors, inverters, flip-flops, latches, multiplexers, and other specialized cells. The first task is defining the physical and electrical characteristics of these cells.

The dimensions and pin placements of the cell needs to be expressed in multiples of the metal pitch, which is defined by the process capabilities. The routing pickup points likewise are determined by the metal pitch, and as many as possible should be placed in the cell to optimize the routing density. The power and ground supplies are designed to minimize the resistive drop to the transistors and to avoid creating excessively high current densities which could lead to early reliability failures due to electromigration. To avoid performance loss due to resistance in the diffusions of the transistors, many metal-to-diffusion contacts need to be used. This is still true even with modern diffusions which use a silicided layer for reducing resistance. Another characteristic of cell design is that the gate resistance combined with the gate capacitance causes a delay of the input signal from the pickup point to the other end of the gate represented by the transistor width. This delay increases as the square of the length of the gate over thin gate oxide. Furthermore, it is a characteristic of the silicidation process that narrower gates form the silicide poorly, resulting in a higher effective sheet resistance, which further aggravates the problem. For this reason, it is necessary to limit the maximum length of gate poly which can be done by using smaller transistors with many legs, by strapping out the poly, or by using pickup points in the center of the gate, between the n-channel and p-channel transistor blocks. All these things impair the routeability of the cell, which needs to be balanced against the performance loss of the poly resistance.

Next, the sizes of the n-channel and p-channel transistor blocks need to be defined. The optimum ratio for speed is in the range of 1.4 to 1.8, for p-channel width relative to n-channel. The switching point will be slightly less than $V_{DD/2}$. This switching point should be the same for all gates, whether nands, nors, or other gates. This means that not all the available transistor width in the cell will be used, but this makes timing simulation using the static timing analyzer more accurate. Cells of different drive strengths are required for optimum timing, but for drive strengths beyond three or four times the minimum, buffer cells should be used. It is also possible to have all the cells have versions optimized for both rising and falling edges, although this will lead to an extensive proliferation of the number of cells.

The design of the flip-flops is optimized for speed and other characteristics, such as minimum hold time and setup time. Dynamic logic can be incorporated into the flip-flops to achieve a performance increase. Another specialized design is to put delay cells into the clock input path of the flip-flop to achieve cycle-stealing or delay transfer between critical paths. Similar strategies can be used with level-sensitive transparent latches. To facilitate testing and debugging, the flip-flops need to have scan designed in. This means adding extra logic and routing scan clocks and the scan data in and scan data out, all of which add cost and complexity. But, there is probably no other way to achieve a high level of fault coverage or to be able to debug the chip when there is a logical bug or a pattern sensitivity.

After building the cells, it is very important to characterize them for timing. The first requirement is to determine the maximum delays for the

characterizing cell timing

frequency-limiting maximum-delay paths. This is done by simulating the cells with the typical process at nominal voltage and worst-case temperature. The propagation delay needs to be determined for each input to each output path or arc. The delay is simulated as a function of the output loading and the input transition time, and is commonly represented as a matrix from which the actual timing delay is interpolated or extrapolated. In the case of state-dependent delays for cells such as exclusive-or gates, the delay of one arc is dependent on the logical state of the other input. This cannot be known to a static timing analyzer, so the worst-case delay needs to be selected. In the case where there are simultaneously switching inputs, such as from a bus, the delay time is again affected. For example, in a nand gate, if all the inputs switch from low to high within a small specified time of each other, the output delay is significantly increased, as compared to the case in which only one input switches while the other inputs stay high.

hold-time requirements

It is also necessary to guarantee that min-path, or hold time requirements, are met. The simulation conditions use the fast process corner at high voltage and low temperature. In the case of state-dependent delays, the shortest delay needs to be selected. Similarly for simultaneously switching inputs, the condition for the fastest output needs to be considered. For example, in the case of the nand again, if all of the inputs switch at the same time from high to low, the load is pulled up by all the p-channel transistors in the nand gate, not just one of them.

The above analysis becomes much more complicated for complex gates such as and-or-invert (AOI) cells and all combinations of input timing need to be exhaustively simulated. Similarly, the logical function needs to be verified in comparison to the Verilog or behavioral model by running an exhaustive combination of all possible inputs. This is especially important for complex gates such as tristate drivers and for AOI gates.

Full-Custom Macro Blocks

The other major category of physical development involves the full-custom designed macro blocks, such as cache memories, register files, input/output drivers, phase-locked loop and clock distribution systems. As with the standard cells, these blocks need to have their timing characteristics and logical function thoroughly specified and verified. The timing is determined after design and layout of the macro blocks by extracting the capacitance of the nodes and resimulating. The functional verification is accomplished by simulating the circuit and comparing the outputs, vector by vector, with the behavioral model.

The design of arrayed structures, such as memories, requires speed to be balanced with the margin of bit-line signal at the sense amps. This is a very carefully balanced race condition, with the sense-amp strobe arriving not too early before the signal has developed on the bit lines and not too late, losing performance. Usual signal requirements at the sense amp are 150 mV at typical timing condition. To guarantee robust design, every race in the circuit needs to be simulated extensively to ensure adequate margin.

Testability is addressed by means of a built-in self test mechanism. Testing a large array solely by means of external parallel vectors or by scan is prohibitively expensive in test time, so an internal engine to generate test vectors is included. It should completely test the array for most of the known failure mechanisms in memories; e.g., such a built-in self-test pattern is the 13N algorithm, which tests the complete array in thirteen passes.

Due to the large area or number of transistors in the design, the yield of regular, arrayed structures (such as memories) can be increased by including redundant rows or columns or both. The regular array is tested and if a defect is found, the defective row is deselected and a spare row is switched in instead.

Among other design features for arrayed structures, it is important to include the ability to bit-map the array for debug purposes, using scan or by using parallel vectors. Some arrayed structures use single-ended bit lines, and in these cases, bit-line coupling needs to be considered and designed. Some designs have used cascade sense amps, but these are too noise sensitive and should be avoided.

Chip Input/Output designs need to match the requirements of the external system at the same time as interfacing to the internal circuitry. Since I/O voltages are often different from the supply voltage used for the rest of the chip, reliable interfaces need to be designed between the two voltage domains, often requiring level shifting. The I/O voltage, being usually higher, imposes special design requirements involving the gate oxide. Excessively high voltage across the gate oxide is a wearout mechanism and a reliability hazard which needs to be addressed.

A special macro block is the phase locked loop, or PLL, which is used for synchronizing the internal clock signal with the external and for multiplying up the external or system bus clock frequency. The requirements are for stability and frequency tracking over a wide range of process conditions. The output frequency of the PLL should be as constant as possible. Jitter, which is variation in the clock period, effectively decreases the amount of time in the cycle available to logic.

The clock distribution system is required to deliver the clock signal to all the flip-flops, latches, and macros in the chip at nearly the same time. *clock distribution* The deviation from this time, called skew, is an important component of the hold time analysis. The main cause of skew in the clock distribution system is local variations in the amount of clock load. After the chip is assembled, this load is extracted and the required number of local clock buffers is programmed in using one of the metal contact layers.

Netlists describe the topology and connectivity of the circuit elements. Netlists usually adhere to a standard format (such as EDIF), which allow them to be used on different computer platforms and enabling various tools to be integrated based on the standard format.

Timing Analysis

Each major functional block of the chip is typically realized as a top-level module based on the gate-level netlists and on the full-custom macro blocks. The initial timing of the gate netlist is accomplished with a static timing analyzer. A default wire load model is used and can be based, for example, on a non linear, statistical capacitive loading model which is a function of fan-out. The module is then floorplanned and the cells placed by hand with the help of some in-house placement programs. Following this, the cells are connected together according to the netlist. Using the placement data, a minpath analysis tool is run using clock skew estimates to ensure hold time constraints are met. After routing, a parasitic-extraction tool is run on the routed database to extract distributed RC delay values. The net delays are computed (e.g., by Ultima Delay Calculator) and input into a timing analyzer. Timing analysis is performed on each top level module, and ultimately on the whole chip. Design rule checks and layout versus schematic checks are run on the completed route. Finally, the database is analyzed for electrical integrity purposes (wire lengths, electromigration, max-transition violations, electrical rules checking, etc.). Any type of undesired results along the design flow causes looping iterations to take place until the entire chip meets all of the design constraints and is ready for tapeout.

The timing analysis and allocation or budgeting methodology is based on gate-level static timing analysis tools, more-accurate RC extraction tools, and delay calculation tools. Various in-house programs are often used to bind all of the above together. The timing analysis and budgeting methodologies are both designed to work together to provide consistency and accuracy throughout the evolution of the chip by making use of as much detailed design information as is available at any given time. As the design evolves, the timing methodology is required to support the following activities. In the early timing phase, time budgeting is done at the block and sub-block level to drive and check the consistency of timing constraints for synthesis or manual design. In the middle timing phase, pre- and post-layout timing analysis of major design blocks is done in the context of the whole chip, before the entire chip is ready to be timed. In the late timing phase, post-layout RC extraction and timing analysis are done on the entire chip.

Cell Placement

Most cells are placed by using text-based directives which are read by an in-house set of programs. A graphical display of the results aids in integration. Most of the chip is placed using these scripts which greatly aid layout productivity and yield density and timing results similar to a full custom design.

The top-level modules are constructed such that they include all logic and any wires passing through their "air-space". The inputs and outputs of each top level module are routed to a predefined I/O footprint which was derived by understanding the routing requirements of each top-level net. This allows most of the chip construction to be done early during the construction of the top level modules. Construction of the chip then consists merely of placing the top level modules and stitching them together with very short final routes.

TI Kilby Noyce

MASK GENERATION, WAFER FABRICATION, AND PACKAGING

Following assembly of the chip, the database goes through an extended release procedure which checks the layout versus schematic and verifies that the drawn geometries match the design rules defined by the process development group. At this point the database is taped out to the mask generation group. At mask generation, the first operation is to size several of the layers according to the latest data from the fab. Here the poly layer is tuned to get the best transistor channel length, for example. A final extended release procedure is done at this step. Following this, the database is fractured, that is, the complex polygons are broken up into rectangles, so that they can be handled by the mask writing hardware. The data are written on to the reticle which is a chrome-covered quartz plate used to project the patterns onto the resist-covered wafer when exposed by ultraviolet light in a machine called a stepper. The data are written onto the reticle using an electron beam machine. The data are then etched in the chrome and the plate inspected. This is repeated for all the mask layers used in the fab.

When the mask plates are shipped to the fab, the wafer fabrication process begins. The initial AMD-K6 processor was fabricated, for example, on a 0.35 micron CMOS process with five layers of metal, shallow trench isolation, tungsten local interconnect, and C4 flip-chip die attach. As is discussed in Chapter 2, the K6 3D design has migrated to a similar 0.25 micron process. The shallow trench isolation is required for tighter active area packing and smaller transistor width variation. The tungsten local interconnect is used to connect poly and diffusion without an intervening contact layer. It provides tighter layout of SRAM cells, standard cells, and custom macros. It is realized by a damascene tungsten process, which means the interconnect pattern is defined by trenches etched in the oxide, filled with tungsten and later polished off. Chemical-mechanical polishing is an integral part of the process, providing planarization, stacked vias, and metalization density unobtainable by any other means. The C4 flip-chip die attach allows better power routing on the chip and low-inductance power supply connections to the package. The process is based on p-epi on a p+ substrate for less susceptibility to latchup. The transistors use a seventy-angstrom-thick gate oxide and the metal pitch is 1.4 microns, 1.8 microns, and 4.8 microns for metal layers 1-3, 4, and 5, respectively.

Following completion of the wafers and the deposition of the lead-tin solder bumps, they are tested by an automatic tester using an instrument called a cobra probe which contacts all the solder bumps with probe pins. The test program consists of a series of routines to verify the operation of every part of the processor. The built-in self-test structures are driven by this procedure to exercise each of the full-custom macros (except the PLL, which is verified by measuring the generated clock signal). There are four scan chains that are used to load the test patterns into the flip-flops. The data is then clocked through, captured in the downstream flip-flops, scanned out and compared with the expected values. In addition to this, the tester applies parallel test vectors to the input and output pins of the processor to complete the test. The test results are then recorded and the wafer is sent for packaging.

The wafers are cut up into separate die and, using a die location map, the good die are mounted onto a ceramic substrate with metalized contacts on the surface for contacting the solder bumps. The solder bumps melt during the refill heating step and make strong mechanical and electrical contact. A potting compound is then forced under the die, between the solder bumps, to make a more rigid assembly which increases reliability. Then decoupling capacitors are attached by reflow. These capacitors provide more stability to the power supply on the chip in the presence of electrical noise. After attaching the lid, the packaged part is sent for final test and measurement of its maximum frequency. Based on their performance, the parts are shipped in various speed grades to the customer.

Video on CD-ROM

 On the companion CD-ROM, there is a tutorial-level video on the steps involved in the fabrication of contemporary microprocessors and chips. There is also a film interview with Bill Siegle, AMD's Chief Scientist, about this technology.

The following video brings together a number of the issues discussed in the section concerning designing and implementing a microprocessor in the context of an actual microprocessor.

VIDEO ON CD-ROM

 Atiq Raza, Executive Vice-President and Chief Technology Officer of AMD answers the following question, "What was the discipline used to design and implement the K6 3D?"

Having completed out overview of the design and implementation of microprocessors, we will not begin our examination of some of the related platform and systems issues.

We stated earlier in this chapter that because the PC platform dominates high-performance microprocessor-based systems, both in terms of unit and dollar volume, it exerts tremendous influence on the design of PC platform compatible processors, such as the K6 3D. Furthermore we noted that the PC-based systems environment is dominated by Microsoft Windows-based PC platforms. Therefore, we explore this environment by providing a guide to the hardware architecture of PC platforms that support Microsoft Windows. The examples used in the platform and systems chapters are based on a PC platform targeted for desktop consumer 3D graphics applications. 3D graphics continues to evolve, presenting a seemingly ever-growing demand on the bandwidth of the platform's buses, peripherals, and sub-systems. We begin our journey into the systems-related issues of PC platforms by giving a high-level hardware overview of a 3D Graphics PC Platform for the consumer market. It is from this point of view that the systems-related chapters will examine the design and implementation of PC platforms and systems.

DESIGNING AND IMPLEMENTING A 3D GRAPHICS PC PLATFORM

PC PLATFORMS: KEY COMPONENTS AND INTERCONNECTIONS

An abstract view of a 3D graphics PC platform and associated system peripherals is provided by Figure 1.2. Consistent with the definition given for platforms on page xiv in the Preface, the platform consists of a number of key components and interconnections on a motherboard and typically includes a high-performance peripheral bus and ports, main memory, an I/O module, a processor module, and appropriate BIOS code. Generally, the processor and I/O modules are not physically distinct components, although the processor module shown in Figure 1.2 roughly corresponds with Intel's Pentium II cartridge and its Slot 1 interface or AMD's proposed K7 Processor Module and its Slot "A" interface (discussed in the Next-Generation Platforms section in Chapter 6). The processor module typically includes the processor, processor local bus, optional external cache, and a controller for the peripheral bus and main memory. The I/O module, as embodied by the South-Bridge shown, typically includes bus controllers and ports for standardized and optional peripherals.

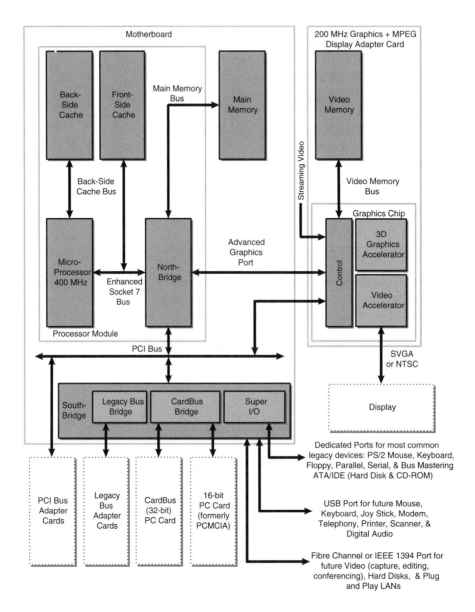

This is a conceptual block diagram of a PC graphics platform for the 1998-1999 time frame. A front-side or back-side cache is generally present on the processor module. Connection to the Display Adapter Card is made via either the Advanced Graphics Port or the PCI Bus. PC Cards are generally found in laptop platforms and not in desktop or server platforms. Conversely, PCI Bus and legacy bus adapter cards are generally found in desktop or server platforms and not in laptops.

Figure 1.2   3D GRAPHICS PC PLATFORM

Legacy Bus Adapter Card Slots
3 x 16-bit ISA Bus Slots

Super I/O

*Connectors for USB, legacy
mouse & keyboard*

Header Connector for legacy FDD

AT-style Power Supply Connector

ATX-style Power Supply Connector

*Header connector for legacy serial ports
(2) and IEEE 1284 parallel port*

PCI Bus Adapter Card Slots
3 x 32-bit PCI Local Bus Slots

AGP Adapter Card Slot

Main Memory Sockets
3 x 168-pin DIMM Sockets

South-Bridge

North-Bridge

Flash BIOS Socket

Microprocessor
in ZIF for Socket 7

Front-Side Cache

*Header connectors for
ATA/IDE drives*

*Dual-Voltage Regulator for
Microprocessor*

Figure 1.3 PHOTOGRAPH OF A 3D GRAPHICS MOTHERBOARD

a. Board Courtesy of Advanced Micro Devices Inc., photo by Smith.

We have printed those features that closely correspond to features shown in Figure 1.2 in regular typeface (but with color accent on the CD-ROM), while new features, or additional feature details, are annotated in italics (and without color accent on the CD-ROM). The microprocessor, front-side cache, and North-Bridge, are implemented directly on the motherboard.

A complete 3D graphics PC system would, consistent with the definition for systems on page xiv in the Preface, consist of extending the foregoing platform descriptions to include an operating system, device drivers including BIOS extensions, other configuration and power management software, and a basic set of applications software. The selection, interaction, configuration and optimization of the components that make up Figure 1.2 and Figure 1.3 is the focus of Chapter 4.

The Microprocessor

The microprocessor, under control of a multi-tasking operating system, carries out interleaved threads of execution for a variety of processes including: the various components of the operating system itself, one or more Application Programming Interfaces (APIs),[3] a number of system-software services and utilities, and one or more user-launched applications.[4] In addition, for 3D graphics-oriented applications, the processor maps graphics scenes to the display's viewport. For this mapping, floating-point operations on vectors are used to perform object modeling, geometry transform, clipping, and lighting calculations. The processor then performs rendering, setup operations, and prepares 3D display (execution) lists in main memory, which contain the mapped scene information and rendering commands for the 3D graphics accelerator. As an alternative to building display lists in main memory, the graphics system may be designed such that the processor directly writes triangle data, parameters, and commands directly to the 3D graphics accelerator.

The processor local bus shown is a 100-MHz Enhanced *Socket 7 Bus* and is discussed in the Processor Bus — Socket 7 section in Chapter 4 and again discussed in the Directions in Optimization of Contemporary Systems section in Chapter 6. The microprocessor is shown mounted in a *Zero Insertion Force (ZIF) socket* compliant with the Socket 7 standard. The term "Socket 7" was introduced in the text inset "Socket 7 Compatible" on page 7.

As discussed further in Chapter 4, many microprocessors today require two power-supply voltages, one for the core and one for the I/O circuitry. Such processors require a dual-voltage regulator, as shown.

ZIF socket, or Zero Insertion Force socket, refers to a socket that permits a device with large numbers of pins to be dropped into the socket rather than requiring pressure insertion.

---

[3]   An API, or Application Programming Interface, is the collection of software routines that comprise a particular system-software facility. Application programs and other system software use API calls to access the services provided by the facility. The API is formally defined by a set of human readable procedure call definitions, including call and return parameters.

[4]   Other than the operating system's user interface, user-launched applications, a few of the utilities and services, and operating system facilities explicitly invoked by the user, the user is generally unaware of the many processes being executed.

The North-Bridge and South-Bridge

Two of the most important components used to couple together the other components on the motherboard are bridge chips referred to as the North-Bridge and the South-Bridge. Here are formal definitions for these components.

DEFINITIONS

Bridge Chips, Chipset, Core Logic, System Logic

In a highly abstract view, *bridge chips* selectively couple (or isolate) two buses. In a more general view, bridge chips couple collections of motherboard components together. Bridge chips historically have been referred to as the *chipset, core logic, or system logic* of the motherboard. The chipset includes control logic for many of the platform components and I/O ports as well as providing data staging and selective coupling among the various buses and components of the platform.

Based on this, we can define the *North-Bridge* and *South-Bridge*.

DEFINITIONS

North-Bridge and South-Bridge

The chipset is frequently partitioned into a North-Bridge device and a South-Bridge device. In the abstract, the North-Bridge selectively couples the processor to the primary peripheral bus (such as the present standard *Peripheral Component Interconnect Bus*, or *PCI Bus*, discussed in the Backplane Bus — PCI section in Chapter 4). More generally however, the *North-Bridge* typically has separate ports (interfaces) to the processor, main-memory, the primary peripheral bus, possibly an external cache, and possibly an AGP (Advanced Graphics Port).

In the abstract, the *South-Bridge* selectively couples the primary peripheral bus with a secondary peripheral bus (such as the ISA Bus, defined shortly in this section). More generally however, the South-Bridge typically has ports coupling the high-performance primary peripheral bus with a number of standard I/O ports and optional peripherals.

 Other perspectives on the principal buses and ports of the North-Bridge and South-Bridge can be found on the CD-ROM in the data sheets for the AMD-640 System Controller and the AMD-645 Peripheral Bus Controller. These devices are the North-Bridge and South-Bridge shown in the motherboard photo in Figure 1.3.

Peripheral Component Interconnect Bus or PCI Bus

The North-Bridge serves a dual role as main memory controller and a bus controller. The bus controller manages the selective coupling of the buses connected to the North-Bridge: the PCI Bus, the AGP (when present), the processor's local bus, and the main memory bus. The bus controller tries whenever possible to isolate these buses in order to maximize the speed of each and to permit concurrent operation of as many buses as possible. However, the bus controller couples buses together whenever a crossing transfer is necessary. The motherboard of Figure 1.3 on page 37 has three 32-bit PCI adapter card slots.

Super I/O is a PC platform component that implements many popular secondary peripheral buses and standard I/O ports.

The South-Bridge typically resides on the PCI Bus and in conjunction with a separate or integrated *Super I/O* module, typically implements the following secondary peripheral buses and standard I/O ports: a legacy Bus (in particular the ISA Bus), dual interfaces for ATA/IDE drives (the most common form of hard disk drive), parallel (compliant with the IEEE 1284 standard), dual legacy serial (compliant with the RS-232 standard), keyboard, legacy Floppy Disk Controller (FDC), and a pointing device (compliant with a PS/2 mouse port). As discussed shortly, support for the ISA Bus is being phased out, support for the Universal Serial Bus (USB) is being added in the near term, and support for the IEEE 1394 (FireWire) is to be added eventually. In laptops, instead of providing legacy bus slots, the South-Bridge is typically used to couple credit-card size adapter cards called PC Cards, via the CardBus, to the PCI Bus. PC Cards come in newer 32-bit, and older 16-bit, versions. All of these I/O ports are again discussed in the PCI-based Ports section in Chapter 4.

The 16-bit PC Cards were originally called PCMCIA cards. A CardBus PC Card is a 32-bit device and is not electrically or physically compatible with the older PCMCIA slots.

REPORT ON CD-ROM

A significant amount of detail regarding the many standard I/O ports associated with the Super I/O component can be found on the CD-ROM in the standard Microsystems Corporation (SMSC) data sheet for their FDC37B78x part, a "128-pin Ultra I/O with ACPI Support and Infrared Remote Control."

Flash EPROM

shadow BIOS

The South-Bridge usually provides access to an external nonvolatile[5] memory, which holds the system BIOS. Increasingly, the nonvolatile memory is in the form of *Flash EPROM*, permitting the BIOS to be upgraded with revisions downloaded from the Internet. Typically, the BIOS is copied during system initialization from the relatively slow nonvolatile memory, to an otherwise unused portion of the faster DRAM that composes main memory. The North-Bridge memory controller subsequently transparently maps requests for BIOS addresses to the *shadow-BIOS* in the DRAM. The South-Bridge also implements the system *Real Time Clock (RTC)* and *CMOS Memory*, a small memory for holding key system hardware configuration parameters. Both the RTC and CMOS memory are provided with independent battery backup, such that they remain functional when power is removed. The large round object between the South-Bridge and the microprocessor in Figure 1.3 on page 37 is the backup battery.

Real Time Clock (RTC)
CMOS Memory

---

[5] Nonvolatile memory retains its contents when power is removed.

Legacy Issues

HISTORICAL COMMENT

Legacy Hardware

The term *legacy* is frequently used as an adjective to describe various PC hardware and software standards that continue to be implemented long after the introduction of better alternatives. The legacy standards live on primarily because of continuing market demand for absolute backward compatibility with earlier generation products. Such compatibility demands persist until the market perceives that the benefits of upgrading overwhelmingly outweigh the costs to upgrade. *legacy*

Generally, legacy PC platform standards are traceable to the *PC/AT (Personal Computer/Advanced Technology)*. This was IBM's very successful 1984 PC-design that firmly established the de facto industry standard for PCs. The PC/AT's broad success has been attributed to the fact that it was perceived to be a largely *open-architecture*[a] [b]design endorsed by the world's largest computer company. The only impediment to copying the PC/AT was its copyrighted BIOS. Soon functionally equivalent but independently developed BIOSes were written and less-expensive PC/AT *clones* were widely available. *PC/AT* *open-architecture* *clones*

Despite numerous and ongoing technology advances, the PC/AT architecture has continued to have a pervasive residual impact on many aspects of the design of PC platforms. A notable example is the existence of several *legacy buses*. The ISA Bus was the peripheral (or expansion) bus used in the PC/AT, although the ISA terminology was not coined until years later. The term *Industry Standard Architecture (ISA) Bus* was coined in conjunction with the 1988 launch of the *Extended Industry Standard Architecture (EISA) Bus*. The EISA Bus was intended to be a relatively open alternative to IBM's 1987 *Micro Channel Bus*, which was perceived to be a *proprietary,* or closed-architecture, design.[c] [d] The Micro Channel Bus was intended as an ISA replacement for IBM's new PS/2 (Personal System/2) line of PCs, which in turn was intended to retake the PC market from the clone-makers. The EISA Bus was an initiative primarily pushed by Compaq and other system vendors. Like the ISA and EISA buses, the Micro Channel Bus is considered a legacy bus, but it is much less common. The ISA Bus is the most important legacy bus as it is found in the majority of desktops already in use. However, beginning in the early 1990s, servers have frequently used the EISA Bus instead. *legacy buses* *ISA Bus* *EISA Bus* *Micro Channel Bus* *proprietary*

[a] A fully open-architecture design is one whose associated intellectual property (such as patents, copyrights and trade secrets) is generally licensed to all interested parties with possibly only modest administrative fees.

[b] The PC/AT design was perceived to be largely open-architecture because it was built entirely from generally available components and sub-systems and key design documentation was not treated as a trade secret. However, IBM had never indicated that the design was freely licensed. IBM later began pursuing licensing fees for PC/AT-related patents from clone-makers that were not otherwise licensed for IBM patents.

[c] A proprietary, or closed-architecture, design is one whose associated intellectual property is not generally licensed. Many "de facto" standards have been "closed" during formulation but have been made "open" later. While very important, the ability to influence the standards development process is often less important than the ability to implement a given "standard."

[d] Key Micro Channel Bus design documentation was treated as trade secret and it was believed that IBM was asking prohibitively high licensing fees to use the intellectual property associated with the new bus.

Legacy Bus Bridge

The ubiquitous PCI Bus has replaced the various legacy buses as the primary peripheral bus in PC platforms. In past desktop and server platforms, a *Legacy Bus Bridge* has been provided in the South-Bridge to selectively couple the PCI Bus and a legacy bus. Such a bus bridge between the PCI Bus and a legacy bus permits the continued use of legacy adapter cards. This hardware compatibility with ISA and EISA adapter cards greatly eased migration to PCI-based platforms, because expensive peripheral upgrades could be deferred.

In spite of the advantages of providing for backward compatibility, industry platform design standards (a key subject discussed in Chapter 4) proscribe certification of systems sold after mid-'98, if the ISA/EISA adapter card slots are populated prior to sale. Legacy adapter card slots are entirely proscribed from all systems sold after mid-'99. There are a number of reasons for this. These cards are discouraged because they generally do not incorporate the latest Plug and Play features (discussed in the Plug and Play Configuration and Maintenance section in Chapter 4), and thereby generally pose system configuration problems. Legacy cards also generally do not have power management features, and have generally narrower bus-widths and generally slower circuitry than do PCI adapter cards. Finally, the use of ISA adapter cards can reduce performance of the execution thread utilizing the card to a small fraction of that possible with PCI cards and may potentially starve other threads from execution while the legacy card is being accessed. As the performance of systems and the reliance on multiple threads of execution (e.g., to implement multi-media and execute background tasks) has increased, this last issue has become the foremost problem with the use of ISA cards.

As discussed above, the Super I/O component provided now largely obviates the need for legacy adapter cards. The Super I/O includes dedicated ports for the most common legacy devices. Generally, integrated ports are provided for a PS/2 mouse, serial devices (for modems and other communications), a keyboard, floppy drives, parallel devices, and bus-mastering ATA/IDE hard disks and CD-ROMs.42

USB, or Universal Serial Bus, is a new standard for low to medium speed serial peripherals designed for hot plug and play connectivity.

From 1998 and onward, platforms will likely provide a *Universal Serial Bus (USB)* port, which is intended by its promoters to obsolete and obviate the need for legacy expansion cards or Super I/O integrated legacy device ports, such as Sound Blaster audio, PS/2 mouse, and PC/AT-style game, serial communications, keyboard, and parallel interfaces. The USB is intended for replacement upgrade devices for the pointer/stylus (mouse), keyboard, joy stick, modem, telephony, printer, scanner, and digital audio devices. USB devices are low to medium speed serial peripherals designed for hot[6] Plug and Play connectivity. In spite of USB promoters intentions, the emergence of general purpose USB devices has

---

[6] "Hot" connectivity indicates that devices can be regularly added or removed while the system is operating normally and without any adverse effects.

been very slow. This is expected to change with the introduction of Windows 98, which has integral support for USB.

Future platforms are also stated to include either an *IEEE 1394* port, or a Fibre Channel port. These ports are for high-speed serial peripherals designed for hot Plug and Play connectivity. For example high-speed devices are video capture, editing, and conferencing units; hard disks; and Local Area Networks (LANs). 1394 has been touted as the serial technology of the future for many years now, yet such devices have not been generally available. With integral support for 1394 in Windows 98, 1394 devices are expected to begin their ascension. The advent of the Device Bay Standard (discussed in the Device Bay section in Chapter 4) should further accelerate the usage of 1394 devices.

IEEE 1394 is a new standard for high-speed serial peripherals designed for hot plug and play connectivity.

DEFINITION

Sealed PC

The USB and 1394 serial ports enable a consumer-oriented easy-to-use sealed PC. The sealed PC ideal is to provide a PC that never needs to be opened for the installation of after-market adapter cards. The name should not be taken too literally.

 The 1394-1995 IEEE Standard for a High-Performance Serial Bus is included on the CD-ROM.

Main Memory

The main memory controller arbitrates access to the main memory bus and main memory from the other buses. By using sophisticated data staging (including caching, prefetching, and posting of write data and commands), the North-Bridge creates the general illusion that the main memory has ports dedicated to each of the other buses.

The main memory uses Dynamic RAM (DRAM)[7] to provide volatile[8] storage of executing code and data. Multiple pairs of 72-pin DRAM *Single Inline Memory Modules (SIMMs)*, with each SIMM supporting a 32-bit (36-bits with parity, a method of detecting single-bit errors) wide memory data width, have typically been installed into platforms via sockets on the motherboard.

SIMM, or Single Inline Memory Module, is a popular type of DRAM packaging that has 72-pins and supports 32-bit wide memory data widths.

---

[7] DRAM memory relies on charge storage techniques and requires periodic refresh (reading and rewriting) to maintain the integrity of its contents. DRAM is known for high-density storage.

[8] Volatile memory loses its contents when power is removed.

DIMM, or Dual SIMM, is an emerging type of DRAM packaging that has 168-pins and supports 64-bit wide memory data widths.

More recently, one or more 168-pin DRAM *Dual SIMMs (DIMMs)* are being used, with each DIMM supporting a 64-bit (72-bits with ECC, or Error Correcting Code, a method of correcting single-bit errors) wide memory data width. The motherboard of Figure 1.3 on page 37 uses three 168-pin DIMM sockets.

Areas in main memory used for code may be allocated to the operating system, APIs, and applications. Areas used for data include system and applications, graphics display lists, and graphics texture maps. Information in both areas is typically dynamically arranged and allocated using a virtual memory management mechanism. 3D graphics related APIs include DirectDraw and particularly Direct3D. Main memory is accessed frequently by the processor and cache, PCI bus-master peripherals, and the AGP. Thus, there are a number of trade-offs to be made when designing a platform centered around minimizing latency to instructions and data while maintaining as high a bandwidth as possible. Memory organizations are extremely important in optimizing system performance. In Chapter 5, we will examine a variety of memory organizations such as the waning mainstream EDO, the waxing mainstream SDRAM, and emerging memory technologies such as Rambus DRAM and SLDRAM.

Caches

A number of microprocessors like the K6 and the Pentium have on-chip L1-Caches. Others, such as the K6 3D, also have on-chip L2-Cache.

DEFINITIONS
L1 Cache, L2 Cache, and External Cache
An *L1-Cache*, or *Level-One-Cache*, is the cache that is placed closest to the processor in the memory hierarchy. An *L2-Cache*, or *Level-Two-Cache*, is one level removed from the processor in the memory hierarchy by the intervening L1-Cache. External caches intervene between the on-chip caches and main memory in the memory hierarchy. Each higher-level of cache is further removed from the processor (and closer to the main memory) and is larger and higher in latency that the caches closer to the processor. Additional external caching typically supplements the on-chip caches, especially in higher performance systems.

External caches are connected to the microprocessor in two basic ways which we will refer to as a *front-side cache* and a *back-side cache*

> ### Definitions
>
> Front-Side Cache and Back-Side Cache
>
> A *front-side cache* is placed on the processor's local bus. A *back-side cache* uses a dedicated bus, separate from the processor local bus. A back-side cache generally operates faster than front-side cache. A back-side cache greatly reduces traffic on the local bus, while permitting more aggressive code and data prefetching from the attached cache. The advantage becomes less pronounced as the size of on-chip cache increases.

The external cache generally uses a variant of Static RAM (SRAM)[9] to hold recently used subsets of the code and data in the main memory. The SRAM provides transfers that are lower in latency, and higher in throughput, than the DRAM-based main memory. Properly managed, the combination of high-speed cache and large main memory virtualizes a single memory that has the capacity of the main memory and approximates the speed of the cache. Because the cache services most accesses, the processor to main memory traffic is reduced. This means that more of the main memory bus bandwidth is available for other sources and destinations, such as PCI bus-masters and the AGP.

Mechanical and Electrical Considerations

PC motherboards are typically oriented in the ubiquitous tower-type (vertically oriented and floor standing) system unit housing such that the board edge shown at the bottom side of the photo is pointing toward the front of the tower and the board edge shown at the left side of the photo is near the bottom of the tower. The board edge shown at the topside of the photo is near the back of the tower, with system chassis access cutouts for the connectors shown in the top-right of the photo. External to the system unit, USB devices, a mouse, and a keyboard are cabled directly to these connectors. Additional cutouts are provided for mechanically securing adapter cards into the various adapter card slots and permitting access to adapter card connectors from the back of the tower. The board edge shown at the right side of the photo is pointing toward the top of the tower, generally just below the system power supply. In full-height towers, the board only occupies the lower portion of the tower.

---

[9] SRAM memory relies on active flip-flop (cross-coupled inverters) storage techniques and does not require refresh. SRAM is known for its high-speed storage.

Connectors are cabled directly to their respective motherboard headers for a pair of legacy Floppy Disk Drives (FDDs) and up to two pairs of ATA/IDE drives, the drives being generally mounted in the front top portion of the tower. (Only one device in each pair mentioned need be populated.) Connectors for the two legacy serial ports and the IEEE 1284 parallel port are generally mounted on the back of the tower either via dedicated cutouts or via covers for unused adapter card slots. These connectors are then cabled directly to their respective headers on the motherboard.

Baby AT form factor

The dimensions of the original PC-AT motherboard are now known as the full AT form factor. The full AT form factor has been largely replaced for some time by a smaller variant (roughly two-thirds the size of the full AT), the *Baby AT form factor*. The Baby AT board shown in Figure 1.3 on page 37 is 8.5" x 12" in size. Recently, several new motherboard standards have been introduced that have new sizes, new board orientation, and new component placements. These include the NLX (New Low-profile eXtension), ATX (AT eXtension), and mini-ATX standards, which are briefly discussed in the Mechanical Design section in Chapter 4. These new motherboard standards require the use of a system chassis that is specifically designed to accommodate the new boards.

An ATX Power Supply is capable of being managed by the platform's BIOS to provide energy savings.

A new power supply configuration was also developed in association with the new ATX boards. The *ATX Power Supply* that is part of the ATX standard specifies a new standby voltage (5VSB), a new power enable control signal (PS-ON), and a power status signal (PW-OK), that enable motherboard BIOS control over the power supply to provide energy savings. New boards still using the Baby AT form factor, but providing BIOS control for power supply management, are also implementing the new ATX-style Power Supply Connector for the new control and status signals. This permits Baby AT form factor boards to work with ATX power supplies, which can be used in a chassis designed for the older Baby AT boards.

DISPLAY ADAPTERS

*Display Adapter
video memory*

The *Display Adapter* card shown in Figure 1.2 on page 36 includes video memory, a 2D/3D graphics accelerator, and a video accelerator. The *video memory* generally uses high-performance or specialty DRAM to provide storage of bit-maps and related parameters. The video memory may include data areas devoted to frame buffers, video buffers, a texture map cache, cursors and sprites, a depth or z buffer, an alpha buffer, and window coordinates. Platform features that access the video memory include the graphics and video accelerators, the streaming video input, PCI bus-master peripherals, and the AGP port.

Integrating some or all of the video memory, graphics accelerator, video accelerator, and AGP functions of the display adapter onto the motherboard and possibly into the north-bridge is tempting. Display adapter integration is commonplace in portable platforms and has been attempted at the low-end of both the consumer and business markets in efforts to increase the functionality of entry-level systems. More importantly, if a baseline for high-performance graphics functionality were established, software developers could rely on the baseline in developing their applications. All applications would benefit from the higher standard and the overall experience of the end user would be enhanced.

Other than portable platforms, where display adapter integration is a practical necessity, such integration is nevertheless generally not done, even for low-end systems. This is due to a number of factors. Historically, there has generally always been a wide range in performance, features, and cost for display adapters corresponding to a large variation in end-user needs. This makes the feature set selection difficult. Also, display technology and software generally are evolving rapidly and a number of competing solutions will exist. This presents both development and marketing risks. It is unlikely that the display adapter market will stabilize anytime soon, so these problems can be expected to continue. In AGP systems, providing both an integrated solution and the ability to later upgrade with an expansion display adapter card may require a revision to the specification. This is due to the extra loading that would exist on an interconnect originally envisioned as having only a source and a single destination.

DEFINITION

Frame Buffer

A *frame buffer* is that portion of the video memory used to compose images for subsequent display. There is a dedicated memory location corresponding to each addressable pixel of the active display area. In a color system, the frame buffer usually consists of separate RGB "planes" for each of the color components. There may also be additional planes for special pixel attributes. Generally, each of the color planes has an 8-bit byte, for a total color depth of twenty four bits.

During image composition, the frame buffer is generally written at random (nonsequential) locations. The frame buffer need only be written when a change is desired in the displayed image.

During display, frame buffer locations are read sequentially, in conjunction with the raster scanning of the attached video display. Because the light emissions from the present phosphor-based CRT displays decay with time, the displayed image needs to be continually refreshed, and hence the frame buffer needs to be continually read.

HISTORICAL COMMENT

Raster Displays

Pixel, or picture element, refers to the smallest resolvable or addressable feature of a computer display.

A *raster display* is characterized as having a rectangular array of discrete *pixels* (picture elements) of varying color or gray-scale intensity. Cathode Ray Tube (CRT)-based displays were the first raster displays. Such raster displays have horizontal and vertical deflection coils that are driven by fixed frequency saw-tooth waveform "sweep" oscillators. The active portion of the beam traces a rectangular scanning pattern on the face of the CRT known as the *raster*. Raster displays are by far the most prevalent paradigm for implementing computer displays. In contrast, vector displays may create images from line segments of generally arbitrary length and orientation. While the underlying technology and low-level electronics is quite different, LCD panels are managed at a high-level like CRTs. Flat LCD panels are expected to eventually replace the CRT for mainstream applications.

raster

Implementations that use a single frame buffer must effectively manage contention between image-building writes, display-refresh reads, and the refresh of the frame buffer's DRAM storage cells. Single frame buffers built from standard DRAMs must generally be written only during periods when the CRT display is undergoing horizontal and vertical retrace. This greatly restricts accesses, generally increasing the latency for performing frame buffer writes and dramatically reducing the effective read and write bandwidth for other than display refresh.

front buffer
back buffer

In contemporary systems there are typically two frame buffers, having the designations front buffer and back buffer. Frames are rendered to the *back buffer* as the display is painted (refreshed) from the *front buffer*. The roles of the buffers are then reversed during the next frame.

video DRAMS or VRAM

High-end frame buffers are often built from two-ported specialty DRAMs known as *video DRAMS* or *VRAM*. One port is a conventional random-access port that is used for the image-building writes. The second port is a serial output port that shifts out sequential locations used by the display refresh function. VRAMs increase the bandwidth available for frame buffer accesses, but are substantially more expensive than conventional DRAM.

2D and 3D graphics accelerators

A *2D graphics accelerator* is a special processor designed to execute the graphics display lists set up in main memory to build and move bit-maps and pixel maps in the video memory. A *3D graphics accelerator* also creates or renders 3D triangles into pixels in the frame buffer, often incorporating texture maps in the process. PCI bus-master capability permits the graphics accelerator to fetch the display commands and data from main memory without further involvement of the processor. Management of the various dedicated areas of the video memory is closely associated with the graphics accelerator.

3D acceleration features provide hardware support for *rasterizing* and *rendering* the 3D objects modeled by the 3D application running on the microprocessor once the objects have been broken down into sets of triangles with screen coordinates, color, and texture data computed by the graphics software. 3D-specific acceleration includes depth queuing and texture, transparency, and shading effects. 2D acceleration features provide hardware for 2D drawing (circles, triangles, lines, and points), raster operations (including window management and acceleration), and VGA (Video Graphics Adapter, a display adapter standard) register and memory compatibility. Display adapters intended for extensive 3D acceleration should make use of the AGP.

rasterizing
rendering

DEFINITION
Advanced Graphics Port (AGP)
The AGP provides a high-bandwidth path between main memory and the display adapter for the large volume of texture data associated with 3D graphics. It also keeps this traffic off of the PCI Bus, increasing the available PCI bandwidth.

The *video accelerator's* primary job is to pump streams of pixel data to the display. Digital pixel data is fetched from the frame buffer or video buffer in video memory, the pixels having been rendered previously by the graphics accelerator or previously received from the streaming video input. The pixel data may be stored in memory in a variety of formats, which have various color depths[10] and associated storage packing densities, color spaces,[11] and degrees of sub-sampling.[12] After being fetched from video memory, the various pixel data memory formats are respectively unpacked, interpolated,[13] color space converted, and scaled (if desired), to convert all pixel data to fully sampled RGB (Red, Green, Blue).

video accelerator

---

[10] "Color depth" relates to the number of available colors that can be explicitly specified for a pixel.

[11] "Color space" relates to different standard paradigms for specifying color.

[12] "Subsampling" is a color-video specific data compression technique.

[13] Interpolation is the inverse of subsampling.

Rasterizing and Rendering

Rasterizing and rendering are terms for related processes. While the two terms are often used synonymously, there are differences between the two. *Rasterizing* is a pixel-centric process of taking image data in any continuous form or model and processing it for storage, transfer, or display as a 2D matrix of modulated-pixel values. *Rendering* may be loosely used to mean simply rasterizing, but it often connotes surface modeling using a more comprehensive process that is image-perception-centric. Specifically, the color or gray-scale intensity of each pixel in the 2D matrix may be established through processing that may rely upon adjacent regions of pixels, textures, depth information, and other sophisticated techniques.

Raster operations (frequently called *RasterOps*) are logical primitives defined for manipulating and moving bit-map and pixel-map data. *BitBLT (Bit-aligned Block Transfer)* is perhaps the most important RasterOp. BitBLT moves a bit-mapped image from a source area at a first bit-origin to an equal sized destination area, having a second bit-origin. BitBLTs are extensively used for *intra* memory transfers from main memory to the back buffer, and intra back buffer transfers. Other RasterOps extend the basic BitBLT via an additional operand that defines various pixel manipulations on the image being transferred. In the most general case, the resulting data may be a function of the source data, the preexisting destination data and the additional operand.

RasterOps

BitBLT (Bit-aligned Block Transfer)

RGB color space model

Just as there are multiple coordinate representations (e.g. cartesian and polar) for physical space, there are multiple coordinate representations for color space. Two popular representations are RGB and YUV. *RGB* is a color space model that is directly usable by hardware at the sensor and display level. If a different color space model is used elsewhere in the system, color space conversion must be performed between the two. *YUV* is a reference to the color video image coding components Y, U, and V, which are formally defined for composite (single signal) analog color video standards such as NTSC, PAL, and S-video. For component (three signal) digital video, as used in computer graphics, the corresponding system is correctly referred to as Y'CbCr. However, in the general PC platform literature, the usage of the term YUV to connote computer digital component video is nearly ubiquitous.

YUV color space model

After digitization and before display, the *YUV color space model* is common for the transmission and intermediate storage of digital "full-motion" video images. YUV is related to RGB color-space via a 3x3-

matrix manipulation, enabling either representation to be derived from the other.

The technology associated with YUV color-coding is complex, relying on the four disciplines of physics, perception, photography, and video. Y' is the luma signal, which is a scaled and gamma corrected (end-to-end-video-path compensated) representation of the luminance information in the video image. A video industry standard defines luminance as an objective definition of brightness, given by $Y' = 0.299R + 0.587G + 0.114B$. The different weightings given to each component take into account human vision sensitivities to power at different visible wavelengths.

Collectively, U' and V' as a pair are representations of the chromatic or chroma information in the video image. In component video, Chroma (C) is a quadrature modulated signal given by $C = U(\cos t) + V(\sin t)$. Individually, U' and V' are scaled and gamma corrected color difference signals. U' is defined to be Blue (B) minus Y', and is sometimes referred to as the Blue Chroma component. V' is defined to be Red (R) minus Y', and is sometimes referred to as the Red Chroma component.

Primes are used to represent that the signals are gamma corrected, which is a compensation necessary due to nonlinear intensity reproduction transfer functions inherent in video systems.

YUV systems often exploit the fact that human perception of color resolution is coarser than perception of luminance resolution. These systems subsample (periodically omit samples of) the chroma in order to transmit and store lower bandwidth signals without any human perceivable degradation. Interpolation is the process of using the sub-sampled chroma information to recreate the missing chroma samples prior to display.

Color depth is the number of bits assigned per pixel to represent its color. The greater the number of bits, the deeper or higher the color depth, and the more colors may be used. Unless further qualified, this view of color depth implicitly means one is talking about RGB pixels in a form ready for processing by the final stages of the video accelerator. In the context of YUV pixels, and sub-sampling, one must find an effective number of bits per pixel.

When used on a PC, the Quick-Time videos on the companion CD-ROM should generally be viewed with 16-bit or greater color depth.

PC color-depth schemes may include 16-color, 256-color, 16-bit color, and 24-bit color modes. The 24-bit color mode is known as the *true color*, and generally corresponds to the highest capabilities of the display adapter. The true color mode is suitable for photographic quality images such as digitized photographs, or the results of photo-realistic graphics rendering, both of which require smooth shading of geometric objects. 16-bit color is known as *high color*, achieving very good quality images, but with some degradation.

true color

high color

The 16-color and 256-color modes are also known as *pseudocolor* or colormapped modes. They are also described as having "palletized" pixels. In the pseudocolor modes, the color pixel value stored in the frame buffer is not itself the ultimately displayed color, but is instead an index into a Color Look Up Table (CLUT), also known as a colormap, or palette. The CLUTs are used to convert palletized pixels to the desired high or true-

pseudocolor

color pixel data. Following color look up, which is required only for the pseudocolor modes, the pixel data streams drive an RGB triplet of Digital to Analog Converters (DACs), for generating analog waveforms suitable for driving the display.

HISTORICAL COMMENT
RAMDAC
CLUTs are often implemented using embedded RAMs and the term RAMDAC was coined to refer to a module that integrated both the CLUTs and the DACs. The term is still used even though much higher levels of integration are common today. Especially at the low-end, display adapter cards frequently consist of little more than video memory, one or two display controller chips, and other minor components.

Thus a palletized pixel value corresponds to a higher true color only via the defined palette mapping, and is otherwise arbitrary. The pseudocolor modes have been analogized[14] to "painting by numbers," where the set of numbers is relatively small, but each individual color can be chosen from the full spectrum of colors. The pseudocolor modes are suitable for artwork such as business presentations and drawn illustrations and for controls and program displays in alphanumeric and GUI (discussed in the Graphical User Interface (GUI) section in Chapter 4) based systems. Pseudocolor modes are very space efficient for such uses. Additionally, special effects may be achieved by dynamic changes to the color palette.

The choice of color mode is usually limited by the finite memory installed in the display adapter in conjunction with the addressable resolution selected. Given that the installed memory is a constant, the addressable resolution must be traded off against color-depth. That is, an increase in one will often demand a decrease in the other.

packed pixels

When low color depth is used, and in particular for hardware with wide data paths, multiple pixels may be *packed* into a single data word. It is also possible for packing to be done in such a manner that pixels straddle word boundaries. *Unpacking* is the process of parsing a data word stream to extract the individual pixels.

unpacking

scaling

Scaling is the magnification or reduction of a raster image. Pixel replication, or decimation, may be used to perform crude integer magnification, or reduction, respectively. Noninteger scaling usually requires special hardware support or else performance may dramatically suffer.

We have now completed an overview of the process of designing and implementing a microprocessor and the issues involved in designing and

---

[14] Charles A. Poynton, *A Technical Introduction to Digital Video*, John Wiley and Sons, 1996, p. 36.

implementing microprocessor-based platforms and systems. Before summarizing the chapter and discussing the road ahead, we have a small but hopefully interesting side-tour to make.

Each year since 1979, the IEEE Computer Society and the Association for Computing Machinery (ACM) have jointly recognized substantial contributions to computer and digital systems architecture by awarding the prestigious Eckert-Mauchly Award to a single individual. We asked a number of the recipients of this award the following two questions:

1. Looking back, what are the most important 5-6 books or articles that affected the way that you approach the central issues in computer architecture?

2. Looking forward, what are the most important 5-6 books or articles that you would recommend all of those interested in the field—student or practitioner—to read because you believe they are concerned with issues that will be increasingly important in future architectures?

Given the sustained contributions these individuals have made to the field and the impact each has had on it, we thought that most readers of this book could benefit from their responses to these questions. As you probably suspect, the answers are both interesting and insightful. The responses are presented in reverse chronological order, starting with the most recent award winner who we approached, and working backwards.

1997 Award Winner, Robert Tomasulo
Award Citation: *For the ingenious "Tomasulo's Algorithm," which enabled out-of-order executive processors to be implemented.*

Looking Back

"Books played a negligible role in my development for two reasons. When I started there were virtually no books in the field. Even useful articles or papers were rare. Books also tend to lag too far behind practice in a rapidly developing field. This is still the case today. By far the most significant influence was the people I worked with and the design community to which we belonged. I learned the ABC's of computer architecture from Amdahl, Brooks and Blaauw, Cocke et al. I learned computer design from Anderson, Sparacio and other colleagues on the Model 91 and subsequent projects.

A powerful external influence was the work of Seymour Cray. A paper on the 6600 and a video lecture (much later) come to mind. Sadly, much excellent early work, even at IBM, was not well documented publicly. Starting with the Model 91 the IBM Journal *has changed that, at least with respect to those of their designs that become products."*

Looking Forward

"I cannot improve on Prof. Flynn's[15] answer to this difficult question but would like to add a greater emphasis on mastering the past. Technology advances in both hardware and software have rendered most Instruction Set Architecture conflicts moot (and I include CISC/RISC). Computer design is focusing more on the memory bandwidth and multiprocessing interconnection problems. Neither of these is new. Even in his special field, Cray realized that problems are ultimately memory (including I/O) limited. The microprocessor field has recapitulated in the last ten years the past forty years of mainframe evolution. Therefore, the problems it faces today were encountered ten or twenty years ago by mainframe designers. A first step toward solving these problems should be an understanding of past attempts, both those that succeeded in their day and, even more importantly, those that failed."

1996 Award Winner, Prof. Yale N. Patt
Award Citation: *For important contributions to instruction level parallelism and superscalar processor design.*

Looking Back

"It is not clear that there are five or six books or articles that have affected how I approach central issues in computer architecture. The fact is, I have been influenced overwhelmingly more by lectures than by books or articles. I have thought about this a lot (on airplanes etc.), trying to identify the books and articles that have mattered to me, and frankly come up with the realization that it was lectures, not books and articles, that mattered far more. One exception: Knuth, Volume 1, *which is not that it related directly to computer architecture, but rather it provided clear insight into what computing is about, where problems are, and how to approach problems.*

As for lectures, I would count the following four, giving me the five that you requested:

1. *Professor W. K. Linvill, Systems Analysis, Stanford, 1964. Taught me to cut through the complexity and big words and get at the heart of the problem. Also taught me the value of analogies to understanding new situations.*

2. *Professor W.K. Linvill, Doctoral Qualifying exam, Stanford, 1963. Taught me that tough problems can be cracked if they can be transformed into problems that I understand.*

3. *Professor Donald Epley, Switching Theory, Stanford, 1962. Taught me that a body of knowledge, if organized systematically and compre-*

---

[15] Note: Prof. Flynn's response appears later in this section.

hensively, lends itself to understanding far better than a collection of badly interconnected ideas.

4. *Professor Michael Harrison, lecture at Duke University, 1973. Taught me that an advancement of knowledge is best explained in the context of simple ideas, and that only after conveying that should one attempt to translate the advancement into heavy mathematics.*

My response departs sufficiently from what you intended that I feel obliged to add a statement, lest some regard it as frivolous. While none of my five are limited to computer architecture, all five have had such a pronounced effect on how I approach everything about computer architecture that they dwarf any computer-architecture-specific books or articles that I could mention.

Looking Forward

1. *"Harold Stone, textbook published by A-W on high-performance computer architecture, because Harold writes lucidly, and provides a careful foundation that is useful to everyone's base of knowledge in computer architecture.*

2. *John Wakerly, textbook on logic design, because one should have a solid grounding in digital logic design if one wishes to deal with computer architecture.*

3. *Martin Graham, textbook on high-performance circuit design, because one should be exposed to the lower levels of implementation as part of one's preparation to work at the higher level of microarchitecture.*

4. *Stephen Melvin and Yale Patt, HICSS 1987, I believe. Hopefully I have transcended the obvious self-serving element of referencing my own work; this paper differentiates hardware/software interface from dynamic/static interface from user/builder interface, and in so doing, focuses on the important problems that must be dealt with to really produce highest performance engines.*

I hope the above is useful."

1992 Award Winner, Prof. Michael J. Flynn
Award Citation: *For his important and seminal contributions to processor organization and classification, computer arithmetic, and performance evaluation.*

Looking Back
"I started in computer design when the field was relatively young. Aside from von Neumann's classic papers [2], most of the books or articles that affected my personal approach to computer architecture were based upon machines themselves—either instruction sets or implementations, or both.

Thus, Buchholz's book on the Stretch computer [1] was an important book describing a deeply pipelined machine and many of the problems which still exist in processor implementations (for instance, speculating on a branch was a feature in the Stretch machine). Other works that emphasized the evolution of instruction sets included System 360's Principles of Operation *[3]. The DEC VAX and PDP-11 instruction sets [4] and the Burroughs B6500 series [5] all illustrated important advances in our understanding of optimizing the executable representation of programs. The Intel x86 instruction set and its evolution was interesting for a different reason. As technology enabled more robust implementations, it also enabled more fully functional instruction sets.*

Machine implementations are equally important, especially machines that were able to break new ground in achieving performance or functionality. Books and papers on the CDC 6600 [6], the IBM System 360 Model 91 [7], and the CRAY-1 [8], all present to me valuable insights.

The reader will note that many of the items mentioned are of some vintage. It is easier to see in the hindsight of, say, a decade, which machines have changed and significantly influenced the field and hence all of our thinking. It is much more difficult to assess the impact of machines introduced in current months. Still, it is no less important to be aware of them."

References:

1. *W. Buchholz and R. S. Ballance,* Planning a Computer System, *McGraw-Hill, 1962.*

2. *John von Neumann,* Collected Works, *Volume V, Pergamon Press, 1963.*

3. *IBM Corporation,* IBM System/360 Principles of Operation, *Technical Report GA22-6821-4, 1970.*

4. *C. G. Bell, J. C. Mudge, and J. E. McNamara,* Computer Engineering: A DEC View of Hardware System Design, *Digital Press, 1978.*

5. *E. Organick,* Computer Systems Organization: The B5700/B6700 Series, *Academic Press, 1973.*

6. *J. E. Thornton,* Design of a Computer: The Control Data 6600, *Scott, Foresman and Co., 1970.*

7. *D. W. Anderson, F. J. Sparacio, and R. M. Tomasulo, "The IBM System/360 Model 91: Machine philosophy and instruction-handling,"* IBM Journal of Research and Development, *11(1):8-24, 1967.*

8. *R. M. Russell, The CRAY-1 Computer System,* Communications of the ACM, *21(1):63-72, January 1978."*

Looking Forward

"It is difficult to predict trends in a field where the technology is rapidly changing, so the architect must be aware of possible avenues of machine implementation. But, underlying these avenues are somewhat more perma-

nent support tools. Computer architecture, like all engineering, is the art of the possible: bringing together ideas for machine implementation with state-of-the-art technology details to provide for the best possible system implementation at a given cost.

I think that the future computer architect is a systems architect, not simply a processor architect; so one must bring together software technology, systems applications, arithmetic, all in a complex system which has a statistical behavior that is not immediately or simply analyzed, so the architect must be aware of current techniques [1]. Here, basic books such as Hayes [2] or Hennessy and Patterson [3] through advanced work by Hwang [4] represent a sampling of the various avenues that the architect should be aware of. But just as importantly, the architect should have basic familiarity with probability and queuing theory, compiler theory, operating systems, and of course VLSI technology. In the more distant future, as the system moves to the chip, the architect needs to know signal processing, graphics, audio, and the human-machine interface."

References:

1. *A good source includes* Microprocessor Reports *or* IEEE Micro.

2. *J. Hayes,* Computer Architecture and Organization, *McGraw-Hill, 1988.*

3. *J. L. Hennessy and D. A. Patterson,* Computer Architecture: A Quantitative Approach, *Morgan Kaufmann, 1990.*

4. *K. Hwang,* Advanced Computer Architecture: Parallelism, Scalability, Programmability, Computer Engineering Series, *McGraw-Hill, 1993."*

1988 Award Winner, Prof. Daniel P. Siewiorek
Award Citation: *For outstanding contributions to parallel computer architecture, reliability, and computer architecture education.*

"In my early career I studied the IBM 360 architectural papers, especially the 360/Model 91 implementation papers, and the CDC 6600. Taken together these were perhaps the first mass-produced, reduced instruction set architectures with high-performance implementations. The concepts in these two architectures fueled high-performance designs for over three decades. The DEC PDP-11 architecture introduced me to the interface between hardware implementation and software (both operating system and application programs). The single most influential book on my early career was C. G. Bell and A. Newell, Computer Structures: Readings and Examples, *McGraw-Hill, 1971. Bell and Newell formalized the hierarchical levels in computer systems, initiated the concept of a computer space (taxonomies of alternatives that made design decisions explicit), introduced ISP as a language to describe*

the programming interface (a language to which many concepts in contemporary hardware description languages can be traced), and the concept of the computer as a system reaching out beyond the data paths and controllers into software and networks.

As you can guess, it is easier identifying historically important articles/ books than predicting the future. Hence there are more entries to your question 1 than to question 2. After I cite each reference, I will make a brief comment about it.

Looking Back

1. *Arthur W. Burks, Herman H. Goldstine, and John von Neumann, "Preliminary Discussion of the Logical Design of an Electronic Computing Instrument," in A. H. Taub (ed),* Collected Works of John von Neumann, *Vol. 5, pp. 34-79, The Macmillan Company, 1963. 'Introduces the basic organization of a processor, instruction set, multiple level storage hierarchy, number representations, reliability (e.g., duplicated processors), and graphics output.'*

2. *T. Kilburn, D. B. G. Edwards, M. J. Lanigan, and F. H. Sumner, "One-level Storage System,"* IRE Transactions, *EC-11, Vol. 2, pp. 223-235, April 1962. 'Introduces the principles of an automatically controlled memory hierarchy.'*

3. *R. M. Tomasulo, "An Efficient Algorithm for Exploiting Multiple Arithmetic Units,"* IBM Journal, *Vol. 11, January 1967, pp. 25-33. 'Introduces basic algorithms for controlling multiple functional units.'*

4. *L. G. Roberts and B. D. Wessler, "Computer Network Development to Achieve Resource Sharing,"* Proc. AFIPS SJCC, *Vol. 36, 1970, pp. 543-549. 'Introduces basic concepts for networking and wide area network goals.'*

5. *Robert M. Metcalfe and David R. Boggs, "Ethernet: Distributed Packet Switching for Local Computer Networks,"* Comm. ACM, *Vol. 19, No. 7, July 1976, pp. 395-404. 'Introduces local area network concepts.'*

6. *C. P. Thacker, E. M. McCreight, B. W. Lampson, R. F. Sproull, and D. R. Boggs, "Alto: A Personal Computer," in D. P. Siewiorek, C. G. Bell, and A. Newell, eds.* Computer Structures: Principles and Examples, *McGraw-Hill, 1982, pp. 549-572. 'Introduces the concept of a single user workstation with bit-mapped graphics, precursor to widely adopted icon, mouse interface with 'what you see is what you get' whole screen editors.'*

7. *C. G. Bell, J. C. Mudge, and J. E. McNamara,* Computer Engineering: A DEC View of Hardware System Design, *Digital Press, 1978.*

'Evolutionary design and computer families.'

8. *M. Y. Hsiao, W. C. Carter, J. W. Thomas, and W. R. Stringfellow,* "Reliability, Availability, and Serviceability of IBM Computer Systems: A Quarter Century of Progress," IBM J. Res. and Development, *Vol. 25, September 1981, pp. 453-465. 'The evolution of reliability techniques.'*

Looking Forward

1. *A. S. Tanenbaum,* Computer Networks, *3rd ed. Prentice Hall, 1996, Upper "Computer networks."*

2. *H. Cragon,* Memory Systems and Pipeline Processors, *Jones and Bartlett Publishers, 1996. "Memory hierarchy and pipelining."*

3. *J. L. Hennessy and D. A. Patterson,* Computer Architecture: A Quantitative Approach, *2nd ed. Morgan Kaufmann, 1996. "Uniprocessor/cache design."*

4. *J. D. Foley and A. van Dam,* Fundamentals of Interactive Computer Graphics, *Addison-Wesley, 1982 "Computer graphics."*

5. D. P. Siewiorek and R. S. Swarz, Reliable Computer Systems: Design and Evaluation, 2nd Edition, Digital Press, 1992. Butterworth Heineman Publishing Co. "System reliability continues to increase in importance."

1986 Award Winner, Prof. Harvey G. Cragon
Award Citation: *For major contributions to computer architecture and for pioneering the application of integrated circuits for computer purposes. For serving as architect of Texas Instruments, scientific computer and for playing a leading role in many other computing developments in that company.*

Looking Back
    "There are two books and two papers that had a profound influence on my early life as a computer architect. The two books are:

1. Planning a Computer System, Project Stretch *edited by W. Buchholz, 1962. "This book spelled out the design decisions that went into Stretch. To a young engineer, learning that design decisions come hard to others was a revelation."*

2. *"The second book is* Design of a Computer: the Control Data 6600 *by J. E. Thornton, 1970. The insight into the causes of dependencies and their solutions in concurrent processors was revealing."*

"For the two papers, I still make reference to:

1. *"Preliminary Discussions of the Logical Design of an Electronic Com-*

puting Instrument" by Burks, Goldstine, and von Neumann." I have a photo copy of the original. The insight shown in this paper is truly astounding. And to think that we still follow this model today with concurrency the only major change."

2. *"The second paper is the collection of papers found in the* IBM Journal of Research and Development, *Vol. 11, No. 1, January 1967. "This collection of papers concerned the design of the IBM S360 91. The paper topics include: floating-point arithmetic, the Common Data Bus, memory system design, and a first look at multiple instruction issue (what we call Superscalar today)."*

Looking Forward

"For contemporary reading, I will mention only two books.

1. *The first is* The Supermen, *by Charles Murray. This is the story of Seymour Cray and all of his machines, both successes and failures. An important story that emerges is the never-ending battle between: higher clock rates leading to higher circuit density leading to higher power density leading to exotic cooling techniques. This is a battle that is still fought today and will in the future as far as I can tell."*

2. *"The second book is the monumental work* Computer Architecture, Concepts and Evolution *by G. Blaauw and Fred. Brooks Jr. This book should be on the desk of an engineer who claims to be a computer architect. The architecture design space that they have pulled together is truly outstanding and is a valuable reference work."*

1985 Award Winner, John Cocke

Award Citation: *For contributions to the high-performance computer architecture through look ahead, parallelism and pipeline utilization, and to reduced instruction set computer architecture through the exploitation of hardware-software trade-offs and compiler utilization.*

Looking Back

"Here are the thoughts you asked me to send to you. First, in 1957 when I was employed by IBM, there were few Computer Science departments and no major books related to Computer Science. I read a 1946 report prepared for the U.S. Army Ordnance Department by Burks, von Neumann, and Goldstine [1]. There were also available journal articles from the ACM, which contained papers related to such things as error correcting codes, etc. The Bell Systems Technical Journal *contained articles by Shannon [2] related to information theory. There was also a book by Richards, [3] which showed how to design adders, etc. Most of the things I learned from people like Fred Brooks and Jim Pomerene, who had worked designing computers at Harvard*

and the Institute of Advanced Study, respectively. Andrew Gleason gave the Stretch Planning Committee some papers related to sorting, which were quite informative. For many years there were no books which would be usable for a Computer Science course, as far as I knew, until Knuth [4] started releasing his books."

Looking Forward

"In answer to the question you asked related to books that I feel are appropriate for the new generation of computer architecture, I would recommend Mike Flynn's [5] Computer Architecture book and the Computer Architecture book by Fred Brooks and Gerrit Blaauw [6]."

1. *Burks, Arthur W., Herman H. Goldstine, and John von Neumann "Preliminary Discussion of the Logical Design of an Electronic Computing Instrument" (Pt. 1. Vol. 1) Report prepared for the U.S. Army Ordnance Department 1946, in A. H. Taub (ed.)* Collected Works of John von Neumann, *Vol. 5, pp. 34-79, The Macmillan Company, 1963.*

2. *Shannon, C. E. "A Mathematical Theory of Communication,"* Bell System Technical Journal, *Vol. 27, pp. 379-423, 623-656, 1948.*

3. *Richards, R. K.,* Arithmetic Operations in Digital Computers, *D. VanNostrand Company, Inc., 1955.*

4. *Knuth, D. E.,* The Art of Computer Programming, Vol. I, *(1968), Vol. II, (1969), Vol. III, (1975), Addison-Wesley.*

5. *Flynn, M. J.,* Computer Architecture, *Jones and Bartlett Publishers, 1995.*

6. *Blaauw, G. and Frederick Brooks,* Computer Architecture Concepts and Evolution, *Addison Wesley Longman, 1997."*

SUMMARY OF CHAPTER AND HOW TO PROCEED

In this chapter, we reviewed the process of designing and implementing a microprocessor in reasonable detail. In particular, we stated that the development of appropriate representative workloads, the subsequent analysis of the resulting performance measurement data, and the use of that analysis in the design and implementation process is the "cornerstone of many, if not most, architectural design decisions." We explained the importance of simulation and testing and emphasized the need for a "golden representation" of the microprocessor. We continued with a discussion of the process of designing and implementing a 3D graphics PC platform. In this section, we identified the key components and interconnections central to contemporary platform architectures. This section will prove fundamental to the discussions that occur in Chapters 4, 5, and 6. Lastly, we benefited from the perspectives of several Eckert-Mauchly Award winners regarding what influenced their individual views of computer architecture and what they think might prove to be important references in the field in the future.

TECHNICAL PRESENTATIONS ON CD-ROM

 Two technical presentations by Bruce Shriver that deal with various topics discussed in this chapter might be of interest to the reader: (1) *An Introduction to Computer Architecture* and (2) *The Design and Implementation Process*.

We recommend that you examine the Table of Contents and then page through each of the chapters to get a sense of the specific topics that are covered and the depth to which the material is presented. Similarly, we suggest you page through the cross-references and the combined glossary/index at the rear of the book.

We suggest you have the companion CD-ROM in your CD-ROM reader as you use the hard copy of the book in order to take advantage of the many hyperlinked and cross-reference features of it. Furthermore, during certain sections of the book, you may want to be connected to the Web as a number of the hyperlinks will connect you to relevant Web sites. We should also mention that the figures and tables that appear in each chapter can be printed out from the *Technical Presentations* road map on the CD-ROM on a chapter-by-chapter basis.

Chapter 2 and Chapter 3 should be read sequentially. However, Chapters 4, 5, and 6 can be read in any order and independently of Chapters 2 and 3.

Chapter 2
A Microarchitecture Case Study

W e pointed out in Chapter 1 that the first half of this book presents a description of the microarchitecture of the AMD K6 3D microprocessor. In attempting to balance between giving you enough detail and too much detail, we will give a layered description of the microarchitecture. In this chapter we discuss the K6 3D's superscalar design and its multiple execution units, instruction buffers, predecode logic, multiple decoders, scheduler, branch resolution logic, operation commit unit, on-chip L1-Cache and L2-Cache, and other aspects of its microarchitecture. We follow this overview with detailed discussions of three of its main elements—its out-of-order, speculative scheduler, its operation commit unit, and its register renaming scheme in Chapter 3.

This chapter is written for all audiences (university professors and students, practitioners, and technical management). However, there are some subsections that have details that will be of more interest and use to practitioners and those in universities. The *road map* for this chapter identifies these sections.

ROAD MAP OF CHAPTER 2

Section	Audience
All major headings in the chapter	All
The following more detailed subsections: Register Number and Name Mappings Special Registers and Model Specific Registers Formats for Decoder Ops LdOps and StOps perform memory accesses and related operations. They have the following format in a decoder OpQuad: RegOp Field Descriptions SpecOp Field Descriptions LIMM Op Field Descriptions	Practitioners, University Professors and Students

63

AN OVERVIEW OF THE K6 3D MICROPROCESSOR

In this section, we give an overview of how the K6 3D microprocessor works: how it fetches instructions and how they are predecoded and then decoded, how multiple internal operations result from this decoding process, how these operations go through a substantial expansion process before they are loaded into its centralized scheduler, how its pipelines are controlled and what type of work they do at each stage, how the decoding of instructions and the execution of the resulting operations are decoupled from one another, what types of caches the processor has on-chip and how they are organized, how operations are issued, and how and when predicted branches are ultimately resolved. The explanation of the particular design approaches taken within the K6 3D requires knowing a bit about the microarchitecture's internal operation set and the internal representation of operations within the scheduler, so some detail of both of these is also presented.

After completing this overview, you should be well positioned to understand the more detailed discussions of the scheduler, operation commit unit, and register renaming given in Chapter 3. Recall that our intent is to give you enough detail to allow you to simulate some important portions of the microarchitecture and associated platform and systems devices. You can gain a much greater understanding of how these chunks of the design actually work by doing such simulations. Such knowledge is basic to understanding the complex mix of cost and performance trade-off involved in taking the microarchitecture and producing a chip from it within a very aggressive time-to-market constraint.

A RANGE OF DESIGN APPROACHES

As stated in Chapter 1, one view of the K6 3D is that it is a high-performance CISC-on-RISC microprocessor. The CISC-component is the x86 instruction set architecture and the underlying RISC-component is known as the Enhanced RISC86 Microarchitecture. The most important technical implication of this constraint is that the K6 3D must be fully x86 binary code compatible, including the MMX multimedia extensions to the x86 instruction set architecture.

SUGGESTED READINGS

Complete Description of the x86 Instruction Set Architecture

For a complete description of the x86 instruction set architecture see the three-volume *The Intel Architecture Software Developer's Manual: Basic Architecture*, Intel Order Number 243190; *Instruction Set Reference,* Order Number 243191; and the *System Programming Guide,* Order Number 243192. These references also describe the x87 (floating-point) instruction set architecture and the MMX extensions.

The K6 3D also supports AMD-developed instruction set extensions to the MMX instructions, called the 3D instructions, which support high-performance 3D graphics, audio, and physics processing. The resulting microprocessor has a decoupled superscalar microarchitecture that uses many advanced design approaches targeted at achieving high performance. Some of the techniques that are employed in the K6 3D design are: instruction predecoding, multiple x86 instruction issue in a single clock cycle, internal single-clock RISC-like operations, superscalar operation (concurrent use of multiple execution units to execute up to six RISC-like operations per clock cycle), out-of-order execution, data forwarding, implicit register renaming, speculative execution, and the use of in-order retirement to ensure precise interrupts

Video Clips on CD-ROM

Greg Favor, Chief Architect of the K6 3D addresses the following two questions on two related video clips, "What were the principle design objectives chosen for the K6 3D microprocessor?" and "What are the key microarchitectural features incorporated into the K6 3D?"

The K6 3D uses a two-level, dynamic branch direction prediction technique that is integral to its ability to execute instructions speculatively. The branch direction prediction logic makes use of a branch history table, a branch target cache, and a return address stack, all of which combine to achieve a predicted address hit rate of better than 95%. These and other design techniques, such as employing a six-stage pipeline, enable the K6 processor to fetch, decode, issue, execute, complete, and retire multiple x86 instructions per clock. The material in this introduction provides a general overview of the K6 3D microprocessor and will be discussed in more detail in Chapter 3.

DESIGN NOTE

K6 3D Code Optimizations

The coding techniques for optimizing peak performance of the K6 3D include many of those recommended for optimizing the performance of the Intel Pentium and Pentium Pro microprocessors. They also include optimizations specific to the K6 3D's implementation of the MMX and 3D instruction set extensions. The use of the K6 3D code optimizations can result in higher delivered performance than off-the-shelf software non optimized code.

A FAMILY OF MICROPROCESSORS

The K6 is a family of microprocessors. The initial member of the family, called the K6 MMX, was introduced (in May 1997) at clock speeds of 166-MHz, 200-MHz, 233-MHz, and 266-MHz, had 8.8 million transistors and was designed in a 0.35-micron process resulting in a 162-mm^2 die-size. These chips have a 66-MHz processor bus. Shrinking to a 0.25-micron process and architectural and microarchitectural enhancements (e.g., the inclusion of the 3D instructions) grew the chip to 9.3-million transistors, yet the die size shrank to 81 mm^2. This later member of the K6 family, called the K6 3D, supports the 3D instruction set extensions. The K6 3D, extended to have a 256-Mbyte L2-Cache on-chip, is called the K6 3D and it is this processor that is discussed in detail in this book. From time-to-time reference will be made to the earlier versions of the K6 family that did not support the 3D instruction set or did not have the L2-Cache on-chip, but the references make clear when this is done. These processors will simply be referred to as the K6 and will be used to describe features that are applicable to both the K6 and the K6 3D.

The characteristics of some of the members of the K6 Family are summarized in the following table. Each family member extends the microprocessor in the row above it.

Table 2.1 K6 FAMILY MEMBERS

Processor	Clock	Bus	Process[a]	Die-Size	TC[b]	Comments
K6 MMX	166-MHz	66-MHz	0.35	162-mm2		original release
	200-MHz	66-MHz	0.35	162-mm2		higher clock
	233-MHz	66-MHz	0.35	162-mm2	8.8	higher clock
	266-MHz	66-MHz	0.35	162-mm2		higher clock
	300-MHz	66-MHz	0.25	68-mm2		K6 MMX shrink
K6 3D	300-MHz	100-MHz	0.25	81-mm2	9.3	K6 with 3D[c] & MMX[d]
	350-MHz	100-MHz	0.25	81-mm2		higher clock
K6 3D	350-MHz	100-MHz	0.25	135-mm2	21.3	K6 3D with L2-Cache on-chip
	400-MHz	100-MHz	0.25	135-mm2		higher clock

[a] in microns

[b] transistor count in millions

[c] also called "AMD-3D Technology"

[d] a superscalar dual-pipeline implementation of the x86 MMX instruction set extensions

The K6 MMX was initially implemented in a 0.35-micron CMOS process and then in a 0.25-micron CMOS process, using five layers of metal, shallow trench isolation, and tungsten local interconnect. C4 solder bump flip-chip technology is used to assemble the die into a ceramic pin grid array (PGA). The high-performance and small die sizes of these microprocessors are achieved using high-speed custom and macro blocks and placed-and-routed blocks of standard cells. The initial 0.25-micron process version of the K6 MMX can operate at a clock speed of 300-MHz, has a 100-MHz processor bus and its chip sets support AGP (Advanced Graphics Port), USB (Universal Serial Bus), and the IEEE 1394 high-performance serial bus (a.k.a. Firewire), all of which are presented in detail in Chapter 5. A die photograph of a recent version of the K6 and an overlay on top of the photograph showing the approximate placement of various K6 components is given in Figure 2.1.

Technical Presentation on CD-ROM

A presentation by Greg Favor, Principal Architect of the K6 3D, on the evolution of the K6 family entitled, "*The AMD-K6 MMX Enhanced Processor Product Roadmap*," can be found on the CD-ROM.

Articles on CD-ROM

To learn more about some of the detailed implementation issues of an early version of the K6 3D processor, see "Circuit Techniques in a 266-MHz MMX-Enabled Processor," by Don Draper, Matt Crowley, John Holst, Greg Favor, Albrecht Schoy, Jeff Trull, Amos Ben-Meir, Rajesh Khanna, Dennie Wendell, Ravi Krishna, Joe Nolan, Dhiraj Mallick, Hamid Partovi, Mark Roberts, Mark Johnson, and Thomas Lee. This article, appeared in the November 1997 issue of the *IEEE Journal of Solid-State Circuits*. To learn more about some of the detailed implementation issues of the 0.35-micron version of the K6, see "An x86 Microprocessor with Multimedia Extensions," by Don Draper, Matthew P. Crowley, John Holst, Greg Favor, Albrecht Schoy, Amos Ben-Meir, Jeff Trull, Raj Khanna, Dennie Wendell, Ravi Krishna, Joe Nolan, Hamid Partovi, Mark Johnson, Tom Lee, Dhiraj Mallick, Gene Frydel, Anderson Vuong, Stanley Yu, Reading Maley, and Bruce Kaufmann 1997 *ISSCC Digest of Technical Papers*. You can find the full test versions of both of the above articles on the companion CD-ROM.

Microprocessor Fabrication Process Mini-Tutorial on CD-ROM

This video clip, in which Bill Siegle, AMD's Chief Scientist, addresses several questions related to the steps involved in the fabrication of contemporary microprocessor chips, effectively becomes a mini-tutorial on the fabrication process.

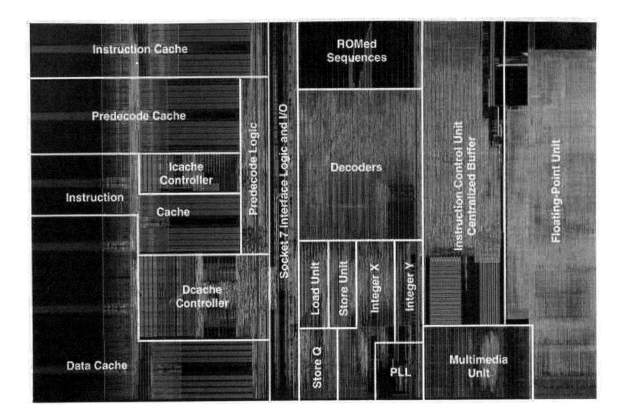

Figure 2.1 K6 Die Photograph and Overlay

K6 3D Block Diagram

Figure 2.2 is a high-level block diagram of the K6 3D microarchitecture. We will give an overview of its operation first, followed by more detail about each of the elements shown in this figure.

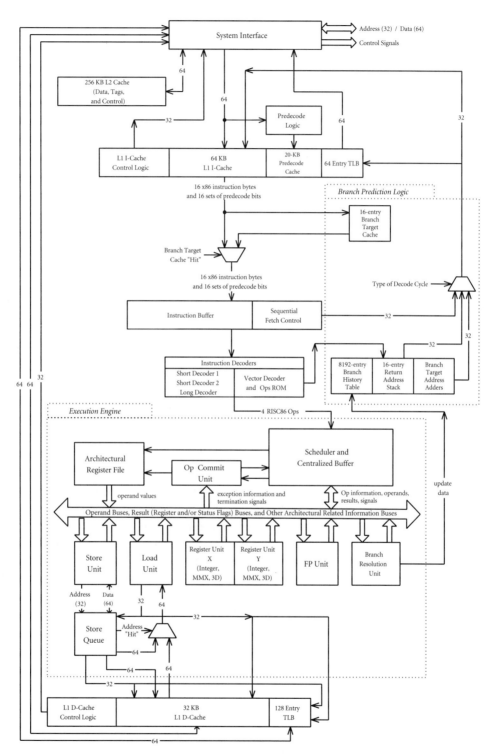

Figure 2.2 K6 3D Block Diagram

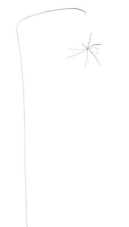

We will, from time to time as appropriate, use the term *bus cycle* when referring to external data transfers and *processor cycle* when referring to operations internal to the microprocessor. There is typically a 3X ratio between these two cycles in the K6.

X86 instructions are stored in the main memory. During each bus cycle, up to eight bytes of x86 instructions are fetched from main memory or the on-chip L2-Cache and loaded into the on-chip *L1 Instruction Cache* (the *L1 I-Cache*) during a cache fill. While they are being loaded into the L1 I-Cache, the x86 instruction bytes are predecoded, using predecoded logic, to assist in later, rapid identification of x86 instruction boundaries.

During each processor cycle, the L1 I-Cache or the Branch Target Cache (BTC) places 16 x86 instruction bytes into a 16-byte instruction buffer which directly feeds the instruction decoders. The multiple instruction decoders (two short decoders, a long decoder, and a vector decoder), taken as an aggregate, will be referred to as the decoders. The decoders, using a combination of the predecoded information and the x86 instruction bytes in the instruction buffer, produce and load four RISC-like operations, called *RISC86 operations*, into the scheduler of the execution engine. RISC86 operations are also called *RISC86 Ops*, *Ops*, or merely *operations*. Our usual term will be Ops. Each cycle, the decoders decode up to two x86 instructions to produce and load a set of up to four RISC86 operations into the scheduler.

HISTORICAL COMMENT

Peter Kogge's Insightful Book

The x86 instruction set architecture began with the Intel 4004 microprocessor, designed in 1969. Architectural innovations such as the use of pipelining, superscalar, speculative, and out-of-order execution were used in a number of mainframe computers at that time. Although these design techniques were not used in early generations of x86 microprocessors, recent members of the x86 family have employed all of them. See Peter M. Kogge's insightful book, *The Architecture of Pipelined Computers*, McGraw-Hill Book Company, 1981, for a detailed technical discussion and an interesting and reasonably complete history of the evolution of these design techniques in many important pre-microprocessor architectures that helped shape many of the current microarchitectural design approaches.

RISC86 Ops are RISC-like, fixed-format, internal Enhanced RISC86 microarchitecture instructions. Taken together, they form the "RISC86 operation set." Generally, all execute in a single clock cycle; register operations have a one-or two-cycle latency and load and store operations have a two-cycle execution latency. RISC86 Ops can be combined, as required, into sequences of Ops to perform every function of the x86 instruction set.

DESIGN NOTE

Enhanced RISC86 Microarchitecture

The Enhanced RISC86 microarchitecture and its underlying RISC86 operation set are optimized for execution of the x86 instruction set architecture, while adhering to the architectural principles of fixed length encoding, regularized fields, and a large register set, common in most RISC architectures.

Some x86 instructions are decoded (translated) into as few as zero Ops (e.g., a RISC86 NoOp) or one Op (e.g., a RISC86 register-to-register add Op). More complex x86 instructions are decoded into several Ops. A more detailed treatment of the operation set is given later in this chapter and Chapter 3. There are six types of Ops:

Table 2.2 TYPES OF RISC86 OPS

Types of Ops	Mnemonic
memory load operations	LdOps
memory store operations	StOps
integer register operations, MMX register operations, and 3D register operations	Integer, MMX, and 3D RegOps
floating-point register operations	FpOps
branch condition evaluations	BrOps
special operations (such as load immediate constant into a register)	SpecOps

When a particular discussion is applicable to both LdOps and StOps, the terms LdStOp or LdStOps will be used, as appropriate. The following simple example gives a series of x86 instructions and corresponding decoded RISC86 Ops using the resources shown in Figure 2.2.

EXAMPLE CODE FRAGMENT

x86 instruction	Type of Op	Comment
MOV CX,[SP+4]	LdOp	The MOV instruction is decoded into a Load Op that requires data to be loaded from memory using the Load Unit.
ADD AX,BX	RegOp	The add instruction is decoded into an ALU Add Op that can be sent to either Register Unit X or Register Unit Y.
CMP CX,[AX]	LdOp, RegOp	The CMP (compare) instruction is decoded into two Ops. A Load Op requiring data to be loaded from memory using the Load Unit followed by an ALU Sub Op that would be sent to either Register Unit X or Register Unit Y. Static flag values produced by the Sub Op reflect the result of the comparison.
JZ TA	BrOp	Conditional branch to "TA" (Target Address) based on Zflag = 1

L1–CACHE, L2– CACHE, STORE QUEUE, AND SYSTEM INTERFACE

The execution engine interfaces to the on-chip 64-Kbyte L1-Cache. This cache is split into the 32-Kbyte L1 I-Cache mentioned earlier and a 32-KByte L1 Data Cache (L1 D-Cache). Split caches, such as these, are sometimes referred to as Harvard Architectures. One of the first references to this term can be found in Cragon, H. G., "The Elements of Single-Chip Microcomputer Architecture," *Computer*, Vol. 13, No. 10, October 1980, pp. 27-41.

Both caches are 2-way set associative with a 64-byte line size and 32-byte subblocking. There are 256 sets in each cache and each set contains two ways (or lines). Cache lines are fetched from main memory or the on-chip Level-2 Cache (L2-Cache). using a burst bus transaction of four octets (or four quadwords in x86 terminology). Bus transactions are discussed in detail in Chapter 4.

The L2-Cache is a 256-Kbyte unified cache, is 4-way set associative, and has a 64-byte line-size with 32-byte subblocking. The L2-Cache employs a true LRU replacement algorithm. A store queue is used in conjunction with the L1 D-Cache. *Abortable* state changes are supported by the scheduler and the store queue through the general technique of temporarily storing (a) register and status results in the scheduler entries and (b) memory write data in store queue entries until the associated Ops are committed and retired.

DEFINITIONS
Abortable and Nonabortable
Abortable refers to changes that can be speculatively performed and later backed out of. Nonabortable changes cannot be backed out of once they are performed,

As will be seen in more detail later, the L1 I-Cache supports single cycle accesses. Both of the K6 3D's L1-Caches are interfaced through the system interface to the L2-Cache. The L1-Cache and L2-Cache are key to the scalability and performance of the K6 as the core frequencies increase.

HISTORICAL COMMENT AND DESIGN NOTES
Cache-Related Issues
In order to increase the access bandwidth, the L1 D-Cache is pipelined. It supports simultaneous loads and stores in a single clock. Bank conflicts are eliminated by performing loads first, followed by stores in a pipelined manner. Each access takes one clock cycle of time; the start of store accesses is offset by half a cycle from the start of load accesses.

Write performance is enhanced using a full write-back policy. Write-back caches are also called copy back, store in, nonstore through, or swapping caches in the literature. When data are written to a specific cache line, its "modified" (or "dirty") bit is set to indicate this. The cache line is actually stored in main memory only when the cache line is replaced. The intent is to reduce the overall traffic on the bus.

In contrast to the K6 3D, the K6 does not have an on-chip L2-Cache. The K6 has full support for an external (off-chip) L2-Cache, including a means for inhibiting the normal operation of its on-chip L1 I-Cache and L1 D-Cache (which are identical to the K6 3D's L1-Caches). This capability allows designers to disable the on-chip L1-Caches while testing the external L2-Cache. A complete description of the K6's L1-Caches and L2-Cache support can be found in the AMD-K6 MMX Processor Data Sheet which is on the companion CD-ROM. This also means that the system interface, shown in Figure 2.2 on page 69 and Figure 2.22 on page 180 for the K6 3D, is somewhat different for the K6.

Cache coherency is maintained using the MESI protocol. More will be said about the L1 and L2 caches later.

As mentioned earlier, during each processor cycle, the L1 I-Cache can place x86 instruction bytes into a 16-byte instruction buffer which directly feeds the decoders. The decoders produce and load four Ops into the scheduler's centralized buffer. The four Ops taken together are called an OpQuad. The scheduler is the heart of the K6 microarchitecture. It contains the logic necessary to manage out-of-order, speculative execution, data forwarding, implicit register renaming, and the simultaneous issue, execution, and retirement of multiple Ops per cycle. The scheduler's centralized buffer can hold up to twenty-four Ops. This is equivalent to six to twelve x86 instructions. The scheduler will be discussed in substantial detail in this book because of its importance and unique design.

SUPERSCALAR DESIGN   Superscalar processors contain a number of execution units that can operate in parallel. The K6 3D is such a processor. It has six specialized execution units that can operate in parallel and are shown in Figure 2.2 on page 69: the Store Unit (SU), Load Unit (LU), Register Unit X (RUX), Register Unit Y (RUY), Floating-Point Unit (FPU), and the Branch Resolving Unit (BRU). As will be seen, RUX and RUY can execute integer, MMX, and 3D instructions.

The non-3D versions of the K6 actually have seven execution units. These microprocessors have a separate MMX unit that overlaps with the operation of RUX. More will be said later about the differences between the versions of the K6 that support the 3D instructions and those which do not, as appropriate throughout this book.

HISTORICAL COMMENT AND SUGGESTED READINGS

x86 Instruction Set Architecture MMX Extensions

Intel publicly released many details of its MMX extensions to the x86 instruction set architecture in March, 1996 in a rather extensive San Francisco news release, "Intel Releases MMX™ Technology Details to Software Community to Drive New Multimedia, Game, and Internet Applications." This news release can be found on the Developers' Insight CD-ROM, Intel Corp., April 1997, Reference SKU #273000, Intel Corporation, 5000 West Chandler Blvd. CH6-413, Chandler, AZ 85226. These extensions consist of new instructions and data types aimed at increasing the performance of x86 processors in multimedia applications. Implementations of the instructions can make use of SIMD (single-instruction stream, multiple-data stream) techniques to process multiple 8, 16, or 32-bits in a 64-bit data path to achieve highly parallel performance in compute-intensive multimedia code. The instruction set extensions consist of 57 new instructions that support addition, subtraction, multiplication, multiply-accumulates, logical or arithmetic shifts, and several other operations that can be executed on all three sizes of data. See *MMX™ Technology Technical Overview* and the *MMX™ Technology Developers' Guide*, both which also are on the Developers' Insight CD-ROM cited above. Another source for related material is the Carole Dulong, David Bistry, Mickey Gutman and Mike Julier book, *The Complete Guide to MMX Technology*, McGraw-Hill, 1997.

We would like to summarize some of the notations used so far. The following sets of terms, listed in alphabetical order for convenience, are used as synonyms in the text and the companion CD-ROM:

1. branch resolving unit and BRU.
2. decoders and instruction decoders.

3. instruction(s) and x86 instruction(s.)

4. K6 3D, K6, K6 microarchitecture, and RISC86® microarchitecture.

5. L1 I-Cache and L1 Instruction Cache.

6. L1 D-Cache, L1 Data Cache, and L1 Dual-Ported Data Cache.

7. operation(s), Ops, RISC86 operation(s), and RISC86 Op(s).

8. 3D Ops.

9. Register Unit X and RUX.

10. Register Unit Y and RUY.

HISTORICAL COMMENT AND SUGGESTED READINGS

K6 3D Technology

K6 3D Technology consists of a set of extensions to the x86 instruction set architecture. Most of these new instructions can be viewed as being floating-point analogs of the MMX instructions discussed in the preceding "Historical Comment and Suggested Reading" inset. Whereas MMX instructions operate on packed sets of 8-bit, 16-bit, and 32-bit fixed point or integer values (within 64-bit wide MMX registers), the 3D instructions operate on packed pairs of 32-bit single-precision IEEE-compatible floating-point values (also within the same 64-bit wide MMX registers). In both cases these are "single instruction stream multiple data stream" or "SIMD" type instructions.

The 3D instruction set extensions were developed with the goal of greatly accelerating floating-point intensive computations, many of which contain substantial parallelism and thus an opportunity to benefit from SIMD floating-point instructions (in contrast to existing scalar x87 instructions within the x86 instruction set architecture). From an application software perspective, the goal was to greatly accelerate a range of multimedia algorithms, particularly in the area of 3D graphics and games. With the increasing use of 3D graphics, hardware accelerators are becoming more popular. These accelerators focus on backend graphics processing, i.e., the triangle/pixel rendering stages of the 3D graphics processing pipeline. Given this, the front-end stages of the graphics pipeline are becoming the performance bottleneck. These stages, which perform geometry transform, clipping, and lighting computations are all floating-point intensive and benefit substantially from the use of 3D instructions. In addition, as games and other multimedia applications evolve toward increasingly more accurate and physics-based modeling of 3D worlds and the interactions between objects in these worlds, the need for even greater levels of floating-point performance continues to grow. Ultimately it is expected that physics-based modeling and simulation computations will equal and surpass the traditional 3D graphics processing pipeline in the amount of floating-point computations and performance that is required. Other areas, such as audio and speech processing, and artificial intelligence/neural network algorithms, will also add to this.

An AMD application note describing the MMX extensions and related optimization, *AMD-K6 MMX Enhanced x86 Code Optimization*, can be found on the companion CD-ROM, as well as a application note related to K6 3D K6 3D optimizations, *AMD-K6 3D Processor Code Optimization*.

The decoders place four Ops in the scheduler's centralized buffer each cycle. The buffer's size, matched to the typical execution lifetime of Ops, allows the decoders to operate largely independently of the execution units. Such a buffer is often called an instruction window, which we formally define below.

The scheduler's issue logic examines the Ops in the buffer, selecting appropriate ones subject to dependencies and resource constraints. It is capable of issuing up to six Ops, out-of-order, each cycle, independently of the decoders. The execution engine can also execute them out-of-order, independently of the decoders. A microprocessor is said to have a decoupled decode/execution microarchitecture when the decode of instructions takes place independently of the issuing and execution of operations. Thus, the K6 is a decoupled decode/execution superscalar processor.

After completion, Ops are committed in-order by the Op Commit Unit (OCU), shown in Figure 2.2 on page 69. The scheduler effectively serves as a re-order buffer to ensure precise exceptions and x86 compatibility.

Historical Comment, Definition, and Suggested Readings

Instruction Windows and Reservation Stations

An instruction window allows a scheduler to optimize the execution of operations by issuing them to the appropriate execution units as the units are available and as various dependencies allow. There are two basic ways to implement instruction windows: centralized or distributed.

Distributed instruction windows, typically called *reservation stations*, are located with each functional unit. The reservation stations at the functional units can be (and often are) different in size from one another. Although their individual sizes are smaller, the aggregate size of the reservation stations is typically larger than the size of the single instruction window to achieve the same amount of instruction look ahead.

Centralized instruction windows provide the storage for both the operands and results of the functional units. The K6 scheduler buffer may be viewed as a type of centralized instruction window. More will be said about this later. Note that we have been using the terminology "x86 instruction" and "RISC86 operation." We will use this terminology consistently throughout this book. The K6's scheduler's buffer can be thought of as providing either an *instruction window* or an *Op window* since x86 instructions are decoded into RISC86 Ops. We will use the term *centralized buffer* or *buffer* when referring to the K6's Op window.

The first article that the authors are aware of that introduced the use of reservation stations was the insightful and seminal article by R. M. Tomasulo, "An Efficient Algorithm for Exploiting Multiple Arithmetic Units," *IBM Journal of Research and Development*, Vol. 11, January 1967, pp. 25-33. The full text version of this article is on the companion CD-ROM. Similarly, the first article we are aware of which uses a form of centralized instruction window is James E. Thornton's article, "Parallel Operation in the Control Data 6600," *Proc. AFIPS Fall Joint Computer Conference*, Part. II, 1964, pp. 33-40, in which the scoreboard of the CDC 6000 is described.

As is seen later, we use the terms *retired*, *committed*, and *removed* in a particular way in this book. Retiring an operation does not imply the results of the operation are either permanent or non permanent. We will use the term *committed* to mean that the results of an operation have been made permanent and the operation retired from the scheduler. *Retiring* means removal from the scheduler with or without the commitment of operation results, whichever is appropriate. Timing-wise, commitment and retirement often happen simultaneously. We will use the term *removed* to mean the operation is retired from the scheduler without making permanent changes.

DEFINITIONS
Decoupled Decode and Execution Decoupled Execution and Commitment A microprocessor is said to have a decoupled decode/execution microarchitecture when the decode of instructions takes place independently of the issuing and execution of operations.   However, microprocessors that support out-of-order execution have an equally important decoupling. In such processors, results are often produced out-of-program-order as the various operations may issue out-of-order and may take different amounts of time to complete. The process of commitment (i.e., making permanent changes in the architecture's state) is decoupled from the execution of the operations. This allows the facility that commits the results to re-order them in program order. A microprocessor is said to have a decoupled execution/commitment microarchitecture when the execution of operations takes place independently of the commitment of the results of these operations.

THE EXECUTION UNITS

As we mentioned when discussing the K6 3D block diagram, we said it has six specialized execution units that can operate in parallel: the Load Unit (LU), Store Unit (SU), Register Unit X (RUX), Register Unit Y (RUY), Floating-Point Unit (FPU), and the Branch Resolving Unit (BRU).

The LU and the SU are pipelined execution units. Before summarizing their functionality, we need to review some aspects of x86 address calculations.

x86 ADDRESS CALCULATIONS

Physical, Virtual and Logical Addresses

The x86 instruction set architecture defines a word as two bytes or sixteen bits. A double word is four bytes or thirty-two bits. The phrase "double word" is often abbreviated as "dword." The x86 architecture treats physical memory as a linear array of bytes. Each byte has a unique address which is known as its *physical address*. Since the x86 instruction set architecture uses byte addressing, memory is organized and accessed as a sequence of bytes. No matter if one or more bytes are being accessed in the x86's address space, a byte address is used to locate the first byte of the set of bytes to be accessed.

Programs that execute on the x86 use a two-part address which is translated, or mapped, into physical addresses. The translation is done by an address translation mechanism and the two-part addresses are often called *virtual addresses* because these addresses do not correspond directly to a physical address, but correspond indirectly to one through the address translation mechanism. Virtual addresses are sometimes called *logical addresses*. The virtual-to-physical mapping mechanism also provides for both memory protection and the determination of a *valid* address (i.e., that an address is present in memory).

The two-part virtual address consists of a 16-bit segment selector and a 32-bit offset. The x86 employs a two-stage mapping mechanism to translate the two-part selector and offset virtual address into a physical address. The virtual address is first translated via a segmentation mapping mechanism into a 32-bit *linear address*. The linear address is then translated into a 32-bit *physical address* via a page mapping mechanism. Thus, the two well-known virtual memory mapping techniques—segmentation and paging—are used. For the specific segmentation and paging techniques defined for the x86 instruction set architecture, see "Programming the 80386," by John H. Crawford and Patrick P. Gelsinger, Sybex, 1987.

Given this brief background in the text inset, we can return our discussion of the LU. The LU performs data memory reads. When the LU unit receives its operand values, it first performs the general calculation,

base register + scaled index register + displacement

yielding the x86 architecturally defined logical address, adds this to the segment base address to produce the architecturally defined linear address which is checked against the segment limit. The linear address is also translated to a physical address by the LU using the data translation lookaside buffer, i.e., data-TLB or D-TLB. The physical address is sent to the store queue and to L1 D-Cache in parallel. Typically data is received from the L1 D-Cache and, assuming a cache hit occurs, the data coming out of the L1 D-Cache is driven onto the LU's result bus. However, if the address matches a store queue entry then the store queue entry takes priority over a hit in the cache and data for the store queue entry is driven onto the LU's result bus. Both the L1 D-Cache and store queue "hit" analyses are based on the comparison of physical addresses received from the data-TLB, even though the D-Cache indexing is based on linear address bits.

We will see later that the LU is pipelined. The LU's pipelined design has the advantage of limiting the penalty for misaligned data loads to a latency of one cycle longer. In the x86 instruction set architecture, a misaligned access occurs either when an 8-byte (a quadword) access is made to an address that is not on an 8-byte boundary, or when a word or a double word access is made to an address that is not on a 4-byte boundary. Misaligned accesses are discussed in more detail later in this chapter, see "Faults, Traps, Abort Cycles, and the Pipelines" on page 168. Data are available from the LU after only two clocks or three clocks in the case of a misaligned access.

DESIGN NOTE

Linearly Indexed and Physically Tagged L1 Cache

Both the L1 I-Cache and the L1 D-Cache are linearly indexed and physically tagged. The L2 Cache is physically indexed and physically tagged. These concepts will be discussed later.

The SU performs address calculations for all store operations as well as for the load effective address and push operations. Logical and linear address calculations and translation to a physical address finish by fetching the memory write data from a register. Upon completion, the SU creates an entry in the store queue to hold the memory write address and data information. The store queue serves to buffer memory writes until they can be committed into the L1 D-Cache. Forwarding of write data from a store queue entry to dependent LdOps is supported. We will learn later that these entries are not valid until the very next cycle after the StOp execution completes. We will also learn the SU is also pipelined

> **DESIGN NOTE**
>
> Memory Aligned and Register Aligned Data
>
> Data stored in the L1 D-Cache and store queue are memory aligned. This means that byte[0] of the 64-bit wide bus always carries bytes where the lower three bits are zero, so they are effectively memory byte addresses. However, data that ends up on the result bus must be register aligned. If a one-byte read is being done, the one valid byte must be on the low byte of the bus, if a two-byte read is being done, then two valid bytes must be on the lower two bytes of the bus, and so on. The K6 employs byte rotators to convert (or map) between these two alignments. See Figure 2.16 on page 165 and Figure 2.19 on page 168.

The RUX (Register Unit X) supports all integer ALU operations—multiplies, divides (signed and unsigned), shifts, and rotates. It can also perform MMX and 3D operations. The RUY (Register Unit Y) can operate on the basic word and double word integer ALU operations—ADD, AND, CMP, OR, SUB, XOR, zero-extend and sign-extend operations. It can also perform MMX and 3D operations. In fact, RUX and RUY share arithmetic resources to execute some of the MMX operations and all of the 3D operations. The relationship between RUX and RUY and the integer, MMX, and 3D operations that each register unit supports is shown in Figure 2.3. The K6 3D has two pipelines for executing integer, MMX, and 3D RegOps.

Generally speaking, RUX and RUY are symmetric pipelines. This means that any Op can issue to either pipeline. The one exception is that some of the integer Ops can only be executed by the RUX pipeline as shown in Figure 2.3.

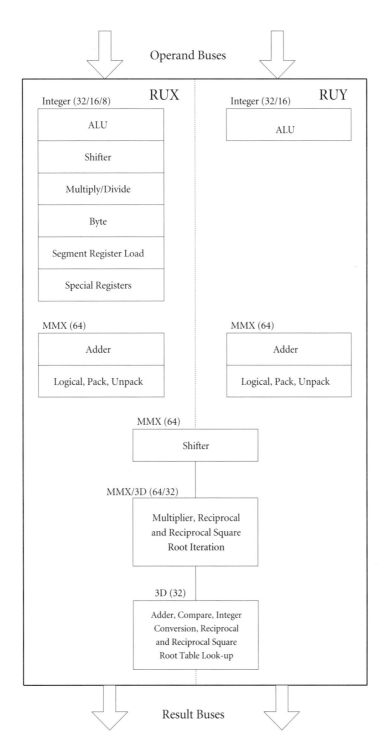

Figure 2.3 RUX AND RUY EXECUTION UNITS

Leaving these Ops aside, the scheduler can issue an Op to either pipeline. Duplicate resources for an Op are either available or they are not available, (e.g., there are two integer ALUs and two MMX adders, but there is only one MMX multiplier). An Op that has duplicate resources available to it can proceed down either pipeline irrespective of what operations may be processing down the other pipeline. In particular, there can be two such Ops simultaneously in execution, one proceeding down each of the two pipelines. Ops that have only one copy of the execution logic available can proceed down the appropriate pipeline. Two such Ops can proceed down both pipelines but cannot start to execute simultaneously which means that one of the OPs incurs a one-cycle *pipeline stall.*

3D instructions can be considered to be a floating-point analog of the integer MMX instructions. Their primary purpose is to provide high-performance floating-point vector operations to enhance performance on 3D graphics-oriented applications. The 3D instructions that operate in a vector fashion operate on two sets of 32-bit single-precision floating-point numbers in parallel. The FPU, in contrast, operates internally on a single pair of floating-point numbers that have an 80-bit representation in accordance with the IEEE floating-point standard (see IEEE Standard for Binary Floating-Point Arithmetic, ANSI/IEEE Standard No. 754, 1988). The 3D floating-point operations are realized in RUX and RUY. All non-3D floating-point operations are executed in the FPU. More will be said shortly about the last of the six execution units, the BRU (Branch Resolving Unit), and the branch direction prediction logic which are shown in Figure 2.3 on page 81.

Historical Comment and Suggested Readings

The K6 Floating-Point Unit

The FPU, in all members of the K6 family of microprocessors, is a direct descendant of the FPU-core that appeared in the NexGen Nx586 microprocessors, which was designed to be instruction set architecture compatible with the Intel x87 floating-point unit. (The x87 instruction set architecture is the instruction set architecture of the x87 floating-point unit.) Thus the K6 family of microprocessors uses some concepts native to the Nx586, such as tags (see the Nx586 Databook cited below). There are a number of important design implications that arise from the decision to use this core. For example, the FPU operates out of its own register file with its own rename registers. The x87 has two 80-bit operands coming in and one 80-bit result coming out in addition to architecturally defined floating-point flag bits that reside in the architecturally defined floating-point status word register. Further, floating-point operations may also modify an architecturally defined top-of-stack pointer field. See *Nx586 Processor Databook*, NexGen Inc., Preliminary, December 6, 1994, Order # NxDOC-DB001-03-W.

LATENCIES

A brief word about *latencies*. In the K6 3D, register operations fall into one of three categories: those that have a latency of one cycle, those that have a latency of two cycles, and those (like divide) that have a latency of more than two cycles. In general, all integer operations and all of the non multiply MMX instructions have a single cycle latency. MMX multiply operations have a two-cycle latency. All of the 3D operations have a two-cycle latency. Subject to dependencies and execution resource contention, two RegOps can start execution each clock regardless of whether they are one-cycle and/or two-cycle operations. For example, a 3D multiply and a 3D add can begin execution each clock cycle. At most one two-cycle latency Op, for which there are not duplicated execution resources (such as an MMX multiply), can be initiated in each cycle. One of the Ops of a pair of Ops wanting to start execution must be delayed if the Ops use a shared execution resource. This results in a delay of one cycle. Back-to-back two-cycle latency Ops that use different execution resources (such as an MMX multiply and a 3D add) can be initiated in the same cycle, one in the RUX pipeline and one in the RUY pipeline. It is important to know instruction latencies when examining instruction dependencies.

Example Code Fragments on CD-ROM

The following two application notes on the CD-ROM contain a number of examples of the timings and latencies of the execution behavior of several code fragments as a function of decode constraints, dependencies, and resource constraints, "AMD-K6 3D Processor Code Optimization," and "AMD-K6 MMX Enhanced Processor x86 Code Optimization."

The details of the inputs and outputs of RUX and RUY on the operand and result buses in Figure 2.3, as well as the inputs and outputs for each of the execution units shown in Figure 2.2 on page 69, will be discussed in later sections of this chapter. Briefly, for example, RUX and RUY take their inputs from the register operand buses, execute the required Ops producing register and status flag result values, and drive them out onto the corresponding register result and status flag buses. It is up to the scheduler to keep track of which result and status flag values are scheduled (or marked) to actually be modified.

STATUS FLAGS, FAULTS, TRAPS, INTERRUPTS, AND ABORT CYCLES

The x86 instruction set architecture supports a register called the EFLAGS register that contains a number of x86 status and control flags (see for example, Intel's publication, the *Intel Architecture Software Developer's Manual, Volume 3: System programming Guide* for a complete listing of all x86 status and control flags, exceptions, and interrupts). The values of these flags are used to control various functions in the processor. The x86 instruction set architecture defines a set of arithmetic status flags and a set of processor control flags. The x86 instruction set architecture also defines and supports exceptions and interrupts, both of which typically result in a transfer of control outside of the currently executing instruction stream. X86 exceptions occur when an unusual or invalid situation is detected during the execution of an instruction. There are two types of x86 exceptions defined, x86 faults and x86 traps. The difference between x86 faults and x86 traps is that an instruction is either aborted (x86 fault) or completed (x86 trap) before the processing of the exception. An interrupt is defined by the x86 instruction set architecture as an event external to the processor. Therefore, interrupts occur asynchronously to the execution of instructions within the processor; i.e., an interrupt has no relation to the specific instruction executing when the interrupt is recognized. X86 exceptions and interrupts are handled at instruction boundaries; that is "in between" two instructions versus within an instruction. Some x86 exceptions and x86 interrupts are given in the following table:

SAMPLE OF X86 FAULT AND TRAP EXCEPTIONS

x86 Exception Name	Type
Divide Error	Fault
Instruction Breakpoint	Fault
Data Breakpoint	Trap
Segment Not Present	Fault
Page Fault	Fault
General Protection	Fault

In particular, note that the x86 instruction set architecture treats an instruction breakpoint as a fault and a data breakpoint as a trap.

It is important to know which execution units can set status flags, which can cause exceptions or traps, and how status flags, faults, traps, and interrupts are treated. *We will always use the preface "x86" to identify an architectural status flag, fault, trap, or interrupt, such as an "x86 trap." Without this modifier, these terms will always be referring to the K6 3D microarchitecture.* Furthermore, we typically will not use the word "exception" but rather use "fault" or "trap" or both, as appropriate. All *x86 faults, x86 traps,* and *x86 interrupts* are ultimately handled by microarchitectural fault and trap handling mechanisms. Interrupts will be discussed later in this chapter.

Only integer RegOps can produce status flag values. At the microarchitecture level, the K6 3D has eight status flags—the six x86 instruction set architecture visible flags and two flags for use within sequences of Ops used in the implementation of complex instructions. All integer RegOps that have a defined behavior for status flags also have the option of modifying the status flags.

A fault or trap at the microarchitectural level causes an abort cycle that then leads to the execution of a sequence of Ops which ultimately turns the abort action into an architecturally defined exception. The only execution units that can produce faults are the LU, the SU, and the FPU. In other words, RegOps can never fault: only LdOps, StOps, and FpOps can fault. RegOps can modify status flag values. The microprocessor must support the x87 architecturally defined floating-point flag bits that reside in the architecturally defined floating-point status word register.

DESIGN NOTE

Microarchitectural Faults and Traps

In addition to supporting all of the x86 architectural exceptions and interrupts, the K6 3D supports some microarchitectural faults and traps which are:

Fault/Trap	Type
Fault Op	Fault
Self-Modifying Code Check	Trap

An abort cycle causes the invocation of a fault handler to determine what caused the fault or trap and act appropriately. Traps are handled somewhat differently than faults. When an x86 trap occurs (such as a data breakpoint trap), information associated with it is loaded into the scheduler and associated with the Op that caused it. Then, when that Op is going to be committed, the Op Commit Unit recognizes that a trap has been detected and sets a pending trap flip-flop. In effect, traps are accumulated as pending traps until the end of an x86 instruction is reached. The Op Commit Unit can recognize that it is retiring the last of all of the Ops associated with a given instruction. If there are any pending traps at the end of the commitment of an instruction, a "fault" is recognized at the beginning of the next instruction which, in turn, causes an abort cycle.

It is useful to think of the microprocessor consisting of an *upper portion* and a *lower portion* when explaining the abort cycle. This is shown in Figure 2.4 where the two portions are shaded differently. When an *abort cycle* is required, the following sequence of actions could occur to

upper and lower portions of the processor

complete the Ops in the scheduler that should be completed, with the non completed Ops being discarded:

1. let all Ops older than the Op that initiated the abort cycle commit and retire by allowing them to naturally progress down to the bottom row of the scheduler's buffer. The commitment of this Op and all younger Ops is inhibited.

2. when all older Ops have been committed, the entire machine, i.e., both the upper portion and the lower portion, can then be flushed.

3. after the flushing has been completed, instruction fetching and decoding can begin at the appropriate point.

DESIGN NOTE

Restarting the Upper Portion of the Processor

Restarting the upper portion of the processor does not affect the operation of the L1 I-Cache, therefore it is not included in the upper portion shown in Figure 2.4 on page 87. Likewise, restarting the lower portion does not affect the L1 D-Cache, so it is not part of the lower portion. If, for example, the L1 I-Cache (or the L1 D-Cache) is processing a "miss," then it is irrevocably committed to the processing of the miss.

This sequence is a direct result of a cost/performance trade-off. It allows for a simplified scheduler design. Several things are happening at the same time that need to be understood to appreciate this statement. On the one hand, the scheduler does not require logic in each entry to determine whether or not the associated Op should be flushed. When the flushing action occurs, all Ops in the scheduler will be marked "invalid." In this design approach, we will learn that a potential latency of one to two cycles in the flush action has been accepted while a simplification in the scheduler circuitry has been achieved.

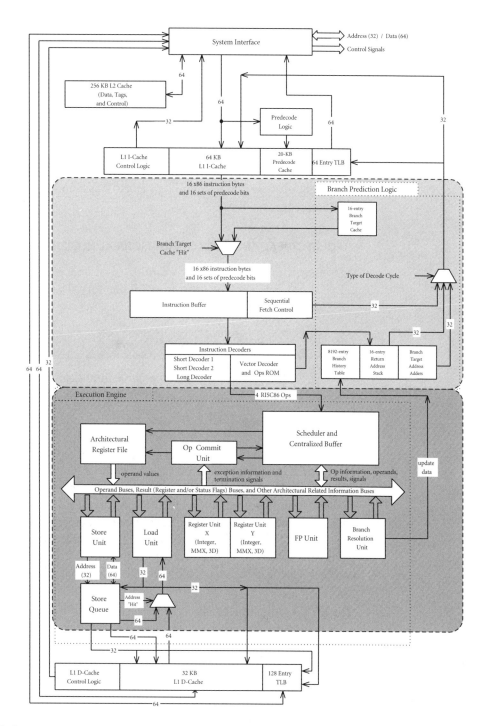

Figure 2.4 UPPER AND LOWER PORTIONS OF THE PROCESSOR

Importantly, for a BrOp-related abort, the K6 modifies the above sequence to reduce the flush performance penalty. The upper portion of the machine can be flushed while the older Ops are being completed. If Ops are generated before the lower portion of the machine can accept them (e.g., the lower portion of the processor may be in the process of invalidating the younger Ops in the scheduler), then these Ops are held until they can be consumed (see the OpQuad Buffer in Figure 2.8 on page 127.) The point is that since the fetch, decode, and execution of the Ops in the execution units are decoupled, the process of fetching and decoding the required instructions can be overlapped (done concurrently) with the completion and flushing of the appropriate Ops. More will be said about this in the section titled "Handling Faults, Traps, and Precise Interrupts" beginning on page 175.

ARCHITECTURAL AND MICROARCHITECTURAL REGISTERS

X86 instructions obtain their operands from and place their results in either the architectural registers or main memory. The execution units, in turn, must access these operands and produce the required results.

DEFINITIONS
Architectural and Microarchitectural Register Files
An architecture has a set of registers accessible by its instruction set for storing values associated with operand values, status flags, and other architectural state-related information. This set of registers is often called the *architectural register set* or *architectural register file*. The values stored in it at any instant in time are called the *architectural machine state* or *instruction set architecture machine state*. The microarchitecture typically has a different number of registers, most often a larger number, that are used not only to store the architectural machine state but also to store *microarchitectural machine state*, i.e., operand values, status flags, and state information that is used exclusively in the microarchitecture and not visible to the instruction set architecture.

The K6 3D must support all of the registers defined by the x86 instruction set architecture. These registers include:

1. eight 32-bit integer general purpose registers.
2. six 16-bit segment selector registers and associated segment descriptor registers.
3. one 32-bit (EIP) instruction pointer register.

4. x87 floating-point unit registers (a stack of eight 80-bit internal floating-point registers, a 16-bit status word register, a 16-bit control word register, and a 16-bit tag word register).

5. eight 64-bit MMX registers which, from an instruction set architecture perspective, are aliased with the eight FPU stack registers.

6. one 32-bit EFLAGS register.

7. five 32-bit control registers.

8. eight 32-bit debug (breakpoint) registers.

9. memory management registers, namely the x86 Global Descriptor Table Register, the Local Descriptor Table Register, the Interrupt Descriptor Table Register, and the Task Register.[16]

The K6 3D supports the 3D registers associated with the 3D instruction extensions to the x86 instruction set architecture. The 3D registers are conceptually and physically one and the same as the MMX registers identified in the above list. In addition, the K6 3D supports a number of special registers which are described in the section titled "Special Registers and Model Specific Registers" beginning on page 94.

Integer Registers

The K6 has twenty-four 32-bit integer registers in the integer architectural/ microarchitectural register file plus it has twenty-four 32-bit integer renaming registers. The twenty-four registers in the integer architectural/ microarchitectural register file consist of eight architecture registers that correspond to the x86 32-bit general purpose registers (EAX, EBX, ECX, EDX, EBP, ESP, ESI, and EDI) and sixteen microarchitecture scratch registers (t0 through t15). The twenty-four renaming registers are located in the scheduler's twenty-four Op entries—one per entry.

The x86's 32-bit integer architectural register set supports addressing, for byte operations, of either of the lower two bytes of half of some, but not all, of the registers. Based on a register size specification, the 3-bit register numbers within x86 instructions are interpreted as either high (H) or low (L) byte registers or as word or double-word registers. The relationship between these interpretations is seen in the following table.

---

[16] For example, the Global Descriptor Table Register holds the 32-bit base address and 16-bit segment limit for the currently active Global Descriptor Table.

Table 2.3   x86 General Purpose Register Names and Sizes

32-Bit Name (dword)	16-bit Name (word)	8-bit Name (high order byte)	8-bit Name (low order byte)
EAX	AX	AH	AL
EBX	BX	BH	BL
ECX	CX	CH	CL
EDX	DX	DH	DL
EDI	DI	—	—
ESI	SI	—	—
ESP	SP	—	—
EBP	BP	—	—

The integer microarchitecture register set also supports similar addressing of the lower two bytes of half of these scratch registers: registers +1 through +4 and registers +8 through +11. This is similar to the way in which byte addressing is supported in the x86 instruction set architecture registers.

The x87 Floating-Point Registers

As noted above, the x86 floating-point unit has eight 80-bit internal floating-point registers, a 16-bit status word register, a 16-bit control word register, and a 16-bit tag word register. The eight data registers are 80-bits wide registers and comply with the IEEE floating-point standard extended precision format. As such, the x87 instruction set architecture views them as 80-bit registers. The K6 FPU does its own local register renaming for all of its registers.

MMX and 3D Registers

The x86 MMX register set consists of eight 64-bit registers which the MMX instructions access directly using the register names MM0 through MM7. Although the eight MMX registers are defined in the x86 instruction set architecture as separate registers, they are aliased to the eight registers in the FPU data register stack. The MMX registers are mapped onto the lower sixty-four bits of the x87 registers, with the upper sixteen bits defined to effectively be all ones. The 3D instructions, being floating-point analogs of the MMX instructions, also use and share the MMX registers with the MMX instructions. Subsequently, we will call these registers the MMX/3D registers.

There are nine MMX/3D 64-bit architecture/microarchitecture registers and twelve MMX/3D 64-bit renaming registers. The nine architectural/microarchitectural registers consist of eight that correspond to the x86 architecture MMX 64-bit registers (MM0 through MM7) and one microarchitecture scratch 64-bit register (MMt1).

DESIGN NOTE

Number of MMX Registers

The K6 has six 64-bit MMX renaming registers which reflects its single-pipeline implementation. The K6 3D, which also supports the 3D instruction set extensions to the x86 instruction set architecture, has twelve 64-bit MMX/3D renaming registers, which reflects its dual-pipeline implementation.

 A presentation by Lance Smith, giving an overview of a non-3D version of the K6, is entitled, "*The AMD-K6 Processor: Microarchitecture Overview and Product Update*," and can be found on the CD-ROM.

REGISTER NUMBER AND NAME MAPPINGS

X86 instructions specify general registers via a 3-bit register number. In the microarchitecture, the K6 adds two leading 0's to the x86's 3-bit register number to form a 5-bit internal architecture/microarchitecture register number. Table 2.4 gives the correspondence between these 5-bit numbers and the various integer, MMX/3D, and scratch registers. The interpretation of a register number as either an integer or an MMX/3D register is, obviously, based on the instruction that is accessing the register. The uses of reg, regm, MMreg, and MMregm are explained in Chapter 3.

Table 2.4 REGISTER NUMBER/NAME CORRESPONDENCE

Register Number	32-bit Register Name	1-Byte Register Name	64-bit MMX/3D Register Name
00000	EAX	AL	MMreg
00001	ECX	CL	MMreg
00010	EDX	DL	MMreg
00011	EBX	BL	MMreg
00100	ESP	AH	MMregm
00101	EBP	CH	MMregm
00110	ESI	DH	MMregm
00111	EDI	BH	MMregm
01000	t1	t1L	MMt1
01001	t2	t2L	—
01010	t3	t3L	—
01011	t4	t4L	—
01100	t5	t1H	—
01101	t6	t2H	—
01110	t7	t3H	—
01111	t0/_[a]	t4H	—
10000	t8	t8L	—
10001	t9	t9L	—
10010	t10	t10L	—
10011	t11	t11L	—
10100	t12	t8H	—
10101	t13	t9H	—
10110	t14	t10H	—
10111	t15	t11H	—
11000	reg	reg	MM0
11001	reg	reg	MM1

Table 2.4 REGISTER NUMBER/NAME CORRESPONDENCE (CONT)

Register Number	32-bit Register Name	1-Byte Register Name	64-bit MMX/3D Register Name
11010	reg	reg	MM2
11011	reg	reg	MM3
11100	regm	regm	MM4
11101	regm	regm	MM5
11110	regm	regm	MM6
11111	regm	regm	MM7

[a] The "t0" and "_" mnemonics are synonymous. "_" is used when an operand or result value is a "don't care." t0 is like the "traditional" RISC R0 register.

DESIGN NOTE
Register Size Specification
In the section titled "Formats for Decoder Ops" beginning on page 142, we will learn that the register size, from an Op perspective, is specified by either the ASz or DSz field of the Op. ASz is used for base and index registers in LdStOps. DSz is used for the data register in LdStOps and the source operand and result or destination registers in RegOps. The scratch integer register set supports addressing of the lower two bytes of half of these registers: t1-t4 and t8-t11.

The combination of the integer architectural/microarchitectural register file and the MMX/3D architectural/microarchitectural file will be called thet Architectural Register File and is shown in Figure 2.2 on page 69. The K6 3D's implicit renaming scheme is discussed in Chapter 3. The microarchitectural and renaming registers just discussed are not the only microarchitectural registers in the K6 3D. There are additional special registers that the scheduler, OCU, and execution units use in many aspects of their work. We will now describe these special registers as some of them are referenced in the pseudo-RTL descriptions that appear in Chapter 3. You may want to skim this section now, but revisit it from time to time when reading Chapter 3.

architectural/microarchitectural register file

SPECIAL REGISTERS AND MODEL SPECIFIC REGISTERS

The special registers shown in the RUX pipeline of Figure 2.3 on page 81 are not accessible from x86 instructions. They are accessible only through special RegOps in OpQuad Sequences. What are OpQuads? The instruction decoders, during a decode cycle, always produce a group of four Ops which is called an *OpQuad* (see Figure 2.6 on page 115). What are OpQuad Sequences? A sequence of OpQuads fetched from an on-chip ROM (called the *OpQuad ROM*) is called an *OpQuad Sequence*. Only the hardware decodes of common/simple instructions produce a single OpQuad. OpQuad sequences result from the decode of more complex instructions. OpQuads and OpQuad sequences are discussed in considerably more detail in the section titled "OpQuad Sequences" beginning on page 137.

Video Clip on CD-ROM

 Greg Favor, Principal Architect of the K6 3D, addresses the following question in this video clip, "Why do you translate x86 instructions into RSIC86 Op sequences?"

The special registers are used for a variety of purposes including internal configuration, debugging, and the processing of traps. Although the special registers are not meant for general use, some of them contain information that is made available to BIOS and operating system implementers via reads and writes to what are termed *model-specific registers.*

SUGGESTED READINGS

Model-Specific Registers

 Discussions of the K6 3D and K6 model-specific registers and the instructions that access the data in them, RDMSR (Read Model-Specific Register) and WRMSR (Write Model Specific Register), can be found in the *AMD K86 Family BIOS Design Application Note* on the CD-ROM.

Some of the special registers reside physically within the RUX, others are external to the RUX in other execution units, other blocks of the machine, or in a special scratchpad memory. In general, when the special registers external to the RUX and in other blocks of the machine are read in an OpQuad Sequence, two reads are required. The first read loads a temporary internal RUX register from the external unit. The second read delivers the data to its destination from this temporary register.

scratchpad memory

The following codes will be used in the "Access" column in the tables that follow:

INTERPRETATION FOR THE ACCESS COLUMN

Access	Interpretation
R	Read-only special registers
W	Write-only special registers
R/W	Readable and writable special registers
E/W	Write-only special registers; readable copy maintained in scratchpad memory

Additionally, all "Reserved" bits are read as zero and should be written with either a zero for forward compatibility with software use of these bits. Some x86 architectural registers (e.g., some of the CRxx, DRxx, and TRx registers plus other registers such as TR and data segment selector registers) are maintained <u>only</u> in scratchpad memory and are thus R/W scratchpad memory locations. Special registers in scratchpad memory are read using a single LdOP versus one or two RegOPs. Such registers are not included in the tables that follow.

Table 2.5 SR0, GENERAL CONTROL AND STATUS REGISTER

Bit	Name	Function	Access
0:1	CPL	Copy of architectural current privilege level (CPL)	R
2	IOS	I/O sensitivity status	R
3	V86	V86 mode = EFlags.VM && CR0.PE	R
4	REAL	Real Mode = !CR0.PE	R
5	EWBE	External write buffer empty	R
6	BusBsy	Indicates if there are any active/asserted internal requests for bus cycles in the processor system bus	R
7	PMSP	POP memory base = SP (from OpQuad Sequence environment)	R
8	FLUSHP	FLUSH# request pending	R
9	SMIP	SMI# request pending	R
10	INITP	INIT request pending	R
11	NMIP	NMI request pending	R
12	INTRP	INTR request pending	R
13	STPCLKP	STPCLK request pending	R
14	VME	Virtual Mode Extension	R/W
15	PVI	Protected Virtual Interrupt	R/W
16	ClrFLUSHP	Clear FLUSH# edge latch	W
17	ClrSMIP	Clear SMI# edge latch	W
18	ClrINITP	Clear INIT edge latch	W
19	ClrNMIP	Clear NMI edge latch	W
20	ClrISTF	Clear INTR/STPCLK# temporary mask flag	W
21	ClrBSNTF	Clear IBrkPt/SMI#/NMI temporary mask flg	W

Table 2.5 SR0, General Control and Status Register (Cont)

Bit	Name	Function	Access
22	NF	NMI mask flag	R/W
23	RIF	Halt instruction fetch	W
24	SMIACT	System management mode active	R/W
25	FERR	Floating-point error pending	R/W
26	StopClk	Allows an OpQuad sequence to stop clock	R/W
27	HaltClk	Allows an OpQuad sequence to stop clock	R/W
28	IGNNE	Ignore CR0.NE	R
29	RBGO	RAM BIST go/initiate	W
30	RBDN	RAM BIST done status	R
31	RBPF	RAM BIST pass/fail status	R

The K6 3D implements various test and debug modes to enable the functional and manufacturing testing of systems and boards that use the processor. In addition, the debug features of the processor allow designers to debug the instruction execution of software components. Some of these test and debug features, which were discussed in Chapter 1, are:

1. built-in self-test (BIST) which is invoked after the falling transition of the x86 RESET signal and runs internal tests that exercise most on-chip RAM and ROM structures, e.g., the L1-Cache, and the TLBs.

2. a tri-state test mode that causes the processor to float its output and bidirectional pins.

3. a boundary-scan test access port (TAP)—which supports the IEEE standard that defines synchronous scanning test methods for complex logic circuits, such as boards containing a processor. The Joint Test Action Group (JTAG) test access function is defined in the *IEEE Standard Test Access Port and Boundary-Scan Architecture*, IEEE 1149.1-1990, IEEE Press.

4. an L1-Cache Inhibit—a feature that disables the processor's internal L1 instruction and data caches.

5. debug support—consists of all x86-compatible software debug features, including the debug extensions.

Boundary-scan testing uses a shift register consisting of the serial interconnection of boundary-scan cells that correspond to each I/O buffer of the processor. This register chain, called a Boundary Scan Register (BSR), can be used to capture the state of every processor pin and to drive every processor output and bidirectional pin to a known state. You will see support for these features in a number of the fields of various special registers, such as the two BIST-related bits in SR0.

The contents of the SR1 register are defined in Table 2.6.

Table 2.6 SR1, FAULT CONTROL AND STATUS REGISTER

Bit	Name	Function	Access
2:0	FID	Fault ID from the OCU	R
3	TSA	TS access fault	R
4	ClrDTF	Clear x86 debug trap pending flag	W
5	ClrSSTF	Clear x86 single-step trap pending flag	W
6	FPF	FpOp fault	R
7	EF	OpQuad Sequence fault	R
10:8	IPFI	Instruction page fault information	R
11	DlyPG	Delay new CR0 PG bit effect	W
14:12	DPFI	Data page fault information	R
15	BIM	Burn-In Mode	R
19:16	DBN	x86 Data Break Point debug status	R
23:20	IBN	x86 Instruction Break Points debug status	R
26:24	SubOpcd	Sub-Opcode (MODR/M[5:3] from OpQuad Sequence Environment)	R
28:27	OCPL	Old CPL (from OpQuad Sequence Environment)	R
29	RBD	RAM BIST Disable	R
30	SSTF	x86 single-step trap pending flag	R
31	SDM	Select Direct Mapped	R

The contents of the SR2 Instruction Page Fault Register are defined as follows:

Table 2.7 SR2, INSTRUCTION AND PAGE FAULT REGISTER

Bit	Name	Function	Access
31:0	—	Logical address of last instruction fetch page fault	R

The contents of the SR3 Data Page Fault Register are defined as:

Table 2.8   SR3, PAGE FAULT REGISTER

BIT	NAME	FUNCTION	ACCESS
31:0	—	Logical address of last operand page fault	R

The contents of the SR4 Fault PC Register are as follows:

Table 2.9   SR4, FAULT PC REGISTER

BIT	NAME	FUNCTION	ACCESS
31:0	—	Logical address of last operand page fault	R

The contents of the SR5 register follow. The SR5 Configuration Register in RUX is write only. There is a readable shadow copy of it kept in the scratchpad memory. An OpQuad Sequence always updates these copies together to keep them in synchronization. There are additional debug features only available via special debug packages used during "silicon" debug. These are in contrast to the test and debug features mentioned on page 97 which are publicly accessible.

Table 2.10   SR5, CONFIGURATION REGISTER (IN RUX)

Bit	Name	Function	Access
0	L1ICD	L1 I-Cache disable	E/W
1	L1DCD	L1 D-Cache disable	E/W
2	L1CI	L1 Cache inhibit (TR12.CI)	E/W
3	DE	Debug extension enable (CR4.DE)	E/W
4	PSE	Page size enable (CR4.PSE)	E/W
5	WAD	Write allocate disable	E/W
6	PDD	Power down disable	E/W
7	NPFCD	NP freeze clock disable	E/W
8	SMO	Strong memory order	E/W
9	VSMO	Very strong memory order	E/W
10	SMCD	Self-Modifying Code trap disable	E/W
11	BPTD	Branch Prediction Table disable	E/W
12	BTBD	Branch Target Buffer disable	E/W

Table 2.10 SR5, CONFIGURATION REGISTER (IN RUX) (CONT)

Bit	Name	Function	Access
13	ROBD	RegOp bumping disable	E/W
14	LCKD	Lock disable	E/W
15	STQFD	STQ forward data disable	E/W
16	DCERLR	D-Cache enable random line replacement	E/W
17	DCSLD	D-Cache speculative load disable	E/W
18	ICERLR	I-Cache enable random line replacement	E/W
19	WBCD	Write back cache disable	E/W
20	SLDD	Speculative load disable	E/W
21	DTBDM	DTB direct mapped	E/W
22	DCDM	D-Cache direct mapped	E/W
23	ICDM	I-Cache direct mapped	E/W
28:24	REGN	Register number	E/W
29	RUYD	RUY disable	E/W
30	BPTNT	When BPTD=1, BPTNT indicates prediction direction; 1 = not taken, 0 = taken	E/W
31	ICPFD	I-Cache prefetch disable	E/W

The copy of the SR13 Instruction Decode Control Register in RUX is write only. There is a read/write shadow copy of it kept in the scratchpad memory. With the exception of setting SetVEC1, an OpQuad Sequence always updates these copies together to keep them in synchronization. Just as with SR5, these are additional debug features used during silicon debug. The contents of the SR13 register are defined as follows:

Table 2.11 SR13, INSTRUCTION DECODE CONTROL REGISTER

Bit	Name	Function	Access
7:0	SDD	Short decode disable bit mask	E/W
9:8	MDD	Multiple decode disable	E/W
10	LDD	Long decode disable	E/W
11	SetVEC1	Set "force HDD for one decode"	W
12	ExtExcpVEC	External OpQuad Sequence exception group	E/W

Table 2.11   SR13, Instruction Decode Control Register (Cont)

Bit	Name	Function	Access
13	ESCDD	ESC (FPU) decode disable	E/W
14	MMXDD	MMX/3D decode disable	E/W
15	SD2D	0F opcode short decode disable	E/W
31:16	ExtVEC	External OpQuad Sequence decode group	E/W

The SDD and SD2D bits, described in the following design note, are also for silicon debug purposes—bypassing broken hardware and/or patching the OpQuad Sequences for complex instructions.

DESIGN NOTE

SDD and SD2D Bits

The SDD and SD2D bits are used in conjunction with the predecoding logic discussed in the section titled "Predecoding Logic" beginning on page 115. *You may want to reread this design note after you have studied that section.* The SDD and Sd2D bits are used to prevent the marking of an instruction as being able to be decoded by one of the short decoders. When an instruction is inhibited from being short-decoded, it is either long decoded or, in most cases, vector decoded. When it is vector decoded, the vector decoder provides an OpQuad Sequence entry point which, by default, is located in the on-chip OpQuad ROM but may be forced to come from the off-chip memory. When the SDD and SD2D bits are changed, the I-Cache and predecode cache should be flushed. Each of the eight SDD bits control two rows of the one-byte x86 instruction opcode map. Thus, SDD[0] controls opcode rows 0 and 1, SDD[1] controls opcode rows 2 and 3, and so on. The SD2D bit controls all opcodes in the two-byte x86 instruction opcode map. Each of the 16 bits in ExtVEC controls two rows in the x86 instruction opcode map. Specifically, the low-order eight bits control the rows of the one-byte x86 instruction opcode map, and the high-order eight bits control the rows of the two-byte opcode map. To have opcodes handled by external OpQuad Sequence entry points, both the appropriate SDD/SD2D bit(s) and the appropriate ExtVEC bit(s) have to be set. An OpQuad Sequence should not update SR13 in the scratchpad memory when the SETVEC1 bit is set, since that bit is not "sticky" in the special registers internal to RUX.

The contents of the SR16 MMX/3D Status Bits Register are defined as follows:

Table 2.12 SR16, MMX/3D STATUS BITS REGISTER

Bit	Name	Function	Access
7:0	MMXD	MMX/3D data register dirty bits	R
8	MMXSTC	MMX/3D store instruction committed	R
31:9	Reserved	—	—

Reading SR16 clears both SR15.MMXD[7:0] and SR15.MMXSTC. Registers SR17 and SR18 are associated with the Time Stamp Counter (TSC) Bits; SR17 with TSC High and SR18 with TSC Low as seen in Table 2.13.

Table 2.13 SR17 AND SR18, TIME STAMP CONTROL REGISTERS

Bit	Name	Function	Access
31:0	TSCL	Must synchronize read and write with TSCH to avoid overflow to TSCH.	R/W
63:32	TSCH	Must synchronize read and write with TSCL to avoid overflow from TSCL.	R/W

The copy of the SR21 Configuration Register RUX is write only. There is a read/write shadow copy of it kept in the scratchpad memory. An OpQuad Sequence always updates these copies together to keep them in synchronization. The contents of the SR21 register are defined as follows:

Table 2.14 SR21, CONFIGURATION REGISTER (IN RUX)

Bit	Name	Function	Access
0	Reserved	—	—
1	NAD	NA# Disable	E/W
2	SIE	Stop Interrupt Enable	E/W
3	FEEC	Force External OpQuad Sequence Cacheable	E/W
4	SSD	String SMI Disable	E/W
14:5	Reserved	—	—
15	INVC	INValidate Caches	E/W
16	WAE15M	Write Allocate Enable 15M-16M	E/W

Table 2.14 SR21, CONFIGURATION REGISTER (IN RUX) (CONT)

Bit	Name	Function	Access
23:17	WAELIM[6:0]	Write Allocate Enable Limit	E/W
24	PDED	Predecode Cache Disable	E/W
31:25	Reserved	—	—

DESIGN NOTE

Upper Limit of Memory

The WAELIM[6:0] defines the upper limit of memory where write allocates are allowed. This is done in 4M quantities as follows: Lower-Limit = 0x0, UpperLimit = WAELIM[6:0] * 4M (max = 508 Mbyte). Excluded areas are: 640K - 1M and, if WAE15M = 0, 15M -16M.

segment not Present

what is N.P.?

The contents of the SR24 NP Presence and Opcode Register are defined as follows:

Table 2.15 SR24, NP PRESENCE AND OPCODE REGISTER

Bit	Name	Function	Access
10:0	FpOpcd	NP opcode register	R/W
30:11	Reserved	—	—
31	NPNotPres	NP Not Present	R

The contents of the SR25 NP Code Selector Register are defined as follows:

Table 2.16 SR25, NP CODE SELECTOR REGISTER

Bit	Name	Function	Access
15:0	FpOpcdSelNP	Code pointer (selector part)	R/W
27:16	Reserved	—	—
31:28	PrfxCnt	Prefix count from the OpQuad Sequence execution environment	R

The contents of the SR26 NP Code Offset Register are defined as follows:

Table 2.17 SR26, NP CODE OFFSET REGISTER

Bit	Name	Function	Access
31:0	FpCodeOffs	NP code pointer (offset part)	R/W

The contents of the SR27 NP Data Selector Register are defined as follows:

Table 2.18 SR27, NP DATA SELECTOR REGISTER

Bit	Name	Function	Access
15:0	FpDataSel	NP data pointer (selector part)	R/W
31:16	Reserved	—	—

The contents of the SR28 NP Data Offset Register are defined as follows:

Table 2.19 SR28, NP DATA OFFSET REGISTER

Bit	Name	Function	Access
31:0	FpDateOffs	NP data pointer (offset part)	R/W

The contents of the SR29 NpCFG (FPU Configuration) Register are defined as follows:

Table 2.20 SR29, NPCFG (FPU CONFIGURATION) REGISTER

Bit	Name	Function	Access
0	ClearBeforeException	Clears the Before Exception (stack fix up) bit in NP	E/W
1	Do Shared State	Allows "share-state" overlapping of p-ops which write their result one cycle after execution, with the following p-op (assuming dependencies are met).	E/W
2	Enable HyperFlg	Enables NPPop[12] (hyper flag). When not set, has the effect of always asserting NPPop[12].	E/W
3	StoreExMode	Used when issuing a "dummy" store (i.e., emulating an FST which does not store to memory). Specifically, inhibits hardware checking of result precision and rounding.	E/W
5:4	Reserved	—	—
6	FastFXCH	Enables single-pop FXCH mode	E/W

Table 2.20 SR29, NPCFG (FPU Configuration) Register (Cont)

Bit	Name	Function	Access
7	false_dependency_suppress	Enhancement to the share-state mechanism which eliminates false dependencies. See bit 1 below.	E/W
8	Disable0Cycle	Disables handling of 0-cycle Ops in NP	E/W
13:9	Reserved	—	—
14	mask_hyperterm	Disables hyper termination for the next p-op only. This bit then resets itself (internal to NP).	E/W
15	Reserved	—	E/W
16	Busy	Force pending error (i.e., always hyper terminate)	E/W
21:17	Reserved	—	E/W
22	UpperTSCWord	Upper 16 bits of 32-bit Tag/Status/Control store will be filled with inverse value of this bit	E/W
31:23	Reserved	—	E/W

Branches in x86 code fit into two categories: unconditional branches, which always change program flow (that is, the branches are always taken), and conditional branches, which may or may not divert program flow (that is, the branches are taken or not-taken based on the evaluation of a specified condition).

Because x86 programs are heavily saturated with conditional branches, branch direction prediction logic is used to avoid execution penalties associated with such changes in program flow. Up to 10% of typical application code consists of unconditional branches and another 10% to 20% conditional branches. The K6 branch direction prediction logic has been designed to handle this type of program behavior and to reduce its negative effects on instruction execution, such as stalls due to delayed instruction fetching and the draining of the processor pipeline.

The K6 handles unconditional branches by redirecting instruction fetching to the target address of the unconditional branch. Branch target addresses are calculated on-the-fly using fast adders during the decode stage (see the Branch Target Address Adders in Figure 2.2 on page 69). The adders calculate all possible target addresses before the instructions are fully decoded and the branch prediction logic then chooses the correct branch target address.

The branch target address for a conditional branch is not immediately known, however, and the K6 uses a dynamic branch direction prediction mechanism to predict the direction of the branch. Target address handling

BRANCH DIRECTION PREDICTION LOGIC AND THE BRANCH RESOLVING UNIT

branch direction prediction logic

branch target address

branch history table
BHT

is similar for both conditional branches (and unconditional PC-relative branches). That is, branch target addresses are calculated on-the-fly using fast adders during the decode stage. As in the unconditional branch case, the adders calculate all possible target addresses in parallel with the determination and selection of the correct target address. The processor then chooses either the predicted target address or the sequential next instruction address adders, based on a prediction of the direction of the branch, as the next address to continue instruction decoding from. The K6's dynamic branch direction prediction logic uses a two-level, adaptive, branch direction prediction algorithm based on the contents of an 8192-entry branch history table (BHT). The BHT is only used to predict the direction of a conditional branch. It stores information about the direction of past conditional branches. It does not store predicted target addresses, nor does it include information about unconditional branches.

branch target cache
BTC

A branch target cache (BTC) is used for both conditional and unconditional PC-relative branches. If a conditional branch is predicted to be not taken, then the processor simply continues decoding and executing the next sequential x86 instruction. When a conditional branch is predicted to be taken or the branch is unconditional, the BTC supplies the first 16 bytes of target instructions directly to the instruction buffer. Assuming the target address hits in this cache, this design approach can avoid a 1-clock decode delay while the first or target I-Cache fetch takes place.[17] The BTC is organized as sixteen entries of sixteen bytes each. Thus, the BTC works with the BHT and delivers instruction bytes directly to the decoders to avoid the otherwise one-clock decode delay for taken branches. The BHT direction prediction rate is estimated to be greater than 95%. The BTC hit rate ranges from 40-60%. In total, the branch prediction logic achieves a predicted branch prediction rate of greater than 95%.

return address stack
RAS

The K6's branch direction prediction logic also employs a 16-entry Return Address Stack (RAS) to minimize fetch and decode stalls associated with subroutine entry (CALL) and exit (RET) instructions. The RAS is specifically designed to optimize subroutine call/return instruction pairs by caching the return address of each call instruction and supplying it as the predicted target address of the corresponding return instruction.

---

[17] Notice the "BTC Hit" control of the instruction multiplexer in front of the instruction buffer in Figure 2.6 on page 115. We will, for the current time, take this control to mean:

      IF (the instruction being decoded is a branch)
        AND (the branch is predicted taken)
        AND (there was a "hit" in the BTC for the target address)
      THEN (select the output of the BTC)
      ELSE (select the output of the I-Cache and Predecode Cache)

Software is typically constructed using subroutines that are invoked from various places in a program. This is usually done to save space. The subroutine is entered with the execution of a CALL instruction. At that time, among other things, the processor pushes the address of the next sequential instruction following the CALL instruction onto the RAS as well as onto the architectural stack in memory. When the processor encounters a RET instruction within or at the end of the subroutine, the branch prediction logic pops the return address from RAS, as well as reading from the stack in memory (for later prediction checking purposes), and speculatively begins fetching from that location.

The Branch Resolving Unit BRU) is separate from the branch direction prediction logic shown in Figure 2.2 on page 69 and enables efficient speculative instruction execution. The BRU gives the processor the ability to execute instructions beyond conditional branches before knowing whether the branch prediction was correct. To accomplish this, the K6 processor does not commit the results of the speculative executed instructions until all preceding conditional branch instructions have been resolved by the BRU. Once the status flag values for evaluating a branch condition are valid, the BRU resolves the conditional branch as either correctly or incorrectly predicted.

branch resolving unit
BRU

If the prediction was incorrect, the processor discards the speculatively executed operations to the point of the mispredicted branch instruction and restores the machine state to that point; execution then continues down the correct branch path.

If the prediction was correct, the BRCOND Op of the branch instruction is so marked and the result of this and the following instructions are allowed to be committed. There are obviously no instruction execution delays in this case. The BRCOND OP represents the branch condition or condition code to be evaluated by the BRU. Equivalently, the BRCOND Op represents the branch condition evaluation operation to be executed by the BRU.

Suggested Readings

Branch Prediction

Because of the importance of branch prediction in achieving high performance, there has been, and continues to be, substantial work in this area. Some articles which, in part, review alternative approaches and are, therefore, of general interest are:

1. Y. N. Patt, W. M. Hwu, and M. Shebanow, "HPS, a New Microarchitecture: Rationale and Introduction," *Proceedings of the 18th Annual Workshop on Microprogramming* (Micro-18), 1985, pp. 103-108.

2. Y. N. Patt, S. V. Melvin, W. M. Hwu, "Critical Issues Regarding HPS, A High Performance Microarchitecture", *Proceedings of the 18th Annual Workshop on Microprogramming* (Micro-18), 1985, pp. 109-116.

3. T. Y. Yeh and Y. N. Patt, "Two-Level Adaptive Training Branch Prediction," *Proceedings of the 24th Annual International Symposium on Computer Architecture* (ISCA), 1991, pp. 124-134.

4. J. E. Smith, "A Study of Branch Prediction Strategies," *Proceedings of the 8th Symposium on Computer Architecture*, 1981, pp. 135-148.

5. D. R. Kaeli and P. G. Emma, "Improving the Accuracy of History-Based Branch Prediction," *IEEE Transactions on Computers*, April 1997.

6. J. K. F. Lee and A. J. Smith, "Branch Prediction Strategies and Branch Target Buffer Design," *Computer*, Vol. 17, No. 1, 1984, pp. 6-22.

7. P. K. Dubey and M. J. Flynn, "Branch Strategies: Modeling and Optimization, *IEEE Transactions on Computers*, Vol. 40, No. 10, 1991, pp. 1159-1167.

8. T. Y. Yeh and Y. N. Patt, "Branch History Table Indexing to Prevent Pipeline Bubbles in Wide-Issue Superscalar Processors," *Proceedings of the 26th Annual International Symposium on Microarchitecture*, (Micro-26), 1993, pp. 164-175.

 You can find the full text versions of the first five articles on the companion CD-ROM.

THE L1 AND L2 CACHES (REVISITED)

The K6 3D on-chip L1 I-Cache has a subblock organization as shown in Table 2.21. Each 64-byte line is configured as two 32-byte subblocks. The two subblocks share a common tag, but have separate pairs of cache coherency protocol bits that are used to track the state of each cache subblock. There is some variability in cache-related terminology applied to specific microprocessors. See, for example, Harvey Cragon's book, *Memory Systems and Pipeline Processors*, Jones and Bartlett Publishers,

1996, where he contrasts some of these differences. The line and subblock organization of the L1-Cache is shown in Table 2.21.

Table 2.21 LINE/SUBBLOCK L1 I-CACHE ORGANIZATION

Tag	Byte 31	Byte 30	...	Byte 1	Byte 0	MESI Bits	Subblock 0
Address	Byte 31	Byte 30	...	Byte 1	Byte 0	MESI Bits	Subblock 1

Suggested Readings

Cache Design

Proper cache design is absolutely central to achieving high performance in systems. Because of this, we have included five articles on the CD-ROM that examine cache-related design, implementation, and performance issues from a variety of perspectives.

1. A. J. Smith, "Cache Memory Design: An Evolving Art," *IEEE Spectrum*, 1987.
2. M. Cekleov and M. Dubois, "Virtual-Address Caches," IEEE Micro, 1997.
3. S. P. VanderWiel and D. J. Lilja, "When Caches Aren't Enough: Data Prefetching Techniques," *Computer*, July 1997.
4. E. van der Deijl, G. Kanbier, O. Temam, and E. D. Granston, "A Cache Visualization Tool," Com*puter*, July 1997.
5. D. Burger, J. R.Goodman and A. Kägi, "Limited Bandwidth to Affect Processor Design," *IEEE Micro*, November/December 1997.

An article which describes several memory consistency models and their relationship to performance, programmability, and portability is given in the article by Sarita V. Adve and Kourosh Gharachorloo, "Shared Memory Consistency Models: A Tutorial," in *Computer*, December 1996

 You can find the full text versions of the above five articles on caches and the Adve article on the companion CD-ROM.

The K6 uses the MESI cache coherency protocol. K6 3D I-Cache lines have only two coherency states, valid and invalid, rather than the full four MESI coherency states of the D-Cache lines. This is a result of the fact that the K6's I-Cache lines are read-only.

<table>
<tr><td colspan="1">

Definition and Suggested Reading
MESI Protocol
MESI = Modified, Exclusive, Shared, Invalid. MESI is a four state cache-coherency protocol that is used in multiprocessor systems in which each processor has one or more caches associated with it and cache consistency must be maintained across these caches. See the article by J. Gallant, "Protocols Keep Data Consistent" *EDN*, Vol. 36, No. 5, March 1991, pp.42-50 and the *International Standard ISO/IEC, ANSI/IEEE Std. 896.I,* 1994 Edition, IEEE, New York, 1994.

</td></tr>
</table>

cache line replacement
cache subblock replacement

Two forms of cache misses and associated cache fills can take place in a cache organized this way—a cache line replacement[18] and a cache subblock replacement. In the case of a cache line replacement, the miss is due to a tag mismatch. In this case, a new cache line is allocated, the required 32-byte subblock is filled from the L2-cache or external memory, and the other 32-byte subblock within the cache line is marked as invalid. In the case of a cache subblock replacement, the tag matches but the requested subblock is marked as invalid. The required 32-byte subblock is filled from the L2-cache or external memory, and the other subblock within the cache line remains in its current state, i.e., its cache coherency bits are not changed. In either case, L1 I-Cache fills are done on a subblock basis.

---

[18] Cache line replacements are also referred to as full-line cache misses.

DESIGN NOTE

L1-Cache Design

The K6 L1-Caches are 32-Kbyte in size and organized as two-way set-associative. This means that the set index is comprised of bits [13:6] of the address. Since the x86 architecture uses linear to physical translation, the physical address is available later than the linear. For timing and performance reasons, the set index needs to use the untranslated bits to start the cache access in parallel to the linear-to-physical translation. In the x86 architecture, only bits[31:12] are translated. Bits[11:0] are identical in linear and physical address spaces. Because of this the K6 3D uses bits [13:6] as the set index. Both ways of a set are physically tagged with the full physical page address (bits [31:12]). Since bits [13:12] are linear, this means that a particular physical cache line can reside in one of a group of 4-sets in the cache. This creates a potential synonym (or aliasing) problem, since a cache lookup indexes into only one of the four possible sets. What happens if the line in question resides in the other three possible sets? The K6 3D deals with this in hardware by avoiding the creation of synonyms in the first place. The tag RAMs of the L1-Caches are designed in a manner that allows all four possible sets to be read out simultaneously. If the line is found in one of the 4-sets, but it is not in the indexed set, it will be invalidated (possibly written back if dirty) and then refetched from the L2 or external memory and put into the indexed set.

The K6 implements a hit-under-miss scheme for both the instruction and data caches. The instruction cache can continue to supply hit data while processing a miss. There are no restrictions. If a new cache access misses in the cache and there is already a pending miss, then the new cache miss is held up until the first miss completes. The L1 D-Cache is similar in its behavior in that it can continue to supply hit data while processing a fill. The only restriction is that the read operation that initiated the fill must have received its data before subsequent read operations can access the cache.

The above behavior provides sufficient performance with a reasonable effort in logic design and implementation. There are more aggressive techniques that are completely nonblocking or nonblocking to a certain depth. For example, if a read operation misses in the L1 D-Cache, the read is allowed to complete without its data (allowing a younger read to advance into the cache lookup stage). The miss can be queued up in a miss queue. The read that completed without its data needs to receive it at a later time when the fill is ready to provide it. Multiple misses will result in more of these types of reads getting completed and queued in the miss queue. While this is all "doable," it creates complicated situations that are more difficult to deal with. The additional effort was not considered worth the increase in performance.

In general many of the microarchitectural performance trade-offs were taken based on a K6 3D trace-driven performance model that was accurate within a few percentage points to the K6 3D's actual behavior. If a particular feature provided a large enough percentage increase in performance, it was carefully considered and usually adopted.

In summary, both the I-Cache and the D-Cache are linearly indexed and physically tagged. Synonyms and aliasing are handled in hardware. At most one synonym at a time is allowed in the caches. Both caches maintain mutual exclusion with respect to each other and, as will be seen, this eases the way in which self-modifying code is handled. The hit-under-miss cache-fill strategy is supported. The L2-Cache on the other hand is physically indexed and physically tagged and thus is not concerned with synonyms and aliasing.

cache prefetching

The K6 performs cache prefetching for L1 I-Cache cache-line replacements. Cache prefetching results in the filling of the required 32-byte subblock first, and a prefetch of the second subblock. However, the prefetch of the 32-byte subblock that is not required is initiated in the forward direction only—that is, the second 32-byte subblock is fetched only if the requested subblock is the first subblock within the cache line. From the perspective of the external bus, the two subblock fills typically appear as two 32-byte burst read cycles occurring back-to-back or, if allowed, as pipelined bus cycles. The K6 3D prefetches both L1 I-Cache and L1 D-Cache subblocks.

The sizes and associativities of the K6 3D's TLBs were selected based on academic studies as well as professional papers. Later, the sizes were looked at in the K6 performance model to guarantee that the choices were appropriate. Larger TLBs, with greater associativity, are generally important in Windows 3.1, Windows 95, Windows NT, and Unix-like environments. The environments that are less stressful are older 16-bit DOS and Windows code and Spec benchmarks.

Suggested Readings

Processor Memory Mismatch Problem

An interesting article by Michael K. Milligan and Harvey G. Cragon, "Processor Implementation Using Queues," *IEEE Micro*, 1995, discusses the evolution of instruction and branch target queues and their relationship to interleaved memory and caches. The article also discusses the use of queues to support variable-length instructions and reduce misalignment problems. The article by Wen-mei Hwu and Thomas M.Conte, "The Susceptibility of Programs to Context Switching," shows the importance of analytical modeling and simulation in cache-related studies.

The L2-Cache is 4-way set associative, with a total of 1K sets. Each set has 4 ways: Way 0, Way 1, Way 2, and Way 3. Each way contains one 64-byte line. Each line has two 32-byte subblocks. Thus, the overall L2 Cache size is 4*1K lines = 4*1K*64bytes/line = 256K Bytes. As noted earlier, the L2-Cache is physically indexed and physically tagged. Bits [15:6] of the physical address determine the set number. The starting byte location within a way is determined by bits [5:0] of the physical address. The L2-Cache uses true LRU replacement within a set. An L2 instruction I-TLB was added to the K6 3D to help out on the instruction TLB misses given the small size of the L1 I-TLB.

The K6 can fetch up to sixteen x86 instruction bytes per clock from either the on-chip L1 I-Cache or the Branch Target Cache as shown in Figure 2.6 on page 115. The fetched x86 instruction bytes along with their corresponding predecode bits are placed into a 16-byte instruction buffer which feeds two instruction registers that supply the decoders. Instruction Register 1 supplies the vector decoder, the long decoder, and short decoder 1, while Instruction Register 2 supplies short decoder 2.

An instruction fetch retrieves sixteen bytes, 4-byte aligned, and all within one 32-byte cache subblock. In the case of branch target fetches after a BTC miss, generally 13-16 useful instruction bytes are retrieved, depending on the byte offset of the target address within the first 4-byte word. This is true except when near the end of a cache subblock.

New instruction bytes are loaded into the instruction buffer as preceding instruction bytes are consumed by the decoders. Instructions are loaded and replaced in the instruction buffer with 4-byte granularity. However, instructions can be consumed from the instruction buffer with byte granularity. This means that the loading and reloading of bytes into the instruction buffer is controlled with 4-byte granularity. This simplifies control logic and eases certain speed-critical logic paths. When a control transfer occurs, the entire instruction buffer is flushed and reloaded with a new set of sixteen instruction bytes.

The K6's decode logic is designed to decode up to two x86 instructions per clock. The decode logic accepts x86 instruction bytes and predecode bits from the instruction buffer, locates the actual instruction boundaries, and generates Ops from the x86 instructions. The Ops are then loaded into a centralized scheduler that controls and tracks all aspects of Op issue, execution, and commitment.

THE INSTRUCTION BUFFER AND INSTRUCTION REGISTERS

instruction buffer
instruction register 1
instruction register 2

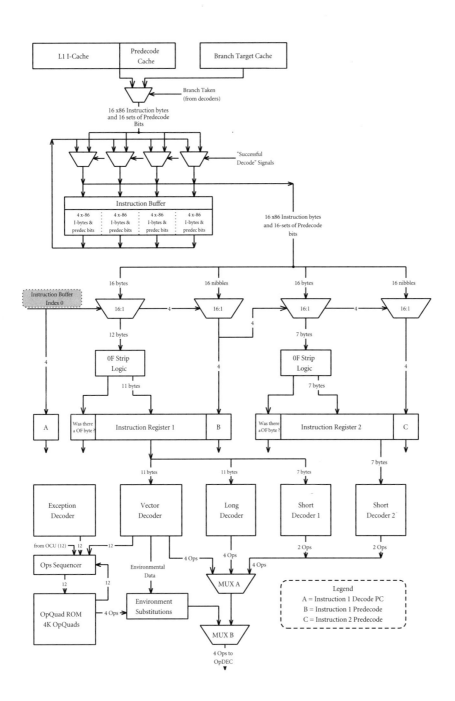

Figure 2.5 INSTRUCTION BUFFER, INSTRUCTION REGISTERS 1 & 2, AND THE DECODERS

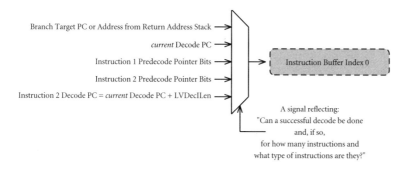

Figure 2.6 INSTRUCTION BUFFER INDEX 0 MULTIPLEXER

Some of the inputs and the control of this multiplexer use information developed by the predecode logic shown in the high-level block diagram of the K6 3D microarchitecture shown in Figure 2.2 on page 69. The predecode logic is discussed in the very next section. This discussion includes an explanation of both Figure 2.6 and Figure 2.6.

PREDECODING LOGIC

As is well documented in the literature, decoding x86 instructions is particularly difficult; see Mike Johnson's book *Superscaler Microprocessor Design,* Prentice-Hall 1991. X86 instructions are variable-length (from one byte to fifteen bytes long) and can have complex addressing modes. They can be modified by one or more prefix bytes, which can appear before any instruction and can affect the instruction's execution. Instruction can have a variable-size *displacement field* of zero, one, two, or four displacement bytes. Instructions can also have a variable-size *immediate field* of zero, one, two, or four immediate bytes. The displacement and immediate fields are both optional and independent—that is, either one or both may be present and they may be of different sizes within an instruction. A number of fields in the first few bytes of x86 instructions are used to indicate whether or not other fields are present. All of this contributes to the difficulty in determining the length of the current instruction which in turn contributes to the difficulty in determining where the next x86 instruction actually begins relative to the current instruction.

The difficulties in decoding instructions and determining their lengths notwithstanding, two primary goals in the design that have a direct impact on performance are: (1) to be able to do multiple decodes per cycle and (2) to make the cycle time as short as possible. The K6 supports the decode of more than one x86 instruction per cycle and employs a predecoding technique to assist in this process. In essence, predecoding annotates each instruction byte with information that later enables the decoders to quickly locate the next instruction boundary and thus to efficiently decode multiple x86 instructions simultaneously. The predecode logic computes five *predecode bits* associated with each instruction byte. This is shown in Figure 2.7.

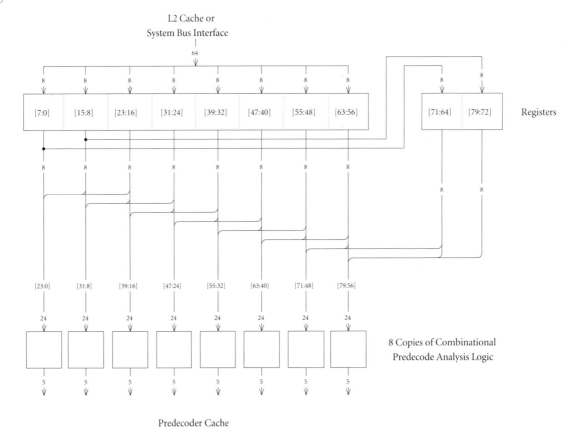

Figure 2.7 PREDECODER LOGIC

PREDECODE BITS

The predecode bits provide a pointer to the first byte of the next instruction. The predecode bits are computed by determining the instruction length and adding this to the low-order PC bits of the predecoded instruction. These bits are stored in a 20-Kbyte predecode cache, separate from the K6's L1 I-Cache. There are five predecode bits per instruction byte and thus the 20-Kbyte for the 32-Kbyte L1 I-Cache. L1 I-Cache lines are filled from main memory or from the L2-Cache using a burst transaction. Each instruction byte is analyzed using the predecode logic on a byte-by-byte basis as an L1 I-Cache line is filled. The analysis consists of assuming the byte under consideration is the beginning of an instruction and then determining the next instruction boundary based on this assumption. Note that the predecode analysis logic in Figure 2.7 can use up to three adjacent instruction bytes in its analysis.

Predecode Cache

The predecode logic produces six predecode bits per instruction byte. One of the six does not need to be stored in the predecode cache as it can be quickly and readily generated as data are read from the predecode cache. Of the remaining five bits:

1. three bits represent the instruction length in the form of a pointer to the first byte of the next instruction (a fourth bit having been discarded).

2. one bit indicates if the instruction length is D-bit dependent.

3. one bit indicates if the instruction is a Mod R/M instruction or not (this bit is only valid for short or long decodable instructions).

The three bits representing the instruction length are, essentially, the low three bits of the linear or physical program counter (PC) of the next instruction. The fourth and most significant bit (MSB) of the pointer is actually generated when the predecode bits are used. This means, in reality, that although five predecode bits are stored in the predecode cache, six predecode bits are used during instruction decode.

If for any reason the predecoder cannot compute the above five bits, it will set the three bits of pointer information to the current instruction. This means, effectively, that the computed instruction length is zero and is, essentially, an *unsuccessful predecode* indication to the decoders.

unsuccessful predecode

COMBINATIONAL PREDECODE ANALYSIS LOGIC

Deciding if an instruction can be decoded by one of the short decoders is done by comparing the lower bits of the instruction's PC (program counter) with the pointer produced by the predecode logic—i.e., the three bits pointing to the first byte of the next instruction as described in the next section. If they are different, the instruction has a length of one to seven bytes (as implied by the difference between these two pointers) and can be decoded by one of the short decoders. If they are equal, implying an instruction length of zero, the instruction cannot be decoded by one of the short decoders and must be decoded by either the long decoder or the vector decoder as appropriate.

COMPARATIVE ANALYSIS AND SUGGESTED READINGS

Predecode Logic

In an interesting article, "Superscalar Instruction Issue," *IEEE Micro*, September/October 1997, by Dezso Sima, he notes:

"Decoding in superscalar processors is a considerably more complex task than in the case of scalar processors and becomes even more so as the issue rate increases. Higher issue rates, however, can unduly lengthen the decoding cycle or can give rise to multiple decoding cycles unless decoding is enhanced. An increasingly common method of enhancement is predecoding. This partial decoding takes place in advance of common decoding, in which instructions are loaded into the instruction cache. The majority of the latest processors use predecoding: the PowerPC 620, PA 7200, PA 8000, UltraSparc, and R10000."

 An audio clip, giving an overview of the predecoding techniques used in the K6 3D, can be found on the companion CD-ROM.

Sima points out that a number of vendors use predecoding in their microprocessor implementations for somewhat different reasons. However, there appears to be conflicting reports about Intel's use of predecoding. Consider the following analysis found in "Intel's Long-Awaited P55C Disclosed," by Michael Slater, *Microprocessor Report*, Vol. 10, No. 14, February 28, 1996, pp. 1-3:

"In the P54C, a tag bit is added to each byte as it is stored in the instruction cache to identify instruction boundaries. The P54C's decoder depends on this bit to feed the two instruction pipelines in a single cycle. The P55C's extra cycle allows instructions to be paired on the fly, eliminating the need for the cache predecode bits and allowing instructions to be paired even on an instruction-cache miss."

continued on the next page.

COMPARATIVE ANALYSIS AND SUGGESTED READINGS (CONT.)

Now contrast this with the following description found in "Centaur Gallops Into x86 Market," by Linley Gwennap, *Microprocessor Report*, Vol. 11, No. 7, June 2, 1997, pp. 1-6:

> *"These caches are simpler than in other competitive chips. For example, virtually all other Pentium-class processors have a dual-ported data cache; to match its scalar core, the C6 has a single-ported data cache, reducing die area. The C6 also has no predecode bits in the instruction cache, a feature found in Pentium (but not Pentium/MMX) and AMD's K5 and K6. These extra bits cause the caches on these chips to consume more die area than the same amount of cache on the Centaur chip."*

So far, the following analysis of the P6 (a.k.a. the PPro) suggests that it does not use predecoding, "Intel's P6 Uses Decoupled Superscalar Design," by Linley Gwennap, *Microprocessor Report*, Vol. 9, No. 2, February 16, 1995, pp. 1-7:

> *"Part of the problem in a superscalar x86 processor is identifying the starting point of the second and subsequent instructions in a group. The K5 includes predecode information in its instruction cache to hasten this process, but the P6 does not, to avoid both instruction-cache bloat and the bottleneck of predecoding instructions as they are read from the L2 cache."*

Predecoding is also used to assist in the attempts to obtain increased code compaction. Here the predecoders are used, in part, to expand compressed code. See, for example, "Embedded Vendors Seek Differentiation: Signal Processing, Code Compression, ASIC Cores Enable Specialization," by Jim Turley, *Microprocessor Report*, Vol. 11, No. 1, January 27, 1997, pp. 1-6:

> *"Following on the heels of ARM's Thumb, MIPS introduced MIPS-16, a similar approach to compressing 32-bit instructions into 16-bit words. Thumb has already begun showing up in products; chips equipped with the MIPS-16 predecoder should roll out by mid-1997."*

See also Deszo Sima, Terence Fountain, and Peter Kacsuk, *Advanced Computer Architectures, A Design Space Approach*, by Addison-Wesley, 1997.

 Copies of the Sima article appearing in *IEEE Micro* and the four referenced *Microprocessor Report* articles which were cited above are on the CD-ROM.

> ### DESIGN NOTE
>
> Unsuccessful Predecode
>
> An *unsuccessful predecode* signal is represented by generating a predecode pointer that points to the beginning of the predecoded instruction (i.e., to the instruction's PC). This implies an instruction length of zero. Thus, the unsuccessful predecode signal is also being interpreted to mean the instruction *"cannot be decoded by a short decoder."* The short decoders only operate on instructions that are less than or equal to seven bytes in length. Therefore, if the combination predecode analysis logic determines that an instruction requires more than seven bytes, it considers this an unsuccessful predecode as well, i.e., it is an instruction that cannot be decoded by a short decoder.

The combinational predecode analysis logic shown in Figure 2.7 on page 116 accomplishes several things as it processes three adjacent instruction bytes. It examines:

1. the instruction's opcode byte to determine if: (a) the instruction is a ModR/M instruction and (b) there are any immediate bytes and, if so, how many.

2. the second byte, the ModR/M byte, and decodes the address mode specified by this byte if the instruction is a ModR/M instruction. This analysis will tell if: (a) there is an SIB byte and (b) there are displacement bytes and, if so, how many.

3. the SIB byte, if one is present, to determine if there is a displacement. This will occur only in certain ModR/M address mode cases.

In most cases the existence of a displacement and its size can be determined from the ModR/M byte. In a small number of cases, which are a subset of when an SIB byte is present, the SIB byte must be examined as well to determine if there is a displacement. These processing steps indicate why the combinational predecode analysis logic must examine at least three instruction bytes. In the most general case, however, up to four bytes must be analyzed since the first instruction byte may have been a preface or "0F" byte. If a "0F" byte is present, the predecode analysis logic looks at the next byte as the "real" instruction opcode byte and then does the processing indicated in the above three steps using three instruction bytes. If the bytes required to do these steps are not available, the combinational predecode analysis logic sets the three predecoder pointer bits to zero (resulting in an "unsuccessful predecode" signal to the decoders).

There are eight sets of predecode logic that get reused four times during an I-Cache fill. Cache fills take place in the form of a burst or block transfer of four octets. In the case where the last octet of the cache line is being predecoded, the predecode logic for the last two bytes modifies its behavior and recognizes that it is predecoding not just the last two instruction bytes of any octet, but the last two bytes of a cache line. The last octet of a cache line is actually the first one to be read. More generally, the octets are read in decreasing or reverse order. The logic takes into account the fact that only one or two bytes are available for predecoding. If the predecode logic needs to examine more than the one or two bytes available to determine the instruction's length, then the three predecode pointer bits are set to imply the instruction is not short-decodable.

While the *average* x86 total instruction length is less than four bytes, when the predecode of an instruction detects a length greater than seven bytes (e.g., the opcode byte plus a ModR/M byte plus a 4-byte displacement value plus a 4-byte immediate value), the instruction's length cannot be represented by the three predecode bits. Consequently, the predecoder logic sets the pointer bits to indicate the instruction is not short-decodable. In summary the combination predecode analysis logic has:

1. preface "0F" byte stripping logic.

2. three chunks of logic to look at the opcode byte and the ModR/M and SIB bytes, if they are present. These chunks of logic each produce "partial length information," The first clump of logic (for the opcode) gives a "base instruction length." The second and third clumps of logic give a "ModR/M and SIB instruction length"— which includes the ModR/M byte (if present) plus the SIB byte (if present) plus the number of displacement bytes, if any. The overall instruction length is the sum of these two lengths. That length added to the instruction's address gives the address of the next instruction. The lower three bits of this address is the predecode pointer.

3. a chunk of logic to (a) determine how many bytes must be examined and if enough bytes are not available to indicate an unsuccessful predecode and (b) determine if the instruction length is less than or equal to seven and, if not, force the outputs to indicate an unsuccessful predecode.

USE OF THE PREDECODE BITS

We now describe how the predecode bits are used during the instruction decode cycle. The predecode bits are used as two of the five inputs to the multiplexer shown in Figure 2.6 on page 115. The output of this multiplexer is used to align the first instruction as shown in Figure 2.6 on page 115. During the decode process, a number of things occur in parallel. For example, for the first instruction, the predecode logic needs to compare its predecode pointer to the Decode PC to determine if that instruction can be decoded by a short decoder. Similarly, for the second instruction, the logic examines the predecode pointer for the first instruction and compares that with the predecode pointer of the second instruction to determine if the second instruction can also be decoded by a short decoder. Based on those two pieces of information, it can be determined: (a) how many instruction bytes of the instruction buffer need to be "valid", starting from the Decode PC, for the first instruction, and (b) how many instruction bytes of the instruction buffer need to be "valid," starting from the end of the first instruction, for the second instruction.

DEFINITION
Decode PC
The term *Decode PC* refers to the pointer into the instruction buffer, shown in Figure 2.6 on page 115, which points to the start of the instruction to be decoded. In particular, it refers to the low four bits of this pointer.

The instruction registers are *blindly* loaded at the beginning of the decode cycle, (based on the predecode bits), and then everything is examined to see whether one or ideally two instructions are, in fact, decodable. Furthermore, all three decoders blindly operate in parallel before knowing what kind of decode, if any, will be possible. If there is a valid instruction in Instruction Register 1 and if it can be decoded by short decoder 1, then short decoder 1 decodes it. Otherwise, the instruction will be sent to the long decoder and see if that decoder can decode it. If so, the long decoder continues processing the instruction. If the long decoder cannot decode the instruction, than by default the instruction vector decoder will process the instruction. A valid instruction will be decoded by short decoder 2 only if it can be decoded by a short decoder and short decoder 1 has decoded a valid, short-decodable instruction.

"valid" signals:
SDEC0_V
SDEC1_V
LDEC_V
VDEC_V

Without giving a complete description of this control logic within the decoders, we point out that there are four key control signals that get generated by this control logic called SDEC0_V, SDEC1_V, LDEC_V, VDEC_V respectively, where the "V" stands for "valid." The use of these signals will aid us in understanding the use of the predecoder information.

Logic within the decoders examines SDEC0_V first, if it is asserted then one short decode can be done. If SDEC1_V is also asserted, then we can do two short decodes, otherwise we'll just settle for one. If SDEC0_V is not asserted, then LDEC_V is examined. If LDEC_V is asserted, a long decode can be done. Otherwise hopefully VDEC_V is asserted so a vector decode can be done. If it is not, then no instruction decode can be successfully done.

There is also "downstream" control logic that looks at SDEC0_V, SDEC1_V, LDEC_V, and VDEC_V. One of the things that emerges from this logic is the control of the 5-to-1 multiplexer shown in Figure 2.6 on page 115, the output of which is the shaded box "Instruction Buffer Index 0" in Figure 2.6 on page 115. If no successful decode of any type can be done, as was just hypothesized, then the control logic will select the current Decode PC, the second input to the multiplexer, to re-circulate its value. If instead a successful instruction decode can be done, then if at most one short decode can be done, then the third multiplexer input will be selected. If, in fact, two short decodes can be done, the fourth input is selected. If no short decodes can be done, but either a long decode or a vector decode can be done, the fifth input is selected. In the case of a branch type instruction being decoded, then the first multiplexer input is used in the following situations: PC relative jumps, calls, conditional branches (as decoded by either short decoder), and the RET instruction. In summary, the logic that controls the multiplexer must address the questions shown in Figure 2.6 on page 115, namely, "Can a successful instruction decode be done and, if so, how many instruction decodes and what types of instructions are they?"

Decoding of x86 instructions begins when sufficient instruction bytes have been fetched into the instruction buffer. A single stage in the K6 3D's six-stage pipeline is used to decode up to two x86 instructions per cycle. The K6 3D uses a combination of decoders to convert x86 instructions into RISC86 Ops. As shown in Figure 2.2 on page 69, this combination consists of three types of decoders—two short decoders (short decoder 1 and short decoder 2), one long decoder, and one vector decoder. However, as shown in more detail in Figure 2.6 on page 115, another decoder, the exception decoder, which we will learn about later, is also involved.

THE DECODERS

HISTORICAL COMMENT AND DEFINITION
Naming the *Vector* Decoder
The *vector* decoder uses "vector" to mean the "address of the location in a ROM where a sequence of Ops begins." We retain the name the K6 designers gave it for historical purposes. We will learn more about OpQuad Sequences in the section titled "OpQuad Sequences and the RISC86 Operation Set" beginning on page 137.

COMPARATIVE ANALYSIS

Pentium II Micro-ops

Intel calls its internal Pentium II microarchitectural operations "micro-ops." The Pentium II has three x86 instruction decoders that can operate in parallel. Two of them (the second and third decoders) handle only "short instructions," each of which produce a single micro-op. As a result, the Pentium II can multiple-decode only very simple instructions. Other reasonably simple instructions such as "ADD reg,mem" can only be decoded in a more limited manner. While this can be a good compromise in the context of new and Pentium II-optimized code, this can be more problematic for decode performance on existing x86 code.

A different approach using two decoders and having each able to decode a larger subset of common instructions was taken within the K6 3D design. This taken as an improvement of an prototype silicon implementation of the processor with three moderately capable decoders able to decode a larger subset of x86 instructions than the two Pentium II simple decoders, but not as large a subset as the final K6 3D decoders. The K6 3D decoders also differ in being nearly symmetric. Most often, one-to-two Op instructions (principally with the exception of x87 floating-point instructions) can be decoded as either the first or the second of a pair of instruction decodes.

What the K6 3D designers found, after analysis of the prototype silicon design and after continuing analysis of a growing variety of instruction traces from PC applications and system software, was the following set of points:

1. a shorter cycle time (and thus higher frequency of operation) was possible by supporting decode of only two versus three x86 instruction decodes.

2. the performance loss due to this change (as judged by instruction traces run through a very detailed and accurate performance model of the design), was far less than the gain in frequency of operation.

3. it was possible to increase the subset of instructions that could be decoded by one of the K6 short decoders without significantly impacting the cycle time. This was because the Op generation by the decoders was not part of the most critical and thus cycle-determining timing paths through the decode logic.

4. significant architectural performance could be gained with just a moderate increase in the size of the short decode instruction subset.

The end result of these realizations was the changeover (in going from the prototype to the final K6 3D design), from having three moderately "simple" decoders to having two more-"sophisticated" decoders. Unlike what is more commonly the case, the frequency of operation and the (net) architectural performance of K6 3D were both significantly improved. Part of this, put differently, is that while the peak decode rate was decreased, the average instruction decode rate was improved!

Each decoder is specialized to handle a specific group of instructions. The use of specialized parallel decoders: (a) significantly improves decode efficiency thereby increasing the decode bandwidth, and (b) enables a shorter clock cycle and thus a higher frequency of operation. The K6 processor classifies short instructions as the most commonly used x86 instructions and those that can be implemented using one or two Ops. These instructions constitute the majority of the x86 instructions and allow the K6 to typically sustain two x86 instruction decodes per cycle. They are handled by the short decoders. Less commonly used instructions, and instructions implemented by three or four Ops, are handled by the long decoder. Finally, x86 instructions that are the least common, the most complex instructions, and instructions that require more than four Ops to be implemented, such as string moves, are decoded using the vector decoder.

The above discussion about the use of the decoders can be expanded in the context of the length of the x86 instructions that are decoded. Short decoder 1 and short decoder 2 decode the most commonly used x86 instructions (e.g., moves, shifts, branches, calls, ALU, MMX, 3D, and FPU instructions) into zero, one, or two Ops each. The short decoders only operate on x86 instructions that are less than or equal to seven bytes in length but can decode up to two such instructions per clock.

The commonly used x86 instructions that are greater than seven bytes in length as well as less commonly used x86 instructions are handled by the long decoder. The long decoder only performs one decode per clock but generates up to four Ops. Both the short decoders and the long decoder can decode instructions longer than seven or twelve bytes when the extra length is due to prefix bytes. The prefix bytes are accumulated and then factored into the one short, long, or vector decode that ultimately occurs.

All x86 instructions that are not handled by either the two parallel short decoders or the long decoder are decoded by the vector decoder (e.g., complex instructions, serializing instructions, interrupts and exceptions, etc.) Short and long decodes are processed completely within their respective decoders. Vector decodes, on the other hand, are started by the vector decoder and then completed by RISC86 OpQuad Sequences fetched from an on-chip OpQuad ROM. The vector decoder logic provides:

OpQuad sequences

1. the initial set of up to four Ops to set up or start execution of the decoded instruction (this initial OpQuad is sometimes referred to as the *vector* OpQuad).

2. a vector (or entry point address) to a sequence of additional Ops stored in the on-chip OpQuad ROM.

No *special* types of RISC86 Ops are stored in the OpQuad ROM; it contains the exact same types of Ops as those that are generated by the hardware decoders.

Articles on CD-ROM

Chapter 4 in the *AMD-K6 3D Processor Code Optimization* Application Note, gives a series of tables showing which decoder and Ops are use for various x86 instructions. This application note is on the CD-ROM.

DECODER COMBINATIONS

All short-decodable integer instructions, as well as the MMX and 3D instructions, can be decoded by either short decoder 1 or short decoder 2. As stated earlier, all of the common, and a few of the uncommon, floating-point x86 instructions are decoded by the short decoders. X86 floating-point instructions are also known as ESC instructions. Such decodes generate a RISC86 FpOp and, optionally, an associated RISC86 floating-point LdOp or StOp. Only the first short decoder, short decoder 1, can be used to decode x86 floating-point instructions. This restriction allows the generation of, at most, one FpOp operation per clock, which matches the single floating-point execution pipeline. Non-ESC x86 instructions can be decoded simultaneously by the second short decoder, short decoder 2, along with an ESC instruction decode in the first short decoder.

All of the x86 MMX and the AMD 3D extensions to the x86 instruction set are also decoded by the short decoders. MMX and 3D instruction decodes generate a RISC86 MMXOp and, optionally, an associated RISC86 MMX LdOp or StOp. Both short decoders can decode MMX and 3D instructions. There are no decoding pairing constraints between integer, MMX, and 3D instructions.

DESIGN NOTE

Simultaneously Decoding ESC and MMX Instructions

Unlike the K6 3D, only the first short decoder, short decoder 1, can be used to decode x86 MMX instructions in the K6. This restriction allows the generation of, at most, one x86 MMXOp per clock and matches the single-pipeline MMX implementation on the K6.

DECODER AND SCHEDULER OPQUADS

A copy of the instruction buffer contents is sent to all of the decoders simultaneously. However, only one of the three types of decoders is used during any one decode clock. As mentioned earlier in this chapter, a group of four Ops called an OpQuad is always produced as the output of the short decoders, the long decoder, the vector decoder, and the OpQuad

ROM. When decodes cannot fill a group with four useful Ops, the empty locations of the group are filled with NoOps. For example, a long-decoded x86 instruction that converts to only three Ops is padded with a single NoOp operation and then passed to the scheduler's buffer. Up to six OpQuads, i.e., twenty-four Ops total, can be in the scheduler's buffer at any given time.

An OpQuad passes through the OpQuad expansion logic just before it is loaded into the scheduler as shown in the following Figure 2.8. MUX A and MUX B in this figure are the same as those that appear in Figure 2.6 on page 115.

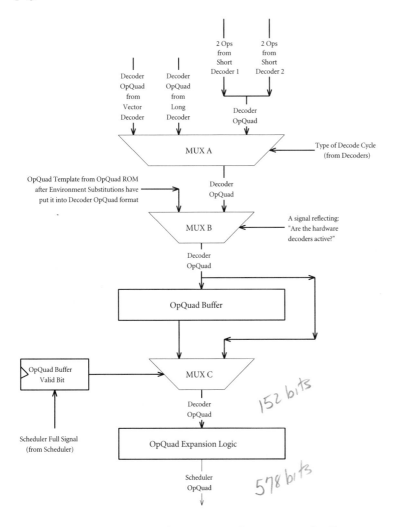

Figure 2.8 Decoder OpQuads and Scheduler OpQuads

To distinguish between the OpQuads produced by the decoders and the OpQuads produced by the OpQuad Expansion Logic, they will be referred to as *decoder* OpQuads and *scheduler* OpQuads respectively. A *decoder* OpQuad consists of four 38-bit Ops to form a 152-bit OpQuad. We will learn in Chapter 3 that a *scheduler* OpQuad consists of a variety of static and dynamic fields that total to 578 bits. OpQuads stored in the OpQuad ROM are essentially 152-bit decoder OpQuads with an additional 14-bit sequencing field associated with them for use with the OpQuad ROM fetch control logic. When they are stored in the OpQuad ROM, these ROM-based OpQuads have an internal 166-bit OpQuad format. However, only their decoder OpQuad component is ever sent to the scheduler. Thus, in all cases, as is shown in Figure 2.8 only 152-bit *decoder* OpQuads are sent to the OpQuad Expansion Logic to be expanded into *578 bit scheduler* OpQuads. The contents and formats of *decoder* OpQuads will be discussed later in this chapter as will all of the resources shown in Figure 2.8. *Scheduler* OpQuads, as noted above, are discussed in Chapter 3.

Before leaving this section, we call your attention to the control signal for the MUX B multiplexer in this diagram. There is some control logic and a single bit of state in the scheduler that is used to distinguish between the use of the hardware decoders and the use of OpQuad Sequences fetched from the OpQuad ROM. We will identify these two states respectively as the "hardware decoders are active" state and the "OpQuad ROM fetch is active" state. Whenever the system is in "OpQuad ROM fetch is active" state, it will remain in the state until the last OpQuad in the OpQuad Sequence, as identified by action in the sequencing field of a ROM-based OpQuad, has completed processing. When this occurs the state will change to the "hardware decoders are active" state. The system will remain in this state until a condition arises, such as a vector decode is encountered or an exception abort is encountered, that require OpQuad Sequences to be fetched from the OpQuad ROM. This will be discussed later in this chapter.

THE SCHEDULER

As mentioned earlier, the scheduler is the heart of the K6 microarchitecture. It contains the logic necessary to manage out-of-order issue, speculative execution, data forwarding, register renaming, and the simultaneous issue, execution, and retirement of multiple Ops. Said differently, the scheduler, shown in Figure 2.9 on page 130, contains logic to track Ops throughout their lifetime, determine dependencies, schedule execution, and commit architecture state. Whenever possible, the scheduler can simultaneously issue Ops to appropriate execution units.

COMPARATIVE ANALYSIS

Combined Reservation Station and Reorder Buffer

The K6's scheduler includes both centralized reservation station and reorder buffer functionality. This is in contrast to other processor designs, such as the Intel Pentium Pro, where these are separate structures.

One of the main components of the scheduler is its centralized buffer. The main advantage of the scheduler and its centralized buffer is the ability to examine the Ops associated with up to twelve x86 instructions at one time. The scheduler examines the contents of the buffer in parallel and performs dynamic scheduling of the Ops for optimized execution. Since the scheduler can issue the Ops out-of-order and speculatively, the corresponding x86 instructions are executed out of order and speculatively. However, the scheduler always retires the Ops in order; thus, the x86 instructions are always retired in order. In total, the scheduler can issue up to six Ops and retire up to four Ops per cycle.

The OCU (Op Commit Unit) is also shown in this figure. It is separated from the scheduler's resources by the dashed line to indicate that it is not part of the scheduler. It has been included in the figure because it will be discussed later in this section in terms of its interaction with the scheduler.

The scheduler's buffer is logically structured as a FIFO (first-in, first-out) queue. Younger Ops (*later in the program order*) enter at the top of the buffer. Older Ops (*earlier in the program order*) are at the bottom of the buffer. Ops enter the top of the buffer four at a time as a *scheduler* OpQuad and are retired up to four at a time (again as a *scheduler* OpQuad) from the bottom. For purposes of this discussion, the buffer will be thought of as either having six elements (each element being a *scheduler* OpQuad) or being six rows deep. The rows are numbered from 0 to 5, with 0 referring to the top row (youngest Ops) and 5 referring to the last row (oldest Ops). Each of the buffer's six rows has four entries, one for each of the four Ops. The entry for an Op is called the Op Entry associated with that Op. A row of four Op entries corresponds to a scheduler OpQuad—the four entries/row correspond to four Ops/row or one scheduler OpQuad/row.

The execution units do not have specialized reservation stations or queues that are blocked if the execution unit itself is stalled. Rather, the pending Ops are in the centralized buffer's Op entries. Many Ops are immediately eligible for execution when they are loaded into the top row of the buffer, but may, in fact, be issued to appropriate execution units from any point in the buffer.

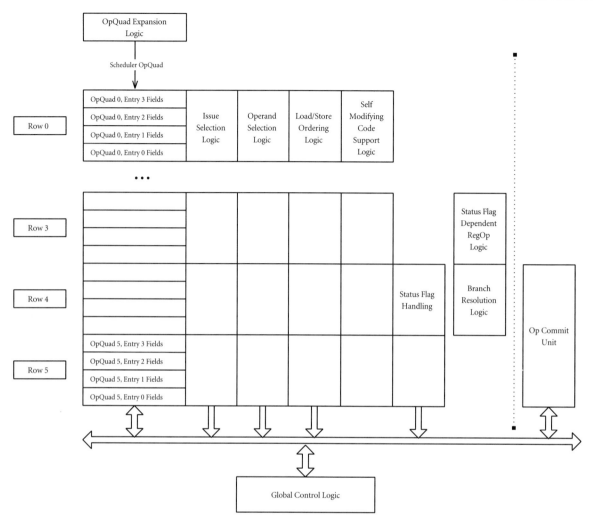

Figure 2.9 The Scheduler and Its Centralized Buffer

State field

Each Op entry has a State field that indicates whether the Op has been issued, is in a specific stage of an execution pipeline, or has been completed.

Video Clip on CD-ROM

 In this video clip, Amos Ben-Meir, Principal Designer of the K6 3D addresses the following question, "How does the K6 3D scheduler work?"

DESIGN NOTE
State and Position are Independent
The state of the Op is independent of its position in the buffer. However, the longer an Op is in the scheduler, the greater the chance that the Op will be issued and completed.

Each clock cycle:

1. new Ops can be loaded into the buffer.

2. existing Ops can be issued, advanced in their execution, and completed (with appropriate updating of their execution state).

3. old and completed Ops can be committed and removed from the buffer.

All LdOps and StOps and most RegOps can execute from any row in the buffer. However, some Ops (such as the evaluation of conditional branches and RegOps that depend on status flags) are executed when the Ops reach a particular row of the buffer. This simplifies and speeds up the hardware by eliminating a design requiring the ability to support execution of these "special" Ops in other rows. Scheduling delays are minimized by selecting the row for executing such operations to be where the necessary operands are likely to be available. For example, Ops that depend on status flags (such as ADD-with-carry) are handled lower in the scheduler at a point where older operations are likely to have completed modification of the status flag values required for the completion of the status flag- dependent operation.

DESIGN NOTE
Execution of Status Flag-Dependent Ops
Additional circuitry that would allow execution of status flag-dependent Ops higher in the scheduler's buffer would provide minimal improvement in Op execution rate because the necessary flags are unlikely to be available when a status flag-dependent Op is in a higher row of the buffer.

The scheduler issues (i.e., dispatches) the Ops to the execution units. The Ops are selected and issued by the issue selection logic according to:

The terms dispatches *and* issues *are used interchangeably in this book.*

1. the type and availability of an execution unit—this means that different types of Ops can be executed out of order with respect to each.

2. sequential program order.

The physical position of an entry in the buffer indicates the program order of the corresponding Op. Each entry contains:

1. storage for the information required for the execution of the associated Op and storage for the result values produced by the execution of the Op.
2. logic for directing the information to the correct execution unit when required.
3. logic for detecting and handling register, status flag, and memory dependencies.

The result values stored in an entry provide the register and status values at the corresponding point in the program order. The buffer's entries are general in the sense that any entry can be used for any type of Op. There is no need for separate, specialized queues for Ops destined for different execution units—the entries in the scheduler are not specialized according to the type of Op that is to be executed.

The determination of dependencies between Ops and the generation of operand forwarding controls takes advantage of the physical ordering of the Ops within the buffer and also depends on the fact that all Ops reside in this central, general entry buffer. Furthermore, as will be seen later, the scheduling and execution of an Op is independent of the grouping of Ops into rows.

DESIGN NOTE

Position in the Scheduler and Program Order

The physical position of an entry in the scheduler's buffer indicates the program order of the corresponding Op. The result values stored in an entry provide the register and status values, produced by that specific Op, at the corresponding point in the program order.

The scheduler retains result values until the OCU determines that no exception and no mispredicted branch precedes the associated operation. After the execution of an abortable operation, the results of the operation are kept in the associated scheduler entry and/or in a store queue. If the OCU determines that the oldest executed operations would be generated in a sequential execution of the program, the results are made permanent by writing them to a register file, a status register, cache, or memory, and the operation is retired. If the OCU determines that a result would not be generated in a sequential execution of the program due to an exception or mis-predicted branch at that point, the operation is retired without making permanent changes.

Abortable state changes are supported by the scheduler and the store queue through the general technique of temporarily storing (a) register and status results in the scheduler and (b) memory write data in store queue entries until the associated Ops are committed and retired. Permanent state changes are made during Op commitment when it is safe and definite for the changes to be made. While these new state values reside in the scheduler and the store queue, they are forwarded to dependent Ops as necessary. Nonabortable state changes, in contrast, occur immediately during execution of certain special RegOPs and the responsibility or burden is placed on the OpQuad Sequences containing these RegOPs to ensure sufficient synchronization with surrounding operations.

Later it will be shown that the scheduler incorporates the functions of a reorder buffer and implied register renaming. Explicit tags indicating the program order of operation results are not used. The physical positions of entries in the scheduler indicate the program order of the corresponding operations. The result values stored in an entry provide the register and status values of the "renamed" registers at the associated point in the program order. Explicit register renaming is not required. Exactly how renaming is accomplished will be discussed in Chapter 3. Briefly, the scheduler's use scan chains which, when directed in the proper physical direction across the scheduler Op entries, locate preceding or older Ops that affect desired register operands and status flags for subsequent operations.

Audio Clip on CD-ROM

 This audio clip gives a summary of the K6 3D's scheduler's functions.

The following is a summary of the role each of the units identified in Figure 2.9 on page 130 play in the scheduler processes just described. Each unit is discussed in detail in Chapter 3.

ISSUE SELECTION LOGIC

The issue selection logic is involved with the selection of the next Ops to enter the LU, SU, RUX, and the RUY processing pipelines—i.e., four Op selections occur every clock. Each cycle, based on the updated state information in the scheduler as of the beginning of the cycle, the issue selection logic performs a selection process to determine the next LdOp, the next StOp, and the next two RegOps to be issued into the corresponding execution unit processing pipelines.

Historical Comment and Suggested Readings

Reorder Buffer

Processors that support speculative and out-of-order execution typically have operations completing execution before they are ready to be committed. The results of such operations are not committed (i.e., producing permanent state change) until it is safe to do so. The collection of storage elements that hold the results of the as-yet-uncommitted operations is often called a reorder buffer, for it is from this buffer that the instructions which have been executed out of order will be reordered and committed in an in-order fashion. A reorder buffer also supports the use and forwarding of results of completed operations as source operands for other dependent operations. The K6 is an example of a microprocessor in which its reorder buffer (included in the scheduler's centralized buffer functionality) also serves as an environment to support register renaming[a]. As we will learn in Chapter 3, the K6's renaming registers hold result register values in the DestVal field of the appropriate Op entries in the scheduler until they are committed. In the K6, a single unified structure, the scheduler's buffer, was designed to hold all information related to the processing of an Op throughout its lifetime. All Ops enter the scheduler after being decoded (or fetched from the OpQuad Sequence ROM) and remain there until the end of their life (i.e., until they are committed or removed). Most out-of-order execution designs utilize separate structures for the functions of a reorder buffer, reservation stations, and possibly other dispatch queues.

 See, "Implementation of Precise Interrupts in Pipelined Processors," by J. E. Smith and A. R. Pleszkum, *Proceedings of the 12th Annual International Symposium on Computer Architecture*, June 1985, pp. 34-44. You can find the full text version of this article on the CD-ROM.

---

[a] See the section titled "Register Renaming" beginning on page 300.

OPERAND SELECTION LOGIC

The operand selection logic is involved with determining:

1. the status of each value, i.e., whether a valid value is or is not available from the designated source.
2. where each of nine operand values actually needs to come from— i.e., from which specific scheduler Op entry, architectural register, or execution unit result bus.

Based on this information, the scheduler determines which Ops will be able to advance in their respective execution pipelines and actually start execution.

LOAD/STORE ORDERING LOGIC

Just as certain execution ordering must be maintained between Ops due to register dependencies, a certain degree of execution ordering must be maintained between LdOps and StOps due to memory dependencies. For example, LdOps cannot freely execute ahead of older StOps. There are two chunks of logic, one associated with the LU pipeline and one associated with the SU pipeline that deal with this ordering and determine when given LdOps and StOps are independent of each other and thus can safely be allowed to execute out of order with respect to one another. These two chunks of logic are collectively referred to as the load/store ordering logic in Figure 2.9 on page 130.

STATUS FLAG HANDLING LOGIC

There is a chunk of scheduler logic, called the status flag handling logic, associated with the fetching and usage of status flag operand values. Two relatively independent areas are involved: the fetching of status flag values for status-dependent RegOps and the fetching of status flag values for the resolution of BRCOND Ops.

STATUS FLAG-DEPENDENT REGOP LOGIC

All status-dependent RegOps, which are referred to as condition code dependent, "cc-dependent," or "cc-dep" Ops, are executed by the RUX or RUY execution units and require their status operand value with the same timing as their register operand values. The status flag-dependent RegOp logic is responsible for ensuring that this happens correctly.

cc-dependent Ops
cc-dep Ops

BRANCH RESOLUTION LOGIC

As is shown in Figure 2.21 on page 175, a BRCOND Ops (BrOp) does not require any actual execution processing. Instead, while a BRCOND Op is outstanding and before it reaches the bottom row of the scheduler's buffer, it must be resolved as to whether the associated conditional branch instruction was correctly predicted or not. This is done for each BRCOND Op, in order, at a rate of up to one per cycle. When the above status flag-handling logic obtains the appropriate status for the next unresolved BRCOND Op, the appropriate set of status flag values is used to determine if the condition code specified within the BRCOND Op is TRUE or FALSE. If valid values for the required status flags are not yet all available, then resolution of the Op is held up.

If the branch condition is FALSE, the BRCOND Op was incorrectly predicted and an appropriate restart signal is immediately asserted to restart the upper portion of the processor at the correct next program address (i.e., the instruction fetch and decode portion—see Figure 2.4 on page 87). The correct address is either the branch target address or next sequential address, whichever was not predicted.

If the branch was correctly predicted, then nothing happens other than BRCOND Op resolution processing advances on to the next

BRCOND Op. The branch resolution logic (also called the BRU earlier) is concerned with resolving these issues.

SELF-MODIFYING CODE SUPPORT LOGIC

The self-modifying code support logic is concerned with the detection and handling of self-modifying code. Logically, in the scheduler, a detection of self-modifying code is treated as a type of an instruction trap (see the section titled "Handling Faults, Traps, and Precise Interrupts" beginning on page 175). The store queue provides the physical address of the store it is preparing to commit. It supplies "linear address" bits which are logically also the "physical address" bits since these bits are only untranslated bits. The bits are compared against the instruction addresses of each following OpQuad. If any OpQuad addresses match, then there may be a write to an instruction which has already been fetched, decoded, and is now in the scheduler. This is a potential self-modifying code situation. Accordingly, the scheduler is then flushed of these following OpQuads and the upper portion is restarted to refetch and redecode the associated x86 instructions, starting with the instruction after the "modifying" instruction.

DESIGN NOTE

False Self-Modifying Code Traps

Due to cycle-time constraints, the self-modifying code logic does not compare all of the address bits. Therefore, an "address" match does not necessarily mean that the code is self-modifying. It is possible for a *false self-modifying code trap* to occur. Since the lower address bits are compared, these false traps can only occur when the memory size exceeds 1Mbyte, and even then they are statistically rare. In this situation, the processor is flushed as with normal trap handling, resulting in a small and transient performance loss.

GLOBAL CONTROL LOGIC

Basically, the global control logic coordinates the overall operation of the scheduler. For example, it issues the control signals to load the pipeline registers and it controls the source operand input multiplexers for each of the execution units.

OPQUAD EXPANSION LOGIC

This chunk of logic, which is shown in Figure 2.8 on page 127, expands *decoder* OpQuads into *scheduler* OpQuads before they are loaded into the top row of the scheduler. A description of what occurs during this expansion process is given in Chapter 3.

Op Commit Unit

The OCU operates in conjunction with the scheduler and generally operates on the Ops within the bottom two rows of the scheduler. During each cycle the OCU examines each of the Ops within the bottom OpQuad and tries to commit the results of as many of these Ops as possible. It is possible for the state changes of all four Ops to be committed in one cycle or for this to take many cycles. If all the Ops of an OpQuad have been committed or are being successfully committed, then the OpQuad is retired from the scheduler at the end of the current cycle. Otherwise, as many changes as possible are committed during the current cycle and the process is repeated on successive cycles until all changes have been committed. In some cases, the OCU will also look ahead into the second from the bottom OpQuad to (a) start committing StOps while RegOps in the bottom OpQuad remain to be committed, or (b) commit, in certain potential deadlock situations, register results while the bottom OpQuad cannot yet be retired from the scheduler. Thus the OCU's principal function is to commit the results of Ops and then to retire them from the scheduler. It also handles mispredicted BRCOND Ops by initiating abort cycles for them.

The performance of a microprocessor that decodes CISC instructions into RISC operations for execution on a RISC microarchitecture depends greatly on the number of RISC operations produced from a single CISC instruction. The decoding of the x86 instructions involves, in part, a mapping of variations of similar instructions into one or more Ops, (e.g., the decoding of the many variations of an x86 ADD instruction into an ADD Op.) A large number of the x86 memory addressing forms of a particular instruction can be converted into load or store Ops (LdOps or StOps) accessing memory in combination with a register-to-register Op (a RegOp).

OpQuad Sequences

OpQuad Sequences and the RISC86 Operation Set

Instruction decoders in superscalar microprocessors such as the Pentium, Pentium Pro, and the K6 often include one or more decoding pathways in which x86 instructions are decoded by hardware logic and a separate decoding pathway which uses an on-chip ROM memory for fetching an OpQuad Sequence that corresponds to a complex or uncommon x86 instruction. OpQuad Sequences may also be initiated as a result of servicing an exception or a trap. There is an important issue centered around an OpQuad Sequence that realizes the semantics of an x86 instruction. X86 instructions are atomic entities in the x86 instruction set architecture. This means that once they begin executing, they complete execution without any interruption. Thus, the x86 instruction's OpQuad Sequence must also be atomic—i.e., it must finish execution without interruption. To achieve this, the hardware decoders are inactive when an OpQuad Sequence from the OpQuad ROM is in the process of executing (see a related comment in the section titled "Use of the Predecode Bits" beginning on page 121).

OpQuad ROM

One problem with using the *OpQuad ROM* for storing OpQuad Sequences is that the process of accessing a ROM is typically slower and less efficient than hardwired decoding of instructions.[19] Another problem is that if a substantial number of x86 instructions are implemented by OpQuad Sequences, a large OpQuad ROM is required for storing them. Obviously, if the OpQuad ROM is large, there is increased circuit complexity for deriving and applying the pointer (vector) into it to identify the appropriate OpQuad sequence. Increased circuit complexity directly relates to increased overhead, which reduces instruction decoding throughput. Furthermore, a large OpQuad ROM increases the size of the processor's circuitry which, in turn, can reduce the manufacturing yields and increase production costs.

Historical Comment and Suggested Readings

Environment Substitution

Designers of some early microprogrammable machines recognized that a number of microcode sequences used to emulate ISAs were quite similar, differing, for example, only in the specific registers manipulated. To take advantage of this situation, the specific registers used in the microcode sequence were specified in auxiliary registers whose values were "merged" with the microcode sequence as it was being executed. Such implementations can be viewed as precursors to the K6's OpQuad Template environment substitution and its use of dynamic fields (see, for example, the article by Gerald Jay Sussman, Jack Holloway, Guy Lewis Steel, Jr., and Alan Bell, "Scheme-79—Lisp on a Chip," in *Computer*, July, 1981, pp. 10-21). For a description of a microarchitecture which dealt with some of these issues and proposed a "snooper" facility for doing both microcode debugging and performance measurements see, B. D. Shriver, "A Description of the Mathilda System," Department of Computer Science, University of Aarhus, Denmark, April 1973.

The approach taken to resolve the issues surrounding the use of an OpQuad ROM and OpQuad Sequences in the K6 was to design a RISC86 Op Set that would:

1. facilitate the decoding of as many x86 instructions as possible into a small (i.e.,"minimum") number of OpQuad Sequences.
2. permit more common x86 instructions to be decoded using hardwired logic, versus being implemented using OpQuad Sequences stored in the OpQuad ROM.

---

[19] It is interesting to note that the K6 has the same Op fetch/generation bandwidth in either case, as will be shown later.

To achieve this, RISC86 Ops are relatively "powerful"—for example, LdOps and StOps support (base + scaled index + displacement) address computations within one Op and executing in one cycle. The K6's OpQuad ROM and its relationship to other resources (such as the instruction vector decoder and the exception vector decoder) is shown in Figure 2.6 on page 115. The relationship is shown in more detail in Figure 2.10.

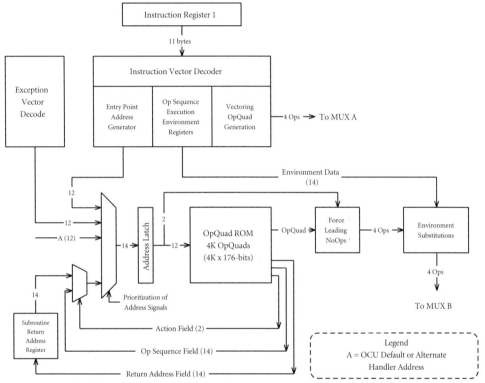

Figure 2.10 OpQuad ROM, Vector Decoder, and Exception Decoder

It is important to understand that *all* x86 instructions have a corresponding OpQuad sequence in the OpQuad ROM. The hardware decoders can be viewed as a performance enhancement over invoking every specific OpQuad sequence when needed. The presence of the hardware decoders also reduces the pressure to maximize the performance of the logic associated with implementing OpQuad sequences.

DESIGN NOTE

Indirect Register Names

The "reg" and "regm" mnemonics in Table 2.4 on page 92 represent indirect register names for the x86's 32-bit integer registers (i.e., AX-DI or AL-BH). They are replaced, at Op decode time, by the current register number (i.e., 00xxx) from the corresponding EmReg or EmRegM execution environment variable. Similarly, the "MMreg" and "MMregm" mnemonics represent indirect register names for the x86's 64-bit MMX registers (i.e., MM0-MM7). They are replaced, at Op decode time, by the current register number (i.e., 11xxx) from the corresponding EmReg or EmRegM environment substitution variable. As was seen in Table 2.4, the indirect register names have multiple encoding. This is done to reduce decode logic.

OpQuad templates

environment substitutions

OpQuad eexecution environment registers

force leading NoOps logic

The K6's RISC86 Op Set is highly regular with a fixed length and format for each Op type. By comparison, conventional x86 instructions are highly irregular, having greatly different instruction lengths and formats. OpQuad Sequences, when required, are implemented in a small OpQuad ROM and exploit the reuse of operation structures for variations that are common among x86 instructions.

The short decoders and the long decoder produce decoder OpQuads. The instruction vector decoder produces an initial decoder OpQuad and an entry point address to an OpQuad Sequence in the OpQuad ROM. The OpQuad Sequence consists of a sequence of *OpQuad templates*. The *environment substitutions* logic, shown in Figure 2.6 on page 115 and Figure 2.10 on page 139, processes various fields in the OpQuad templates and outputs decoder OpQuads. An OpQuad Sequence environment is maintained in the *OpQuad Execution Environment Registers* in the instruction vector decoder and includes default address and data sizes for the code segment and the register numbers from the x86 instruction. The environment variables allow a section of an OpQuad Sequence to be re-used for different x86 instructions by proper replacement of field values with environmental variables appropriate for the code section and x86 instruction. Importantly, the OpQuad ROM contains OpQuad Sequences where not all of the Ops in the OpQuads are actually part of the implementation of one specific x86 instruction. Such Ops are changed to NoOps by the *Force Leading NoOps logic* as required for the x86 instruction being decoded. The use of the execution environment substitution achieves encoding of the x86 instruction set architecture functionality while substantially reducing the number and size of the code sequences in the OpQuad ROM. Correspondingly, this approach also reduces the size and cost of required circuitry.

The exception vector decoder and the OCU produce entry point addresses into the OpQuad ROM, but do not produce an initial vectoring OpQuad as the hardware instruction vector decoder does. Concurrent with an abort cycle, the OCU also vectors the machine to one of two possible OpQuad Sequence entry point addresses—either the "default" OCU fault handler address or an "alternate" OCU handler address (see "A" in Figure 2.10). The setting of these addresses is supported by the LDDHA Op (load *default handler address*) and the LDAHA Op (load *alternate handler address*). The default fault handler address is initialized by the processor reset OpQuad Sequence and the alternate handler address is specified within OpQuad sequences for some x86 instructions and for some cases of exception processing. Alternative handler addresses remain active from execution of the LDAHA Op (a) until the end of the instruction or exception processing OpQuad sequence, or (b) until another LDAHA Op executes. At this point, control for subsequent faults reverts to the default fault handler addresses.

Design Note

Decoder OpQuads, *Scheduler* OpQuads, and OpQuad Templates

As was mentioned earlier and as shown in Figure 2.8 on page 127, the *decoder* OpQuads produced by the decoders pass through the OpQuad Expansion Logic to produce *scheduler* OpQuads prior to being loaded into the scheduler's buffer. When we use the term "RISC86 Ops," we are referring to the Ops in *decoder* OpQuads and the fields and formats of these Ops. The differences between the contents of *decoder* OpQuads and *scheduler* OpQuads is discussed in Chapter 3. The OpQuad ROM stores OpQuad Templates that are changed into *decoder* OpQuads by the environmental substitution logic.

There are a few additional resources in Figure 2.10 on page 139 that we should explain to give you a more complete understanding of the decoding process and OpQuad ROM work.

The Op Sequence and Action Fields

Every OpQuad *must* specify a branch, even if it is only a branch to the next sequential instruction in the ROM. Branches in OpQuad sequences are specified by a combination of the SpecOp Type field (discussed later in Table 2.39 on page 155), the *Op Sequence field* and the *action field*, both of which are shown in Figure 2.10. There is a single Op Sequence field and a single action field for each OpQuad in the OpQuad ROM. The action field specifies the type of branch. The branches may be conditional. Thus, in addition to the Op sequence and action fields, the OpQuad may also contain a BRCOND Op. If there is a BRCOND Op, then the OpQuad sequence branch is considered to be a conditional branch. If it does not, then the OpQuad sequence branch is considered to specify an unconditional branch. The exception to this is the OpQuad sequence subroutine branch (BSR), discussed below, which is always unconditional, yet always requires a BRCOND Op in the OpQuad to supply the return address in the *Return Address Field*. You can have four Ops plus a branch in a single OpQuad if the branch is unconditional, but only three Ops plus a branch in an OpQuad if the branch is conditional (or is a BSR branch).

OpQuad Sequence Subroutines

An OpQuad sequence can branch to a subroutine in the OpQuad ROM by executing the BSR branch described above. The Subroutine Return Address Register represents a one-deep OpQuad Sequence return address stack. This allows one level of subroutine nesting within OpQuad sequences. Being only one entry, this allows extremely simple control logic (for example, no actual top-of-stack pointer needs to be maintained, particularly in the face of mispredicted OpQuad sequence branch and exceptions). In practice this proves sufficient for most all OpQuad sequences across the entire x86 instruction set architecture functionality. OpQuad sequence subroutines need not return to the OpQuad following the caller.

Initial Vector OpQuad Generation Logic

The Initial Vector OpQuad generation logic handles the generation of an initial four Ops during an instruction vector-decode cycle (in parallel with generation of a ROM entry point address of the appropriate instruction OpQuad Sequence). During successive clock cycles, additional OpQuads are supplied by the ROM. The initial vectoring OpQuad varies between instructions. There are special cases for certain specific instructions, but most are grouped into a small number of categories or cases. For each of these general cases (e.g., for the register and for the memory forms of x86 mod R/M instructions), the Ops in the vectoring OpQuad primarily serve to set up various immediate displacement, and/or effective memory address values in scratch integer registers (via LIMM Ops). The fourth of the four Ops is typically the address of the next sequential instruction.

Address Latch

And finally in Figure 2.10 on page 139 there is the *Address Latch*. This latch is simply a registered address input to the ROM. This holds the ROM fetch address from the end of one clock cycle to the start (and completion) of the fetch itself in the next cycle.

FORMATS FOR DECODER OPS

A *decoder* OpQuad consists of four 38-bit Ops. Decoder OpQuads can contain LdOps and StOps, RegOps, SpecOps, and LIMMOps. The formats for these Ops are shown in Table 2.22 on page 143, Table 2.30 on page 150, Table 2.38 on page 155, and Table 2.42 on page 158, respectively. Although some of the fields are similar, there are a number of differences among these Op formats. Having an understanding of these fields will help you understand the mappings between the decoder OpQuads and scheduler OpQuads that the OpQuad Expansion Logic implements. The following diagram indicates how we will cover these topics:

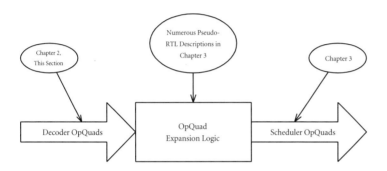

The *decoder* Op formats are presented in this section. The *scheduler* OpQuad formats are discussed in Chapter 3. Explanations of various chunks of the OpQuad Expansion Logic exist in numerous pseudo-RTL descriptions running throughout Chapter 3. We'll begin by looking at the format of LdOps and StOps.

LdOp and StOp Field Descriptions

LdOps and StOps perform memory accesses and related operations. They have the following format in a *decoder* OpQuad:

Table 2.22 Decoder OpQuad LdOp and StOp Format

37 36	35 32	31 30	29 26	25 24	23 22	21 17	16	15 12	11 4	3 0
0 1	Type	ISF	Seg	ASz	DSz	Data	LD	Base	Disp8	Index

We now describe each of the fields in this table: Type[3:0], ASz[1:0], DSz[1:0], Data[4:0], Seg[3:0], Base[3:0], Index[3:0], ISF[1:0], LD, and Disp8[7:0]. The Type[3:0] field specifies the specific type of LdOp or StOp to be performed according to the following table:

Historical Comment and Suggested Readings

Expanding Microinstructions

The technique of expanding a "smaller" microinstruction into one or more "larger" microinstructions has a long history of use in processor design. The Nanodata QM-1 is typical of two-level emulation systems. The machine had both a control store for holding microinstructions and a nanostore for holding nanoinstructions. The control store consisted of from 2K to 65K 16-bit words and the nanostore consisted of up to 1K 342-bit words. A microinstruction (usually) consisted of a 6-bit opcode field and two 5-bit address parts. Microprograms consisted of sequences of microinstructions. Microinstructions can be viewed as pointers in nanostore. A nanoinstruction consisted of a 38-bit constant field and four 76-bit T-fields. Execution progressed from the first T-field, then to the second T-field and so on and then returned to the first T-field. A nanoinstruction could specify a branch to another nanoword specified by a 10-bit subfield of the K-field. T-fields can be skipped. These features allowed a microinstruction to be realized by: (1) the execution of one-to-four T-field operations in a single nanoinstruction, (2) a nanoprogram consisting of the iterative execution of a single nanoinstruction, (3) a nanoprogram consisting of the successive execution of multiple nanoinstructions, (4) a nanoprogram combining nanoprograms of types 2 and 3. One can view the 16-bit microinstructions being expanded in place into a set of 342-bit nanoinstructions during the execution of a microprogram. Given this, there are two interesting features to mention in this historical comment: (a) there could exist nanowords that were common to more than one microinstruction and (b) one could essentially use some of the fields of a microinstruction as parameters to the nanoprogram. The QM-1, like other microprogrammable machines, made extensive use of residual data and control. This allowed microinstructions to set up an environment for execution by other microinstructions. In the case of the QM-1, this meant for nanoprograms as well. Of interest is the fact that (a) the mapping of microprogram-accessible registers' host resources could be statically established upon entry to an emulator or dynamically altered by reestablishing bus address mappings within microprograms, and (b) the addresses of interrupt-specific nanoprograms were specified in a set of registers so they could be dynamically changed by the nanoprogrammer (see, for example, the articles by Robert F. Rosin, Gideon Frieder, and Richard H. Eckhouse, Jr., "An Environment for Research in Microprogramming and Emulation," in *Communications of the ACM*, Vol. 15, No. 8, August 1972, pp. 748-760, and by Michael J. Flynn and Robert F. Rosin, "Microprogramming: an Introduction and a Viewpoint," *IEEE Transactions on Computers*, July, 1971, pp. 721-731).

For an interesting discussion of various vertical, diagonal, and horizontal single-level and two-level microinstruction formats for a variety of different processors see the book, *Foundations of Microprogramming*, by Ashok K. Agrawala and Tomlinson G. Rauscher, Academic Press, 1976. A number of early papers dealing with microcode verification can be found in *Firmware, Microprogramming and Restructurable Hardware*, by Gerhard Chroust and Jorg R. Muhlbacher, North-Holland Publishing Company, 1980.

mov mask [BX][SI], 2Ch — memory immediate
disk   Base Index

Table 2.23   LDOP AND STOP TYPE(3:0) FIELD

Type(3:0)	Op Symbol	Type of LdOp or StOp to be Performed
0000	LD, LDL	Load integer data
0001	LDF	Load floating-point data
0010	LDST	Load integer data with store check
0011	LDM	Load MMX or 3D data
0100	CDAF(X)	CDA (see below) plus flush cache line(s)
0101	LDPF	Load Prefetch (prefetches a block)
0110	LDSTL	Load integer data with store check, locked
0111	LDMSTL	Load MMX or 3D data with store check, locked
1000	ST	Store integer data
1001	STF	Store floating-point data
1010	STUPD	Store integer data and update base register
1011	STM	Store MMX or 3D data
1100	CDA	Check "data" effective address (segment and page protection)
1101	CIA	Check "instruction" effective address (segment protection only)
1110	TIA	TLB invalidate address (based on TLB index only)
1111	LEA	Load effective address

The LDL Op is a synonym for LD which is used as the first of a pair of LD Ops used to read an 8-byte segment descriptor. All LdStOps, except for ST, STF, and STM, produce a result that is stored in a general register. LdOps load a general register (the data register) with data from memory. For CDA, CIA, TIA, and LEA StOps, the data register is loaded with the calculated effective (logical) address. In both of these cases, the register modification size is based on the DSz field. For STUPD StOps, the base address register is loaded with the calculated effective (logical) address (i.e., "store and update"). The register modification size is also based on the ASz field instead of the DSz field.

The ASz[1:0] field specifies the address calculation size (in bytes) before and after the environment substitutions described above and according to the table on the following page:

Table 2.24   LᴅOᴘ ᴀɴᴅ SᴛOᴘ ASᴢ(1:0) Fɪᴇʟᴅ

ASz(1:0)	Address Calculation Size Before Environment Substitution	Address Calculation Size After Environment Substitution
00	Asize	2 Bytes
01	Ssize	—
10	4 Bytes	4 Bytes
11	Dsize	—

The DSz[1:0] field specifies the size of the data (in bytes) before and after the environment substitutions described above and according to the following two tables. The first table is for all LdOp and StOp operation Types other than LDF, STF, LDM, and CDAF(X):

Table 2.25   DSᴢ(1:0) Fɪᴇʟᴅ ꜰᴏʀ LᴅSᴛOᴘs ᴏᴛʜᴇʀ ᴛʜᴀɴ LDF STF, LDM, & CDAF

DSz(1:0)	Data Size Before Environment Substitution	Data Size After Environment Substitution
00	1 Byte	1 Byte
01	2 Bytes	2 Bytes
10	4 Bytes	4 Bytes
11	Dsize	—

The second table is only for the LdOp and StOp operation Types LDF, STF, LDM, and CDAF(X):

Table 2.26   DSᴢ(1:0) Fɪᴇʟᴅ ꜰᴏʀ LᴅSᴛOᴘs LDF, STF, LDM & CDAF

DSz(1:0)	Data Size Before Environment Substitution	Data Size After Environment Substitution
00	FpDSize	—[a]
01	2 Bytes	2 Bytes
10	4 Bytes	4 Bytes
11	8 Bytes	8 Bytes

[a]   LDF and STF only.

The Data[4:0] field specifies the general register to be used by an Op. The register field encodings can be found in Table 2.4 on page 92. If the Op is a LdOp, the specified register should be thought of as a "destination" register. If the Op is a StOp, it should be thought of as the "source" register of the data to be stored. The Seg[3:0] field specifies the segment register to be used by this Op for the "segment descriptor."

Table 2.27 LDOP AND STOP SEG(3:0) FIELD

Seg(3:0)	Register	Description
0000	ES	x86 architectural ES register
0001	CS	x86 architectural CS register
0010	SS	x86 architectural SS register
0011	DS	x86 architectural DS register
0100	FS	x86 architectural FS register
0101	GS	x86 architectural GS register
0110	HS	microarchitectural temporary segment register
0111	—	reserved
100x	TS	"descriptor table segment register" for accessing the x86 architectural global and local descriptor tables (GDT and LDT respectively)
1010	LS	"linear segment register" (i.e., the segment base = 0)
1011	MS	"special memory" memory segment register (the special memory contains the "scratchpad" memory, as well as other special address spaces—I/O, cache flush, and special bus cycles)
11xx	OS	effective x86 architectural operand segment register

The Base[3:0] field specifies the general register containing the base address operand for this Op. The Index[3:0] field specifies the general register containing the index address operand for this Op. The Base and Index register fields only refer to the low half of the general register set, i.e., to AX-DI and t0-t7. The mapping between the set of x86 architectural registers and the set of microarchitectural physical registers is discussed in detail in Chapter 3.

DESIGN NOTE
Expanded Segment Register Address Space
The segment register address space has been expanded to four bits, allowing additional special microarchitectural segment registers to be supported. The segment OS register is replaced when the environment substitution occurs by 0xxx, where xxx is the register number from the OpQuad Sequence environment.

Note the use of the scaled index in Figure 2.17 on page 166. The ISF[1:0] field specifies the index register scale factor according to the following table:

Table 2.28 LDOP AND STOP ISF(1:0) FIELD

ISF(1:0)	Index Register Scale Factor
00	1 X
01	2 X
10	4 X
11	8 X

The LD (large displacement) field specifies what field is to be used as the displacement according to the following table:

Table 2.29 LDOP AND STOP LD (LARGE DISPLACEMENT) FIELD

LD	Field to Use as the Displacement
0	Use the Disp8 field of this Op.
1	Use the 32-bit displacement from the appropriate decoder displacement bus

In order to understand what the choice means when LD = 1, we need to revisit Figure 2.8 on page 127. A modified version of it appears as Figure 2.11, below.

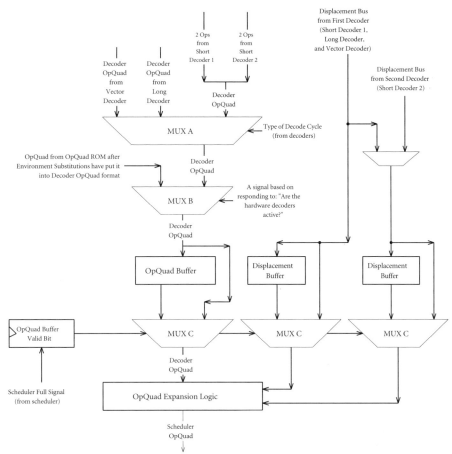

Figure 2.11 Displacement Buses from Decoder

Whenever an instruction that specifies a long displacement is decoded by either the short decoders or the long decoder, that 32-bit (or sign-extended 16-bit) displacement is passed along with the decoder OpQuad through a multiplexer similar to MUX A. In order to keep Figure 2.11 simple, this multiplexer is not shown. If one of the short decoders or the long decoder is selected as the output of MUX A and if the decoder OpQuad is selected as the output of MUX B, then the 32-bit displacement is either:

1. loaded into the displacement buffer if the corresponding decoder OpQuad is loaded into the OpQuad buffer or

2. immediately sent to the OpQuad Expansion Logic via the displacement register if the corresponding decoder OpQuad is sent directly to the OpQuad Expansion Logic.

If LD = 1, this 32-bit displacement is then used in the OpQuad expansion and is stored in the DestVal field of the corresponding Op entry. The Disp8[7:0] field specifies an 8-bit value which is sign-extended to 32-bits when used as the displacement, otherwise it is ignored. The LD field specifies whether to use the Disp8 field or not.

REGOP FIELD DESCRIPTIONS

RegOps perform register operations. They have the following format in a *decoder* OpQuad.

Table 2.30 DECODER OPQUAD REGOP FORMAT

37	36	35	30	29	26	25	24	20	21	17	16	12	11	10	9	8	7	0
0	0	Type		Ext		RX	DSz		Dest		Src1		—		SS	I	Imm8/Src2	

We now describe each of the fields in this table: Type, Ext, RX, DSz, Dest, Src1, SS, I, and Imm8/Src2. The Type field specified the type of RegOp operation to be performed according to the encodings in the following four tables. Table 2.31 is for ALU (arithmetic logic unit) type operations:

Table 2.31 REGOP TYPE(5:1) FIELD GENERAL ARITHMETIC OPERATIONS

Type(5:1)	DSz Other Than 1 Byte	DSz = 1 Byte	cc-dep	RUX Only
00000	ADD, INC, CADD	ADD, INC	—	—
00001	MOV, OR, EOR	OR, EOR	—	O
00010	ADC	ADC	X	X
00011	SBB	SBB	X	X
00100	AND, EAND, BAND	AND, EAND	—	—
00101	SUB, ESUB, DEC, CSUB	SUB, DEC, ESUB	—	—
00110	XOR, EXOR	XOR, EXOR	—	—
00111	CMP	CMP	—	—

In the above table, Type[0] = 0 for all of the RegOp except for BAND for which Type[0] = 1.

DESIGN NOTE
Interpretation of RegOp Type Field
As is seen in Table 2.31, the RegOp Type field is interpreted differently based on the DSz field of the RegOp. One set of operations is implemented by hardware for byte-size operations, and a different set for 2-byte and 4-byte (i.e., 16-bit and 32-bit) operations. This distinction is made at Op execution time, after the DSz field has been resolved into an absolute Op size specification.
The "cc-dep" column means that the RegOp is dependent on a condition code as described in Chapter 3. All RegOps with Type = xx01x are treated by the hardware as being condition-code-dependent and are synchronized by the status operand forwarding logic discussed in Chapter 3. The "RUX Only" column means that the operation can only be executed in the RUX pipeline; see Figure 2.3 on page 81. Finally, the BAND ALU Op differs from AND Op in the generation of the CF status result.
The other RegOps sharing the same Type encoding only differ in the value put into the EXT field as the status modification bits as described later.

Table 2.32 is for Shift and MMX Ops. All MMX register operations share one RegOp Type. The individual MMX operations are distinguished by a separate MMX opcode (or operation type) that is passed to and decoded by the MMX execution units at Op execution time.

Table 2.32   REGOP TYPE(5:1) FIELD SHIFT AND MMX OPERATIONS

Type(5:1)	DSz Other Than 1 Byte	DSz = 1 Byte	cc-dep	RUX Only
01000	SLL, BLL	SLL	—	X
01001	SRL	SRL	—	X
01010	SLC, RLC	—	X	X
01011	SRC, RRC	—	X	X
01100	SLA	SLA	—	X
01101	SRA	SRA	—	X
01110	SLD, RLD	RLS	—	X
01111	SRD, RRD, MMX	RRS	—	—

In the above table, Type[0] = 0 for all of the Shift and MMX Ops except for BLL and MMX for which Type[0] = 1.

DESIGN NOTE
Difference in BLL and SLL Op
The BLL Shift Op differs from the SLL Op in that the masking of the shift amount is DSz-dependent.

The third table is for other arithmetic RegOps:

Table 2.33   REGOP TYPE(5:1) FIELD FOR OTHER ARITHMETIC REGOPS

Type(5:1)	DSz Other Than 1 Byte Type(0)= 0 Type(0)=1		DSz = 1 Byte Type(0)= 0 Type(0)=1		cc-dep	RUX Only
10000	ZEXT8	SEXT8	—		—	X
10001	ZEXT16	SEXT16	—		—	X
10010	RDFLGS		DAA	DAS	X	X
10011	MOVcc	MOVcc	—		X	X
10100	MUL1S	MUL1U	—		—	X
10101	MULEH	MULEL	—		—	X
10110	DIV1	DIV2	—		—	X
10111	DIVER	DIVEQ	—		—	X

DESIGN NOTE
ZEXT8, SEXT8, ZEXT16, and SEXT16 RegOp
For the ZEXT8, SEXT8, ZEXT16, and SEXT16 RegOps, only the low one or two bytes of the source operand is required to be valid, even if DSz is two or four bytes. Further, for the ZEXT8 and SEXT8 RegOps, the source operand register number is interpreted as specifying a byte register. Note, the other source operand is not used by these Ops.

The fourth and last RegOp Type table is for special RegOps:

Table 2.34 RegOp Type(5:1) Field for Special RegOps

Type(5:1)	DSz Other Than 1 Byte		DSz = 1 Byte		cc-dep	RUX Only
	Type(0)= 0	Type(0)=1	Type(0)= 0	Type(0)=1		
11000	RDxxx	RDxxx	—		—	X
11001	RDFLG	BSWAP	—		—	X
11010	RDSEG	RDSEG	—		X	X
11011	—		—		—	—
11100	WRDR	WRDL	—		—	X
11101	WRxxx	WRxxx	—		—	X
11110	WRIP	WRDLIP	—		—	X
11111	CHKS	WRDH	—		—	X

Design Note

Valid Source Operand Bytes for CHKS and WRDR

Only the low two bytes of the source operands are required to be valid for the CHKS and WRDR RegOps, even if DSz is equal to four bytes.

The Ext[3:0] (Extension) field combines with or extends the meaning of the Type field as follows:

Table 2.35 RegOp Ext(3:0) Field

Type of Ops	Field Combination	Used to Specify
MOVcc	Type[0] Ext[3:0]	a 5-bit condition code
RDxxx and WRxxx	Type[0] Ext[3:0]	a 5-bit special register number
RDSEG	Type[0] Ext[3:0]	a 5-bit segment descriptor register number
(other) Ops with SS = 1	Ext[3:0]	four status flag modification bits stored in the scheduler
(other) Ops with SS = 0	Ext[3:0]	not used

What are the ops?

For the WRFLG WRxxx Op, the special register number specifies the x86 EFLAGS register. The low four bits of this register number is also identical to the desired four status modification bits for loading the status flag bits of EFLAGS, when SS = 1.

The DSz[2:0] field specifies the size of the data (in bytes) for the Op according to the following table:

Table 2.36 REGOP DSZ(2:0) FIELD

DSz(2:0)	Data Size Before Environment Substitution	Data Size After Environment Substitution
000	1 Byte	1 Byte
001	2 Bytes	2 Bytes
010	4 Bytes	4 Bytes
011	Dsize	—
100	Asize	—
101	Ssize	—
110	—	—
111	—	—

The Dest[4:0] field specifies which general register the Op will use to store its results in (i.e., the destination register). The Src1[4:0] field specifies which general register the Op will use to obtain its first operand from (i.e., the source register Src1). The SS field (Set Status field) specifies whether the Op affects status flags. If it does, then the status modification bits in the Ext field indicate which groups of flags are affected. The I field (Immediate field) indicates if the second operand of the Op is an immediate value or is obtained from a general register. It is interpreted in conjunction with the Imm8/Src2 field according to the following table:

Table 2.37 REGOP I (IMMEDIATE) FIELD

I Field	Imm8/Src2	Source for Second Operand
0	Imm8/Src2[4:0]	a general register to be the source register Src2
1	Imm8/Src2[7:0]	an 8-bit immediate value that is extended to the DSz size

Lastly, bits [11:10] of a RegOp are unused and should be set to "00".

SpecOp Field Descriptions

SpecOps perform a variety of special operations. They have the following format in a decoder OpQuad:.

Table 2.38 Decoder OpQuad SpecOp Format

37 35	34 31	30 26	25 24	23 22	21 17	16 0
1 0 1	Type	CC	—	DSz	Dest	Imm17

We now describe each of the fields in this table: Type, CC, DSz, Dest, and Imm17. The Type field specifies the type of SpecOp to be performed according to the following table:

Table 2.39 SpecOp Type(3:0) Field

Type(3:0)	Op Symbol	Type of SpecOp
00xx	BRCOND	Branch condition
0100	LDDHA	Load default handler address
0101	LDDHAB	Load binary default handler address
0110	LDAHA	Load alternate handler address
0111	LDAHAB	Load binary alternate handler address
1000	LDK	Load constant
1001	FPOP	Floating-point Op
1010	LDKD	Load DSz-modified constant
1011	FPOPE	Floating-point Op from the OPQuad Sequence Environment
11xx	FAULT	Unconditional fault

As discussed in the section titled "The Op Sequence and Action Fields" beginning on page 141, every OpQuad *must* specify a branch, even if it's only a branch to the next sequential instruction in the ROM. It was also noted that branches in OpQuad sequences are specified by a combination of the SpecOp Type field (discussed above) and the Op Sequence and Action Fields shown in Figure 2.10 on page 139.

Further, the OpQuad may or may not also contain a BRCOND Op. If there is a BRCOND Op, then the OpQuad sequence branch is considered to specify a conditional branch, otherwise it is considered an unconditional branch. The exception to this that was mentioned is the subroutine branch (BSR), which is always unconditional, yet always requires a BRCOND Op in the OpQuad to supply the return address (remember that OpQuad sequence subroutines need not return to the OpQuad following the caller).

You can have four Ops plus a branch in a single OpQuad if the branch is unconditional, but only three Ops plus a branch in an OpQuad if the branch is conditional (or is a BSR branch). In tabular form, this discussion can be summarized as follows:

MORE DETAILED ANALYSIS OF OPQUAD SEQUENCE BRANCH TYPES

Action Field	BRCOND in OpQuad	Branch Type
00	No	BR
00	Yes	BRcc
01	No	*Illegal*
01	Yes	BSR
10	No	ERET
10	Yes	ERETcc
11	No	SRET
11	Yes	SRETcc

The CC[4:0] field specifies the particular condition to be tested for in the case of BRCOND SpecOps. CC[4:1] specifies the condition to be tested according to the following table: CC[0] specifies whether the condition or its complement is to be tested. CC[0] = 1 complements the condition.

Table 2.40 SPECOP CC(4:1) FIELD

CC(4:1)	Mnemonic	Condition to be Tested	Usage
0000	True	1	Always TRUE
0001	ECF	ECF	OpQuad Sequence Carry Flag
0010	EZF	EZF	OpQuad Sequence Zero Flag
0011	SZnZF	EZF | ~ZF	Early termination of string instructions due to debug trap or hardware interrupt
0100	MSTRZ	~EZF & ~IP & ~ (DTF | SSTF | MDD)	String instruction exit condition
0101	STRZ	~EZF & ~IP & ~ (DTF | SSTF | MDD)	String instruction exit condition
0110	MSTRC	~EZF & ~IP & ~ (DTF | SSTF | MDD)	String instruction exit condition
0111	STRZnZF	~EZF & ~IP & ~ (DTF | SSTF | MDD) & ZF	String instruction exit condition

Table 2.40 SPECOP CC(4:1) FIELD

CC(4:1)	Mnemonic	Condition to be Tested	Usage
1000	OF	OF	Overflow Flag
1001	CF	CF	Carry Flag
1010	ZF	ZF	Zero Flag
1011	CvZF	CF | ZF	Used for "below or equal", "not below or equal", "above", "not above" conditions
1100	SF	SF	Sign Flag
1101	PF	PF	Parity Flag
1110	SxOF	SF ∧ OF	Used for "less", "not less", "greater or equal", "not greater or equal" conditions
1111	SxOvZF	(SF ∧ OF) | ZF	Used for "greater", "not greater", "less or equal", "not less or equal" conditions

The DSz[1:0] field specifies the size of the data (in bytes) for the SpecOp according to the following table:

Table 2.41 SPECOP DSz(1:0) FIELD

DSz(1:0)	Data Size Before Environment Substitution	Data Size After Environment Substitution
00	1 Byte	1 Byte
01	2 Bytes	2 Bytes
10	4 Bytes	4 Bytes
11	Dsize	—

The Dest[4:0] field specifies the general register the SpecOp will use to store its results (i.e., the destination register).

The Imm17[16:0] field is used as either (a) a 17-bit signed constant (for LDK or LDKD SpecOps), (b) a 14-bit Op address (for BRCOND or LDxHAx SpecOps), or (c) to specify a specific type of FpOp for FPOP SpecOps.[20] In the latter two cases, only bits [13:0] of this field are used. Lastly, bits [25:24] of a SpecOp are unused and should be set to "00".

---

[20] Imm7 is not used for FPOPE SpecOps as the OpQuad sequence environment specifies the specific type of FpOp.

LIMM Op Field Descriptions

LIMM Ops perform a 32-bit load immediate operation. They have the following format in a decoder OpQuad.

Table 2.42 Decoder OpQuad LIMM Op Format

37	36	35	21	20	17	16	0
1	1	ImmHi		Dest		ImmLo	

Bits [37:36] indicate a LIMM Op; there is no further Type field. ImmHi[15:0] and ImmLo[15:0] together specify a 32-bit immediate value. Dest[3:0] is a 4-bit destination register specifier. Like LdStOp base and index registers, this can only specify the low half of the full 5-bit register space.

DESIGN NOTE
Definition of a NoOp
Register t0 serves as a "bit bucket" for writes as it always returns "0" for reads. A NoOp is defined as a LIMM Op into t0.

EXECUTION PIPELINES

The LU, SU, RUX, and RUY execution units are all implemented as multi-stage pipelines. The LU execution unit is a six-stage pipeline. The SU execution unit is a seven-stage pipeline. The RUX and RUY execution units are either six- or seven-stage pipelines, depending on the type of Op being executed. Each stage in the pipelines nominally requires one processor clock cycle. An Op can be held up in one of the stages for stage-specific reasons or because an Op is held up in the next consecutive pipeline stage. For most Ops, the Op's position in the scheduler is independent of the Op's stage of execution in one of the pipelines.

An overview of the design and implementation of the RUX and RUY pipelines is given as an example of various microarchitectural characteristics of the K6 3D that come into play in the design and implementation of the execution unit pipelines. Both RUX and RUY have identical pipelines, which we will call the RUX/RUY pipeline" or the "RegOp pipeline." Figure 2.12 is used to describe the RUX/RUY pipeline for integer RegOps and single-cycle MMX Ops.

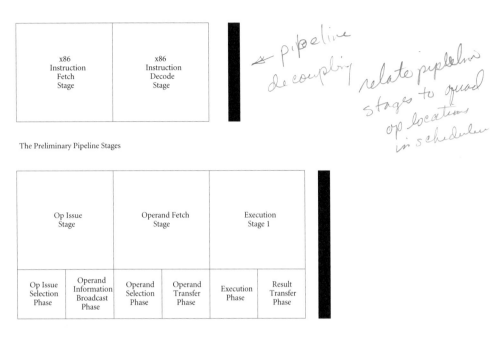

The Preliminary Pipeline Stages

The Intermediate RUX/RUY Pipeline Stages for Integer and Single-Cycle MMX Ops

The Commit Stage

Figure 2.12 INTEGER AND SINGLE-CYCLE MMX RUX/RUY PIPELINE STAGES

A pipeline consists of one or more pipeline stages. Figure 2.12 shows the RegOp pipeline having six pipeline stages: two preliminary pipeline stages, three intermediate or *execution* stages, and a *results* commit stage. Moreover, there is the normal buffering that one would find in between the stages of a pipeline implementation. Results from one stage are captured in pipeline registers or latches for use in the next stage. A typical connection between showing the pipeline register explicitly could have been represented by the following diagram.

RegOp pipeline
preliminary pipeline stages
intermediate stages
commit stage
pipeline registers
pipeline latches

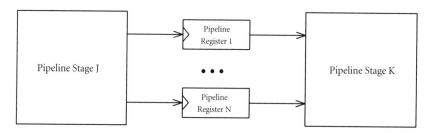

Figure 2.13 GENERIC PIPELINE STAGES

Explicit representation of these registers, as well as other inputs and outputs to various pipeline stages, would have made Figure 2.12 (and the other pipeline figures in this section) overly complex for the current discussion and therefore we did not show them. Each boundary between adjacent stages represents as many pipeline registers as are needed to hold and transfer information to the next stage. Some of these registers are explicitly shown in more detailed figures for the LU and SU pipelines that appear later in this section. The global control logic, shown in Figure 2.9 on page 130, is directly involved with controlling the loading of the pipeline registers.

We emphasize the buffering between the two preliminary pipeline stages and the three intermediate stages and the buffering between three intermediate stages and the commit stage by the dark vertical bars in the Figure 2.12. We do this to draw your attention to the fact that the buffering in between the preliminary pipeline stages and the intermediate pipeline stages is part of the support for the *decoupled decode/execution structure* of the microarchitecture. Similarly, the buffering in between the preliminary pipeline stages and the commit stage is part of the support for the *decoupled execution/commitment structure* of the microarchitecture. Both of these types of decoupling were discussed earlier in this chapter, see "Decoupled Decode and Execution Decoupled Execution and Commitment" on page 77.

instruction fetch stage
x86 instruction decode stage
commit stage

The x86 Instruction Fetch Stage, the x86 Instruction Decode Stage, and the Commit Stage are common to all execution unit pipelines. During the x86 Instruction Fetch Stage, up to 16 bytes of x86 instructions and associated predecode bits are fetched from the L1 I-Cache into the instruction buffer. During the x86 Instruction Decode Stage the decoders decode up to two x86 instructions out of the instruction buffer and form an OpQuad that is loaded into the top row of the scheduler's buffer.

Historical Comment and Suggested Readings

Design and Implementation of High-Performance Pipelines

There is a rich history of the design and implementation of very high-performance pipelines. Indeed, the use of deep pipelines (often termed superpipelines) is high on the list of design alternatives of both architects and microarchitects. The basic elements in pipeline design are the chunks of logic to do the computation within each stage, the mechanism to capture the outputs of one stage for use in the next stage, and the approach used to control the pipeline. Clock signals are typically used to synchronize the inputs to the stages and inhibit signals are used to halt the flow within a pipeline.

The partitioning of the functions to be performed within the pipeline into specific stages, the subsequent control of the stages, and the pipeline's interface to the memory and caching hierarchy are the most important parts of pipeline design at the microarchitectural level. For excellent treatments of these and related issues see Harold Stone's book, *High Performance Computer Architecture*, 3rd Edition, Addison Wesley, 1993, pp. 143-148 and pp. 169-192. Harvey Cragon's book, *Memory Systems and Pipeline Processors*, Jones and Bartlett Publishers, *1996*, pp. 294-309 and Michael Flynn's *Computer Architecture*, Chapters 4 and 7, Jones and Bartlett Publishers, *1995*. Issues such as how to deal with pipeline hazards (stalls), exceptions, and traps and how to support operand forwarding must factor into the design of the pipeline. The overall objective is to achieve as simple a design as possible while meeting the cost/performance goals.

The analysis to determine the number of pipeline stages to employ runs along the following line. The performance of the pipeline basically rests on the designer's ability to break up the functions to be performed into stages of equal duration. The greater the number of stages in the pipeline means less work per stage. Less work per stage means fewer levels of logic per stage. Fewer levels of logic means a faster clock. A faster clock means faster program execution. For deep pipelines (i.e., those with many stages) this analysis must be tempered by the facts that: (a) a long delay to both flush and fill the pipeline occurs, impacting the overall performance and (b) the memory and cache hierarchy interface must match the higher performance of the pipeline. For short pipelines (i.e., those with few stages) the analysis must be tempered by the facts that: (a) the stages are more complex and require more levels of logic to implement, particularly during mispredicted branches and (b) the clock will be slower. Importantly, regardless of whether a short, intermediate, or deep approach is taken, the memory and cache interface needs to support the total number of operand and results accesses required by the pipeline performance in a non conflicting way and at the required rate and data bandwidth. It should not come as too much of a surprise that increasing the number of stages does not always increase the overall performance of the processor. What this means is that the pipelines and the memory and cache hierarchies must be designed together. However, this is not the end of the story. The actual performance of the implementation of a pipeline can depend heavily on variations in logic circuit delays and in clock skew. Thus, attention to the physical circuit interconnections, the electrical characteristics of the circuits, the effect of loading on the components, and the techniques employed to distribute the clock signal must often be taken into consideration,. The implementation solutions employed may very well impact the design of the pipeline at the microarchitectural level, (e.g., such implementation considerations might dictate whether or not pipeline latches are actually used at specific stage boundaries or for all of the outputs at a given boundary). This is another example of where the microarchitects and the logic designers must work closely together.

Additional readings: Peter M. Kogge, *The Architecture of Pipelined Computers*, McGraw-Hill Book Company, 1981 and Harvey Cragon, cited above, both give brief but interesting histories of the use of pipelines in processors. The LARC, co-designed by IBM and Univac and delivered to Lawrence Livermore Laboratory in 1959, had a four-stage pipeline. Descriptions of a number of pipelined machines can be found in C. Gordon Bell and Allen Newell, *Computer Structures: Readings and Examples*, McGraw-Hill Book Company, 1971, and Daniel P. Siewiorek, C. Gordon Bell, and Allen Newell, *Computer Structures: Principles and Examples*, McGraw-Hill, 1982.

The scheduler then controls the Op Issue Stage and the Operand Fetch Stage for all LdOps, StOps, RegOps other than branch operations (BrOps) and floating-point operations (FpOPs). During the Op Issue Stage, which consists of an Op Issue Selection Phase and an Operand Information Broadcast Phase, the scheduler scans the entries in its buffer (instruction window) and issues up to six Ops to appropriate execution units if an unissued Op for the type of execution unit is available.

Operands for the Ops issued during the Op Issue Stage are forwarded to the execution units in Operand Fetch Stage which consists of an Operand Selection Phase and an Operand Transfer Phase. For many types of RegOp, the operation completes in the one clock cycle identified as Execution Stage 1, which, as seen in Figure 2.12 on page 159, consists of:

1. an Execution Phase in which the integer, MMX, or 3D execution sub-units within the register execution processes the source operands of the RegOp (according to the type of RegOp being executed).

2. a Result Transfer Phase in which result values and status flag values from one of the register execution sub-units are stored back in the scheduler entry corresponding to the RegOp being executed.

Register and status flags result values, stored in the Op's scheduler entry, are subsequently committed to the architectural register file and the architectural status flag register if and when it is safe to do so. Internal microarchitectural state is also changed as appropriate. After an Op completes and there are no preceding exceptions or mispredicted branches the following actions occur during the Commit Stage:

1. the Op's results can be committed.

2. the Op can be retired by moving the OpQuad containing the Op out of the scheduler's buffer, once all of the Ops within the OpQuad are ready to be retired.

The register and status flag result values from an Op can be used by the scheduler as operands for execution of dependent Ops between the execution completion and results commitment times of that Op.

This brief introduction to the K6 3D pipelines and their operation will be continued later in this and the next chapter. A diagram for 2-Cycle MMX and 3D RegOps is given in Figure 2.14.

Diagrams for the LU pipeline (also called the LdOp pipeline), the SU pipeline (also called the StOp pipeline), and the BRU pipeline (also called the BRU pipeline (also called the BrOp pipeline) are shown as Figure 2.15 through Figure 2.21 on page 175 respectively.

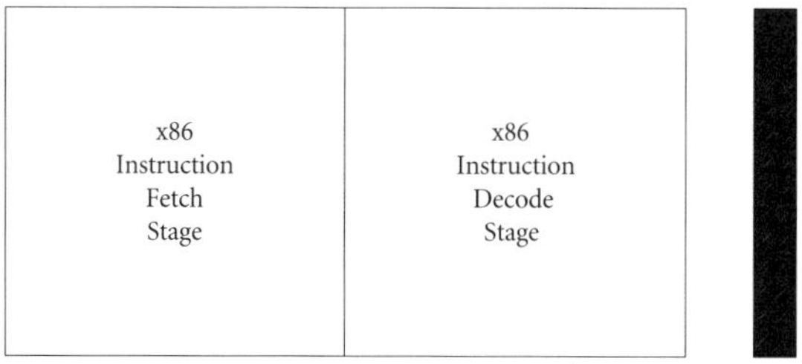

The Preliminary Pipeline Stages

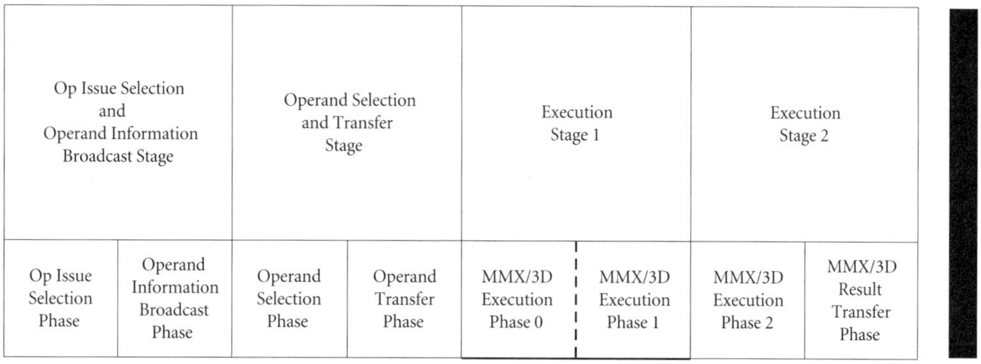

The Intermediate RegOp Pipeline Stages for 2-Cycle MMX and 3D Ops

The Commit Stage

Figure 2.14 2-Cycle MMX and 3D RUX/RUY Pipeline Stages

They are included here, with some brief remarks, to let you see some of the differences in the various pipelines. Both the LU pipeline and SU pipeline are shown in more detail immediately after their high-level pipeline diagram. Further explanations of these figures are in Chapter 3.

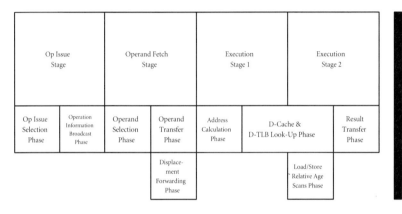

The Preliminary Pipeline Stages

The Intermediate LU Pipeline Stages

The Commit Stage

Figure 2.15 LU Pipeline Stages

Both Figure 2.16 on page 165 and Figure 2.19 on page 168 contain a shaded box which is labeled "Sources of Segment Base, Base, Index, and Displacement." The logic contained in this box is the same for both of these figures and is shown separately in Figure 2.17. The logic identified as "SLC" in Figure 2.16 refers to the Segment Limit Violation Check logic which is discussed later in this section.

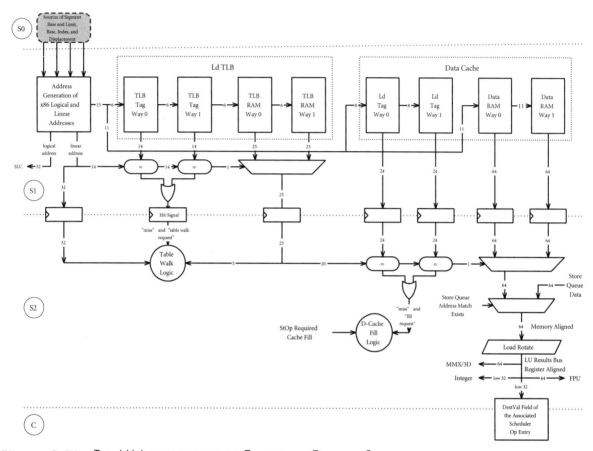

Figure 2.16 THE LU INTERMEDIATE OR EXECUTION PIPELINE STAGES

We have introduced some textual abbreviations in Figure 2.16, Figure 2.19 on page 168, and Figure 2.20 on page 169 to reduce the visual clutter in these three already crowded figures. Using Si to stand for stage and Ci to stand for commit, we introduce the notation Si and Ci at the left-hand side of these figures.

S = stage
C = commit

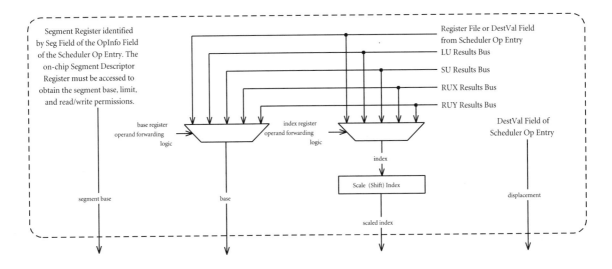

Figure 2.17 SOURCES OF SEGMENT BASE AND LIMIT, SCALED INDEX, AND DISPLACEMENT VALUES

The notations correspond in the following fairly obvious way:

Table 2.43 PIPELINE NOTATIONAL CORRESPONDENCE

Figure 2.16 and Figure 2.19	Figure 2.12, Figure 2.14 and Figure 2.18
S0	Operand Fetch Stage
S1	Execution Stage 1
S2	Execution Stage 2
C	Commit Stage

The use of C1, C2, and C3 in Figure 2.20 on page 169 reflects the fact that the overall Commit Stage for StOps is composed of several "stages." We will find this useful when discussing the operation of the store queue commit L1 D-Cache Access logic. The registers shown in Figure 2.16, Figure 2.19, and Figure 2.20 in between the pipeline stages (i.e., S0, S1, S2, C, C1, and C2) are the pipeline registers discussed earlier in this section.

> ## DESIGN NOTE
>
> ### Dual Ported TLB
>
> The D-TLB shown in Figure 2.2 on page 69 and Figure 2.22 on page 180 is actually designed to be "dual ported," i.e., to translate both a load address and a store address per cycle. Thus it is shown in Figure 2.16 on page 165 and Figure 2.19 on page 168 as logically consisting of two TLBs, the Ld-TLB and the St-TLB, that are copies of each other.

The three SU pipeline figures corresponding to the three LU pipeline figures follow:

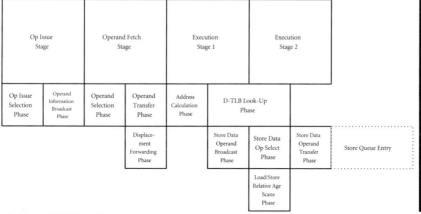

Figure 2.18 SU PIPELINE STAGES

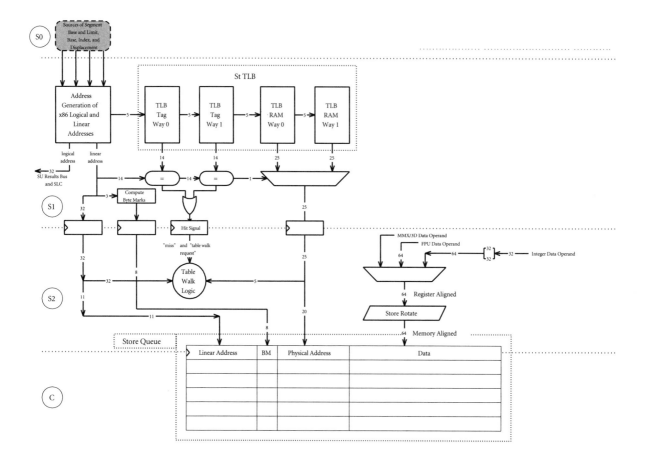

Figure 2.19 THE INTERMEDIATE OR EXECUTION SU PIPELINE STAGES AND STORE QUEUE ACCESS

FAULTS, TRAPS, ABORT CYCLES, AND THE PIPELINES

When the execution units were introduced, we discussed how the K6 deals with exceptions, traps, and abort cycles. The mechanisms employed are extremely important in the design of the pipeline. In fact, there are those who believe that these issues are among the difficult ones to resolve and are central to "what makes pipelining hard to implement," see Patterson and Hennessy, *Computer Architecture: A Quantitative Approach*, 2nd Edition, Morgan Kaufmann Publishers, Inc. 1996, pp. 178-187. You may want to review the section titled "Status Flags, Faults, Traps, Interrupts, and Abort Cycles" beginning on page 83 before proceeding. We will expand on our explanations there by taking a look in more detail at how the K6 deals with these issues by looking at how it handles a misaligned access while executing a LdOp or a StOp.

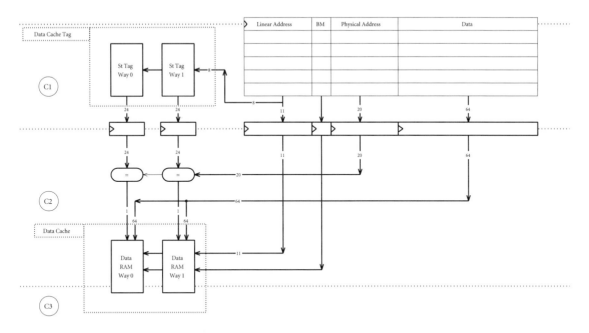

Figure 2.20 STORE COMMIT PIPELINE STAGES

In the x86 instruction set architecture, a misaligned access occurs either when an 8-byte (a quadword) access is made to an address that is not on an 8-byte boundary, or when a 2-byte (a word) or a 4-byte (a double word) access is made to an address that is not on a 4-byte boundary. We'll first look at how traps are handled and then examine the misaligned access. The x86 instruction set architecture has an alignment check bit which, if set, enables the generation of a misaligned access fault when a misaligned access occurs. This feature is generally disabled as it has limited, if any, use under contemporary operating systems.

FAULT AND TRAP HANDLING

When a fault (such as a segment violation or page fault exception) occurs during the execution of a LdOp or a StOp, the OCU is immediately notified and an abort cycle typically is eventually initiated for the associated Op. Later, we will discuss faults that do not cause an abort cycle. The abort cycle results in a fault handler getting invoked which determines what caused the fault and then initiates an appropriate response. Traps, in contrast to the treatment of faults, are handled differently.

When a trap occurs, trap information is loaded into the scheduler in the entry associated with the Op that caused the trap. Later, when the OCU analyzes if it can commit that Op, it recognizes that the Op caused a trap and it sets a pending trap flip-flop. In effect, traps are accumulated as pending traps until the end of an instruction is reached. Recall that instructions decoded by either of the short decoders or the long decoder produce at most one OpQuad and instructions that are decoded by the vector decoder produce OpQuad sequences that end with an "ERET" Action Field value within the sequencing field of its last OpQuad.

The OCU can recognize that it is retiring the last of all of the Ops that are associated with a given instruction. If there are any pending traps at the end of the commitment of an instruction, the OCU will initiate an exception (i.e., a fault) at the beginning of the next instruction—i.e., an abort cycle will occur at the beginning of the next instruction whenever the pending trap flip-flop is set. This discussion points out that the abort cycle is central to the handling of both faults and traps. So, let's take a closer look at it.

LDOP ABORT CYCLES

Typically a LdOp, like all Ops, finishes execution successfully. But there are a number of faults that can arise that cause the LdOp to be "held up" in the last execution stage of the LU pipeline. Whenever one of these situations occurs, the LU sends a signal to the OCU indicating that there is a LdOp held up in Stage2 of its pipeline because the Op has a violation associated with it.

Eventually, when the OCU examines the Ops in the bottom OpQuad of the scheduler, it attempts to commit the LdOp for which the LU has sent the violation signal. The OCU then recognizes that the LdOp is not going to complete. It will retire any older Ops in the OpQuad and initiate an abort cycle which will flush both the upper and lower portions of the machine and vector the processor to a fault handler address in the OpQuad ROM. Simultaneously, a snapshot of information in the LU is written into the OCU's Fault ID Register. This information is readable from SR1[2:0] by the OCU, i.e., bits [2:0] of Special Register 1 (see Table 2.6 on page 98). The fault handler OpQuad Sequence examines the fault information in the SR1 through the use of a special RegOp that allows the Special Registers to be read by an OpQuad sequence to determine what caused the fault.[21] Based on this, the fault handler branches to an appropriate OpQuad sequence that will process the specific type of fault encountered.

Fault ID register

---

[21] For some interrupts and "exceptions," an x86 error code is constructed and ultimately placed on the architectural interrupt stack (see, for example, Chapter 5 in Intel's publication, *The Intel Architecture Software Developer's Manual, Volume 3: System Programming Guide*).

DESIGN NOTE

Default Handler Address and Alternate Handler Address

As explained in Chapter 3, concurrent with the abort cycle, the OCU vectors the machine to one of two possible OpQuad sequence entry point addresses—either the OCU default handler address or an OCU alternate handler address; see Figure 2.10 on page 139. The setting of these addresses is supported by the LDDHA Op (Load Default Handler Address) and the LDAHA Op (Load Alternate Handler Address). The default fault handler address is initialized by the Reset OpQuad Sequence and the alternate handler address is specified within some instruction and exception processing OpQuad sequences.

Now that we have explained how faults and traps are handled and what occurs during an abort cycle, we can examine how the misaligned access is handled.

LdOp Misaligned Accesses

Since the size of the access is known when the LdOp begins execution, it can be determined if an access is misaligned when the computed address is available at the end of the address calculation phase of Stage1 of the LU pipeline.

If the access is misaligned, the hardware in LU pipeline Stage1 splits the LdOp into a cloned pair of LdOps. One of the cloned LdOps handles the first half of the access (the lower byte addresses) while the other cloned LdOp handles the upper half of the access (the high byte addresses). Thus, the two cloned LdOps have different addresses and access sizes. The LdOp accessing the lower half proceeds into Stage2 while the LdOp accessing the upper half is left immediately behind it in Stage1. The two cloned LdOps now progress down the LU pipeline back-to-back and get processed individually—(e.g., each LdOp will get separately translated by the Ld-TLB, and each will get separately looked up in the D-Cache). The two LdOps are guaranteed to access data within neighboring aligned octets of memory. The assembly of the output of the back-to-back accesses into the originally required access is done in the assembly buffer register on the output of the 2:1 multiplexer, just before the rotator, shown in Figure 2.16 on page 165. When the first LdOp completes, its data is loaded into the assembly buffer. When the second LdOp completes, its data are combined with the data in the assembly buffer and the correctly combined group of bytes is input to the rotator.

DESIGN NOTE

Transparency of Cloned LdOps

The forming of the cloned LdOps and their progression through the remaining LU pipeline stages are essentially transparent to the scheduler, which only has a single Op entry for the original LdOp that caused the misaligned access. The exception to this statement is a signal generated within the LU pipeline and used in the scheduler's LdOp and StOp relative age determination process. This situation is discussed in Chapter 3.

DESIGN NOTE

LdOp Worst Case Misaligned Access

The worst case misaligned access occurs when both of the cloned LdOps each require an Ld-TLB fill and a D-Cache line fill. The processor will basically do a Ld-TLB fill followed by a D-Cache fill followed by the second Ld-TLB fill followed by the second D-Cache fill. The two cloned LdOps are effectively executed by the majority of the LU pipeline just the same as two unrelated LdOps would be.

The approach taken in the K6 to handling misaligned access effectively results in a one clock penalty for such accesses. We will now examine how a misaligned access is handled when executing a StOp since there are some important similarities and differences from the above discussion for LdOps.

STOP ABORT CYCLES

Both the logical and linear address are calculated in the address calculation phase of Stage1 of the SU pipeline, using a) the base, scaled index, and displacement, b) the segment base, and c) taking into account the requirement of producing either a 16-bit style or a 32-bit style address. The lower twenty bits of the linear address is sent to the St-TLB, while the 32-bit logical address is sent to the Segment Limit and Access Check logic, along with the segment limit and access right bits. A page-related access check is also done, assuming a St-TLB hit. If there is a miss in the St-TLB then a table walk request to the table walk logic in the system interface unit initiates a table walk to retrieve the appropriate page translation and load it into the St-TLB and Ld-TLB (see Figure 2.22 on page 180).

If there is a fault in the processing of a StOp in the SU pipeline, the StOp will "stick" in Stage2 of this pipeline, just as was the case in the processing of a LdOp in the LU pipeline. The SU will then signal that along with the information about the fault to the OCU. Again, just as with the signal from the LU, when the OCU examines Ops in the bottom OpQuad of the scheduler and eventually attempts to commit the StOp for which the SU has sent the violation signal, the OCU recognizes that the StOp is not going to complete. It will retire any older Ops in the OpQuad and initiate an abort cycle which will flush both the upper and lower portions of the machine and vector the processor to a fault handler address in the OpQuad ROM. Just as was the case with a LdOp abort cycle, a snapshot of information in the SU is written into the OCU's Fault ID Register. As before, this information is readable from the OCU as SR1[2:0]. The fault handler OpQuad sequence examines the fault information and branches to the appropriate OpQuad sequence to handle this particular type of fault.

StOp Misaligned Accesses

The issues with misaligned StOp accesses are quite similar to those for misaligned LdOp accesses. Since the size of the access is known when the StOp begins execution, it can be determined if an access is misaligned when the computed address is available at the end of the address calculation phase of Stage1 of the SU pipeline.

If the access is misaligned, the reference is split by the SU into two memory writes and two associated store queue entries. The hardware in SU pipeline Stage1 splits the StOp into a cloned pair of StOps. One of the cloned StOps handles the first half of the access (the lower byte addresses) while the other cloned StOp handles the upper half of the access (the high byte addresses), and access sizes. Thus, the two cloned StOps have different addresses. The StOp accessing the lower half proceeds into Stage2 while the StOp accessing the upper half is left immediately behind it in Stage1. The two cloned StOps now progress down the SU pipeline back-to-back and get processed individually—(e.g., each StOp will get separately translated by St-TLB, and each will get separately looked up in the D-Cache). The two StOps are guaranteed to access data within neighboring aligned octets of memory. Unlike misaligned LdOps, each of these StOps creates a separate store queue entry which ultimately results in two separate writes into the D-Cache and/or out onto the system bus to main memory.

DESIGN NOTE

Transparency of Cloned StOps

The forming of the cloned StOps and their progression through the remaining SU pipeline stages is transparent to the scheduler, which only has a single Op entry for the original StOp that caused the misaligned access. Further, the OCU, when committing the original StOp from its scheduler Op entry, recognizes that it has two associated store queue entries and commits both entries before viewing the original StOp as having been committed. The OCU is able to do this since the first store queue entry of a related pair of entries is so marked within the store queue entry itself. If the StOp has a fault then it must be aborted without retirement of either store queue entry. This issue is discussed in some detail in Chapter 3.

DESIGN NOTE

StOp Worst Case Misaligned Access

The worst case misaligned access occurs when both of the cloned StOps require both a St-TLB fill and a D-Cache line fill. The processor will basically do a St-TLB fill followed by a D-Cache fill followed by the second St-TLB fill followed by the second D-Cache fill. The two cloned StOps are effectively executed by the majority of the SU pipeline just the same as two unrelated StOps would be.

BRU PIPELINE

Before leaving this section, we present the pipeline diagram for a BrOp. This pipeline is described in some detail in Chapter 3 and is presented in this section with the RUX/RUY, LU, and SU pipelines for completeness.

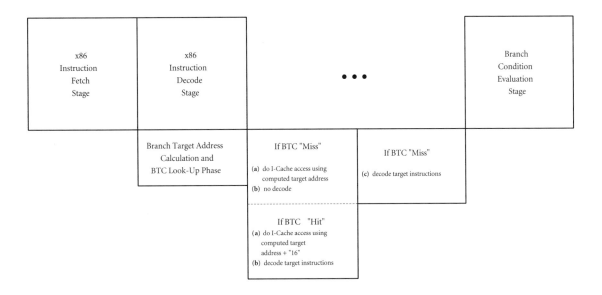

Figure 2.21 THE BRU PIPELINE STAGES

We discussed the handling of faults and traps in two earlier segments of this chapter—the section titled "Status Flags, Faults, Traps, Interrupts, and Abort Cycles" beginning on page 83 and the section titled "Faults, Traps, Abort Cycles, and the Pipelines" beginning on page 168. You may want to review these sections before proceeding. As we pointed out in these sections, handling faults and traps in speculative, superscalar, pipelined processors can be difficult. There are several problems to contend with: (1) faults and traps can occur at various stages within a pipeline, (2) the results of operations that were issued and executed speculatively may no longer be valid after the fault or trap occurs, and (3) appropriate machine state must be saved in the event of faults or traps that abort a series of operations. There must be a relatively efficient mechanism to restore the state and restart execution at that point. The execution pipelines, various queues, and other processor resources may have to be flushed. Depending on the microarchitecture, this can be done either sequentially or in an overlapped fashion. The microarchitect basically attempts to minimize the latency incurred in restating execution while reducing the overall microarchitectural complexity in achieving this goal. Some simple examples of faults are a segment limit violation and a page fault. A simple example of a trap is the data breakpoint trap.

The K6 uses a uniform mechanism to handle faults, traps, and interrupts. In the K6, there are some faults that are detected at decode time by the hardware decoders, some that are detected in the scheduler by the OCU, and some that are detected during the execution of an OpQuad sequence by "manual" checks (and corresponding conditional branches) within the OpQuad sequence.

As just indicated, some faults are detected at decode time and some are detected at Op commit time. An "instruction length greater than sixteen bytes" fault is an example of a fault detected at decode time while a "memory-related" fault is a common example of a fault recognized at Op commit time (although initially detected at Op execution time). During each decode cycle, the decoders check for several x86 instruction set architecture-specific exception conditions, including a code segment overrun, an instruction fetch page fault, an instruction length greater than sixteen bytes, a nonlockable instruction with a "lock" prefix, and a floating-point not available condition. At the same time, the decoders also check for the assertion of any pending hardware interrupts, including INTR, NMI, SMI, STPCLK, INIT, and FLUSH. Some conditions are evaluated only during a successful decode cycle; other conditions, including all hardware interrupts, are decoded irrespective of any other possible decoding actions during the cycle.

When an active fault condition is detected, all short, long, and vector instruction decode cycles are inhibited and an exception vector decode cycle occurs in the following decode cycle. During this exception vector decode cycle, a special fault OpQuad sequence vector address is generated in place of a normal instruction vector address. The fault vector address is a fixed value except for low-order bits that are used to identify the particular fault condition that has been recognized and needs to be handled. Other than a different vector address, this behaves just like any instruction vector decode. There is no special synchronization within the scheduler with respect to the OpQuads already in the scheduler. The handling of this decoder-detected exception is naturally processed in the normal and proper program order. When multiple fault conditions are simultaneously detected, the faults are prioritized and the highest priority fault is recognized. In-order decode ensures precise fault handling for decoder-detected faults.

Faults that are detected during the execution of an OpQuad sequence do not insert an OpQuad into the top of the scheduler. A branch abort occurs due to a mispredicted BRCOND Op based on status flag values that were set by a preceding RegOp which performed some type of "check." The abort cycle results in a redirection to an alternate OpQuad sequence.

RE-EXAMINING THE ABORT CYCLE

When discussing the abort cycle in the earlier sections of this chapter cited above, we introduced the notion of flushing and restarting the upper and lower portions of the processor; the former is part of the BRCOND

Op resolution cycle and the latter is part of the abort cycle in the case of branch aborts.

When a "flush" occurs, all Ops in the bottom portion of the machine are basically discarded, all abortable state is discarded, and the "valid bits" of all Ops in the scheduler are set to invalid. In the case of a mispredicted branch, the upper portion of the machine is flushed and then restarted to begin fetching from the mispredicted path. This is done as part of the resolution of the branch versus as part of the abort cycle. The restarting of the upper portion of the processor consists of reloading the PCs (program counters) in the decoders and sending the mispredicted fetch address to the I-Cache.

"Exception" aborts, discussed above, are different in that there is no "resolution" stage, only an abort cycle. During the abort cycle, the bottom portion of the machine is also flushed similar to the case of a mispredicted branch and the upper portion is flushed and restarted. In this case the scheduler vectors to the start of a "fault handler" OpQuad sequence in the OpQuad ROM.

PRECISE INTERRUPTS AND PRECISE EXCEPTIONS

As discussed earlier, interrupts are asynchronous events that occur independently of the synchronous activity within the microprocessor. The x86 instruction set architecture employs a precise interrupt model. This model holds that an interrupted process can resume correct execution after the interrupt has been serviced. When the microprocessor detects an interrupt, it:

1. halts the execution of the current instruction stream (i.e., the current process).
2. saves enough of the state of the machine so processing can resume at the point the interrupt was detected.
3. activates an interrupt handling routine to service the interrupt.
4. resumes processing after the interrupt has been serviced and after the saved state has been restored.

A precise exception model is implemented for program-related exceptions; see the section titled "Status Flags, Faults, Traps, Interrupts, and Abort Cycles" beginning on page 83. The issues that apply to precise interrupts can be equally challenging to resolve as those dealing with precise program exceptions. The following discussion is couched in the context of precise interrupts and can be extended to precise exceptions.

Let us use $state_{resume}$ to be the machine state that is required to resume processing if an interrupt occurs. And, let us use $state_{no\ interrupt}$ to be the state that is required to continue processing if no interrupt occurred. What must be done to support precise interrupts is to guarantee that $state_{resume} = state_{no\ interrupt}$ which essentially means that the saved machine state that exists after the interrupt has been serviced is that same saved state that would have existed if the interrupt had not occurred at all. This is reasonably straightforward to do in conventional, nonpipelined, in-order processors. It's a bit more difficult in pipelined processors, particularly those that support out-of-order execution.

Suggested Readings

Precise Interrupts

 We have included three articles on the CD-ROM that deal either wholly or in part with the issue of providing for precise interrupts in pipelined processors. The article by Smith and Pleszkum, is considered by many as a classic paper in this area. The second article, by Walker and Cragon, develops a taxonomy of design strategies for providing precise interrupts based on a detailed examination of fifteen processors that support concurrent instruction execution. The third article, by Moudgill and Vassiliadis, gives an interesting treatment of the topic of precise interrupts.

1.   James E. Smith and Andrew R. Pleszkum, "Implementation of Precise Interrupts on Pipelined Processors," in *Proceedings of the 12th Annual International Symposium on Computer Architecture,* June 1985, pp. 34-44.

2.   Wade Walker and Harvey G. Cragon, "Interrupt Processing in Concurrent Processors," *Computer,* Vol. 28, No. 6, June 1995, pp. 36-46.

3.   Mayan Moudgill and Stamatis Vassiliadis, "Precise Interrupts," *IEEE Micro,* Vol. 16, No. 1, February 1996, pp.58-67.

We also suggest a paper by Hwu and Patt that presents an interesting hardware checkpointing scheme to support precise interrupts, W. M. Hwu and Y N. Patt, "Checkpoint Repair for Out-of-Order Execution Machines," *Proceedings of the 14th Annual International Symposium on Computer Architecture,* 1987. Similar checkpointing schemes have been widely used in software systems.

Smith and Pleszkum identify three conditions that must hold to support precise interrupts:

1.   all instructions that issued prior to the instruction that was executing when the interrupt was detected have completed and have modified the process state correctly.

2.   all instructions after the one indicated by the saved program counter execute only after control is returned to the interrupted process.

3.   if the interrupt were caused by an instruction (versus some activity external to the processor), then the saved program counter must point to that instruction.

The K6 supports the x86 instruction set architecture precise interrupt model. An interrupt, when detected, is directed to the decoders. As described in the preceding pages, hardware interrupts are just cases of exception vector decodes. Once the appropriate interrupt handling OpQuad sequence is initiated, the K6 goes through the details of storing the appropriate program state as defined by the x86 instruction set architecture. This state is restored through execution of an IRET instruction at the end of the x86 interrupt handler before returning control to the interrupted instruction stream.

SYSTEM INTERFACE

All transactions involving the system bus are mediated by the system interface unit shown in Figure 2.2 on page 69. However, transactions may involve the L2-Cache only, the system bus only, or both. System bus transactions can proceed concurrently with L2-only transactions. L2-only transactions may complete out of order with respect to system bus-only transactions.

Requests are presented to the system interface over six separate interfaces that are shown in Figure 2.22:

1. L1 I-Cache read interface, IC.
2. L1 D-Cache read interface, DC.
3. L1 D-Cache write back interface.
4. L2-Cache write back interface.
5. Table Walk Unit read/write interface, TW.
6. Write Pipeline/Merge Unit interface, PM.

Each interface shown in this figure consists of:

1. request and handshake signals.
2. an address bus.
3. a data bus.
4. various attribute and status signals.

Data transfers may involve 1 or 4 octets, where an octet is eight bytes or sixty-four bits. As mentioned earlier, standard Socket 7 pinouts and protocols are implemented and are discussed in more detail in Chapter 4. Also, operation of the system bus at 100-MHz is supported. The bus operates at a whole or half-integer divisor of the core frequency (e.g., 3.5X for a 350-MHz processor and a 100-MHz system bus). Because the L2-Cache is on-chip, it runs at the core speed of the microprocessor itself. The L2-Cache has separate read and write ports, allowing one read and one write per cycle.

Neither inclusion nor exclusion is enforced between the L1- and L2-Caches. L2-Cache line misses that result in an L2-Cache line fill cause simultaneous L1- and L2-fill operations. A given line is never marked modified in both the L1- and L2-Caches.

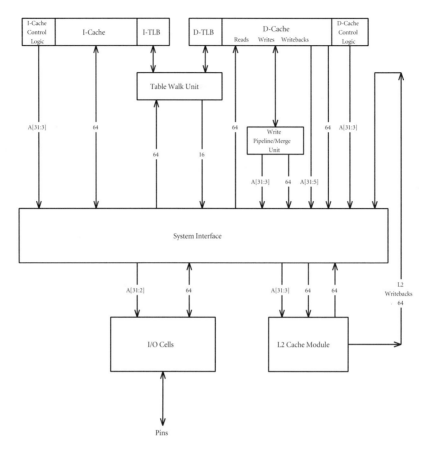

Figure 2.22 SYSTEM INTERFACE UNIT

table walk unit

The table walk unit undertakes x86-based page table walks in response to requests from either the I-Cache TLB or the D-Cache TLB. It contains an 8-entry PDE cache (page directory entry) to reduce the average table walk time from a 2-level table walk to just a single table read. Request for such a table walk are shown in the LdOp Pipeline and L1 D-Cache Access diagram shown in Figure 2.16 on page 165 and in Figure 2.19 on page 168 for the StOp pipeline and store queue access.

The write pipeline/merge unit handles all single-octet writes from the D-Cache, merging and pipelining them onto the system bus wherever possible. The system bus supports 2-deep bus transaction pipelining.

The critical importance of how the microprocessor is integrated into the other elements that make up a typical system (i.e., platform) is one of the central themes of this book and is dealt with in a number of the following chapters.

A general overview of the K6 3D microarchitecture has been given. In particular, we examined a number of the design choices that were made which were part of the decisions that ultimately led to the K6 3D's microarchitecture. Some of these choices were centered around

1. the predecode scheme which is done (a) at cache fill time, outside of the fetch/decode/execute pipeline and (b) without knowledge of the actual instruction boundaries.

2. the number and types of decoders used.

3. the unification of most major control requirements (e.g., reservation stations, reorder buffer, and register renaming) into one structure— the scheduler and its centralized buffer.

4. the focus on short pipelines and short latencies, (e.g., short branch prediction, fetch redirection, execution latencies, short branch misprediction penalty, and short misaligned memory access penalty).

5. the use of an internal RISC-like microarchitecture in conjunction with the translation of x86 instructions into corresponding short or long sequences of RSIC-like Ops (OpQuads and OpQuad sequences).

In fact, as pointed out in Chapter 1, this case study provides a detailed and coherent context for studying the wealth of design problems encountered in processor design that are covered in conventional textbooks in computer architecture. Hopefully, the rich set of design issues that result from the above set of topics and other design choices discussed in this chapter have helped you understand the interrelationships and dependencies that exist among them.

Suggested Readings

Instruction Level Parallelism

Many of the approaches discussed in this chapter are discussed in the literature under the general phrase "instruction level parallelism (ILP)". Two articles we recommend, in addition to those already cited, are given here. The article, "The 16-Fold Way: A Microparallel Taxonomy," by Barton J. Sano and Alvin M. Despain, *Proceedings of the 26th Annual International Symposium on Microarchitecture,* 1993, presents an interesting taxonomy for processors that have multiple-instruction processing capabilities, including some of those discussed here. Additionally, the article, by Roger Espasa and Mateo Valero, "Exploiting Instruction- And Data-Level Parallelism," *IEEE Micro,* 1997, describes a design approach which combines ILP design approaches with data-level parallelism techniques (i.e., vectorization techniques). Both of these articles are on the CD-ROM.

Additionally, two presentations by Bruce Shriver related to these issues are on the CD-ROM. Their titles are, "*Instruction Level Parallelism,*" and "*The Evolution of High-Performance ISAs.*"

Now that we have given an overview of the K6 3D's microarchitecture, we will, in the next chapter, examine three of the major aspects of the it microarchitecture in considerably more depth to aid you in understanding some of the implementation issues associated with specific design approaches.

Chapter 3
The K6 3D Microarchitecture

I n this chapter, we will explore three main aspects of the microarchitecture of the K6 3D in more detail: its scheduler, its operation commit unit, and its register renaming scheme. As specific microarchitectural concepts are introduced, pseudo-RTL code is given for typical chunks of logic that could be used to implement these concepts.

ROAD MAP OF CHAPTER 3

Section	Audience
All sections in this chapter	Practitioners, University Professors and Students
Chapter Summary	All

In Chapter 2 we showed that the scheduler:

THE SCHEDULER: AN EXPANDED DESCRIPTION

1. is tightly coupled to the execution units.
2. is tightly coupled to the OCU.
3. maintains information concerning Ops in multiple execution pipelines.
4. issues Ops to the execution units for execution.
5. provides the Op information to the execution units at the times required.
6. does register and status flag dependency checking.
7. forwards results as required for the execution of dependent Ops.
8. holds the results from completed Ops until the results are committed or aborted.
9. deletes Op information as required.

In accomplishing this the scheduler can initiate, among other things:

1. four Op issues, to Load Unit, Store Unit, Register Unit X, and Register Unit Y.

2. nine register operand "fetches": two each for Load Unit, Registrant X, and Register Unit Y and three for the Store Unit, including immediate values for Register Unit X and Register Unit Y.

3. two displacement "fetches," for Load Unit and Store Unit.

4. outputs to nine register operand buses.

5. one status operand fetch, for Register Unit X.

6. BRCOND Op resolution and mispredicted branch handling.

7. LdOp and StOp ordering and relative age determination for pipeline Stage 2 LdOps and StOps.

We will now examine how all of this is done.

LOADING THE SCHEDULER

It might be useful at this point for you to review the scheduler diagram given in Figure 2.9 on page 130 and the three diagrams related to the decoder, i.e. Figure 2.6 on page 115, Figure 2.8 on page 127, and Figure 2.10 on page 139.

As OpQuads are loaded into the scheduler, they pass through the OpQuad Expansion Logic discussed in the "Decoder and Scheduler OpQuads" section in Chapter 2 and shown in Figure 2.8 on page 127. The OpQuad Expansion Logic expands the *decoder* OpQuads into *scheduler* OpQuads. *Decoder* OpQuads are 152 bits wide and *scheduler* OpQuads are 578 bits wide. Different types of processing occur during the expansion of *decoder* OpQuads:

1. a few Op fields are simply passed through unchanged.

2. some Op fields are modified based on the values contained in other fields.

3. some Op fields are replaced by physically different fields.

4. new fields are derived from existing ones.

As explained in the section titled "Execution Pipelines" beginning on page 158 and as shown in Figure 2.8 (cited above), Figure 2.6 on page 115 and Figure 2.10 on page 139, OpQuad Templates, fetched from the OpQuad ROM, are translated into *decoder* OpQuads in the environment substitution logic preceding the OpQuad Expansion Logic.

Whatever its source, the *scheduler* OpQuad formed by the OpQuad Expansion Logic is loaded into the scheduler whenever Row 0 (the top row) of the scheduler's buffer is empty or contains an OpQuad that is shifting to Row 1. If no scheduler OpQuad is available when the OpQuad in the top row shifts down, an *invalid* OpQuad is loaded into Row 0.

In Figure 2.9 on page 130, the scheduler's centralized buffer[22] is repre-   *scheduler entry*
sented as consisting of six rows, each row having four entries—one entry
for each Op in the scheduler OpQuad stored in that row. Each of these
entries includes:

1. a number of static and dynamic fields, i.e., values stored in storage
   elements.

2. various portions of logic dedicated to specific scheduler functions—e.g., the *issue selection* logic, the *operand selection* logic, the
   load/store ordering logic, and the *self-modifying code support* logic.

The entries in Rows 3, 4, and 5 in Figure 2.9 also contain status flag-   *static and dynamic fields*
dependent RegOp synchronization logic, branch resolution logic, and sta-
tus flag fetch logic. All twenty-four Op entries are otherwise essentially
identical.

Most of each entry's storage elements contain values of static fields.
These fields are initialized when the Op is loaded into the scheduler and
maintain their value until the Op is retired. Their contents can never
change from their initial values. Other storage elements for an entry contain values of dynamic fields which can be reloaded with new values before
the Op is retired.

Finally, other storage elements store values for fields, referred to as   *OpQuad fields*
OpQuad fields that are associated with a scheduler OpQuad taken as a
whole. Most OpQuad fields are static; however, some OpQuad fields are
dynamic.

DEFINITION

Static Fields and Dynamic Fields

Some fields in an Op entry in the scheduler's buffer retain the same value
throughout execution of the Op and are called static fields. Other fields
can be changed as the Op proceeds through the scheduler and are called
dynamic fields.

When taken on an OpQuad basis, the scheduler's storage elements
can be thought of as forming a shift register that is six rows deep. Each
clock cycle, an OpQuad that is not held up in a row shifts down to the next
row if the next row is empty or contains an OpQuad that is also shifting
downward. The OpQuad in the bottom row shifts out of the scheduler if
all operations associated with the bottom row have been committed or
aborted.

---

[22] Instruction windows, reservation stations, and centralized buffers were introduced in the section titled "Superscalar Design" beginning on page 74.

Historical Comment and Suggested Readings

Early Environment Substitution Techniques

Designers of some early microprogrammable machines recognized that a number of microcode sequences used to emulate instruction set architectures were quite similar, differing, for example, only in the specific registers manipulated. To take advantage of this situation, the specific registers used in the microcode sequence were specified in auxiliary registers whose values were "merged" with the microcode sequence as it was being executed. Such implementations seem to be precursors to both OpQuad Template environment substitution and to the use of dynamic fields. See, for example, "Scheme-79—Lisp on a Chip," by Gerald Jay Sussman, Jack Holloway, Guy Lewis Steel, Jr., and Alan Bell, in *Computer*, July 1981, pp. 10-21.

The entries in the scheduler's buffer store information regarding the Ops that are awaiting execution, being executed, or have completed execution. How and when the information in the storage elements is modified is central to the operation of the scheduler. For example, the value of the State Field of an entry changes as an Op proceeds through the scheduler to indicate if the Op has been issued, is in a specific stage of execution, or has been completed.

Notation

OpQuad (without a modifier)

From now on the term "OpQuad" will be used without the modifier "*decoder*" or "*scheduler,*" unless either is needed for clarity. It should be clear from the context if it refers to a *decoder OpQuad* or a *scheduler OpQuad*. In the current section, we are discussing scheduler OpQuads.

The scheduler issues Ops, provides Op information to the execution units at a specific time when required, holds the results from completed Ops until the results are committed or aborted, and forwards the results for the execution of other Ops as required. Each scheduler entry holds the register and status flags results from its associated Op. Each dynamic field storage element must be able to be loaded both from the appropriate preceding storage element and from a relevant data source. Further, the loading of data into a storage element and the shifting of the present or new data into a different storage element must be able to happen simultaneously (during the same cycle) and independently (from a control perspective).

SHIFTING OPFIELDS FROM ROW TO ROW

Figure 3.1 on page 187 shows portions of the scheduler's buffer that represent parts of an entry in Row 3 and its connection to Rows 2 and 4. Figure 3.1 shows a storage element for one of that entry's static fields while Figure 3.2 on page 191 shows a storage element for one of its dynamic fields. Both storage elements are edge-triggered flip-flops. Row 3 contains identical storage elements for every bit of each dynamic and static field for all four entries in Row 3 (i.e., the four Ops in Row 3). What this figure represents then is one of the four Ops (and the same Op) in each of the three rows. The other rows in the buffer are similar or identical to Row 3 and are connected in series with Row 3.

Let's look into this example in more detail. In Figure 3.1, flip-flops A, B, and C store one bit of the same static field in Rows 2, 3, and 4. This bit value shifts from flip-flop A to flip-flop B to flip-flop C as the OpQuad shifts from Row 2 to Row 3 to Row 4. The global control logic generates signals LdEntry[i], one for each row to control whether shifts to the corresponding rows occur or not. Thus, the LdEntry[i] signals can be thought of as the OpQuad shift control signals.

LdEntry[i] signals

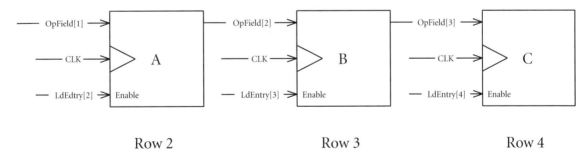

Row 2   Row 3   Row 4

Figure 3.1 EXAMPLE OF ONE BIT OF A STATIC FIELD

The rows are shifted at the rising edge of the clock signal CLK. For example, a signal LdEntry[3] either enables or disables flip-flop B, and a signal LdEntry[4] either enables or disables flip-flop C. When an OpQuad is held up in Row 4, signal LdEntry[4] is deasserted so that flip-flop C retains its value. The independence of signals LdEntry[i] allows filling of empty OpQuad entries above a held-up OpQuad. For example, even though an OpQuad is held up in Row 4, signal LdEntry[3] can be asserted so that a value OpField[2] from Row 2 shifts into Row 3 at the rising edge of clock signal CLK. Empty rows may result if the decoder is unable to provide an OpQuad every cycle—due to a branch target cache miss, for example. Empty rows are created only as a result of the decoder being unable to provide an OpQuad and by an abort cycle. Empty rows are never created by shifting lower OpQuads down while holding higher non-empty OpQuads in place since, in such cases, all the rows below the row being held will also be held from shifting.

NOTATION

OpQuadY, OpQY, and OpX

We will, from time to time, use the following notation to refer to *scheduler* OpQuads: OpQuadY, where Y = 0 to 5. For example, OpQuad1 identifies the OpQuad in Row1 of the scheduler, OpQuad2 the OpQuad in Row 2, etc. Additionally, we will use the following notation to refer to scheduler Op entries: OpX, where X = 0 to 23. For example, X = 0 identifies the youngest Op in the scheduler and X = 23 identifies the oldest Op in the scheduler. Thus OpQuad4, for example, contains Op16, Op17, Op18, and Op19. Moreover, the notation OpQuadY may be abbreviated OpQY in some contexts.

PSEUDO-RTL DESCRIPTIONS

As was mentioned in Chapter 1 and reinforced in Chapter 2, in order to assist you in understanding exactly how the microarchitecture realizes some of its functions (as well as to encourage you to simulate various chunks of logic), we give pseudo-RTL descriptions of the operation of portions of circuitry implementing specific functions. We believe the pseudo-RTL descriptions are intuitive. The first such example will be an RTL description for the operation of the circuitry implementing the shifting of data from one static field storage element to another, as shown in Figure 3.1. Such descriptions played a very important part in the overall design and simulation of the microprocessor as described in Chapter 1. First, a word about notation.

Notation

Pseudo-RTL Descriptions

A pseudo-RTL description may use signals described in other pseudo-RTL descriptions without further explanation or reference to the other descriptions since such references should be reasonably obvious from the context. Signals given in the descriptions are asserted or active high unless expressly indicated otherwise. The following notation is used in the pseudo-RTL descriptions in this text:

Signals connected via a "Þ", " ", and "&" are combined as a logical AND such as could be implemented by an AND gate. Signals connected via a "+" are combined as a logical OR such as could be implemented by an OR gate. Signals connected via a "^" are combined as a logical exclusive OR such as could be implemented by an XOR gate. "~" indicates the complement or inverse of a signal such as would be provided by an inverter.

Either if (a) x = b else x = c or if x = (a) ?b:c indicate a multiplexer with an output signal x equal to signal b if signal a is asserted and an output signal x equal to c otherwise. If "else x = c" is omitted, the signal x is unaffected if signal a is low (i.e., signal a forces signal x to a value if and only if a is asserted, otherwise signal x maintains its value as determined thus far, by preceding assignments to x. Another notation which represents a multiplexer is:

```
  x = switch (A) case A1: x1
                 case A2: x2
                 ...
                 case An: an
```

where output signal x has values x1 or x2 or ... xn depending on the value of a multi-bit select signal A.

The notation "xxOp.yyy" refers to an input signal to the Op decoder indicating a value from a field yyy defined for an Op of type xxOp. For example, "RegOp.Src1" refers to bits in an operation at the same position as the Src1 field of a RegOp.

Most signals described change each clock cycle. The notation "@clk:" indicates a signal is latched into a register at an edge-of-signal clock for use in a subsequent clock cycle.

Finally, it should be clear that the logic described by the pseudo RTL-descriptions can be implemented in a variety of ways.

Suggested Readings

Digital and Integrated Circuit Design

For readers who have little or no background in electronic circuits, we recommend reading a copy of the small but very well done introduction to the subject by Niklaus Wirth, *Digital Circuit Design for Computer Science Students, An Introductory Textbook*, Springer-Verlag, 1995. Wirth, as many of the readers know, designed a number of popular programming languages, among them Pascal and Modula. In this book he uses an easy-to-understand hardware description language called Lola.

For electronic, electrical, and computer engineers who would like an introduction to the myriad of tools and techniques used in the design, manufacture, and test of integrated circuits, we recommend Peter R. Shepherd's book, *Integrated Circuit Design, Fabrication and Test*, McGraw-Hill, 1996.

STATIC FIELD STORAGE ELEMENT SHIFTING OPERATION

The following pseudo-RTL description defines the operation of circuitry for the shifting of data from one static field storage element to another, as shown in Figure 3.1.

PSEUDO-RTL DESCRIPTION

Shifting Data from One Static Field Storage Element to Another

```
@clk: if (LdEntry[i])              // OpQuad shift control
         OpField[i] = OpField[i-1]; // conditionally shift in preceding
                                    // OpField Value
```

DYNAMIC FIELD STORAGE ELEMENT OPERATION

Dynamic fields, shown in Figure 3.2, are more complicated to handle than static fields because new data from outside the buffer may be inserted into a dynamic field while the OpQuad is being shifted or re-circulated.

Two independent events are happening here, so let's expand on them to clarify this last statement:

1. the value of a dynamic field may or may not take on a new value.

2. the OpQuad may or may not shift to the next row.

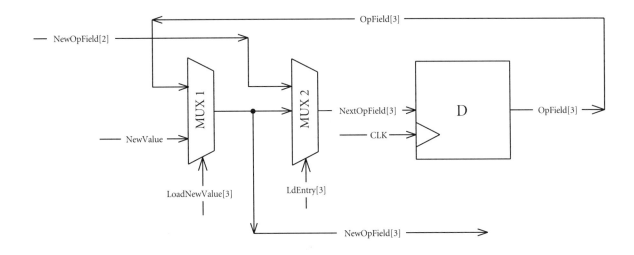

Row 3

Figure 3.2   EXAMPLE OF ONE BIT OF A DYNAMIC FIELD

In the example discussed here and shown in Figure 3.2, the dynamic field is called OpField and its value is stored in flip-flop D. A chunk of logic outside the scheduler generates the NewValue[23] and LoadNewValue[3] signals. If a NewValue has been generated, the LoadNewValue[3] signal selects it as the output of the MUX 1 multiplexer, otherwise the old value of OpField[3] is selected as the output. Obviously, selecting the old value is equivalent to saying that the dynamic field did not change. The output of the MUX 1 multiplexer is called NewOpField[3]. The NewOpField[3] output could have been called *Potentially_Changed_Dynamic_OpField[3]* to reflect more precisely what we just explained, but that would have been too unwieldy a name to be used in the figure.

The MUX 2 multiplexer selects whether or not the OpQuad shifts. If OpQuad[2] can shift from Row[2] to Row[3] and become OpQuad [3], then the LdEntry[3] signal selects the NewOpField[2] value from OpQuad[2] as the output of the MUX 2 multiplexer and the shift occurs at the rising edge of the clock signal CLK. Otherwise, the NewOpField[3] value is selected as the output and no shift occurs. The output of the MUX 2 multiplexer in Figure 3.2 is called NextOpField[3]. It could have been called *Potentially_Shifted_OpQuad*, to reflect more precisely what we just explained. The LdEntry[3] signal will be discussed shortly. First, it will

---

[23] The signal NewValue can be a signal common to all twenty-four Op entries or may be specific to each Op.

be useful to summarize the actions that occur when a valid OpQuad either shifts or does not shift:

1. *the shift occurs*: This means that OpQuad[2] shifts from Row[2] to Row[3] and OpQuad[3] shifts from Row[3] to Row[4]. By definition, all of the static and dynamic fields of OpQuad [3] take on the values of those same fields from OpQuad[2]. And, all of the static and dynamic fields of OpQuad[4] take on the values of those same fields from OpQuad[3]. Note that the value of the dynamic field OpField[3] of OpQuad[3] is sent to Row 4, via the output of the MUX 1 multiplexer.[24]

2. *the shift does not occur*: This means that OpQuad[2] stays in Row[2] only if it is valid; if it is invalid, it will be replaced with whatever is in OpQuad[1]. OpQuad[3] stays in Row[3]. This in turn means that the output of the MUX 2 multiplexer is NewOpField[3] from OpQuad[3] and not NewOpField[2] from OpQuad[2].

In summary, MUX 1 is used to conditionally choose the NextOpField value and MUX 2 is used to conditionally advance the OpQuad through the buffer. The following pseudo-RTL description defines the operation of the circuitry implementing the operations associated with dynamic fields. It should be reasonably obvious how one could have written the following description, given Figure 3.2. However, the figure represents only one implementation strategy to realize the description.

PSEUDO-RTL DESCRIPTION

Dynamic Field Operation

```
if (LoadNewValue[i])                // logic to conditionally
 NewOpField[i] = NewValue[i];       // select a value for the
else                                // dynamic field
  NewOpField[i] = OpField[i];

if (LdEntry[i])                     // logic to conditionally
  NextOpField[i] = NewOpField[i-1]; // advance the OpQuads
else
  NextOpField[i] = NewOpField[i];

@clk: OpField[i] = NextOpField[i]   // simple flip-flop
```

---

[24] The output of the MUX 1 multiplexer in Row[3] is an input to the MUX 2 multiplexer in Row[4].

Let's summarize what we have learned so far. The scheduler can be viewed as a shift register in which OpQuads are loaded into the top, gradually shift downward from row to row, and eventually unloaded from the bottom. However, the scheduler is not quite exactly controlled as a true shift register since each scheduler row has its own independent shift control signal, LdEntry[i]. We will now examine these signals in more detail.

Simulators on CD-ROM

One way to test your understanding of the above concepts is to simulate the chunk of logic described by the previous two pseudo-RTL descriptions. To encourage you to do this, we have provided three simulators on the CD-ROM. Each has an extensive reference manual with it.

THE LdENTRY SIGNALS: SHIFTING THE OPQUADS

The LdEntry[i] signals determine if the OpQuad in Row[i-1] shifts into Row[i]. In general, OpQuads always shift down whenever there is space below. That is, as long as there is at least one empty row below a given OpQuad, or the bottom row of the scheduler is being unloaded, then the OpQuad can shift down to the next row, the OpQuad above can shift down into the given OpQuad's row from above, and so on. However, situations can exist that prevent OpQuads from shifting. The situations that can hold up OpQuads basically fall into five categories:

1. OpQuads containing Ops that are dependent on status flags as part of their processing, i.e., BRCOND Ops and cc-dependent RegOps.
2. OpQuads that contain nonabortable RegOps.
3. OpQuads that are being considered for commitment by the OCU and contain one or more Ops that have not yet completed execution.
4. OpQuads containing multiple StOps in an OpQuad.[25]
5. OpQuads above the bottom row of the scheduler that cannot shift.

We will examine each of these categories separately:

1. *1st Category*: It was pointed out in the section titled "The Scheduler" beginning on page 128 that "... some Ops (such as the evaluation of conditional branches and RegOps that depend on status

---

[25] More than one StOp in an OpQuad does not guarantee a hold up since, as we will see later, the OCU can look ahead into the second OpQuad row from the bottom to get a "head start" on committing StOps.

flags) are executed when the Ops reach a particular row of the buffer." Conditional branches, for example, are held in Row[3] until they are resolved and only then are they allowed to advance. If the branch is resolved as correctly predicted, processing proceeds normally. However, if the branch is resolved as mispredicted in Row[3], an appropriate restart signal is asserted that causes the upper portion of the machine to be flushed and then restarted to begin fetching instructions from the not-predicted path. The flushing of the upper portion is done as part of the resolution of the branch versus as part of the abort cycle since the abort cycle will be initiated later when the OpQuad reaches the bottom of the scheduler. If Ops are generated before the lower portion of the machine can accept them, then these Ops are held until they can be loaded into the scheduler. The BrAbort signal is asserted when the OpQuad containing a mispredicted branch reaches the bottom row of the scheduler. CC-dependent RegOps are also held in Row[3] until the necessary status flag operand value(s) are successfully obtained, and only then are they allowed to advance or shift down into lower rows.

2. *2nd Category*: There are four nonabortable RegOps, WRDR, WRDL, WRxxx, and WRDLP. Nonabortable RegOps that cannot yet proceed into the Execution Stage of the RegOp pipeline are held when they reach Row[4] until they can execute.

3. *3rd Category*: Because of the out-of-order execution nature of the processor, or due simply to execution latencies and serial dependencies between Ops, an Op might reach the bottom row of the scheduler before the other Ops associated with the OpQuad have completed execution. It must wait there while the other Ops are still executing.

4. *4th Category*: Consider a situation in which there are four StOps, two in each of two consecutive OpQuads. The first StOp will commit from OpQuad4, the second from OpQuad5 (the first OpQuad retires without delay), the third and fourth from OpQuad5 and thus shifting of the second OpQuad out of the scheduler is delayed for one cycle.

5. *5th Category:* There can be instances when OpQuads cannot shift because all rows below contain valid OpQuads and they are not able to shift. Conversely, an OpQuad is generally able to shift if there is an invalid OpQuad immediately below it or if all of the OpQuads below it are able to shift down.

The pseudo-RTL description that follows summarizes the equations determining which OpQuad can advance at the next clock cycle boundary. The code reflects the five categories discussed above as constraints on the

LdEntry signals that advance the OpQuads. While it may be apparent to some readers, what might not be obvious to others that there is the potential for some "deadlock" situations to occur. For example, you do not want to hold OpQuad[4] or OpQuad[5] if a branch has been detected as mispredicted or it will never reach the bottom row of the scheduler to initiate the abort cycle.

A few words about the notation for signals in the description are in order. The LdEntry[i], SC_MisPred, BrAbort, and trap pending flag have all been introduced in the preceding paragraph. The Q4PendLdStAbort signal indicates that there is a LdOp or a StOp in OpQuad4 which has a pending exception waiting to be recognized by the OCU (once it gets into OpQuad[5]) and then cause an abort cycle. The OpQV[i], $i = 0$ to 5, signals represent the state of valid bit of OpQuad[i]. The OpQRetire signal originates from the OCU and, if asserted, indicates when a valid OpQuad in the bottom scheduler can be retired. The HoldOpQ45 signal, if asserted, holds up both OpQuad[4] and OpQuad[5]. HoldOpQ3 and HoldOpQ4A correspond to BRCOND resolution and cc-dependent RegOps, both of these situations are in Category 1 above. The HoldOpQ4B signals correspond to Category 2 above. Both Category 3 and Category 4 are handled via the OpRetire signal. Category 5 is handled via the OpV[i] signals.

The scheduler generates signals that indicate whether it will be able to accept a new OpQuad at the end of the current cycle. This is shown in the following pseudo-RTL description.

PSEUDO-RTL DESCRIPTION
Advancing OpQuads in the Scheduler

```
HoldOpQ45 = (HoldOpQ3 | HoldOpQ4A | HoldOpQ4B) &
            ~(SC_MisPred | Q4PendLdStAbort | "trap pending")

LdEntry[5] = (OpQRetire | ~OpQV[5]) & ~HoldOpQ45

LdEntry[4] = (OpQRetire | ~OpQV[5] | ~OpQV[4]) & ~HoldOpQ45

LdEntry[3] = LdEntry[4] | ~OpQV[3]

LdEntry[2] = LdEntry[4] | ~OpQV[3] | ~OpQV[2]

LdEntry[1] = LdEntry[4] | ~OpQV[3] | ~OpQV[2] | ~OpQV[1]

LdEntry[0] = LdEntry[4] | ~OpQV[3] | ~OpQV[2] | ~OpQV[1] |
             ~OpQV[0] | BrAbort
```

The signal "~LdEntry[0]" indicates that OpQuad[0] is full and not shifting and thus the scheduler does not have enough room to accept a new OpQuad. The signal "SC_MisPred & ~BrAbort" indicates that there is a pending mispredicted branch and while the upper portion of the processor has been restarted and may have a new OpQuad ready, that the scheduler cannot accept it until the abort cycle is started.

PSEUDO-RTL DESCRIPTION
SchedFull and SchedEmpty Signals
`SchedFull = ~LdEntry[0]	SC_MisPred & ~BrAbort`
`SchedEmpty = ~(OpQV[0] | OpQV[1] | OpQV[2] | OpQV[3] | OpQV[4] | OpQV[5])`

We will now look at the static, dynamic, and OpQuad fields in more detail.

STATIC AND DYNAMIC FIELDS

The static and dynamic fields in an entry are shown in Table 3.1 and Table 3.2 respectively. These fields are related to but not identical to the fields of the associated *decoder* OpQuad Op formats shown in Table 2.22, "Decoder OpQuad LdOp and StOp Format," Table 2.30, "Decoder OpQuad RegOp Format," Table 2.38, "Decoder OpQuad SpecOp Format," and Table 2.42, "Decoder OpQuad LIMM Op Format." Indeed, if we return to the following diagram given in Chapter 2, we see that the relationship between these fields is established by the OpQuad expansion logic:

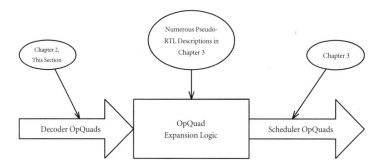

The eleven static fields require a total of 45 bits per Op entry. The sixteen dynamic fields require a total of 65 bits per Op entry.

Table 3.1 STATIC FIELDS PER OP ENTRY

Field Identifier	Bits/Entry
Type[2:0]	3
Imm	1
Src1Reg[4:0]	5
Src2Reg[4:0]	5
DestReg[4:0]	5
SrcStReg[4:0]	5
Src1BM[1:0]	2
Src2BM[1:0]	2
Src12BM[2]	1
SrcStBM[2:0]	3
OpInfo[12:0]	13

— BMs bytemark - indicate word size.

Table 3.2 DYNAMIC FIELDS PER OP ENTRY

Field Identifier	Bits/Entry
State[3:0]	4
ExecX	1
DestBM[2:0]	3
DestVal[31:0]	32
StatMod[3:0]	4
StatVal[7:0]	8
OprndMatch LUsrc1	1
OprndMatch LUsrc2	1
OprndMatch SUsrc1	1
OprndMatch SUsrc2	1
OprndMatch SUsrcSt	1
OprndMatch RUXsrc1	1
OprndMatch RUXsrc2	1
OprndMatch RUYsrc1	1
OprndMatch RUYsrc2	1
DBN[3:0]	4

Additionally, the OpQuad fields, which are also stored in the buffer on a per OpQuad basis, are shown in Table 3.3. The thirteen OpQuad fields require a total of 138 bits.

Table 3.3 OPQUAD FIELDS PER OPQUAD

Field Identifier	Static/Dynamic	Bits/OpQuad
Emcode	static	1
Eret	static	1
FaultPC[31:0]	static	32
BPTInfo[14:0]	static	15
RASPtr[2:0]	static	3
LimViol	dynamic	1
OpQV	dynamic	1
OpQFpOp	static	1
ILen0[2:0]	static	3
Smc1stAddr	static	20
Smc1stPg	static	20
SMC2ndAddr	static	20
Smc2ndPg	static	20

Thus, a scheduler OpQuad requires a total of 45*4 + 65*4 + 180 = 578 bits.

The initial values of the static and dynamic fields depend on the corresponding Op loaded into that entry. As mentioned earlier, the OpQuad Expansion Logic modifies some fields from the Op based on other fields, derives new fields from existing ones, replaces some fields with physically different fields, and passes a few fields through unchanged. The OpQuad fields are generated from information corresponding to the OpQuad as a whole.

AN OP ENTRY'S STATIC FIELDS IN MORE DETAIL

Each scheduler entry contains the following eleven static fields:

1. Type[2:0]
2. Imm
3. Src1Reg[4:0]
4. Src2Reg[4:0]
5. SrcStReg[4:0]
6. DestReg[4:0]

7. Src1BM[1:0]
8. Src2BM[1:0]
9. Src12BM[2]
10. SrcStBM[2:0]
11. OpInfo[12:0]

In the following discussion, all signals are actively high. Before proceeding, we make an additional comment about notation.

Notation
Decoder OpQuad Field Notation
There are many references to various decoder OpQuad fields in the pseudo-RTL description. We believe the notation identifying them, such as: 1. RegOp.Src1 (the Src1 field of the RegOp) 2. LdStOp.Data (the Op Data field of the LdOp or StOp) 3. SpecOp.Dest (the Op Dest field of the SpecOp) 4. LdOp.Type[1] (bit 1 of the Type field of the LdOp) is quite intuitive if the reader examines the decoder OpQuad Op formats cited above.

Static Field Type[2:0]

The static field Type[2:0] specifies the type of Op for the entry, particularly for issue selection purposes. Possible types include: a SpecOp; a LdOp; a StOp which references memory or generates a faultable address; a RegOp executable only by RUX; and a RegOp executable by either RUX or RUY. Floating-point operations (FpOps) are a type of SpecOp executed by the floating-point unit. This can be summarized in the following table:

Table 3.4 OP TYPE SPECIFIED BY THE TYPE FIELD

Type[2:0]	Type of Op
000	a SpecOp—not issued to an execution unit
010	a LdOp—issued to the Load Unit
10x	applies to all StOps
100	a StOp that does not reference memory—issued to the Store Unit
101	a StOp that references memory or at least can result in a memory fault—issued to the Store Unit
110	a RegOp that can only be executed by RUX—issued to RUX
111	a RegOp that can be executed by RUX or RUY—issued to either RUX or to RUY

The pseudo-RTL description that follows defines the chunk of circuitry in the OpQuad Expansion Logic that generates a value for the static field Type. In the equations in the description, fields in the *scheduler* OpQuad appear on the left-hand side of the equations and fields from the *decoder* OpQuad appear on the right-hand side. For example, in the description below the equation Type[2] = LdStOp.Type[3] means that bit three of the Type field of the *decoder* LdStOp is assigned to bit two of the static field Type of the *scheduler* Op entry. "RUYD" is a signal from a special register bit that inhibits use of the second register unit RUY for silicon debugging purposes; see Table 2.11 on page 88.

PSEUDO-RTL DESCRIPTION
Static Field Type

```
switch(OpId)
  case RegOp:
    Type[2:1] = 2'b11
    Type[0]   = ~(RegOp.R1 | RUYD)
  case LdStOp:
    Type[2] = LdStOp.Type[3]
    Type[1] = ~LdStOp.Type[3]
    Type[0] = LdStOp.Type[3] & ~(LdStOp.Type[2] &
              LdStOp.Type[1])
  default:
    Type[2:0] = 3'b000
```

Static Field Imm

For RegOps, the static field Imm indicates that the Src2 operand is an immediate value (being temporarily held in the DestVal field of the Op entry) instead of a register. For LdStOps, the static field Imm is not used.

PSEUDO-RTL DESCRIPTION
Static Field Imm

```
Imm = RegOp.I  // don't care if not RegOp
```

Static Fields Src1Reg[4:0], Src2Reg[4:0], & SrcStReg[4:0]

Some Ops can have up to two input values (obtained from registers). StOps, which actually write to memory, have a third input value, the data to be stored.

Articles on CD-ROM

Chapter 3 of the AMD application note, *AMD-K6 3D Processor Code Optimization*, gives several examples of address register operands, data register operands, and store data register operands. This application note is on the CD-ROM.

Fields Src1Reg[4:0], Src2Reg[4:0], and SrcStReg[4:0] hold register numbers identifying the registers which an Op uses. Src1Reg[4:0] holds the register number of the first source operand Src1, Src2Reg[4:0] the register number of the second source operand Src2, and SrcStReg[4:0] the register number of the store data operand in the case of StOps. The following three pseudo-RTL descriptions define the circuitry in the OpQuad Expansion Logic that generates values for the static fields Src1Reg, Src2Reg, and SrcStReg:

PSEUDO-RTL DESCRIPTIONS

Static Fields Src1Reg, Src2Reg, and SrcStReg

```
// Field Src1Reg
if (OpId = RegOp)
  Src1Reg[4:0] = RegOp.Src1
  Src1Reg[2] &= ~(LdStOp.DSz=1B)      // do byte register conversion
else
  Src1Reg[4:0] = {1'b0,LdStOp.Base} // don't care if not RegOp or LdStOp

// Field Src2Reg
if (OpId = RegOp)
  Src2Reg[4:0] = RegOp.Src2
  Src2Reg[2] &= ~(LdStOp.DSz=1B)      // do byte register conversion
else
  Src2Reg = {1'b0,LdStOp.Index}       // don't care if not RegOp or LdStOp

// Field SrcStReg
SrcStReg[4:0] = LdStOp.Data
SrcStReg[2] &= ~(LdStOp.DSz=1B & LdStOp.DataReg=t0)
// don't care if not StOp
```

Static Field DestReg[4:0]

Static Field DestReg[4:0] holds a register number identifying the destination register of the Op. The following pseudo-RTL description defines the circuitry in the OpQuad Expansion Logic that generates a value for the static field DestReg:

PSEUDO-RTL DESCRIPTION

Static Field DestReg[4:0]

```
if (OpId = LIMMOp)
  DestReg[4:0] = {1'b0,LIMMOp.Dest}
elseif ((OpId = LdStOp) & (LdStOp.Type = STUPD))
  DestReg[4:0] = {1'b0,LdStOp.Base}
else
  DestReg[4:0] = LdStOp.Data
  DestReg[2] &= ~(LdStOp.DSz=1B) // do byte register conversion
                                 // don't care if non-STUPD StOp
```

Static Fields Src1BM[1:0], Src2BM[1:0], & Src12BM[2]

The x86 instruction can operate on individual bytes and 16-bit words as well as 32-bit double words and, correspondingly, can modify just parts of 32-bit registers. The K6 3D's microarchitecture reflects this ability. Static fields Src1BM[1:0], Src2BM[1:0], and Src12BM[2] specify the sizes and locations of the operands. The "BM" is used as an abbreviation for the phrase "byte marks" and these three fields indicate which bytes of operand registers Src1 and Src2 must be "valid" for execution of the Op that will use values from these registers—i.e., which fields in the source registers must have correct, up-to-date values in them so the Op can proceed.

Src12BM functions as both Src1BM[2] and Src2BM[2]. A "0" in Src12BM means that the high-order 16-bits of neither source register will be used. A "1" in Src12BM[2] specifies that the high-order 16-bits of *both* source registers will be used. That is, a "1" for a BM indicates that the corresponding register part *will* be used as it is presumed to be "valid." The Src1BM and Src2BM fields indicate if the byte positioned at bit [15:8] in the Src register or the byte positioned at bits [7:0] will be used if they contain a valid value. The byte positioned at [15:8] is specified by a "1" and the byte positioned at [7:0] is specified by a "0." Thus, bits 2, 1, and 0 of the SrcBM fields correspond to bits [31:16], [15:8], and [7:0] respectively. The following pseudo-RTL description defines the OpQuad Expansion Logic circuitry that generates values for the Src1BM[1:0], Src2BM[1:0], and Src12BM[2] fields.

PSEUDO-RTL DESCRIPTIONS

Static Fields Src1BM, Src2BM, and Src12BM

```
if (OpId = RegOp)
  Src1BM[0] = ~(RegOp.DSz = 1B) | ~RegOp.Src1[2]
  Src1BM[1] = ~(RegOp.DSz = 1B) |  RegOp.Src1[2]
  Src2BM[0] = ~(RegOp.DSz = 1B) | ~RegOp.Src2[2] |  RegOp.I
  Src2BM[1] = ~(RegOp.DSz = 1B) |  RegOp.Src2[2] & ~RegOp.I
  if (RegOp.Type = 6'b10001x)
    Src2BM[1] = Src1BM[1] = 1'b0 // if ZEXT,SEXT
    Src12BM[2] = (RegOp.DSz = 4B)
    if ((RegOp.Type = 6'b10001x) | (RegOp.Type = 6'b111x00))
      Src12BM[2] = 1'b0  // if ZEXT,SEXT,CHKS

else// else LdStOp or don't care
  Src1BM[1:0] = Src2BM[1:0] = 2'b11
  Src12BM[2] = (LdStOp.ASz = 4B)  // don't-care if LIMM

if (LdStOp.Type = 4'bx0xx) { // STxxx Ops
  SrcStBM[0] = ~(LdStOp.DSz=1B) | ~LdStOp.Data[2]
  SrcStBM[1] = ~(LdStOp.DSz=1B) |  LdStOp.Data[2]
  SrcStBM[2] =  (LdStOp.DSz=4B)
} else
  SrcStBM[2..0] = 3'b000// CDA,CIA,LEA Ops
// don't care if not StOp
```

Static Field SrcStBM[2:0]

Static Field SrcStBM[2:0] indicates which bytes of the store data operand are required for completion of a StOp. The bit correspondence is the same as for Src1BM or Src2BM. The following pseudo-RTL description defines the circuitry in the OpQuad Expansion Logic that generates a value for the static field SrcStBM:

PSEUDO-RTL DESCRIPTION

Static Field SrcStBM

```
if (LdStOp.Type = 4'bx0xx) // STxxx Ops
  SrcStBM[0] = ~(LdStOp.DSz = 1B) | ~LdStOp.Data[2]
  SrcStBM[1] = ~(LdStOp.DSz = 1B) |  LdStOp.Data[2]
  SrcStBM[2] =  (LdStOp.DSz = 4B)
else
  SrcStBM[2:0] = 3'b000// CDA,CIA,LEA Ops
  // don't care if not StOp
```

Static Field OpInfo[12:0]

The static field OpInfo[12:0] holds additional information about the Op for either the execution units or the OCU depending on whether the operation is executable or not. OpInfo is the union of three possible field definitions, depending on whether the Op is a RegOp, a LdStOp, or a SpecOp:

1. for a RegOp, field OpInfo contains a concatenation of the following bits from the Op template: six bits from the Op Type field; four bits from the Op Ext field; the Op R1 field; and two bits indicating an effective data size DataSz for the operation.

Table 3.5 OPINFO DATA FOR A REGOP

Op Template	Description
Type[5:0]	copy of the original Op Type field
Ext[3:0]	copy of the original Op Ext field
R1	copy of the original Op R1 field
DataSz[1:0]	effective data size of the Op (one, two, or four bytes)

2. for a LdStOp, field OpInfo contains a concatenation of the following bits from the Op template: four bits from the Op Type field; two bits from the Op ISF field; four bits from the Op Seg field; two bits indicating the effective data size DataSz for the operation; and a bit AddrSz indicating a 16-bit or a 32-bit effective address size for the address calculation.

Table 3.6 OPINFO DATA FOR A LDSTOP

Op template	Description
Type[3:0]	copy of the original Op Type field
ISF[1:0]	copy of the original Op ISF field
Seg[3:0]	copy of the original Op Seg field
DataSz[1:0]	effective data size for the memory transfer
AddrSz	effective address size for the address calculation

3. for a SpecOp, the OpInfo field contains a concatenation of the following bits from the Op template: four bits from the Op Type field and five bits from the Op CC field.

Table 3.7 OPINFO DATA FOR A SPECOP

Op template	Description
Type[3:0]	copy of the original Op Type field
CC[4:0]	copy of the original Op CC field

The following pseudo-RTL description defines the OpQuad Expansion Logic circuitry that generates a value for the OpInfo Static field:

PSEUDO-RTL DESCRIPTION

Static Field OpInfo

```
OpInfo[12] = Op[35]
             // prevent LIMM from looking like various exception Ops

OpInfo[11:8] = (OpId = LIMMOp) ? 4'b1111 : Op[34:31]
OpInfo[7:0] = {Op[30:25],Op[23:22]}
```

AN OP ENTRY'S DYNAMIC FIELDS IN MORE DETAIL

The entry's dynamic fields are initialized by the operation decoder but can then change during execution of Ops. Typically, each entry contains logic for changing the values in dynamic fields as required. Each scheduler entry contains the following eight dynamic fields:

1. State[3:0].
2. Exec1.
3. DestBM[2:0].
4. DestVal[31:0].
5. StatMod[3:0].
6. StatVal[7:0].
7. OprndMatch_XXsrcY.
8. DBN[3:0].

These fields are discussed in the following paragraphs:

Dynamic Field State[3:0]

The dynamic field State[3:0] indicates an operation's execution state with respect to the execution unit pipelines. In Figure 2.16 on page 165 and Figure 2.19 on page 168, the stages S2, S1, and S0 are alternate signal names for State[3:0]. The State[3:0] bits are updated as the Op is successfully issued or advances out of a pipeline stage. The updating can be viewed as shifting a field of ones across four bits.

Table 3.8 INTERPRETATIONS OF THE STATE FIELD

S3	S2	S1	S0	Indicates the Op is
0	0	0	0	unissued / not yet issued
0	0	0	1	in operand fetch stage
0	0	1	1	in execution stage 1
0	1	1	1	in execution stage 2
1	1	1	1	completed

Most Ops enter the scheduler with field State set to 0000 (unissued). The dynamic field State changes after the operation issues to an execution pipeline. Upon completion of the execution pipeline, State is set to 1111 (completed) while the Op awaits to be committed or retired. The state field of every scheduler entry is set to 1111 during abort cycles. Some Ops (e.g., load constant LDK or load 32-bit immediate LIMM) have an initial state field value of 1111 and thus are already completed when loaded into the scheduler. The following pseudo-RTL description defines the circuitry in the OpQuad Expansion Logic that initializes dynamic field State and the circuitry in the scheduler entries that modify field State during execution of the associated operation. Note that "OPQV" in the pseudo-RTL descriptions for the dynamic fields is the OpQuad Valid bit associated with the incoming decoder OpQuad and not the OpQV field of a scheduler OpQuad. The OpQuad Expansion Logic initializes field State[3:0] either as 0000 (unissued) or 1111 (completed) according to the OpId field. Signal SC_Abort is asserted to abort execution of Ops currently in the scheduler. The signal "Issue Op[i] to XXX" are generated during the Op issue selection scan process; see the section titled "Issue Selection Logic" beginning on page 228.

PSEUDO-RTL DESCRIPTION

Dynamic Field State

```
State[3:0] = (~OpQV |
              (OpId = SpecOp) &
              ((SpecOp.Type = LDKxx) | (SpecOp.Type = LDxHA)) |
              (OpId = LIMMOp)) ? 4'b1111 : 4'b0000
```

Field State (signals S0, S1, S2, and S3) changes during operation execution as follows.

```
if (S0Enbl) S0 = ~BumpEntry | SC_Abort
if (S1Enbl) S1 = S0 & ~BumpEntry | SC_Abort
if (S2Enbl) S2 = S1 | SC_Abort
if (S3Enbl) S3 = S2 | S1 & RU | SC_Abort

BumpEntry = RU & ~S1 & S0 & (Exec1 & BumpRUX | ~Exec1 & BumpRUY)

S0Enbl = "Issue Op[i] to " & CHP_LUAdv0 |
         "Op[i] to SU " & CHP_SUAdv0  |
         "Issue Op[i] to RUX" & CHP_RUXAdv0 |
         "Issue Op[i] to RUY" & CHP_RUYAdv0 |
         SC_Abort | BumpEntry

S1Enbl = LU & CHP_LUAdv0 |
         SU & CHP_SUAdv0 |
         RU & (Exec1 & CHP_RUXAdv0 | ~Exec1 & CHP_RUYAdv0) |
         SC_Abort

S2Enbl = LU & CHP_LUAdv1 | SU & CHP_SUAdv1 | RU | SC_Abort
S3Enbl = LU & CHP_LUAdv2 | SU & CHP_SUAdv2 | RU | SC_Abort
```

Abort Handling (revisited)

The signal SC_Abort in the above pseudo-RTL description warrants special attention. When an abort cycle occurs, the entire scheduler is flushed. All OpQuad entries are invalidated by clearing all of the OpQuad Valid fields (OpQV) and certain fields of all Op entries are also cleared to innocuous values. The latter is necessary since OpQV only affects the control of scheduler OpQuad entry loading and shifting. All other operations within the scheduler ignore OpQV and simply assume that Op entries are always valid and sufficiently well defined.

DESIGN NOTE

Representation of an Invalid Op

An invalid Op within the scheduler is represented as a valid but innocuous Op. Its State field is set to completed so the Op will not be executed. Its DestBM and StatMod fields are set to indicate that it does not modify any register bytes or status flags. All other fields, in these circumstances, can have any values without causing any "harm" (side effects). An invalid Op is effectively a NoOp.

One important aspect of abort cycle handling within the scheduler occurs after mispredicted BRCOND Ops. In this case, a new OpQuad may be loaded into the scheduler during the abort cycle. This OpQuad is not associated with any of the outstanding OpQuads that all need to be flushed. It is logically the first new OpQuad after the abort. In all other cases, there will be a delay to the reception of the first new OpQuad after abort cycles due to exception conditions.

As discussed in the section titled "Loading the Scheduler" beginning on page 184, in the section titled "Static Field Storage Element Shifting Operation" beginning on page 190 and the section titled "Dynamic Field Storage Element Operation" beginning on page 190, the storage elements within the scheduler are fully synchronous and do not change state in response to inputs until the next cycle boundary. Thus, the following sequence of events occur at the end of the abort cycle. First, certain Op entry fields are changed to innocuous values. Then all, some, or none of the OpQuad entries shift down one position and a new OpQuad is loaded into the top scheduler entry. The shifting of any OpQuads other than OpQuad[0] during an abort cycle is a "don't care" situation. In the case of exception-related aborts, this new OpQuad is also invalidated. In the case of BRCOND-related aborts, this new OpQuad is allowed to be valid and reloading of the top scheduler OpQuad entry is forced.

To improve the clock frequency, there is both an "early" and a "late" version of the abort signal. The late version is logically the same as the early version, but delayed by one cycle using a flip-flop. The late version is called SC_Abort, and the early version is called SC_EAbort. SC_EAbort is used to flush the scheduler immediately; SC_Abort is used to flush the execution pipelines—this is not performance critical since there will be at least two cycles after SC_EAbort before an Op can possibly be ready to enter Stage 1 of a pipeline. The SC_Abort signal was "split off" of SC_EAbort to reduce the fanout/loading on a critical signal and to also make the longer distance usages non-timing critical. In short, this was done for timing improvement on a critical signal.

Dynamic Field Exec1

If the Op is a RegOp, the Exec1 field indicates that register unit RUX (versus RUY) is executing it. This field is set when the Op has successfully been issued to RUX or RUY. The OpQuad Expansion Logic initializes the Exec1 field to low (it is actually a "don't care" before the RegOp is issued). The following pseudo-RTL description defines the logic which sets and changes field Exec1. The signals "Issue Op[i] to RUX" are generated during the Op issue selection scan process; see the section titled "Issue Selection Logic" beginning on page 228.

PSEUDO-RTL DESCRIPTION
Dynamic Field Exec1
`if (S0Enbl) Exec1 = "Issue Op[i] to RUX"`

Dynamic Field DestBM[2:0]

The dynamic field DestBM[2:0] specifies which bytes of the register specified by the DestReg field are modified by the Op. DestBM[2], DestBM[1], and DestBM[0] correspond to bits [31:16], [15:8], and [7:0], respectively. The DestBM field is initialized by the operation decoder and may be cleared during an abort cycle. The logic associated with dynamic field DestBM is given in the following pseudo-RTL description. As in the case of the Src1/2BM fields, "BM" is used as an abbreviation for "byte marks." The equations shown are for integer results. There are similar 64-bit MDestVal fields (one per pair of Ops) for MMX/3D register results.

Dynamic Field DestVal[31:0]

The dynamic field DestVal[31:0] holds the register result value which has resulted from execution of the Op and is to be committed to DestReg. DestBM indicates which bytes of the result value are valid after the execution of the Op. The DestVal field is loaded when the Op completes execution stage 1 or 2 (depending on the type of Op). For non-executed Ops (e.g., the load constant operation LDK), DestVal is initialized with the appropriate register result value. DestVal can be used for temporary storage before register results are stored when an Op is completed. DestVal initially holds immediate values for RegOps, displacement values for LdStOps, and the alternate (sequential or target) branch program counter (PC) value for a BRCOND Op.

PSEUDO-RTL DESCRIPTION

Dynamic Field DestBM

```
Initialization by OpQuad Expansion Logic:

if (OpId=LIMMOp)
  if (LIMMOp.DestReg = t0)
    DestBM[2:0] = 3'b000
  else
    DestBM[2:0] = 3'b111
elseif (OpId=LdStOp LdStOp.Type = STUPD)
  DestBM[1:0] = 2'b11
  DestBM[2] = (LdStOp.ASz=4B)
else
  DestBM[0] = ~(LdStOp.DSz=1B) | ~LdStOp.Data[2]
  DestBM[1] = ~(LdStOp.DSz=1B) | LdStOp.Data[2]
  DestBM[2] = (LdStOp.DSz=4B)

if (~OpQV | (DestReg[4:0] = 5'b01111) | // invalid or dest is t0
    ((OpId = LdStOp) & (LdStOp.Type = ST/STF)))  // stores have no dest reg
  DestBM = 3'b000

if (SC_Abort)
  DestBM = 3'b000
```

The DestVal field plays an important role in the K6's implicit renaming strategy. The OpQuad Expansion Logic circuitry used to initialize the DestVal field and the scheduler circuitry logic associated with dynamic field DestVal is given in the following pseudo-RTL description:

PSEUDO-RTL DESCRIPTION

Dynamic Field DestVal

```
The OpQuad Expansion Logic generates the DestVal field according to
the following logic:

DestVal[31:0] = switch(OpId)
                case RegOp:  sext(RegOp.Imm8)
                case LdStOp: sext(LdStOp.Disp8)
                case LIMMOp: {LIMMOp.ImmHi[16:0],LIMMOp.ImmLo[16:0]}
                case SpecOp: if (SpecOp.Type=BRCOND & ~DEC_OpQSel_E)
                                 DEC_AltNextIPC[31:0]
                             else
                                 sext(SpecOp.Imm17)


Following execution of the Op, the DestVal field changes as follows:

if ((~S2 | LU) & ~S3 & S1)
  DestVal[31:0] = switch (Type)
                  case LU:              DC_DestRes
                  case SU:              SU1_DestRes
                  case (RU & Exec1):    RUX_DestRes
                  case (RU & ~Exec1):   RUY_DestRes

where signals DC_DestRes, SU1_DestRes, RUX_DestRes, and RUY_DestRes are the
LU, SU, RUX, and RUY result buses, respectively.
```

Dynamic Field StatMod[3:0]

Status flag bits EZF, ECF, OF, SF, AF, PF, and CF may be modified by RegOps. This field specifies which groups of status flags can be modified by the Op as shown in the following table:

Table 3.9 STATUS FLAGS GROUPS SPECIFIED BY THE STATMOD FIELD

StatMod bit	Status Flags Groups that can be Modified by RegOps
3	{EZF, ECF}
2	{OF}
1	{SF, ZF, AF, PF}
0	{CF}

[handwritten margin notes:]
Overflow
Sign
Zero
Aux Carry
Parity
Carry

Direction – string ops
Trap / dbg trace
Interrupt enable

EZF and ECF are separate "zero" and "carry" flags for use within OpQuad Sequences. When set, they are set in the same way as the architectural ZF and CF flags. The StatMod field is initialized to all zeroes for non-RegOp Ops and is cleared during abort cycles. The logic associated with dynamic field StatMod is given in the following pseudo-RTL description:

PSEUDO-RTL DESCRIPTION

Dynamic Field StatMod

```
Initialization by OpQuad Expansion Logic:

StatMod[3:0] = (~OpQV & (OpId=RegOp) & RegOp.SS) ? RegOp.Ext : 4'b0000

Logic in the scheduler clears field StatMod during an abort:

if (Exec1 & ~S3 & S1 & RUX_NoStatMod | SC_Abort)
   StatMod[3:0] = 4'b0000
```

Dynamic Field StatVal[7:0]

Like the StatMod field, the StatVal field is significant only for RegOps. The StatVal dynamic field stores the Op's status flag results value which are to be committed to status register EFLAGS. StatMod indicates which bits are valid after the RegOp completes execution stage 1. The StatVal[7:0] field is loaded when the RegOp completes execution stage 1. The logic associated with dynamic field StatVal is given in the following pseudo-RTL description. Note that there are no two-cycle RegOps that produce status flag results.

PSEUDO-RTL DESCRIPTION

Dynamic Field StatVal

```
Field StatVal is initially set to zero (i.e StatVal = 8'b00000000) and
changes when a RegOp completes execution pipeline Stage 1.

if (~S3 & S1)
   StatVal[7:0] = Exec1 ? RUX_StatRes[7:0] : RUY_StatRes[7:0]
```

Dynamic Fields OprndMatch_XXsrcY

This set of dynamic fields is associated with the control of transient information that is passed between two adjacent pipeline stages; see, for example, Figure 2.15 on page 164. In the notation, OprndMatch_XXsrcY, XX is either the Load Unit, the Store Unit, RUX, or RUY, and Y is either 1 or 2.

The logic associated with dynamic field OprndMatch_XXsrcY is given in the following pseudo-RTL description:

PSEUDO-RTL DESCRIPTION

Dynamic Fields OprndMatch_XXsrcY

```
match with operand XXsrcY:
OprndMatch_XXsrcY =(busReg[4:0] = DestReg[4:0]) &
                   (busBM[1] & DestBM[1] | busBM[0] & DestBM[1])
```

where XXsrcY takes on the values LUsrc1, LUsrc2, SUsrc1, SUsrc2, RUXsrc1, RUXsrc2, RUYsrc1, and RUYsrc2, and "bus" refers to OprndInfo_XXsrcY. The byte mark checking does not include BM[2], as a simplification, since (BM[2] = 1'b1) implies (BM[1] & BM[0]); thus, if (bus.BM[2] = 1'b1), then a match will be signaled irrespective of DestBM[2].

Dynamic Field DBN[3:0]

The DBN[3:0] dynamic field holds four data breakpoint status bits Bn (for n = 0 to 3) for a LdStOp. This field is initially all zeroes. When the associated LdStOp executes, the breakpoint bits from the appropriate execution unit are recorded for later trapping. Field DBN is initialized to zero (DBN[3:0] = b0000). Scheduler circuitry changes it during execution as shown in the following pseudo-RTL description:

PSEUDO-RTL DESCRIPTION

Dynamic Field DBN

```
if ((AdvLU2 | AdvSU2) & ~S3 & S2)
  DBN[3:0] = (DBN_LU[3:0] & LU) | (DBN_SU[3:0] & SU)
```

THE OPQUAD FIELDS IN MORE DETAIL

In addition to the static and dynamic fields for each Op entry in a row, the scheduler contains fields that are associated with the OpQuad as a whole. Most of these OpQuad fields are static; however, some are dynamic. Logic in each row of the scheduler changes the dynamic OpQuad fields as required. We will now examine the OpQuad fields that were given in Table 3.3 on page 198 in more detail.

OpQuad Field Emcode

The Emcode field indicates if the OpQuad was fetched from the OpQuad ROM or if it was generated from the hardware decoders. The scheduler logic associated with field Emcode field, which is a static field, is given in the following pseudo-RTL description:

PSEUDO-RTL DESCRIPTION
OpQuad Field Emcode

```
Emcode = DEC_OpQSel_E | DEC_Vec2Emc
    // treat initial vectoring OpQuad as part of an
    // OpQuad Sequence
```

OpQuad Field Eret

The Eret field indicates the OpQuad was fetched from the OpQuad ROM and that it is marked as the last OpQuad in an OpQuad Sequence. The scheduler logic associated with the Eret field, which is a static field, is given in the following pseudo-RTL description:

PSEUDO-RTL DESCRIPTION
OpQuad Field Eret

```
Eret = DEC_OpQSel_E & EDR_Eret
```

OpQuad Field FaultPC[31:0]

Field FaultPC[31:0] holds the logical x86 instruction fault program counter value associated with Ops in the OpQuad. In the case of a dual hardware decode, the FaultPC field holds the value of the PC associated with the first of the two instructions. The OCU uses the FaultPC field when handling fault exceptions for any of the Ops in the OpQuad. The logic associated with the FaultPC field, which is a static field, is given in the following pseudo-RTL description:

PSEUDO-RTL DESCRIPTION
OpQuad Field FaultPC

```
FaultPC = DEC_IPC // the logical PC for the first
                  // decoded x86 instruction in the
                  // OpQuad.
```

OpQuad Field BPTInfo[14:0]

The BPTInfo[14:0] field holds branch prediction table-related information from when the OpQuad was generated. The BPTInfo field is defined only for OpQuads generated by the hardware decoders which contain a BRCOND Op; it is not defined for OpQuads fetched from the OpQuad ROM. The logic associated with field BPTInfo field, which is a static field, is given in the following pseudo-RTL description:

PSEUDO-RTL DESCRIPTION
OpQuad Field BPTInfo
`BPTInfo = DEC_BPTInfo  // information from the` `                    // current BPT access.`

OpQuad Field RASPtr[2:0]

The RASPtr[2:0] field points to the top of the return address stack as of when the OpQuad was generated. The RASPtr field is defined for all Opquads but is significant only for OpQuads that contain a BRCOND Op. When a mispredicted BRCOND Op occurs, the RASPtr field is used to restore the decoder's top of Return Address Stack (RAS) pointer to its value as of the mispredicted branch. Note, the K6's RAS is used only for the implementation of x86 RET instructions. A separate one-deep return address stack is implemented in hardware to support one level of OpQuad Sequence subroutine nesting. The logic associated with the RASPtr field, which is a static field, is given in the following pseudo-RTL description:

PSEUDO-RTL DESCRIPTION
OpQuad Field RASPtr
`RASPtr = DEC_RASPtr` `        // the current return address stack pointer.`

Historical Comment and Suggested Readings

Return Address Stacks in Microprogrammable Processors

Standard Computer Corporation's MLP-900 was among the early dynamically microprogrammable processors that supported return address stacks for microcode-level subroutines. The MLP-900 return address stack was also used in the processing of interrupts by automatically saving the return address before branching to the control store address where the class of interrupts to be serviced was located. Additionally, the MLP-900 supported a reasonably complete set of micro-operations that used the return address stack in relatively obvious ways, (e.g., branch and enter a subroutine, conditional branch or return, and branch and increment or decrement). See Harold W. Lawson, Jr.'s. and Burton K. Smith's article "Functional Characteristics of a Multi-Lingual Processor," in the *Preprints of the 3rd Annual Workshop on Microprogramming*, Buffalo, New York, October 12-13, 1970.

OpQuad Field LimViol

The LimViol field indicates that the OpQuad contains the decode of a transfer of control instruction for which a code segment limit violation was detected on the target address. The LimViol field is actually loaded one cycle later than all of the other fields above (i.e., during the first cycle that the new OpQuad is resident and valid within the scheduler). For most rows, field LimViol is static; however, this field can be changed in the first row and therefore the field must be considered a dynamic field. The logic associated with the LimViol field is given in the following pseudo-RTL description. The LimViol field is initialized to zero (LimViol = 1'b0). The description reflects the fact that LimViol is loaded one cycle later:

PSEUDO-RTL DESCRIPTION

OpQuad Field LimViol

```
LdLV = LdEntry[0] & ~DEC_OpQSel_E  // a simple flip-
                                   // flop

if (LdLV) LimViol = DEC_LimViol
```

OpQuad Field OpQV

The OpQV field indicates whether the row contains a valid OpQuad. The OpQV field is used by the global control logic when shifting the OpQuads. Invalid OpQuads may be overwritten if an OpQuad lower in the scheduler is held up. The fields in a row containing an invalid OpQuad have the same values as an aborted OpQuad. An OpQuad can become invalid as a result of an abort.

The OpQuad Expansion Logic initially sets the OpQV field to indicate whether the OpQuad loaded into the top of the scheduler is valid. The logic associated with the OpQV field, which is a dynamic field, is given in the following pseudo-RTL description:

PSEUDO-RTL DESCRIPTION
OpQuad Field OpQV
| ```
OpQV = (DEC_OpQSel_E ? EDR_OpQV : DEC_OpQV ) &
       ~ExcpAbort & ~(SC_MisPred & ~BrAbort)

Field OpQV can later be cleared after an abort to
invalidate an OpQuad and prevent execution or commitment.

if (SC_Abort) OpQV = 1'b0
``` |

OpQuad Field FPOP

The FPOP field indicates that the OpQuad contains a floating-point operation (an FpOP). The associated pseudo-RTL description is as follows:

PSEUDO-RTL DESCRIPTION
OpQuad Field FPOP
| ```
FPOP = DEC_NPPopV  // indicates that Opquad contains
                   // a floating-point op
``` |

OpQuad Field ILen0[2:0]

In the case of OpQuads produced from dual hardware decodes, the field ILen0 holds the length in bytes of the first of the two decoded x86 instructions. For all other OpQuads, this field is forced to indicate a zero length. The ILen0 field is used to calculate the proper instruction address for faults on the third or fourth Ops within an OpQuad (i.e, as FaultPC + ILen0). The logic associated with the ILen0 field, which is a static field, is given in the following pseudo-RTL description:

PSEUDO-RTL DESCRIPTION
OpQuad Field ILen0

```
ILen0 = DEC_ILen0   // instruction length of first
                    // short-decoded instruction
```

OpQuad Fields Smc1stAddr, Smc1stPg, Smc2ndAddr, and Smc2ndPg

The fields Smc1stAddr, Smc1stPg, Smc2ndAddr, and Smc2ndPg hold the first and, if there are instructions from more than one cache line in the OpQuad, the second cache-line addresses covered by the instruction bytes of the instruction associated with the OpQuad. These fields are used in the detection of self-modifying code, which consists of writes to any of the bytes of the current instructions. The logic associated with the Smc1stAddr, Smc1stPg, Smc2ndAddr, and Smc2ndPg fields, which are static fields, is given in the following pseudo-RTL description:

PSEUDO-RTL DESCRIPTION
OpQuad Fields Smc1stAddr, Smc1stPg, Smc2ndAddr, & Smc2ndPg

```
Smc1stAddr[11:5] = DEC_Smc1stAddr[11:5]   // page and address from first
Smc1stPg[24:12]  = DEC_Smc1stPg[24:12]    // cache line
Smc2ndAddr[11:5] = DEC_Smc2ndAddr[11:5]   // page and address from second
Smc2ndPg[24:12]  = DEC_Smc2ndPg[24:12]    // cache line
```

THE SCHEDULER PIPELINE   Physically the scheduler is a large storage structure, holding most of the fields of information describing the Ops that are outstanding in the machine at any point in time. This includes both (a) the static state derived from the original Ops as fetched from ROM or generated by the decoders, and (b) the dynamic state resulting from the processing of these Ops. From a control perspective, however, an alternative and perhaps better view of the scheduler is to view it as a pipelined datapath that generates various bits of control information related to the execution of the Ops through their respective execution unit processing pipelines.

The functioning of the scheduler pipeline and the generation of the appropriate control signals are based on the State field associated with each scheduler entry. As we saw in the section titled "Dynamic Field State[3:0]" beginning on page 205, the bits in an entry's State field reflect the progress of that Op through the appropriate execution unit pipeline.

All changes to the processor state are synchronous with the clock in a very strict manner, (i.e., all state changes effectively occur on the rising edge of the clock). This means, among other things, that processor state changes do not occur in the middle of a cycle and multiple changes to a given element of state do not occur within one cycle or, if they do, the one that occurs on the rising edge of the clock will take effect. In essence, the scheduler, at this level of abstraction, can be thought to be comprised of edge-triggered flip-flops for all storage elements that store processor state information.

The pipelined nature of the processing of Ops is reflected in the structure of the scheduler itself. The overall scheduler and, correspondingly, each Op entry can be divided into many distinct, independent portions (chunks) of logic, each of which is directly associated with a specific processing pipeline stage of a given type of Op or execution pipeline. Correspondingly, from the perspective of a particular processing pipeline, there is a chunk of scheduler logic associated with each pipeline stage that provides key control information for the processing done in that stage and/or for determining when that stage can successfully complete. From the perspective of a given pipeline stage, as viewed across all processing pipelines (at least for the first few common pipeline stages), there are n sets of similar chunks of logic that perform the same function for each pipeline or for each Op source operand of each pipeline.

Suggested Review

It might be useful at this point for you to review several pipeline diagrams shown in Chapter 2 (Figure 2.12, Figure 2.14, Figure 2.15, Figure 2.18, and Figure 2.21) and the text that accompanies them as well as the scheduler diagram, Figure 2.9, and its related discussion.

Each Op goes through a multistage pipeline as it is processed and transitions between several states:

1. the first two pipeline stages are common to all Ops and represent Op Issue stage and Operand and Operand Transfer stage.
2. the last one or two stages are the actual execute stages.

For integer RegOps there is a single execute stage, corresponding to the fact that all RegOps execute in a single cycle. Further, once an integer RegOp enters this stage, it always successfully completes and exits this stage at the end of the cycle. Some MMX/3D RegOps take two cycles and some can be held up in execute Stage 1. For LdStOps there are two execute stages, during which address calculation, segment and page translation and protection checking, and D-Cache accessing (in the case of LdOps) all take place. Furthermore, LdStOps can be held up for arbitrary periods of time in either stage. Most reasons for holdups apply to the last stage, most notably D-Cache and D-TLB misses, and faults. Holdups in the first of the two execute stages stem typically from misaligned memory references[26] and the second execute stage being occupied and blocked, (i.e., not advancing).

The scheduler has limited involvement with the control of the execute stages of the processing pipelines; it simply keeps track of the state of each Op as it is executed and captures resultant register and status values as and when appropriate. Because of its usefulness at this point, Figure 2.9 is reprinted here:

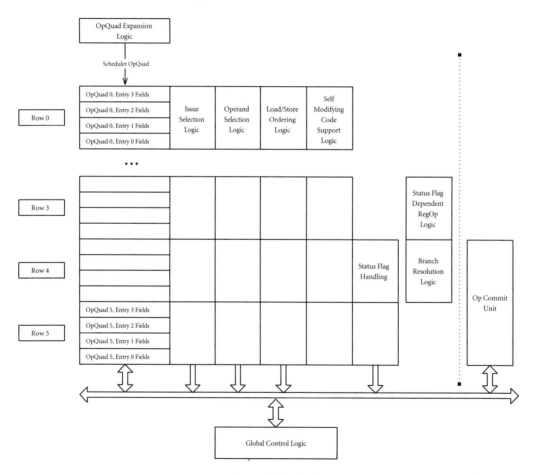

REPRINTING OF FIGURE 2.9, THE SCHEDULER AND ITS CENTRALIZED BUFFER

---

[26] Actually there are some miscellaneous additional cases that occur during cache and TLB fill which are not worth describing in any detail. The idea was to give you an example that already appeared in Chapter 2.

The various chunks of scheduler logic shown in this figure, namely the

1. issue selection logic
2. operand selection logic
3. load/store ordering logic
4. status flag handling logic
5. status flag dependent RegOp logic
6. branch resolution logic
7. self-modifying code support logic
8. global control logic

will be summarized and then discussed in more detail using this pipeline framework in the following sections. We will show how the information in the static and dynamic fields in the scheduler is used during the processing of instructions.

An inspection of Figure 2.12, Figure 2.14, Figure 2.15, and Figure 2.18 shows the scheduler processing in the first two common pipeline stages, where each stage consists of two phases. Each phase nominally occurs during the first and second halves of a cycle. These common stages are shown in Figure 3.3.

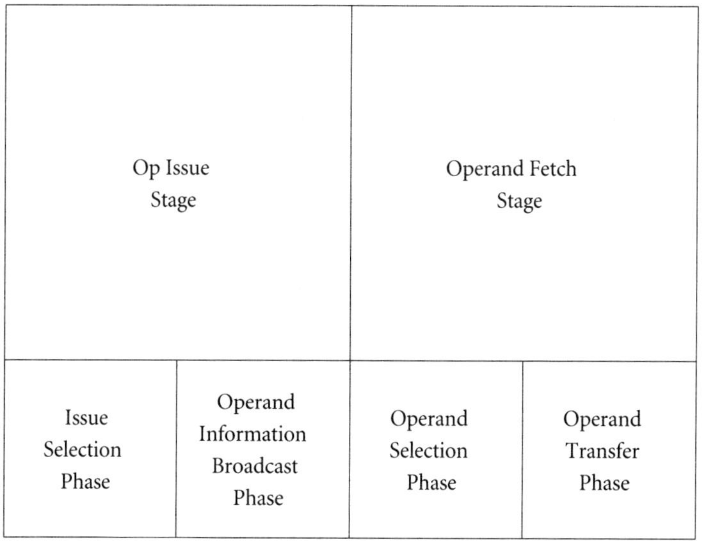

Op Issue Stage		Operand Fetch Stage	
Issue Selection Phase	Operand Information Broadcast Phase	Operand Selection Phase	Operand Transfer Phase

Figure 3.3 COMMON PIPELINE STAGES FOR ALL REGOPS, LDOPS, AND STOPS

The Issue Selection Logic and the Operand Selection Logic shown in Figure 2.9 are directly related to the Op Issue Stage and the Operand Fetch Stage, respectively.

Recall that we introduced some textual abbreviations in Figure 2.16, Figure 2.19, and Figure 2.20 that help reduce the visual clutter of those already crowded figures. Using "S" to stand for stage and "C" to stand for commit, we introduced the notation S_i at the left hand side of Figure 2.16 and Figure 2.19 and the notation C_i in Figure 2.20. We then summarized these pipeline notational correspondences in Table 2.43. We now extend that table to reinforce the fact that neither Figure 2.16 nor Figure 2.19 show the Op Issue Stage.

Table 3.10 ADDITION OF NEW ROW TO TABLE 2.43

Figure 2.16 and Figure 2.19	Figure 2.12, Figure 2.14 and Figure 2.18
Not shown in either figure	Op Issue Stage
S0	Operand Fetch Stage
S1	Execution Stage 1
S2	Execution Stage 2
C	Commit Stage

The use of C1, C2, and C3 in Figure 2.20 reflects the fact that the overall Commit Stage for StOps is composed of several "stages." We will find this useful when discussing the operation of the Store Queue Commit and L1 D-Cache Access logic. The registers shown in Figure 2.16, Figure 2.19, and Figure 2.20 in between the pipeline stages (i.e., S0, S1, S2, C, C1, and C2) are the pipeline registers discussed earlier in this section.

OP ISSUE STAGE LOGIC OVERVIEW

The Issue Selection Stage Logic supports the requirements of both the Op Issue Selection Phase and the Operand Information Broadcast Phase.

Issue Selection Phase

During the Op Issue Selection Phase, the scheduler selects the next Ops to enter the LU, the SU, the RUX, and the RUY processing pipelines—(i.e., four Op selections occur). Each cycle, based on the updated State field of all the scheduler Op entries as of the beginning of the cycle, the scheduler performs a selection process to determine the next LdOp, StOp, and the next two RegOps to be issued into the corresponding execution unit processing pipelines. This will be discussed in detail later in this section.

Operand Information Broadcast Phase

During the Operand Information Broadcast Phase of the cycle, information is broadcast to all scheduler entries and to external logic about each operand required by the Ops that were selected in the Op Issue Selection Phase. The Operand Information Broadcast Phase sets the scheduler up for actually locating where the appropriate operand values need to come from: (a) a scheduler Op entry, (b) the architectural register file, or (c) the results buses of the execution units (i.e., the *bypass* case). Since each of the four Ops may have up to two operands, a total of eight operand values might be involved. The store data operand for StOps represents a ninth register operand to be fetched, but this operand is not fetched until later in the SU pipeline, (i.e., at the latest possible moment before execution completion).

results buses

find operands

upto 9 operands

OPERAND FETCH STAGE LOGIC OVERVIEW

The Operand Selection Logic supports the requirements of both the Operand Selection Phase and the Operand Transfer Phase.

Operand Selection Phase

During the Operand Selection Phase, the scheduler determines:

1. where each of eight operand values actually needs to come from—including which specific scheduler Op entry, architectural register, or execution unit result bus.

2. the status of each value, (i.e., whether a valid value is or is not available from the designated source).

discuss these how related to other ops.

valid?

Based on this information, the scheduler determines which of the current Stage0 Ops will be able to advance into Stage1 of their respective execution pipelines. This determination is made independently for each Op. Only explicit operand dependencies constrain the order with which Ops are actually executed. Different types of Ops are processed through their respective execution unit pipelines in arbitrary order with respect to other types of Ops after explicit operand dependencies are taken into account.

Operand Transfer Phase

During the Operand Transfer Phase, eight operand values are transferred from the designated sources over the operand buses to the LU, SU, RUX, and RUY execution units. The transfers occur irrespective of whether the values are valid or not. If a value is invalid, then the value will not be used by the execution unit since the associated Op will not have advanced. Once an Op enters pipeline Stage1, the associated execution unit has latched its required operand values and will hold them as long as it remains in Stage1.

operand buses

displacement buses

Also during the Operand Transfer Phase, two displacement operand values are transferred over the displacement buses to the Load Unit and the Store Unit execution units (one to each unit). The displacements are 32-bit values and always come from scheduler Op entries; in particular, from the DestVal field of the LdStOp's associated scheduler Op entry; see the section titled "The DestVal field plays an important role in the K6's implicit renaming strategy. The OpQuad Expansion Logic circuitry used to initialize the DestVal field and the scheduler circuitry logic associated with dynamic field DestVal is given in the following pseudo-RTL description:" beginning on page 210. The selection of the source entries occurs during the Operand Selection Phase in a relatively trivial manner. When a LdOp or a StOp enters pipeline Stage1, the transferred displacement values are latched by the Load Unit or the Store Unit execution unit along with the associated register operand values.

Immediate values, which can exist as Src2 operands of RegOps, are handled as part of the operand transfer mechanism. In such cases, forwarding of a register value is inhibited and the immediate value is forwarded in its place, using the operand buses, directly from the DestVal field of the scheduler entry holding the Op requiring the immediate value.

DESIGN NOTE

Store Data Register Value for a StOp

In addition to the above process for obtaining the source operands of the next Ops that will start execution, a similar process is performed for obtaining the store data register value for a StOp. The process is virtually identical to that just described. The only difference is that the four phases—the Issue Selection Phase, the Operand Broadcast Phase, the Operand Selection Phase, and the Operand Transfer Phase—occur in synchronization with pipeline Stage1 and pipeline Stage2 of the StOp. In this case, issue selection is interpreted as the trivial selection of the StOp currently in the SU pipeline Stage1. In essence, store data is fetched in parallel with StOp execution. The actual data value is obtained concurrent with completion of StOp execution. If a valid value is not available yet, then the StOp is held up in Stage2. When a StOp successfully completes execution and exits Stage2, this data and the associated store address is put into the Store Queue as part of creating a new Store Queue entry for this StOp. Effectively, the Store Queue entry is created at the end of pipeline Stage2 and exists as a valid entry starting with the next clock cycle. We will revisit this topic later.

LDOP-STOP ORDERING LOGIC OVERVIEW

There are two chunks of logic, one associated with the LdOp pipeline and one associated with the StOp pipeline, that comprise the LdOp-StOp Ordering Logic. Just as certain execution ordering must be maintained between Ops due to register dependencies, a certain degree of execution ordering must be maintained between LdOps and StOps due to memory dependencies. For example, LdOps cannot freely execute ahead of older StOps.

Only a relatively limited amount of ordering is maintained between LdOps and StOps and it is enforced only at Stage2 of the two execution pipelines. This occurs in the form of holding up a LdOp or a StOp in Stage2 until it is acceptable or safe to allow the Op to complete. Up until this point, no ordering is maintained between the two processing pipelines. Further, LdStOps are generally allowed to complete out of order when memory independence can be proved based on partial address comparisons with older LdStOps that are somewhere in the other pipeline, (i.e., when the least significant, untranslated physical address bits are reliably available for such a comparison).

The word "safe" in the above paragraph means the LdOp and StOp in question access a disjoint set of memory bytes. The word "independent" is used as a synonym in this context. Given the splitting of misaligned StOps into pairs of StOps, this can be determined simply by the comparing of 28-bit octet addresses and the 8-bit byte marks. The Ops in question are independent if any part of the address bits don't match or if the two sets of byte marks and non-overlapping (i.e., the bit-wise AND of the two sets of byte marks equals all zeros). Clearly a comparison of a subset of address bits can be sufficient to show two LdStOps are independent; however, all address bits may need to be examined to prove either independence or dependence. Although dependence checks between LU Stage2 and SU Stage2 use full-address and byte mark comparisons, dependency checks between Stage2 and Stage1 pipeline stages use partial-address and full-byte-mark comparisons to determine independencies in the majority of cases (statistically speaking).

The actual address comparisons associated with dependency checking are external to the scheduler, within the LU and SU. However, scheduler support is required for determining the relative age of the LdOps and StOps in the Load Unit and Store Unit execution pipelines. This is necessary so that only the appropriate address comparisons are considered in determining whether a given LdOp or StOp can be allowed to complete. The two chunks of logic referred to are used in these comparisons. The chunk of logic associated with the LdOp pipeline Stage2 determines the age of any LdOp in that stage with respect to any StOps in the StOp pipeline Stage1 or Stage2 and any other StOps which are in earlier stages of processing. The chunk of logic associated with the StOp pipeline Stage2 determines the age of any StOp in that stage with respect to any LdOps in the LdOp pipeline Stage2 and any other LdOps which are in earlier stages of processing.

In the case of a LdOp in LU Stage 2 and older StOps before SU Stage1 (i.e., not having started execution yet), not even a partial-address comparison can be performed. In such cases, which statistically are not performance critical, the temporary conservative assumption is made that these Ops may be dependent and consequently the LdOp is held up in LU Stage2 until a better dependency check can be performed. Similarly, in the case of a StOp in SU Stage2 and older LdOps before LU Stage2, the StOp is *blindly* held up in Stage2. Address comparison with LU Stage1 is not supported since this has minimal performance benefit and saves LdOp-StOp ordering logic in the scheduler.

STATUS FLAG HANDLING LOGIC OVERVIEW

Lastly, in addition to the chunks of scheduler logic associated with Op issue, register operand fetch, and LdOp-StOp ordering, there is a chunk of scheduler logic associated with the fetching and usage of status flag values. Three relatively independent areas are involved: the fetching of status flag values for status-dependent RegOps, the fetching of status flag values for the resolution of BRCOND Ops, and the synchronization of nonabortable RegOps with surrounding Ops. There is no *explicit* synchronization with BRCOND Ops per se. Instead, this synchronization roadway simply enforces that nonabortable RegOps will always execute in OpQuad[4] of the scheduler and not above or below OpQuad[4]. This, combined with appropriate OpQuad Sequence coding rules and the fact that nonabortable RegOps occur only in OpQuad Sequences, allows the OpQuad Sequence programmer to efficiently achieve the necessary synchronization or serialization with any surrounding dependent or potentially affected Ops (both preceding as well as following).

STATUS FLAG DEPENDENT REGOP LOGIC OVERVIEW

cc-dependent Ops
cc-dep Ops

All status-dependent RegOps, which are referred to as condition code dependent, "cc-dependent," or "cc-dep" Ops, are executed only by RUX and require their status operand value with the same timing as their register operand values, (i.e., by the end of pipeline Stage0). Unlike the fetching of register values, though, the entire status fetch process is not pipelined and occurs in one cycle, (i.e., entirely during RUX pipeline Stage0). Further, a common set of logic serves to fetch appropriate up-to-date status flag values for both cc-dependent RegOps and for resolution of BRCOND Ops. In the former case these values are simply passed on to the RUX execution unit while validity of the status values needed by the RegOp is checked. If valid values for the required status flags are not yet all available, then the RegOp is held up in pipeline Stage0, just as is done for register operand values not yet available when needed.

BRANCH RESOLUTION LOGIC OVERVIEW

As is seen from Figure 2.21 on page 175, BRCOND Ops do not require any actual execution processing. Instead, while a BRCOND Op is outstanding and before it reaches the bottom row of the scheduler's buffer, it must be resolved as to whether it was correctly predicted or not. This is done for each BRCOND Op as it passes through OpQuad4 of the scheduler, in order, at a rate of up to one per cycle. When the above status fetch logic obtains the appropriate status for the next unresolved BRCOND Op, the set of status flag values is passed to condition code evaluation logic which determines whether the condition code specified within the BRCOND Op is TRUE or FALSE. If valid values for the required status flags are not yet all available, then resolution of the Op is held up.

If the branch condition is FALSE, the BRCOND Op was incorrectly predicted. In this case, the BRCOND Op is marked as mispredicted and the appropriate restart signal is asserted to restart the upper portion of the processor at the correct branch address (see Figure 2.4 on page 87). Only the upper portion is restarted at this point. The scheduler and the rest of the lower portion are not flushed and restarted until the branch abort cycle. The correct branch direction is the alternative or not-predicted branch direction and the resulting address may be either the sequential or the target address. If the branch was correctly predicted, then nothing happens other than the BRCOND Op is marked as predicted correctly and BRCOND resolution processing advances on to the next BRCOND Op.

This treatment for handling BRCOND Ops applies to BRCOND Ops from the hardware decode of x86 conditional branch instructions and from within OpQuad Sequences. The only difference is whether the alternative address is an x86 instruction address or an OpQuad Sequence address.

The State of BRCOND Ops is initially set to *unissued* (0000). When the Op is resolved, it is left in this state if it is mispredicted or it is changed to *complete* (1111) if it is predicted correctly. Later, based on the state of the Op, the OCU knows whether a branch abort cycle is necessary or not. Typically, RegOps and BRCOND OPs are "trivially" handled by OpQuad Sequences avoiding placing two such Ops in the same OpQuad. As a result, only one of these executes or resolves in any given clock. These executions/resolutions are naturally strictly ordered in OpQuad Sequence programming order. Further, a nonabortable RegOp in the next OpQuad after a BRCOND Op is kept from executing if the BRCOND Op was mispredicted, by the SC_MisPred flip-flop being set (i.e., by that signal being asserted). The case of a nonabortable RegOp and a BRCOND Op in the same OpQuad is allowed (and sometimes actually done) when the

BRCOND is status-flag-dependent on the nonabortable RegOp (since this ensures that the BRCOND Op is not resolved and the SC_MisPred flip-flop possibly set until after the nonabortable RegOp has executed.

GLOBAL CONTROL LOGIC OVERVIEW

Basically, the global control logic coordinates the overall operation of the scheduler. For example, among other things it is involved with: RegOp Bumping, the control of the source operand input multiplexers for each of the execution units, validity of each operand value being transferred, and generation of the pipeline advance signals that enable the pipeline registers for each pipeline stage.

SELF-MODIFYING CODE SUPPORT LOGIC OVERVIEW

Logically, in the scheduler, a detection of self-modifying code is treated as a "kind" of trap of the modifying instruction and factors into the K6's "trap pending" logic. The self-modifying code support logic detects the existence of such situations and deals appropriately with them.

ISSUE SELECTION LOGIC

As mentioned above, each cycle, based on the updated State fields of all the scheduler Op entries as of the beginning of the cycle, the scheduler performs a selection process to determine the next LdOp, StOp, and the next two RegOps to be issued into the corresponding execution unit processing pipelines. This selection is based solely on the State field and the Type field within each Op entry and essentially results in an in-order issue selection to each type of execution pipeline. The selection is not based on any consideration of the register, status, or memory dependencies that each Op may have on older Ops since such dependencies are not yet known (or at least not within the context of a reasonably short clock cycle time).

This selection process is physically performed simultaneously and independently for each of the four pipelines. The selection algorithms for all four pipelines are similar—the next unissued Op, as indicated by its State field, of the given type of Op is chosen. In other words, the next unissued LdOp is selected for the Load Unit, the next unissued StOp is selected for the Store Unit, and the next two unissued RegOps are selected for RUX and RUY, the first to RUX and the second to RUY. Conceptually, as described earlier in this chapter, the issue selection for RUY is dependent on RUX, but physically is performed in parallel with RUX issue selection. Also as was discussed earlier, some RegOps are only issueable to RUX and thus the Op selected for issue to RUY is the next RegOp that is in fact issueable to RUY. The following describes the selection algorithm in generic terms:

The Selection Algorithm

Each scheduler Op entry generates a signal that represents whether that Op is currently eligible for issue selection to the appropriate pipeline. These signals,

> "Issueable to XXX" =
>   (State = Unissued) AND ("Executable by XXX")

and their pseudo-RTL description were discussed earlier. The selection process consists of a scan, from the <u>oldest scheduler Op entry to the youngest</u>,[27] to locate the first entry with its "Issueable to XXX" signal asserted. The first such Op located is the one selected for issue to execution unit XXX. For RUY issue selection, it is the first such Op after the Op selected for RUX that is selected. The terms in the "Issueable to XXX" equation use information from the State field and Type fields of an Op entry. Specifically, "State = Unissued" = ~S0. The Type field, as shown in Table 3.4 on page 199, indicates if an Op is "Executable by XXX" where XXX = LU, SU, RUX, RUY for the execution pipelines Load Unit, Store Unit, RUX, and RUY respectively. This process can be shown abstractly in the Figure 3.4:

Ops are eligible for issue selection immediately after being loaded into the scheduler which means that <u>an Op can be issued during its first cycle of residence within the scheduler</u>. In such cases, only the Type field and State[0] need to be valid at the beginning of the cycle. All other bits comprising an Op entry can be generated as late as during the issue selection phase (i.e., up to one half cycle later); they only need to be valid within a scheduler entry and set up for the next phase of the processing pipeline.

If an Op selected for issue does not actually advance into pipeline Stage0, then effectively it was not successfully issued. During the next cycle its state will continue to indicate *unissued*. During the next cycle, it will recompete for issue and will be available to be selected again. In the case of RegOps, it is not guaranteed that the Op will be immediately reissued due to the implementation of "RegOp bumping" which is described in the section titled "RegOp Bumping" beginning on page 254.

[handwritten margin note: timing related to generality & loading sched ops opnd fetch stage]

---

[27] That is, from the bottom row of the scheduler to the top row.

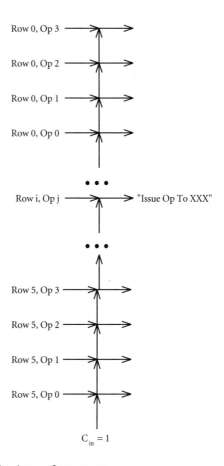

Figure 3.4 OP ISSUE SELECTION

Scan Chains

The scheduler's scanning process can be viewed from an implementation perspective as a simple form of carry chain. The carry-in, C_{in}, is injected into the beginning of the scan chain at the bottom of the scheduler at the start of the cycle. $C_{in} = 1$ and begins to advance through each bit position either propagating or being *killed*:

Kill = ~Propagate = "Issue To XXX".

The C_{in} to each bit position (i.e., to each Op entry) indicates whether that entry can be selected:

"Selected for issue to XXX" = "Issueable to XXX" & ($C_{in} = 1$)

A "ripple-carry" style implementation of this process is shown in Figure 3.5 below:

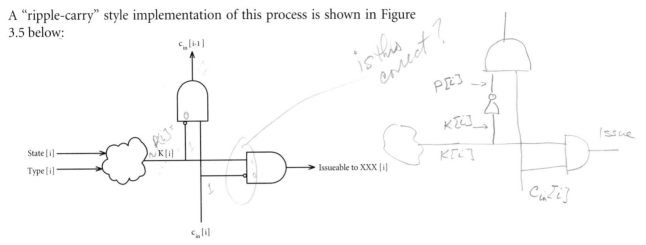

Figure 3.5   Scan Chain Style Implementation of Op Selection

The final C_{out} from the youngest Op entry is also used by peripheral scheduler logic to indicate whether any Op was found and selected for issue. The scan chain for RUY is more complicated and is discussed below. While a serial scan implementation is very simple, a substantially faster implementation was necessary for the K6 given the central role this scan algorithm plays in issue selection. As with conventional carry chains, carry lookahead techniques can be applied.

lookahead techniques

The following discussion provides a more concrete description of each scan chain in terms of carry lookahead equations analogous to the traditional Generate-Propagate-Kill equations used in traditional adders. For the LU, SU, and RUX scan chains, the bit-level K terms are defined, the G (generate) terms are all zero, and the P (propagate) terms are the complement of the associated K (kill) terms; i.e., as defined earlier,

generate, propagate, kill signals and equations

$$G[i] = 0, P[i] = \sim K[i].$$

For the RUY scan chain a more complex set of lookahead equations is necessary to do the scan in parallel with the RUX scan, instead of being dependent on it. Four terms are needed: G, P, K, and O. The first three terms are analogous to the conventional terms. At the bit level, the O and G terms are identical and are the same as the bit-level K terms for the RUX scan chain. The K terms are analogous to the K terms for the other chains and the P terms are again the complement of the associated K terms. The overall lookahead equations are extended forms of the conventional ones. The following bit-level G, P, K, and O terms are based on the State and Type fields of an Op entry. The operative definition of the Type field stems from its usage here, i.e. LU = 1 for LdOps, SU = 1 for StOps, RU = 1 for all RegOps, and RUY = 1 for RegOps executable by RUY. These bits are generated by the OpQuad Expansion Logic as Ops are loaded into the scheduler. This is trivially done without any logic since a bit in the RegOp format indicates this.

PSEUDO-RTL DESCRIPTION

Scan Chain Equations

Bit-level or Op entry equations
```
LU:   ~P = K = LU ~S0
SU:   ~P = K = SU ~S0
RUX:  ~P = K = RU ~S0
RUY:  ~P = K = RUY ~S0
 O = G = RU ~S0
```

Group lookahead equations (based on four-bit groups)
```
LU,SU,RUX: Pgrp = P0 P1 P2 P3
      CIn0 = Cin
          CIn1 = CIn P0
          CIn2 = CIn P0 P1
          CIn3 = CIn P0 P1 P2
          COut = CIn P0 P1 P2 P3
RUY: Pgrp = P0 P1 P2 P3
     Ogrp = O0 + O1 + O2 + O3
     Ggrp = G0 P1 P2 P3 + ~O0 G1 P2 P3 + ~O0 ~O1 G2 P3 +
            ~O0 ~O1 ~O2 G3
CIn0 = CIn
CIn1 = CIn P0          + G0
CIn2 = CIn P0 P1       + G0 P1      + ~O0 G1
CIn3 = CIn P0 P1 P2 + G0 P1 P2 + ~O0 G1 P2 + ~O0 ~O1 G2
COut = CIn P0 P1 P2 P3 + G0 P1 P2 P3 + ~O0 G1 P2 P3
       + ~O0 ~O1 G2 P3 + ~O0 ~O1 ~O2 G3
```

Issue selection equations
```
Issue OPi to LU  = LUchain.CINi  LUchain.Ki
Issue OPi to SU  = SUchain.CINi  SUchain.Ki
Issue OPi to RUX = RUXchain.CINi RUXchain.Ki
Issue OPi to RUY = RUYchain.CINi RUYchain.Ki
```

OPERAND INFORMATION BROADCAST

During the Operand (information) Broadcast Phase of the Op Issue Stage of the four processing pipelines, information about each of the four selected Ops is broadcast to all scheduler entries and to external logic. This information describes the two source register operands required by each Op. In addition, other information about each selected Op is also sent to external logic for use later by the associated execution units when they execute the Ops.

In total there are eight operand information buses that run through the scheduler. Each is driven by an issue-selected Op and goes to comparison logic within each Op entry. The total number of comparisons is equal to (8 * the number of Op entries). The results of all of these comparisons are 1-bit signals that control the actions that occur during Operand Selection Phase, which is the next processing phase.

operand information buses

Each operand information bus is eight bits wide and carries the five-bit register number and the three byte marks for a source operand. For each Op that has been selected for issue, the Src1Reg, Src2Reg, Src1BM, Src2BM, and Src12BM fields of its scheduler entry are driven, during the operand broadcast phase, onto the pair of operand information buses corresponding to the processing pipeline that the Op has been selected to be issued to. The following pseudo-RTL description summarizes the equations determining which operand information buses, if any, are driven by a scheduler Op entry during this phase of a cycle:

PSEUDO-RTL DESCRIPTION

Operand Information Bus Equations

```
Src1Info[7:0] = {Src1BM[1:0], Src12BM[2], Src1Reg[4:0]}
Src2Info[7:0] = {Src2BM[1:0], Src12BM[2], Src2Reg[4:0]}

OprndInfo_Lusrc1  = "Issue Op to LU"   ? Src1Info : 8'bZ
OprndInfo_Lusrc2  = "Issue Op to LU"   ? Src2Info : 8'bZ
OprndInfo_Susrc1  = "Issue Op to SU"   ? Src1Info : 8'bZ
OprndInfo_SUsrc2  = "Issue Op to SU"   ? Src2Info : 8'bZ
OprndInfo_RUXsrc1 = "Issue Op to RUX"  ? Src1Info : 8'bZ
OprndInfo_RUXsrc2 = "Issue Op to RUX"  ? Src2Info : 8'bZ
OprndInfo_RUYsrc1 = "Issue Op to RwUY" ? Src1Info : 8'bZ
OprndInfo_RUYsrc2 = "Issue Op to RUY"  ? Src2Info : 8'bZ
```

During the latter part of the operand broadcast phase, every Op entry monitors the operand information buses and checks for matches between its Op's destination register and any of the source operands about to be fetched. This comparison logic checks both for matching register numbers and for overlapping byte marks as some or all of the bytes required for an operand are or will be modified by this Op. The following pseudo-RTL description summarizes the generic comparison equation:

PSEUDO-RTL DESCRIPTION

Destination Register & Source Operand Comparisons

```
match with operand XXsrcY:
OprndMatch_XXsrcY =(bus.Reg[4:0] = DestReg[4:0]) &
                  (bus.BM[1] & DestBM[1] | busBM[0] & DestBM[1])

where XXsrcY takes on the values LUsrc1, LUsrc2, SUsrc1, SUsrc2,RUXsrc1,
RUYsrc2, and RUYsrc2, and "bus" refers to OprndInfo_XXsrcY.

The byte mark checking does not include BM[2], as a simplification, since
(BM[2] = 1'b1) implies (BM[1] & BM[0]); thus, if (bus.BM[2] = 1'b1), then a
match will be signaled irrespective of DestBM[2]
```

---

pipeline registers match signals

The results of these comparisons represent the output of the operand broadcasting phase and are captured in pipeline registers for use in the Operand Selection Phase of Stage0, which is the very next pipeline stage. This is done concurrently within each and every Op entry—within each entry, eight match signals (the values of the comparison results) are captured in pipeline registers to be used in the entry's operand selection logic. All of the match signals remain local to each Op entry. In essence, within each entry, eight operand information bus comparators feed eight "control" signals (the match signals) to eight chunks of Operand Selection Logic. We will learn later that the match signals within each Op entry in the bottom row of the scheduler are masked by additional signals associated with the committing of the results of the Ops in this OpQuad to the architectural register file.

The loading of the pipeline registers that capture the match signals is not controlled by logic within the entry. Instead, the registers within each entry associated with the two load unit operands are controlled by global control signals generated by scheduler peripheral logic. For example, all pipeline registers within the scheduler associated with the LU pipeline Stage0 are controlled by the global signal LUAdv0. The global control signal is a function of whether an Op selected for issue to the LU can advance into pipeline Stage0. Similarly, the registers across all entries that are associated with the SU, RUX, and RUY Stage0 are controlled by SUAdv0, RUXAdv0, and RUYAdv0,respectively.

Besides the internal use of the values on the operand information buses, these values are also latched into external pipeline registers for use by peripheral logic. Additional information about each selected Op, namely the OpInfo field, is also read out of the scheduler during this phase and latched into external pipeline registers; see the section titled "Static

Field OpInfo[12:0]" beginning on page 204. The following summarizes the equations representing this readout of OpInfo fields:

PSEUDO-RTL DESCRIPTION

OpInfo Field Readout

```
OpInfo_LU  = "Issue Op to LU"  ? OpInfo: 13'bZ
OpInfo_SU  = "Issue Op to SU"  ? OpInfo: 13'bZ
OpInfo_RUX = "Issue Op to RUX" ? OpInfo: 13'bZ
OpInfo_RUY = "Issue Op to RUY" ? OpInfo: 13'bZ
```

All of these external pipeline registers are controlled in the same way as the above internal registers, (i.e., by the XXAdv0 signals). The Src1Reg, Src2Reg, Src1BM, Src2BM, and Src12BM fields are used for a number of purposes during the next two pipeline phases, (i.e., during pipeline Stage0). The OpInfo fields are simply passed "down the pipeline" to the corresponding execution units through a second set of pipeline registers controlled by the corresponding XXAdv1 signals.

Operand Selection Logic

Each cycle, based on the values of the match signals in the pipeline Stage0 operand match registers as generated by the above Op issue stage chunk of logic, the scheduler performs a selection process to determine which Op entry, if any, will supply the operand value for each register operand being "fetched". This is called the Operand Selection Phase. It must also be determined during this phase whether each operand's value will come from the scheduler or the architectural register file. The architectural register file is the default source for these values if there is no matching Op entry to supply the value. As with the Op selection process in the Op issue stage pipeline, the operand selection process is independently and simultaneously performed for each operand being fetched. Thus there are eight chunks of Operand Selection Logic. The operand selection process is very similar to the Op issue selection process. During the next Stage0 phase, the Operand Transfer Phase, the operand values from the selected scheduler entries or register file will be driven onto the operand buses and transferred to the associated execution units.

For each operand, there is an operand match register bit in each Op entry (see the section titled "Dynamic Fields OprndMatch_XXsrcY" beginning on page 212). There are a total of (8 * "# of Op entries" = 192) such operand match register bits. The selection algorithm is to find the youngest Op entry with a match which is older than the Op entry containing the Op whose operand is being selected (i.e., fetched).

DESIGN NOTE, HISTORICAL COMMENT, AND SUGGESTED READINGS

Operand Forwarding and Register Bypassing

During each cycle, the selection process determines what needs to be done to forward appropriate operand values during that cycle in case the Op successfully advances into pipeline Stage1 after this cycle. If an Op, whose operands are being selected, does not advance out of pipeline Stage0, then the selection process will be performed again the next cycle. Since an Op's state and location within the scheduler can change each cycle, the outcome of the new selection may be different from the current cycle's outcome.

The terms *operand forwarding* or *register bypassing* are typically applied to a design that allows a result value produced by an operation to be used at an earlier stage in a pipeline than it would normally be able to be used by forwarding the output directly from the producing unit to the unit that requires the value as a source operand, bypassing an intermediate load of a register from which it would be subsequently read. See, for example, Michael J. Flynn, *Computer Architecture Pipelined and Parallel Processor Design*, Jones and Bartlett Publishers, 1995.

(in state S0) ?

This can be viewed as a scan, from the Op entry containing the Op whose operand is being fetched and in the direction of older entries, for the first entry with its operand match bit set. This Op is selected as the supplier of the required operand value and thus as the driver of the associated operand bus during the operand transfer phase. As mentioned earlier, if no older matching entry exists, then the register file, by default, is selected to supply the operand value.

The scan to find the appropriate source for an operand value can be viewed, like the Op issue selection scans, as a form of carry chain. In this case, though, the scan chains cannot be simple "propagate-kill" chains. In fact, it turns out that an operand selection scan chain is directly analogous to a traditional carry or "generate-propagate-kill" chain. Furthermore, the scan is in the direction of older Ops which is the opposite direction of the Op issue selection scans.

The initial C_{in} into the least significant bit of the chain is set equal to 0 while a carry generate occurs at the Op entry position corresponding to the Op whose operand is being fetched. Carry kills occur at all Op entries with set operand match bits. Carry propagates occur at all other positions. The Op entry with both a set match bit and a $C_{in} = 1$ is the selected entry. The final C_{out} from the oldest Op entry is also used by peripheral scheduler logic to determine if any entry was selected and thus whether the architectural register file should instead be selected—if $C_{out} = 1$, then use the value in the architectural register file. The selected operand value source drives the corresponding operand bus during the operand transfer phase, (i.e., the latter part of the cycle).

As with the issue selection scan chains, a carry-lookahead-based implementation will be necessary for speed. The following pseudo-RTL description provides a concrete definition of the operand selection scan chain in terms of carry-lookahead equations similar to the traditional generate-propagate-kill equations:

```
              PSEUDO-RTL DESCRIPTION

                Operand Selection Scan Chain

Bit-level or Op entry equations:

LUsrc1:  ~P = K = OprndMatch_LUsrc1
          G = LU & ~S1 & S0
LUsrc2:  ~P = K = OprndMatch_LUsrc2
          G = LU & ~S1 & S0


SUsrc1:  ~P = K = OprndMatch_SUsrc1
          G = SU & ~S1 & S0
SUsrc2:  ~P = K = OprndMatch_SUsrc2
          G = SU & ~S1 & S0


RUXsrc1: ~P = K = OprndMatch_RUXsrc1
           G = RU & Exec1 & ~S1 & S0
RUXsrc2: ~P = K = OprndMatch_RUXsrc2
           G = RU & Exec1 & ~S1 & S0 & ~Imm


RUYsrc1: ~P = K = OprndMatch_RUYsrc1
           G = RU & ~Exec1 & ~S1 & S0
RUYsrc2: ~P = K = OprndMatch_RUYsrc2
           G = RU & ~Exec1 & ~S1 & S0 & ~Imm


Group lookahead equations (based on four-bit groups)

Pgrp = P0 & P1 & P2 & P3
Ggrp = G0 & P1 & P2 & P3 | G1 & P2 & P3 | G2 & P3 | G3
CIn0 = CIn
CIn1 = CIn & P0 | G0
CIn2 = CIn & P0 & P1 | G0&P1 | G1

continued on the next page ...
```

Pseudo-RTL Description (cont.)

Operand Selection Scan Chain

```
CIn3 = CIn & P0 & P1 & P2 | G0 & P1 & P2 |
        G1 & P2 | G2
COut = CIn & P0 & P1 & P2 & P3 | G0 & P1 & P2 & P3 |
        G1 & P2 & P3 | G2 & P3 | G3

Operand selection equations:

"Supply Op[i] result value to LUsrc1"  =
    LUsrc1chain.CIN[i] & LUsrc1chain.K[i]
"Supply Op[i] result value to LUsrc2"  =
    LUsrc2chain.CIN[i] & LUsrc2chain.K[i]
"Supply Op[i] result value to SUsrc1" =
    SUsrc1chain.CIN[i] & SUsrc1chain.K[i]
"Supply Op[i] result value to SUsrc2"  =
    SUsrc2chain.CIN[i] & SUsrc2chain.K[i]
"Supply Op[i] result value to RUXsrc1" =
    RUXsrc1chain.CIN[i] & RUXsrc1chain.K[i]
"Supply Op[i] result value to RUXsrc2" =
    RUXsrc2chain.CIN[i] & RUXsrc2chain.K[i]
"Supply Op[i] result value to RUYsrc1" =
    RUYsrc1chain.CIN[i] & RUYsrc1chain.K[i]
"Supply Op[i] result value to RUYsrc2" =
    RUYsrc2chain.CIN[i] & RUYsrc2chain.K[i]
```

Operand Transfer Logic

During the Operand Transfer Phase of Stage0 of the four processing pipelines, appropriate values for each of the eight register source operands being fetched are transmitted over the eight operand buses to input operand registers of the associated execution units. Integer operand values are always 32-bit quantities; some bytes may be undefined and an execution unit may not use all four bytes. Undefined operand bytes will never be used by an execution unit if the processor is functioning properly. As previously described, each operand bus can be driven by any scheduler Op entry or by the register file. Conversely, any Op entry could drive any or all of the buses or none of them.

During the preceding phase (8 * "# of Op entries" = 192) operand selection signals and eight scan chain carry-outs (C_{out}) were generated. The pseudo-RTL description for the Operand Information Bus Equations on page 233 summarizes the equations that determine which operand information buses, if any, are driven by a scheduler Op entry or the register file during this phase of a cycle.

The operand values transferred over the eight operand buses are captured in pipeline registers at the inputs of the four execution units for use in the next pipeline stage, which is the first execution unit pipeline stage, Stage1. The loading of these pipeline registers is controlled by global control logic signals generated by scheduler peripheral logic as was described earlier for the Stage0 pipeline registers. The LU pipeline Stage1 source operand registers are controlled by global signal LUAdv1; similarly, the SU, RUX, and RUY Stage1 operand registers are controlled by SUAdv1, RUXAdv1, and RUYAdv1, respectively. The signals are a function of whether an Op in a pipeline Stage0 can advance into pipeline Stage1.

MMX/3D operands are handled similarly to integer operands and, notably, they use the same logic. To accomplish this, the following modifications are utilized:

1. the 64-bit MMX/3D registers are treated like 4-byte reads and writes of integer registers insofar as source and destination byte marks, (i.e., all three byte marks are set for MMX/3D registers).

2. separate 5-bit register numbers are used for MMX/3D registers (twenty-four numbers are used for integer registers and eight numbers are used for MMX/3D registers). Consequently, register number comparisons between integer and MMX/3D registers never match, (i.e., operand match and selection logic equations readily handle, without change, both integer operands for integer Ops and MMX/3D operands for MMX/3D-related Ops).

3. copies of the integer operand selection signals are also used as MMX/3D operand selection signals. Similarly, copies of integer operand bypass control signals are also used as MMX/3D operand bypass control signals.

During the operand transfer phase of Stage0, information about each of the Ops selected to provide an operand value is also read out of the scheduler. Each operand bus can be viewed as having an associated operand status bus that carries information describing the "origins" of the value being fetched. This information is used during this phase, by external logic, to determine the availability of a valid operand value and where the operand came from.

operand status bus

Each operand information bus is ten bits wide and contains a number of fields. The following summarizes these fields as taken directly from or derived from fields of the Op entry that is providing the operand value:

OprndStat[9:0] = {State[3:0], DestBM[2:0], Type[2:1], Exec1}

The following pseudo-RTL description summarizes the equations describing this readout of OprndStat information. These equations determine how and when the operand status buses, if any, are driven by a scheduler Op entry during this phase of a cycle. It can be easily seen that they directly correspond to the operand bus driver enable equations just given.

PSEUDO-RTL DESCRIPTION

OprndStat Information

```
OprndStat_LUsrc1 =
  "Supply Op result value to LUsrc1" ? OprndStat : 10'bZ
OprndStat_LUsrc2  =
  "Supply Op result value to LUsrc2" ? OprndStat : 10'bZ
OprndStat_SUsrc1  =
  "Supply Op result value to SUsrc1" ? OprndStat : 10'bZ
OprndStat_SUsrc2  =
  "Supply Op result value to SUsrc2" ? OprndStat : 10'bZ
OprndStat_RUXsrc1 =
  "Supply Op result value to RUXsrc1" ? OprndStat : 10'bZ
OprndStat_RUXsrc2 =
  "Supply Op result value to RUXsrc2" ? OprndStat : 10'bZ
OprndStat_RUYsrc1 =
  "Supply Op result value to RUYsrc1" ? OprndStat : 10'bZ
OprndStat_RUYsrc2 =
  "Supply Op result value to RUYsrc2" ? OprndStat : 10'bZ
```

Just as with the operand buses, there is a similar set of drivers at the output of the register file. As default drivers of these buses, they ensure that the operand status buses always carry defined values and, in these cases, that the values result in appropriate behavior by the external logic using this information. The pseudo RTL-description for OprndStat Information on this page summarizes the equations describing how and when the operand status buses are driven by the register file.

Completion Of Operand Transfer

The source operand value that is eventually delivered to an execution unit can come from any one of three possible sources:

1. a scheduler Op entry.
2. the architectural register file.
3. the result bus coming from the output of this or another execution unit.

The first case is covered by the Operand Transfer Logic described in the section titled "Operand Transfer Logic" beginning on page 238. In the second case, the register file is accessed during the operand selection phase of Stage0. As we learned, the register number of the desired architectural register is read out of the associated Op entry during the operand information broadcast phase of the Op Issue Stage and passed to the appropriate read port of the register file. For both of these cases, the resultant source operand value is transferred, during the Operand Transfer Phase, to the execution unit's operand input via a dedicated operand bus (Oprnd_XXsrcY) where it is multiplexed into the unit's operand register. The selection of whether a scheduler Op entry or the register file is enabled to drive the operand bus is determined by the scheduler during the preceding operand selection phase, as described at the end of the preceding section. The operand registers are controlled/enabled by the XXAdv1 global pipeline control signals. There are five-to-one (5:1) multiplexers which are used to select between the operand bus from the scheduler and the four buses from the LU, SU, RUX, and RUY execution units.

In the third case above, the value on the operand bus is ignored by the execution unit and, instead, the value on the appropriate result bus (Result_XX) is directly multiplexed into the unit's operand register. Thus, five operand buses run to each operand input of each execution unit, namely the operand bus for that operand input plus the four execution unit result buses. Since there are a total of eight operand fetches per cycle, there are twelve (8 + 4 = 12) buses carrying register values to and from the execution units. There is one additional operand bus, described later, for the store data operand of StOps, see the section titled "Store Data Operands" beginning on page 244.

The control for the 5:1 multiplexer at operand input of each execution unit is generated by the scheduler during the operand transfer phase of Stage0. The scheduler determines if the desired operand value is or may just be coming available, in which case the appropriate result bus is bypassed into the execution unit; otherwise, the operand bus is selected as the input. The validity of the desired operand value is an independent issue that only affects whether the associated Op in pipeline Stage0 will be allowed to advance into pipeline Stage1 and thus actually enter the execution unit.

Displacement Operand & Immediate Value Forwarding

We will consider the logic associated with displacement operands and the logic associated with immediate values separately as there are important differences between them.

Displacement Operand Forwarding

During the operand transfer phase of the Load Unit and the Store Unit processing pipelines, in addition to the register operands for each of these units, displacement operands are fetched and forwarded. The Load Unit and the Store Unit each have three operand buses carrying two register operands and one displacement operand. Displacement operands are always 32-bit quantities that are sign-extended from 8-bit quantities, as need be, when loaded into the scheduler from the decoders.

displacement buses

Displacement values are handled within the scheduler in a manner similar to Op register result values. Until they are used, displacement values are stored within the 32-bit DestVal fields of Op entries. They are driven onto displacement buses during the operand transfer phase of Stage1 of the LU and the SU pipelines. Displacement values are always supplied from scheduler Op entries. They are never forwarded from the register file. This usage of the DestVal field of a LdStOp does not conflict with its normal usage by LdOps and some StOps since result values are not loaded into the scheduler Op entry until after the displacement value is used.

As noted above, all displacements are stored in the DestVal field. Small (8-bit) displacements are expanded during Op decode. The selection between this expanded displacement and the 32-bit dedicated displacement bus occurs during Op decode and the final, effective 16/32-bit displacement value is loaded into the Op's DestVal field.

The selection of DestVal values to drive onto the displacement buses during each cycle does not require a scanning process across scheduler Op entries. Instead, each Op entry enables the drivers of its DestVal field onto the appropriate displacement bus based on its State and Type bits. The following pseudo-RTL description summarizes the equations enabling the displacement bus drivers within each Op entry:

PSEUDO-RTL DESCRIPTION
Displacement Value Selection

```
Disp_LU  =  (LU & ~S1 & S0 & ~LD) ? DestVal : 32'bZ
Disp_SU  =  (SU & ~S1 & S0 & ~LD) ? DestVal : 32'bZ
```

Immediate Values Forwarding

Immediate values can only exist as Src2 operands of RegOps. They are handled in a manner similar to displacements but as part of the operand transfer mechanism. Like displacement values, they are stored in the DestVal fields of Op entries; like register operands they are forwarded over register operand buses, specifically the RUXsrc2 and RUYsrc2 operand buses.

Only small (8-bit) immediate values need to be handled and are treated just like small displacement values in that they are stored in the DestVal field of the Op entry holding the RegOp using the immediate value. The are stored after suitable sign extension by OpQuad Expansion Logic before being loaded into the DestVal field. Comments regarding storage of displacement values in DestVal fields also apply to storage of immediate values.

Src2 operand immediate values are forwarded to respective RegOp execution units during the operand transfer phase of pipeline Stage0 in place of any register value. The selection of any register value source (a scheduler Op entry or the architectural register file) is inhibited and the RegOp in question directly drives its DestVal field onto the appropriate Src2 operand bus.

The inhibition of any RUXsrc2 or RUYsrc2 operand selection is done during the operand selection phase through masking of the generate signal that would normally be asserted by the Op entry holding the RegOp whose operands are being fetched. This is done separately and independently for RUXsrc2 and RUYsrc2. This prevents selection of any Op entry by the RUXsrc2 and RUYsrc2 scan chain and selection of the register file as the default operand source and is reflected in the previous operand selection scan chain equations.

The selection of immediate DestVal values to drive onto the RUXsrc2 and RUYsrc2 operand buses during each cycle does not require a scanning process across scheduler Op entries. Instead, each Op entry enables the drivers of its DestVal field onto the appropriate operand bus simply based on its State and related bits. These are the same drivers that are used for normal register value forwarding; there is simply an additional term in each enable equation for handling immediate operands. The following pseudo-RTL description summarizes these terms as separate equations enabling separate bus drivers within each Op entry:

PSEUDO-RTL DESCRIPTION
Immediate Value Selection

```
Oprnd_RUXsrc2 =  (RU &  Exec1 & ~S1 & S0 & Imm) ? DestVal : 32'bZ
Oprnd_RUYsrc2 =  (RU & ~Exec1 & ~S1 & S0 & Imm) ? DestVal : 32'bZ
```

When an Op entry drives an immediate DestVal onto an operand bus, it must also drive the associated operand status bus. This is handled in the same manner as it is with the operand buses, (i.e., the same bus drivers and driver input values as for normal operands are used for immediate values). There is simply an additional term in each enable equation—the same additional terms as given above in the immediate value selection equations.

The following summarizes these terms as separate equations enabling separate bus drivers:

PSEUDO-RTL DESCRIPTION
OprndStat Information for Immediate Values

```
OprndStat_RUXsrc2 = (RU &  Exec1 & ~S1 & S0 & Imm) ? OprndStat : 10'bZ
OprndStat_RUYsrc2 = (RU & ~Exec1 & ~S1 & S0 & Imm) ? OprndStat : 10'bZ
```

Store Data Operands

StOps are rather special in that they have three register source operands and (typically) no register destination. This is in contrast to all other Ops, which have up to two register source operands and one register destination. A STUPD Op is an exception insofar as it also has a destination. The data is only needed for completion of the Op. Certain StOps, such as STUPD Ops and LEA Ops, are an exception insofar as they also have a register destination. For LEA Ops there is no store data operand.

As a result, the fetching of StOp data operand values is performed in a manner similar to that for all other register source operands, but it is synchronized with the Store Unit pipeline Stage2 (see Figure 2.18 on page 167 and Figure 2.19 on page 168). Whereas the "normal" operand fetch process occurs during the Op Issue and Stage0 stages of processing for an Op, the store data fetch process occurs during Store Unit pipeline Stage1 and Stage2. If a data value is not yet available, this is realized during Store Unit Stage2 and the associated StOp is held up there.

Given that the data fetch process is largely the same as described in previous sections, the following section simply describes the two principal differences and summarizes all of the corresponding equations that support this process. Thus, this section describes logic within each scheduler Op entry.

The first difference is that the selection of an Op to issue is more simply the selection of the StOp currently in the Store Unit pipeline Stage1. A scan across scheduler entries to choose between multiple selection candidates is unnecessary. The second difference is that the OpInfo field of the StOp does not need to be read out during the operand broadcast phase. Instead, the OpInfo value read out when the StOp was issued is retained and used during the following two data fetch phases. The OpInfo value read out during the Store Unit Op Issue Stage is essentially passed down the Store Unit pipeline through Stage0, Stage1, and Stage 2.

PSEUDO-RTL DESCRIPTION

Store Data Operand Fetching

```
Store Unit stage 1: Op Selection

"Select for store data fetch" = SU & ~S2 & S1

Store Unit stage 1: Operand Info Broadcast

SrcStInfo[7:0] = {SrcStBM[2..0],SrcStReg[4..0]}

OprndInfo_SUsrcSt = "Select for store data fetch" ? SrcStInfo : 8'bZ

"match with operand SUsrcSt':
  OprndMatch_SUsrcSt = (busReg[4:0] = DestReg[4:0]) &
                       (busBM[1] & DestBM[1] | busBM[0] & DestBM[1])

  where "bus" refers to OprndInfo_SUsrcSt.

This match signal is then latched into a pipeline register bit within each
Op entry:

if (SUAdv2) OprndMatch_SUsrcSt = "match with operand SUsrcSt"

Store Unit stage 2: Operand Selection

Bit-level scan equations:
  ~P = K = OprndMatch_SUsrcSt
   G = SU & ~S3 & S2

Group-level scan equations:
  same as for other operand selection scan chains

"Supply OPi result value to SUsrcSt" =
  SUsrcStchain.CIN[i] & SUsrcStchain.K[i]
```

continued on next page ...

Pseudo-RTL Description (cont.)

Store Data Operand Fetching

```
Store Unit stage 2: Operand Transfer

Enable for driver within each Sched Op entry:
  Oprnd_SUsrcSt =
    "Supply Op result value to SUsrcSt'? DestVal : 32'bZ
  OprndStat_SUsrcSt =
    "Supply Op result value to SUsrcSt" ? OprndStat:10'bZ

Enable for driver at output of register file:
  Oprnd_SUsrcSt =
    SUsrcStchain.COUT ? SUsrcStRewgVal : 32'bZ
  OprndStat_SUsrcSt =
    SUsrcStchain.COUT ? {7'b1111111,3'bxxx} : 10'bZ
```

---

store data operand bus, Oprnd_SUsrcSt bus

The store data operand value transferred over the source data operand bus (the Oprnd_SUsrcSt bus) is captured in a pipeline register at the input of the Store Queue. The operand status value read out is used by external control logic during this phase. There is the same sort of 5:1 multiplexer at the input of the Store Queue like those for the other operand inputs to the execution units.

REGOP BUMPING

When Ops are issued to a given execution unit processing pipeline, they typically progress down it in order with respect to other Ops issued to that pipeline. When an Op is held up in pipeline Stage0 the Op currently being selected for issue to that pipeline also gets held up. The scheduler generally manages the execution unit processing pipelines based on in-order issue selection and processing.

When a RegOp is bumped out of either the RUX or RUY pipeline Stage0, the following RegOp selected for issue to that register execution unit advances into Stage0, immediately taking the place of the bumped RegOp. This allows the issue-selected RegOp to "pass by" without delay. Simultaneously, the bumped RegOp is immediately eligible for reselection and Op issue.

out of order issue

> **DESIGN NOTE**
>
> *RegOp Bumping*
>
> Although Ops can readily pass each other when they are in different processing pipelines, including the two RegOp pipelines, Ops cannot pass each other within any given processing pipeline. One exception is made to this general rule. When a RegOp is held up in pipeline Stage0 of either RUX or RUY due to one or more unavailable operand values, it may be both acceptable (insofar as not causing unnecessary Op execution delays) and desirable (insofar as having positive performance benefit) to bump the RegOp out of its processing pipeline. This *RegOp bumping* is accomplished by clearing the Stage0 valid bit for the RegOp and by resetting its state in the associated scheduler Op entry to *unissued*.

The bumping of a stalled RegOp is generally applicable to all RegOps and is subject only to the following two constraints:

1. a RUX-only RegOp cannot be bumped if a RUX-only RegOp is currently being selected for issue to RUX. Bumping the stalled RegOp would violate the principle that RUX-only RegOps are guaranteed to execute in order with respect to each other. This fact is taken advantage of in many OpQuad Sequences to accomplish various serialization and synchronization purposes (e.g., for multiply, divide, and segment register loading instructions).

2. a RegOp should only be bumped if it is guaranteed to be stalled for more than one cycle, otherwise it is generally better to leave the RegOp in pipeline Stage0 waiting to advance in Stage1. This avoids the additional execution delay and thus detrimental performance impact that could result from bumping a RegOp that only needed to wait one clock before being able to advance into Stage1 and start execution.

The implementation of RegOp bumping is reflected in the equations controlling the S1 State bit of an Op's scheduler entry; see the section titled "Dynamic Field State[3:0]" beginning on page 205. The implementation is also reflected in additional peripheral control logic that generates the global bump signals BumpRUX and BumpRUY and forces assertion of the RUXAdv0 and RUYAdv0 signals.

BumpRUX
BumpRUY

```
                       Pseudo-RTL Description

                       BumpRUX/Y Equations

// Inhibit Bumping of RUX
  InhBumpRUX =
    OpInfo_RUX_0.RegOp.R1 & OpV_RUX_Iss & OpInfo_RUX.RegOp.R1

// RUX Time Out
  RUXTimeOut = (RUXTimeOutCnt[2:0] == 0x0)

// Bump RUX Stage0 Op
  BumpRUX =
    (!OprndStat_RUXSrc1.State[0] ||
     !OprndStat_RUXSrc1.State[1] && !OprndStat_RUXSrc1.Type[1] ||
     !OprndStat_RUXSrc2.State[0] ||
     !OprndStat_RUXSrc2.State[1] && !OprndStat_RUXSrc2.Type[1] ||
     RUXTimeOut) &&
    !InhBumpRUX && !RegOpBumpDisable

// RUY TimeOut
  RUYTimeOut = (RUYTimeOutCnt[2:0] == 0x0)

// Bump RUY Stage0 Op
  BumpRUY =
    (!OprndStat_RUYSrc1.State[0]  ||
     !OprndStat_RUYSrc1.State[1]  && !OprndStat_RUYSrc1.Type[1]  ||
     !OprndStat_RUYSrc2.State[0]  ||
     !OprndStat_RUYSrc2.State[1]  && !OprndStat_RUYSrc2.Type[1]  ||
     RUYTimeOut) &&
    !RegOpBumpDisable
```

LOAD/STORE ORDERING LOGIC

In this subsection, we will deal with two important issues: (1) the determination of the relative order or age, within the scheduler, between certain LdOps and certain StOps; (2) the process of maintaining proper execution ordering between dependent LdOps and StOps.

LdOp-StOp Ordering Determination and Control Logic

The scheduler provides key support for maintaining a sufficient degree of execution ordering between LdOps and StOps. This is necessary so that related memory-dependency handling logic can ensure appropriate forwarding of memory data from memory writes to memory reads. As described earlier, only a limited amount of ordering is maintained and is done so only at Stage2 of the Load Unit and the Store Unit execution pipelines. Further, this only applies to StOps which actually reference memory or at least generate fault addresses (i.e., CIA and CDA StOps), although these latter Ops are included only for design simplification reasons. There is no execution-ordering constraint on or with respect to LEA Ops. No LdOps are excluded since all LdOps reference memory.

relative age of LdStOps

The actual LdOp-StOp ordering control logic is based on partial address comparisons between LdStOps in pipeline Stage1 and Stage2 of their respective pipelines. The scheduler provides information about the relative age of such LdStOps so that only the appropriate comparisons are considered in determining whether to hold up a pipeline Stage2 LdOp or StOp. These comparisons are separately performed for any LdOp in Load Unit pipeline Stage2 and for any StOp in the Store Unit pipeline Stage2.

1. in the former case, the scheduler determines the age of any Stage2 LdOp with respect to any StOps in Store Unit Stage1 or Stage2, and any other StOps that are in earlier stages of processing. The purpose in this case is to prevent LdOps from completing execution ahead of Store Queue entries being created for older StOps that the LdOp is or may be dependent on.

2. in the latter case, the scheduler determines the age of any Stage2 StOp with respect to any LdOps in Load Unit pipeline Stage2 and any other LdOps that are in earlier stages of processing. The purpose in this case is to prevent StOps from completing execution and creating Store Queue entries ahead of older LdOps that would eventually look up in the Store Queue and falsely appear dependent on these StOps.

The Relative Age Determination Process

Thus the two cases are not symmetric. The actual relative age determination process is similar to the Op issue selection and operand information broadcast process described earlier and involves the use of scan chains. During the first phase of pipeline Stage2 for a LdStOp, propagate-kill style scans (three scans for LdOps and two for StOps) are performed across all the scheduler Op entries from the oldest to the youngest. Each of the scan chains has its initial carry-in signal (C_{in}) set to 1. The initial Cin is the Cin injected into the beginning of the scan chain. Carries are "killed" by certain LdStOps which are different for each scan chain. During the second phase of Stage2 the C_{in} of the Stage2 LdStOp is selected or read out via a multiplexer, effectively broadcasting its C_{in} values out to peripheral scheduler logic. The value of these signals indicates the desired relative age information.

In the case of either a Stage2 LdOp or a misaligned Stage1 LdOp (for which the first half then is in Stage2 while the second half is in Stage1[28]), three scan

---

[28] See the section titled "LdOp Misaligned Accesses" beginning on page 171.

chains are needed since their age relative to the following three categories of StOps must be determined:

1. any Stage2 StOp or Stage1 StOp performing the second half of a misaligned StOp.
2. any Stage1 StOp.
3. any pre-Stage1 StOps.

Each scan chain handles one of these cases and each scans for the oldest StOp with a given state. The value of the carry at any point in the scan chain reflects whether a StOp of given state has been found yet. Thus, the LdOp in question can determine its relative age to any StOps in a given category simply by examining the value of the corresponding scan chain C_{in} to its Op entry. If the carry has not been killed yet (i.e., $C_{in} = 1$), then no older StOp of the given state exists. Based on these indications, LdOp ordering control logic can determine which Store Unit pipeline Stage1 or Stage2 address comparators to examine and then whether to hold up the Stage2 LdOp in question.

In the case of either a Stage2 StOp or a misaligned Stage1 StOp (for which the first half then is in Stage 2 while the second half is in Stage 1[29]) performing the second half of a misaligned StOp, only two scan chains are needed since their age relative to only two categories must be determined:

1. any Stage2 LdOp or Stage1 LdOp performing the second half of a misaligned LdOp.
2. any pre-Stage2 LdOps.

Relative age determination for Stage2 LdOps is possible, at the cost of a third scan chain, but proves to be of insignificant performance benefit. This is because StOps: (a) have less opportunity to try to and execute ahead of older LdOps and (b) often do not have following dependent LdOps that would benefit from earlier StOp execution.

As in the Op issue selection scans, each scan handles one of the cases identified above. Then, based on the value of the carry-in signals to the Op entry holding the StOp in question, StOp ordering control logic can determine whether to examine the Load Unit pipeline Stage2 address comparator and then whether to hold up the StOp.

The scan chains are simple propagate-kill chains, scanning from the oldest scheduler Op entry to the youngest. The following pseudo-RTL description describes each of the five scan chains in terms of carry lookahead equations. The bit-level P and K terms are based only on the State and Type fields of an Op entry (see the section titled "Dynamic Field State[3:0]" beginning on page 205 and the section titled "Dynamic Field Exec1" beginning on page 209, respectively). For the three LdOp scan chains, the ST Type field value (101) is used instead of the SU Type field value (10X) as this distinguishes the StOps which

---

[29] See the section titled "StOp Misaligned Accesses" beginning on page 173.

actually reference memory from LEA Ops, which only generate logical addresses. LUst2, LUst1, LUst0, SUld2, and SUld1 denote the five scan chains.

PSEUDO-RTL DESCRIPTION

Ld-St Ordering Determination Logic

```
Bit-level or Op entry equations:

LUst2:~P = K = ST & ~S3 & (S2 | S1 & SU2_FirstAddrV)
LUst1:~P = K = ST & ~S2
LUst0:~P = K = ST & ~S1
SUld2:~P = K = LU & ~S3 & (S2 | S1 & LU2_FirstAddrV)
SUld1:~P = K = LU & ~S2


Group lookahead equations (based on four-bit groups):

Pgrp = P0 & P1 & P2 & P3


CIn0 = CIn// note: Op 0 is oldest Op within a quad
CIn1 = CIn & P0
CIn2 = CIn & P0 & P1
CIn3 = CIn & P0 & P1 & P2


Lookahead among Quads:

CinGrp5 = 1// note: Quad 5 is oldest quad
CinGrp4 = Pgrp5
CinGrp3 = Pgrp5 & Pgrp4
CinGrp2 = Pgrp5 & Pgrp4 & Pgrp3
CinGrp1 = Pgrp5 & Pgrp4 & Pgrp3 & Pgrp2
CinGrp0 = Pgrp5 & Pgrp4 & Pgrp3 & Pgrp2 & Pgrp1


During the second phase of pipe stage 2 for a LdStOp, the two/three Cin's to
the Op entry holding the LdStOp are combined with a 24:1 mux as follows:

LUAges[2:0] = 3'b000
SUAges[1:0] = 2'b00

for (all Ops)
 LUAges[2:0] |=
    (LU & ~S3 & (S2 | S1 & LU2_FirstAddrV)) ?
      {~LUst2chain.CIN,~LUst1chain.CIN,~LUst0chain.CIN} : 3'b0
  SUAges[1:0] |=
    (SU & ~S3 & (S2 | S1 & SU2_FirstAddrV)) ?
      {~SUld2chain.CIN,~SUld1chain.CIN} : 2'b0
```

Scheduler Op Entry Fields Read Out During Operand Transfer

During the Operand Information Broadcast and the Operand Transfer Phases of fetching operand values, a variety of information is read out from the associated Ops for use by external control logic. For most operands this occurs during the Op Issue Stage and pipeline Stage0 of the processing pipelines. For the store data operand of StOps this occurs during SU pipeline Stage1 and Stage2.

During the operand information broadcast phase, information about the Op whose operands are being fetched is read out onto the appropriate OpInfo bus. In parallel, the SrcReg and SrcBM fields of the Op's scheduler entry are read out onto the two associated OprndInfo buses. In the case of the store data operand for a StOp, there is not an associated OpInfo bus transaction since this information is retained from when the StOp was issued. The OprndInfo information is used during the next couple of phases. The OpInfo data is simply passed down the pipeline to the actual execution units; in the case of RUX and RUY, the two source BM[0] bits from the OprndInfo buses are also passed down the pipeline to the execution units.

During the operand transfer phase, information about the status of each Op that is the source of an operand value is read out onto the OprndStat bus associated with each Oprnd bus. This information is only used during operand transfer phase. The following pseudo-RTL description summarizes all of the information that is read out of the scheduler, at various times, for external use. In these equations, XX = {LU, SU, RUX, RUY} and Y = {1, 2}.

PSEUDO-RTL DESCRIPTION

Scheduler Information for External Use

```
During Operand Information Broadcast phase:
    OprndInfo_XXsrcY[7:0]
    OprndInfo_SusrcSt[7:0]
    SrcYReg[4:0]
    SrcYBM[2:0]
    OpInfo_XX[12:0]

During Operand Transfer phase:
    OprndStat_XXsrcY[9:0]
    OprndStat_SUsrcSt[9:0]
    State[3:0]
    DestBM[2:0]
    Type[2:1]
    Exec1
```

GLOBAL CONTROL LOGIC

During the descriptions of the logic, storage elements, and buses comprising the core of the scheduler, there has been reference to a modest but critically important amount of peripheral control logic that coordinates the overall operation of the scheduler and the "feeding" of Ops to the four execution pipelines. The section describes each piece of this peripheral logic in its order of significance within the four phases of the first two pipeline stages.

During the issue selection phase the only external question to resolve is whether any Op had been selected for issue to the various execution unit processing pipelines. For each issue selection that did not find an eligible Op, the corresponding OprndInfo and OpInfo buses will not be driven by a scheduler entry. In such cases, the values on these buses and the operation of the scheduler during the following three phases for this execution unit processing pipeline in question is a "don't care." The only requirement is that the scheduler must know if it should treat pipeline Stage0 as still being empty or not. This is accomplished by using OpValid bits, one for each pipeline stage.

The Stage0 OpValid bits are called OpV_LU_0, OpV_SU_0, OpV_RUX_0, and OpV_RUY_0. Thus the OpValid bit passed into pipeline Stage0 must be zero for this pipeline stage is to be treated as still being empty. The OpValid bits for each processing pipeline are generated from the final carry-out (C_{out}) of the issue selection scan chains out of the youngest Op's scheduler entry. The OpValid bits are loaded into pipeline registers controlled by the XXAdv0 global signals. In addition, during abort cycles these registers are unconditionally cleared. The following pseudo-RTL description summarizes these equations:

OpValid bits:
OpV_LU_0
OpV_SU_0
OpV_RUX_0
OpV_RUY_0

PSEUDO-RTL DESCRIPTION
Op_XXX_Iss Signals

```
OpV_LU_Iss  = ~LUchain.COUT
OpV_SU_Iss  = ~SUchain.COUT
OpV_RUX_Iss = ~RUXchain.COUT
OpV_RUY_Iss = ~RUYchain.COUT
```

During the Operand Information Broadcast Phase there is no significant peripheral logic other than the pipeline registers which latch the OprndInfo and OpInfo values read out of the scheduler for external use. During the operand selection phase two external activities take place:

1. the SrcYReg fields of the latched OprndInfo values (i.e., the source register numbers read out during the preceding phase) are used to access the architectural register file. This is done blindly and in

parallel with operation of the operand selection scan chains within the scheduler.

2. the determination is made for each operand bus of whether the register file or the scheduler is to drive the bus with an operand value during the next phase. Each scheduler Op entry directly determines for itself whether it should drive the bus or not, so the only issue is determining whether the register file should be enabled to drive the bus. This decision is simply based on whether any Op entry was selected during this phase or not. If no Op entry was selected, as indicated by the final C_{out} of the associated operand selection scan chains, then the register file is enabled. This is done independently for each operand bus and the equations describing this are summarized in the operand selection section.

DESIGN NOTE

Architectural Register File Ports

Since there are up to nine source operands[a] to be fetched each cycle, there are nine corresponding read ports to the architectural register file, each port being associated with a source to one of the operand buses. The register fields presented to these ports are SUsrcSt and XXsrcY, where XX = {LU, SU, RUX, RUY} and Y = {1, 2}.

---

[a]   Eight Stage0 operands plus the store data operand.

During the operand transfer phase there are a number of external control functions that occur:

1. RegOp bumping.
2. control of all the execution unit operand input multiplexers.
3. validity determination for each operand value being fetched.
4. generation of the HoldXX0 signals.[30]

Each of these situations will now be discussed

RegOp Bumping

As described in the section titled "RegOp Bumping" beginning on page 246, the implementation of RegOp bumping is split between logic within each scheduler Op entry and peripheral logic which generates the global

---

[30]   The HoldXX0 signal factor into the generation of the XXAdv0 global pipeline register control signals.

bump signals BumpRUX and BumpRUY and forces assertion of the
RUXAdv0 and RUYAdv0 signals. The generation of the BumpRUX and
BumpRUY signals are based on the OprndStat values that are read out of
the scheduler, during the operand transfer phase, for each of the register
unit source operands—i.e., the four values OprndStat_RUXsrcY, where X,
Y = {1, 2}. In particular, the State and Type fields for each operand source
are examined to determine whether the sourcing Op is at least two cycles
away from being able to (possibly) provide a valid operand value. If this is
the case for either sourcing Op, then the dependent RegOp is bumped out
of pipeline Stage0.

DEFINITION
Sourcing Op
A Sourcing Op is an Op that has been selected to be the source of an operand value.

The following pseudo-RTL description summarizes the BumpRUX and
BumpRUY equations and includes an additional term in each equation
(the RUXTimeout and RUYTimeout signals) to handle what could otherwise be deadlock situations:

PSEUDO-RTL DESCRIPTION

RegOp Bumping Logic

```
Inhibit if RUX-only stage 0 RegOp and valid RUX-only issue stage RegOp:

InhBumpRUX = OpInfo_RUX(RegOp).R1 & OpV_RUX_Iss & OpInfo_RUX_0(RegOp).R1


// "~S0 | ~S1 & LU | timeout"
BumpRUX = ~InhBumpRUX &
         (~OprndStat_RUXsrc1.State[0] |
          (~OprndStat_RUXsrc1.State[1] & ~OprndStat_RUXsrc1.Type[1]) |
          ~OprndStat_RUXsrc2.State[0] |
          (~OprndStat_RUXsrc2.State[1] & ~OprndStat_RUXsrc2.Type[1]) |
          RUXTimeout)

// "~S0 | ~S1 & LU | timeout"
BumpRUY =   ~OprndStat_RUYsrc1.State[0] |
    (~OprndStat_RUYsrc1.State[1] & ~OprndStat_RUYsrc1.Type[1]) |
     ~OprndStat_RUYsrc2.State[0] |
    (~OprndStat_RUYsrc2.State[1] & ~OprndStat_RUYsrc2.Type[1]) |
     RUYTimeout
```

The RUXTimeout and RUYTimeout terms are generated by 3-bit counters associated with Stage0 of the RUX and RUY pipelines. Taking RUX as an example, whenever RUX Stage0 is loaded, irrespective of whether with a valid or invalid Op, the associated counter is reset to a start value; during all other cycles the counter is decremented. If the counter reaches 000, then RUXTimeout is asserted.

The BumpRUX and BumpRUY signals force the reload of Stage0 of the RUX and RUY pipelines, and reset the State bits to unissued within the scheduler Op entries corresponding to the RegOps being bumped. They also deassert the Stage0 OpValid signals and thus prevent a Stage0 RegOp, while being bumped, from also advancing into pipeline Stage1. For example, RUXTimeout immediately forces $OpV\_RUX\_0 = 0$. Recall that if the Stage0 OpValid bit appears to be zero, the pipeline stage will be treated as being empty. $OpV\_RUX\_0 = 0$ then causes assertion of the RUXAdv0 pipeline control signal and thus reloading of RUX Stage0.

Control of All Execution Unit Operand Input Multiplexers

The second peripheral function occurring during the operand transfer phase is generation of the controls for each of the source operand input multiplexers of each of the execution units. There are nine such multiplexers, one for each of the eight Stage0 operands plus one for a store data operand. As described in an earlier section, there is a 5:1 multiplexer associated with each operand fetch that selects a value from either the corresponding operand bus or one of the four execution result buses, to load into the execution unit's operand register.

The control for each of these multiplexers is based on the OprndStat values that are read out of the scheduler, during operand transfer phase, for each of the operands being fetched, i.e., OprndStat_XXsrcY and OprndStat_SUsrcSt, where XX = {LU, SU, RUX, RUY} and Y = {1, 2}. In particular, the State and Type fields for each operand source are examined to determine whether the sourcing Op has already completed execution or, if not, then which unit it is being executed by. The case of a RegOp sourcing a Src2 immediate value to itself is also appropriately handled. The following pseudo-RTL description summarizes the five input select equations for each operand multiplexer:

PSEUDO-RTL DESCRIPTION

Operand Multiplexer Logic

```
// RUXsrc2 OprndStat values
RUXsrc2Imm = (Type[1:0]=2'b11) & ~S1 & S0 &  Exec1

// RUYsrc2 OprndStat values
RUYsrc2Imm = (Type[1:0]=2'b11) & ~S1 & S0 & ~Exec1

// "S3 | S2 & ~LU"
SelOprndBus_XXsrcY = State[3] | State[2] & Type[1]

// above is for all SelOprndBus signals except the two below
SelOprndBus_RUXsrc2 = State[3] | State[2] & Type[1] | RUXsrc2Imm
SelOprndBus_RUYsrc2 = State[3] | State[2] & Type[1] | RUYsrc2Imm

SelLUDestRes_XXsrcY  = ~SelOprndBus_XXsrcY & ~Type[1]
SelSUDestRes_XXsrcY  = ~SelOprndBus_XXsrcY &  Type[1] & ~Type[0]
SelRUXDestRes_XXsrcY = ~SelOprndBus_XXsrcY &  Type[1] &  Type[0] &  Exec1
SelRUYDestRes_XXsrcY = ~SelOprndBus_XXsrcY &  Type[1] &  Type[0] & ~Exec1
```

Validity Determination for Each Operand Value Being Transferred

The third peripheral function occurring during the operand transfer phase is determination of the validity of each of the nine operand values being presented to execution unit source operand registers. A signal is generated for each source operand that indicates whether its current value is valid or not. As with the control of the associated execution unit input multiplexers, the signal is based on the State and Type fields of the Oprnd-Stat values that are read out of the scheduler. The sourcing Op must either have completed execution or currently be completing execution. In addition, the DestBM field of the OprndStat value is compared with the Src1BM or Src2BM field of the latched OprndInfo value for the operand being fetched. The sourcing Op's byte marks must be a superset of the required byte marks. The case of a RegOp sourcing a Src2 immediate value to itself is also appropriately handled, but in the HoldXX0 equations described below instead of being factored into the appropriate equations for the OprndInvld signals. The following pseudo-RTL descriptions summarize the OprndInvld equations:

PSEUDO-RTL DESCRIPTION

OprndInvld Signals

```
//~S1* | LU & (~S2 | ~S3 & ~LUAdv2)
OprndInvld_XXsrcY= ~State[1] |
                   ~Type[1] & (~State[2] | ~State[3] & ~CHP_LUAdv2) |
                   SrcYBM[2] & ~DestBM[2] |
                   SrcYBM[1] & ~DestBM[1] |
                   SrcYBM[0] & ~DestBM[0]
```

Generation of the HoldXX0 Signals

The fourth and last peripheral function occurring during the operand transfer phase is generation of the HoldXX0 pipeline control signals. The following summarizes the equations for generating these signals:

PSEUDO-RTL DESCRIPTION

HoldXX0 Pipeline Control Signals

```
SC_HoldLU0  = OprndInvld_LUsrc1 | OprndInvld_LUsrc2
SC_HoldSU0  = OprndInvld_SUsrc1 | OprndInvld_SUsrc2
SC_HoldRUX0 = OprndInvld_RUXsrc1 | OprndInvld_RUXsrc2 & ~RUXsrc2Imm |
              StatusInvld_RUX | NonAbSync
SC_HoldRUY0 = OprndInvld_RUYsrc1 | OprndInvld_RUYsrc2 & ~RUYsrc2Imm
SC_HoldSU2  = OprndInvld_SUsrcSt & ~SU2_FirstAddrV
```

STATUS FLAG HANDLING LOGIC, STATUS FLAG DEPENDENT REGOP LOGIC, BRANCH RESOLUTION LOGIC, AND NONABORTABLE REGOP LOGIC

The handling and usage of status flags, both architectural status flags and K6 microarchitectural flags, involves three areas of functionality:

1. fetching of status flag operand values for cc-dependent RegOps.
2. fetching of status flag values for and the resolution of BRCOND Ops.
3. synchronization of the execution of nonabortable RegOps.

Unlike the handling of register operands and LdOp-StOp ordering constraints, the logic for supporting these functions is not spread across all scheduler Op entries. Status flag handling for related Ops can only occur while they are within certain rows of the scheduler. In the case of cc-dependent RegOps, they must be in Row 3 during the RUX pipeline Stage0 cycle (i.e., the cycle in which status operand fetching occurs). In the case of BRCOND Ops and nonabortable RegOps, they must be in Row 4 during their resolution or RUX Stage0 cycle, respectively.

DESIGN NOTE

Simplifications and Reductions in Logic

Condition code dependent and nonabortable RegOps are held up in RUX Stage0 if they have not yet shifted down to scheduler Row 3 or 4, respectively. Conversely, such Ops are held up at these positions by inhibiting OpQuad shifting until they are successfully able to advance into RUX Stage1. These restrictions enable all of the associated logic to be simpler and much smaller. For example, the fetching of appropriate status flag values for condition code dependent RegOps and BRCOND Ops only occurs across the bottom three scheduler rows and can be performed independently for each of the four groups of status flags. One set of this status fetching logic can be shared or utilized for both condition code dependent RegOp status operand fetching and BRCOND Op resolution.

In addition, the direct bypassing of status flag values directly from either RegOp execution unit to a condition code dependent RegOp entering the RUX execution unit, is not supported. The result is a minimum one-cycle latency between the execution of a RegOp that modifies status flags[a] and the execution of a following cc-dependent RegOp. The overall performance impact of this is found to be minimal. In cases where an OpQuad Sequence is being executed, the impact might very well be eliminated through appropriate Op scheduling.

[a] Such RegOps are termed ".cc" RegOps.

To further aid the simplification and reduction of logic, a number of restrictions are placed on where condition code dependent RegOps, BRCOND Ops, and nonabortable RegOps can occur relative to each other within OpQuads. Many of the relevant Ops can only occur in OpQuad Sequences. The restrictions generally translate into OpQuad Sequence coding rules and in some cases also constrain the decoding of multiple x86 instructions in one cycle. In particular, the restrictions are as follows:

1. no ".cc" RegOps after a BRCOND Op within an OpQuad.
2. no cc-dependent RegOps after a ".cc" RegOp within an OpQuad.
3. no nonabortable RegOps in the same OpQuad as a BRCOND Op.

4. only one cc-dependent RegOp within an OpQuad.

5. only one BRCOND Op within an OpQuad.

The following describes each of the pieces of logic: for status value fetching, status forwarding to condition code dependent RegOps, BRCOND resolution, and nonabortable RegOp synchronization

The Fetching of Status Flag Operand Values for CC-Dependent RegOps and BRCOND Ops

During each cycle, the effective set of status flag values at the boundary between scheduler Rows 3 and 4 is computed by examining all the RegOps in OpQuads 4 and 5. Since it is possible for each RegOp to modify only a subset of the flags, this process is performed independently for each of four groups of status flags, corresponding to the four StatMod bits within each scheduler Op entry (see the section titled "Dynamic Field StatMod[3:0]" beginning on page 211). The result, within each group, is a set of flag values and state information from the youngest RegOp with its StatMod bit set for that set of flag values. The validity of the flag values is directly implied by the associated state information.

The end result or output of the status flag fetch logic is eight flag values and four associated valid bits. These are passed to the logic handling condition code dependent RegOps and to the logic handling BRCOND Op resolution, where the flag values are evaluated and the valid bits are examined to determine whether the required flag values are, in fact, valid. Based on the latter information, appropriate pipeline and scheduler shift control signals are generated. The correspondence between the StatMod[3:0] bits and the status flags was given in Table 3.9 on page 211.

NOTATION (REPEATED FOR CONVENIENCE)
OpQuadY and OpX
We will, from time to time, use the following notation to refer to scheduler OpQuads: OpQuadY, where Y = 0 to 5. For example, OpQuad1 identifies the OpQuad in Row 1 of the scheduler, OpQuad2 the OpQuad in Row 2, etc. Additionally, we will use the following notation to refer to scheduler Op entries: OpX, where X = 0 to 23. For example, X = 0 identifies the youngest Op in the scheduler and X = 23 identifies the oldest Op in the scheduler. Thus OpQuad4, for example, contains Op16, Op17, Op18, and Op19.

A process somewhat similar to that for fetching register operand values is used within each status flag group to obtain the appropriate flag values, i.e., the most recent new values relative to Op15 in the scheduler. A propagate-kill-style scan from Op16 to Op23 locates the first Op with its Stat-Mod bit for this flag group set, and that Op entry's Completed State bit (i.e., S3) and the appropriate set of flag values are read out; the valid bit for this group is simply the State bit. In the case that no such Op is found, the desired flag values are read from the architectural status flags register along with S3 = 1. The following pseudo-RTL descriptions give the equations for the status flag fetch logic for each flag:

PSEUDO-RTL DESCRIPTION

Status Flag Fetching Logic

```
for (j = 16 to 23) {
  Op[j]:StatInfo_3[1:0] = {Op[j]:StatVal[7],  Op[j]:S3} //OF
  Op[j]:StatInfo_2[4:0] = {Op[j]:StatVal[6:3],Op[j]:S3} //SF,ZF,AF,PF
  Op[j]:StatInfo_1[1:0] = {Op[j]:StatVal[2],  Op[j]:S3} //CF
  Op[j]:StatInfo_0[2:0] = {Op[j]:StatVal[1:0],Op[j]:S3} //EZF,ECF
}

FlgStatInfo_3[1:0] = {StatFlags[7],  1'b1} //OF
FlgStatInfo_2[4:0] = {StatFlags[6:3],1'b1} //SF,ZF,AF,PF
FlgStatInfo_1[1:0] = {StatFlags[2],  1'b1} //CF
FlgStatInfo_0[2:0] = {StatFlags[1:0],1'b1} //EZF,ECF

for (i = 0 to 3) {
  // i indexes flag group corresponding to StatMod[i]
  StatSel16_[i] =  Op16:StatMod[i]
  StatSel17_[i] = ~Op16:StatMod[i] & Op17:StatMod[i]
  StatSel18_[i] =
    ~Op16:StatMod[i] & ~Op17:StatMod[i] & Op18:StatMod[i]
  StatSel19_[i] =
    ~Op16:StatMod[i] ... ~Op18:StatMod[i] & Op19:StatMod[i]
  StatSel20_[i] =
    ~Op16:StatMod[i] ... ~Op19:StatMod[i] & Op20:StatMod[i]
  StatSel21_[i] =
    ~Op16:StatMod[i] ... ~Op20:StatMod[i] & Op21:StatMod[i]
  StatSel22_[i] =
    ~Op16:StatMod[i] ... ~Op21:StatMod[i] & Op22:StatMod[i]
  StatSel23_[i] =
    ~Op16:StatMod[i] ... ~Op22:StatMod[i] & Op23:StatMod[i]
  StatSelFlg_[i]=
    ~Op16:StatMod[i] ... ~Op22:StatMod[i] & ~Op23:StatMod[i]
}
continued on next page ...
```

Pseudo-RTL Description (cont.)

Status Flag Fetching Logic

```
StatInfo_3[1:0] =   {2{StatSel16_3}} & Op16:StatInfo_3[1:0] |
                    {2{StatSel17_3}} & Op17:StatInfo_3[1:0] |
                    {2{StatSel18_3}} & Op18:StatInfo_3[1:0] |
                    {2{StatSel19_3}} & Op19:StatInfo_3[1:0] |
                    {2{StatSel20_3}} & Op20:StatInfo_3[1:0] |
                    {2{StatSel21_3}} & Op21:StatInfo_3[1:0] |
                    {2{StatSel22_3}} & Op22:StatInfo_3[1:0] |
                    {2{StatSel23_3}} & Op23:StatInfo_3[1:0] |
                    {2{StatSelFlg_3}} & FlgStatInfo_3[1:0]

StatInfo_2[4:0] =   {5{StatSel16_2}} & Op16:StatInfo_2[4:0] |
                    {5{StatSel17_2}} & Op17:StatInfo_2[4:0] |
                    {5{StatSel18_2}} & Op18:StatInfo_2[4:0] |
                    {5{StatSel19_2}} & Op19:StatInfo_2[4:0] |
                    {5{StatSel20_2}} & Op20:StatInfo_2[4:0] |
                    {5{StatSel21_2}} & Op21:StatInfo_2[4:0] |
                    {5{StatSel22_2}} & Op22:StatInfo_2[4:0] |
                    {5{StatSel23_2}} & Op23:StatInfo_2[4:0] |
                    {5{StatSelFlg_2}} & FlgStatInfo_2[4:0]

StatInfo_1[1:0] =   {2{StatSel16_1}} & Op16:StatInfo_1[1:0] |
                    {2{StatSel17_1}} & Op17:StatInfo_1[1:0] |
                    {2{StatSel18_1}} & Op18:StatInfo_1[1:0] |
                    {2{StatSel19_1}} & Op19:StatInfo_1[1:0] |
                    {2{StatSel20_1}} & Op20:StatInfo_1[1:0] |
                    {2{StatSel21_1}} & Op21:StatInfo_1[1:0] |
                    {2{StatSel22_1}} & Op22:StatInfo_1[1:0] |
                    {2{StatSel23_1}} & Op23:StatInfo_1[1:0] |
                    {2{StatSelFlg_1}} & FlgStatInfo_1[1:0]

StatInfo_0[2:0] =   {3{StatSel16_0}} & Op16:StatInfo_0[2:0] |
                    {3{StatSel17_0}} & Op17:StatInfo_0[2:0] |
                    {3{StatSel18_0}} & Op18:StatInfo_0[2:0] |
                    {3{StatSel19_0}} & Op19:StatInfo_0[2:0] |
                    {3{StatSel20_0}} & Op20:StatInfo_0[2:0] |
                    {3{StatSel21_0}} & Op21:StatInfo_0[2:0] |
                    {3{StatSel22_0}} & Op22:StatInfo_0[2:0] |
                    {3{StatSel23_0}} & Op23:StatInfo_0[2:0] |
                    {3{StatSelFlg_0}} & FlgStatInfo_0[2:0]
```

continued on next page ...

Pseudo-RTL Description (cont.)

Status Flag Fetching Logic

```
// OF; SF,ZF,AF,PF; CF; EZF,ECF
Status[7:0] =
  {StatInfo_3[1],StatInfo_2[4:1],StatInfo_1[1],StatInfo_0[2:1]}

StatusV[3:0] =
  {StatInfo_3[0],StatInfo_2[0],StatInfo_1[0],StatInfo_0[0]}
```

CC-Dependent RegOp Synchronization

During each cycle, the four Ops within scheduler Row 3 are examined (for) — *awkward* whether any of them is a condition code dependent RegOp. If one is found, then the specific type of the RegOp is decoded to determine which groups of status flags are needed, and the Status valid bits are checked to determine whether all of those groups are, in fact, valid. Concurrently, bits Status[7:0] are blindly passed to the RUX execution unit.

If all of the required flag groups are currently valid, then the RegOp is allowed to advance into RUX pipeline Stage1, at least insofar as the status operand fetch is concerned. If the RegOp does not immediately advance into Stage1, though, then shifting of scheduler OpQuad3—and thus Opquad4-OpQuad5—are inhibited. If any of the required flag groups are not currently valid, then the RegOp is held up from advancing into RUX Stage1 and shifting of scheduler OpQuad3-OpQuad5 is inhibited.

If there is no unexecuted cc-dependent RegOp in scheduler OpQuad3, but there is a cc-dependent RegOp in RUX pipeline Stage0, then the RegOp is unconditionally held up in Stage0 until it also arrives in OpQuad3. If there is a cc-dependent RegOp in OpQuad3 that has not yet executed, but there is no cc-dependent RegOp in RUX Stage0 or there is an unexecuted cc-dependent RegOp in scheduler OpQuad4, then shifting of OpQuad3-OpQuad5 is inhibited.

There is an additional input called RUX_NoStatMod from the RUX unit pipeline Stage 1. RUX_NoStatMod indicates that the Op being executed there does not modify status flags despite it being marked as modifying status flags. This is necessary to handle certain architectural situations where a RegOp does not modify status flags for certain zero operand values. A cycle-delayed version, called NoStatMod, is used in control logic. The following pseudo-RTL description gives the equations for synchronizing or coordinating the execution of cc-dependent RegOps:

PSEUDO-RTL DESCRIPTION

CC-Dependent RegOp Synchronization Logic

```
CCDepInRUX_0 = (OpInfo_RUX_0(RegOp).Type[3:2] = 2'b01) & OpV_RUX_0

UnexecCCDepInQ3 = OP12:(RU & OpInfo(RegOp).Type[3:2]=2'b01 & ~S1) |
                  OP13:(RU & OpInfo(RegOp).Type[3:2]=2'b01 & ~S1) |
                  OP14:(RU & OpInfo(RegOp).Type[3:2]=2'b01 & ~S1) |
                  OP15:(RU & OpInfo(RegOp).Type[3:2]=2'b01 & ~S1)

if (~OpInfo_RUX_0(RegOp).Type[5])
  StatV = StatusV[1]  //need CF for ADC,SBB,RLC,RRC Ops

elseif (OpInfo_RUX_0(RegOp).Type[1:0] = 2'b10)
  StatV = StatusV[0]  //need EZF,ECF for MOVcc Op

else                 //need OF,...,CF for MOVcc,RDFLG,DAA,DAS Ops
  StatV = StatusV[3] & StatusV[2] & StatusV[1]

// keep track of when an unexecuted cc-dep RegOp
// is in Sched Op quad 3:

StrtExecCCDep = CCDepInRUX_0 & SC_AdvRUX0 & ~BumpRUX

// keep track of when an unexecuted cc-dep RegOp
// is in Sched Op quad 4
if (LdEntry4 | StrtExecCCDep | SC_EAbort)  // enabled flip-flop
  UnexecCCDepInQ4 = LdEntry4 & UnexecCCDepInQ3 &
                    ~StrtExecCCDep & ~SC_EAbort
// hold copy of status flag values at input to
// RUX execution unit:
SC_HoldStatus = UnexecCCDepInQ4

// hold RegOp execution if ...:
StatusInvld_RUX = (CCDepInRUX_0 & ~UnexecCCDepInQ4) &
  ~(UnexecCCDepInQ3 & StatV & ~NoStatMod)

// hold Op quad from shifting out of Sched quad 3 if ...:
HoldOpQ3 = UnexecCCDepInQ3 & ~(CCDepInRUX_0 & StatV & ~NoStatMod) |
           UnexecCCDepInQ4
```

BRCOND Op Resolution Logic

In the "Branch Resolution Logic" section of Chapter 2, we explained that a BRCOND Op must be resolved as to whether the associated conditional branch instruction was correctly predicted or not while the BRCOND Op is outstanding *and* before it reaches the bottom row of the scheduler's buffer. By way of review, we will summarize that discussion before presenting the pseudo-RTL description which gives the equations for the BRCOND Op resolution logic. We also recommend that you review the placement of the Branch Resolution Unit (a.k.a. the branch resolution logic) in Figure 2.2 on page 69 and in Figure 2.9 on page 130.

BRCOND Op resolution is done for each branch operation, in order, at a rate of up to one per cycle. The appropriate set of status flag values is used to determine if the condition code specified within the BRCOND Op is TRUE or FALSE when the status flag handling logic obtains the appropriate status for the next unresolved BRCOND Op. If valid values for the required status flags are not yet all available, then resolution of the BRCOND Op is held up.

If the branch condition is FALSE, the BRCOND Op was incorrectly predicted and an appropriate restart signal is immediately asserted to restart the upper portion of the processor at the correct next program address (i.e., the instruction fetch and decode portion—see Figure 2.4 on page 87). The correct address is either the branch target address or next sequential address, whichever was not predicted.

If the branch was correctly predicted, then nothing happens other than BRCOND Op resolution processing advances on to the next BRCOND Op. The branch resolution logic is concerned with resolving these issues.

With this review as background, we will now give some additional, more detailed comments, to aid in understanding the pseudo-RTL description of the resolution process.

During each cycle, the four Ops within scheduler OpQuad4 are examined for whether any of them (at most one) is a BRCOND Op. If one is found, then the Condition Code field of that Op entry is decoded to select one of thirty-two condition values and associated valid bits. The value and validity of the selected condition are then used to inhibit scheduler shifting of OpQuad4-OpQuad5 or to assert pipeline restart signals when appropriate.

In the case that a BRCOND Op is found to be mispredicted, a pipeline restart is required. The appropriate restart signal is asserted based on whether the BRCOND Op has been produced by the decoders or is from an OpQuad Sequence. If the BRCOND Op is from an OpQuad Sequence, the signal also depends on whether it is from an internal (OpQuad ROM-based) or external (external memory-based) sequence. In addition to generating the restart signal, an appropriate x86 instruction address or OpQuad Sequence vector address must be generated.

For the benefit of the logic handling synchronization between non-abortable RegOps and preceding BRCOND Ops, a record is also maintained of the occurrence of a mispredicted BRCOND Op until an abort cycle occurs via the SC_MisPred flip-flop. Further, the existence of an outstanding mispredicted BRCOND Op is used to hold up the loading of new OpQuads into the scheduler from the "restarted" decoders until the abort cycle occurs.

In the case that a BRCOND Op was correctly predicted, the only action taken is to set the BRCOND Op's S3 State bit. The following pseudo-RTL equations describe all of this logic. Reference is made below to the DTF and SSTF signals used to indicate pending data breakpoint and single-step traps, respectively. There is also a signal called MDD ("multiple decode disable") which can be used for silicon debugging to prevent more than one instruction from being decoded into each OpQuad. The following pseudo-RTL description gives the equations for the BRCOND Op resolution logic:

Pseudo-RTL Description

BRCOND Op Resolution Logic

```
BRCOND16 = OP16:(Type=SpecOp & OpInfo(SpecOp).Type=BRCOND & ~S3)
BRCOND17 = OP17:(Type=SpecOp & OpInfo(SpecOp).Type=BRCOND & ~S3)
BRCOND18 = OP18:(Type=SpecOp & OpInfo(SpecOp).Type=BRCOND & ~S3)
BRCOND19 = OP19:(Type=SpecOp & OpInfo(SpecOp).Type=BRCOND & ~S3)

BRCONDInQ4 = (BRCOND16 | BRCOND17 | BRCOND18 | BRCOND19) & OPQ4:OpQV

CondCode[4:0] = {5{BRCOND16}} & Op16:OpInfo(SpecOp).CC[4:0] |
                {5{BRCOND17}} & Op17:OpInfo(SpecOp).CC[4:0] |
                {5{BRCOND18}} & Op18:OpInfo(SpecOp).CC[4:0] |
                {5{BRCOND19}} & Op19:OpInfo(SpecOp).CC[4:0]

CondV = switch (CondCode[4:1])
          case 0000:  1'b1
          case 0001:  StatusV[0]
          case 0010:  StatusV[0]
          case 0011:  StatusV[0] & StatusV[2]
          case 0100:  StatusV[0]
          case 0101:  StatusV[0]
          case 0110:  StatusV[0]
          case 0111:  StatusV[0] & StatusV[2]
          case 1000:  StatusV[3]
          case 1001:  StatusV[1]
          case 1010:  StatusV[2]
          case 1011:  StatusV[2] & StatusV[1]
          case 1100:  StatusV[2]
          case 1101:  StatusV[2]
          case 1110:  StatusV[3] & StatusV[2]
          case 1111:  StatusV[3] & StatusV[2]

// any active hardware interrupt requests?:
IP = SI_NMIP | SI_INTRP
```

continued on next page ...

Pseudo-RTL Description

BRCOND Op Resolution Logic

```
CondVal = switch (CondCode[4:1])
          case 0000: CondCode[0] ^ 1'b1
          case 0001: CondCode[0] ^ Status[0]
          case 0010: CondCode[0] ^ Status[1]
          case 0011: Status[1] | (CondCode[0] ^ ~Status[5])
          case 0100: CondCode[0] ^ (~Status[1] & ~IP & ~(DTF|SSTF|MDD))
          case 0101: CondCode[0] ^ (~Status[1] & ~IP & ~(DTF|SSTF|MDD))
          case 0110: CondCode[0] ^ (~Status[0] & ~IP & ~(DTF|SSTF|MDD))
          case 0111: ~Status[1] & ~IP & ~(DTF|SSTF|MDD) &
                     (CondCode[0] ^ Status[5])
          case 1000: CondCode[0] ^ Status[7]
          case 1001: CondCode[0] ^ Status[2]
          case 1010: CondCode[0] ^ Status[5]
          case 1011: CondCode[0] ^ (Status[5] | Status[2])
          case 1100: CondCode[0] ^ Status[6]
          case 1101: CondCode[0] ^ Status[3]
          case 1110: CondCode[0] ^  (Status[7] ^ Status[6])
          case 1111: CondCode[0] ^ ((Status[7] ^ Status[6]) | Status[5])

// the definitions of CondCode[4:1] is as follows
// (bit 0 flips the sense):

True    4'b0000
ECF     4'b0001
EZF     4'b0010
SZnZF   4'b0011
MSTRZ   4'b0100
STRZ    4'b0101
MSTRC   4'b0110
STRZnZF 4'b0111
OF      4'b1000
CF      4'b1001
ZF      4'b1010
CvZF    4'b1011
SF      4'b1100
PF      4'b1101
SxOF    4'b1110
SxOvZF  4'b1111
```

continued on next page...

Pseudo-RTL Description (cont.)

BRCOND Op Resolution Logic

```
// hold Op quad from shifting out of Sched quad 4 if ...:
HoldOpQ4A = BRCONDInQ4 & ~CondV

SC_Resolve = BRCONDInQ4 & CondV & ~SC_MisPred & ~NoStatMod & ~OPQ4:Emcode

// remember resolution of a BRCOND Op in quad 4:
Resolved = ~LdEntry4 & (SC_Resolve | Resolved)// simple flip-flop

// terminate REP MOVS OpQuad Sequence loop if almost done:
// use CS "D" bit supplied by RUX to aid termination in 16-bit case
TermMovs = BRCONDInQ4 & CondV & ~NoStatMod & ~SC_MisPred &
            // CondCode=MSTRC ... | CondCode=MSTRZ ...
            ((CondCode[4:1] = 4'b0110) & (OP19:DestVal[15:0] = 16'h5) &
             ((OP19:DestVal[31:16] = 16'h0) | RUX_D) |
             (CondCode[4:1] = 'b0100) (OP23:DestVal[15:0] = 16'h6) &
             ((OP23:DestVal[31:16] = 16'b0) | RUX_D))

TermedMOVS = ~LdEntry4 & (TermMOVS || TermedMOVS)// simple flip-flop

SC_TermMOVS = TermMOVS | TermedMOVS

// get OpQuad Sequence or instruction vector address for
// handling mispredicted branch
BrVecAddr[31:0] = {32{BRCOND16}} & Op16:DestVal[31:0] |
   {32{BRCOND17}} & Op17:DestVal[31:0] |
   {32{BRCOND18}} & Op18:DestVal[31:0] |
   {32{BRCOND19}} & Op19:DestVal[31:0]

// supply old RAS TOS ptr to decoders for restoring
// if BRCOND Op mispredicted:
SC_OldRASPtr[2:0] = OpQ4:RASPtr[2:0]

// supply old BPT info to decoders for restoring
// if BRCOND Op mispredicted:
SC_OldBPTInfo[14:0] = OpQ4:BPTInfo[14:0]

// supply either fault PC or alternate branch address to
// decoders if BRCOND Op mispredicted:
SC_RestartAddr[31:0] = ExcpAbort ? OpQ5:FaultPC :
   (OpQ4:Emcode ? OpQ4:FaultPC[31:0] :
        BrVecAddr[31:0])
```

continued on next page ...

Pseudo-RTL Description (cont.)

BRCOND Op Resolution Logic

```
// initiate restart if BRCOND Op mispredicted:
BrVec2Emc = SC_Resolve & ~CondVal & OpQ4:Emcode
BrVec2Dec = SC_Resolve & ~CondVal & OpQ4:~Emcode

// remember misprediction:
if (SC_Resolve | SC_Abort)
  SC_MisPred = ~SC_Abort & (~CondVal | SC_MisPred) // enabled flip-flops

// mark BRCOND Op as Completed if correctly predicted:
// enabled flip-flops
if (SC_Resolve & CondVal & BRCOND16) Op16:S3 = 1'b1
if (SC_Resolve & CondVal & BRCOND17) Op17:S3 = 1'b1
if (SC_Resolve & CondVal & BRCOND18) Op18:S3 = 1'b1
if (SC_Resolve & CondVal & BRCOND19) Op19:S3 = 1'b1
```

A BRCOND Op that is being successfully resolved may sit in scheduler OpQuad3 for more than one cycle due to OpQuad4 and OpQuad5 not being able to shift and thus OpQuad4 is not able to shift down. During this time SC_Resolve = 1 and one of the BrVec2XXX signals remains asserted for the entire time, versus for just the first cycle. This is all right since the x86 instruction fetch and decode or OpQuad Sequence fetch areas of the machine which are in the process of being restarted will simply keep on restarting each cycle until the BrVec2XXX signal deasserts. All of the other associated signals such as the vector address will maintain their proper values throughout this time.

Nonabortable RegOp Execution Synchronization Logic

During each cycle, the four Ops within scheduler OpQuad4 are examined for whether any of them is a nonabortable RegOp. If one is found, then it is checked whether there are any preceding mispredicted BRCOND Ops. Due to the OpQuad Sequence coding constraints, any preceding BRCOND Ops must be in a lower scheduler OpQuad (i.e. ,OpQuad5) and thus have all been resolved.

If no such mispredicted BRCOND Ops exist, then the RegOp is allowed to advance into RUX pipeline Stage1. If there is no unexecuted nonabortable RegOp in OpQuad4, but there is a nonabortable RegOp in RUX pipeline Stage0, then the RegOp is unconditionally held up in Stage0. If there is a nonabortable RegOp in OpQuad4 that has not yet executed, but there is no nonabortable RegOp in RUX Stage0, then shifting of

OpQuad4 (and OpQuad5) is inhibited. The pseudo-RTL descriptions that give the equations which describe this logic follow:

PSEUDO-RTL DESCRIPTION

Nonabortable RegOp Execution Synchronization Logic

```
NonAbInRUX_0 = (OpInfo_RUX_0(RegOp).Type[5:2] = 4'b1110) & OpV_RUX_0

UnexecNonAbInQ4 = Op16(RU & OpInfo(RegOp).Type[5:2]=4'b1110 & ~S1) |
                  Op17(RU & OpInfo(RegOp).Type[5:2]=4'b1110 & ~S1) |
                  Op18(RU & OpInfo(RegOp).Type[5:2]=4'b1110 & ~S1) |
                  Op19(RU & OpInfo(RegOp).Type[5:2]=4'b1110 & ~S1)

// hold RegOp execution if ...:
NonAbSync = NonAbInRUX_0 & (~UnexecNonAbInQ4 | SC_MisPred | "trap pending")

// hold Op quad from shifting out of Sched quad 4 if ...:
HoldOpQ4B = UnexecNonAbInQ4
```

SELF-MODIFYING CODE SUPPORT LOGIC

Logically, in the scheduler, a detection of self-modifying code is treated as a trap and it factors into the "trap pending" logic. The Store Queue provides the physical address of the store it is preparing to commit. Most of the bits of this address are compared against the instruction address or addresses, if the instructions were from two different (logically consecutive) cache lines of each scheduler OpQuad. If any OpQuad addresses match, then there may be a write to an instruction which has already been fetched, decoded, and is now present in the scheduler—i.e., there must be self-modifying code. Accordingly, the scheduler is then flushed and the fetch/decode process is restarted from the last committed instruction, namely, the modifying instruction.

The following equations describe this functionality. Not all of the address bits need to be compared. A partial-address comparison reduces logic and improves speed while resulting in a very low incidence of "false" matches. In particular, several of the most significant bits and a few least significant bits are not compared. STQ_LinAddr[11:5] are untranslated address bits and thus are the same as STQ_PhysAddr[11:5]. The logic is conceptually only doing a comparison between physical address bits.

PSEUDO-RTL DESCRIPTION

Self-Modifying Code

```
for (i=0; i < 5; ++i) {
    Match1st =
        (STQ_LinAddr[11:5] = OpQi:Smc1stAddr) &
        (STQ_PhysAddr[19:12] = OpQi:Smc1stPg)
    Match2nd =
        (STQ_LinAddr(11:5) = OpQi:Smc2ndAddr) &
        (STQ_PhysAddr(19:12) = OpQi:Smc2ndPg)
    MatchSMC[i] = (Match1st | Match2nd) & OpQi:OpQV
}

SmcHit =
    "STQ store is not a special memory access" &
    ("self-modifying code detected" |
    MatchSMC[0] | MatchSMC[1] | MatchSMC[2] |
    MatchSMC[3] | MatchSMC[4]);
```

THE OCU: AN EXPANDED DESCRIPTION

The OCU operates in conjunction with the scheduler and generally operates on the Ops within the bottom two rows of the scheduler. Its principal function is to commit the results of the execution of the Ops within the bottom OpQuad and then to retire the OpQuad from the scheduler. The OCU also handles mispredicted BRCOND Ops and various types of exceptions by initiating abort cycles for them.

> **DESIGN NOTE**
>
> Committing and Retiring OpQuads (revisited)
>
> One of the differences between committing the results of an Op and the retiring of an OpQuad from the scheduler in the K6 3D is that the actions of commitment and retirement may or may not happen on the same cycle. If some, but not all, of the Ops in an OpQuad can be committed in a given cycle, whatever can be committed is committed. The OpQuad is not retired and removed from the scheduler until all its Ops are committed, so the Ops that were committed will still be in the scheduler. Typically the commitment of all of the Ops in an OpQuad and the retirement of the OpQuad all happen simultaneously.
>
> It is important to note that when result values (both the register value and status flag bits) of an Op are committed, the corresponding byte marks and status modification bits are cleared in the scheduler's Op entry.

There are many types of results or state changes that can stem from the execution of an Op. The principal types of changes are abortable (i.e., they can be speculatively executed and backed out of later) and encompass the following:

1. general register results.
2. status flag results.
3. memory writes.

We include in "general register results" the possibility of partial register modifications and "superset" register dependencies that arise from register forwarding being supported from only one source at a time.[31]

All other state changes are nonabortable (i.e., they cannot be backed out of once executed) and are limited to being the result of RegOp executions. These include changes to:

1. segment registers.
2. non-status EFLAGS bits.
3. special registers, both architectural registers and K6 3D microarchitectural registers.

With respect to general register commitment, the OCU only looks at one OpQuad at a time. It looks at OpQuad5 in the bottom row if it is not all

---

[31] All needed bytes must come from either one scheduler entry, a result bus, or from the architectural register file.

committed. Otherwise, it looks at OpQuad4 in the second from the bottom row. This is necessary to avoid deadlock situations in which OpQuad3-related or OpQuad4-related synchronization logic is preventing shifts of OpQuad4 and OpQuad5. These situations result from an Op in OpQuad3 or OpQuad4 waiting directly or indirectly for an Op in OpQuad4 to execute or commit before it can execute. Status commitment is always from OpQuad5 (since full forwarding of individual status flag bits is provided). To achieve better performance, store commitment is only loosely coupled with register commitment, (i.e., the OCU can start committing StOps in OpQuad4 while still committing register results from OpQuad5). Given one store commit per clock, this lets the store commit get a head start which is useful when there is more than one StOp in an OpQuad.

In general it is possible for the OCU to commit the state changes of all four Ops in OpQuad5 in one cycle. However, this may take additional cycles. If all the Ops of an OpQuad have been committed or are being successfully committed, then the OpQuad is retired from the scheduler at the end of the current cycle. Otherwise, as many changes as possible are committed during the current cycle and the process is repeated on successive cycles until all changes have been committed.

DESIGN NOTE

Abortable, Permanent, and Nonabortable State Changes

Abortable state changes are supported by the scheduler and the Store Queue through the general technique of temporarily storing (a) register and status results in the scheduler Op entries and (b) memory write data in Store Queue entries until the associated Ops are committed and retired. Permanent state changes are made during Op commitment when it is safe and definite for the changes to be made. While these new state values reside in the scheduler and the Store Queue, they are forwarded to dependent Ops as necessary. Nonabortable state changes, in contrast, occur immediately during RegOp execution and the responsibility or burden is placed on OpQuad Sequences to ensure sufficient synchronization with surrounding operations.

COMMITMENT CONSTRAINTS

The commitment of the results of the execution of an Op is constrained by:

1. the Op's execution state—it must be completed.
2. the status of any preceding faultable Ops—these Ops must be completed, which implies that they are fault-free.

3. the status of any preceding conditional branch Op—the associated BRCOND Op's State must be *completed* (versus *unissued*), which implies that it was correctly predicted.

In the case of StOps which generated a memory write there is the additional constraint that only one write can be committed per cycle from the Store Queue into the D-Cache. However, StOps can commit despite preceding not completed RegOps since RegOps can never result in a fault exception.

DESIGN NOTE

Independent Commitments

The commitment of register results, status flag results, and memory writes are performed independently. For Ops that have multiple results (e.g., a RegOp with both a register result and a status flag result, or a STUPD Op with a register result and a memory write), the various results will not necessarily be committed simultaneously. The commitment of one type of state change can generally get ahead of or behind the commitment of another type of state change. The overall commitment of an Op is considered to occur when the last of all the necessary result commitments associated with that Op occurs. Finally, the commitment of results from multiple Ops is performed without regard to whether the Ops are part of one x86 instruction or separate x86 instructions.

Typically the OCU will commit and retire an OpQuad from the scheduler every cycle. It has the capability to commit up to four register and four status results per cycle and one memory write per cycle. An OpQuad can sit unretired at the bottom of the scheduler for more than one cycle only if it contains multiple memory write StOps or if some of the Ops are sufficiently delayed in their execution that they are not yet completed.

If an Op in the bottom OpQuad needs to be faulted, then all of the succeeding Ops (i.e., Ops higher in the scheduler) are inhibited from being committed. Once all preceding Ops (i.e., Ops lower in the scheduler) within the OpQuad have been committed or are being successfully committed, then the OCU initiates an abort cycle. The abort cycle flushes the entire scheduler and all the execution units of all outstanding Ops.

Concurrent with the abort cycle, the OCU vectors the machine to one of two possible OpQuad Sequence entry point addresses—either the OCU default handler address or an OCU alternate handler address; see Figure 2.10 on page 139. The setting of these addresses is supported by the LDDHA Op (LoaD Default Handler Address) and the LDAHA Op (LoaD Alternate Handler Address). Both of these Ops are loaded into the scheduler in a *completed* State and are recognized and "executed" by the OCU

LDDHA, load default handler address

LDAHA, load alternate handler address

reset OpQuad Sequence

when they reach the bottom of the scheduler. The default fault handler address is initialized by the Reset OpQuad Sequence and the alternate handler address is specified by OpQuad Sequences for some instructions and some exception processing cases.

FAULT OPS AND LDSTOPS WITH PENDING FAULTS

Only certain types of Ops can be faulted, namely LdOps, StOps (except for LEA Ops), and FAULT Ops. For a LdOp or StOp, faults are determined by the second stage of the LU or SU execution pipe respectively. If a fault is detected, the LdStOp is held up in pipe Stage2 indefinitely until either an associated or an unrelated abort cycle flushes it. This results in the characteristic that completed LdStOps are guaranteed fault-free.

The OCU is able to differentiate between a faulting LdStOp and a LdStOp that simply has not yet completed. This is done using signals from the LU and the SU indicating when a faulting Op is stuck in their respective second pipe stages. When the OCU attempts to commit the next uncompleted LdStOp and the associated execution unit is signaling that it contains a faulting Op, then these two Ops must be one and the same. Thus, this Op has encountered a fault. If, instead, the associated execution unit's signal is not asserted, then nothing definite can be determined. In this case, the OCU must continue to wait for the LdStOp to complete.

FAULT Ops are special Ops that are handled somewhat differently by the OCU since they do not execute. They are loaded into the scheduler in an *unissued* state and unconditionally always fault. The handling, though, with respect to commitment and abortion of surrounding Ops is the same as for LdOps and StOps. The *not-completed* state of a FAULT Op is key in causing all of this handling to fall out "naturally"—i.e., without explicit special logic.

DEBUG TRAPS AND SEQUENTIAL AND BRANCH TARGET LIMIT VIOLATIONS

In addition to faults on specific Ops, the OCU also recognizes various debug traps. As discussed in the the section titled "Status Flags, Faults, Traps, Interrupts, and Abort Cycles" beginning on page 83, traps are recognized at the end of the instigating instruction. In the case of instructions decoded to an OpQuad Sequence, the traps are accumulated and remembered up until the end of an OpQuad Sequence. Traps are processed on the first OpQuad of the next instruction, which may or may not come along to the OCU in the next clock. This is done so that the FaultPC of the next instruction can be used as the value of the desired TrapPC. Recall that OpQuad sequences end with an "ERET" action field value within the sequencing field of the last OpQuad of the sequence. When such an OpQuad is retired, any accumulated traps are then recorded as now being a pending trap exception or waiting for the first valid OpQuad of the next instruction to come along.

Lastly, the OCU recognizes both sequential and branch target limit violation conditions which, while occurring with just certain Ops within an OpQuad, is associated with the OpQuad as a whole. This is done since the instruction(s) associated with the OpQuad are partially or wholly part of the end of the current code segment limit. If such a violation is detected, it unconditionally causes an abort cycle to be initiated as if a fault was recognized on the first Op within the OpQuad. This bit of OCU functionality handles both sequential and hardware-decoded branch target code segment limit violations.

ABORTS FOR MISPREDICTED BRCOND OPS

While the OCU is primarily concerned with all the types of Ops that generate abortable state changes, it is also concerned with mispredicted BRCOND Ops. BRCOND Ops are resolved before they reach the bottom of the scheduler and, when mispredictions are detected, the instruction fetch and decode portions of the machine are immediately reset and restarted from the proper instruction address. Therefore, when an OpQuad containing a mispredicted BRCOND Op reaches the bottom of the scheduler and the OCU tries to commit it, the OCU initiates an abort cycle to flush the scheduler and all the execution units of all the older Ops, but does not also restart the upper portion of the processor. This abort cycle also allows new OpQuads to start loading into the scheduler and Ops to immediately be issued.

Aborts for mispredicted BRCOND Ops are similar to aborts for Op faults. For example, for mispredicted BRCOND Ops the commitment of all following Ops is inhibited, pending initiation of an abort cycle. Furthermore, the mispredicted BRCOND Op abort cycle is not initiated until all preceding Ops within the OpQuad, relative to the BRCOND Op, have been committed or are being successfully committed. However, mispredicted BRCOND Op aborts and Op fault aborts are different in that no vectoring to an OpQuad Sequence is initiated for mispredicted BRCOND Op aborts. As mentioned earlier, vectoring to an OpQuad Sequence in the case of a BRCOND Op from an OpQuad Sequence or restarting the x86 instruction fetch and decode in the case of a BRCOND Op hardware decode of a conditional branch instruction has already occurred. If a BRCOND Op is correctly predicted when it reaches the bottom of the scheduler, no action is necessary to "commit" the Op.

The BRCOND Op can be viewed as being either trivially committed or aborted by the OCU—the choice of action is based on the BRCOND Op's scheduler Op entry State. If a BRCOND Op was correctly predicted when it is resolved, its scheduler Op entry State is changed to 'b1111 (effectively completed). However, if it was mispredicted it is left in its initial State of 'b0000. Thus, the prediction status of a BRCOND Op is implied by whether it is completed or not. Treating the state of a BRCOND Op in this way is key in allowing the commitment and abortion of surrounding Ops to occur without explicit special logic.

THE TIMING OF RESULT COMMITMENTS

The actual timing of Op result commitments is relatively simple and can be viewed as happening during the latter part of the commit cycle. In a typical case, an OpQuad reaches the bottom row of the scheduler during some cycle, is committed during that cycle, and is retired from the scheduler at the end of the cycle. During this cycle, while results are being written to the corresponding architectural registers, operand values continue to be forwarded to all dependent Ops from the scheduler (versus from the architectural registers).

MEMORY WRITES

The commit process for memory writes is actually a two-stage process implemented in the form of a two-stage write commit pipeline (see Figure 2.20 on page 169). The first stage of this pipe corresponds to the OCU's commit cycle for a StOp. As far as the OCU is concerned, the StOp has been committed when it enters the second stage of this pipeline (this includes the case of the StOp possibly having been retired from the scheduler). The StOp must enter the second write commit pipe stage before or concurrent with retirement of the associated OpQuad from the scheduler. If a StOp cannot enter this second stage, then the StOp is viewed as not yet being committable and retirement of the OpQuad is held up.

THE TIMING OF ABORTS

When the OCU initiates an abort cycle due to an Op fault, the abort signal SC_Abort and its associated OpQuad Sequence vector address are asserted during the commit and retire cycle of the OpQuad containing the faulting Op. During the next cycle the scheduler will have been flushed and the fetch of the first or target OpQuad from the OpQuad Sequence is started. In the case of internal K6 microarchitectural OpQuad Sequences, the scheduler will be empty for exactly this one cycle.

In the case of aborts for mispredicted BRCOND Ops, the abort signal is also asserted during the commit and retire cycle of the associated OpQuad. Since instruction fetch and decode has already been restarted, the scheduler can be reloaded with a new OpQuad as early as the very next cycle. In this case, the scheduler will typically not sit empty for even one cycle.

DESIGN NOTE
Multiple Ops Within an OpQuad Requiring Abort Cycle Processing When the OCU recognizes multiple Ops within an OpQuad as requiring abort cycle processing, it chooses the first such Op and initiates appropriate abort actions with respect to that Op, at the appropriate time for that Op. The following Ops requiring an abort are flushed along with all other Ops following the chosen Op.

The following sections detail each aspect of OCU operation. It begins by discussing issues that arise for the various types of Ops that can produce the abortable state changes identified at the beginning of the current section, namely:

1. general register changes produced by all RegOps, LdOps, some StOps (LEA and STUPD), LIMM Ops, and LDK Ops.

2. status flag changes produced by RegOps.

3. memory writes produced by memory-writing StOps.

GENERAL REGISTER COMMITMENT

Probably the most obvious function of the OCU is to manage and control the commitment of register result values to the architectural register file. Such values are generated by most types of Ops, e.g., general register changes result from RegOps, LdOps, LIMM Ops, LDKxx Ops, and STUPD StOps. During any given cycle, the OCU examines OpQuad5 and possible OpQuad4 as described earlier in this section to determine which, if any, of the register results can be written into the architectural register file. This is done during the latter part of the cycle via four independent write ports. Each of these writes is performed based on the associated register byte marks, DestBM[2.0], from the appropriate scheduler Op entry. This process applies equally to the architectural registers and to the K6 3D's temporary microarchitectural registers. If an Op is not yet completed and committable, then the associated register file write is inhibited for this cycle.

> **DESIGN NOTE**
>
> Clearing Byte Marks (Part 1)
>
> If an Op is of a type which conceptually does not generate a register result, then the byte marks will be all clear and the register number possibly undefined. This results in no bytes being modified during the register file write. If t0 is specified as the destination register for an Op, the byte marks will again be all clear. In both of these cases the byte marks were forced to 3'b000 when the Op was loaded into the scheduler. See the K6 3D Design Note, "Clearing Byte Marks (Part 2)," below.

MULTIPLE SIMULTANEOUS FULL AND PARTIAL WRITES

In general, when there are multiple enabled file writes, the possibility of contention—in the form of multiple simultaneous writes to the same register—exists. The desired result is that the youngest write succeeds and the other, older writes are inhibited or effectively ignored. Achieving this result is handled within the register file itself, separate from the OCU's control of the register commitment process. It is based simply on the presented register numbers and associated write enables to the register file.

contention resolution logic

Further, if the contending writes are such that the older writes modify register bytes which are not modified by the youngest write, then the effective register file write must be of the appropriate combination of bytes from each of the possible source Ops. For example, if the first (oldest) Op modifies bytes {3,2,1,0}, the second Op modifies bytes {1,0}, and the third (youngest) Op modifies byte {1}, then the actual register file write takes bytes {3,2} from the first Op, byte {0} from the second Op, and byte {1} from the third Op. This effect is handled locally by the register file's write control logic. The contention resolution or prioritization logic operates on the basis of individual bytes instead of 32-bit words.

In addition, the nine "match with operand XXsrcY" signals associated with a scheduler Op entry must be forced to indicate no match at the same time that the DestBM bits within that Op entry are about to be cleared (see the section titled "Dynamic Fields OprndMatch_XXsrcY" beginning on page 212. This is due to the pipelined nature of the register operand fetch process within the scheduler. The DestBM bits of an Op entry are used in both stages of this process and must be consistent across both cycles.

Clearing Byte Marks (Part 2)

The write enable signals for all four Ops are generated in parallel. For each Op, if it is completed and all preceding Ops are completed (which includes no FAULT OPs and mispredicted BRCOND Ops), and all other "preceding" conditions that can inhibit commitment (e.g., a pending trap exception from the preceding x86 instruction), are inactive, then the associated write enable is asserted. Further, the associated DestBM bits are cleared to reflect the fact that the scheduler entry for this Op no longer needs to provide a register value to dependent Ops. Such values may now be obtained from the register file. Clearing the DestBM field is also necessary in the case of partial register writes since a dependent Op will be held up in a pipe Stage 0 until it can obtain more or all the bytes of the register from the register file if it cannot obtain all its required bytes from this Op. See the K6 3D Design Note, "Clearing Byte Marks (Part 1)," above.

As discussed in the "Register Renaming" section later in this chapter, Op register writes may also take place from OpQuad4 when all the Ops in OpQuad5 have completed. This is accomplished through the use of a 2:1 multiplexer between OpQuad4 and OpQuad5 and by generalizing the RegOp write enable logic to consider either the four Ops in OpQuad5 or the four Ops in OpQuad4. The Ops of the selected OpQuad are renamed OpA through OpD in place of Op0 through Op3 or Op4 through Op7.

Continuous Numbering of Ops

Sometimes the twenty-four Ops in the scheduler are numbered continuously from Op0 to Op23. Op0 corresponds to the *youngest* Op (i.e., at the top of the scheduler) and Op23 corresponds to the *oldest* Op (i.e., at the bottom of the scheduler). When this is done, Op0 corresponds to OpQuad0[Op3], Op2 to OpQuad0[Op2], Op3 to OpQuad0[Op1], Op4 to OpQuad0[Op0], Op5 to OpQuad1[Op3], Op6 to OpQuad1[Op2], and so on with Op23 corresponding to OpQuad5[Op0]. Note that this numbering scheme is similar to the numbering of OpQuads from OpQuad0 to OpQuad5 and is in contrast to the numbering of Ops within an OpQuad from 0 to 3, where Op0 is the first (and oldest) Op in the OpQuad and Op3 is the last (and youngest) Op in the OpQuad.

The following pseudo-RTL description summarizes the register file write enable equations and the modified DestBM and "match with operand XXsrcY" equations for each Op of the bottom two OpQuads of the scheduler, where Op0 is the oldest Op and Op3 is the youngest Op. These equations ensure the in-order commitment of register results, although not necessarily the simultaneous commitment of these results.

PSEUDO-RTL DESCRIPTION

Register File Write Enable

```
RegCmtSel = Op0:S3 & Op1:S3 & Op2:S3 & Op3:S3 &
    (Op0:DestBM = 3'b0) & (Op1:DestBM = 3'b0) &
    (Op2:DestBM = 3'b0) & (Op3:DestBM = 3'b0)

OpA = RegCmtSel ? Op4 : Op0
OpB = RegCmtSel ? Op5 : Op1
OpC = RegCmtSel ? Op6 : Op2
OpD = RegCmtSel ? Op7 : Op3

CmtInh = OpQ5:LimViol | "trap pending"

RegCmtInh = CmtInh | RegCmtSel & (OpQ4:LimViol | ~StCmtSel[2] | SetTrapPend)

WrEnbl0 = ~(RegCmtSel ? OpQ4:LimViol : OpQ5:LimViol) & OpA:S3
WrEnbl1 = ~(RegCmtSel ? OpQ4:LimViol : OpQ5:LimViol) & OpA:S3 & OpB:S3
WrEnbl2 = ~(RegCmtSel ? OpQ4:LimViol : OpQ5:LimViol) &
          OpA:S3 & OpB:S3 & OpC:S3
WrEnbl3 = ~(RegCmtSel ? OpQ4:LimViol : OpQ5:LimViol) &
          OpA:S3 & OpB:S3 & OpC:S3 & OpD:S3

// enabled flip-flops:
if (WrEnbl0)              Op0:DestBM = 3'b0
if (WrEnbl1)              Op1:DestBM = 3'b0
if (WrEnbl2)              Op2:DestBM = 3'b0
if (WrEnbl3)              Op3:DestBM = 3'b0
if (WrEnbl0 & RegCmtSel)  Op4:DestBM = 3'b0
if (WrEnbl1 & RegCmtSel)  Op5:DestBM = 3'b0
if (WrEnbl2 & RegCmtSel)  Op6:DestBM = 3'b0
if (WrEnbl3 & RegCmtSel)  Op7:DestBM = 3'b0
```

continued on the next page ...

Pseudo-RTL Description (cont.)

Register File Write Enable

```
// dynamic field flip flops
Op0:"effective match with Operand XXsrcY" =
  Op0:"match with Operand XXsrcY" & ~WrEnbl0
Op1:"effective match with Operand XXsrcY" =
  Op1:"match with Operand XXsrcY" & ~WrEnbl1
Op2:"effective match with Operand XXsrcY" =
  Op2:"match with Operand XXsrcY" & ~WrEnbl2
Op3:"effective match with Operand XXsrcY" =
  Op3:"match with Operand XXsrcY" & ~WrEnbl3
Op4:"effective match with Operand XXsrcY" =
  Op4:"match with Operand XXsrcY" & ~(WrEnbl0 & RegCmtSel)
Op5:"effective match with Operand XXsrcY" =
  Op5:"match with Operand XXsrcY" & ~(WrEnbl1 & RegCmtSel)
Op6:"effective match with Operand XXsrcY" =
  Op6:"match with Operand XXsrcY" & ~(WrEnbl2 & RegCmtSel)
Op7:"effective match with Operand XXsrcY" =
  Op7:"match with Operand XXsrcY" & ~(WrEnbl3 & RegCmtSel)
```

STATUS FLAG COMMITMENT

The second function of the OCU is to manage and control the commitment of status flag result values, as generated by status flag modifying RegOps (a.k.a. ".cc" RegOps) to the architectural status flags register. Unlike the commitment of register results, none of the four groups of status results within the bottom OpQuad are written into EFLAGS until the OpQuad is about to be either retired or aborted. In the meantime, full forwarding of individual status flag values is performed as needed. In the normal case, when all the Ops within the OpQuad have been fully committed or are being successfully committed, then the cumulative or overall result of all four status results is written into EFLAGS at the end of the cycle as the OpQuad is retired from the scheduler. In the case of an OpQuad containing a faulting Op or a mispredicted BRCOND Op, only the status results from the Ops before the faulting or BRCOND Op are committed and this cumulative result is written at the end of the abort cycle.

architectural status flags register

The above process applies to both the architectural status flags and the K6 microarchitectural status flags. In essence, the architectural EFLAGS register is extended to thirty-four bits to make room for the extra two microarchitectural status flags, EZF and ECF. The RDFLG (ReaD FLaG) and WRFLG (WRite FLaG) RegOps reference only the standard 32-bit portion of this extended EFLAGS register.

The generation of the cumulative status result is based on the status bit marks StatMod[3:0] from each of the four Op entries within the bottom scheduler OpQuad (see the section titled "Dynamic Field StatMod[3:0]" beginning on page 211, and the section titled "Dynamic Field StatVal[7:0]" beginning on page 212). As discussed in these sections, the eight x86 status flags are divided into four groups for modification marking purposes instead of having eight individual bit marks. This provides sufficient status modification control within the context of implementing the x86 instruction set architecture. As with updates to a general register within the register file, the possibility of contention exists, i.e., of multiple modifications to the same group of status flags. The desired result, of course, is to take the youngest modification values for each group of status flags as was done for register results.

The generation of the cumulative status result is also based on whether the State of each of the four Ops is *completed* or not. The following pseudo-RTL description summarizes the equation to perform this cumulative result generation or selection process for a status group, which is applied independently for each status group.

No explicit control or constraint on Op commitment and retirement is required for status flag results. Since status flag state changes only results from RegOps and since all RegOps generate register state changes (even if just to microarchitectural register t0), an OpQuad cannot be retired until all RegOps within it are completed and thus also have valid status result values. Consequently, when an OpQuad is ready to retire, it is guaranteed that all status results are available and thus ready to be committed. There is also no need, given the fully unconstrained forwarding of status flag values to BRCOND Ops and "cc-dependent" RegOps, for any clearing of StatMod fields within the Ops of the bottom scheduler OpQuad.

PSEUDO-RTL DESCRIPTION

Status Flag Generation and Selection

```
NextStatFlags[x1..x2] =
  if (Op3:StatMod[x] & Op0:S3 & Op1:S3 & Op2:S3)
    Op3:StatVal[x1..x2]
  elseif (Op2:StatMod[x] & Op0:S3 & Op1:S3)
    Op2:StatVal[x1..x2]
  elseif (Op1:StatMod[x] & Op0:S3)
    Op1:StatVal[x1..x2]
  elseif (Op0:StatMod[x])
    Op0:StatVal[x1..x2]
  else
    StatFlags[x1..x2]
```

StOps and Memory Write Commitment

The third function of the OCU is to commit StOps, particularly StOPs performing actual memory writes. We contrast these types of StOPs with those that do not perform memory writes, such as LEA, CDA, and CIA Ops. LEA Ops do not require any additional commitment handling past commitment of their register results. CIA and CDA Ops do, however, because like normal memory-writing Ops, each of these Ops can result in memory access-related faults. The process of writing data values to "memory"—i.e., to either the D-Cache, the main memory, or the L2-Cache—differs from the commitment of register and status results in a number of ways:

1. StOp commitment involves, in most cases, a memory write and thus an associated store queue entry.

2. at most one memory write can be committed per cycle.

3. the memory write commitment process is a two step process implemented in the form of a two-stage commit pipeline.

4. the OCU looks across the bottom two OpQuads of the scheduler to find StOps with memory writes to commit.

5. the possibility of faults on the associated StOps exists.

When a StOp completes execution, the associated memory address and store data is entered into the store queue. Later, when the memory write of a StOp is committed, this entry is read and retired from the store queue. Since StOps are executed in order and later committed in order, the store queue is managed as a simple FIFO and the matching of store queue entries with associated scheduler StOps is straightforward.

The Commitment Process

The actual commitment process is relatively complicated. We make reference to Figure 2.19 on page 168 to aid in the explanation. A two-step process is required in which the oldest store queue entry is first read and the address looked up in the L1 D-Cache. Then, based on the status of this lookup, the store data is written into the L1 D-Cache or out to memory. In the latter case, the data and address are loaded into the Write Buffer and written out to memory later. From the OCU's perspective the commit process is largely viewed as a single-cycle, single-stage action that either succeeds or is delayed (like the commit process for register and status results). However, it is actually implemented as a two-stage write commit pipeline. The first commit stage C1 corresponds to the commit cycle of register and status results. During this stage no control decisions are made. The L1 D-Cache tag lookup is performed and the accessed tag data is latched for examination during the second commit stage C2. When a write does enter commit stage C2, the associated StOp can be retired from the scheduler and the remainder of the commit process proceeds completely asynchronous to the OCU and the scheduler.

DESIGN NOTE

One Memory Write Per Cycle

The implication of this "one memory write per cycle" implementation is that OpQuads containing multiple StOps have to sit at the bottom of the scheduler for multiple cycles. In the case of OpQuads containing at most one memory-writing StOp, we have the possible commitment and retirement of an OpQuad each and every cycle, subject to the same sort of constraints that stem from the commitment of register state changes. A corresponding number of cycles is required to commit all the StOps in the OpQuad. For long bursts of StOps, this will typically result in fewer—but still extra—cycles of OpQuads being held up at the bottom of the scheduler before being retired. For short bursts, due to the OCU sometimes being able to get a "head start" by committing StOps from OpQuad4, and due to there sometimes being other retirement delays, there are often times when there are no additional delays due to needing extra cycles to commit the burst of StOps.

The fact that an OpQuad could sit at the bottom of the scheduler for many cycles is partially mitigated by providing support for committing memory writes associated with StOps in the second to bottom scheduler OpQuad as well as the bottom OpQuad. Given that memory writes are committed in order, the OCU can get a "head start" on multiple write OpQuads when the bottom OpQuad does not contain any StOps or when it is held up but otherwise empty of uncommitted memory writes. This helps to better match the OCU's one write per cycle commitment capability to the average number of writes per OpQuad, which is less than one per OpQuad.

Commitment Criteria

During each cycle the OCU's memory write commit logic searches the bottom two scheduler OpQuad entries for the oldest uncommitted memory-writing StOp, i.e., for the next StOp and associated write to try and commit. This selected Op corresponds to the current oldest Store Queue entry. Concurrently, the address of this Store Queue entry is presented to the L1 D-Cache and a tag lookup initiated. The tag lookup is done without consideration of whether the associated StOp is presently committable. If the selected StOp is, in fact, committable, and if this write commit is able to advance into the commit pipe stage C2, then the StOp is considered by the OCU to be committed. In the next cycle the OCU will search for and move on to the next memory-writing StOp.

The criteria for StOp commitment are similar to those for register result commitment:

1. the selected StOp must be completed (in the case of misaligned writes; this also means that both associated Store Queue entries have been created).

2. all older LdStOps within the OpQuad, and possibly the preceding OpQuad if this StOp is in the second to last scheduler OpQuad, must also be completed.

3. there must not be an older mispredicted conditional branch Op.

As mentioned earlier for register commitments, there are other "miscellaneous" conditions as well, but the above serve to illustrate the points that need to be made here. A write commit is able to advance into commit pipeline stage C2 when that stage is either empty or is successfully completing commitment of a write.

If the selected StOp is not committable and this is only because it is not completed, then the OCU examines the signal from the store unit pipeline Stage2 indicating whether a StOp is "stuck" in that stage with a detected fault condition. If there is any such Op, then it is the same StOp as the one being unsuccessfully committed by the OCU, and thus must be aborted by the OCU. An appropriate abort cycle will not be initiated, though, until the StOp is in the bottom scheduler OpQuad, all preceding Ops within the OpQuad have been committed, and there is no preceding mispredicted BRCOND Op. This set of conditions is essentially an extension of the condition for StOp committability. The OCU will remain in this state until an abort cycle is initiated for a preceding Op.

Handling CIA and CDA Ops

While the OCU is primarily concerned with memory-writing StOps, it must also handle CIA and CDA Ops. This is necessary since these Ops generate faultable memory addresses and thus must be examined and committed by the OCU. In the normal case of such an Op having executed fault-free, the OCU trivially spends a cycle on committing the Op and simply moves on to committing the next StOp in the next cycle. Since no store queue entry was created during execution of the Op, no entry is retired from the store queue. If, instead, a fault was detected during execution of the CIA or CDA Op, then it is "stuck" in the store unit pipeline Stage2 and the OCU aborts it in exactly the same fashion as for memory-writing StOps.

Memory References Crossing Alignment Boundaries

The OCU must accommodate the situation that arises when a StOp's memory reference crosses an alignment boundary, eight bytes for eight-byte accesses and four bytes for two-and four-byte accesses.[32] When this occurs, the reference is split by the SU into two memory writes and two associated store queue entries during its execution. In such situations,[33] the OCU takes two cycles to retire the two store queue entries and does not officially commit the StOp until the end of the second cycle. If the StOp has a fault then it must be aborted without retirement of either store queue entry.

The OCU's Write Commit Logic

The following pseudo-RTL description summarizes the functionality of the OCU's write commit logic (where Op0 is the oldest Op and Op3 is the youngest Op in the bottom/last scheduler OpQuad, Op4-Op7 are the corresponding Ops in the second to last scheduler OpQuad, and Op8-Op11 are the corresponding Ops in the third to last scheduler OpQuad).

Its operation is based on a set of CmtMask[7:0] mask bits which represent the OCU's progress in committing memory-writing StOps within the last two scheduler OpQuads. The first several bits, starting from bit 0, are clear, indicating that the OCU has already committed any StOps up to the last such Op position, which contains the next StOp to be committed. All Ops corresponding to the remaining, set, mask bits have yet to be examined for

---

[32] This irregularity is due to the fact that this is how alignment boundary crossing is defined in the x86 instruction set architecture.

[33] The OCU is able to distinguish aligned versus misaligned StOps because the first Store Queue entry of a misaligned access pair is specially marked as such via a bit that is part of each Store Queue entry.

committable StOps. In addition, from cycle to cycle the OCU maintains a set of UncmtStOp[7:0] bits indicating which Op positions contain uncommitted memory-writing StOps.

During each cycle the OCU selects the next uncommitted StOp and generates a new set of CmtMask mask bits based on the position of this Op. The unmasked Ops (i.e., those with their mask bit set to 0) are examined to determine whether:

1. the selected StOp is presently committable (i.e., is it *completed* and all preceding OPs are fault-free).

2. an abort cycle needs to presently be initiated.

In the former case, if the selected Op is committable and if Stage 2 of the commit pipeline is able to accept a new write commit at the end of the cycle, then the StOp is "committed" and the UncmtStOp bits are updated with new values. The UncmtStOp bits are also updated (shifted) to match any shifting of the last two OpQuads within the scheduler.

Pseudo-RTL Description

Write Commit Logic

```
// StCmtSel = 0000 if OP0 selected (highest priority)
//    "     = 0111 if OP7 selected (lowest priority)
//    "     = 1111 if no Op selected
StCmtSel[3:0] =
  priority_encode((OPQ5:OpQV & UncmtStOp[0]), ... ,
                  (OPQ5:OpQV & UncmtStOp[3]),
                  (OPQ4:OpQV & UncmtStOp[4]), ... ,
                  (OPQ4:OpQV & UncmtStOp[7]))

// this generates a field of zeroes from bit 0 up to and including
// the bit pointed at by StCmtSel[2:0], and a field of ones past
// this up to bit 7
CmtMask[7:0] = {(StCmtSel[2:0] < 3'b111),..., (StCmtSel[2:0] < 3'b000)}

CmtCiaCda =
    (~CmtMask[7] & Op7:Type[2]) |
    (~CmtMask[6] & CmtMask[7] & Op6:Type[2]) |
    (~CmtMask[5] & CmtMask[6] & Op5:Type[2]) |
    (~CmtMask[4] & CmtMask[5] & Op4:Type[2]) |
    (~CmtMask[3] & CmtMask[4] & Op3:Type[2]) |
    (~CmtMask[2] & CmtMask[3] & Op2:Type[2]) |
    (~CmtMask[1] & CmtMask[2] & Op1:Type[2]) |
    (~CmtMask[0] & CmtMask[1] & Op0:Type[2])

continued on the next page ...
```

PSEUDO-RTL DESCRIPTION

Write Commit Logic

```
StCmtInh = CmtInh |
        StCmtSel[2] & (OpQ4:LimViol | SmcHit & ~CmtCiaCda | "trap pending")

StCmtV = ~StCmtSel[3] & ~StCmtInh &
        (CmtMask[7] | Op7:S3) &
        (CmtMask[6] | Op6:S3 | Op6:RU) &
        (CmtMask[5] | Op5:S3 | Op5:RU) &
        (CmtMask[4] | Op4:S3 | Op4:RU) &
        (CmtMask[3] | Op3:S3 | Op3:RU) &
        (CmtMask[2] | Op2:S3 | Op2:RU) &
        (CmtMask[1] | Op1:S3 | Op1:RU)

Q5StCmtV = ~StCmtSel[2] & ~CmtInh &
          (CmtMask[3] | Op3:S3) &
          (CmtMask[2] | Op2:S3 | Op2:RU) &
          (CmtMask[1] | Op1:S3 | Op1:RU) &
          (CmtMask[0] | Op0:S3 | Op0:RU)

StAdv = ~STQ_FirstAddr & ~DC_HoldSC1 & CHP_AdvSC2 | CmtCiaCda

StRetire = StCmtV & StAdv

Q5StRetire = StAdv & Q5StCmtV

NewUncmtStOp[7:0] = {(CmtMask[7] & Op7:Type=ST), ... ,
                    (CmtMask[0] & Op0:Type=ST)}

// indicates when all memory-writing StOps have been
// committed or are being successfully committed in the
// bottom Sched Op quad

AllStCmt = StCmtSel[2] | Q5StRetire &
          ~NewUncmtStOp[3] &...& ~NewUncmtStOp[0]

// update UncmtStOp bits:
NextUncmtStOp[7:0] = (StRetire) ? NewUncmtStOp[7:0] : UncmtStOp[7:0]
NextUncmtStOp[11:8] =
  {Op11:Type=ST, Op10:Type=ST, Op9:Type=ST, Op8:Type=ST}

// mux followed by a flip-flop:
UncmtStOp[7:4] = LdEntry4 ? NextUncmtStOp[11:8]: NextUncmtStOp[7:4]
UncmtStOp[3:0] = LdEntry5 ? NextUncmtStOp[7:4] : NextUncmtStOp[3:0]
```

continued on the next page ...

Pseudo-RTL Description (cont.)

Write Commit Logic

```
SC_HoldSC1 = ~StQCmtV | CmtCiaCda

StAbort = ~StCmtSel[2] SUViol &
         ((StCmtSel[1:0] == 2'b00) & ~Op0:S3 |
          (StCmtSel[1:0] == 2'b01) & ~Op1:S3 & Op0:S3 |
          (StCmtSel[1:0] == 2'b10) & ~Op2:S3 & Op1:S3 & Op0:S3 |
          (StCmtSel[1:0] == 2'b11) & ~Op3:S3 & Op2:S3 & Op1:S3 & Op0:S3)
```

MEMORY READ FAULT HANDLING

LdOps normally do not require any special handling by the OCU since they only result in general register state changes. Like most StOps, though, they can also encounter faults during their execution. When this occurs, it is recognized by special logic and handled in the same manner as for StOp faults. To determine whether a faulting LdOp exists in the bottom scheduler OpQuad, the OCU examines each Op in the OpQuad for the following conditions:

1. it is a LdOp.
2. all older Ops are completed and fully committed.
3. there is no preceding mispredicted BRCOND Op.

Again there are other "miscellaneous" conditions as well and, again, the above conditions serve to illustrate the points that need be made here. The conditions identified ensure that all preceding Ops are properly committed. The OCU also examines the signal from the LU pipeline Stage2 indicating whether a LdOp is stuck in that stage with a detected fault condition. At most one of the Ops in the OpQuad satisfies all of these conditions. If one does and the signal from the LU pipeline Stage2 is asserted, then a faulting LdOp is recognized by the OCU and an appropriate abort cycle is initiated immediately to abort this Op and all following Ops. The following pseudo-RTL description summarizes the OCU's LdOp fault handling logic:

PSEUDO-RTL DESCRIPTION

LdOp Fault Handling Logic

```
LdAbort = LU2_LUViol &
 (Op0:(Type=LU & ~S3) |
  Op1:(Type=LU & ~S3) & Op0:S3 & ~CmtMask[1] |
  Op2:(Type=LU & ~S3) & Op0:S3 & Op1:S3 & ~CmtMask[3] |   // [3]==[2]!
  Op3:(Type=LU & ~S3) & Op0:S3 & Op1:S3 & Op2:S3 & ~CmtMask[3]
 )
```

FAULT Op COMMITMENT

OpQuad Sequence constraints

In addition to commitment of abortable state changes associated with all the normal types of Ops, there are a few special Ops—the FAULT, LDDHA, and LDAHA Ops—that require additional, special commitment handling. None of these Ops are issued to and executed by an execution unit and they have no execution dependencies with other Ops. They are significant only to the OCU.

The FAULT Op is similar to a faulting LdStOp in that it is handled by the OCU in the same way—an abort cycle is initiated along with vectoring to the current OpQuad Sequence OCU fault handler. Unlike faulting LdStOps, though, there is no problem in determining whether there is a fault to recognize and of when to initiate the abort cycle.

To simplify the OCU's logic for handling FAULT Ops, the following constraints are placed upon OpQuad Sequences:

1. FAULT Ops must be located in the first Op position of an OpQuad.

2. all following Ops in the OpQuad must be NoOps.

3. the next OpQuad to be executed must not contain any memory-writing StOps.

The latter constraints ensure that the OCU's StOp commitment logic can operate blindly of the presence of FAULT Ops, (i.e., without any special consideration). Moreover, the last constraint has no negative effect on performance since the next OpQuad will be unconditionally aborted when the FAULT Op executes, (i.e., the next OpQuad could not have done useful work anyway). In practice, OpQuad Sequences are written so that FAULT OpQuads branch to themselves.

The state of a FAULT Op is initialized to *unissued* when it is loaded into the scheduler. When it reaches the bottom of the scheduler, this inhibits the OCU's OpQuad retirement logic from retiring the containing

OpQuad while the OCU's FAULT Op commit logic immediately initiates an abort cycle. The specifics of this abort cycle are the same as for faults on LdStOps; the only difference is the generation of a unique fault id. The following equation summarizes the OCU's FAULT Op handling logic:

PSEUDO-RTL DESCRIPTION
FAULT Op Handling Logic
`FltAbort = OpQ5:OpQV & Op0:(Type=SpecOp & (OpInfo(SpecOp).Type=FAULT))`

LDDHA AND LDAHA OP COMMITMENT

The LDDHA and LDAHA Ops enable OpQuad Sequences to set and to change the OpQuad ROM address to which OCU-recognized exceptions are vectored. The OCU maintains two vector address registers: the first holds a default handler address and the second holds an alternate handler address. The first register is set once by the Reset OpQuad Sequence via an LDDHA Op and is active, by default, for most OpQuad Sequences (for both instructions and exception processing). The second register is set during certain sections of OpQuad Sequences via a LDAHA Op.

For OpQuad Sequences that do not contain an LDAHA Op, any faults recognized by the OCU result in vectoring to the address in the default handler address register. For OpQuad Sequences that contain an LDAHA Op, faults on Ops in OpQuads before the one containing the LDAHA Op still result in vectoring to the default address, while faults on Ops in the OpQuad containing the LDAHA Op or in any following OpQuads up to and including the last OpQuad of the sequence (i.e., the OpQuad containing the ERET), result in vectoring to the address in the alternate handler address register. The retirement of the ERET OpQuad, as well as the occurrence of an abort cycle, reactivates the default handler address register for all following OpQuads, until the next occurrence of a LDAHA Op.

To simplify matters for the OCU, LDDHA and LDAHA Ops are constrained to be located in the first Op position in an OpQuad. Valid Ops are allowed in the following Op positions of the OpQuad (in contrast to FAULT OpQuads where this is not allowed). The following pseudo-RTL descriptions summarize the OCU's LDDHA and LDAHA Op handling logic:

PSEUDO-RTL DESCRIPTION

LDDHA and LDAHA Op Handling

```
if (OpQ5:OpQV & Op0:(Type=SpecOp & (OpInfo(SpecOp).Type=LDDHA)))
  DefFltVecAddr[13:0] = Op0:DestVal[13:0]// enabled flip-flOp

LdAltAddr = OpQ5:OpQV & Op0:(Type=SpecOp & (OpInfo(SpecOp).Type=LDAHA))

if (LdAltAddr)
  AltFltVecAddr[13:0] = Op0:DestVal[13:0]// enabled flip-flop

// This implements the requirement for faults on Ops
// within the same Op quad as a LDAHA Op to be vectored
// to the new alternate handler address.
EffAltFltVecAddr[13:0] = (LdAltAddr) ? Op0:DestVal[13:0] :
                                    AltFltVecAddr[13:0]

// OpQ refers to an Op quad field
if (NextOpQ5:Eret & NextOpQ5:OpQV & ~BrAbort | LdAltAddr | ExcpAbort)
  FltVecMode = ~ExcpAbort &
               ~(NextOpQ5:Eret & NextOpQ5:OpQV & ~BrAbort) &
               LdAltAddr// enabled flip-flop

CurFltVecAddr[14:0] =
  (FltVecMode | LdAltAddr) ? EffAltFltVecAddr[14:0] :
                        DefFltVecAddr[14:0]
```

SEQUENTIAL AND BRANCH TARGET SEGMENT LIMIT VIOLATION HANDLING

In addition to the commitment of state changes associated with each of the Ops within an OpQuad, the OCU also recognizes a special condition tagged with an OpQuad as a whole. Right after the decoders have generated an OpQuad and it has been loaded into the scheduler, if a sequential code segment limit overrun violation is detected, or if a transfer control instruction was just decoded and a code segment limit violation is detected on the target address, the OpQuad is marked to indicate that a code segment limit violation was detected in association with the instruction decode that produced the OpQuad.

When the OpQuad reaches the OCU and is to be committed, the set tag bit (called LimViol) is recognized and an abort cycle is initiated without commitment of any state changes from the Ops within the OpQuad. Effectively the entire OpQuad is faulted. The effect is similar to that which would have occurred if there had been a FAULT Op in the OpQuad. The following equation summarizes the OCU's logic for handling branch target limit violations:

Pseudo-RTL Description
Branch Target Limit Violations
`LimAbort = OpQ5:(OpQV & LimViol)`

MISPREDICTED BRCOND OP HANDLING

Besides the commitment of abortable state changes and the handling of various special cases, the OCU handles the generation of abort cycles for mispredicted BRCOND Ops. The restart of both the instruction fetch and decode portions of the machine occurs before the BRCOND Op reaches the bottom row of the scheduler (when the branch was resolved as correctly predicted or not, while the BRCOND Op passed through scheduler OpQuad4). The scheduler simply needs to generate an abort cycle and to ensure that only preceding Ops are committed and, as with the generation of abort cycles for Op faults, the abort must not be initiated until all preceding Ops have been committed. The following pseudo-RTL description summarize the OCU's mispredicted BRCOND Op handling logic. The commitment of following Ops is inhibited by the State of the BRCOND Op.

Pseudo-RTL Description
Handling Mispredicted BRCOND Ops
| ```
BrAbort = Op0:(Type=SpecOp & ~S3) |
   Op1:(Type=SpecOp & ~S3) & Op0:S3 & ~CmtMask[1] |
   Op2:(Type=SpecOp & ~S3) & Op0:S3 & Op1:S3 &
         ~CmtMask[3] | //[3]==[2]!
   Op3:(Type=SpecOp & ~S3) & Op0:S3 & Op1:S3 & Op2:S3
         & ~CmtMask[3]
``` |

OPQUAD RETIREMENT

The OCU retires the bottom OpQuad from the scheduler at the end of the cycle when all of the abortable state changes of the Ops within it have been committed or are being successfully committed. Since this process removes this OpQuad from the scheduler, it also allows the next OpQuad to shift into the bottom row of the scheduler and all earlier OpQuads to shift down as well. During cycles in which not all such Op results have yet been committed, the bottom OpQuad is not retired and either it is retained into the next cycle for further commitment processing or it is
```

invalidated due to an abort cycle. In the latter case, the abort cycle would be in response to some fault having been recognized on one of the Ops within the OpQuad.

DESIGN NOTE

OpQuad Retirement

The retirement of an OpQuad requires that all register results, status results, and memory writes are committed, and that there is no FAULT Op or mispredicted BRCOND Op in the OpQuad. Removal of an OpQuad also immediately occurs if the OpQuad is marked as invalid, a situation taken care of by the scheduler shift control logic.[a] Status results are all committed together in conjunction with retirement or abortion of the OpQuad. Register results are guaranteed to be committed or currently committing if the associated Ops are completed.

---

[a]   See the pseudo-RTL description in the section titled "Dynamic Field Storage Element Operation" beginning on page 190.

The following pseudo-RTL description summarizes the OCU's OpQuad retirement control logic:

PSEUDO-RTL DESCRIPTION

OpQuad Retirement Control

```
OpQRetire = Op3:S3 & Op2:S3 & Op1:S3 & Op0:S3 &
            AllStCmt

if ((OpQRetire | SC_Abort) & ~OpQ5:LimViol)
  StatFlags[7:0] = NewStatFlags[7:0]
  // enabled flip-flop
```

OpQRetire may be asserted for multiple cycles for the same OpQuad. This will occur when shifting of the bottom scheduler entries is inhibited for other unrelated reasons.

ABORT CYCLE GENERATION

The OCU generates abort cycles in two situations, recognition of:

1.   an Op fault on a LdOp, StOp or a FAULT Op.
2.   a mispredicted BRCOND Op.

Preceding sections have covered the generation of signals initiating an abort cycle: LdAbort, StAbort, FltAbort, LimAbort, and BrAbort. This section describes the generation of the general abort signal[34] and related information.

The Abort signal is simply a combination of all the individual abort signals associated with commitment of specific types of state changes or Ops. The associated OpQuad Sequence vector address, which is used only for fault-related aborts and not BRCOND-related aborts, is simply the currently active fault handler vector address as described earlier.

The Abort signal, itself, flushes the bottom portion of the machine— the scheduler and all execution units—of all outstanding Ops and reinitializes these areas in preparation for receiving fresh new Ops from the upper portion of the machine—the instruction fetch and decode areas. For BRCOND-related aborts this is sufficient since the upper portion of the machine was already restarted earlier by the BRCOND Op resolution scheduler logic.

For exception-related aborts, though, the upper portion of the machine also needs to be restarted at the above OpQuad Sequence vector address. This is accomplished by assertion of the appropriate restart signal SC_Vec2XXX. When the instruction fetch and decode restarts are signaled simultaneously for both a mispredicted BRCOND Op and an Op exception, the latter is given higher priority and the restart vector address and restart signals are generated accordingly.

When a fault-related abort occurs, the OCU also latches information about the fault, namely the x86 instruction fault Program Counter, i.e., the logical address of the x86 instruction associated with the Op being faulted; in other words, the address of the instruction effectively being faulted. The following pseudo-RTL description summarizes the abort cycle generation logic:

---

[34] SC_EAbort and SC_Abort, where the latter is simply a one-cycle delayed version of the former.

Pseudo-RTL Description

Abort Cycle Generation

```
ExcpAbort = LdAbort | StAbort | FltAbort | LimAbort | TrapAbort | SCReset
SC_EAbort  = ExcpAbort | BrAbort
SC_Abort = SC_EAbort// simple flip-flop

if (TrapAbort)
  FaultId[2:0] = (DTF | SSTF) ? 3'h1 : 3'h0
else if (LimAbort)
  FaultId[2:0] = 3'h2
else
  FaultId[2:0] = LdAbort ? LU2_ViolType : SU2_ViolType

// latch into SR4:
if (ExcpAbort)
  SC_FID[2:0] = FaultId[2:0]// enabled flip-flop
  SC_SR4[31:0] = OPQ5:FaultPC[31:0]// enabled flip-flop

// select OpQuad Sequence vector address:
if (SCReset)
  SC_VecAddr[13:0] = 14'h2200
  ExtEmcVecAddr      = SCExtReset
else
  SC_VecAddr[13:0] =
    (ExcpAbort) ? CurFltVecAddr[13:0]  : BrVecAddr[13:0]
  ExtEmcVecAddr =
    (ExcpAbort) ? CurFltVecAddr[14]  : BrVecAddr[14]

SC_Vec2ROM = (ExcpAbort | BrVec2Emc) & ~ExtEmcVecAddr
SC_Vec2RAM = (ExcpAbort | BrVec2Emc) &  ExtEmcVecAddr
SC_Vec2Dec = ~ExcpAbort & BrVec2Dec
```

Avoiding Deadlock

There is a difference between committing the results of an Op and retiring an Op from the scheduler. Often these actions happen on the same cycle but this is not always the case. If some, but not all, of the Ops in an OpQuad can be committed in a given cycle, whatever can be committed is committed. The OpQuad cannot be removed from the scheduler until all of its Ops are committed, so committed Ops will still be in the scheduler. When result values (both the register value and status flag bits) of an Op are committed, the corresponding byte marks and status modification bits are cleared in the scheduler's Op entry.

Ops can modify all or just part of a register with a result value (specifically, either of the lower two bytes, both lower bytes, or all four bytes, corresponding to one,-two,-and-four byte size operations). When a scan is being made for the supplier of an operand value required by an Op in pipeline Stage0 or a StOp in SU Stage2), the scan must take into account which bytes of the register are required and which bytes are modified by each of the older Ops that modify the required register. The scan only identifies those Op entries for which there is an overlap between which bytes are needed and which bytes are modified. Destination byte mark (DestBM[2:0]) bits keep track of which parts of a result register are modified by an Op. The result of the OCU clearing these bits during Op commitment is that the scan logic realizes that this Op no longer looks like it modifies the required register and the particular bytes, if needed, can be supplied by the architectural register file.

Why is it that the OCU needs to be able to commit some of the Ops in an OpQuad even though it cannot commit all of them? This approach is in contrast to simply waiting until you can commit all of the Ops in the OpQuad before committing any of them—i.e., commit and retire all of them at the same time. The answer has to do with avoiding potential deadlock situations.

Suppose that one of the Ops in OpQuad3 or OpQuad4 cannot get its source operands and, because it is a cc-dependent regOp, a nonabortable RegOp, or a BRCOND Op, this causes shifting of this OpQuad and the one or two below it to be inhibited as discussed earlier. If an older Op, say in OpQuad4, is producing some of the required register operand value, but not all of it, the scheduler needs to wait for the OCU to commit the older Op. But, if it cannot get to the bottom of the scheduler to be committed because the scheduler cannot shift, then the scheduler and OCU are deadlocked.

For example, suppose the Op that gets stuck in OpQuad3 or OpQuad4 requires all four bytes of the AX register as one of its source operands. Let's assume that two of these bytes are modified by an Op lower down in the scheduler, one of the remaining required bytes is modified by a different Op lower down in the scheduler, and the final required byte is in the architecture register file. The K6 does not support being able to source or forward some of the bytes from one Op entry and some of the bytes from another Op entry and some of the bytes from the architectural register file. In general, all required bytes must be forwarded from just one source. In this case, the scheduler will have to wait until the OCU can commit to two Ops lower down in the scheduler, so that all of the required bytes can be obtained from the architectural register file. But, since the scheduler cannot shift, these Ops will never get committed.

Another, but more subtle example, is the deadlock that might arise within a single OpQuad. even if it is already in OpQuad5 of the scheduler.

Suppose one of the later Ops in the OpQuad is partially dependent on the results of an earlier Op in the same OpQuad. Unless the OCU can commit the earlier Op so that the required operand can be obtained from the architectural register file, the dependent Op will never be able to execute.

To resolve such potential deadlock situations, the OCU is able to commit whichever Ops in an OpQuad that can be committed, instead of having to wait for all of the Ops to be able to be committed. Further, the OCU is able to commit Ops from both OpQuad4 and OpQuad5 (the bottom two rows of the scheduler).

Since these deadlock situations arose from the fact that the scheduler cannot provide a set of required register bytes from a collection of sources—if four bytes of a register are required, the scheduler cannot get one byte from one place, one byte another place, and the other two bytes from a third place—an alternative solution would be to provide the resources to allow the scheduler to do this. This approach, however, proves to be much more costly (somewhat in speed and very much in size) than providing the OCU the flexibility just described.

REGISTER RENAMING

Programs are written under the assumption that their constituent instructions will execute sequentially. For architectures that support the out-of-order execution of instructions, this assumption is not true and certain conflicts may arise that need to be avoided to ensure proper program behavior. Since the issues discussed in this introductory section are applicable to the x86 instruction set architecture and the K6 3D microarchitecture, the term *command* is used in this section to mean either an *x86 instruction* or a *RISC86 operation*. In general, a command either:

1. requires and "reads" zero, one, or more operand values to be operated upon from some form of storage such as registers or memory.

2. produces one or more result values and "writes" them into some form of storage such as registers or memory.

There are potential conflicts between various combinations of reading operand values and writing result values from and to common storage locations when they are allowed to occur out of their sequential program order. There are four basic combinations of reading and writing of operand and results values from and to the registers and memory locations for two commands.

Table 3.11 POTENTIAL CONFLICTS WHEN READING/WRITING OPERAND/RESULT VALUES

1st command	2nd command	Notation or Terminology	Example of Potential Conflict
Read	Read	RAR Read After Read	In this case, both commands use the same result, produced by some previous command. There is no conflict and the two commands can be executed in any order.
Read	Write	WAR Write After Read	In this case, the 1st command reads a result produced by some previous command from a specific storage location and then the 2nd command writes to the same storage location. A conflict exists if the 2nd command writes a new result to the storage location in question before the 1st command reads the older, previous result value from it.
Write	Read	RAW Read After Write	In this case, the 2nd command uses the result produced by the 1st command. A conflict exists if the 2nd command reads the result's storage location before the 1st command has written its result to the storage location in question as the 2nd command will be reading the wrong result value—the result produced by some other command.
Write	Write	WAW Write After Write	In this case, the 1st command writes its result value to a specific storage location and then the 2nd command writes its result to the same storage location. A conflict exists if the 2nd command's write occurs before the 1st command's write as the storage location is left with the wrong result. Subsequent reads to the storage location will read this wrong value.

IMPLICATIONS FOR PIPELINE OPERATION

Pipeline operation, can be affected by the presence of these conflicts as execution will be stalled until such conflicts, when they exist, are resolved. As Hennessy and Patterson point out in the last reference cited in the following "Historical Comment and Suggested Readings" inset, commands that use registers and have a potential Write-After-Read conflict or a potential Write-After-Write conflict can execute out of order if the registers are renamed (see Section 4.1 of the Hennessy and Patterson text). It is therefore relatively important that a high-performance method of supporting register naming be an integral part of the processor's core.

HISTORICAL COMMENT AND SUGGESTED READINGS

Pipeline Design

There is a range of terminology used to describe the conflicts that arise in the design of pipelines and the techniques used in both processor design and compilers to resolve them. They have been called, among other things, "dependencies" or "hazards" in various architecture-and compiler-related work. For a treatment of the issues from an architecture point of view, see Peter M. Kogge's book, *The Architecture of Pipelined Computers*, McGraw-Hill Book Company, 1981, and Harold Stone's book, *High-Performance Computer Architecture*, 3rd Edition, Addison-Wesley Publishing Company, 1993. Kogge's book gives a rich history of the resolution of these conflicts in pipelined computers. His discussions of Thorton's scoreboarding technique used in the CDC6600 and Tomasulo's algorithm used in the IBM 360/91 are quite interesting.

For a compiler-related treatment of these issues see: "Local Microcode Compaction Techniques," Dave Landskov, Scott Davidson, Bruce Shriver, and Pat Mallet, *ACM Computing Surveys*, Vol. 12, No 3, September, 1980; "Microcode Compaction: Extending the Boundaries," Dave Landskov, Josh Fisher and Bruce Shriver, *International Journal of Computer and Information Sciences*, Vol. 13., No. 1, February, 1984; "Microcode Compaction: Looking Backward and Looking Forward," Josh Fisher, David Landskov and Bruce Shriver, *Proceedings of the National Computer Conference*, NCC '81, AFIPS Press, Chicago, Illinois, May, 1981.

Since pipelining is typically an integral part of current microarchitectures, there is an extensive treatment of the issues involved in classifying and resolving these conflicts in this literature as well. See, for example, the article by Wen-Mei Hwu, Richard E. Hank, David M. Gallagher, Scott A. Mahlke, Daniel M. Lavery, Grant E. Haab, John C. Glyllenhaal and David I. August, "Compiler Technology for Future Microprocessors," *Proceedings of the IEEE*, Vol. 83, No. 12, 1995, pp. 1625-1640. You can find the full text version of this article on the CD-ROM. See also Mike Johnson's, *Superscalar Microprocessor Design*, Prentice-Hall, 1991; and John Hennessy and Dave Patterson's *Computer Architecture: A Quantitative Approach*, 2nd Edition, Morgan Kaufmann Publishers, Inc., 1996.

An architecture's instruction set accesses a set of registers that are used for storing values associated with general registers, status flags, and other architectural state-related information. This set of registers is often called the architectural register set or architectural register file[35] (see the section titled "Architectural and Microarchitectural Registers" beginning on page 88). The values stored in it at any instant in time are called the architectural machine state or instruction set architecture machine state. The microarchitecture typically

---

[35] Although separate register files are often used for each of the various types of state, e.g., a separate register in the case of status flags distinct from the architectural register file for general registers.

has an additional number of registers used to store additional microarchitectural machine state, (i.e., operand values, status flags, and state information that is used exclusively in the microarchitecture and not explicitly visible to the instruction set architecture). Further, the microarchitecture typically has a different number of physical registers, most often a larger number, that are used to store uncommitted as well as committed values in these architecture and microarchitecture registers. Before proceeding in this section, we recommend you consider the following review:

Suggested Review

It might be useful at this point for you to review the following sections in Chapter 2 that are particularly relevant to the issues in register renaming: the section titled "Architectural and Microarchitectural Registers" beginning on page 88, the section titled "Register Number and Name Mappings" beginning on page 91, and the section titled "Special Registers and Model Specific Registers" beginning on page 94.

From the sections identified in the above "Suggested Review" inset, we recall that the K6 3D has twenty-four 32-bit integer registers in the integer architectural register file. The K6 3D also has twenty-four 32-bit integer renaming registers. The twenty-four integer registers in the integer architectural register file consist of eight registers that correspond to the x86 architecture 32-bit-general purpose registers (EAX, EBX, ECX, EDX, EBP, ESP, ESI, and EDI) and sixteen microarchitecture scratch registers (t0 through t15). The twenty-four renaming registers are located in the scheduler's twenty-four Op entries—one per entry. The K6 3D also has nine MMX/3D 64-bit architecture registers and twelve MMX/3D 64-bit renaming registers. The nine architectural registers consist of eight that correspond to the x86 architecture MMX 64-bit registers (MM0 through MM7) and one microarchitecture scratch 64-bit register (MMt1).

Register mapping is the process of associating one set of registers with another set of registers. The mapping can be static (bound before execution) or dynamic (done at execution time). If the process is dynamic, (i.e., "renaming" (re-mapping) occurs during execution, it is called register renaming.

In the K6 3D, both the x86 architectural registers (e.g., AX-DI, MM0-MM7, CF, ZF, SF, OF, PF, and AF) and the microarchitectural registers (e.g., t0-t15, MMt1, ECF, and EZF) are renamed to physical registers. Thus, in the context of the K6 3D, register mapping is the process of associating the set of x86 architectural registers and the set of K6 3D microarchitectural registers with specific physical registers which actually store the register values. As this process is dynamic, it is appropriate to call this process register renaming. The renaming is such that each x86 architectural register and each K6 3D microarchitectural register having a valid value has a corresponding physical register mapped to it.

Register renaming is often accomplished through the use of tags that are used to identify the various registers. The tags can be thought of as register numbers or register identifiers. When an architectural or microarchitectural register identifier is presented to the mapping mechanism (e.g., a mapping table), the current corresponding physical register identifier is output. We will discuss two types of register renaming schemes, explicit and implicit. The mappings must be complete, i.e., each architectural register having a valid value must have a corresponding microarchitectural register mapped to it at each point in time when a valid value is associated with the architectural register.

EXPLICIT REGISTER RENAMING

Some architectures implement an explicit register renaming scheme. In such schemes there is an explicit mapping or translation of architectural registers into physical registers. These schemes employ a translation or mapping mechanism that:

1. maintains a list of which physical register numbers are currently not in use and thus available to be allocated.

2. assigns a physical register number to be associated with an architectural number; results that are to be held in the architectural register are held in the associated physical register.

3. produces or outputs the physical register number associated with a given architectural register number.

Such schemes often require additional information such as an indication of the validity of the data value a register contains. A copy of the mapping information is typically required to be able to restore the machine state when an exception, abort, or mispredicted branch is encountered. We will now discuss two basic approaches that are used to implement explicit renaming schemes.

Suggested Review

It might be useful at this point for you to review several pipeline diagrams shown in Chapter 2 (Figure 2.12 on page 159, Figure 2.14 on page 163, Figure 2.15 on page 164, Figure 2.18 on page 167, and Figure 2.21 on page 175) and the text that accompanies them, as well as the scheduler diagram Figure 2.9 on page 130 and its related discussion.

Using One Pool of Registers

One type of approach used in explicit register renaming schemes is to have a general pool of physical registers that can be used to hold both committed and uncommitted values in the registers of the architectural/microarchitectural register set. A tag associated with each of the physical registers points to the specific architectural or microarchitectural register that it is currently assigned to. Similarly, there is a tag associated with each architectural or microarchitectural register pointing to the physical register that it is mapped to. At a specific instant in the instruction stream, the set of values of all such tags is the *current mapping* of the architectural and microarchitectural register numbers onto the physical register numbers. This means that the physical registers identified hold the latest or current values for the architectural and microarchitectural registers identified. At that specific instant in time, some of the other physical registers may be free while others might be holding older values of various architectural and microarchitectural registers.

The tags are located in a centralized resource, say a mapping register or renaming table. Copies of older versions of mapping information are also required to be able to restore the machine state when an exception or a mispredicted branch is encountered. If there is a 1-to-1 correspondence between each operation and a corresponding register modification (i.e., each operation modifies at most one register), the number of physical registers required is roughly (X + Y + Z) where:

1. X is the number of architectural registers.
2. Y is the number of microarchitectural; registers.
3. Z is the number of speculative copies of architectural and microarchitectural register values (i.e. computed register values that are not yet committed).

In the explicit mapping approach, when instructions are decoded the architectural register identifiers or numbers used in the instructions must be translated to the current corresponding physical register identifiers. The current corresponding physical register numbers are used in the internal operations associated with the decoded instructions. The mapping information is modified in the decoding process and in the commitment process. For example, assume the following instruction is decoded:

AX <— AX + BX

(i.e., the value contained in AX is added to the value contained in BX and the result replaces the original value contained in the AX). Assume that the mapping information indicates that the current values of the architectural registers AX and BX are in physical *Register 3* and *Register 7,* respectively.

Assume that physical *Register 24* is currently free and unused. During the decode process a physical register is allocated to hold the result of the add instruction so that the previous value of AX is not immediately lost when the operation is speculatively executed. In this example, physical *Register 24* is assigned to hold the result of the addition and the mapping information is modified to reflect this assignment. The resulting operation will read physical *Register 3* and *Register 7* for its two source operands and then put the result of the addition into physical *Register 24*.

At this point, the most recent value of AX is held in physical *Register 24* and its previous value is held in physical *Register 3*. The next instruction that references AX will read from physical *Register 24* and not from physical *Register 3* as the mapping information has been modified to reflect this. When a mispredicted branch or an exception occurs, all following instructions that have been decoded will need to be flushed out of the machine. Correspondingly, the mapping information needs to be restored to a set of mappings corresponding to the point where execution will be restarted. If the example instruction had been executed speculatively and a mispredicted branch occurred such that the instruction should not have been executed, the mapping information would have to be restored to reflect that the current value for AX is in physical *Register 3* and not physical *Register 24*. When a register is committed (i.e., its results are made permanent in the architectural register file), the mapping information needs to reflect that the most recent value of the register is the current value and any registers that were holding older values are now free to be reallocated as new instructions are decoded.

Using Two Pools of Registers

A variation of the approach just described is now given. Instead of having just one general pool of physical registers you might have two pools. One pool is a set of registers which is used as a *committed architectural/microarchitectural* register file. The other set is used to hold register values until they are committed, i.e., an *uncommitted register set*.[36] As with the preceding approach, architectural register numbers are converted into physical register numbers at decode time and then the mapping information is updated. Operations can reference either (or both) the committed and uncommitted register files.

When a register value is committed, the value needs to be written from the uncommitted register file to the committed register file. In terms of the previous example, after the add operation executed, *Register 24* in the uncommitted register file was holding the new value of AX. At the time

---

[36] The term *register set* is used to reflect the fact that these registers do not form a register file in the conventional sense of one register per register address.

of commitment, the value from this register is written to the AX register in the committed architectural register file. At this point, *Register 24* in the uncommitted register file is also freed up to get reallocated as new instructions are decoded.

IMPLICIT REGISTER RENAMING

In contrast to such explicit renaming schemes, the K6 uses an implicit register renaming scheme. This implicit scheme is similar to the immediately preceding scheme (*Using Two Pools of Registers*) in having two pools of physical registers, committed and uncommitted register files. We will first explain how this is done for integer instructions and then for MMX and 3D instructions.

The scheduler uses forty-eight physical registers when processing the (up to) twenty-four Ops that can be in the scheduler at any point in time. The registers consist of two register groups, twenty-four committed state registers and twenty-four renaming registers. The twenty-four general registers consist of eight registers that correspond to the x86 general-purpose registers—(i.e., EAX, EBX, ECX, EDX, EBP, ESP, ESI and EDI), and sixteen microarchitectural scratch registers for use within OpQuad Sequences. These twenty-four registers are located in the Architectural Register File, shown in Figure 2.2 on page 69. The twenty-four renaming registers correspond to the twenty-four DestVal fields in the scheduler, one DestVal field per scheduler Op entry as discussed in the section titled "The DestVal field plays an important role in the K6's implicit renaming strategy. The OpQuad Expansion Logic circuitry used to initialize the DestVal field and the scheduler circuitry logic associated with dynamic field DestVal is given in the following pseudo-RTL description:" beginning on page 210. The renaming registers hold result register values while they are not yet committed. We repeat, for your convenience, part of a "Historical Comment and Suggested Reading" inset titled Reorder Buffer on page 134:

> ### Excerpt from an Earlier Historical Comment and Suggested Reading
>
> #### Reorder Buffer
>
> Processors that support speculative and out-of-order execution typically have operations completing execution before they are ready to be committed. The results of such operations are not committed (i.e., producing permanent state change) until it is safe to do so. The collection of storage elements that holds the results of the as-yet-uncommitted operations is often called a reorder buffer, for it is from this buffer that the instructions which have been executed out of order will be committed in an in-order fashion. A reorder buffer also supports the use and forwarding of results of completed operations as source operands for other dependent operations. The K6 is an example of a microprocessor in which its reorder buffer (i.e., included in the scheduler's centralized buffer functionality) also serves as an environment to support register renaming. Its renaming registers hold result register values until they are committed. It holds these values in the DestVal field of the appropriate Op entries in the scheduler.

As seen in the first portion of this chapter, each scheduler Op entry holds one RISC86 operation which can modify at most one register. At this point, in contrast to earlier sections, we are talking about general registers, i.e., excluding "status flag" registers. Fields Src1Reg, Src2Reg, and SrcStReg in the Op entry hold the register numbers identifying the registers for the first source operand Src1, the second source operand Src2, and the store data operand (which exists only for StOps) of the Op. The register result of the operation is stored in the Op entry's 32-bit DestVal field.[37] The DestVal field is effectively the Op entry's register result renaming register. The architectural register identity of the renaming register within the Op is specified by value in the DestReg field of that Op (see the section titled "Static Field DestReg[4:0]" beginning on page 201). The DestVal field could also be called the *local implicit renaming register*. Since there can be up to twenty-four Ops outstanding in the scheduler at any time, each having a DestVal field, the K6 has twenty-four local implicit renaming registers.

---

[37] This is for the integer case. The MMX and 3D cases will be examined shortly.

The Basic Scheme

As was seen earlier in this chapter, when Ops are committed the value in the Op entry's local renaming register is written into the architectural register file, as was done in the *Using Two Pools of Registers* explicit renaming schemes just discussed. The K6 3D design exploits the following features of the microarchitecture that were discussed in Chapter 2:

1. the 3-bit architectural register numbers are trivially converted to 5-bit microarchitectural register numbers effectively implementing a fixed mapping between x86 registers and eight corresponding K6 microarchitectural registers.[38]

2. the K6 has twenty-four microarchitectural registers (eight corresponding to x86 architectural registers) and the others are scratch registers (for use within instruction OpQuad sequences).

3. the twenty-four microarchitectural registers are renamed using forty-eight physical registers.

The implicit renaming scheme is based on the fact that the scheduler contains a physically ordered list of Op entries and thus a physically ordered list of locally implicit renaming registers. Renaming is achieved by dynamically determining from where the required source register operand values are supplied. These values can be supplied from scheduler Op entries or, by default, the architectural/microarchitectural register file. Starting from the Op entry that requires a register operand value, a scan is made down the scheduler toward the bottom row of the scheduler (i.e., toward the older Op entries) looking for the first Op that modifies the required register *and* the required bytes of that register. Essentially, the scan compares the value in the Op's Src1Reg, Src2Reg, or SrcStReg field, as appropriate, with the value in the DestReg field of the older Ops. If a match occurs, (i.e., such an Op is found), it will be the supplier of the operand value, as it is the most recent older modifier of the required register. If such an Op is not found, then by default the architecture/microarchitecture register file is the supplier of the required register operand value.

Assume an Op is found. If the State field of that Op entry indicates the Op has already completed execution, then the value in that Op entry's DestVal field (i.e., its renaming register) can be read out onto the appropriate operand bus and used as the required source operand value. If instead the State field indicates that the Op is currently completing execution, then it is possible to "bypass" the desired operand value off of the appropriate result bus. If the State field indicates that the Op entry has not

---

[38] See the section titled "Architectural and Microarchitectural Registers" beginning on page 88.

yet started execution or is not finished completing execution, then an operand value is not yet available. In any case either:

1. during the operand scan/selection process, an Op is identified as a source or supplier for each of the required source operand register values.

2. if the scan cannot find any older relevant Op entries, then by default the architectural/microarchitectural register file is the supplier of the required register operand value. This means that what is used is, in fact, the oldest and committed value for the required register.

Once the register operand values are available and supplied and the appropriate execution unit is available, the Op is executed and the register result value gets loaded into the Op entry's DestVal field.

THE MMX AND 3D REGISTERS

As mentioned earlier, the K6 3D has twenty-four 32-bit integer registers in the architectural/microarchitectural register file and twenty-four 32-bit integer renaming registers. The latter registers correspond to the twenty-four Op entries within the scheduler.

The MMX/3D instructions operate on 64-bit values and share usage of the eight architectural MMX registers. In contrast there are nine 64-bit MMX/3D registers in the architectural/microarchitectural register file and twelve 64-bit renaming registers. The nine architectural registers consist of eight that correspond to the x86 architecture MMX registers, plus one microarchitectural scratch register. Before indicating where the twelve renaming registers are located, let's first discuss why there are twelve of them.

Recall from Figure 2.3 on page 81 that the RUX and RUY can execute any combination of MMX and/or 3D instructions that do not involve the simultaneous use of the same shared execution logic in the two pipelines. Further, the decoders can decode up to two MMX or 3D instructions per cycle. These instructions each produce zero or one MMX or 3D RegOps for a maximum possible of two MMX/3D RegOps in an OpQuad. Similarly, each instruction may produce up to one LdOp. From an architectural perspective, each instruction can produce Ops with at most one register result. Consequently, each instruction, although able to produce up to two Ops, only requires up to one MMX/3D renaming register. (The case of a "LdOp;RegOp" combination is finessed by taking advantage of the fact that the LdOp register result is only used by the RegOp and that the two Ops are guaranteed to execute in sequential order. This allows one physical renaming register to be used by both Ops without actual conflict.)

If two MMX/3D instructions are decoded, the first pair of Ops in the OpQuad corresponds to the first MMX or 3D instruction and the second pair of Ops in the OpQuad corresponds to the second MMX or 3D instruction. Since the K6 3D requires only one MMX/3D renaming register per instruction, the scheduler contains one MMX/3D renaming register for the first pair of Ops in an OpQuad and a second MMX/3D renaming register for the second pair of Ops in an OpQuad. Given that there are six OpQuads in the scheduler, this means a total of twelve MMX/3D renaming registers are needed.

In the basic implicit renaming scheme just discussed, the scan for source operands examines the DestReg fields to look for a match with each of the SrcReg fields in the Op that require a source operand. The MMX/3D renaming registers are located within the scheduler itself according to the following algorithm. There is a 32-bit DestVal per Op entry and a 64-bit MDestVal per pair of Op entries. There is no physical sharing or reuse of the integer DestVal fields to hold MMX/3D register values.

But, how are these registers identified, i.e., what are their register numbers? Recall that the static fields Src1Reg[4:0], Src2Reg[4:0], and SrcStReg[4:0] hold the register numbers that identify registers which respectively hold the first source operand Src1, the second source operand Src2, and the store data operand of an Op, while the static field DestReg[4:0] holds a register number identifying the destination register of the Op. Each of the register number fields are five bits wide which means that thirty-two microarchitectural registers can be uniquely identified. A design decision was made that of the thirty-two possible registers, twenty-four of them were to be used for the twenty-four integer (micro)architectural registers and that the remaining eight would be used to identify eight of the nine MMX/3D architectural registers. The register number for the ninth register, the MMX/3D scratch register MMt1, was chosen to be the same register number as that of the integer register t1. This results in the constraint that MMt1 and t1 cannot be used in such a way that both are "live" at the same time, holding both an integer value and an MMX value for use by following integer and MMX/3D Ops.

The Basic Implicit Renaming Scheme Revisited

The MMX and 3D instructions do not deal with partial register modifications as do many of the x86 instructions. The bottom line is that the same exact scan process (and, in fact, the exact same logic) is used in renaming the MMX and 3D registers as was described earlier, taking into account that partial register modifications cannot occur. A scan to locate an MMX/3D operand will result in the 64-bit operand value located in the "MDestVal field" of two adjoining Op entries being driven onto the appropriate operand bus if a match is made on the DestReg field of either

Op entry. If no match results, the operand value is located in the MMX/3D architectural register file.

The handling of operand scan and selection and forwarding for integer and MMX/3D register values is unified within the scheduler—the same scheme and, in fact, the same scheduler logic and generated control signals function for handling both. This is enabled by having the twenty-four integer and nine MMX/3D registers use the same 5-bit register identifier space and by the appropriate setting of fields (such as the source and destination byte marks), and by the pair-wise OR'ing of per-Op-generated DestVal read/write/etc. control signals to produce the associated per pair of Ops MDestVal control signals.

DESIGN NOTE

FPU Register Renaming

The K6 renaming scheme does not apply to the floating-point unit. As discussed in the section titled "The Execution Units" beginning on page 77, the floating-point unit is essentially the core of the FPU from the Nx586 and is considered a "mini" microprocessor with a simple interface to the scheduler. It has its own Op queue, floating-point Op decoder, register file and register renaming scheme, control logic, dependency checking, and abort handling.

DIFFERENCES BETWEEN THE IMPLICIT AND EXPLICIT REGISTER RENAMING SCHEMES

There are a number of different issues that can form the basis of discussing differences between the implicit and explicit register renaming schemes. Among them are: the complexity of the solution, dependency checking, operand forwarding, dealing with partial register modifications, the amount of registers and logic required, and the scalability and flexibility of the scheme. There are a variety of approaches taken to implement renaming schemes. To do a good classification would be difficult because of the number of variables involved; however, some coarse comparisons can be made.

Complexity of the Solution

Let's consider what has to be done in any renaming scheme somewhere around instruction decode time, or shortly thereafter, if multiple decodes are supported. Multiple decodes means, in general, that multiple register renamings will be required. Since there may be data dependencies among instructions, the multiple renamings may be interdependent. If an explicit renaming scheme is being used, some mechanism is required to reflect these dependencies in the mapping information and to accommodate them during the multiple decode process itself as well as during an abort cycle. No such mechanism is required in the K6 3D's implicit renaming scheme.

On the other hand, when it comes time to actually obtain an operand, explicit schemes are somewhat simpler. If *Register 5* is needed, there's only one other Op in the machine that can be modifying *Register 5*. In an explicit renaming scheme, each older modifier of an architectural register, say AX, looks like it is modifying a different physical register. Suppose the value in AX is required. In the explicit scheme where there is one pool of registers, there is one physical register mapped into the AX register at any point in time, say *Register 5*, and that is the required register. That value may be a committed value or not but there's only one such required register. In the two pools scheme, either there is some register that contains a new value for the AX register, say *Register 7* (and there is only one of these at most) or, if no such register exists,[39] then the value for AX must be in the architectural register file. In either scheme, there is only one supplier for the required value and there is no need to distinguish between potentially many modifiers of a register as is required in the K6 3D.

The K6's implicit scheme is realized within the framework of a centralized scheduler buffer, not within a framework of distributed reservation stations. It is not clear how easily it extends to a distributed environment. Explicit schemes are, however, implemented in both centralized and distributed instruction window environments. Also note that handling of partial register results is relatively straightforward with the K6 3D's implicit scheme. This can be trickier and more involved with explicit schemes.

Resources Required

In an explicit scheme there needs to be some mechanism for keeping track of which physical registers are free and which are mapped to specific architectural registers for holding speculative, uncommitted results and what those mappings are. Multiple copies of such mappings need to be retained to accommodate aborts back to the architectural register state corresponding to just before or after any of the recent, still speculatively executed instructions. The specifics of what is needed depend, of course, on the particular explicit scheme employed and its implementation. In the K6, the renaming registers are contained within the scheduler Op entries. Therefore, no lists need to be maintained to identify free registers. The renaming registers are available to Ops as they are loaded into the first row

---

[39]   That is, neither Register 7 nor any other register holds a value for AX.

of the scheduler. Further, no mappings or multiple copies of mappings are required due to the way aborts are handled.

The number of registers required to do register renaming is basically identical for both approaches. As identified earlier, a total $X+Y+Z$ registers are required. In the explicit scheme, additional registers are required for the various copies of the mapping information (current table and history tables) and logic to do the mapping, multiple decodes, abort cycle handling, etc. In the centralized buffer, implicit scheme, no additional information is required for such mapping information. Logic is required to do the scan, but no special logic is required to handle multiple decodes or abort cycles.

SUMMARY OF THE CHAPTER

A detailed examination of three main aspects of the microarchitecture of the K6 3D in more detail—its scheduler, its operation commit unit, and its register renaming scheme—has been given in this chapter. As specific microarchitectural concepts were introduced, pseudo-RTL descriptions were given for typical chunks of logic that could be used to implement these concepts. Hopefully, the combination of "diagram, text, and pesudo-RTL descriptions," augmented by independent simulations by the reader, helped bring about an understanding how a contemporary superscalar microprocessor—with its multiple execution units, predecode logic, multiple decoders, scheduler, operation sequences, branch resolution logic, operation commit unit, register renaming scheme, and on-chip L1-Cahce and L2-Cache—might be designed and implemented. We intended Chapters 1 and 2 to provide a detailed and coherent context for the reader to study and understand microarchitecture elements and their impact on the overall design of a microprocessor. We now begin the second part of this book in which we attempt to provide a detailed and coherent treatment for understanding a wide range of platform-related and systems-related issues.

Chapter 4
Technology Components of Platform Architecture

T his chapter and the two chapters that follow are intended to provide the technology environment and platform context in which the microprocessor of Chapters 2 and 3 functions. The material here in Chapter 4 examines the interactions between the microprocessor and the balance of the platform, including hardware and software relationships, but it continues to be hardware centric. Chapter 5, Platform Memory Technology, examines memory types, memory controllers, and concludes with sections on Rambus and SLDRAM. Chapter 6, Platform Optimizations and Directions, ties together the material in Chapters 4 and 5, and examines performance issues and forces that are driving platform evolution.

This chapter builds on the platform overview provided in Chapter 1 (which we suggest you review at this point) and provides background information and overviews for the important technologies, standards, and initiatives impacting PC platforms. It should provide literacy with respect to the technologies examined and thereby facilitate further in-depth study of each technology. It will also act as an introduction to less-accessible industry standards. This chapter also provides the reader with information on the groups that control and publish the various platform standards and how the standards may be obtained.

This chapter is built around three major sections: PC Design Metastandards, Platform-Level Technology, and Component-Level Technology. The PC Design Metastandards section introduces the on-going series of industry endorsed PC Design Guides and Specifications, and describes the Microsoft logo certification process. The Platform-Level Technology section focuses on technologies, standards, and initiatives that have a major impact on multiple components or subsystems or the system as a whole. The Component-Level Technology section focuses on technologies, standards, and initiatives that tend to be centered in a single or few components or subsystems. The intended audience for each section in the chapter is indicated in the Road Map below.

ROAD MAP OF CHAPTER 4

Section	Audience
PC Design Metastandards	
Forces Driving Platform Architecture PC Design Guides and Specifications	Students and Faculty
Platform Categories	Those unfamiliar with PC platforms

Platform-Level Technology
    Enhanced User Experience
    Appliance-Like Operation
    Total Cost-of-Ownership
    Connectivity
	Those unfamiliar with PC industry initiatives

Component-Level Technology
    Processors
    General-Purpose Buses
    Device-Specific Buses and Ports
	Practitioners, managers, students, and faculty who want to study outside their area of specialization

PC DESIGN METASTANDARDS

PC platform technology is being driven forward by underlying economic and technology forces and by recent PC industry metastandards and certification programs for PC design. The economic and technology forces were present long before the industry standards and certification were in place and would continue to drive the platform forward in the absence of the standards. Nevertheless, one should not underestimate the importance of the present PC Design Specifications. Unlike previous PC industry attempts at metastandards, the present PC Design Specifications are more than just a codification of what PCs already are. They are now co-driving the PC technology evolution by aggressively raising the mandatory baseline functionality that PC platform designers must implement. The underlying economic and technology forces are still there, but the evolution is being driven faster in the short term than it would be otherwise, as a direct result of the PC Design Specifications and the certification process.

FORCES DRIVING PLATFORM ARCHITECTURE

From its inception, the PC platform has been perceived as a very flexible, but basic, programmable machine that the owner or user could customize via application software. This view was typified by early use of the platform as a near-dedicated word processor, spread sheet, data terminal, instructional aid, or game machine. The continuous but largely uncoordinated efforts at improving the PC platform's diverse roles as a publishing tool, a business machine, a tool for personal productivity, a self-instruction education device, or an entertainment machine, have been long established primary forces evolving the architecture. Another well established primary force behind platform evolution has been the necessity to overcome severe installation, configuration, and reliability problems stemming from the way in which the original I/O architecture was defined and used. More recently, PC platforms in different specialty forms have been emerging as preferred tools and appliances for the creation, collaboration, storage, distribution, retrieval, and presentation of content. The efforts to accelerate the realization of this vision are becoming additional primary forces.

Secondary Forces Driving Platform Architecture

Several secondary forces have driven and continue to drive the PC platform. A first of these is the economics of advancing semiconductor and magnetic-recording technologies, which have provided dramatically increased performance at constant and generally decreasing prices.

Another force is the keen desire of the PC and related industries to continue to grow the PC platform market at a double-digit rate. For at least the semiconductor sector, strong growth is necessary to offset continued decreasing sales prices and to finance the enormous investments required in factory and tooling costs. Strategies for accomplishing such growth are to increase platform affordability, accessibility, and acceptability in the general population, and to capture market share from other recreational pursuits. Platform affordability is improved by providing increased baseline functionality at constant or decreasing prices. Accessibility and acceptability are addressed by making platforms similar to appliances in their ease of operation, convenience, and unobtrusiveness. Market share capture from other recreational pursuits is accomplished by offering superior experiences or comparable experiences at a better value.

Additional secondary forces driving platform architecture include the adoption of the PC as a standard piece of office equipment, keen industry competition, and the transition of the platform to an item of mass production. Keen competition is most prevalent in common applications software, packaged systems, and such components as memory, hard disks, and system logic. Mass production has the expected volume-pricing benefits, but it also has attendant compatibility burdens. These burdens arise because standards with a large installed base are difficult to supplant with new standards, even when the new standards are superior.

PC Platform Evolution

The PC platform has evolved in many ways from the PC/AT archetype. Mainstream users interacted with the original ISA-Bus-based platform predominantly via a 23-row by 80-column character-only display and a keyboard. The keyboard was required for communicating commands and file names to the operating system and applications. The keyboard was also the principal means of moving the data entry point about the display screen. Printer output was also predominantly character oriented. Dial-up communications were available, but modems were expensive and slow.

The Rise of Graphics, Multimedia, and Networking

The later half of the 80's saw the augmentation of the mainstream PC platform with capabilities for graphics, multimedia, networking, and content distribution. The open architecture of the ISA Bus contributed to the availability of affordable peripherals, which in turn facilitated the adoption of new capabilities and the success of the platform as a whole. Following in the footsteps of the Apple Macintosh, graphics features were applied to the control of the operating system and applications and for the creation of documents and other works. These features included the ability to display, create, and print graphics; to move and select screen objects via a hand-held pointer; to use a wide range of typeface styles and sizes; and the ability to imbed both images and text on the same page.

These new graphics features were motivated by a desire to make computers easier to use and to enable *desktop publishing*. Desktop publishing required the capability to create virtually any kind of printed work and to have the final printed form of the work match exactly what was created on the screen.[40] These features required a migration to high-resolution color graphics displays and printers, larger hard-disks, new applications, and support from the operating system.

Multimedia features included the ability to have simultaneous use of text, images, video, and audio and sound effects. Multimedia features were motivated by the desire to exploit, experiment with, and be entertained by a new genre of dynamic and interactive works that was much more effective at communication than the static printed page. Multimedia offered exciting games, attention grabbing education, and compelling business presentations. Multimedia required high data-transfer rates and it was soon realized that the ISA Bus had insufficient bandwidth headroom to provide quality results. The data storage requirements for multimedia works were also high and necessitated the widespread adoption of the CD-ROM as a storage peripheral to augment the hard disk.

---

[40] This ability to have print output exactly match the screen is known as *What You See Is What You Get* (WYSIWIG).

During this same period, networking evolved from a specialty add-on to an integral component of the operating system. In addition, consumer use of modem communications rose PC in tandem with improving speeds and the availability of dial-up services providing consumer oriented content.

The System Resource Crisis

The rise of graphics, multimedia, and networking features frequently resulted in what was perceived to be a shortage of available system resources. These resources included expansion slots, certain classes of control lines, and other system resources[41] generally necessarily assigned to each peripheral for proper operation. The I/O paradigm from the beginning of the PC platform was that each expansion device generally used a dedicated interrupt resource to signal the microprocessor that it needed servicing in a timely fashion. There was no defined way of sharing interrupts that ensured that conflicts would not result, or that each of the devices sharing the interrupt would be serviced within any particular time interval. While expansion slot availability was solved in part by integrating some popular expansion peripherals into the standard logic of the system, the shortage of other system resources continued. The resource shortage resulted in considerable loses in productivity and goodwill toward the PC platform, due to difficulties in installation and maintenance and instabilities and unreliability due to marginal operation. The perception arose that in addition to its performance limitations, the small number of critical resources defined for the ISA Bus's I/O architecture was going to ultimately limit the success of the platform.

Focus on Performance for Graphics and Multimedia

The early 90's saw continued advancements in the performance of the PC platform in many areas and attempts to address the system resource configuration problem. PCs became highly connected, with ubiquitous networking for office PCs and ubiquitous modem communications for home PCs. Graphics acceleration became common for speeding complex screen updates. The PCI Bus was added to provide improved peak bandwidth for high speed peripherals, such as high speed hard disks and the new graphics accelerators. The PCI Bus also provided needed low latency capability and bandwidth headroom for the multiple latency-intolerant-processes associated with multimedia. The view arose that one used the PCI Bus for

---

[41] The control lines mentioned are associated with the ISA Bus's interrupt request and Direct Memory Access features. The other system resources mentioned included areas in the I/O address space and reserved areas in the memory address space.

high performance peripherals, but one could continue to rely on the ISA Bus for inexpensive low-performance devices.

Early Automatic Configuration Efforts

The system-resource configuration-problem was partially mitigated through an industry initiative known as Plug and Play, which placed new requirements on both hardware and software. Hardware devices, whether integrated in the system logic or on expansion cards, were required to report their resource needs to the operating system and be flexibly configurable under operating system control. Application programs were required to be as flexible as possible and the operating system managed the assignment of resources.

Call for Abandonment of Legacy I/O

In spite of a lessening of configuration problems due to the Plug and Play initiative, the installation, maintenance, and reliability of the PC platform continues to be a serious problem that is blamed on legacy-based I/O. Furthermore, the perception has arisen that as performance requirements have increased, the ISA Bus is not merely inadequate in performance, but the very use of the ISA Bus for low performance peripherals is limiting the performance realizable from the system as a whole.

Recently, new peripheral bus architectures, including the Universal Serial Bus and IEEE 1394, have emerged that redefine the use of system resources and physical connections to the platform in a far more efficient manner than legacy I/O. In the new paradigm of resource allocation, many diverse devices communicate via packet messaging to a host controller in the PC. The communications protocol of these buses are defined to ensure that any device that so requires it may be serviced within guaranteed maximum latencies. With these new buses, individual interrupts per device are neither required nor available.

To ensure completely that no conflicts or instabilities arise due to legacy peripherals, the present PC Specifications require not only the adoption of the new buses, but the complete abandonment of legacy I/O architecture devices and the ISA Bus. This radical departure from legacy hardware compatibility also ensures that the use of legacy I/O devices will no longer limit system performance or create installation and maintenance difficulties. The new peripheral bus architectures are also much more versatile, supporting carefree attachment and removal of peripheral devices. Such events required significant reconfiguration and loss of productivity in the legacy I/O architecture.

Constants of Change

Throughout the evolution of the PC platform, speeds have continually increased for processors, memory, and peripherals, as have memory and storage capacities. These advances have been partially offset by the demands of increasingly sophisticated operating systems and applications. The practical and reliable operation of both types of software would not be possible without the attendant increases in processors and memory speed and the capacity of memory and storage.

PC DESIGN GUIDES AND SPECIFICATIONS

The PC Design Guides and Specifications are a running series of published guides and specifications that have become the overarching standards governing all aspects of PC platform architecture. The PC 98 guide was over 600 pages in length, although a summary appendix provides a condensed requirements checklist of slightly over 30 pages. The specifications consist of the published guides in conjunction with amendments and associated compliance schedules. The PC Specifications are followed closely by all major PC manufacturers.

While the first two guides were authored solely by Microsoft, Microsoft and Intel began co-authoring the guides starting with the *PC 98 System Design Guide*. Recent guides have been initially posted on the Web in draft form and reviewers from the general industry have been encouraged to provide feedback and suggested changes that help mold the final specification. The guides systematically detail requirements for performance, interoperability, ease of use, and ergonometrics. These requirements cover all of the platform's subsystems, buses, and devices. This section examines why the guides and specifications have achieved the significance they have and provides an overview of their organization.

AUDIO ON CD-ROM

Legacy Software Compatibility: The CD-ROM includes a short audio-segment that describes some implicit PC platform requirements.

Logo Certification

The PC specifications and their associated design guides have achieved their stature as a result of Microsoft's "Designed for Windows" logo certification program. Microsoft permits hardware vendors to use special Microsoft logos in the marketing of products that meet the specification guidelines. The Microsoft "Designed for Windows" logo is a very desirable

Microsoft's "Designed for Windows"

Win32 operating systems include the Windows 95, Windows 98, and Windows NT 32-bit operating systems.

marketing feature for system vendors and other Independent Hardware Vendors (IHVs).

Burned by incompatibilities and difficult installations, many consumers and corporate buyers rank products with the logo well above those products that do not have it. At Microsoft's WinHEC '97[42], Microsoft said that 273 PC manufacturers, 348 hardware vendors, and 267 software vendors had been certified to use a Microsoft *Designed for Windows* logo for its Win32 operating systems.

The product-by-product license to use Microsoft's "Designed for" logos and listing of the vendor's product on Microsoft's Windows Hardware Compatibility List (HCL), occurs only after the vendor's product passes qualification by Microsoft's Windows Hardware Qualification Labs (WHQL). The WHQL develops its Hardware Compatibility Tests (HCT) from the requirements in the design guide, amendments to the guide, and a compliance schedule. The amendments and compliance schedule are posted on Microsoft's Web site. Passing the HCT involves significant effort on the part of the vendor, including self pretesting, satisfying the Test Submission requirements (including providing pretest logs and many duplicates of the system or device to be tested), signing the relevant logo license agreements, and payment of test fees.

Each subsequent guide often incorporates, by reference, sections from earlier guides in the series. To design a compliant system and fully understand each guide, you generally need access to more than the most recent guide.

Products submitted for testing on or after July 1st of each year must meet the PC Specifications for that year as detained in the PC Design Guides and as amended online. However, several requirements usually are often not enforced until a later date. This occurs when it is perceived that the requirements are too aggressive for earlier enforcement. The compliance schedules for such postponed enforcement items are also posted online.

Report on CD-ROM

To learn more about Microsoft Windows Logo Certification, see the article by Peter N. Glaskowsky, "WinHEC Shows Road to Memphis," *Microprocessor Report*, Vol. 11. No. 6, May 12, 1997, on the CD-ROM.

Summary of Principal System Requirements

The core system requirements for certification of PCs for several of the past specifications are shown in Table 4.1. The staged phasing-out of legacy devices, the elimination of the ISA Bus, and the adoption of replacement peripheral buses are quite evident. The continued evolution of

---

[42] WinHEC is Microsoft's Windows Hardware Engineering Conference, which is held twice a year.

increased processor performance, memory size, and graphics capabilities are unmistakable as well. Note that generally the changes between each year's requirements are incremental. Recommendations are used to signal future major design shifts, with major technology components usually being been phased in (or out) over multiple years. The requirement trends for performance and feature attributes that have changed rapidly in the past (e.g., processor performance, main memory size, and graphics resolution) also likely will continue and designers can extrapolate these trends and make expectations for future requirements.

Platform Category Definitions

Figure 4.1 shows a Venn diagram of the subcategories defined by the PC Specifications and the various groupings into which they are associated. The overall consumer category includes the Consumer PC and Entertainment PC subcategories. The overall business category includes the Office PC, Mobile, Workstation, and NetPC subcategories. Each of these subcategories is explained below in the Platform Categories section.

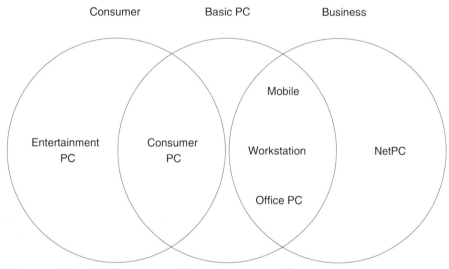

Figure 4.1 PC PLATFORM CATEGORIES AND SUBCATEGORIES

A Basic PC meta-category is defined to include the Consumer PC, Office PC, Mobile, and Workstation subcategories. These Basic PC platforms all generally share many common hardware characteristics and more importantly what has become the basic operating paradigm for PC platforms. To the extent that this is so, the Basic PC category serves as a useful abstraction, and acts to distinguish the Entertainment and NetPCs as truly distinct species from conventional PC platforms.

Basic PC

Table 4.1 COMPARISON OF CORE SYSTEM REQUIREMENTS FOR DIFFERENT PC SPECIFICATIONS

Feature[a]	PC 95[b] [c]	Basic PC 97	Basic PC 98	Basic PC 99
Equivalent Processor Performance	80386, 33 MHz 80486 recommended	120 MHz P5	200 MHz P55C (with MMX)	300 MHz PII (with MMX)
Main Memory Size	4 MB, 8MB recommended	16 MB, 32 MB recommended	32 MB, 64 MB at 66 MHz recommended	32 MB, 64 MB at 100 MHz recommended
External Cache	(not mentioned)	recommended	256 KB	256 KB
Graphics	640 x 480 x 8 bits per pixel (bpp) recommended, high-speed bus (not ISA) recommended	800 x 600 x 16 bpp, uses high-speed bus, does not use ISA, multiple display adapters and monitors supported	1024 x 768 x [8,15,16] bpp and lower Video Electronics Standard Association modes, otherwise same as PC 97	same as PC 98, AGP 2.0 recommended
2D or 3D Graphics Acceleration	(not mentioned)	(not mentioned)	if present, 2D/3D rendering must have double buffering for up to 800 x 600 x 16 bpp. 3D rendering must also have a Z buffer [d] and 1.25 MB local texture cache or equivalent AGP capability	same as PC 98, Z buffer must be at least 16-bits
ISA Bus	ISA devices must be Plug and Play compliant, 16-bit I/O decoding required	same as PC 95, but not recommended for any device	no populated ISA slots when sold, not recommended for motherboard devices	No ISA slots or motherboard devices
High-speed Expansion Bus	recommended, PCI must be Revision 2.0 compliant	recommended, PCI must be Revision 2.1 compliant	SCSI or IEEE 1394 recommended, PCI must be Revision 2.1 compliant	IEEE 1394 recommended, PCI must be Revision 2.2 compliant
Universal Serial Bus	(not mentioned)	required, 2 user accessible ports recommended	1 user accessible port required, 2 recommended	2 user accessible ports required
IEEE 1394 Bus	(not mentioned)	recommended	recommended	required, recommended as a secondary host controller
Device Bay	(not mentioned)	(not mentioned)	recommended	recommended

[a]   Each of SCSI, IEEE 1394, the Universal Serial Bus, and Device Bay are discussed later in this chapter.

[b]   There was no PC 96 guide.

[c]   Platform designers must rely on official guides as amended online. See http://www.microsoft.com/hwdev/.

[d]   A *Z buffer* is a memory used in 3D rendering to facilitate the relative foreground-to-background ordering of modeled objects.

The Consumer PC is essentially a desktop platform targeted at and optimized for the consumer market segment. Consumer PC platforms are expected to have Internet connectivity via dial-up modem, be used primarily for entertainment, education, and personal productivity applications, have strong graphics capability, and be digital-TV and audio ready.

The Office PC is essentially a desktop platform targeted at and optimized for the commercial market segment. Such platforms are connected to a Local Area Network (LAN) and run productivity applications. Each Office PC has manageability features, such as Advanced Configuration and Power Interface support, centralized administration, and is upgradable for remote boot capability. It is intranet, Microsoft Zero Administration Initiative for Windows (ZAW), and conferencing ready. AGPI is discussed in the Appliance-Like Operation section. ZAW is discussed in the Total Cost-of-Ownership section.

Consumer PC

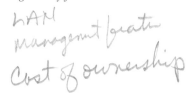

Office PC

manageability features

INDUSTRY STANDARDS

PC Design Guides

The most recent guides are available in most technical bookstores and can be ordered direct from Microsoft Press at URL:

> http://mspress.microsoft.com/

Microsoft provides free access to formatted text files and online navigable versions of the guides, along with up-to-date information about logo compliance dates, under the following URL:

> http://www.microsoft.com/hwdev/desguid/

> Microsoft "Designed for Windows" Logo Qualification Standards

More information about the Hardware Compatibility Tests (HCT) Test Suite and how to order a CD-ROM containing the suite is at URL:

> http://www.microsoft.com/hwtest/

SUGGESTED READINGS

PC Design Guides

The past design guides can provide additional understanding and collectively they chronicle an important era in the evolution of the PC platform:

1. *Hardware Design Guide for Microsoft Windows 95*, Microsoft Press, 1994.
2. The *PC 97 Hardware Design Guide,* Microsoft Press, 1996.
3. The *PC 98 System Design Guide,* Microsoft Press, 1997.

PLATFORM CATEGORIES

This section surveys conventional platform types and market segments, and platform categories as defined by the PC Specifications. The relationships and distinctions between each of these is important to understanding the PC marketplace and our analysis of industry initiatives and platform-and component-level technologies.

Platform Types

New content and connectivity uses constitute new subsegments of platform and market types. The continual redefinition of platform types and market segments is discussed in the discussed in the Contemporary Platform Strategic Issues section of Chapter 6.

A specific PC is designed primarily for use as a desktop, workstation, server, mobile, entertainment appliance, or network PC. These distinctions between platform types are idealizations that are often blurred in practice. For example, mobiles are frequently used as desktop surrogates. Desktops are pressed into service as low-price servers, particularly in small office peer-to-peer networking situations.

Desktops

Desktops (including consumer and office desktops, mini-towers, and towers) are typically used predominantly by one person, for one or a few key applications, such as word-processing, database entry or management, or Web browsing. Desktops are available in a wide range of features, performance, and price. Currently, desktop platforms come in single-and-multiple processor configurations, have a wide range of advanced memory technology, have different levels of I/O integration, and offer multiple types of system and microprocessor buses.

Workstations

Workstations are high-end desktops, virtually always used by professional knowledge workers engaged in some form of critical intellectual property or content creation, be it software development, large desktop publishing projects, elaborate multimedia works, or engineering simulations.

Servers

A *server* is a networked high-performance PC that is a gateway for other PCs to one or more desired resources or concentrations of data. Specialized server categories included *Workgroup Servers, Departmental Servers,* and *Enterprise Servers.* Often a variant of the workstation class, *workgroup servers* may be found distributed throughout offices to provide file and printer sharing, often organized around the teams reporting to first-line managers and the staffs of higher-level management.

workgroup servers

departmental servers

Departmental servers are generally used in organized collections of servers used in divisional or secondary data centers, supporting site intranets, project databases, and departmental services such as e-mail and remote access dial-in and dial-back modem connections. Departmental servers are often packaged for mounting in racks with other servers or networking equipment, and may share switched monitors, keyboards, and mice, among several other servers.

Enterprise servers are an extension of departmental servers, but designed for use in the principal data centers of large enterprises. These servers support corporate intranets, large transactional databases, and other applications requiring centralized processing or control. They are characterized by the use of tightly coupled multiprocessors within the same platform, loosely coupled platform clusters, ultra high-capacity storage, and very high speed network connections.

Mobiles

Mobile PCs (including portables, laptops, systems having integrated digital phones and future systems incorporating Personal Communication Services (PCS) features) are machines that can easily be moved about. A *portable* is a personal computer that is capable of being carried, and in which the motherboard, keyboard, pointing device, and display are generally integral to a single package. A *mobile* is a portable computer that can be used solely on batteries or directly or indirectly on 12V. A *laptop* is a mobile computer that can be used on one's lap. While these distinctions were once important, today the terms are used almost interchangeably because virtually all portable computers sold today meet the above definition of a laptop.

Entertainment PCs

Entertainment PCs are being positioned through industry design initiatives to become the favored centerpiece of consumer free-time activity. An offshoot of consumer desktops, the Entertainment PC was first introduced in PC 97 as the Entertainment Platform (EP), and was described as an "interactive multimedia system optimized for games, education, personal communications, and video playback."

The Entertainment PC is intended to be the ultimate PC for audio/visual and game enthusiasts, with the best graphics, video, and audio of any platform class. It is to be the platform of choice for cutting-edge applications, characterized by engaging rich detail and realism. The Entertainment PC will be the vehicle used to enhance TV via interactivity and better image quality, and it provides advanced e-mail, voice mail, and telephony. These latter applications require that this platform be as easy or easier to use than present consumer appliances found in the home.

enterprise servers

portable

mobile

laptop

Network PC

The PC Specifications require that Net PCs have hard disks. However, the hard disks are not used for resident storage of either system or application software or data, but for data caching to improve performance and reduce network traffic.

Network PCs or NetPCs are an emerging category envisioned as providing the lowest cost-of-ownership for massive commercial PC installations while addressing the typical needs of most knowledge and service workers. These *thin clients* rely on networked servers for most or all of their data storage and are designed specifically for remote configuration and management.

AUDIOS ON CD-ROM

	Additional information about each Platform Type is included on the CD-ROM:
	· Desktops · Mobiles
	· Workstations · Entertainment PC
	· Servers · Network PC

Market Segments

Market segments are a device for abstracting the buying patterns and decisions of groups of PC buyers who tend to behave in a like manner. The PC Market was once simply conceptually divided between the Consumer and Commercial market segments. New platform uses have grown the market steadily to encompass new segments. For example, today the Commercial market may be considered to include Enterprise Computing, Workgroup Computing, Internet Service Provider, and Small Business and Emerging Markets Computing Segments. Across the various segments there is a wide variation in the scale of infrastructure for computing, storage, networking, and communications.

Consumer Segment

The *Consumer* segment has always been centered on providing entertainment or amusement, self-paced education (especially for school-age children), and enhancing personal productivity, while meeting acute cost sensitivities. Important subsegments are the gaming and Small Office/Home Office (SOHO) markets. Future subsegments are anticipated for home servers, computing appliances, and hybrid TV/PCs.

Commercial Segment

Enterprise Segment

The segments of the *Commercial* Business market are centered on enhancing the profits or service of companies and organizations via cost-effective personal-productivity and information-management tools. The *Enterprise Segment* characteristically has a client-server galaxy managed and linked via a large routing and switching network. The network is used to logically integrate application and data resources and provide distributed and remote computing services including Internet and intranet access.

The *Workgroup Segment* focuses on peer-to-peer networking within a local site, while providing connectivity to the centralized computing resources of a parent Enterprise. The *Internet Service Provider* Segment focuses on managed storage servers and Telephone Company ("Telco") access. The *Small Business and Emerging Market Segment* focuses on ease of use and the Internet access.

Workgroup Segment

PLATFORM-LEVEL TECHNOLOGY

This major section and the one that follows (Component-Level Technology) examine the key standards, initiatives, and technologies that define present and emerging platform architecture. We distinguish platform-level technologies from component-level technologies by their scope. Platform-level technologies have a major impact on multiple components or subsystems or the system as a whole. Component-level technologies have a focus that is generally limited to a single type of component or subsystem.

It is also the case that we view the platform-level technologies as representing technology directions. This contrasts with the component-level technologies that we view as generally representing specific technology destinations. Accordingly, we examine a number of platform-level standards, initiatives, and technologies organized under four categories that are our abstraction of the most significant thrusts in platform hardware. These four thrusts are the deliverance to the platform user or owner of an *Enhanced User Experience*, *Appliance-like Operation*, reduced *Total Cost-of-Ownership (TCO)* and *Connectivity* to networks and other platforms.

As will come out in the individual discussions, many of the standards and initiatives have attributes that fall in multiple categories.

ENHANCED USER EXPERIENCE

Sell more Windows NW –

This section focuses on the efforts by the PC industry to improve the experiences that users accrue. These experiences are key to the continued growth of the PC market. Manufacturers are counting on users to be enthusiastic proponents of the platform to potential users, they want users to continually upgrade, and they want users to consider buying multiple PCs for diverse purposes, including supplanting other consumer entertainment electronics.

Continually upgrade = bloatware

Providing enhanced user experiences is progressing along several fronts. The advent of Windows 3.X and Windows 95, brought great strides to the PC platform through a greatly improved user interface (UI) technology (discussed below) compared to the earlier command-line-oriented operating systems. The improved UI provided user ease of use and presentation quality, at levels previously unseen in the PC platform. Ease-

of-use features serve to improve PC usability and productivity for users. This greatly minimizes the intimidation and frustration experienced by novice users and enhances productivity for all users for applications that are just being learned or which are used infrequently. Presentation quality features enable users to rapidly generate business-quality documents and presentations.

Enhanced user experience features go beyond ease of use and presentation quality. New technologies are being incorporated to engage the user with dazzling and sophisticated audio, video, and rich 3D graphics effects. Plug and Play technology is reducing the very negative experiences that users have had in PC platform configuration and maintenance. New interconnect technologies (e.g., USB and IEEE 1394) will further this by eliminating legacy resource limitations that had been a source of much user configuration frustration. Reliability, compatibility, and performance are being improved through software initiatives including the introduction of the Win32 Driver Model (WDM) and the DirectX API. Also essential to improved performance and reliability is the eventual elimination of legacy ports.

Summary of Key User Interface Technology

These fundamental sections are intended for those who are relatively new to PC platforms. PC veterans will want to skip ahead.

The user interface paradigms and enabling technologies reviewed in this section promote ease of use and presentation quality.

Graphical User Interface (GUI)

Today's principal operating systems (OSs, such as Windows 95 and Unix) and associated applications for PC platforms use a *Graphical User Interface (GUI).* GUIs are typified by the use of on-screen menus and icons (stylized graphical objects) to represent programs, program controls, and data objects. The objects are activated by a button-press while using a hand-held pointer (typically a mouse) to position a cursor over the object. This provides a *point-and-click interface* for *navigation* (locating and selecting programs and data) and primary control (activating, opening, copying, moving).

Windows[43]

PC platform OSs and applications also manage complexity by organizing the display as arbitrarily sized and opaquely overlapping rectangular display regions or *windows,* each generally associated with an individual pro-

---

[43] A reference in this chapter simply to "Windows" refers to the generic windows described in the section associated with this footnote. A reference to an operating system product will give a specific product name (e.g., Windows NT) or will include the vendors name (e.g., Microsoft) in close proximity.

gram, data file, status message, or control selection. The user is generally permitted wide latitude in the placement and organization of these windows. Windows promote awareness by the user of the computer's multiple ongoing activities and permit quick shifts in the user's focus to any of the activities.

High-Resolution Color BitMaps

PC platform OSs and applications also generally use a *bitmap* to permit the definition of window boundaries and other screen graphics with resolution that is conceptually the same as the pixel resolution of the display screen. High-resolution color monitors, printers, and scanners for high-quality bit-mapped images greatly augment and enhance GUIs, by providing displays and hard-copy output with graphics, drawings, and pictures.

When using analog displays (e.g., a CRT monitor) the frame buffer resolution is typically somewhat higher than the realizable resolution of the display screen. See the section on Graphics and Video Adapters later in this chapter for information on graphics standards.

HISTORICAL COMMENTS

Bit-Mapped Graphical User Interfaces (GUIs) with Windows

Bit-mapped Graphical User Interfaces (GUIs) with Windows of today's PCs share many similarities with concepts investigated in Ted Nelson's, multi-decade long, 1965-initiated Project Xanadu and further developed in the Xerox Palo Alto Research Center (PARC) Alto personal computer in 1973. Apple founder Steve Jobs was so impressed with a demonstration of the Alto that he hired away several key designers to develop similar machines for Apple. Apple subsequently introduced the unsuccessful Lisa personal computer in 1982 and the wildly successful Macintosh in 1984.

"insanely"

Portable Document Format (PDF)

PDF is a standard file format for distributing presentation-quality formal documents having both images and text, such as datasheets, manuals, technical reports, and journal papers. Via the PDF standard, creators of documents continue to compose works with their favorite content creation tools (typically desktop publishing and graphics programs). The work is then converted using a special writing tool and distributed in the.pdf format. Users are not required to have the same creative tool used by the publisher in order to view and print the work, yet the document appears identical across all output devices.

INDUSTRY STANDARDS

Portable Document Format (PDF)

The PDF is a proprietary standard of the Adobe Corporation. The Adobe Acrobat Reader, which permits viewing and printing of .pdf files that will look in the final reproduction as the creator intended, is available free to download over the Internet. Adobe benefits by selling the writing tools necessary to create the .pdf files.

The Acrobat Reader is included on the companion CD-ROM. Generating PDF files requires purchasing the full Adobe Acrobat package.

See http://www.adobe.com/prodindex/acrobat/ for information about Adobe Acrobat and the Adobe Acrobat Reader.

Hypertext Documents

Hypertext Documents are Windows-GUI documents containing point-and-click activated text or graphics objects. The reader activates these objects to move within the same document, to go to a new machine-readable document, to activate file transfers and content delivery, activate an embedded program, or activate other arbitrary functions.

HISTORICAL COMMENT

Hypertext

Hypertext has similarities with the "memex" information system described in a 1945 article in *The Atlantic Monthly*, by Vannevar Bush, entitled *As We May Think*. Doug Englebart demonstrated a system using hypertext at the 1968 Fall Joint Computer Conference.

Interactive Assistance and Automation

Sophisticated interactive assistance and automation is common in today's applications for desktop publishing, word processors, presentations, spreadsheets, databases, and design graphics. These features enable individual workers to more efficiently generate, manipulate, and communicate information.

Audios on CD-ROM

Additional tutorial information about several of these Key User Interface Technologies is included in several audio clips on the CD-ROM.

- Graphical User Interface (GUI)
- High-Resolution Color Bitmaps
- Hypertext Documents
- Interactive Assistance and Automation

Multimedia Technology

Multimedia is the ability to augment a static program display with music, sound effects, informational audio messages, video clips, or dynamic graphics and animation, and particularly the simultaneous combination of these. The information presented by the additional media enhances the user experience by providing background information, different perspectives, and other supplemental material, and by grabbing and keeping the user's attention through its dynamic presentation. Multimedia applications are facilitated by the data density of CD-ROMs, or by more expensive high-bandwidth data communications network connections. Multimedia requires additional hardware, such as sound-cards, external speakers and microphones, and interfaces to audio and video sources. Multimedia processing is characterized by the use of intensive, recurring, computations and data-independent recurring memory-accesses on large volumes of small native data types.

CD-ROM and DVD-ROM

CD-ROMs permit volumes of locally held content to be streamed through the platform to the user at data rates that if held remotely would require network connections that are presently prohibitively expensive for many users. These characteristics make this inexpensive removable optical media ideal for software and data distribution via mail and archival storage. The read-only CD-ROM drive is widely available with good performance at low prices and has become a standard feature in all platforms, including the mobile platform. The DVD-ROM is expected to supplant CD-ROM over time, but is being hindered by the existence of multiple competing formats and slow acceptance by some sectors of the entertainment industry.

Streaming Media

Digitization and digital signal processing are discussed in the next subsection.

Audio and video interact with the user as streams of information in analog form. PC platforms employ any of a number of popular digital audio and video standards for capturing and digitizing analog sources for later reconstruction prior to output. The digitized data also exists as streams of information, this time in sequential bit patterns. More generally, streaming data could be any serial sequence of digitized analog signals, such as telemetry from an instrumented process or event. Such a sequence might originate from a CD-ROM drive or other mass storage device, from a video digitizer coupled to a television-like source, or from a high-speed network. Digitized data streams may be compressed, edited, filtered, or otherwise processed using digital signal processing techniques.

Signal processing on streaming data may be done either by the primary processor or dedicated audio and video hardware accelerators (data pumps). Video processing requires input and output peripherals and processing power of significantly higher bandwidth, sophistication, and expense, than for analog. Trade-offs frequently must be made between fidelity and bandwidth.

The processing of streaming data by the processor requires special considerations compared to general-purpose data processing. Unlike other types of data processing, the processing ordering of the data streams generally matters. To prevent acute performance degradation, special care should be taken to prevent the transient streaming data from causing the rapid displacement of other (non-streaming) data from the caches. The most straightforward solution to this problem is to treat streaming data as noncacheable.

DEFINITION
Real-Time Data Processing
Real-time processing of streaming data requires information capture, storage or transmission, processing, or timely generation of responses, for events that are impractical, undesirable, or impossible for the system to temporarily stop or run at a slower rate. A system is effectively a real-time system for a given processing task if it is fast enough to perform its desired function, while processing information at least as fast as it is being naturally generated (or needed) by the evolving event.

Capture, playback, and live conferencing must be performed such that noticeable delays, lack of synchronization, or lost data are minimized. Capture must always be performed in real time. Coding to achieve efficient file sizes involves compression techniques that for video often cannot be performed in real time, especially if dedicated accelerators are not used. Playback, including digital decoding, generally must be performed in real time. For interactive or multimedia applications, real-time processing should not introduce any processing artifacts noticeable to the user, such as unexpected delays, gaps or abrupt changes in the output, or out-of-sync multimedia.

Digitization Digital Signal Processing

Pulse Code Modulation (*PCM*) and derivative techniques perform digitization of real-world analog signals; intermediate transmission, storage, and signal processing in the digital domain; and eventual analog reconstruction. The arbitrary processing (filtering or other manipulation) of signals in the digital domain is known as Digital Signal Processing (DSP).

Digitization is the sampling and coding of an analog signal into a digital word. *Sampling* uses a sample-and-hold circuit to repetitively capture analog domain (continuous) voltage levels at discrete time intervals. *Coding* maps the continuous voltage level of each sample to one of the discrete voltage levels representable by the fixed bit-width of the digital word output. The mapping is frequently and intentionally non-linear. The Analog-to-Digital conversion (ADC) and front-end signal processing is called *Coding* and is done by a Coder (sometimes Encoder). Sometimes the sampling step is integral (or implied to be) to the coding step. The inverse Digital-to-Analog conversion (DAC) with back-end signal processing is called *Decoding* and is done by a Decoder.

A Coder/Decoder, or *Codec*, is a method, a hardware device or subsystem, or signal processing software that combines both a Coder and Decoder. Historically and in most dedicated or high-performance applications, the Codec is implemented in special-purpose hardware. However, depending on the pass-band frequencies of interest, processors can execute Software Codecs to perform the compression and decompression functions in software.

Software-based Codecs and other DSP routines can consume considerable processor power, particularly for digital video. If DSP functions are used simultaneously with other major applications, or on a regular basis, the platform may need to increase processor speeds, make use of appropriate MMX or AMD-3D instruction sets, or resort to the appropriate acceleration hardware, in order to deliver acceptable performance.

Broadly speaking, a Codec is a standard for implementing digital audio (e.g., AC-3, AC 97) or video (e.g., Indeo, Cinepak). Each standard defines applicable attributes such as the bit-width of the digital words, the sample-rate (and thereby the effective analog pass-band), stereo/mono capability, full/half duplex capability, and the characteristic "law" or "curve" used to map (generally non-linearly) between the analog continuous voltage values and the digital discrete data values.

PCM

*digitization
sampling*

coding

decoding

Codec

Software Codecs

Digital Audio

Digital audio is music, voice, and sound effects that are at least partially created, transmitted, stored, or received, using PCM techniques. Digital audio also encompasses the use of Musical Instrument Digital Interface (MIDI) and three-dimensional audio. These are each discussed in turn.

Music and Sound Effects Synthesis

FM Synthesis

Sound Blaster is a series of sound cards originally produced by Creative Labs. Its popularity resulted in its becoming a register-level hardware standard for audio cards. Sound Blaster and compatible products relied on *FM Synthesis* to emulate musical instruments and generate sound effects by artful combination and control of many analog oscillators, mixers, and special wave-shaping analog signal processing circuits.

Wavetables

Digital PCM-based Wavetable Synthesis, already popular for portable and compact musical instruments, is supplanting analog FM synthesis methods in the PC platform as well. "*Wavetables*" are sets of digitized samples of musical instruments and other real-world sounds that are stored in ROM or downloaded into RAM. High-fidelity music and audio are then reconstructed from the wavetable samples. Commercial providers can offer wavetables digitized under ideal conditions, sampling notes over the entire range of a perfectly tuned, studio-quality instrument.

Musical Instrument Digital Interface (MIDI)

Musical Instrument Digital Interface (*MIDI*) is a protocol and interface standard for the flexible control and operation of music synthesizers. MIDI files can control both the FM and Wavetable Synthesizer used by PCs to generate music. MIDI-support is a common standard or optional feature on PC sound cards. MIDI has been commonly used for quite some time by portable and "compact" musical instruments and in PC-based games. It is used on Web pages as a low-bandwidth means to add musical content.

MIDI files are the modern day enhanced equivalent of a player-piano song paper-roll. Music is represented by a sequence of digital words. The digital values specify "voice" (choice of a particular mode on the target musical instrument) and musical notes with associated attributes (amplitude, start, duration, and optional special effect). The current General MIDI (GM) specification calls for support for 128 voices and 24 simultaneous notes.

Three-Dimensional Audio

3D Audio, 3D Sound, or Positional Audio, describes multi-channel audio systems that employ signal processing to enhance or emphasize positional or dimensional effects for simulating reflections, depth and spaciousness, and directionality of sounds. Positional audio directional effects include pinpoint sounds that can be moved arbitrarily around the listener.

Dolby Surround AC-3 (for Audio Coding 3), also known as Dolby Surround Digital, or simply AC-3, is the 3D-audio codec used by DVDROMs. It is the Dolby Labs specification for a "5.1" channel PC implementation of Dolby's Surround Sound movie-theatre sound technology. The 5.1 channel designation refers to AC-3's five 3Hz-20kHz channels, for rear-left-side "surround", left, center, right, and rear-right-side "surround;" and one 3-120Hz channel for an arbitrarily placed sub-woofer

Plug and Play Configuration and Maintenance

PC platforms are noted for their relatively cheap peripherals that are sometimes trivial to install and configure. Once set up, PCs are usually stable and do not require significant maintenance. In contrast, adding new software or hardware is fraught with setup sensitivities, interactions, and inconsistencies. Making a seemingly minor change in software or hardware can wreak havoc, making a PC partially or wholly unusable. One reason the PC platform has been so successful is that PC novices usually don't find out how bad things really are until sometime after they have made a sizable investment in time and money with their system.

Small-business owners and consumers must either maintain their own system, or pay for others to do so. Yet, configuration problems may take hours to resolve for someone who is a senior EE/CS-type and a PC veteran user. Novice PC users without deep pockets and PC-savvy friends may try in vain until they give up in despair and disgust. Small-business owners who have developed a reliance on their PC are usually forced to seek (and pay) for outside help. Such experiences can leave them bitter and hostile toward the PC industry. Tenacious veteran users will resort to exhaustive trials of various combinations (often relieving the tension by cursing a certain software magnate).

The expansion of the PC into both consumer and commercial markets will continue to be limited until this situation is resolved. Potential purchasers are (rightly) scared by the configuration horror stories they hear. They are not completely blind to the fact that such configuration difficulties add to the cost of ownership and subtract from the promised productivity gains.

The problematic nature of PC configuration is often blamed on lack of foresight in early PC architecture decisions leading to acute resource limitations. However, shortcomings in addressing installation and service needs are also to blame. Devices often have a bewildering number of poorly documented configuration parameters. There is typically a near total absence of diagnostic information to aid in isolating what device (or software routine), device parameter, or incompatible interaction between devices, is at the root of the problem. Furthermore, it is generally difficult or time-consuming to get competent support either via telephone, Internet, or computer bulletin-board systems (BBSs).

Dolby Surround AC-3

not clear

"We have been successful in spite of ourselves." – Andy Grove, Chairman of Intel, in reference to the poor ease of use of PCs.

Configuration by guess

REQUIREMENTS SUMMARY FOR **PC** PLATFORM GENERIC DEVICES
• Every device driver[a] meets requirements specific to its device-class
• Provided companion applications are Win32 compliant
• Every device meets power management requirements specific to its device-class, including class specific support for OnNow and wave-up events[b]
• Provided device drivers meet installation requirements, including unattended installation and help files for special parameters
• Device connectors are labeled with defined icons
• Every device meets Plug and Play requirements specific to its device-class, including unique device ID, auto resource assignment and dynamic-disable[c]

[a] A *device driver* is low-level software that interfaces device independent I/O routines in the OS to a specific type or specific instance of a peripheral device. Short of a custom written application that directly accesses the device, the device cannot be used with the OS without an appropriate device driver.

[b] See the *OnNow and ACPI* section of this chapter.

[c] See the *Plug and Play Configuration and Maintenance* section of this chapter.

REQUIREMENTS SUMMARY FOR **PC** PLATFORM AUDIO
• Generic device requirements apply
• Only required in Entertainment platform
• Does not use ISA Bus
• Device drivers support Win32 Driver Model[a]
• Full-duplex support for mono or stereo, at 2 data widths, and 6 sample rates
• Provides externally accessible I/O ports
• Reports sample position for stream synchronization with 1ms accuracy
• Meets specific frequency response, dynamic range, distortion, voltage level, and cross-talk requirements for playback, recording, and end-to-end analog
• If DVD Video present, audio specs must be comparable to stand-alone DVD player
• If PCI Bus, must be digital ready (capable of routing final output to OS using bus master[b] transfers for mixing, streaming, sampling rate conversion, and transfer to Universal Serial Bus or IEEE 1394 devices)[c]

[a] See the *Win32 Driver Model (WDM)* section in this chapter.

[b] See the *Backplane Bus — PCI* section in this chapter.

[c] See specific sections in this chapter for discussions of the PCI Bus, Universal Bus, and IEEE 1394.

Plug and Play and Elimination of Legacy Resource Limitations

Plug and Play (Plug-n-Play or PnP) and similar initiatives are intended to ease the frustration and complexity that is typical of installing and configuring hardware for PC platforms.

Plug and Play-compliant devices must have the capability to uniquely identify themselves and their device drivers, state the services they provide and the resources they require, and permit themselves to be programmatically configured by system software. These capabilities, in conjunction with Plug and Play-compliant drivers and OSs, enable the management of peripheral cards for the optimal system assignment of I/O addresses, Interrupt Request (IRQ) select line, and Direct Memory Access[44] (DMA) channels.

It is now possible to buy "Plug and Play" and Microsoft "Designed for Windows" logo devices that supposedly only require insertion (plug), answers to on-screen configuration questions, and the new device is ready for use (play). Such simplicity is designed to reduce returns, minimize customer support costs, and reduce end-user cost of ownership. Plug and Play generally makes installation of new devices easier. However, the installation of devices requiring legacy IRQ and DMA assignments in fully loaded systems is still often difficult. Until all legacy dependencies are removed, the goal of ease of configuration and maintenance remains elusive.

INDUSTRY STANDARDS

Plug-N-Play Specifications

Plug and Play is actually a family of specifications for the system BIOS and various device classes, including buses and ports. A compilation of links to many of the PnP specifications is found at URL:

> http://www.microsoft.com/hwdev/respec/pnpspecs.htm

SUGGESTED READINGS

Plug and Play

The book by Tom Shanley, *Plug and Play System Architecture*, Addison-Wesley, 1995, gives a clear and detailed explanation of the concepts behind Plug and Play.

---

[44] DMA is described in the section on Legacy Direct Memory Access (DMA).

Mechanical Design

As we discussed in the Mechanical and Electrical Considerations section of Chapter 1, the ATX motherboard standard has introduced a new size and orientation and component placement. Figure 4.2 provides an example ATX motherboard layout. Figure 4.3 shows an example connector placement at the rear of the ATX motherboard. Relative to the Baby AT board form factor shown in Figure 1.3 on page 37, the ATX motherboard is intended to reduce system assembly time and costs for manufacturers, increase ease of use for end users, and lower technical support needs. It does this by attention to detail with respect to the placement of the microprocessor and connectors.

ATX places the microprocessor near the power-supply. The ATX power-supply fan blows air onto the microprocessor, instead of out of the system unit as in an AT-style chassis. This eliminates the need for a fan-heatsink on the processor. In addition, the microprocessor is out of the path of any full-length expansion boards that might obstruct access to the microprocessor. This ensures that processor upgrades do not require removal of any expansion boards.

The floppy and ATA/IDE connectors are at the front of the board and closer to the peripherals, permitting reduced cable lengths. Integrated I/O connectors on the rear of the board obviate the need for cabling between the motherboard and connectors mounted on the system unit. The power-supply connector is also a single piece, instead of the two-piece connector used in an AT-style chassis.

REPORTS ON CD-ROM

REPORT

The following AMD technical documents on the CD-ROM are related to ATX motherboards and electrical and thermal system design issues:

- *ATX Reference Design for AMD-640 Chipset*, Users Guide Publication 21265, June 1997.
- *ATX Reference Design for AMD-640 Chipset*, Technical Specification Publication 21264, June 1997.
- *AMD-K6 MMX Enhanced Processor Power Supply Design*, Document 21103, June 1997.
- *AMD-K6 MMX Enhanced Processor Thermal Solution Design*, Document 21085, June 1997.

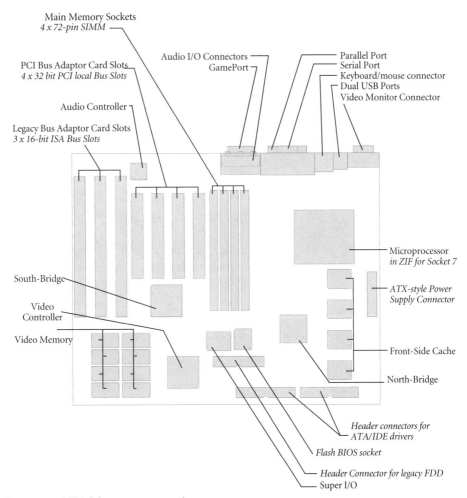

Main Memory Sockets
4 x 72-pin SIMM

PCI Bus Adaptor Card Slots
4 x 32 bit PCI local Bus Slots

Audio Controller

Legacy Bus Adaptor Card Slots
3 x 16-bit ISA Bus Slots

Audio I/O Connectors
GamePort

Parallel Port
Serial Port
Keyboard/mouse connector
Dual USB Ports
Video Monitor Connector

Microprocessor
in ZIF for Socket 7

*ATX-style Power
Supply Connector*

South-Bridge

Video
Controller

Video Memory

Front-Side Cache

North-Bridge

*Header connectors for
ATA/IDE drivers*

Flash BIOS socket

Header Connector for legacy FDD
Super I/O

Figure 4.2 EXAMPLE ATX MOTHERBOARD LAYOUT

Adapted with permission of Advanced Micro Devices Inc., from *AMD ATX Reference Design Technical Specification,* Copyright 1997.

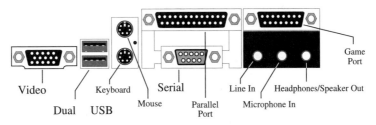

Video

Dual USB

Keyboard

Mouse

Serial

Parallel
Port

Line In

Microphone In

Headphones/Speaker Out

Game
Port

Figure 4.3 EXAMPLE ATX CONNECTOR PLACEMENT VIEWED FROM REAR OF BOARD

Adapted with permission of Advanced Micro Devices Inc., from *AMD ATX Reference Design Technical Specification,* Copyright 1997.

S TANDARDS ON CD-ROM

The following Intel authored motherboard and system specifications are included on the CD-ROM:

- *NLX Motherboard Specification.*
- *ATX Specification Version 2.01.*
- *microATX Motherboard Interface Specification Version 1.0.*
- *SFX Power Supply Design Guide Version 1.0 Release*

Win32 Driver Model (WDM)

Driver problems are considered the most significant contributor to poor consumer experiences with the PC. Problems arise from bugs, compatibility problems, and unintended side effects from driver upgrades. The Win32 Driver Model (WDM) is a planned Microsoft architecture for device drivers, which hierarchically splits device drivers into OS-provided device-class drivers and IHV-provided minidrivers. The WDM interface resides above bus and device drivers, and below PnP, power management, and I/O executives.

WDM is intended to improve device driver quality and consistency, while reducing the burden of device driver development by IHVs. Late '90s Windows 95 and Windows NT releases will be based on the NT 5.0 Kernel and will ship with common device-classes drivers. Earlier drivers will not be WDM compliant, but Windows 98 will be backward compatible. WDM-compliant device drivers updates are envisioned as being distributed via the Web.

WDM provides a common set of I/O services and binary-compatible drivers for Windows 98 and Windows NT 5.0. WDM supports Windows NT Plug and Play and power management, USB, IEEE 1394, OnNow power management, Streams (video, video camera, CD-ROM or DVD sourced), Audio, still image (camera or scanner) capture, and Human Interface Device (HID – keyboard, mouse, game pad).

DirectX and ActiveX

DirectX is the name of low-latency and high-performance Win32 APIs, which give the performance effect of writing directly to hardware, while maintaining register-level independence. DirectX supports "transparent" hardware acceleration, wherein APIs automatically make use of any available hardware acceleration, without any special effort by the application programmer. Applications that are written using these APIs, instead of being written for a specific hardware register set, will run on any hardware that provides the user with drivers appropriate to the user's OS. DirectX has been described as game extensions to Microsoft Windows.

[handwritten margin note: does the softwr OS require this security]

DIRECTX CLASSES

CLASS NAME	ASSOCIATED FUNCTIONS
Direct3D	3D graphics accleration
DirectDraw	2D graphics acceleration, foundation for more complex video services, including Direct3D
DirectInput	input devices, including keyboards, mouse-like pointing devices, and joysticks
DirectPlay	communications for multi-PC and multi-player games
DirectSound	audio, including mixing
DirectVideo	full-motion video overlays
DirectMPEG	MPEG full-motion video codec

INDUSTRY STANDARDS
DirectX
Information about DirectX, including Software Development Kits (SDKs) and Device Driver Kits (DDKs), can be found at:
http://www.microsoft.com/directx/
Information on "Meltdown," an annual software/hardware compatibility testing event, can be found at:
http://www.microsoft.com/hwdev/meltdown.htm

ActiveX is the name of Microsoft time-based APIs used for creation, coordination, and management of synchronized multimedia streaming data. ActiveX is intended to find use particularly in Web-based applications over networks (including intranets and the Internet), where latencies and bandwidth are unpredictable and time-varying. ActiveX includes support for the reusability, coexistence, and interoperability of remote and local files and objects. ActiveX also provides support for unified browsing. Built on top of the DirectX APIs, ActiveX has been described as Internet extensions to Microsoft Windows.

APPLIANCE-LIKE OPERATION

Appliance-like operation describes a PC platform that is unobtrusive, always ready yet energy efficient, and extremely simple to install, operate, maintain, and upgrade. Simply Interactive Personal Computer (SIPC) is the umbrella initiative that defines the vision of "simple, convenient, and approachable" appliance-like operation. Device Bay, OnNow, and ACPI are key standards and initiatives that will enable SIPC to eventually be a reality.

Simply Interactive Personal Computer (SIPC)

Simply Interactive Personal Computer (SIPC) is a broad Microsoft system-oriented vision of future PCs that encompasses the OS, applications, platforms, and peripherals. The SIPC proposal integrates a number of Microsoft and industry initiatives and standards.

SIPC machines are to have the ease of use of established consumer devices, such as a TV or VCR. This will be accomplished in part by virtually grafting a consumer electronics user interface onto SIPC platforms. Microsoft's vision is that a user can do the most common PC tasks envisioned for the future without any prior experience. Such tasks include "playing a game; watching a movie; writing an email, letter, or invitation; browsing the Internet, hooking up a device (such as a digital camera or camcorder); and listening to voice messages."[45]

Like other consumer devices, SIPC platforms should be sealed-case devices as far as the user is concerned. This means that peripherals and communications devices can be hooked and unhooked, and basic upgrades can be performed, without opening the case. This is to be accomplished by reliance on USB, IEEE 1394, and Device Bay. Instant-on capability is also required, to enable users to interact with the machine with more spontaneity, yet conserve power when not active. SIPC power features are addressed by OnNow and ACPI technologies. SIPC is also consumer-entertainment-focused, calling for large screens, DirectX-and ActiveX-based multimedia, DVD-ROM-based movies, and AC-3-based three-dimensional audio.

INDUSTRY STANDARDS
Microsoft's Simply Interactive Personal Computer (SIPC) Initiative
Information on the SIPC initiative can be found at URL:
http://www.microsoft.com/hwdev/desinit/sipc.htm

---

[45] *Making The PC An Appliance*, presented by Bill Gates at WinHEC '96.

REPORT ON CD-ROM

To learn more about the SIPC initiative, see Peter N. Glaskowsky's article, "PCs Head Toward Appliance Status," *Microprocessor Report*, Vol. 10, No. 6, May 6, 1996, on the companion CD-ROM.

Device Bay

Device Bay is an initiative intended to make installation of new peripherals "as easy as inserting a game cartridge." Hard-disk drives, modems, network adapters, CD drives, DVD drives, and other electronic devices can be Plug and Play hot-swapped into a "sealed-case" PC with the same convenience that floppy disks and other removable media presently offer. Figure 4.4 illustrates the Device Bay concept.

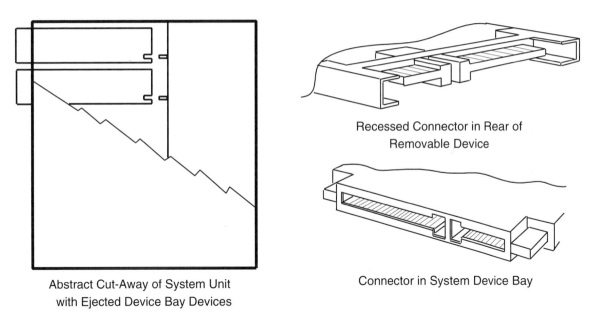

Recessed Connector in Rear of
Removable Device

Connector in System Device Bay

Abstract Cut-Away of System Unit
with Ejected Device Bay Devices

Figure 4.4 DEVICE BAY CONCEPTUAL DRAWINGS

On the left is shown a cut-away view of a system unit with two ejected Device Bay devices. All Device Bay compatible devices will have a standardized recessed connector and connector placement. The mating connector is correspondingly mounted within the system-unit. These self-aligning connectors are drawn to the right of Figure 4.4. Platform customization of peripherals should also prove faster and easier. Its promoters claim that Device Bay will provide platform scalability over the next 5-10 years via trivial peripheral additions and upgrades. Support for Device Bay is scheduled for Windows NT 5.0 and in a secondary release of Windows 98.

A Device Bay mobile hard disk will provide the advantages offered today by removable media in easily moving working files between machines. Typical examples include disk transfers for commuting between home and office or for business trips between laptop and workstation.

Electrically, Device Bay relies on a hybrid combination of the USB and IEEE 1394 buses. Each bay includes multi-voltage DC power, a USB port, and an IEEE 1394 port. Presently the 1394 port operates at 400 Mbps,[46] but later will be upgraded to 1 Gbps when devices based on the 1394B standard are available. The Device Bay specification defines the physical and electrical interfaces, desktop and mobile form factors (size), and OS response to device insertion and removal.

INDUSTRY STANDARDS

The Group Known as Device Bay

The Device Bay Specification is being developed and controlled by Compaq, Intel, and Microsoft. The Device Bay group maintains a Web site, with downloadable copy of the draft specification and a variety of useful technical documents. The main URL is:

> http://www.device-bay.org/

The draft Device Bay specification is downloadable free from URL:

> http://www.device-bay.org/tech/spec.htm

OnNow and ACPI

An OnNow PC is a platform that appears to be turned off, yet immediately responds when called upon by the user (or other devices). It is also an industry initiative and standard for enabling OS awareness of power use and requirements for all system components, as well as power control of the components. OnNow initiative goals include reducing typical power consumption to one-third of present levels and achieving a 5-second or less "warm-up" delay. The OS will have the ability to dynamically enable subsystems, whether on the motherboard or in attached peripherals. This requires "OnNow awareness" by platform hardware, expansion peripherals, applications, the OS, and the BIOS.

The Advanced Configuration and Power Interface (ACPI) is a specification and language that enables OS power control over installed devices. The OS is made aware of the power functions and requirements of installed devices through ACPI-compliant device drivers. Intel, Microsoft,

---

[46] We use "bps" for bits per second and "Bps" for bytes per second.

and Toshiba created ACPI in support of the OnNow initiative. ACPI is compliant with both VxD and WDM device driver models.

INDUSTRY STANDARDS

OnNow Specifications

The OnNow area of Microsoft's Web site includes device-class power management specifications, ACPI Source Language Assembler (Asl.exe), the Microsoft Windows Hardware Compatibility Tests for ACPI, and information about fast-boot BIOS and Simple Boot Flag specification. Power management reference specifications are available for each device class and bus. The main URL is:

> http://www.microsoft.com/hwdev/onnow.htm

Requirements for OnNow system designs were originally published in the *PC 97 Hardware Design Guide*. Information about obtaining this guide was included earlier in the chapter. Clarifications and changes subsequent to the release of the PC 97 guide are found at URL:

> http://www.microsoft.com/hwdev/desguid/onnowpc97.htm

TOTAL COST-OF-OWNERSHIP

Total Cost-of Ownership (TCO) of PC installations is an important facet of the commercial market segment. Reducing TCO is viewed as an enabler of increased commercial sales. TCO includes capital costs; administration; technical support; and end-user training, applications development, data management, supplies, and other miscellaneous costs. This section surveys two management initiatives held up as solutions to reduce TCO. Specifically, these initiatives are designed to help increase platform control, improve interoperability, increase user productivity, reduce the need for user support, and reduce capital and administrative costs.

The Desktop Management Initiative defines a very general operating-system-and device-independent means to interface management (control) applications with controllable devices. Management applications include network, telecom, Microsoft Windows kernel processes, DMI processes, and other unspecified applications that may need to control a device. The Microsoft Zero Administration Initiative for Windows (ZAW) is Microsoft's comprehensive management vision that integrates a number of management technologies and initiatives, including DMI.

INDUSTRY STANDARDS
Microsoft's Total Cost-of-Ownership (TCO) Initiative
Information on the TCO initiative can be found at URL:
http://www.microsoft.com/windows/platform/info/tco.htm

Desktop Management Initiative (DMI)

The Desktop Management Initiative (DMI) specification requires that an ASCII text file database be set up for all controllable devices. The files contain the "manageable attributes" of the devices in a language called *Management Information Format (MIF)*, which has a grammar and syntax. The files are called MIF files. A continuously running background task called the Service Layer manages the MIF database, compiling MIF file data, and servicing database queries from management applications. The DMI enables users and technical support personnel to retrieve a wealth of information about a PC, including processor type, installation dates, installed peripherals, power sources, and maintenance history. DMI 2.0 incorporated Remote Procedure Calls (RPC) to permit technical support to retrieve the management data remotely over a network. The *Common Interface Model (CIM)* is an object-oriented version of DMI that permits cross-platform interoperable management over intranets and the Internet.

INDUSTRY STANDARDS
Desktop Management Task Force (DMTF)
The Desktop Management Task Force sees itself as "*Driving industry standards for systems management to reduce total cost of ownership. (DMTF) is the industry consortium chartered with development, support and maintenance of management standards for PC systems and products, including DMI, the most-widely used management standard today.*" DMTF membership is $2,500 or $10,000 per year, depending on level of participation. The DMTF maintains the following Web site:
http://www.dmtf.org/
DMI Specification
The DMI specification and other DMTF standards are downloadable for free at the following URL:
http://www.dmtf.org/tech/specs.html

The Zero Administration Initiative for Windows (ZAW)

Microsoft's Zero Administration Initiative for Windows (ZAW) is an umbrella initiative for other Microsoft management initiatives, including Web-Based Enterprise Management (WBEM), Microsoft Windows Management Interface (WMI), Net PC, and Hydra (a Microsoft Windows terminal). In general these initiatives attempt to reduce TCO via reduced needs for user support, increased centralized but flexible control, automation of administrative tasks, while maintaining or increasing user productivity.

The WBEM Initiative supports the sharing of management data across network, desktop DMI, telecom, and Microsoft Windows applications. WBEM incorporates DMI and has provisions for power management, full system monitoring, and remote configuration. WMI defines a low-level instrumentation layer for efficient development of management-instrumented drivers.

NetPC platforms implement OnNow power management and perform auto detection and configuration of all buses and devices via ACPI protocols. Net PC systems perform automatic network configuration and then implement centralized configuration of the Net PC desktop via pre-configured system policies, user profiles, and setup scripts. "Roaming" and easy machine replacement are made possible by maintaining all application and data storage (centralized state) on the network server.

Users are not allowed access to system files and features, cannot install unapproved applications, and are otherwise prevented from performing end-user operations that may require technical support to correct. "Task Oriented" workers (e.g., clerks or bank tellers) are configured into *TaskStation Mode*, in which the Net PC machine boots into a single management-specified dedicated application, such as a Web browser or a business application. "Knowledge" workers are configured into *AppStation Mode*, in which the user may run any one of multiple management-selected business applications.

TaskStation Mode

AppStation Mode

INDUSTRY STANDARDS
Microsoft's Zero Administration Initiative for Windows
Information about ZAW and other Microsoft Windows Management Initiatives can be found at the following URL:
http://www.microsoft.com/management/
Information about ZAW and other Microsoft Windows Total Cost of Ownership Initiatives can be found at the following URL:
http://www.microsoft.com/windows/innovation/

Hydra describes a client that is thinner than the Net PC. All applications run on the server. (HID) inputs are uploaded to the server, which downloads each display screen to a terminal. The user sees a Window 95 User Interface

CONNECTIVITY

Connectivity describes the interconnection of PC platforms (particularly with servers) via data communications and network technologies. Interconnection may be point-to-point with other platforms, but is increasing via a network, including workgroups, intranets, and the Internet. The first subsection on *Data Communications and Networking* surveys fax, "data," Integrated Services Digital Network, and Asymmetric Digital Subscriber Line modem technologies; Ethernet and derivative networks; and compares bandwidths for a variety of channels and links. The second subsection, on the *Internet*, provides a short technical overview of Internet access and Internet-based applications and uses.

Data Communications and Networking

Reducing file sizes via compression prior to transmission facilitates transfer (over any connection) of large files at low data rates. Received files are restored to original form via decompression prior to use. These complementary processes can be done in express steps on the entire file, respectively performed before sending and after receipt, using zip and unzip utilities. Communications protocols and publishing standards are increasingly incorporating compression and decompression as integral components of the end-to-end transfer. The PDF format discussed earlier incorporates text and image compression.

Medium-speed (14.4kbps-54kbps) fax and dial-up data communications hardware, software, and related services are now integral platform components for home and business. On the hardware side, "high-speed" serial ports and progressively faster high-speed data and fax modems support the trend toward faster connectivity. Increased connectivity has resulted in additional home and business phone lines to avoid the unavailability of normal voice use that would otherwise occur from high dial-up usage.

Data Communications and FAX and Data Modems

Data modems[47] provide access to a variety of data communications services via the public telephone-switching network ("on-line" or "dial-up" services) to Internet Service Providers (ISPs), consumer online services, and subscription news and database providers. Generally these services insure that their subscribers have all the necessary software for HTML browsing or for accessing the services proprietary content.

Modems supporting common fax standards are available for minimal additional cost over that of non-fax modems. Such fax-modems typically are bundled with supporting software, enabling the associated platform to replace a conventional fax machine for receiving faxes, while providing

---

[47] Modem is short for modulator-demodulator, a device that encodes a digital data stream into analog tones for transmission over an analog communications link and decodes received tones back to digital form. The term is also loosely and widely used for any adapter between a computer and a communications link regardless of whether a modulator-demodulator is present or not.

additional features only available in very expensive standalone fax machines, or only available on a PC. Fax-equipped PCs are commonly used to permit viewing with optional printing, archiving of fax images, delayed fax sending, maintenance of address books, and broadcasting to distribution lists. For sending faxes, either an optional scanner must be used, or messages must be composed on the computer.

INDUSTRY STANDARDS

International Telecommunications Union (ITU)

Modem modulation standards are promulgated by and only available from the International Telecommunications Union (ITU). The modem standards are known as *ITU-T Series V Recommendations*. The "-T" stands for Telecommunications. Series V covers all ITU-T standards for data communication over the telephone network.

The ITU-T Series V Recommendations can be downloaded in zipped Word or PostScript formats via a secure credit-card payment server. Prices, in French francs, vary with each standard. The V.34 standard was roughly $6 as of this writing. The standards, listed by number and title, may be ordered from the following URL:

http://www.itu.int/itudoc/itu-t/rec/v.html

Recent important standards include:

ITU-T Rec. V.17 for 14,400 bps class 1 & 2 FAX modems.

ITU-T Rec. V.32 bis for 14,400 bps data modems.

ITU-T Rec. V.34 for 33,600 bps data modems.

ITU-T Rec. V.90 for 56,000 bps data modems.

REQUIREMENTS SUMMARY FOR PC PLATFORM MODEM DEVICES

- Generic device requirements apply
- Required, if no network adapter[a]
- Devices use the Universal Modem Driver (Unimodem), which uses vendor supplied INF files to characterize the device to the OS
- Hayes an early, popular modem compatible command set
- 33.6 Kbps minimum using V.34, V.42, and V.42bis
- Pulse Code Modulation modems (e.g., X2, K56flex) are V.90 compliant
- Fax modems support 14.4 Kbps (V.17) with Class 1 command set
- Controller supports the diagnostic command; has a 60 character minimum command buffer; reports connection status including rate, error control, and data compression; and is software upgradable
- Devices on power-managed buses support wake-up on incoming ring
- ISDN modems (discussed next) have additional special requirements

---

[a] See the *Ethernet and Derivatives* section in this chapter.

Other Data Communications Technologies

Integrated Services Digital Network (ISDN) is the name of a family of switched (dial-up) digital telephone services that use existing telephone wiring. Some of these services include burglar alarm monitoring and virtual PBC telephone services. For PC platform applications, the most common type of ISDN is the Basic Rate Interface (BRI), which consists of two independent 64-Kpbs (56-Kbps in some places) "B" channels for data and a "D" channel for control.

ISDN has established a reputation for being limited in general availability to sites close (18,000 feet) to telephone company Central Offices in major metropolitan areas, difficult and expensive to install and configure, and costly to use. It is however an established technology, including built-in support in the most recent releases of Microsoft Windows. Furthermore, short of leasing a dedicated frame relay or T1 phone line, as of this writing it is the fastest way (other than satellite modem, discussed next) to connect to the Internet for major metropolitan users. It is estimated that there were 1.7 million ISDN subscribers in 1997.[48] ISDN may soon become obsolete in face of the newer technologies discussed below.

MICROSOFT WINDOWS SUPPORT FOR ISDN
Microsoft maintains an area on its Web site dedicated to ISDN. General information on ISDN, geographic availability, and a facility for requesting ISDN service, are found at URL: http://www.microsoft.com/windows/getisdn/

Consumer satellite modem systems have been made recently available. These use a data modem (e.g., V.34 or ISDN), for low-or medium-speed (28.8-128 Kbps) client-to-provider data over conventional telephone lines, coupled with a special satellite downlink data modem for medium-speed (400 Kbs) provider-to-client data. Such systems are targeted at Web browsing, where such asymmetric bandwidth is typical. These systems find particular application in areas where other high-speed services are not available.

Cable Modems

Cable modems use specially conditioned segments of the existing cable TV infrastructure to provide bidirectional high-bandwidth communication channels for Internet connectivity. Cable modems are currently undergoing trials in several metropolitan areas in the

---

[48] Mo Krochmal, "ISDN Dukes It Out in Bandwidth Battle," *TechWeb*, January 25, 1998.

U.S., with roughly 100,000 households participating.[49] At present, many competing and incompatible cable-modem interface standards are being used. As a result, local cable companies with cable modem service require the subscriber to lease a cable modem. This ensures that the cable modem is interoperable with the modulation methods and interface protocols chosen for the cable company's headend servers. Because volumes of these diverse modem types is low, their costs have stayed high ($300-$1500), and installation and service rates are not yet to levels affordable by the masses. Standardization efforts are attempting to address this problem.

INDUSTRY STANDARDS

The Data Over Cable Service Interface Specifications (DOCSIS)

The Data Over Cable Service Interface Specifications (DOCSIS), also known as the MCNS specifications, is a family of interoperability certification standards for cable modems that are based on TCP/IP[a] protocols. MCNS stands for Multimedia Cable Network System (MCNS) Partners, L.P., a group consisting of four major cable providers that originally started the effort. The project, which is now managed by CableLabs discussed below, is implementing a certification program for cable modems so that cable operators can be assured that a given modem will be interoperable with DOCSIS-compliant headend equipment. The project also plans to work with the Society of Cable Telecommunications Engineers (SCTE) to eventually submit a DOCSIS-based standard for approval by ANSI and the ITU. The DOCSIS Project has a web site. An overview, answers to frequently asked questions, and member links, are available at URL:

> http://www.cablemodem.com/

Public releases of DOCSIS technical specifications may be freely downloaded at URL:

> http://www.cablemodem.com/public/pubtech.html

Cable Television Laboratories, Inc. (CableLabs) is a research and development consortium of cable television system operators. Vendors of cable equipment, other telecommunications providers, and the general public are not eligible. Member companies pay dues based on their subscriber base. Cable Labs manages the DOCSIS Project, discussed below. CableLabs operates a web site. Tutorial publications on cable modems and the cable industry in general are available at URL:

> http://www.cablelabs.com/Publications.html.

[a] TCP/IP, or Transmission Control Protocol/Internet Protocol.

---

[49] Seth Schiesel, "Three Giants of PC World Turn Focus to Speed," *New York Times*, January 26, 1998.

While present cable modem designs are coupled to PCs via 10BaseT interfaces, having 10Mbps nominal rates, entry-level service plans start with advertised asymmetrical rates of 500Kbps downstream and 100Kbps upstream for $100 per month. Symmetrical rates or higher bandwidths (e.g., 1Mbps advertised) cost more, $300 and $500 per month, respectively. It is hoped that competition with Digital Subscriber Line (DSL) connectivity (discussed next) will rapidly lower these monthly charges.

Like any other network, effective data rates are actually a function of loading on the local cable operator's network and the cable operator's connection to the Internet. Under light loads some users have reported effective rates within the same local cable network limited only by the capabilities at which contemporary PCs can process TCP/IP protocols, said to be approximately 4Mbps.[50] Conversely, skeptics have expressed concerns as to whether there is enough bandwidth headroom on the local nets if a significant number of cable subscribers sign up. Also, like getting service from any other form of Internet Service Provider, users are advised to inquire as to what bandwidth the cable service provider has to the Internet backbone, and how many users are sharing that bandwidth.

Emerging DSL and ADSL Modems

ADSL

Digital Subscriber Line (DSL) modems promise to offer fast (1.5 Mbps-8 Mbps) connections to the home in the near future. It is estimated that there may be 1 million DSL subscribers by the year 2000.[51] A number of DSL variants exist and are undergoing development and field trials. Asymmetric DSL (*ADSL*) is one variant that may be the first to see widespread use. ADSL downstream and upstream rates are different, due to cost-benefit compromises in engineering a low-cost, high-data-rate solution for the masses. Maximum rates are said to be 9 Mbps downstream and 800 Kbps upstream, depending upon line length and conditions. [52]

In one ADSL implementation being proposed by the Universal ADSL Working Group (UAWG), a consortium led by Microsoft, Intel, Compaq, and several Baby Bells, downstream rates are 1.5 Mbps and upstream rates are 384 Kbps. Since by far most users will consume much more data than they generate, and since the upstream rate will still be roughly an order of magnitude improvement over analog modems, its promoters do not perceive the disparity in upstream and downstream bandwidths as being a problem.

---

[50] www.cnet.com/Content/Features/Techno/Cablemodems/

[51] Mo Krochmal, "ISDN Dukes It Out in Bandwidth Battle," *TechWeb* (http://www.techweb.com/), January 25, 1998.

[52] ADSL Forum.

In addition to improved performance, the UAWG claims several advantages of the technology will speed its global acceptance. Universal ADSL is also known as a *Spliterless ADSL* or *Lite ADSL* version of DSL. ADSL does away with a splitter device that other versions of ADSL require to be installed at the point of entry into each home, reducing time and costs for installation. Microsoft promises to incorporate simplified setup for Universal ADSL in future versions of Microsoft Windows. Finally, Universal ADSL is being proposed as an "always-on" service. "Always-on" connectivity eliminates connection delays and will enable continuous Web services and e-mail delivery.

Universal ADSL

Spliterless ADSL
Lite ADSL

INDUSTRY STANDARDS

Asymmetric Digital Subscriber Line (ADSL) Forum

The *ADSL Forum* is a 200-member group formed in 1994 to educate and promote ADSL technology to telephone companies and their suppliers. Membership costs $1500-$5000 depending on company size and level of participation in Forum activities. The ADSL Forum maintains a Web site. Information on joining and tutorial papers are available at URL:

http://www.adsl.com/

The Universal ADSL Working Group (*UAWG*), composed of PC industry, networking, and telecommunications companies, is developing a compatible extension to the present ANSI standard T1.413 for ADSL. Their proposal is to be submitted to the International Telecommunication Union (ITU) G.Lite subcommittee. The UAWG has set up a Web site at URL:

http://www.uawg.org/index.html

ADSL Specifications

ANSI T1.413-1995, *Telecommunications - Network and Customer Installation Interfaces - Asymmetric Digital Subscriber Line (ADSL) Metallic Interface*, $135, must be ordered directly from ANSI. ANSI standards can be ordered through their online catalog, searchable at URL:

http://www.ansi.org/catalog/search.html

Networking and Local-Area Networks

This section overviews Ethernet and its derivative technologies (Fast Ethernet and Gigabit Ethernet) and considers network applications enabled by Ethernet. Such applications include workgroup computing, the client-server paradigm, departmental and Enterprise servers, and intranets.

Ethernet and Derivatives

Media Access Control (MAC)

Ethernet is the most popular of several *Media Access Control (MAC)* methods used for LANs. *Media* refers to the physical infrastructure that comprises the communications network. *Access Control* refers to how the media is shared among multiple nodes that request to use the media, often at the same time. Developed at Xerox PARC in 1976.

Carrier Sense Multiple Access with Collision Detection

Ethernet uses a MAC method known as *Carrier Sense Multiple Access with Collision Detection (CSMA/CD)*. Essentially, each node with data to transmit checks the status of the media and begins transmitting if the media is not in use, or waits if the media is already busy. Each node also checks to make sure that a *collision* (simultaneous transmission attempt) did not occur with another node. If a collision is detected, then both nodes wait for random intervals before starting over with checking the media status before transmitting. In the absence of a collision, the transmitting node gets the exclusive use of the media to transmit its data. Ethernet later became the IEEE 802.3 (dot3) standard. Ethernet has a number of variations. The topology for three of these variations is shown in the left half of Figure 4.6 on page 359.

10Base 5
Thick Ethernet

The initial physical implementation of the 802.3 standard was known as 10Base-5, which is a reference to its 10Mbps rate, reliance on baseband (non-frequency shifted) data signaling, and 500-meter range. *10Base-5* is also known as *Thick Ethernet*, due to its use of thick 50-ohm coaxial cable. Thick coax is expensive and its coiling radius makes it difficult to work with inside small clearance areas. Thick Ethernet is prevalent at many sites, but newer Ethernet variants have supplanted it for new installations. In 1984, a variant known as *10Base-2*, was standardized. 10Base-2 (having a 185-meter range) is also known as *Thin Ethernet*, due to its use of thin 50-ohm coaxial cable and BNC-type connectors. Figure 4.5 compares the diameter of the two coax types.

10Base 2

Thin Ethernet

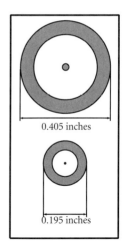

0.405 inches

0.195 inches

Figure 4.5

COMPARISON OF THICK AND THIN COAXIAL CABLES USED FOR ETHERNET

10Base T
Twisted-Pair Ethernet

In 1990, another variant known as 10Base-T was standardized as IEEE 802.3i. 10Base-T is also known as *Twisted-Pair Ethernet* due to its use of Unshielded Twisted Pair (UTP) and RJ-45 connectors. UTP is a type of telephone-wiring-like cabling that is available in a range of performance categories. More recently, a 100Mbps extension, known as *100Base-T*, or *Fast Ethernet*, was standardized as IEEE 802.3u. Variants include 100Base T2, T4, and TX. IEEE 802.3z is a proposed 1000Mbps extension, known as *Gigabit Ethernet*.

100Base T
Fast Ethernet

Gigabit Ethernet

A Medium Attachment Unit (MAU, also known as a transceiver) couples a LAN controller in the Data Terminal Equipment (DTE, e.g., computers or data terminals) to the network. The MAU and LAN controller combination comprise a *network adapter*. For 10Base-5 and 10Base-2, the MAU couples the DTE to a *trunk* coaxial cable, which function as a distributed data bus. For 10Base-5, each trunk can be no more than 500 meters in length and have no more than 100 nodes attached. Five trunks can be coupled using four repeaters for a maximum length of 2,460 meters, although source and destination nodes must be no more than two repeaters apart.

A *repeater* extends a logical LAN segment[53] by regenerating transmissions observed on a first subnetwork onto a second subnetwork. For 10Base-2, each trunk can be no more than 186 meters in length and have no more than thirty nodes attached. Five trunks can be coupled using four repeaters for a maximum length of 910 meters, although again no more than two repeaters may exist between source and destination nodes. In both coaxial Ethernet forms, each far-end must have a 50-ohm *terminator* (termination resistor). The terminator reduces unwanted signal reflections on the trunk and ensures proper operation.

For 10Base-T, the MAU couples the DTE via transmit and receive twisted-pairs to a *hub* (also known as a *concentrator*), which functions as a logical data bus. Workgroup-class hubs commonly come with up to twelve ports. Up to twelve Workgroup-class hubs may be connected to an Intermediate-class central hub.

In all three Ethernet variants, LAN segments are usually limited to significantly less than the maximum number of nodes to avoid network congestion. Multiple LAN segments are then bridged, routed, or switched to form larger departmental or enterprise networks. A *bridge* selectively links two network segments and will forward Ethernet transmissions to a second segment only if the destination address specified by the transmission and the second segment match. A *router* selectively couples many network segments and can perform sophisticated filtering and best-path selection in addition to simple address matching.

The MAU for each Ethernet type is shown in the right half of Figure 4.6. The MAU consists of a network interface (either to coax or twisted-pairs), an *Attachment Unit Interface (AUI)*, a transceiver for coupling signals between the two interfaces, and some means to provide DC isolation between the two interfaces. The AUI includes separate differential signal-pairs for transmit data (TD) receive data (RD) and transmit collision status (COL). The MAU passes received data from the network to the LAN controller and broadcasts transmit data from the LAN controller onto the network. It also detects collisions between its transmit data and activity on the network and notifies the LAN controller of any detected collisions.

Medium Attachment Unit (MAU)
transceiver

network adapter

repeater

hub
concentrator

bridge

router

Attachment Unit Interface (AUI)

---

[53] A network segment is a portion of a network having a unique address. Different network segments necessarily have different addresses.

transceiver cable

AUI connector

When collisions occur, the LAN controllers involved in the collision reschedule their transmissions after a random interval. For 10Base-2 and 10Base-T expansion cards designed for the PC platform, the MAU is usually integrated with the LAN controller on the card. However, if the MAU is external, an *AUI cable* or *transceiver cable* couples the DTE to the AUI connector of the MAU. The MAU transceiver has an associated power supply run off 12 volts supplied over the AUI cable or integrated interface.

For Thick Ethernet, a *tap connector* frequently attaches the MAU onto the thick coax without need to interrupt network operation to cut the cable and install connectors. Figure 4.7(a) has end-on views of male and female *Type-N* connectors, which may be used instead of a piercing tap. Figure 4.7(b) shows a segment of thick coax with a male Type-N connector that has been screwed onto a Type-N barrel (double-female) connector. The barrel is required to re-couple segments previously cut in two for installation of a MAU using connectors.

Figure 4.7(c) and (d) are an end-on and side view, respectively, of the 15-pin male *AUI connector* (also known as a DIX-type connector). The male connector is essentially a common D-shell-type connector with added retaining posts. The female AUI has a sliding clamp used to retain the posts of the male connector. Figure 4.7(e) and (f) are views of the female AUI connector with the clamp in the unlocked and locked positions, respectively.

Figure 4.7(g) is a view of male (top) and female (bottom) BNC connectors, used for Thin Ethernet. Figure 4.7(h) is a view of a BNC T-connector with a segment of thin coax connected on the left of the T and a BNC 50-ohm terminator shown on the right of the T. Thus, the illustration corresponds to a node at one of the far-ends of a Thin Ethernet network. The center of the T would connect to a MAU.

Figure 4.7(i) is a view a UTP cable with the outer insulation removed to show the four twisted-pairs contained within. Some variations of Ethernet use all four pairs per node. Figure 4.7(j) and (k) are views of an 8-pin modular RJ-45 plug connector and its mating socket connector, respectively.

INDUSTRY STANDARDS

Ethernet and Fast Ethernet Manufacturers

A plethora of technical information and white papers is available from the numerous manufacturers of Ethernet (10-Mbps) and Fast Ethernet (100-Mbps) products. The main URL is:

http://www.gigabit-ethernet.org/

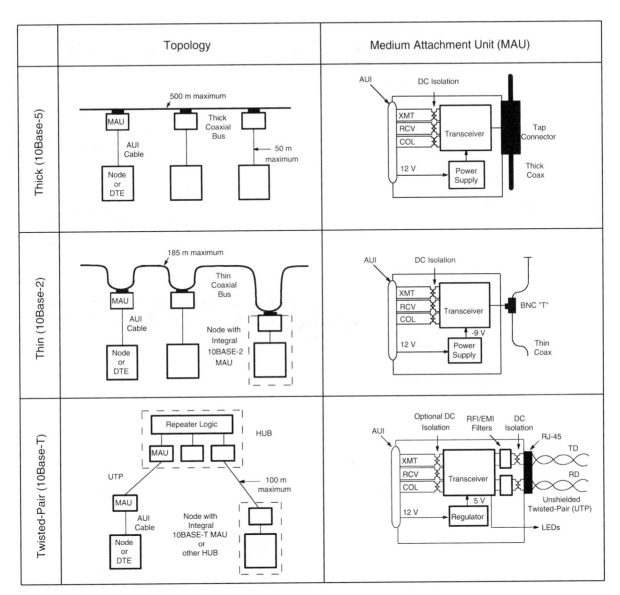

Figure 4.6 COMPARISON OF ETHERNET TYPES

Adapted with permission of Advanced Micro Devices, Inc., from "AM79C960 PCnet-ISA Technical Manual," Copyright 1992,

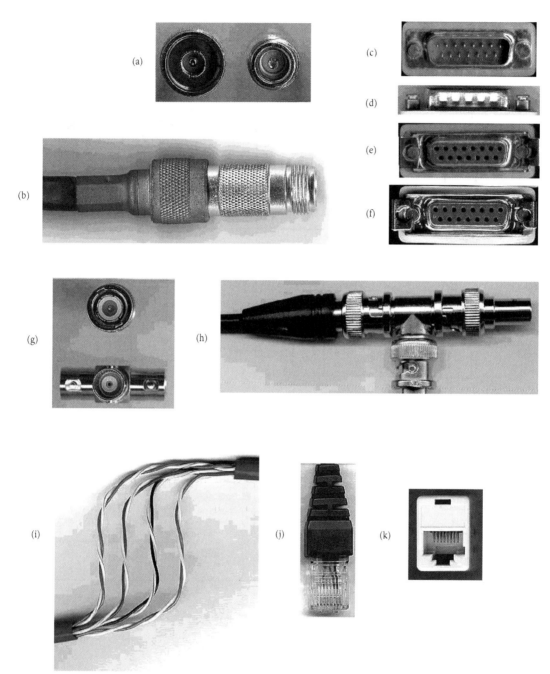

Figure 4.7 COMMON ETHERNET CONNECTORS AND CABLES

IEEE Standards on CD-ROM

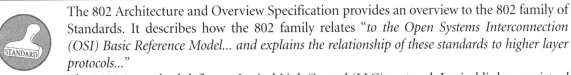

The 802 Architecture and Overview Specification provides an overview to the 802 family of Standards. It describes how the 802 family relates *"to the Open Systems Interconnection (OSI) Basic Reference Model... and explains the relationship of these standards to higher layer protocols..."*

The 8802.2 standard defines a *Logical Link Control (LLC)* protocol. Logical links are *virtual circuits* that establish a communication session between two nodes. The standard defines various types of communication services over logical links. The LLC protocol applies to any Media Access Control method, not just Ethernet.

The 8802-3 standard defines the implementation of CSMA/CD methods for different media types including coax, twisted-pair, and fiber-optic cables.

A copy of several Ethernet Standards documents standard are included on the CD-ROM.

- *802-1990 IEEE Standards* for Local and Metropolitan Area Networks: Overview and Architecture Information Technology—Telecommunications and information exchange between systems—Local and Metropolitan area networks—Specific requirements.
- *8802-2: 1994* (ISO/IEC) [ANSI/IEEE 802.2, 1994 Edition] Part 2: Logic Link Control.
- *8802-3: 1996* (ISO/IEC) [ANSI/IEEE Std 802.3, 1996 Edition] Part 3: Carrier Sense Multiple Access with Collision Detection (CSMACD) Access Method and Physical Layer Specifications.

REQUIREMENTS SUMMARY FOR PC PLATFORM NETWORK DEVICES

- Generic device requirements apply
- Device driver compliant with Network Driver Interface Standard (NDIS) version 5.0, which implements much of the Media Access Control (MAC) protocol in the OS. The vendor supplies only a miniport driver tailored to the device, only makes NDIS defined library calls to the kernel, and uses new INF files to characterize the device
- Works correctly with Microsoft's implementations of the popular TCP/IP, IPX/SPX, and NetBEUI protocols
- Driver supports modes of operation to enable network monitoring by administrative applications
- Automatic sensing and appropriate configuration for full-duplex operation, transceiver type, and connection to network
- To prevent the adapter buffer from overburdening software with packet alignment, the adapter performs byte alignment on transmission and performs quadword alignment, or smaller, on receive
- Adapter supports push technology via hardware filtering (match detection) of a minimum of 32 multicast addresses
- If used to install the OS on a new PC, must support the Dynamic Host Configuration Protocol (DHCP) standard.
- Device supports wave-up on match to specified network address
- ISDN, ADSL and other adapters have additional special requirements

Applications of Networks

LANs, such as *Ethernet*, provide a means to electronically transfer files at high speeds (commonly 10 Mbs migrating to use of 100 Mbs) between interconnected PC platforms within the confines of small offices or workgroups. The file transfer can be of an explicit nature, such as when electronic mail is used, a disk backup is performed, or when someone wants to copy or move files from one networked platform to another. The file transfer can also be of an implicit nature, such as when a disk drive at a remote node is mounted for use over the network.

workgroup computing

LANs have enabled *workgroup computing*, which includes the ability to send electronic mail to colleagues on the LAN; to selectively share data files, directories, or entire disks; and to share expensive peripherals. The shared peripherals may include high-end color printers, high-capacity backup resources, and high-speed access ports (gateways) to other networks, including the Internet. Electronic mail can be simple bulletins and messages, or it can include *attachments*, of logically separate files, such as graphics, word processing files, or programs.

attachments

Platforms on LANs are frequently characterized as *servers, clients,* or *peers.* A platform that has a shared resource attached is referred to as a server for that resource. For example, one speaks of disk or file servers and printer servers. The platforms that connect to the server to make use of the server's resource are *clients.* The larger the client population, the more important and economically pragmatic it is that the server be a high-end platform equipped with the most superlative features available. In small office environments, the distinction between clients and servers is usually blurred, and peer-to-peer networking between desktop platforms is the norm.

clients

peer-to-peer networking

Multiple LANs can be coupled and interconnected via a variety of techniques to encompass an entire site or multiple sites at a large company. Such an interconnection is often referred to as an *Enterprise Network.* Within an isolated site, networking addressing and protocols must be compatible, but can be largely arbitrary. Beyond an isolated site, different sites may be linked together via either private or public high-bandwidth communications channels. Networking more than one site requires destination addresses to be coordinated and properly assigned and a common communications protocol to be used.

Enterprise Network

intranet

An *intranet* is an Enterprise Network that uses the Internet standard Transmission Control Protocol/Internet Protocol and related HTTP addressing standard. By supporting the same Web browsers and other tools used for Internet access, software license and training costs are minimized. Intranets are used for intra-company departmental and corporate-headquarters Web sites, enabling easy company-wide access to standards, publications, and services.

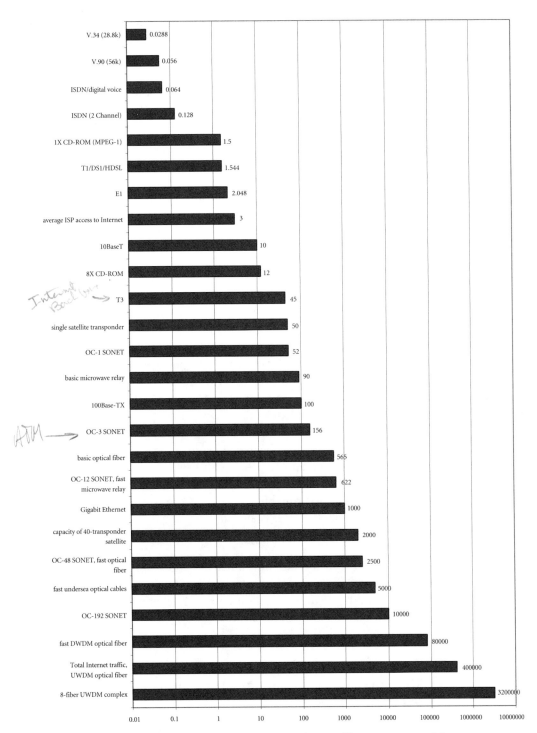

Figure 4.8 Bandwidth of Channels and Links (Bandwidth in Mbits per second, Logarithmic Scale)

Comparison of Communication and Network Bandwidths

Figure 4.8 on page 363 provides a comparison of bandwidths (shown in Mbps) for a variety of common channels and links.[54] A number of interesting observations can be made from this figure, where orders of magnitude differences in bandwidth are readily apparent. The present total Internet traffic is shown at 400 Gbits per second. This is also the capacity of an Ultra Dense Wave Division Multiplexed (UWDM) single optical fiber. *Wave Division Multiplexing* (WDM) techniques are being used to substantially increase the capacity of many existing installed fibers, by modulating multiple light sources of different wavelengths. The 8-fiber UWDM complex represents the state-of-the-art in optical network systems at the time of this writing.[55] With continued reference to Figure 4.8, we will next examine the different Ethernet variations against the various data communications rates found in the telephone network and against CD-ROM transfer rates.

Wave Division Multiplexing

10BaseT

Note that 10BaseT is only roughly five times slower than the T3 leased phone line rate at which most Internet backbones operate. 10BaseT is also roughly three times faster than the average rate at which Internet Service Providers connect to the backbone. Medium and small-size businesses often are connected to the Internet via dedicated T1 leased phone lines, which are then coupled to individual office PCs on multiple 10BaseT segments. For light loads on both the LAN and the T1, each PC should enjoy basically the equivalent of their own T1 connection. Under today's normal business-user loads of light Web browsing, periodic e-mail transmissions, and occasional large file downloads, a single T1 line could support over fifty simultaneous users with V.34 (28.8k) equivalent performance. However, video is another matter. A single MPEG-1 bit stream from a 1X CD-ROM is roughly the same as the bandwidth of the T1. A modern 8X or better CD-ROM can deliver more bandwidth than 10BaseT.

100BaseTX

A single satellite transponder has sufficient bandwidth to support a single commercial-quality color TV broadcast. A basic microwave relay has sufficient bandwidth to support a thousand voice channels. 100BaseTX has comparable bandwidth to both of these.

---

[54] Many of the more obscure link names in this figure are described in the following section on the Internet.

[55] *Lucent Technologies delivers record-breaking optical networking capacity; five times greater than current systems,* Lucent press release, January 26, 1998. Dense Wave Division Multiplexing (DWDM) was a precursor to UWDM.

Gigabit Ethernet

Gigabit Ethernet has roughly half the bandwidth of an entire 40-transponder satellite. Thus its raw bandwidth compares to that of 20 color TV channels. Or, you could compare it to ten-thousand voice channels! Gigabit Ethernet also exceeds the bandwidth of the OC-12, the fastest rate planned for near-term upgrades to most Internet backbones.[56]

The Internet

Internet Access

The *Internet* is the name given to an interconnected conforming system of networks used for global file transfer and data communications. The Internet enables PC platforms to run applications that support global e-mail, Web browsing, and audio and video conferencing. The Internet in its current form was enabled by the advent of the HTML document (Web page) publishing standard, the HTTP Web navigation standard, and the proliferation of HTML readers (Web browsers). The number of people with access to the Internet is growing rapidly, supplanting the use of both electronic bulletin boards systems (BBSs) and other limited/proprietary access services. Responsible for this growth is the perception of readily available quality content and the now widespread availability of low-cost Internet connections.

In the U.S., the Internet is a meta-network interconnection of more than a dozen major national high-speed networks and another dozen major regional high-speed networks independently operated by competing communications companies (network providers). The major national and regional networks consist of data links and packet routers that are logically structured around one or more 45 Mbs (known as *T3*), or higher, *backbone* links, which couple, ring, or span, major metropolitan areas. The backbones of the national and regional providers are interconnected at multiple high-bandwidth junctions called peer interconnect points. In the U.S. there are a dozen major peer interconnect points.

backbone

Depending on the provider and usage, a 45-Mbps T3 leased line costs between $20,000-60,000 per month at the time of this writing, while a 1.544-Mbs T1 leased line costs between $1,400-3,000 per month.[57] These costs do not include setup and required interface equipment. Nearly all backbone providers have migration plans that include backbones at 155 Mbs (*OC-3*), and at 622 Mbs (*OC-12*). In addition to the backbones, these

---

[56] Optical Carrier Level One (OC-1) is the basic building block channel capacity for the Synchronous Optical Network (SONET) standard. Each OC level is corresponding multiple of the OC-1 rate of 51.84 Mbps.

[57] All statistics in this section are based on data from the *Boardwatch Magazine Directory of Internet Service Providers*, Fall 1996.

networks will also have dozens to hundreds of 1.544-Mbs (*T1*)[58] links to serve the metropolitan areas surrounding the major metropolitan nodes of the backbones. Both the backbones and the lesser links may be owned by the backbone providers or leased from the major long-distance exchange carriers and the local telephone companies.

The national and regional network providers lease dedicated 58 Kbps-45 Mbps Internet access to major corporations, institutions, and over 3000 independently operated Internet Service Providers. The three national providers MCI, Sprint, and UUNET provide backbone access to 79% of the ISPs. ISPs on average have access to a backbone at 3 Mbs. The ISPs in turn provide Internet access to businesses and consumers via over 11,000 "points of presence" (POP), to which dedicated leased lines are connected, or as needed dial-up connections may be made.

Internet-Based Applications and Uses

The Internet uses the standardized TCP/IP (Transmission Control Protocol/Internet Protocol) for all communications links, routers, connected platforms, and compatible communications applications programs. TCP/IP requires messages to be logically partitioned into multiple "packets." Multiple data links are connected to routers, which attempt to relay the packets closer to their destination, based on an associated address. The packets may pass through an arbitrary number of data links and routers on their path from source to destination. Furthermore, not all packets from the same source message need take the same path. TCP/IP permits point-to-point electronic messaging, file transfers, and remote access log-in, wherever such privileges are enabled, throughout an arbitrarily sized network.

Commonly used Internet-based application programs and associated TCP/IP-compliant sub-protocols include: electronic mail (e-mail) using Simple Mail Transfer Protocol (SMTP), Post Office Protocol 3 (POP3) and newer protocols; interactive teletypewriter-like network access to remote computer systems via TELNET; file transfer using File Transfer Protocol (FTP); exchange of Users Network (USENET) "newsgroups" (electronic conferences) via Net News Transfer Protocol (NNTP); and Web publishing using Hyper Text Markup Language (HTML) and Web navigating using Hyper Text Transfer Protocol (HTTP).

---

[58] *E1* is a European variant of T1.

INDUSTRY STANDARD

Internet Protocol Standards

TCP/IP and other Internet-related protocol standards are developed by the Internet Engineering Task Force (IETF) and recommended by the Internet Engineering Steering Group (IESG), both subsidiary groups of the Internet Architecture Board (IAB). Information on the IETF can be found at

http://www.ietf.org/

RFC 1920, "Internet Official Protocol Standards," is an overview of Internet standards and the standards process. Links to this overview (contained in the file "std1.txt") and the Internet protocol standards themselves can be found in the /in-notes/std/files subdirectory at URL:

http://info.internet.isi.edu/

Other Internet protocols are found in the /pub/WWW/Protocols/ subdirectory at URL:

http://www.w3.org/

SUGGESTED READINGS

Data Communications and Networking

Two texts that provide good tutorial overviews of data communications and networking technology and standards are:

1. Tom Sheldon, *LAN TIMES Encyclopedia of Networking*, Osborne McGraw-Hill, 1994.
2. John G. Nellist, *Understanding Telecommunications and Lightwave Systems, an Entry Level Guide*, 2nd Edition, IEEE Press, 1996.

COMPONENT-LEVEL TECHNOLOGY

We have defined component-level technologies as those standards, initiatives, and technologies that have a focus generally limited to a single type of component or subsystem. Component-level technologies are often enabling technologies for the platform-level technologies just examined. For example, the new USB and IEEE 1394 buses, surveyed in this section, are key to the Device Bay and Plug and Play initiatives previously discussed.

Our survey of component-level technologies is carried out in four subsections: *Processors*, *Storage Devices*, *General-Purpose Buses*, and *Device-Specific Buses and Ports*. Of course, each of these technologies has its own field of study to which volumes of texts have been devoted. We examine them here to provide a broad view from an overall platform architecture perspective and to ensure that the reader is literate with respect to the most important components and subsystems used in platforms. The detailed structure of this section is as follows.

SUGGESTED READINGS

Additional Resources: Mindshare and Annabooks are two companies that write books and sponsor seminars on various aspects of platform technology. Each operates a web-site. The URLs are:

http://www.annabooks.com/

http://www.mindshare.com/index1.html

PROCESSORS

Processor performance is generally not an issue for basic word-processing and data-entry applications.

Computation performance is important to application and system software emphasizing presentation quality and ease-of-use features, new 3D graphics applications, software-based DSP, and many scientific and engineering applications. Presentation quality and ease of use are now baseline features of PC platform application and system software. These features greatly enhance user accessibility and productivity, as outlined earlier, but add significant computational overhead to the platform's primary processor.

Real-time processing requirements or extensive data filtering and manipulation often characterize 3D graphics, DSP, and other scientific and engineering applications, leading to increased processor performance requirements. In these areas, the time until results are obtained is often directly proportional to processor performance. In some applications this can be merely a matter of productivity. For 3D graphics and DSP human interface applications, processor performance is usually directly proportional to the quality of the result. Higher quality results mean more realistic simulations that do a better job of engaging the user.

To support the initiatives for *Enhanced User Experience*, discussed earlier in this chapter and as a reflection on trends in PC platform applications, processor performance is being increased through Instruction Set Architecture, physical design, and microarchitecture enhancements. Particular x86 Instruction Set Architecture, enhancements include the MMX and AMD-3D instruction sets for communications, multimedia, and 3D geometry functions. Processor clock rates are being increased steadily due to continual advances in circuit design and semiconductor processing, as illustrated in Figure 4.9.

The number of instructions per clock cycle (IPC)[59] has also increased as advanced microarchitectural techniques (both new and old) are applied to microprocessors. These techniques attempt to increase resource concurrency and utilization, reduce the frequency of pipeline stalls and flushes, and attempt to exploit the full extent of instruction level parallelism (ILP) in the program being executed.

Techniques used to increase processor performance in the K6 3D are discussed in detail in Chapters 2 and 3.

ARTICLES ON CD-ROM

 Michael Bekerman's and Avi Mendelson's article,, "A Performance Analysis of Pentium Processor Systems," *IEEE Micro*, pp. 72-83, October 1995, describes a performance study made by Intel on the P5 architecture and speculates on how to improve it.

The rate of continued increases in microarchitectural performance (in terms of SPECint92 benchmark results normalized by clock speed) is shown in Figure 4.10.

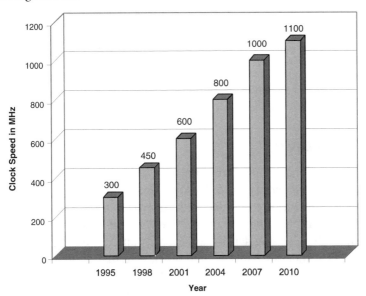

Figure 4.9 EXPECTED GROWTH IN MICROPROCESSOR CLOCK SPEED

Based on Semiconductor Association (SIA)Forecast

The graph suggests that the rate of microarchitectural performance growth is slowing and is presently in a range of 10% growth per year. Overall future platform performance growth will thus likely come mostly from frequency and system architectural improvements, the latter

---

[59] The reciprocal of IPC, Cycles per Instruction (CPI), is also a frequently used metric.

including optimized connectivity and increased bandwidth to other processing and data storage resources.

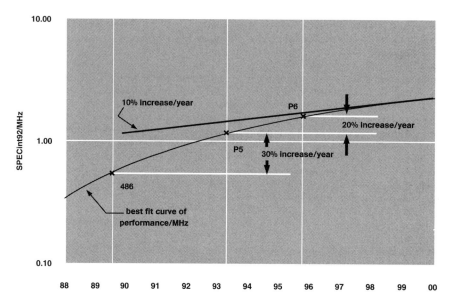

Figure 4.10 Microarchitectural Performance vs Time

Adapted with permission of Advanced Micro Devices Inc., from *Competing with Intel*, Copyright 1997.

Storage Devices

For mobile devices, hard-disk power consumption and management is also a key concern.

In conventional PC platforms, the hard disk is absolutely crucial to system operation and performance. The hard disk is the repository for system and application software and data sets, and holds virtual memory pages not presently in main memory. Fortunately, recent history has delivered hard disks with increasing density and capacity and decreasing costs.

The raw performance of hard disks, in terms of both rotational latency and sustained throughput, is proportional to the rotational speed of the platters. Also significantly impacting hard-disk performance is the chosen electrical interface, of which there are several. Because each of these interfaces can be used for a number of different device types besides hard disks, we have chosen to treat the interfaces separately. Readers are encouraged to separately examine the interface sections on SCSI, ATA/IDE, and the emerging USB, IEEE 1394, and Device Bay standards, according to their interests.

From a system perspective, hard-disk performance is optimized through data staging techniques, in particular the use of a disk cache, and the management of the disk cache using write-back techniques. Hard-disk performance is also optimized by careful attention to the block size and per block latencies, for large file transfers. Finally, the system as a whole is performance optimized when hard disks are managed using a bus-mastering controller. These optimization techniques are discussed in a more general context in the Overall System Architecture Performance Optimization of Chapter 6.

Besides the hard disks discussed above, other common platform storage devices include floppies, tape drives, CD-ROMs and DVD-ROMS, and a number of removable media technologies (removable hard disks). The section that follows will examine CD-ROM and DVD-ROM technology in more detail. .

REQUIREMENTS SUMMARY FOR PC PLATFORM STORAGE DEVICES

- Generic device requirements apply
- Device and controller support bus master operation
- Removable media supports media status notification
- System BIOS or Option ROM support for Int 13H Extensions (includes high capacity drives and consistent drive-letter mapping across OS operating modes), and in CD-ROM or DVD systems, the controller must support the El Torito standard for the CD-ROM or DVD installation process
- Device and file system run in protected mode[a] following installation
- Driver for partitioned media supports all Windows partition types
- IDE hard drives must be compliant with Self-Monitoring, Analysis, and Reporting Technology (SMART) IOCTL API Specification, Version 1.1, or higher

[a] A privileged, or system, mode of the processor that protects unprivileged or user mode execution threads from each other.

REQUIREMENTS SUMMARY FOR PC PLATFORM OPTICAL STORAGE DEVICES

- General storage requirements apply
- Rewriteable drives meet SFF 8070i specification
- A CD-ROM drive uses CD-Enhanced compatible support to mount multisession CD-ROM discs; is compatible with CD Red, Yellow, White, and Blue Book logical format standards; meets SFF 8020i, Version 1.2 or higher (requirements for ATAPI devices); and provides 8x (12Mbits/s throughput) or higher performance
- A DVD (if present) uses a high-speed expansion bus; is compatible with CD Red, Yellow, White, and Blue Book logical format standards; supports the Universal Disk Format Specification (UDFS), Version 1.02, or higher; its device driver meets the SFF 8090 specification; and it supports CSS copyright protection to enable decryption and prevent duplication of CSS protected media

---

INDUSTRY STANDARD

Small Form Factor (SFF) Committee Specifications

The Small Form Factor (SFF) Committee was formed in 1990 to quickly promulgate standards for small devices, such as those typically found in PC platforms. It is administered by ENDL Publications. Observers may joint for $300/year and full membership is $1,800/year. There is a SFF related FTP-site. The URL is:

ftp://fission.dt.wdc.com/pub/standards/SFF/specs/

GENERAL-PURPOSE BUSES

This section surveys interconnect designs that support communication between many arbitrary devices. These buses are distinguished from the next subsection on *Device-Specific Buses and Ports*, which generally couple only a very few (often, just two) devices or subsystems, and frequently implement device-specific protocols.

Distributed Peripheral Buses

The buses in this section are designed to couple multiple devices over distributed and user-extensible paths that are long compared to conventional system expansion buses. These buses are a synthesis of the conventional expansion buses and LANs. The emerging USB and IEEE 1394 buses, and their hybrid combinations in the form of Device Bay and the Enhanced Video Connector (EVC), are key technologies enabling the Plug and Play and SIPC initiatives discussed in the platform-level technology section. SCSI is an established technology with ongoing enhancements. SCSI plays a key role in high-performance hard disks, particularly for server applications.

Universal Serial Bus (USB)

The Universal Serial Bus (USB) is a serial protocol bus intended to support trivial hookup of low-to-medium-bandwidth peripherals. Typical devices include input devices, control functions, telephony/modems, audio, scanners, and printers.

host controller

USB interconnections employ a daisy-chained multi-ported hub star topology, superficially similar to a twisted-pair Ethernet connection between a PC and an Ethernet hub. Each hub in the daisy-chain represents a "tier," of which a maximum of 6 tiers are allowed with no more than 5 meters between segments.   Signals are repeated across all tiers of the network without any storage delay. Up to a maximum of 127 simultaneous devices are possible in such a "tiered-star topology." Figure 4.11 on page 373 shows a PC system in which a 5-port external hub is connected to a *host controller* (resident in each PC) and 4 other peripherals. The host also acts as a hub, connecting with the external hub and to the keyboard.

Each segment is a bidirectional, half-duplex link, with error detection and recovery. The connectors are 4-pin, and the cables are 4-wire. 3.3V signaling differential signaling is used with NRZI coding and bit stuffing. 5V at 100 to 500ma (depending on the hubs) is available to supply low-power peripherals. Figure 4.12 on page 373 gives a close-up of a USB connector and a pair of USB sockets. Figure 4.13 is an abstract drawing of the internal detail of the connector and port.

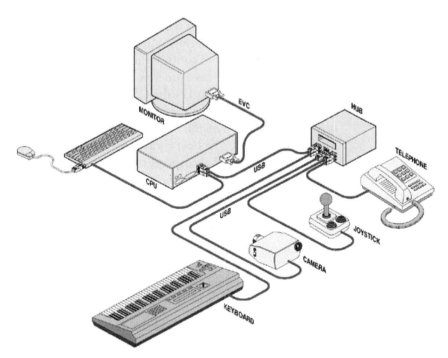

Figure 4.11 EXAMPLE USB INTERCONNECT USE IN A SMALL SYSTEM
Copyright 1997, Molex Inc., used with permission.

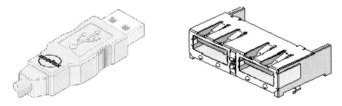

Figure 4.12 USB CONNECTOR AND PORT
Copyright 1997, Molex Inc., used with permission.

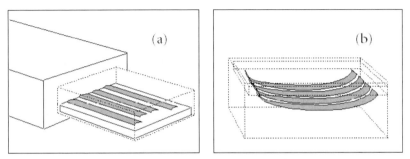

Figure 4.13 DRAWING OF USB CONNECTOR AND PORT INTERNAL DETAIL

Microsoft recommends that any peripheral that consumes more than 30% of the available USB bandwidth should use IEEE 1394 instead.

The host controller manages the bus in many ways. It issues tokens with unique device addresses, to which addressed devices may respond by presenting read data or accepting write data. Transfer types include bulk, isochronous, interrupt, and control transfers. The host controller detects the attachment of new devices, queries the device, determines its capability, assigns it an address, invokes the OS to load the driver corresponding to the device, configures the device, and signals the OS to start the device driver. It performs dynamic reconfiguration in response to any insertion or removal activity. The host controller performs power management for the bus by issuing global suspend/resume commands. It also dynamically allocates the bus bandwidth, including the assignment of isochronous use of the bus, with an aggregate maximum rate of 12 Mbps.

The ability to communicate with 127 devices through only a single connection on a PC platform is a key aspect of the appeal of USB. Such leverage is particularly appealing for laptops, but it also permits a reduced footprint[60] for desktops. Other key aspects include the ability to perform hot insertion and removal of connections, and to perform the connections on the outside of a sealed-case PC.

INDUSTRY STANDARDS

Universal Serial Bus Implementers Forum (USB-IF)

The USB-IF describes itself as "is a support organization formed by the seven promoters of USB to help speed development of high quality compatible devices using USB." Intel administers the USB-IF. USB-IF membership is $2500/year.

The USB-IF maintains a Web site. Useful information on joining, white papers, conference presentations, and free download access to the USB specification and clarifications and enhancements is best found in the technical area, under URL:

http://www.usb.org/developers/

REPORT ON CD-ROM

To learn more about Universal Serial Bus (USB), see the article by Michael Slater titled, "Universal Serial Bus to Simplify PC I/O," *Microprocessor Report*, Vol. 9, No. 5, April 17, 1995, on the CD-ROM.

---

[60] Footprint refers to the amount of furniture-top surface area required by a PC.

INDUSTRY STANDARDS

VESA Enhanced Video Connector (EVC)

The Enhanced Video Connector is a hybrid combination of IEEE 1394, USB, digital audio, and both analogy and digital display monitor drive signals. The EVC permits peripheral devices mounted in the monitor to attach to these individual buses yet only requires a single cable between the monitor and the system unit. The following standards define EVC:

- *VESA Enhanced Video Connector (EVC) ™ Pinout and Signal Standards, Version 2* establishes the electrical pinout and signals for the EVC connector.
- *VESA Enhanced Video Connector (EVC) ™ Physical Connector Standard, Version 1, Revision 2* establishes the physical features of the EVC connector.

VESA standards are only available to VESA members. A complete list of VESA standards with a brief abstract of each is available at URL:

> http://www.vesa.org/ve00013.html

The Video Electronics Standards Association (VESA) is discussed in more detail in the section on Graphics and Video Adapters later in this chapter.

SUGGESTED READINGS

USB

Don Anderson's book, *Universal Serial Bus System Architecture*, MindShare, Inc., Addison-Wesley, 1997, gives a clear and detailed explanation of the concepts behind USB.

REQUIREMENTS SUMMARY FOR PC USB DEVICES

- Required
- Generic device requirements apply
- All devices compliant with USB Specification, Version 1.0
- The host controller must be compliant with the Open Host Controller Interface (OpenHCI) or Intel's Universal Host Controller Interface (UHCI)
- The host controller can wake the system

IEEE 1394

IEEE 1394 is a PC 98 required high-speed serial protocol bus that provides easy hookup of high-bandwidth peripherals, such as video cameras,

VCRs, video or audio conferencing channels, hard disks, or CD-ROMs and DVD-ROMs. It is cited by many as being a replacement for the present ATA/IDE interface as well as small LANs.

IEEE 1394 offers speeds of 100, 200, and 400 Mbps on the same cable with dynamic speed negotiation between source and destination. Transfers are strictly between source and destination and do not require the involvement of a host. Transfers can be made with guaranteed bandwidth and known latency.

Dynamically assigned device identifiers let each bus support up to 63 devices, connected in a point-to-point fashion. Splitters permit branching at any point, in any direction. Intermediate devices need not be powered and all connections are hot-swappable. Removal or insertion of a device results in transparent dynamic reconfiguration of addresses. Any non-loop topology is permitted, provided that node-to-node distances are a maximum of 4.5m and no more that 16 hops exist between any two nodes. Bus identifiers permit bridging of up to 1023 buses. Figure 4.14 shows an IEEE 1394-1995 external port and plug connector.

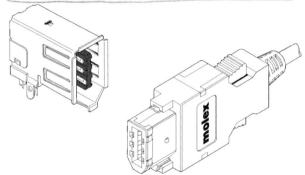

Figure 4.14 Six-Wire External Port and Plug Connector
Copyright 1997, Molex Inc., used with permission.

These are 6-wire connectors, consisting of one pair of power conductors and two pairs of signal conductors. Low-power devices can take power from the cable, up to a cumulative 60 watts maximum. Another external connector pair (not shown) is a 4-wire Audio-Visual (AV) connector that does away with the power conductors. There are also internal device connectors, suitable for motherboard mounting for the mating of either daughterboards or cables.

IEEE Standard on CD-ROM

A copy of the IEEE 1394-1995 standard is included on the CD-ROM.

INDUSTRY STANDARDS

IEEE 1394 Trade Association (1394 TA)

In its own words, "The 1394 Trade Association actively promotes the proliferation of the IEEE 1394 Serial Bus standard technology into the computer, consumer, peripheral, and industrial markets to enable a truly interoperable, standardized, universal I/O and backplane interconnect." Membership fees in 1394 TA are $4000 or $8000/year, based on gross revenues. The 1394 TA maintains a Web site with information on joining, a mailing list, and links to conference presentations and papers. The main URL is:

http://www.1394ta.org/

TECHNICAL PRESENTATION ON CD-ROM

 Two IEEE 1394 technical presentations are included on the CD-ROM. The first gives numerous quality illustrations of the various connector types used for IEEE 1394 and its hybrid forms, including the Enhanced Video Connector discussed earlier. The second is an outstanding presentation that gives a detailed overview of the IEEE 1394 protocol.

- Max Bassler, *IEEE 1394 Interface Technology.*
- Michael D. Johas Teener, *IEEE 1394-1995 High Performance Serial Bus.*

REPORTS ON CD-ROM

 To learn more about IEEE 1394, see the following reports on the companion CD-ROM:

- Michael Teener, *New Technology in the IEEE P1394 Serial Bus—Making it Fast, Cheap and Easy to Use,* March 31, 1998.
- Curtis P. Feigel, "FireWire Brings Fast Serial Bus to Desktop," *Microprocessor Report*, Vol. 8, No. 3, March 7, 1994.
- Michael Teener, *A Bus on a Diet—The Serial Bus Alternative: An Introduction to the P1394 High Performance Serial Bus,* December 14, 1993.

REQUIREMENTS SUMMARY FOR **PC** PLATFORM **IEEE 1394** DEVICES

- General device requirements apply
- Devices support a peak data rate of 400 Mb/s, minimum
- Controllers must be compliant with the Open Host Controller Interface (OpenHCI) for 1394, which defines standard register addresses and functions, data structures, and DMA models and promotes performance, security, and error handling
- Recommended for all devices needing high-bandwidth and Plug and Play connectivity
- The controller must exhibit robust response to topology faults, including surprise removal, safe removal (device is switched off prior to removal from bus), more than 16 cable hops, or more than 63 devices
- Devices capable of initiating peer-to-peer communications must support a programming language that enables them to be remotely controlled by the platform
- A configuration ROM compliant with a number of special requirements is required to enable the PC to uniquely identify each device on the bus, determine and configure its requirements, and load the correct device driver
- Devices and controllers must comply with the Cable Power Distribution Specification and the IEEE 1394 Specification for Power Management
- Devices must keep their physical interface (PHY) powered at all times when otherwise powered down to enable the device to perform the repeater function
- Devices that consume or source power must report such characteristics and must notify the bus power-manager if the device is switched off
- AC-powered platforms must source power to the bus
- Self-powered devices propagate the power bus through each connector
- Each source supplies a minimum of 20 volts at 15 watts
- Cable and self-powered devices must allow a bus manager to control their power state
- End user cabling purchases and decisions are reduced by generally requiring devices to use a standard 6-pin connector
- Single-port, leaf-node, devices may use the 4-pin connector intended for hand-held devices
- Multiple port devices use all 6-pin connectors, all connectors propagate the power bus, all ports support a common peak data rate, and all cabling supports 400 Mb/s

ARTICLES ON CD-ROM

The first article in the following set provides yet another perspective on the IEEE 1394 architecture. The last two articles describe how consumer video applications can make use of IEEE 1394.

- Stephen L. Diamond, "IEEE 1394: Status and Growth Path," *IEEE Micro*, Vol. 16, No. 3, June 1996.
- Alan T. Wetzel and Michael R. Schell, "Consumer Applications of the IEEE 1394 Serial Bus, and a 1394 DV Video Editing System," *ICCE*, June 1996.
- Adam J. Kunzman and Alan T. Wetzel, "1394 High Performance Serial Bus: The Digital Interface for ATV," *IEEE Transactions on Consumer Electronics,* Vol. 14, No. 13, August 1995.

Small Computer System Interface (SCSI)

The Small Computer System Interface (SCSI) has been a popular interface for peripheral devices and particularly so in high-end platforms. SCSI is second only to the IDE/ATA interface in popularity for attachment of hard disks. Variants (and their theoretical peak bandwidths) include SCSI-1 (5 MBps), SCSI-2 (5 MBps), Fast SCSI-2 (10 MBps), Wide SCSI-2 (20 MBps), Ultra SCSI or SCSI-3 (20 MBps), and Wide Ultra SCSI (40 MBps). SCSI is frequently used for high-performance hard disks, CD-ROMs, other media, and scanners. SCSI bus mastering controllers were widely available earlier than with IDE/ATA. Consequently, SCSI has been adopted for some time as the preferred hard disk interface in file servers, where the ability to have multiple simultaneous file-transfers and other execution processes is essential. SCSI shares attributes with LAN technologies, in that node devices (up to 8, or up to 16 for Ultra SCSI) are coupled over an extendable distributed bus, often at least partially external to the host platform. Figure 4.15 shows commonly used SCSI connectors.

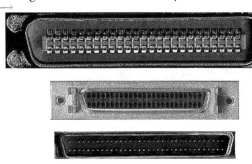

50-pin Centronics-style male

50-pin high-density female

68-pin high-density male

Figure 4.15 COMMON SCSI CONNECTORS

The 50-pin Centronics-style connector was used for SCSI-1 devices. The 50-pin high-density connector is used for SCSI-2 and 8-bit Ultra SCSI devices. The 68-pin high-density connector is used for Wide SCSI-2 and Wide Ultra SCSI. The PC Specifications plan to supplant the SCSI interface with IEEE 1394, which offers enhanced expansion capabilities and performance.

INDUSTRY STANDARDS
SCSI Trade Association
The SCSI Trade Association is involved in promoting and explaining the technology. The SCSI Trade Association operates a Web site with information on joining and downloadable white papers and technical presentations. The main URL is: http://www.scsita.org/

REQUIREMENTS SUMMARY FOR PC SCSI DEVICES

- General device requirements apply
- Bootable controllers must support the El Torito standard for the CD-ROM installation process
- Controllers must support virtual DMA services (including scatter/gather)
- Controllers must include support for SCSI-3 defined DIFFSENS, which senses and configures for either differential or single-ended peripherals, and also support SCSI-3 automatic termination, which permits external devices to be added without opening the case
- External connectors must be a high-density connector according to the SCSI-2, or higher, specification
- Connectors must clearly identify the bus as SCSI and external connectors must display the SCSI icon connectors
- Peripherals must implement on the parity SCSI bus
- Cabling must meet clause 6 of the SCSI-3 spec, shielded device connectors must meet SCSI-2 or higher spec, users must be prevented from incorrect cabling of either internal or external devices, and external devices must use automatic termination or an externally accessible switch
- hardware supports the SCSI-2 spec defined STOP/START UNIT command used by software to conserve power or resume normal operation

INDUSTRY STANDARDS

SCSI Specifications

Approved SCSI-related standards are available only by purchase from the American National Standards Institute (ANSI). The available standards include:

SCSI-2 CAM Transport and SCSI Interface Module X3.232:1996

SCSI-3 Architecture Model (SAM) X3.270:1996

SCSI-3 Controller Commands (SCC) X3.276:1997

SCSI-3 Fast-20 Parallel Interface (Fast-20) X3.277:1996

SCSI-3 Interlocked Protocol (SIP) X3.292:1997

SCSI-3 Parallel Interface (SPI) X3.253:1995

SCSI-3 Primary Commands (SPC) X3.301:1997

Small Computer System Interface - 2 (SCSI-2) X3.131:1994

SSA SCSI-2 Protocol (SSA-S2P) X3.294:1996

ANSI maintains a Web site with a searchable online catalog and electronic ordering of specifications. Prices of each specification vary. The main URL is:

http://www.ansi.org/

Secondary SCSI Technical Documents

Draft SCSI-related specifications are available from the T10 Web site. The main URL is:

http://www.symbios.com/x3t10/

The ISA Bus

DEFINITION
Industry Standard Architecture Bus (ISA Bus)[a]

The ISA Bus is the 1984 PC/AT bus that was a 16-bit extension of the 8-bit bus used in the 1981 IBM PC. The IBM PC bus was a near derivative of the processor bus signals generated by an Intel 8088[b] in conjunction with an Intel 8288 bus controller. Similarly, the ISA Bus is a near derivative of the processor bus signals generated by the Intel 80286 used in the original PC/AT. Like these Intel processors, the ISA Bus supports a memory address space and a separate I/O address space,[c] which are nominally used for memory and I/O peripherals, respectively.[d] In addition to basic cycles for accessing memory and I/O, the ISA Bus architecture is considered to include a number of other facilities associated with the programmer visible features of the PC/AT architecture. These features include its interrupt controller, DMA, RTC, CMOS Memory, Keyboard and mouse controller, and system timers.

[a]   The derivation of the ISA Bus name was given in Chapter 1.

[b]   The Intel 8088 has the same 16-bit internal microarchitecture as an Intel 8086, but has an 8-bit external data bus.

[c]   While PC platforms make extensive use of the peripherals, partially or wholly memory-mapped peripherals are also common.

[d]   The MEMR# and MEMW# signals are asserted for memory space reads and writes, respectively. The IOR# and IOW# signals are asserted for I/O space reads and writes, respectively.

Figure 4.16 shows the 8-bit portion of an ISA slot, just above the nickel. The ISA edge connector detail is visible on an 8-bit ISA card that is lying on its side above and adjacent to the slot and aligned with it. There are thirty-one contact positions on each side of the 8-bit edge connector, for sixty-two total bus lines. These include 20-bits of address and 8-bits of data, 6 interrupt request (IRQ) lines, and 3-pairs of DMA handshake lines. The full 16-bit ISA slot extended this with an additional eighteen contact positions on each side of another edge connector segment. The additional thirty-six bus lines brings the total number of 16-bit ISA slot bus lines to ninety-eight. The 16-bit extension included the following additional signals: 4-bits of address, 8-bits of data, five additional interrupt lines, and three additional DMA pairs.[61] The new edge connector segment is

---

[61]   A fourth additional DMA pair appears on the motherboard, but not on the ISA bus.

collinear with the original 8-bit edge connector in a manner that permits the reliable use of 8-bit ISA cards in the 16-bit ISA slot.

Figure 4.16   VIEW OF 8-BIT ISA CARD EDGE ADJACENT TO 8-BIT PORTION OF ISA CARD SLOT

DEFINITION
The X-Bus (The Extended ISA Bus)
The ISA Bus per se connects only to the ISA expansion slots. However, motherboard implemented 8-bit-wide discrete memory and I/O devices may use the *X-Bus*, or *Extended ISA Bus*, a buffered extended variation of the ISA Bus.

In the PC/AT, X-Bus discrete motherboard peripherals included the ROM BIOS, the RTC, the CMOS Memory, the Keyboard and mouse controller, the DMA controller, and the interrupt controller. Today, the Super I/O module, itself often integrated into the South-Bridge, integrates all of these former X-Bus functions save for the ROM BIOS. (The backup-battery for the RTC and the CMOS Memory also still remains on the motherboard.) Moving the contents of the ROM BIOS into DRAM on power-up initialization is now one of the last remaining uses of the X-Bus on the motherboard.

Protocol

> ### DEFINITION
>
> #### Bus Protocols
>
> A *bus protocol* is the method the bus uses to communicates address, data, command, and status information between source and destination devices. Two fundamental attributes of bus protocols are whether they are *clocked* and whether they make use of any *handshakes* between the source and destination. A clocked bus includes a clock signal among the bus signals to provide a reference for the sequential logic associated with the bus interfaces at both the source and destination. The buses used for expansion cards on PC platforms are clocked. Peripheral buses are often not clocked. Handshakes are additional status signals frequently included among the bus signals to pace the progress of transfers over the bus. The extent of handshaking varies considerably with different bus protocols. Whether or not a bus handshaken is totally independent of whether it is clocked or not, and vice versa.
>
> *clocked*
> *handshakes*
>
> The terms *synchronous* and *asynchronous* are also often used to describe bus protocols. Unfortunately, neither of these terms is used consistently in the literature. The reader must generally deduce what is meant from the context in which these terms appear. Synchronous may mean clocked, and asynchronous may mean not clocked. This usage is consistent with general usage in logic design.[a] However, in bus protocols, asynchronous may be used to mean handshaken, independent of whether the bus is clocked or not. Likewise synchronous may be used to mean a bus that is not handshaken, independent of whether the bus is clocked or not.
>
> *synchronous*
> *asynchronous*
>
> A *semi-synchronous protocol* is one that makes use of optional handshakes. When the optional handshakes are not used, the semi-synchronous bus is said to use *passive termination*, and operates in an entirely synchronous (i.e., not handshaken) fashion using the defined default bus cycle timings.
>
> *semi-synchronous protocol*
>
> Clocked buses perform transactions in integer multiples of the reference clock cycle. Generally, different transaction types have different *bus-cycle timings*, in that the number of cycles varies with the transaction type. For handshaken buses, each transaction type has a nominal-case[b] bus cycle timing corresponding to the case when both source and destination are ready to proceed at the nominal rate for that transaction. This nominal-case timing can be lengthened by the introduction of additional bus clock cycle multiples via the bus's handshake mechanism. Each additional bus clock cycle introduced beyond the nominal-case timing is referred to as a wait state or a wait cycle.

[a] Unfortunately, synchronous and asynchronous may also be used to describe the extent to which two clocked signals maintain frequency or phase relationships of particular interest.

[b] The nominal-case timing is usually the best-case timing. This is usually greater than a single bus clock period.

An 8.33MHz bus clock (BCLK) is the reference for ISA Bus timing. The ISA Bus has two types of control signals that may be respectively used to optionally shorten or lengthen default bus cycle timings. Thus, the ISA Bus uses a clocked semi-synchronous protocol.

REPORTS ON CD-ROM

ISA Bus Detailed Operation

 Two data sheets included on the CD-ROM have valuable supplemental information on the ISA Bus.

From the AMD-645 Peripheral Bus Controller Data Sheet:

- Section 2.2 on pp. 2-3 through 2-5 gives an overview of the ISA Bus controller functions of the South-Bridge.

- Section 4.2 on pp. 4-4 through 4-10 describe each of the ISA bus signals.

- Section 4.4 on pp. 4-13 and 4-14 describe each of the X-Bus signals.

- I/O Read/Write cycles and timing diagrams for ISA Slaves[a] are discussed in Section 5.2.3 on pp. 5-3 through 5-5.

- Memory Read/Write cycles and timing diagrams for ISA Slaves are discussed in Section 5.2.4 on pp. 5-4 through 5-14.

- Memory Read/Write cycles and timing diagrams for DMA ISA Masters[b] are discussed in Section 5.4.1 on pp. 5-18 through 5-10.

- Memory and I/O Read/Write cycles and timing diagrams for non-DMA ISA Masters are discussed In Section 5.4.2 on pp. 5-20 through 5-22.

- Table 9-7 through 9-11 and figures 9-3 through 9-8, on pp. 9-8 through 9-17. These tables and figures provide detailed ISA interface timing diagrams and associated parameters for ISA Masters, ISA 16-bit Slaves, ISA 8-bit Slaves, and ISA Master-to-PCI Accesses.

---

[a] Slaves, or targets, are devices that respond to transactions initiated by other devices.

[b] Masters are devices that initiate transactions to which other devices must respond.

REPORTS ON CD-ROM (CONT.)

> ### ISA Bus Detailed Operation
>
> - Tables 9-12 through 9-14 and figures 9-8 through 9-10, on pages 9-18 through 9-23. These tables and figures provide detailed DMA interface timing diagrams and associated parameters for DMA read, DMA write, and Type F DMA cycles.
> - Table 9-15 and figure 9-11, on pages 9-24 and 9-25. This table and figure provide a detained X-Bus interface timing diagram and associated parameters for X-Bus operation.
>
> *From the ATX Reference Design for AMD-640 Chipset Technical Specification*:
>
> - Table 2-7, on pp. 29-30 maps the ISA Bus signals to the specific pin locations on the slot connectors.

Performance

Using fast 16-bit peripherals, the fastest ISA transaction transfers two bytes in two BCLK cycles. Thus, 8.33 MBytes per second is the theoretical maximum transfer rate for the ISA Bus. However, the default timing for 16-bit transfers is three BCLK cycles (5.55 MBytes per second). Furthermore, many peripherals are only 8-bits wide. The best timing for 8-bit transfers is three BCLK cycles (2.77 MBytes per second) and the default timing is six BLCK cycles (1.38 MBytes per second). Note that every datum transferred over the ISA Bus requires an associated address broadcast. The more efficient transfer of multiple data items for a single address is discussed in the section below on PCI.

Typical transfer-rates using the ISA Bus are well below the theoretical maximum of 8.33 MBytes per second.

The rate of continued increases in microarchitectural performance (in terms of SPECint92 benchmark results normalized by clock speed) is shown in Figure 4.10. The graph suggests that the rate of microarchitectural performance growth is slowing and is presently in a range of 10% growth per year. Overall future platform performance growth will thus likely come mostly from frequency and system architectural improvements, the latter including optimized connectivity and increased bandwidth to other processing and data storage resources.

Legacy Direct Memory Access (DMA)

DMA controller

DEFINITION
Direct Memory Access (DMA)
Direct Memory Access (DMA) uses dedicated DMA *controllers* to transfer blocks of data between memory and peripherals. Once initialized and initiated by the processor, DMA transfers are carried out by the DMA controller, *theoretically* freeing the processor for other activities. To use DMA, The processor may program the DMA controller with a start address and the number of bytes to transfer. The DMA controller will execute the transfer and notify the processor via interrupt when the operation is complete.

As originally implemented, Legacy DMA required the processor to relinquish the processor's local bus in order for the DMA controller to access main memory. This meant that concurrency between the DMA controller and the processor was severely limited. The processor could only proceed to the extent that it could execute instruction out of its prefetch buffers and internal cache. In a later section on Legacy I/O Issues, pointers are provided to materials that describe how Legacy DMA is implemented in current PCI Bus systems.

Suggested Readings
ISA Bus
The following texts are extensive references on the ISA Bus. The first is a very well organized and clear presentation of all basic concepts. The second is a very comprehensive discussion of low-level design issues. 1. Tom Shanley and Don Anderson, *ISA System Architecture*, 3rd Edition, Addison-Wesley, 1995. 2. Edward Solari, *ISA & EISA Theory and Operation*, Annabooks, 1993.

Elimination of the ISA Bus

 Generally, the history of the PC platform has been one of absolute compatibility with legacy software and hardware. Yet, as we indicated in the Legacy Issues section of Chapter 1, the legacy ISA Bus is being eliminated from new mainstream platform designs. In this instance, compatibility has been subordinated to the ability to provide a system that is substantially higher performing, better behaved, and easier to support.

As we will see in the discussion of the PCI Bus and the AGP, the bus-width, bus-timings, and effective rate of transfer for the ISA Bus are but a small fraction of what is available with the newer buses. These new buses were developed because the ISA Bus is totally insufficient to satisfy the needs of emerging 3D graphics acceleration and other high performance peripherals.

Equally important, the problems frequently caused by ISA cards are not limited to the card or the application using the card, but may adversely affect the entire system. ISA-based legacy peripherals may cause performance degradation to all threads of execution on today's highly multi-tasked systems. Additionally, the system as a whole may develop obscure and difficult to diagnose problems due to ISA cards that do not have Plug-n-Play automatic resource configuration or power-management capability.

The issue can be also be easily viewed from a support context. The relationship between the use of ISA cards and such systemic problems is neither obvious nor easily explainable to the naïve end-user. Furthermore, asking an end-user to remove an installed ISA card to help debug a problem, or asking him to forgo use of an ISA card that the user is presently dependent on, are not practical solutions.

While clearly a drastic move, eliminating ISA slots altogether does away with the aforementioned performance, poor-behavior, and support problems. The burden to the user of excising the ISA slots is mitigated by the integration of much of the common peripheral functionality into the Super I/O component of the South-Bridge. The burden will be further mitigated by the growth of peripherals making use of the USB and IEEE 1394 buses and the Device Bay initiative.

Backplane Bus — PCI

Through the 80's and early 90's, PC/AT memory subsystems were operated off the processor's increasingly faster local bus, while display adapter cards and other expansion peripherals were generally operated off the ISA/ EISA Bus. To insure compatibility with earlier peripherals, the speed of the ISA Bus was left unchanged. Bus transceivers isolated the processor local bus and the ISA Bus, coupling the two only when necessary. This permitted certain programs or program segments that were not heavily I/O oriented to run much faster as processor and memory speeds increased. By the early 90's however, growing interest in multimedia applications, which are heavily I/O oriented, was creating additional performance demands beyond increased processor speed. Multimedia applications need an expansion bus with high effective data-transfer rates, support for burst transfers, support for concurrent subsystems, support for bus-mastering peripherals, and guaranteed low-latency access to the bus.

DEFINITIONS

Bus Features for Multimedia Applications

High effective data-transfer rates are essential for full-motion video due to the need to move high frame rate, large size, high-resolution color bit-maps, or related data and commands, to the display adapter. While the requirement is most acute for the display adapter, graphics-related data needs to be moved about between various other system components, including the processor, main memory, hard disks, and communications adapters.

Support for large numbers of data transfers per address, or long burst mode transfers, is key to high effective data-transfer rates. Burst mode transfers realize the highest data-transfer rates and make the most efficient use of the available bus bandwidth. Burst mode writes for transferring data into the video memory are an important performance feature, as the video memory holds both the frame buffer and command information for the display adapter.

Support for concurrent subsystems is inherent in the very nature of presenting the user with multiple simultaneous types of media. Furthermore, concurrent subsystems are necessary to provide multimedia augmentation without compromising the performance of the fundamental data processing and control flow requirements of the application program.

Support for bus mastering peripherals is key to concurrent subsystems. Bus mastering peripherals may autonomously carry out transfers, permitting the processor to carry out another task while the bus-master transfer is on going. Bus mastering peripherals are frequently, but not limited to, peripherals with bus-mastering DMA controllers. Bus mastering DMA is an important performance feature for display adapters, hard drives, and high-speed networking.

Guaranteed low-latency access is necessary because devices on the expansion bus generally cannot be held off the bus indefinitely or else noticeable visual or aural anomalies will be experienced by the user and data being recorded may be irretrievably lost.

HISTORICAL COMMENT

The VESA Local Bus (VL Bus)

In the early 90's, the display adapter was the peripheral subsystem where it was most apparent that peripheral speeds needed to be improved over those possible with ISA Bus. Interest arose is adding slots to the processor local bus for display adapter cards, and in 1992, the Video Electronics Standards Association (VESA) announced the VESA Local Bus (VL Bus, or VLB) standard. This formally defined slots for adding display adapter cards and other high-speed peripherals to a bus that was designed electrically to be a compatible derivative of the Intel 80486 (486) processor local bus, then used in most new PC platforms.

Definitions were included for a type "A" nonbuffered single VL Bus slot version and a type "B" buffered version for up to three slots. Physically the VL Bus standard called for two collinear connectors, one specific to the expansion bus (i.e., ISA, EISA, or Micro Channel) and another specific to the VL standard. This permitted VL Bus cards to optionally have separate connections to both buses. A typical 33-MHz PC platform might have one 8-bit ISA slots, five 16-bit ISA slots, and two VL Bus/ISA Bus hybrid slots for eight slots total. The hybrid slots could also be used for regular ISA cards.

A one slot VL Bus at 33-MHz was capable of an transfer rate of 106 MBytes per second for 16-byte burst reads[a]. However, this was only possible if the bytes were cacheable, aligned on a cache-line boundary, and the VL Bus card supported the 486 cache-line burst mode. Non-burst Reads and Writes to 32-bit devices can be performed at 66 MBytes per second. Since writing into the video memory is a dominant display-adapter use, the general transfer rate for display adapters on the VL Bus was likely closer to the non-burst transfer rate than the burst read rate.[b]

While the VL Bus provided needed higher bandwidth, it did not address the other needs of multimedia applications, as presented above. It also suffered from a number of other weaknesses. It placed significant loading on the processor local bus, due to their tight coupling. This meant that only two VL Bus slots were possible for 33-MHz machines, while 66-MHz machines were limited to one slot. Furthermore, the buffered multi-slot implementation required additional wait states over the single-slot version.[c] As a result, a multi-slot 33-MHz VL Bus was likely to have an transfer rate of no more than 44 MBytes per second for Non-burst Reads and Writes, or 88 MBytes per second for burst reads.

[a]   16-bytes in 5-cycles at 33MHz.

[b]   Because data is being transferred to the display adapter only a fraction of the time, the overall throughput for a display adapter card is a corresponding fraction of the available transfer rate.

[c]   Tom Shanley and Don Anderson, *PCI System Architecture,* 3rd Edition, Mindshare, Inc., 1995, p. 27.

The VESA Local Bus (VL Bus)

Several factors unique to its time also seriously compromised the VL Bus's chances for long term survival. First, any VL Bus compatible product needed to be designed solely for use in one of the three popular expansion-buses then in use. Second, VL Bus products designed for the more prevalent 33-MHz machines were not necessarily compatible with the emerging 60 and 66-MHz machines. Finally, products designed for a 486-based VL Bus bus, were not directly compatible with a different processor local bus, such as that of the highly anticipated Pentium.

VESA has implemented a number of important standards for PC Platforms. The Section on Graphics and Video Adapters gives a brief discussion of some of these standards and a pointer to the VESA organization.

Factors Leading to the Success of PCI

The PCI Bus has recently gained strong acceptance in several RISC architectures, enabling them to exploit the wide availability of relatively inexpensive high-performance peripherals designed for the higher-volume PC platform.

The PCI Bus was introduced in mid "93 and was rapidly adopted as the primary expansion bus for post-486 PC Platforms. Its success is attributable to a number of factors:

- Many PC buyers were keenly interested in multimedia applications and were willing to pay for new high-performance hardware,
- the ISA Bus was clearly inadequate for high performance multimedia and the higher performance of the then new Intel Pentium processor further highlighted the need for a new primary systems bus,[a]
- the roll-out of the PCI Bus coincided fairly closely with the roll-out of the 486-socket-incompatible Pentium and buyers needed a new motherboard anyway,
- PCI was an open architecture with wide industry backing, and
- PCI addressed the needs of multimedia applications better than did the VL Bus.

[a] The 64-bit processor local bus of a 66 MHz Pentium had a peak burst bandwidth of 528 MBytes per second and a transfer rate of 264 MBytes per second for non-burst reads and writes.

The PCI Connector

Figure 4.17 shows two views of the 32-bit PCI edge card connector. The right close-up view provides details of both the connector and the matching card edge of a PCI card. The card is on its side but is otherwise aligned with the connector, as it would be inserted. Figure 4.18 is a composite image[62] that provides a same scale comparison of slots for the ISA, VL, and PCI Buses, and AGP. The AGP is a variation of the PCI Bus that has been customized specifically for display adapter use. The AGP is discussed briefly later in this section and in the later section on Graphics and Video Adapters. A reference line representing the rear edge of a motherboard has been provided toward the right edge of the image. The slots are placed horizontally with respect to the reference line, in a manner that is representative of their relative alignment on a motherboard. A 16-bit ISA Bus slot is at the upper right with a collinear 32-bit VL Bus slot on the upper left. A 32-bit PCI Bus slot is in the lower middle. An AGP slot is at the bottom of the figure.

Figure 4.17 VIEWS OF PCI CARD SLOTS AND PCI CARD EDGE

---

[62] While theoretically possible, VL Bus slots normally are not present in systems with PCI.

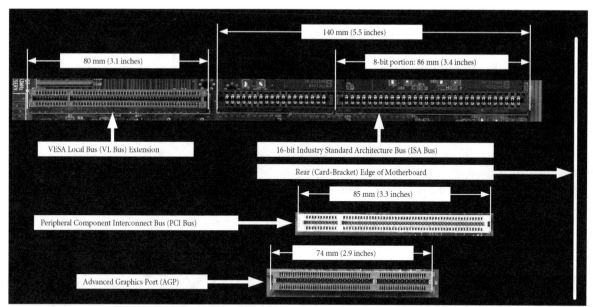

Figure 4.18 COMPARISON OF POPULAR CARD SLOTS

This is a same scale comparison. Horizontal placement is representative of relative alignment on a motherboard. Dimensions are approximate.

Key Features of the PCI Bus

The PCI Bus provides good support for multimedia applications via high-bandwidth, long burst transfers, well-done support for multiple bus-masters, guaranteed low-latency access. Additionally, PCI offers a number of other outstanding features including a processor independent bus architecture, scalable performance via bridged multiple buses, low power operation via Reflected-Wave Switching technology, and automatic configuration support for the Plug-n-Play initiative.

High-Bandwidth and Long Burst Transfers

A 32-bit PCI bus operating at 33MHz is capable of peak transfer rates of 132 MBytes per second. A 64-bit PCI bus at 33MHz, has a 264Mbyte per second peak transfer rate. Finally, a 64-bit PCI bus at 66MHz, has a 528 MByte per second peak transfer rate. Sustained rates are also more effectively realizable, at roughly 60-75%[63] of the peak rate, because the PCI bus is capable of long burst-mode transfers.

---

[63] Anthony Cataldo, "PC makers say Intel's 440LX chip set won't deliver sufficient performance—Compaq, Micron roll core logic for workstations," *EE Times TechWeb News*, August 18, 1997.

DEFINITIONS

Burst Cycles and Burst Transfers

Burst cycles, or burst-mode transfers, transfer multiple data items for a single address. Burst cycles may be viewed as being composed of a *lead-off*, or initial, transfer and subsequent *burst transfers*. The address and first data item is sent during the lead-off. Burst transfers consist of contiguous data transfers sent without their associated address information. Generally, each data item sent in a burst transfer requires only a single bus clock cycle, while the lead-off transfer requires a larger number bus clock cycles. As a result of their compressed timing, burst transactions generally realize much greater effective data transfer rates than non-burst transactions and thus make more efficient use of available bus bandwidth.

For relatively short bursts, such as cache line fills, burst transfer performance is often described using notation of the form *W-X-Y-Z*. W is the number of bus clock cycles for the lead-off transfer, and X, Y, and Z are the number of bus clock cycles for the subsequent burst transfers.

lead-off
burst transfers

Processor Independent Bus Architecture

The PCI Bus is designed as a processor independent expansion bus. Neither the processor's local bus nor its speed directly affects the operation of the PCI Bus. A bus bridge[64] is customized for each local bus architecture to selectively couple the processor local bus with the PCI Bus for *crossing-transfers*. Unlike the simple transceivers used to isolate the processor local bus and the ISA Bus, this bridge has separate bus mastering controllers that implement the bus protocols unique to the processor local bus and the PCI Bus. The bridge may also be augmented with bi-directional (dual) first-in-first-out (FIFO) command and data buffering, which further reduces the coupling duration as perceived by the faster processor local bus.

crossing-transfers

Concurrent Subsystems, Bus Masters, and Guaranteed Low-Latency Access

The processor-to-PCI bus-bridge provides default isolation between the processor and peripherals on the PCI Bus. It also implements a PCI Bus arbiter, selectively granting the PCI bus to bus masters that request it. The PCI Bus permits any peripheral[65] to be a bus master, enabling peripherals to

---

[64] This is the North-Bridge of Figure 1.3.

[65] This is in contrast to the ISA architecture where a centralized DMA controller is generally the only bus master other than the processor.

readily carry out transfers on the isolated PCI Bus while the processor is carrying out other tasks on the processor local bus. PCI bus-masters are designed such that burst transfers that have exceeded a predetermined length can be momentarily suspended and subsequently resumed, should another bus master need to perform a transfer. This mechanism enables long burst transfers to attain high effective transfer rates yet ensures that every bus master will gain access to the bus within a desired interval.

Bus-Mastering DMA

Bus-Mastering DMA controllers reside on peripherals attached to the expansion bus and are dedicated to use by the associated peripheral. PCI Bus-mastering DMA is far superior to the centralized Legacy DMA mechanism. For bus-master DMA transfers between two PCI devices, the processor continues to have access to its external cache, to main memory, and to the AGP. This means that truly concurrent independent operation can take place by the Bus-master DMA controller and the processor. Examples include transfers between two hard disks, transfers between a hard disk and a network adapter, and transfers between a video capture device and either a hard disk or a display adapter. For bus-master DMA transfers between a PCI peripheral and main memory or AGP, the processor continues to have access to its external cache. While limiting, this is still greatly improved over having access only to the prefetch buffers and the internal cache as was the case with the original implementation of Legacy DMA. Because Bus-master DMA controllers are dedicated to a peripheral, the peripheral need not contend for scarce, shared DMA resources. Bus-mastering DMA controllers also generally have reduced microprocessor configuration requirements, because they can be custom-tailored to the needs of the associated peripheral and never need to be reconfigured for use with a different peripheral.

Scalable Performance via Bridged Multiple PCI Buses

Multiple instances of the PCI Bus may be bridged together via *PCI-to-PCI Bridges*. This provides scalable PCI performance. Standard PCI Bus implementations are generally limited to three or four slots. PCI-to-PCI Bridges permit servers and workstations to have larger numbers of expansion devices or greater bandwidth capacity. Since the available bandwidth of each bus must be shared among all slots, multiple bridged PCI buses permits greater flexibility in allocating the total available bandwidth. Specifically, a peripheral that has unusually high bandwidth requirements can be used in a lightly loaded bus, which is normally isolated from heavily loaded buses populated with multiple peripherals having lower bandwidth requirements. While generally the number of PCI Buses bridged together has been limited to a few, there are development efforts to bridge together as many as 256 PCI Buses.[66]

---

[66] Terry Costlow, "Startup stretches PCI bandwidth," *Electronic Engineering Times*, Nov. 10, 1997, p. 16.

Bridged Special Purpose PCI Variants

CardBus and AGP are two special cases of bridging different types of PCI Buses. Each of these is a variant of PCI for special applications. CardBus is an PCI Bus variation that is used in laptops as a second expansion bus dedicated to removable PC Cards. The CardBus is bridged to a standard PCI Bus for non-CardBus peripherals.

AGP is also a PCI Bus variation that is dedicated to a single high bandwidth peripheral, the display adapter. This permits the display adapter to have essentially the entire bandwidth of an enhanced PCI Bus for 3D graphics texture data traffic between main memory and the display adapter. This is traffic that in a sans AGP single-PCI platform would otherwise dilute the bandwidth available to other PCI peripherals. AGP is discussed again in the section on Graphics and Video Adapters.

Reflected-Wave Switching

Electrically, the PCI Bus employs a switching technique called *Reflected-Wave Switching*. The signal traces, which act as transmission lines at the frequencies involved, are carefully laid out and purposefully *unterminated* to cause significant *reflected* waves to occur along the traces. A carefully designed driver creates an *incident* wave of half the desired switching voltage. The incident and reflected waves add together to create the desired switching voltage, which is sampled by the destination devices on the clock cycle following the driving of the incident wave. In contrast, the ISA Bus and VL Bus used a traditional *Incident-Wave Switching* propagation technique, in which bus drivers drive the signal traces to the final switching voltage and the traces are terminated and laid out to minimize reflected waves. Reflected-Wave Switching reduces driver size and peak currents by half, for the same performance as Incident-Wave Switching.

Plug and Play

PCI Bus devices are required to have automatic configuration registers. These registers appear in a PCI configuration address space that is separate from the memory and I/O address spaces. The registers are programmed on system initialization at each power up, by a Plug and Play compliant System BIOS. The Plug and Play BIOS largely relieves the user or system administrator from the burden of avoiding conflicts in the assignment of system resources. The BIOS assigns each PCI card with the system resources it requires. Generally, such system resources would include a DMA channel, an interrupt request line, I/O addresses, and memory addresses. This also eliminates the need for manually changing jumpers or switches on the card. Plug and Play was discussed in the section on Plug and Play Configuration and Maintenance earlier in this chapter.

Initiator
Target

PCI Bus Protocol

The PCI Bus is a clocked bus using handshakes to pace the progress of each bus cycle. PCI uses the term *Initiator* for bus master devices and the term *Target* for slave devices. Initiator Ready (IRDY#) and Target Ready (TRDY#) are handshakes that if not asserted will introduce wait cycles. Unlike the ISA and VL-Bus, the PCI bus multiplexes its address and data on a common set of signal lines. This is a factor contributing to the small size of the PCI connector.

REPORTS ON CD-ROM

PCI Bus Detailed Operation

Two data sheets included on the CD-ROM have valuable supplemental information on the PCI Bus.

From the AMD-640 System Controller Data Sheet:

- Section 4.2 on pp. 4-5 through 4-7 describe each of the PCI Bus signals.

- The introduction to Section 5.4 on pp. 5-30 and 5-31 gives an overview of the PCI Bus controller functions of the North-Bridge.

- Sections 5.4.1 through 5.4.7 on pp. 5-31 through 5-52 discusses bus cycles and timing diagrams for PCI Bus Initiator transactions, PCI Target transactions, arbitration, configuration, accesses by other Initiators, fast back-to-back cycles.

- Section 7 describes the Configuration Registers for the North-Bridge. Section 7.1 describes the PCI Configuration Mechanism used to access the Configuration Registers.

- The two data sheets discussed earlier in the ISA Bus Section also have valuable information on the PCI Bus.

From the ATX Reference Design for AMD-640 Chipset Technical Specification:

- Table 2-6, on pp. 26-28 maps the PCI Bus signals to the specific pin locations on the slot connectors.

PCI Card Types

There are a number of different configurations for PCI cards. Figure 4.19 is a matrix of PCI card edge connector silhouettes. A pair of 32-bit and 64-

bit card types exist for each of the 5V and 3.3V signaling voltages. In addition, a pair of 32-bit and 64-bit Universal card types exist that are compatible with either signaling voltage. Beneath each card silhouette are the slot types that the card is compatible with. The 5V PCI and 3.3V PCI cards have a *key* cut into the edge connector that corresponds to a keyway, or *key segment*, in their associated slot. This insures that a card can only be inserted into a bus that operates with the signaling voltage to which the card was designed. The 5V and 3.3V 32-bit slots (but not the 64-bit slots) are physically identical except for orientation. Universal cards are cards that have two keys in the edge connector in order that they will fit into either a 5V or a 3.3V slot.

A 64-bit PCI slot will accept either 64-bit or 32-bit cards having signaling voltage keying compatible with the slot. In a nicely done forward compatibility feature, a 32-bit slot will accept either 32-bit or 64-bit cards[67] with compatible signaling voltage keying. All 32-bit cards identify themselves as such during transfers, which are dynamically adjusted to match the card bit-width, regardless of the slot bit-width. All 64-bit cards in 32-bit slots configure themselves for 32-bit transfers.

It is not possible to mix 5V and 3.3V slots on a given PCI Bus segment. All cards on a given segment must use the same signaling voltage. Universal cards use I/O buffers that can be compliant with either signaling voltage, detect the type of slot into which they are plugged, and adapt their signaling voltage accordingly. The signaling voltage used is independent of the power-supply power rail voltages used by card components. 5V, 3.3V, and Universal cards all have connections defined to both 5V and 3.3V power rails, and are permitted to have any mix of components powered from the two rails.

Use of lower operating voltages provides advantages in energy savings and are generally required by present day higher density IC processes. The intent is for all PCI cards to eventually be 3.3V cards. While all this was known at the time the PCI specification was developed, it was also the case that the state of the industry was such that PCI chipsets were only going to be initially available with 5V signaling. The scheme of Figure 4.19 was devised to enable a migration from 5V technology to 3V technology.

All initial PCI cards and slots were designed for 5V signaling. Vendors are encouraged to use Universal cards for all new designs. While Universal cards are increasingly available, presently 5v-only cards are still the norm. Once Universal cards are widely available, it is envisioned that 3.3V slots will begin to replace 5V slots in new designs.

---

[67] 32-bit slots have associated "keep-out areas" to permit unobstructed insertion of 64-bit cards.

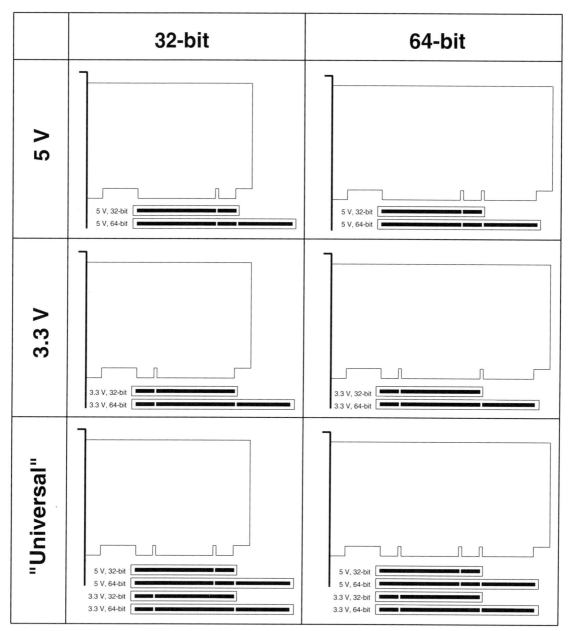

Figure 4.19 MATRIX OF PCI CARD TYPES AND ASSOCIATED COMPATIBLE SLOTS

The initial version of PCI was designed for operation at 33 MHz. Revision 2.1 of the PCI specification extended PCI buses with 3.3V signaling (but not 5V signaling) to optional operation at 66 MHz. If a 66 MHz PCI card is installed in a 33 MHz bus (theoretically including 66 MHz Universal cards in 5V slots), the device will configure itself to operate at 33 MHz. If a

33 MHz PCI card is installed in an otherwise 66 MHz bus, the bus will configure itself to operate at 33 MHz. 66 MHz PCI buses thus necessarily use 3.3V slots. One or two 66 MHz 3.3V slots are beginning to appear in high-end workstations and servers. These are augmenting existing 5V slots that are still needed for compatibility with the large installed base of 5V PCI cards. This is accomplished by using multiple bridged PCI bus segments, one segment for the 66MHz 3.3V slots and one or more segments for 33 MHz 5V slots.

Legacy I/O Issues

One thing that the PCI specification does not directly address is the handling of legacy I/O. Legacy software that assumes that the ISA Bus is present, expects to be able to use legacy locations in the DMA, Interrupt, I/O, and memory spaces. As these peripherals are integrated into the Super I/O module residing off the PCI Bus, and the ISA Bus eliminated, legacy references must be claimed by PCI devices. See the section on PCI-based Ports in this chapter for examples of PCI-based Legacy I/O implementations. The following documents describe in greater detail how Legacy I/O on the PCI Bus is done to ensure backward software compatibility.

TECHNICAL PRESENTATION ON CD-ROM

The following presentation overviews the migration of legacy peripherals from the ISA Bus to the PCI Bus and introduces the Distributed DMA and Serialized IRQ approaches to legacy I/O: Richard Wahler, *Preserving Legacy DMA's and IRQ's on the PCI Bus.*

STANDARDS ON CD-ROM

The full text of three industry standards for implementing legacy I/O on the PCI Bus are included in their entirety on the CD-ROM:

- *Common Architecture, Desktop, PC/AT systems.*
- *Distributed DMA Support for PCI Systems.*
- *Serialized IRQ Support for PCI Systems.*

Recent and Future PCI Developments

Hot Plug capabilities will permit PCI cards to be inserted and removed without incident while a system is running, and is directed mainly toward mission-critical servers, where downtime is costly. PCI power management will permit PCI cards to power down when not in use and power up on demand. Vital Products Data (VPD) will permit the storage of manufacturer, warranty, and serial number data for use by system administrators and support personnel.

PCI is expected to be the primary expansion bus in desktops for some time. Nevertheless, in the next five years it may be supplanted in high-end Symmetric Multi-Processing (SMP) server clusters by multi-Gigabit per second serial buses currently under development.[68] One or more of the serial buses are proposed as links between processor, memory, and I/O and between multiple processors both in a local cluster and over significant distances.

INDUSTRY STANDARDS

Peripheral Component Interconnect Special Interest Group (PCI SIG)

The PCI SIG describes itself as "an unincorporated association of members of the microcomputer industry set up for the purpose of monitoring and enhancing the development of the Peripheral Component Interconnect (PCI) architecture." Membership is $2,500 per year.

The PCI SIG maintains a Web site with information on joining, a mailing list, and how to order the specifications it controls. The main URL is:

http://www.pcisig.com/

PCI-related specifications are available only by mail from the PCI SIG. A bundled hard-copy and Acrobat copy of the main specification is sold for $25. Ordering information is found at URL:

http://www.pcisig.com/specs.html

SUGGESTED READINGS

PCI Bus

The following books are valuable as additional references for the PCI Bus. The first gives extensive low-level design details. The second gives a clear and well-organized explanation of the principal concepts.

1. Edward Solari and George Willse, *PCI Hardware and Software Architecture & Design*, 2nd Edition, Annabooks, 1995.

2. Tom Shanley & Don Anderson, *PCI System Architecture*, 3rd Edition, Addison-Wesley, 1995.

---

[68] Rick Boyd-Merritt, "Gigabit Bus Carries Intel Into Communications Territory," *EE Times*, March 9, 1998.

> ## REQUIREMENTS SUMMARY FOR PC PCI BUS DEVICES
>
> - General device requirements apply
> - Devices and controller must comply with PCI 2.1 specification
> - PCI chips sets implement general DMA controllers according to SFF 8020i, which defines the hardware and software requirements for ATAPI devices, while PCI-based ATA controllers implement Ultra ATA[a]
> - Buses, devices, and functions define a three dimensional coordinate space in which multiple functions per card are OK, but *ghost cards* (single cards that appear at multiple coordinates) are not allowed
> - PCI-to-PCI bridges that don't implement internal memory or I/O regions must proactively close (inhibit decoding to) any I/O or memory windows by configuring the *Base Address Registers (BARs)* according to the PCI to PCI Bridge Specification
> - Controller requirements include that multifunction devices generally do not share writable configuration space bits, all expansion cards may be bus masters, and the Plug and Play write-data configuration-port-address must be propagated during power up and system reset to all ISA Buses that may contain Plug and Play cards (to enable Plug and Play configuration during the boot process)
> - Plug and Play specific requirements include special configuration space register and configuration space requirements; supplemental subsystem device identifiers; interrupt routing must be ACPI compliant; BIOS must configures the boot device IRQ to a PCI-based IRQ; and device hot swapping must be compliant with an ACPI-based insert/remover notification mechanism
> - All devices comply with PCI Bus Power Management Specification

ghost cards

Base Address Registers (BARs)

[a] See the *IDE/ATA* section in this chapter for a discussion of ATAPI, ATA and Ultra ATA.

DEVICE-SPECIFIC BUSES AND PORTS

The interconnects studied in this subsection generally have a minimum number of devices connected, typically just two devices or subsystems, and frequently implement device-specific protocols between the two devices. We will examine in turn the Socket 7 Processor bus, so-called Super I/O ports coupled to the PCI Bus, and graphics and video adapters. Our discussion of graphics and video adapters will include an examination of the Advanced Graphics Port (AGP) and its impact on the graphics subsystem.

PCI-based Ports

See the Legacy I/O Issues section for a discussion of how Legacy I/O should be implemented on the PCI Bus.

A number of ports are associated with controllers that are coupled to the PCI Bus. With reference to Figure 1.2 on page 36 in Chapter 1, a Super I/O block is shown coupled to the PCI Bus. The Super I/O typically has dedicated ports for legacy devices, including one or two PS/2 pointing-device/keyboard ports, floppy disk controller port, IEEE 1284 parallel port, legacy parallel ports, legacy serial ports, and ATA/IDE interfaces. A CardBus Bridge and a Legacy Bus (ISA or EISA) Bridge may also be coupled to the PCI Bus. Figure 1.2 on page 36 shows a South-Bridge containing all of these previously discussed components. Actual implementations may vary, with one or more of the CardBus Bridge, Super I/O, and Legacy Bus Bridges being implemented as individual chips.

REPORT ON CD-ROM

	To learn more about PCI-based Ports, see the following data sheets on the CD-ROM: • *AMD-645 Peripheral Bus Controller Data Sheet.* • *128 Pin Ultra I/O with ACPI Support and Infrared Remote Control,* FDC37B78x, Rev. December 8, 1997.

The PC Specifications allow legacy PS/2, serial (COM), and parallel (LPT) ports implemented on the PCI Bus. However, pointing devices and modems may not be connected using the legacy serial ports. No device except printers may be provided that are connected to the legacy serial and parallel ports. The preference is for the mouse (and keyboard) to be connected via USB, the modem via USB or Device Bay, and the printer via USB or IEEE 1394.

REQUIREMENTS SUMMARY FOR I/O DEVICES
• General device requirements apply
• Required external devices include serial, parallel, keyboard, and pointing device ports
• Multiple keyboards attached to mobile devices do not conflict with each other
• game control devices and drivers must support the USB Human Interface Device Class Specification, Version 1.0 or higher
• Legacy serial port specific requirements include that the mouse must not use a legacy serial port and any legacy serial port must use a 16550A Universal Asynchronous Receiver Transmitter (UART) and support up to 115.2 Kbaud[a]
• Legacy parallel port specific requirements include that the Enhanced Parallel Port (EPP) must support flexible I/O addressing; ports must support IEEE 1284-1984 defined compatibility and nibble modes as well as Enhanced Capabilities Port (ECP) protocols; and Ports must, at a minimum, use IEEE 1284-I defined connectors

[a] A baud is a measure of signal changes per second. The baud rate is usually less than the effective bit per second rate due to the use of signal encoding techniques.

IEEE STANDARD ON CD-ROM

The IEEE 1284 Standard covers asynchronous, fully interlocked, bidirectional parallel communications between hosts and printers or other peripherals. It is included in its entirety on the companion CD-ROM.

1284-1994 IEEE Standard Signaling Method for a Bidirectional Parallel Peripheral Interface for Personal Computers.

The IEEE 1284.1 Standard defines a vendor-independent standard protocol for the control of printers. It includes provisions for automatic identification and configuration of printers and messaging from the printer to a monitoring host computer.

1284.1-1997 IEEE Standard for Information Technology--Transport Independent Printer/System Interface (TIP/SI).

IDE/ATA

The AT Attachment (ATA) Interface and its variants (e.g., IDE, ATA-2, ATAPI, E-IDE, Fast ATA, all discussed below) are presently the most common method of interfacing storage media to the PC Platform. Integrated

Drive Electronics (IDE) is a tradename for ATA products made by Western Digital. The name was intended to emphasize that most of the drive's low-level electronics were integrated in the drive in contrast to earlier drive interfaces. The distinction between ATA and IDE is often lost, and IDE is more prevalent in the PC platform literature.

An ATA Interface is implemented between minimal control logic and two drives. The control logic resides on an expansion bus and operates under the control of the system's microprocessor. The interface standard includes definitions for a bus, a register set within the drive, a command set executed by the drive, and a physical connector and cable for coupling the drive to the controller. The bus is a variant of the ISA Bus. It is a 16-bit data bus using single-ended TTL compatible drivers. The bus is clockless. Seven bus control signals generated by the controller select which of roughly two dozen I/O registers are selected for read and write transfers of commands, data, status, and various drive-address attributes (drive, cylinder, head, and sector number). Roughly 40 commands may be given to the drive. A 40-pin connector and a 40-conductor non-shielded flat ribbon cable are used.

DEFINITION
Programmed I/O (PIO)
Programmed I/O, or *PIO*, refers to peripheral reads and writes carried out by the processor. This is a fundamental method of I/O transfer and is the preferred method for relatively small byte-count transfers. In a general sense it refers to either memory or I/O address space accesses. As applied to hard disks it usually literally refers only to I/O space accesses.

PIO is also often done for transfers of large data blocks between memory and a peripheral using the processor as an intermediary. PIO is generally performed via program loops. String[69] instructions may be used, if the peripherals are memory-mapped. As discussed in Chapter 6, the effective data transfer performance may be substantially reduced by overhead delay associated with the transfers. PIO Overhead delays take two forms. The first is the inner loop delay of the routine that actually performs the transfer. Thus, it is very important to programmed I/O block transfer rates for the program loop executing the transfer to be tight. The second overhead delay is the turnaround time between executions of the transfer routine. If interrupts and associated interrupt service routines, or other significant

---

[69] String instructions are complex instructions that transfer data byte sequences between source and destination memory locations. Instruction operands include the source and data locations and the number of bytes to transfer.

processor activity intervenes between executions of the transfer routine, the turnaround time can be large.

The ATA specification (as opposed to the later variants) includes the definition of three *Programmed I/O (PIO) modes and one Multiword DMA mode.*[70] In all modes, single word control and status transfers are common, but data transfers between the drive and the controller occur in *sectors*, which are groups of 512 bytes. Data transfers are normally 16-bits. Once a sector transfer is initiated the data transfer is not handshaken and proceeds at a rate determined solely by the host processor. In the PIO modes, the system microprocessor is responsible for accessing the drive's 16-bit wide data register to transfer data to or from the drive's sector buffer using I/O instructions. PIO Modes 0, 1, and 2, define data transfer cycles of 600, 383, and 240 ns, respectively. These correspond to peak transfer rates of 3.3, 5.2, and 8.3 MBps, respectively.

sectors

Transactions at a procedural-level are handshaken, in that the system's I/O routines are paced by status signals from the drive. The following is an example of the PIO protocol used on reads. The microprocessor initializes the drive by writing the appropriate parameters for the desired read. The microprocessor then sends a command to initiate the drive to process the read request. The drive asserts BSY (Busy) and begins reading the data and loading the drive's sector buffer. Once a sector is available in the drive's sector buffer, it asserts DRQ (Drive Request), lowers BSY, and asserts Interrupt Request (INTRQ) to interrupt the microprocessor. Once the sector is read by the host, INTRQ is deasserted, then DRQ is deasserted. An optional multiple sector mode permits the transfer of blocks of 2, 4, 8, or 16 (and possible greater) sectors before the drive interrupts the microprocessor. In order to minimize the overhead delay associated with sector transfers, it is clearly desirable to maximize the number of sectors transferred per interrupt.

In the Multiword DMA mode, a bus-mastering DMA controller in the ATA control logic is initialized by the microprocessor prior to initiating a multi-sector transfer command. The sectors are then transferred by the DMA controller and the processor is not interrupted until all sector transfers are completed. Multiword DMA Mode 0 defines a data transfer cycle of 480 ns, corresponding to a peak transfer rate of 4.2 MBps. The DMA mode theoretically allows the microprocessor to do other work instead of performing the data transfers and significantly reduces the interrupt servicing overhead for large sector count transfers.

ATA-2

Subsequent to the ATA standard, ATA-2 defines two additional PIO modes and two additional Multiword DMA modes. PIO Modes 3 and 4, define data transfer cycles of 180 and 120 ns, respectively. These correspond to

---

[70] Singleword DMA modes also exist, but are generally not used.

peak transfer rates of 11.1 and 16.6 MBps, respectively. In addition, these modes require that an IORDY handshake be implemented to permit the drive to pace the data transfers. Thus, PIO Mode 3 and 4 data transfers are optionally handshaken with passive termination. Multiword DMA Modes 1 and 2, define data transfer cycles of 150 and 120 ns, respectively. These correspond to peak transfer rates of 13.3 and 16.6 MBps, respectively. ATA-3 is and extension of ATA-2, but no additional PIO or DMA modes were added. ATA-2 and ATA-3 devices are marketed under the tradenames Enhanced-IDE (E-IDE) and Fast ATA. In the fastest modes, the maximum effective rate realizable in PC platforms was 7.8 MBps. The reduction was due to a confluence of a system intra-read latency and disk rotational latency effects that resulted in missed sector-read opportunities that effectively increased the data transfer cycle time. This became the limiting factor in ATA-based disk subsystem performance as the raw data rate capability of drives now exceeds 10MBps.[71]

Ultra ATA

Ultra ATA (also known as Ultra DMA/33) is an ATA extension that defines an additional multiword DMA mode. Multiword DMA Mode 3 defines an effective data transfer cycle of 60 ns, corresponding to a peak transfer rate of 33.3 MBps. This rate is temporarily more than raw drive data rates and it avoids the disk rotational effects that plagued the ATA-2 DMA modes. Multiword DMA Mode 3 actually uses the 120 ns cycle of Multiword DMA Mode 2, but redefined the signaling to transfer data on both edges of the data strobes instead of just the rising edge as on previous modes. In addition, the data strobe is sent by the data source instead of always by the drive controller as on previous modes. Such *source synchronous signaling* reduces clock skew between the timing reference (here the strobe) and the data and contributes to the reduced cycle time. Ultra ATA also adds a Cyclic Redundancy Check (CRC) to all transfers between the drive and drive controller to insure data integrity.

Use of ATA DMA Modes

From the advent of the PC/AT until just recently, the PIO modes have been exclusively used for ATA devices in PC platforms. The use of an ATA DMA mode requires a drive that supports it, compatible hardware, and software to manage the hardware and interact with the application programs that want to access the associated peripherals. The hardware necessary includes a compatible bus-master DMA controller in the ATA controller and a high-performance bus that supports bus-mastering DMA. The ISA Bus did not support bus-mastering DMA and the legacy DMA associated with the ISA Bus was limited to a peak transfer rate of

---

[71] *Ultra DMA, A Quantum White Paper*, Copyright 1998, Quantum Corporation.

2MBps. Thus, legacy DMA does not support ATA DMA mode 0 and later modes.

It has always been possible to use custom bus-master DMA hardware and a custom written application that directly controls the DMA hardware. However, to make the DMA modes transparently usable by all applications requires generally available hardware and support from the operating system and a device driver tailored to the ATA controller. Until the advent of Ultra DMA, the ATA Modes inherently did not offer any performance improvement over the PIO modes and there was no demand for either hardware or software support. Also, unless the OS is capable of multi-tasking and applications with multiple execution threads are used, there is no apparent performance benefit to the use of the DMA modes.

Ultra ATA is now the preferred mode to use on an ATA interface in new platforms. All the necessary components to both enable and motivate its use are present. The enabling components include available bus-mastering DMA chipsets, the PCI Bus, Microsoft Windows, and device drivers. The motivation comes from multimedia and other graphics intensive applications that have multiple real time threads of execution.

AT Attachment Packet Interface

The AT Attachment Packet Interface (ATAPI) is a compatible an extension to the ATA protocol. It defines a packet protocol for CD-ROM and Tape devices, which permits them to coexist on and ATA interface with traditional ATA devices.

Requirements Summary for **IDE/ATA** Devices
• Generic device requirements apply
• Controller is ATA-2 compliant
• Bootable controllers must support the El Torito standard for the CD-ROM installation process
• Any sharing of hardware between the channels of a Dual channel IDE adapter is transparent to all system software
• System BIOS and devices support the Logical Block Address (LBA) standard for accessing high capacity drives
• PCI Bus Mastering DMA requirements include that the DMA's register set and the drives must comply with SFF 8038i and must support Ultra ATA
• Controller and peripherals must use keyed and shrouded connectors and cables must have pin 1 designated, to avoid incorrect cabling
• Devices support the ATA STANDBY command to spin up devices after being placed in a power saving state

Graphics and Video Adapters

Graphics adapters and Advanced Graphics Port (AGP) have been covered fairly extensively in other parts of the text. Specifically, see the Display Adapters section in Chapter 1 and *Performance Optimization Specifics in a Contemporary 3D Graphics Platform* in Chapter 6. As covered in both of the cited sections, AGP is a system topology wherein the memory controller (within the North-Bridge) incorporates an additional port (the AGP) in the group of ports that are arbitrating for main memory access. The AGP is used for a direct high-bandwidth connection between the memory controller and the graphics/video adapter. The AGP supports higher throughputs between the graphics/video adapter and main memory than possible over the PCI Bus, while simultaneously eliminating major traffic on the PCI Bus, thus increasing its bandwidth availability to other platform devices. To some extent, AGP reduces the amount of video memory that would otherwise be required, as the fast connection to main memory can be thought of as effectively increasing the available video memory. Its primary motivation however, is to enable 3D rendering processes to exploit a ready availability of a wealth of textures that can be preloaded and manipulated in main memory for on-demand transfer to the 3D graphics accelerator, while keeping the texture traffic between memory and the display adapter off of the PCI Bus.

There are currently three defined AGP modes: AGP (1-mode), 2 AGP (also 2-mode or 2x mode), and 4 AGP (4x mode). 2 AGP increases transfer rates to 533 MBps, 4AGP offers 1GB/s transfers.

Figure 4.21 on page 409 illustrates the 124-pin single-signaling-voltage AGP connector. The AGP card edge is seen close up in the right of the figure. Depending on the orientation of the key segment, the connector is used for AGP cards with 3.3V signaling or for AGP cards with 1.5V signaling. A 132-pin universal voltage AGP connector also exists that will accept AGP cards designed for either 1.5V or 3.3V signaling. AGP card types and their associated compatible connectors are illustrated in Figure 4.20.

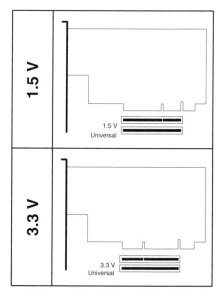

Figure 4.20   AGP CARD TYPES AND ASSOCIATED COMPATIBLE CONNECTORS

REPORT ON CD-ROM

To learn more about AGP, see the article by Yong Yao, "AGP Speeds 3D Graphics," *Microprocessor Report*, Vol. 10, No. 8, June 17, 1996, on the CD-ROM.

Figure 4.21   VIEWS OF AGP SLOT AND AGP CARD EDGE

REQUIREMENTS SUMMARY FOR GRAPHICS ADAPTER DEVICES

- Adapter uses high-speed bus
- System exploits processor *write combining* (dynamic opportunistic batching by the processor of multiple individual byte writes within a single larger write), when available
- Primary adapter works with Window's default VGA mode driver
- Adapter and driver support multiple adapters and multiple monitors
- Adapter supports all VESA standard timings for refresh and for resolutions up to 1024 x 768 x 16 bpp
- All supported color depths are enumerated by the driver and its associated INF file
- Only *relocatable* (arbitrarily reassignable to new locations) registers should be used for dynamic graphics operations
- Multiple-adapter/multiple-monitor use requires all extended (non-VGA) resources to be dynamically relocatable after system boot and VGA resources to be capable of being disabled
- Adapter supports downloadable RAMDAC entries, which are used for transition effects, palette switches, and gamma correction for color matching between the display and output devices
- Adapter supports Display Data Channel Standard (DDC), Version 2.0, in support of software management of the display
- Additional requirements apply to video playback, 2D and 3D hardware acceleration, television output, BIOS and option ROMs, AGP, PCI-based adapters, and device drivers and installation

---

INDUSTRY STANDARDS

Video Electronics Standards Association (VESA)

VESA is an organization that supports and sets industry-wide interface standards for the PC, workstation, and computing environments. VESA promotes and develops timely, relevant, open standards for the video electronics industry, ensuring interoperability and encouraging innovation and market growth. Annual membership dues run $500 to $5000, depending on company structure and revenue. The main URL is:

http://www.vesa.org/

VESA Monitor Standards

VESA standards are only available to VESA members. Some of the more important video standards include:

- *Discrete Monitor Timings (DMT) Standard 1.0*: Timing standards for display monitors for resolutions from 640 x 350 to 1280 x 1024 with refresh rates from 60 Hz up to 85 Hz.

- *VESA Display Data Channel (DDC) ™ Standard, Version 3*: This standard defines a communications channel between a computer display and a host system for configuration and display control information and for uses as a data channel for peripherals connected to the host via the display.

A complete list of VESA standards with a brief abstract of each is at URL:

http://www.vesa.org/ve00013.html

Processor Bus — Socket 7

Another motherboard configuration, seen in earlier 486 platforms, is to provide an empty socket for an "upgrade" processor, obviating the need to remove the original processor. Intel calls its upgrade processors OverDrive Processors.

Desktop motherboards for Pentium-class and higher performance x86 processors are generally manufactured and originally sold with empty ("unpopulated") sockets for the processor and DRAM main memory. Socketing, while expensive and bulky, provides great flexibility for both manufacturers, system vendors, technicians, and end users. Sockets permit the same motherboard to be used in a range of system performance determined largely by the speed of the chips chosen to populate the sockets. Socketing facilitates system diagnosis and repair and decouples the motherboard manufacturer and vendor from the volatile and generally rapidly decreasing prices for processors and DRAM. Sockets are the only practical way to enable a consumer end user to replace large pinout chips as part of a processor upgrade.

Socketed x86 processors use plastic and ceramic *Pin-Grid-Array_(PGA)* packages with hundreds of pins, suitable for through-hole board permanent mounting. PGAs, turned pins up, are reminiscent of a "bed-of-nails." These flattish, generally square, packages have a processor die in the center cordoned by regularly spaced rows of nested pins (perpendicular to the package) arranged in horizontal and vertical (grid-like) pattern. The grid can be standard or interstitial. In a *standard grid*, all pin rows/columns are collinear. In an *interstitial grid*, alternating pin rows/columns are collinear, while adjacent pin rows/columns are offset by half the pin-spacing. A PGA using an interstitial grid is also referred to as a *Staggered PGA (SPGA)*. Figure 4.22 shows a 321-pin SPGA.

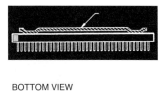

Pin-Grid-Array (PGA)

BOTTOM VIEW

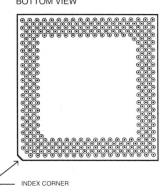

INDEX CORNER

standard grid

interstitial grid

Figure 4.22 321-PIN SPGA PACKAGE

Adapted with permission of Advanced Micro Devices Inc., from *AMD-K6 Processor Data Sheet*, Copyright 1997.

Staggered PGA (SPGA)

Due to the force multiplication from hundreds of pins, the flexibility of socketing the processor is best realized by the use of specially designed and relatively expensive *Zero-Insertion-Force (ZIF) sockets*. ZIF sockets generally have a lever (handle), which must be manipulated to socket the processor. When the lever is moved to the "off" (up or open) position, there is no force constraining the processor pins, and easy insertion or replacement is possible. When the lever is moved to the "on" (down or closed) position, reliable physical and electrical contact is achieved, and the system is ready for normal operation. Figure 4.23 shows an empty ZIF socket with the lever in the off position

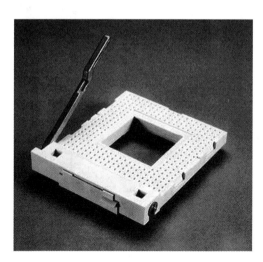

Figure 4.23   AMP ZIF

Reprinted with the permission of AMP.

Industry-Standard Sockets

Due to their popularity, x86 sockets and their associated pin assignments (pinouts) and electrical buses become de facto industry standards. The moniker "Socket 7" (or 4, or 5) has come to more generally signify the collective of physical and electrical interfaces associated with the socket. Socket 4, Socket 5, and Socket 7 are three related Pentium-bus standards associated with three notable classes of Pentium processors.[72] These three sockets are illustrated in Figure 4.24.

---

[72] Socket 6 defines a 3V 486DX4.

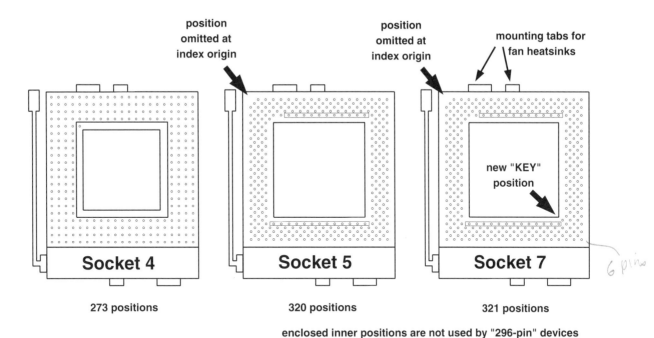

position omitted at index origin

position omitted at index origin

mounting tabs for fan heatsinks

new "KEY" position

Socket 4

Socket 5

Socket 7

6 pins

273 positions

320 positions

321 positions

enclosed inner positions are not used by "296-pin" devices

Figure 4.24 SAME SCALE COMPARISON OF SOCKETS 4, 5 AND 7

DESIGN NOTE

Distinguishing Socket 4, 5 and 7 Devices

You can tell apart the major Pentium-bus packaged device pinouts at a glance by examining the nested rows of pins on the underside of the package. 273-pin Socket 4 devices align pins on a regular grid. Socket 5 (296-pin and 320-pin) and Socket 7 ("296-pin" and 321-pin) devices align pins on an "interstitial" grid that staggers alternate rows. A 296-pin device has 4 nested pin rows on two opposite sides, and 5 nested pin rows on the other two opposite sides. 320-pin and 321-pin devices have 5 nested pin rows on all four sides. Along the major diagonal opposite the package's index corner (the corner with the 45-degree chamfer, establishing the origin that pin assignments are referenced from), a Socket 7 device has six pins (includes the electrically not-connected KEY pin), compared with five pins (no KEY pin) for a Socket 5 device.

While thinking of these Pentium-bus Sockets as industry standards is a useful abstraction, there have been numerous variants within each socket type. Manufacturers have used a wealth of combinations, including variations in bus frequency, core frequency, minimum timing and frequency spreads, unified versus split core and I/O power supplies, core operating voltages and ranges, boundary-scan support, and multi-processor (MP) support. Not all combinations are offered in each socket type or by all manufacturers. Beyond the bus electrical and functional variations discussed in the main text, manufacturers may market further variants based on chip-package type, processor revision (tooling and process stepping), level of testing, OEM shipping trays versus consumer cartoning (so-called *boxed processors* often bundled with fan/heatsinks), and instruction-set support.

Socket 4

Socket 4 was used for Intel's CPU Family 5, Model 1, also designated by the part number substring 80501, and widely known by the (once internal) Intel code name *P5*. Intel has marketed P5 processors with core frequencies of 60 and 66 MHz. The Pentium Overdrive Processor at a core frequency of 133 MHz was designed as a Socket 4 upgrade for the 60-and 66-MHz P5 processors. Socket 4 uses a 273-pin-position ZIF. Socket 4 specifies a (non-staggered) PGA having pins arranged on a 21 x 21 grid with 0.10-inch standard grid spacing. The power supply pins for the Socket 4 bus are defined for a single supply, of roughly 5V. Different P5-compatible parts have used a variety of voltage ranges including 4.75-5.25V, 4.90-5.25V, 4.90-5.40V, and 5.15-5.40V. Pentium Overdrive Processors at core frequencies of 63, 83, and 133 MHz were designed as Socket 4 upgrades for the 60-and 66-MHz P5 processors.

Socket 5

Socket 5 was used for Intel's CPU Family 5, Model 2, also designated by the part number substring 80502, and widely known by the Intel code name *P54C*. Intel has marketed P54C processors with core frequencies of 75, 90, 100, 120, 133, 150, 166, and 200 MHz. Strictly speaking, P54C describes only the Socket 5, 0.5-micron BiCMOS, Pentium processors (at core frequencies of 75, 90, and 100 MHz), while P54CS describes Socket 5, 0.35-micron BiCMOS, Pentium processors (those with core frequencies of 120 MHz and above). The additional "S" reportedly being a mnemonic for a process "shrink." However, the distinction is not generally made, as the term P54C is loosely used for the P54CS parts as well. There are no substantive bus changes between the P54C and P54CS. Pentium Overdrive processors, Intel code named the *P54CT*, at core frequencies of 125, 150, and 166 MHz were designed as Socket 5 upgrades for the 75-,90-,and 100-MHz P54C processors. Socket 7 later became the recommended upgrade socket for new platforms designed around the same processors.

Socket 5 uses a substantially different layout than Socket 4. Socket 5 uses a 320-pin-position ZIF. Socket 5 specifies an SPGA having pins arranged on a 19 x 19 grid with a 0.05 x 0.10-inch interstitial grid spacing. Intel's P54C processors for new installations used 296 of Socket 5's 320 pin positions. As a result, Socket 5 is often misdescribed as having 296 pins. However, Intel's Pentium OverDrive processors use all of Socket 5's 320 pin-positions.

Most of the forty-seven new pins on Socket 5 were provided for future expansion options and unassigned in the P54C. Six of the new pins are for Dual Processor support, one for Functional Redundancy Checking, and three for an Advanced Programmable Interrupt Controller module (APIC). (Two of Socket 4's interrupt-related signals are dynamically redefined, when a Dual Processor system is present.) One new pin is used to put the processor in a "stop clock" low-power mode that is cache coherency aware. One Socket 5 pin was also defined to program a clock multiplication ratio, setting the ratio of the frequencies of operation for the processor core and the external bus. Four instruction-tracing-related signals defined for Socket 4 were deleted in Socket 5.

The new Socket 5 pins are used in Socket 7, as well, and are individually discussed in detail later in the main text.

Socket 5 processors are marketed in a number of power supply variations and designations. Socket 5 processors marketed primarily for the desktop are unified-plane processors. *Unified-plane processors* have a single positive power supply to which both the core and the I/O circuitry are commonly connected. Unified-plane Socket 5 processors with an Intel *Standard (STD) operating voltage* designation have a 3.3V nominal voltage, but are guaranteed to operate over a range from 3.135 to 3.6V (3.3V -5%, 3.5V +100mV). Unified-plane Socket 5 processors with an Intel *Voltage Regulated (VR) operating voltage* designation have a reduced voltage specification of 3.300-3.465V (3.3V -0%, +5%). Unified-plane Socket 5 processors with an Intel *Voltage Regulated Extension (VRE) operating voltage* designation have a reduced and shifted voltage specification of 3.40-3.60V (3.5V -/+ 100mV).[73] Intel was able to produce profitable yields and increased clock speeds of VR and VRE parts in advance of STD parts, permitting OEMs to get systems to market earlier and at less cost than would otherwise have been possible. All Socket 5 processors have operating voltages reduced from 5V, but are required to have 5V-tolerant clock inputs.

Split-plane processors have separate core and I/O positive power supplies. These generally permit compatibility with standard 3.3V I/O chip-sets, while ensuring reliable operation for submicron core circuits and permitting reduced power consumption. The power dissipation of the core, which dominates overall chip power dissipation, is proportional to the square of the core operating voltage, so the payback from reducing the core operating voltage is dramatic. Care should be taken that split-plane Socket 5 parts not be used in motherboards configured for a single power

---

[73] The 3.135-3.6V range for STD, and the 3.40-3.60V range for VRE, are true for Intel's C2-step and later Pentium processors. B-step parts had a STD range of 3.135-3.465V (3.3V -/+ 5%), and a VRE range of 3.45-3.60V(3.5V-50mV,+100mV).

supply, as such operation overstresses the core, generally reducing reliability and life expectancy.

The positive power supply pins in unified-plane Socket 5 processors are labeled with V_{CC}. In split-plane Socket 5 and Socket 7 processors, the core pins are labeled V_{CC2}, while the I/O pins are labeled V_{CC3}. Socket 5 assigns the core (V_{CC2}) pins and I/O (V_{CC3}) pins generally on opposite halves of the socket. The "unified" and "split" terminology arises because the common (unified) V_{CC} power plane used on motherboards for single-supply processors is (fairly neatly) partitioned (split) into two power planes for the dual-supply processors. This is apparent in Figure 4.25, which illustrates the separate power planes for V_{CC2} and V_{CC3}, and associated decoupling capacitors, in an under-the-socket layout for a Socket 5 processor printed circuit board. Socket 5 processors have no means to identify to the motherboard whether they are unified or split-plane processors.

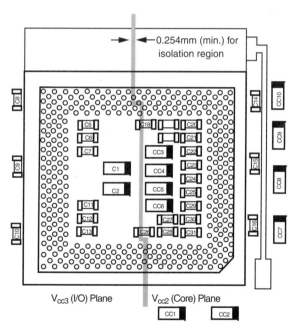

Figure 4.25 SPLIT POWER PLANES FOR DUAL-SUPPLY PROCESSORS
Copyright 1997, Advanced Micro Devices Inc., used with permission.

Split-plane Socket 5 processors were initially marketed primarily as mobile processors, where power conservation is especially critical. Split-plane processors with an Intel *Voltage Reduction Technology (VRT) operating voltage* designation have 3.3V I/O and 2.9V core nominal voltages. Split-plane processors with an Intel *3.1V operating voltage* designation are VRT processors with 3.3V I/O and 3.1V core nominal voltages. Both classes of

VRT processors have 25 V_{CC2} pins, 28 V_{CC3} pins, 53 V_{SS} pins, and 296 pins total.

In addition to the split-plane technique, *mobile* Socket 5 processors generally have other significant variations from the *desktop* Socket 5 parts. These mobile parts generally do not support the Upgrade, Dual Processing (DP), Functional Redundancy Checking (FRC), and the Advanced Programmable Interrupt Controller (APIC) features, and do not support two optional signals included primarily for L2 caches.

Intel targeted its Pentium OverDrive processors to be consumer upgrade products. Other than the 200Mhz part, these parts are compatible with a Socket 5 pin out with a single 3.3V power supply, typical of most older Pentium desktop motherboards. The 200Mhz OverDrive processor requires Socket 7. The Socket 5 OverDrive parts work just as well in the Socket 7 upgrade socket found in newer boards. The Intel Pentium Over-Drive processors at 125, 150, and 166 MHz are unified-plane processors with STD operating voltages. Pentium OverDrive processors with MMX Technology (Intel code-named the *P54CTB*) at 125, 150, 166, and 180 MHz are internally split-plane designs that work in unified-plane motherboards, because of an *internal* voltage regulator powering the core from the external unified supply.

OverDrive processors also require a +5V supply for their required fan heatsink.

Unlike other Socket 5 processors with 296 pins, the 320-pin Pentium OverDrive processors have twenty-four pins in positions near the center of the Socket 5 SPGA grid. Four of these extra pins are No Connects (NC). Twenty of the extra pins are used for extra power supply pins. Additionally, the Pentium OverDrive uses two power supply pins that are defined as No Internal Connection (NIC) pins on the 54C. In total there are sixty V_{CC} and sixty-eight V_{SS} pins. This is twenty-two power supply pins more than the fifty-three V_{CC} and fifty-three V_{SS} pins of the P54C.

Socket 7

Socket 7 uses a substantially similar layout to Socket 5. Socket 7 also specifies an SPGA having pins arranged on a 19 x 19 grid with a 0.05 x 0.10-inch interstitial grid spacing. However, Socket 7 uses a 321-pin-position ZIF. Socket 7 standardizes for the first time the placement of the ZIF's integral clips (tabs) for the mounting of fan heatsinks. Designed as a superset of the various Socket 5 variations, Socket 7 is backward compatible with most Socket 5 processors.

Socket 7 adds one new pin, KEY, required of all Socket 7 processors. The KEY pin prevents Socket 7 devices from being inserted into a Socket 5 socket. Yet, Socket 5 processors may be inserted in Socket 7's socket without difficulty.

Socket 7 defines all positive power-pins using split-plane definitions in a manner that compatibly merges the power supply definitions used for the 296-pin split-plane Socket 5 VRT processors and the 320-pin unified-plane Socket 5 OverDrive processors. Specifically, in 296-pin Socket 7

Intel's P55C processors used only 296 of Socket 7's 321 pin positions. As a result, Socket 7 is often misdescribed as having 296 pins. The AMD-K6 uses all of Socket 7's 321 pin positions.

implementations, the definitions for the core (V_{CC2}) and I/O (V_{CC3}) pins previously used in the 296-pin split-plane Socket 5 VRT processors are adopted. As discussed earlier, such processors have 25 V_{CC2} pins, 28 V_{CC3} pins, and 53 V_{SS} pins.

Although optionally implemented, Socket 7 also defines the twenty-two extra power pins used previously in the 320-pin Socket 5 OverDrive processors, but with new distinction made for which are for the core (V_{CC2}) and which are for I/O (V_{CC3}). The new definitions continue the assignment of core pins and I/O pins generally on opposite halves of the socket. A full 321-pin implementation of Socket 7 has 28 V_{CC2} pins, 32 V_{CC3} pins, and 68 V_{SS} pins.

Compatible with standard chipset I/O, V_{CC3} is 3.3V. V_{CC2} in the initial Socket 7 processors was roughly 0.5V below V_{CC3}, but V_{CC2} is being reduced with each processor version implemented in smaller geometry processes. The 0.25-micron K6 has a nominal V_{CC2} of 2.2V. Socket 7 revises the specification for the clock inputs (CLK and PICCLK), requiring them to be driven only by 3.3V clock drivers.

DESIGN NOTE
VCC2DET
In both the K6 and the Pentium processor with MMX Technology (a.k.a. P55C), VCC2DET is always logic 0.

The most significant change over Socket 5 is that Socket 7 standardized a means for optional automatic detection of unified-plane versus split-plane processors and configuration of motherboard supplies for the core supply and I/O supply pins. This enables motherboards designed with Socket 7 to be configurable to accept either unified-plane (e.g., P54C or current Pentium OverDrive processors) or split-plane processors. This was accomplished by redefining a previous Socket 5 No-Connect (NC) pin as a V_{CC2} Detect (VCC2DET) output pin that is to be externally tied to a pull-up resistor and to the control input of a selectable-output voltage regulator. VCC2DET indicates whether the core and I/O supplies are to be unified (logic level 1) or split (logic level 0).

Flexible motherboards and VRMs are discussed in more detail in Intel's AP-579 (order 243187-001) Pentium Processor Flexible Motherboard Design Guidelines.

A Socket 7 motherboard capable of being configured for either split-plane or unified-plane processors is called a *flexible motherboard*. Flexible motherboards may use VCC2DET with automatic configuration, may be configured at manufacturing build or assembly time (by installation of particular voltage regulator components, including jumpers), may use a *Voltage Regulator Module (VRM)*, which is a modular DC-to-DC converter having an integral *header* connector, or combinations of the above.

If a Socket 7 device sinks VCC2DET low, a flexible motherboard with VCC2DET capability can automatically configure the supplies for a split-plane processor. If a device lets VCC2DET go high, as all pre-Socket 7 devices will, the supplies are configured for a unified-plane processor. Desktop Socket 5 processors, the majority of Socket 5 processors, will have their supplies properly configured when used in a motherboard having VCC2DET and automatic configuration capability. However, the "mobile" split-plane Socket 5 devices will not.

All new-installation Socket 7 processors to date have been split-plane processors. Socket 7 is *required* for the AMD-K6 MMX Enhanced Processor. AMD has marketed AMD-K6 processors at bus frequencies of 60, 66, 83, and 100 MHz and core frequencies of 166, 200, 233, 250, 266, and 300 MHz. Socket 7 is also *required* for Intel's CPU Family 5, Model 4, also designated by the part number substring 80504, and widely known by the Intel code name *P55C*. Intel has marketed P55C Pentium processors with MMX technology at core frequencies of 166, 200, and 233 MHz.

Newer platforms designed around Pentium processors (P54C) at 75, 90, 100, and 120 MHz were *recommended* to use Socket 7 as the upgrade socket. Pentium processors (P54C) at 133, 150, 166, and 200 MHz were *required* to use Socket 7, in order to accept their intended Pentium Over-Drive processors with MMX technology.

The split-plane AMD-K6 MMX Enhanced Processor has a nominal I/O voltage of 3.3V, with a range of 3.135-3.465V (3.3 V -/+ 5%), and a nominal core voltage of 2.9V, with a range of 2.755-3.045V (2.9V -/+ 5%). Split-plane Intel desktop and mobile Pentium processors with MMX (P55C) have a nominal I/O voltage of 3.3V, with a range of 3.135-3.60V (3.3V -5%, 3.5V +100mV). The desktop processors have a nominal core voltage of 2.8V, with a range of 2.7-2.9V (2.8V -/+ 100mV). The mobile processors have a nominal core voltage of 2.45V, with a range of 2.285-2.665V (2.45V-165mV, +215mV).

Performance

The Socket 7 bus is designed for high performance and supports a peak throughput 8 bytes every cycle. Thus at speeds of 66, 75, 83.3, and 100 MHz, the bus offers a peak throughput of 528, 600, 664, and 800 MBps, respectively. These peak rates are only approached when the system can exploit the bus cycle pipeline of the bus and burst cache line fill features.

The Socket 7 bus is known as a *fractional speed bus*. This means it supports core clock multiplication controls, such that the core can operate at fractional multiples greater than the bus speed. This enables the processor core to execute significantly faster than the bus, while keeping the motherboard low cost and easy to design due to its slower speed.

fractional speed bus

The transfers on the Socket 7 data bus consist of 64-bit (8-byte) wide objects. Because the 8086 used 16-bit registers, the x86 architecture has historically referred to a 16-bit object as a "word" and a 32-bit object as a "doubleword." Thus, a 64-bit object transferred on the Socket 7 bus is called a "quadword."

Basic Bus Operation

A dedicated 64-bit wide data bus is organized as 8 selectively enabled, byte wide data buses, for optimal use with 8-byte wide memory systems. Separate 32-bit addressing is provided by 8 byte-enables and 29 address-bits (A31..A3). The 8 byte-enables provide the same address range as 3-bits of address, but with the capability of selecting multiple arbitrary bytes within an 8-byte group. Cache line block fills of 32-bytes are supported, which are filled using 4, 8-byte bursts, that only require a single start address.

INDUSTRY STANDARD

Big and Little Endian Byte and Bit Ordering

In multiple-byte data objects, the relative significance of individual bytes that compose the object is an arbitrary characteristic of the processor's architecture. The bit-ordering within bytes is generally consistent with the byte-ordering convention. The two standard conventions use monotonic orderings that are known as the Little and Big Endian orders.

The K6 and other X86 processors use Little Endian ordering, in which the address of the object corresponds to the least significant byte, and bytes of greater significance within the object correspond to higher byte addresses. In a Big Endian ordering, the address of the object corresponds to the most significant byte, and bytes of less significance within the object correspond to higher byte addresses.

The terms Little and Big Endian were suggested by D. Cohen in an analogy drawn to the argument in Gulliver's Travels over whether an egg should be opened from the "little end" or the "big end." See "On holy wars and a plea for peace," by Cohen, *IEEE Computer*, October 1981, pp. 48-54.

The *M/IO! (Memory/IO!)* signal is output by the processor to distinguish accesses to the memory address space versus the I/O address space. I/O address space is intended for system I/O ports and is the target address space whenever I/O instructions are executed. All other instructions target the memory address space. The *D/C! (Data/Control! or Data/Code!)* signal is output by the processor to distinguish access to data versus program code (instructions). The *W/R! (Write/Read!)* signal is output by the processor to distinguish write accesses versus read accesses.

Platform Chip-sets use M/IO! for decoding between the memory and I/O address spaces and W/R! to command the addressed memory and I/O devices to accept or provide data. In addition to the generic purposes described individually for these signals, two reserved combinations of M/IO!, D/C!, and W/R!, are used to define the Interrupt Acknowledge and Special Cycles. Chip-sets must employ decoders to monitor for the reserved combinations in order to appropriately respond to such cycles.

Socket 7 can perform read and write cycles as either *single transfers* or *burst transfers*. In both cycle types, the processor outputs only a single address at the beginning of the cycle. Single transfers end after only one transfer. Burst transfers, without additional addresses, end only after four transfers have occurred. Due to their efficient bus usage, burst transfers are the preferred method of performing transfers, but are made only under select conditions. The four transfers of a burst occur according to a predetermined address order, or burst order.

Support for burst transfers by the external memory system is *mandatory*, as Socket 7 directly associates burst transfers with cacheable data or code, and vice versa. If data or code is cacheable, then it is *only* brought into the processor (read or prefetched) via a burst transfer. If data cached in the processor has been modified and needs to be written back to the Level 2 cache, then it is *only* output from the processor (written) via a burst transfer. Burst transfers are not used for non-cacheable data or code, for Interrupt Acknowledge, or I/O Cycles.

The *CACHE!* signal output serves different purposes, depending on whether a read or write is indicated. Assertion of CACHE! on prefetches or reads indicates that the processor considers the code or data to be cachable and is prepared to perform a four transfer burst *cache-line fill*.

Caches are organized as linear arrays of entries, known as "cache-lines." Socket 7 implicitly calls for cache-lines of 32-bytes in width (8 doublewords, or 4 quadwords). K6 also organizes every two cache-lines to share a common tag address, the collection being referred to as a cache "sector."

critical-item

critical-item first burst order

linear burst order

round-robin burst order

486-compatible burst order

INDUSTRY STANDARDS

Burst Orders

Cache-line reads are initiated when a request is made to any data location that falls within the bounds of the cache-line. The requested location is called the critical-item. Frequently the critical-item is not the first location within the cache-line. Socket 7 processors using *critical-item first burst orders*, retrieve the critical-quadword first, passing it immediately to the CPU, permitting the processor to continue execution in parallel with the retrieval of the remaining (3) cache-line locations. In a strict *linear burst order*, each quadword in the cache line is fetched in sequential order, generally low-to-high, without regard for the location of the critical-quadword.

Critical-item-first burst orders include the round-robin variant of the linear burst order and the 486-compatible (Intel) burst order. A *round-robin burst order* begins with the critical quadword and then proceeds sequentially, modulo the cache-line width, generally from low-to-high, but always sequencing in the same direction.

The *486-compatible (Intel) burst order* is a round-robin burst order that was used in the 486, where the sequence direction is a function of the even/odd status of the critical quadword. If the critical quadword is even (A3 is zero), the burst order sequences up, modulo the cache-line width. If the critical quadword is odd (A3 is one), the burst order sequences down, modulo the cache-line width.

The 486-compatible order arguably has advantages for use with certain memory banks organizations that access two 64-bit banks (representing one-half of a cache-line) in parallel. The 486-compatible burst order will sequence such that each-half of the cache-line need only be retrieved once.

Whether such bank organizations are actually used or not is largely irrelevant, if the processor supports only the 486-compatible burst order. The chip-set must use a compatible (identical) burst order to the processor. Some chip-sets only support the 486-compatible burst order.

For code prefetches or data reads, deassertion of CACHE! indicates that the processor will perform a single data transfer that will not be cached. This occurs when the L1 cache is disabled, the paging unit has determined the code or data address to be non-cachable based on the cache disable page attribute bits, TLB replacements, and locked cycles. CACHE! is likewise deasserted and only single transfers are used for Interrupt Acknowledge, Special, or I/O Cycles.

KEN! (Cache Enable) is an input to the processor, of consequence only for reads for which CACHE! is asserted. KEN! is ignored for writes and for reads when CACHE! is deasserted. KEN! is generated collectively by the L2 cache controller and *Non-Cachable Address (NCA)* logic within the chipset. KEN! is asserted on hits to L2, and on misses when the address is decoded to fall outside one or more programmable non-cachable address regions. On reads, if CACHE! and KEN! are both asserted, the final determination of cachability, the present cycle will be a four transfer burst. If the addressed location is a miss and is decoded by the NCA logic as noncachable, KEN! will be returned deasserted, and the cycle will consist of only a single data transfer that will not be cached.

In support of a *write-back cache management protocol*, on writes, CACHE! indicates that the processor will perform a burst transfer modified-cache-line write-back. The write-back may be prompted by the *replacement process* used to manage the Level 1 Cache. The write-back may also be necessitated by the *MESI shared-memory coherency protocol*.

The *ADS! (Address Status or Address Strobe)* output is asserted by the processor to indicate the first clock of a new active bus cycle, and is kept deasserted otherwise. ADS! assertion within a given clock period signals the validity within the same clock period of the following signals (some of which are yet to be discussed): A31-A3, AP, BE7!-BE0!, CACHE!, LOCK!, M/IO!, W/R!, D/C!, SCYC, PWT, PCD.

Valid sig

The *BRDY! (Burst Ready)* input is generated by the external memory system to indicate that the external system considers the current transfer complete. For reads, BRDY! signals to the processor that the data being provided to the processor by the external system is valid. For writes, BRDY! signals to the processor that the data being provided by the processor has been accepted by the external system. The processor monitors for the assertion of BRDY! in each clock cycle for which there is an on-going transfer. Hence there is one assertion of BRDY! in single transfer bus cycles, and four assertions for burst transfer bus cycles. The assertion of BRDY! on the last transfer of a bus cycle is considered to terminate the current cycle and defines the validity of the following signals sampled during the same clock cycle: KEN!, WB/WT!, NA!, EWBE!, data and data parity.

The absence of a BRDY! assertion constitutes a *wait-state* request. For each contiguous clock cycle in which the external system cannot complete the current transfer within the clock-cycle, BRDY! is kept deasserted. The processor inserts wait-states as required, suspending the termination of the bus cycle until the external system asserts BRDY! for each transfer of the bus cycle. This wait-state mechanism means Socket 7 is a semisynchronous bus, which normally operates with the speed of a synchronous bus.

The use of wait-states is common in PC platforms, arising due to disparities between the period of the bus clock and the timing of affordable memories. There are number of potentially different memory timings of interest, of which at least one usually requires wait-states. The different timings arise because the external memory system consists of a relatively fast SRAM-based Level 2 Cache, used whenever possible, and a slower DRAM-based main memory, used on L2 cache misses and for non-cachable data. Furthermore, each of these memory types has generally different read and write access times, and typically different timings for lead-off and burst operation. Finally, the timing for I/O space accesses is unrelated to the memory system timings and may vary with each I/O device.

If any of these memory timings is not less than the bus clock period by a comfortable margin, one or more wait-states must be added as required to insure a valid transfer. The memory and cache controllers of the external system collectively must dynamically generate the BRDY! timing according to the different memory timings and as a function of the hit/miss status of the L2 cache, the read/write status of the bus cycle, and whether the transfer is a lead-off transfer or a subsequent burst transfer. The different memory timings are usually programmed into non-volatile storage on the motherboard by a setup program run after the memory is installed.

address pipelining

bus-cycle pipelining

Under certain conditions, Socket 7 permits *address pipelining*, the overlapping of (at most) two bus cycles. The external system must request such *bus-cycle pipelining*, via the assertion of the processor's *NA! (Next Address)* input. During overlapped bus cycles, ADS!, which defines the validity of the address and transfer type and the beginning of the next cycle, is asserted before the last assertion of BRDY! in the current bus-cycle, which defines the current bus-cycle's completion.

When bus cycles are not overlapped, ADS! can be asserted no sooner than the first clock-cycle after the last BRDY! assertion in the previous bus-cycle. This results in an idle state between bus cycles. Memory controllers that support (by latching the address and transfer type) and request bus cycle pipelining, increase the efficiency of the bus by reducing the number of idle states between bus cycles.

REPORTS ON CD-ROM

 More detailed descriptions regarding Socket 7 are available in the following items on the companion CD-ROM. The first document includes a detailed description of every bus signal. In particular see Chapter 5, *Signal Descriptions,* and Chapter 6, *Bus Cycles.* The second document describes models that are available to simulate accurately the I/O drivers in circuit simulations of systems built around the processor. The third document provides additional insight into interfacing with a Socket 7 bus processor. In particular see section 5.1, *Processor Interface.* In addition, Section 4.1, *Processor Interface Signals*, describes the processor bus signals in summary form.

- *AMD-K6 Processor*, 20695H/0-March 1998.

- *Application Note AMD-K6 MMX Enhanced Processor I/O Model*, Document 21084, June 1997.

- *AMD-640 System Controlle*r, 21090C/10-June 1997.

Suggested Readings

Processor Local Buses

The following books provide detailed information on processor local buses and associated sockets and slots:

1. Tom Shanley, *Pentium Pro Processor System Architecture*, Addison-Wesley, 1997.
2. Don Anderson & Tom Shanley, *Pentium Processor System Architecture*, Mindshare Press, 1993.
3. Tom Shanley, *80486 System Architecture, 3rd Edition*, Addison-Wesley, 1995.
4. *Understanding x86 Microprocessors*, Ziff-Davis Press, 1987.

CHAPTER SUMMARY

This chapter has presented the standards, metastandards, platform-level technologies, and component-level technologies that play important roles in PC platform architecture. Chapter 5 extends the examination of component-level technologies to memories and their control.

Chapter 5
Platform Memory Technology

I n this chapter we continue our examination of the platform context in which contemporary microprocessors function. Here we focus on memory technology, an absolutely critical technology for high-performance platforms. Our study will begin with a survey of the memory types most common to new platforms (Fast Page Mode, Extended Data Out and Synchronous DRAM). After a brief introduction to emerging memory types (Direct Rambus and SLDRAM), we then proceed to examine memory controllers for main memory in some detail. The memory controller material will discuss the differences in support for the asynchronous and synchronous memory types, consider the consequences of multiple memory banks, and detail memory controller low-level functions. Such functions include the state machine control of memory timing signals, address processing, data routing and staging, and programmable configuration of DRAM type and size.

ROAD MAP OF CHAPTER 5

Section	Audience
All major headings in the chapter	All

The following more detailed subsections:
 	
Basic Memory Technologies
    Asynchronous DRAM
    Synchronous DRAM
	Students and those unfamiliar with the internal distinctions between Fast Page Mode, Extended Data Out, and Synchronous DRAM.

BASIC MEMORY TECHNOLOGIES

DRAMs have traditionally used clockless interfaces. Such asynchronous DRAMs were used in all PC platforms until only recently, when high-end platforms began using DRAMs having clocked interfaces. Having a clocked interface simplifies the control of the DRAM while making it easier to optimize the performance of accesses with main memory. Improvements in main-memory performance are necessary to support continued increases in transfers rates between main memory and PCI-Bus peripherals and between main memory and the AGP. Improved main-memory data-rates are also necessary to reduce latencies on cache line replacements and thereby support continued increases in instruction fetch and data transfer rates of the processor. Consequently, synchronous DRAMs are now generally supplanting the use of asynchronous DRAMs in new platforms. However, the industry is still in a state of transition between these two types of DRAM, and present memory controllers support both types.

ASYNCHRONOUS DRAM

Page Mode, Fast Page Mode, and Extended Data Out DRAM are minor variations of asynchronous DRAM. These devices consist of little more than a core memory array with row and column selects generated by address decoders. Figure 5.1 is a typical asynchronous DRAM block diagram. Figure 5.2 is an abstract view of the DRAM analog Core that makes up the memory array block.

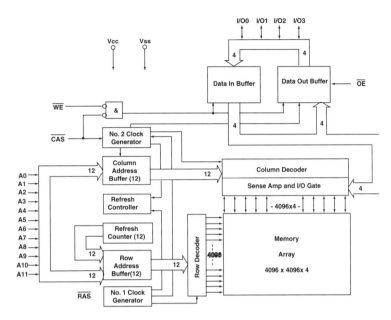

Figure 5.1 ASYNCHRONOUS DRAM BLOCK DIAGRAM

Reprinted by permission from *16M x 4 12/12 EDO DRAM*, Copyright 1996, by International Business Machines Corporation.

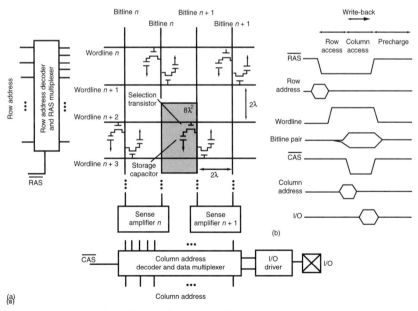

Figure 5.2 ABSTRACT VIEW OF DRAM ANALOG CORE

Copyright 1997, *IEEE Micro*, Nov/Dec 1997, used with permission.

Idiosyncrasies of the DRAM Core

All Dynamic RAM have a basic core of analog-esque functional circuits. Central to this core is a rectangular array of capacitor-based storage cells in which the stored charge must be periodically refreshed. DRAM chips have traditionally parsed the overall memory address into "row" and "column" components, and multiplexed these components over a reduced pin interface. The row address and column address normally correspond to higher order and lower order address bits, respectively. The row address is often thought of as representing a page within the memory, while the column address represents locations within the page. *Row- and column-address strobes*, generally known as *RAS!* and *CAS!*, respectively, are active-low control signals used to latch the row and column addresses within the DRAM for accessing the internal rectangular storage matrix. Write-enable, WE!, is an active-low control signal used to indicate that data is to be written into the addressed location. If WE! is deasserted, data is read from the addressed location. A data input/output signal, MD (also I/O or DQ), conveys the data input to and output from the DRAM for writes and reads, respectively.

During a row access interval, assertion of RAS! activates one *wordline* in the array corresponding to the decoded row address. Since the activated wordline is merely the unencoded row address, the activated wordline and its associated storage cells correspond to a currently addressed page in the memory. Wordline activation enables every storage cell in the addressed page to be coupled to its adjacent *bitline*. During row access, the coupled storage cells perturb the bitlines from specially precharged voltage levels. Due to charge sharing between the necessarily small capacitance of the minimum-geometry storage cells and the large parasitic capacitance of the lengthy bitlines, the impact of the stored charges on the bitline voltages is small. During a column access interval, assertion of CAS! activates a *sense amp* on each bitline to quickly produce a voltage level suitable for output to other circuits. The column address is decoded to select with a multiplexer which column's data is coupled to the memory's I/O.

As used in DRAM, a sense amp is a dynamic logic circuit that has two terminals coupled to cross-coupled circuitry. Either its two terminals are explicitly coupled to differential signal lines (as is done in Figure 5.2 on page 429), or one terminal is explicitly coupled to a signal line and the other implicitly coupled to a reference voltage. During a *precharge* time interval, corresponding to the deassertion of RAS!, every sense amp and its associated bitline is *precharged* to voltage levels ideal to their operation during the subsequent row access and column access intervals. This bitline evaluation by the sense amp during the column access also serves to *refresh* (restore, or write-back) the charge in the storage cell. Since all bitlines in a row are precharged and evaluated simultaneously, any access within a page acts to refresh all storage cells within the page.

Row- and column- address strobes

RAS! and CAS!

wordline

bitline

Page Mode DRAM

The overall *cycle time* for back-to-back memory cycles is the *access time* (the combined row and column access intervals) plus the precharge interval. It is possible in certain DRAM to accesses multiple locations anywhere within the same page by changing the column address (by strobing CAS!) while leaving the row address unchanged (and keeping RAS! asserted). Such accesses merely select a different, but already evaluated, bitline for coupling to the output drivers. Thus, same page accesses do not require the precharge and row access intervals. Consequently, the cycle time of such *page-mode accesses* is reduced. The capability to exploit page-mode accesses requires the memory controller to alter dynamically its RAS! and CAS! generation based on access patterns. A *Page Mode (PM) DRAM* is a DRAM that permits page-mode accesses, which has been a baseline requirement in PC platforms since page-mode support became common in highly integrated memory controllers.

cycle time

access time

page-mode accesses

Fast Page Mode DRAM

In both original PM DRAM and later Fast Page Mode (FPM) DRAM, CAS! activation serves to latch the column address, enable sense amp evaluation, and enable the data output buffer. The difference between these parts lies in when column address decoding is begun. PM parts do not couple the multiplexed row/column address inputs to the column decoders until CAS! is activated. In FPM parts, a transparent (type D) latch clocked by CAS! couples the output of the address multiplexer to the column address decoders. The output of the row/column address multiplexer flows through the latch, with CAS! deasserted, and its value is captured, when CAS! is asserted. As a result, the necessary delay for column address set-up begins from stable and valid column addresses, and is overlapped with the end of the row access interval. Thus, column address decode begins earlier than the later CAS! activation of the earlier PM parts, which reduces the column access interval, and hence the cycle time and the page-mode cycle time.

Extended Data Out DRAM

The relationship of the output drivers and the CAS! signal is a key difference between FPM DRAM and *Extended Data Out (EDO) DRAM*. In FPM DRAM, the column data multiplexer is coupled directly to the bidirectional transceiver buffers that drive the I/O lines. On reads, the output drivers are only active during active CAS! and CAS! must therefore be kept active from assertion until the end of the memory cycle. Because the column address decoders and column data multiplexer include dynamic circuitry that is precharged between CAS! assertions, there is a minimum interval during which CAS! must be held inactive. Because CAS! must be held active in FPM parts until the end of the memory cycle, in order to enable the output drivers, the minimum CAS! precharge time can delay CAS! assertion for subsequent accesses.

In EDO DRAM, an output transparent latch clocked by the compliment of CAS! couples the column data multiplexer to the I/O buffers. The output of the column data multiplexer flows through the latch, with CAS! asserted, and its value is captured, when CAS! is deasserted. The output drivers are designed to go off *only when both CAS! and RAS! are deasserted*. Bringing CAS! inactive by itself, does not turn off the output drives and the data remains valid until the next falling edge of CAS!. The ability to return CAS! inactive while continuing to transfer data enables the CAS! precharge for the next column access to begin earlier and to overlap with the valid data output for the previous column access. As a result, EDO cycle timing is generally one CPU CLK faster than the cycle timing for FPM DRAM. In addition, the output data is generally valid for larger portion of the memory cycle than with FPM parts.

REPORT ON CD-ROM

To learn more about EDO see the IBM Application Note, *EDO (Hyper Page Mode)*, August 27, 1996, on the companion CD-ROM.

Accessing FPM and EDO DRAM

For asynchronous DRAM, the DRAM's clockless analog core is essentially directly accessed. The FPM and EDO inputs may directly (or with minor buffering or inversion) act as clock strobes of internal latches (for the row and column addresses), act as unlatched inputs to combinational functions (address decode for row select), control pass-transistor signal routing and power-activation, act as level-sensitive enables for gating other control signals, or activate dynamic circuit operations (such as column sense-amp evaluation or pre-charge). RAS!, CAS!, the multiplexed row and column address components, and WE!, are output from the memory controller to the DRAM. Memory data (MD) is input or output from the memory controller, for writes and reads, respectively. Figure 5.3 illustrates these signals.

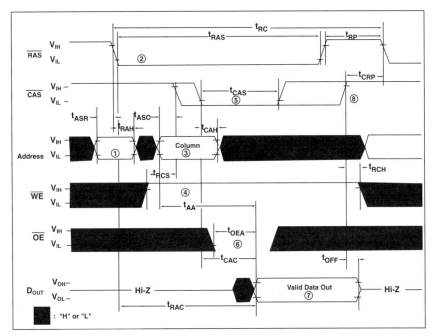

Figure 5.3 SIMPLIFIED ASYNCHRONOUS DRAM READ TIMING

Reprinted by permission from *Understanding DRAM Operation*, copyright 1996, by International Business Machines Corporation.

Synchronous Main Memory Access

Does use of asynchronous DRAM in PC platforms mean that the main memory is being operated asynchronously? The answer depends on where you look and which definition of asynchronous[74] you use. With asynchronous DRAM, there is no explicit clock coupled to the memory chips, the DRAM access and cycle timings are multiples of the CPU clock, the DRAM access timings vary depending on the history of accesses, and the initiation and control sequencing of DRAM accesses must be dynamically modified due to various time-out intervals. The above factors might suggest to some that the main memory is operated asynchronously.

Other factors suggest that asynchronous DRAM are operated synchronously in PC platforms, in spite of the foregoing. The memory controller's RAS! and CAS! strobes are generated synchronous to the CPU clock, and their transitions are used to effectuate the internal operation of the DRAM. Addresses and optional write data and write enables are set up and held synchronous with the CPU clock for a pre-programmed and pre-determined number of CPU clock periods. Likewise, read data is always clocked into the memory controller synchronous with the CPU clock at

---

[74] See the Protocol section in Chapter 4.

the end of a preprogrammed and predetermined number of CPU clock periods. Finally, in spite of its demanding idiosyncrasies, asynchronous DRAM always operates in a fashion that is completely predictable by the memory controller, so there is no need for a handshake mechanism for the DRAM to dynamically alter the predetermined DRAM timing.

ARTICLES ON CD-ROM

To learn more about Asynchronous DRAM, see the following IBM documents on the companion CD-ROM:

- *16M x 4 12/12 EDO DRAM Data Sheet.*
- *Understanding DRAM Operation.*

SYNCHRONOUS DRAM

Synchronous DRAM (SDRAM) interposes a modest but higher-level encoded and clocked interface between the memory controller and the core, which in SDRAM is generally organized and operated as two or more interleaved arrays. The SDRAM-clocked interface internally generates the low-level unencoded direct control of the core as part of its execution of any of a rich repertoire of commands available to the memory controller. The SDRAM interface causes a minor increase in latency on acceses to random off-page locations compared to the FPM and EDO parts. In return, however, the clocked command interface permits system optimizations through access pipelining, long highly efficient burst transfers, and the shifting of responsibility for DRAM-specific low-level control details to the DRAM and away from the memory controller.

In contrast to asynchronous DRAM, SDRAM isolates the analog core behind a clocked interface. Generally, an SDRAM core is similar in technology to the FPM and EDO parts, but employs two or more internal interleaved arrays instead of one. SDRAM inputs and outputs are isolated from the inner core via clocked latches, and the control inputs are encoded (have defined combinations) to represent a rich variety of commands that the control interface translates into internal signals that control the core. The control interface generates the internal control signals using its own internal state machine controller. It is the SDRAM interface logic's responsibility to meet the setup and hold times of all the SDRAM basic core control signals. The interface carries out commanded accesses, including internal generation of addresses for burst transfers as required. SDRAM can perform burst transfers up to a page in size without signaling after command initiation. If necessary, burst transfers can be aborted prior to completion. The interface performs access pipelining in that it can accept the starting address and command for a second access while executing a first access command. The refresh function can be automatically or semi-automatically performed by on-chip circuitry ancillary to the interface logic.

REPORTS ON CD-ROM

A wealth of information on SDRAM is contained in the IBM 64Mb Synchronous DRAM Data Sheet, included on the CD-ROM. In particular, see:

- A block diagram, on p. 6, which illustrates this part's internal 4-bank organization;
- A functional description of each I/O pin, on p. 4;
- Definition of control fields for the operating mode and other control registers, on p. 9;
- A truth table for the encoded command functions, on pp. 30-32;
- A truth table for the internal state machine, on pp. 33-36; and
- 19 timing diagrams of various operations, on pp. 44-62 (a list of these appears on p. 43).

Rambus and SLDRAM are emerging memory design technologies that incorporate a more sophisticated system-level perspective that tightly couples memory and memory controller operation. These technologies incorporate many advanced technologies, including clock forwarding to eliminate clock skew, special attention to packaging and board design to minimize transmission line effects in optimized voltage signaling, highly efficient packetized command protocols, split-transaction operation, and sending and receiving data on both clock edges.

EMERGING MEMORY TECHNOLOGIES

ARTICLES ON CD-ROM

To learn about the factors motivating these and other DRAM technologies, see "Trends in Semiconductor Memories," by Yasunao Katayama, *IEEE Micro*, 1997, included on the companion CD-ROM.

RAMBUS

Rambus Channel

Rambus Interface

Rambus DRAM (RDRAM)

Rambus is a technically sophisticated, multi-disciplined, proprietary approach to implementing highly optimized memory systems for board-level platforms. Rambus systems consist of masters and slaves coupled to a *Rambus Channel*, each via its own *Rambus Interface*. Masters can be microprocessors, accelerators, memory controllers, or other core logic or ASIC devices. The prototypical master is a memory controller. Slaves can include any of the obvious memory types such as DRAMS, SRAMs, and Flash EPROM, or other devices such as RAMDACs. The prototypical slave is a *Rambus DRAM (RDRAM)*, which couples a Rambus Interface to one or more banks constructed from conventional DRAM cores. Figure 5.4 shows a simplified view of Rambus DRAM, coupled via a Rambus Interface to a Rambus Channel. Rambus memory systems offer a fundamentally different approach to platform design. Memory controllers are designed to the Rambus Channel specs, not for specific DRAMs. RDRAMs in turn are expected to meet Rambus Channel specs for timing and pinout.

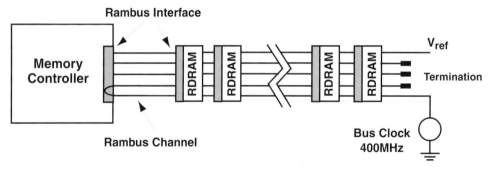

Figure 5.4 PRIMARY ELEMENTS OF A RAMBUS-BASED SYSTEM

Copyright 1997, Courtesy Rambus, Inc.

Direct Rambus Channel

In low-end platforms in particular, RDRAMs provide high bandwidth using small packages and pin count relative to other DRAM technologies. In the present version of Rambus, known as Direct Rambus, RDRAMs are coupled to the *Direct Rambus Channel* via a two-byte width of 16 or 18 bits. The Direct Rambus Channel and data transfers are made on both edges of the Bus Clock. As a result, RDRAMs have a burst transfer rate in MB/sec that is four times the clock rate in MHz. The present clock rate is 400MHz, yielding a peak data transfer rate of 1.6 GBps.

Features and Philosophy

The Rambus Channel is at the center of Rambus-based designs. The channel efficiently communicates between masters and slaves at high data transfer rates using a split-transaction packet protocol that bundles control, addressing, and data into transaction packets that are physically transported over a narrow bus. Controlled-impedance transmission line techniques are used to achieve predictable bus delays. Sophisticated synchronous clocking methods guarantee minimal skew. Primary Channels are designed to support up to thirty-two RDRAMs. A bridge called an RTransceiver may be used to increase the effective number of slaves. Up to ten Secondary Channels (each supporting up to thirty-two RDRAMs) may be coupled to a Primary Channel via such bridges. Thus a Primary Channel can accommodate up to 320 RDRAMs through the use of bridged Secondary Channels.

The Rambus Channel also has an associated philosophy that includes a design philosophy and a design and implementation discipline. Rigid adherence to the Rambus Channel philosophy ensures consistent and reliable high bandwidth in systems making use of memory controllers and DRAM from multiple vendors. A key aspect of the Rambus philosophy is that the channel's data width is intended to be held narrow regardless of memory population. Bandwidth is instead scaled by use of multiple channels or through increasing the clock frequency. The architecture of the basic channel is intended to be relatively constant over multiple generations. Similarly, system designers are discouraged from making independent modifications to the bus architecture.

Details of the Rambus Channel

The Rambus Channel achieves its high bandwidth partly by signaling over high-quality transmission lines. The topology of the channel connections, shown in Figure 5.5, plays a key role in achieving quality characteristics. The master is located at one end of the channel. At the other end of the channel, terminators are used, matched to the same characteristic impedance as the signal traces. Slaves are placed only between the master and the terminators. A disciplined implementation also contributes to the transmission line quality. The Rambus Channel is intentionally a dense/narrow bus, having only thirty-five active signals. Figure 5.1 details all signal types on the Rambus Channel. All signals are carried via controlled impedance traces, free of discontinuities. Short, dense packaging with minimized parasitics is employed. All trace loading is uniform in distribution and matched in value.

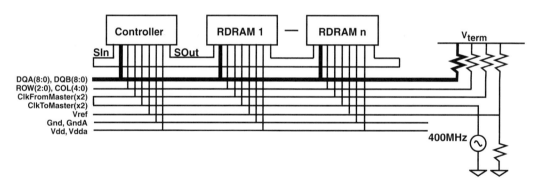

Figure 5.5   Topology Details of the Rambus Channel

Copyright 1997, Courtesy Rambus, Inc.

Table 5.1   Rambus Channel Pins and Signal Types

Pin	Signal Type and Notes
DQA, DQB (16 to 18bits)	"active" RSL (low-voltage Rambus Signaling Logic); data
ROW	"active" RSL; row commands
COL	"active" RSL; column commands
ClkToMaster (and compliment)	"active" RSL; differential sync for data from slaves
ClkFromMaster (and compliment)	"active" RSL; differential sync for data from master
SIn and SOut	"active" TTL; address configuration and refresh
Vref	Voltage reference for all RSL signals
Gnd, Vdd	power
GndA, VddA	"analog" power for PLLs

Rambus Signaling Logic (RSL)

The proprietary active-low *Rambus Signaling Logic (RSL)* defines the signaling protocol of the Rambus Channel. As shown in Figure 5.6, low voltage swings (800-mv) are differentially sensed about a bused Voltage Reference signal (Vref) of approximately 1.4V. Logic 0 corresponds to the voltage of the termination resistors (Vterm!), which is roughly 1.8V. Logic 1 corresponds to a VOL of approximately 1.0V. The differential sensing provides common-mode noise immunity, while the low voltage swings result in reduced EMI and less ground bounce.

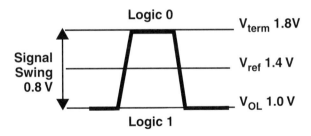

Figure 5.6 RAMBUS CHANNEL SIGNALING

Copyright 1997, Courtesy Rambus, Inc.

The Rambus Channel achieves virtually skewless data clocking by propagating clocks and data in parallel, down matched transmission lines. A clock signal known as ClkToMaster originates from a clock generator on the terminator side of the Channel. ClkToMaster is propagated down a transmission line toward the master end of the Channel. Slaves use the ClkToMaster signal, referred internally to the Slave as the TxClk, to synchronize data being sent to a master. The ClkToMaster is looped back at the master and propagates anew down a separate transmission line as a signal known as the ClkFromMaster. Masters use the ClkFromMaster signal to synchronize data being sent to slaves. Slaves use the ClkFromMaster signal, referred internally to the Slave as the RxClk, to synchronize data being sent from a master. Each master or slave on the Channel has separate PLLs for extracting internal clock signals synchronized to the ClkToMaster and the ClkFromMaster.

The Rambus Interface

Integral to all masters and slaves is the Rambus Interface, the I/O logic and circuitry which enables coupling with the Rambus Channel. Rambus makes available to licensees a reference Rambus Interface module, known as the *Rambus ASIC Cell (RAC)*. Figure 5.7 illustrates a generic Rambus Interface between a Rambus Channel and a Rambus-based memory controller. The interface module shown presents the memory controller with a simplified 128-bit (with 144-bit "9th-bit byte" option) interface operating at 100MHz. Whether based on the RAC, or based on a custom design, the Rambus Interface must perform a number of specific functions. Electrically, it performs signaling conversion between the RSL voltage levels and the voltage levels required by the CMOS-core of the attached device. The PLLs, which synchronize the transfer of data with the off-chip Rambus Channel propagated clocks, also reside in the Rambus Interface. Logically, the Rambus Interface generates for masters, and decodes for

Rambus ASIC Cell (RAC)

slaves, the request packets that are key to the master/slave packet protocol. Likewise, the acknowledge protocol is implemented here, and includes the proper handling of multiple byte transfers. For memory array slaves, the Rambus Interface also selectively couples the addressed memory location from the array sense amp latch to the channel.

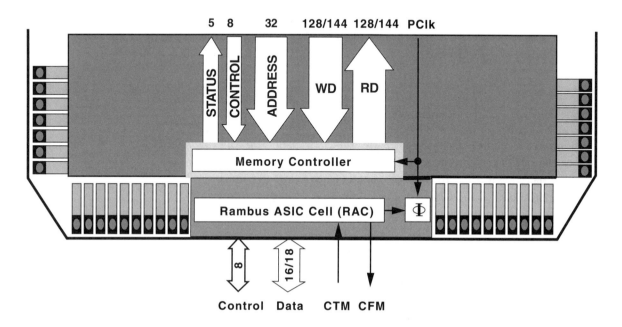

Figure 5.7 EXAMPLE RAMBUS INTERFACE WITH MEMORY CONTROLLER

Copyright 1997, Courtesy Rambus, Inc.

Other Rambus Architectural Features

Rambus devices support a register space having both programmable control registers and read-only status registers. Read-only registers provide such information as device type, size, and manufacturer's ID. Programmable control registers enable system designer configuration of address mapping, power management, refresh, and transaction timing. Rambus devices also are linked together via a serial daisy-chain using the SIn and SOut pins. This link is used to configure the base memory address of each slave during initialization, and to initiate system refresh requests during power down.

Pros and Cons of Rambus-based Systems

A principal factor in the appeal of designing a platform to use Rambus is its characteristic high bandwidth in small capacity and small pinout memory systems. A high ratio of bandwidth-to-memory capacity reduces the need to widen the memory system with additional memory solely to achieve a desired level of memory bandwidth. Such additional memory may increase the memory capacity and the associated cost of the base system configuration beyond what is otherwise necessary. A high ratio of bandwidth-to-memory capacity also reduces the need for special memory architectures, which might include SRAM caches or VRAM, depending on the application. Rambus's high ratio of bandwidth-to-memory capacity in small capacity systems makes it particularly well suited to dedicated video memories and low-end *Unified Memory Architecture (UMA)* platforms, in which the video memory is just a region within the main memory and not a dedicated subsystem.

Unified Memory Architecture (UMA)

Another factor in the appeal of Rambus relates its narrow bus width. Rambus's high ratio of bandwidth-to-pinout results in smaller packaging and routing without the need to resort to special packaging technologies, such as Multi-Chip Modules (MCMs). The low pin count associated with the narrow bus also permits a Rambus-based memory controller to be integrated more readily with other logic. Thus as processing technology advances, systems using Rambus have an advantage over other system approaches in combining system functions into fewer chips. Also, due to the byte-wide organization, memory can be added to a Rambus system with finer granularity (a smaller increment in capacity) and correspondingly lower cost, compared to a more typical 4- or 8-byte wide memory bus organization.

In contrast to the foregoing, Rambus's appeal diminishes with increases to the slave population of the Rambus Channel. Since the bandwidth of the Rambus Channel does not scale with the number of RDRAMs, there is a decrease in the ratio of bandwidth-to-memory capacity as the number of RDRAMs increases. Furthermore, as the number of masters and slaves increases, there is increased likelihood for contention for the single narrow bus. Finally, while not an issue with only a few masters and slaves, larger systems must deal with the cumulative power dissipation from the multiple PLLs in each chip's Rambus Interface.

Additional information about Rambus technology and the company is accessible at http://www.rambus.com/.

ARTICLE ON CD-ROM

 To learn more about Direct DRAM, see the article "Direct Rambus Technology: The New Main Memory Standard," by Richard Crisp, *IEEE Micro*, 1997, on the companion CD-ROM.

The following presentation gives an overview of the original Rambus architecture:

Rambus and Direct DRAM, by Bennett Smith.

Synchronous-Link DRAM (SLDRAM)

Synchronous-Link DRAM (SLDRAM), like Rambus, is a high-performance interface for efficiently coupling DRAM with memory controllers. Unlike Rambus, SLDRAM is an open standard (IEEE Standard P1596.7), developed by a consortium of memory manufacturers that promote its use. This is in contrast to the proprietary Rambus interface, which requires the payment of licensing or royalty fees, or other compensation, for its use in either DRAMs or memory controllers.

Additional information about SLDRAM technology and the SLDRAM organization is accessible at http://www.sldram.com/.

SLDRAM has a clocked handshakeless interface, terminated low-voltage signaling, and a packet protocol. It uses burst-mode transfers, returns data on both clock edges, and is designed to make effective use of memories having multiple internal banks. SLDRAM uses a unidirectional *CommandLink* bus for command and address packets and a bi-directional *DataLink* bus for read and write data packets. SLDRAM is a parallel interface variant of *RamLink (IEEE Standard 1596.4)* a point-to-point memory interface standard. RamLink, in turn, is a memory specific reduced command set variant of the *Scalable Coherent Interface* protocol *(SCI, IEEE Standard P1596).*

A detailed overview of the SLDRAM architecture an operation is provided in the Peter Gillingham's and Bill Vogley's article "SLDRAM: High-Performance, Open-Standard Memory," *IEEE Micro,* November/December 1997, which is included on the companion CD-ROM.

REPORTS ON CD-ROM

We have included two reports about SLDRAM on the companion CD-ROM. The first item is an SLDRAM data sheet. The second item is an SLDRAM white paper.

- *4M x 18 SLDRAM Pipelined, Eight Bank, 2.5V Operation.*
- *SLDRAM Architectural and Functional Overview,* Peter Gillingham, MOSAID Technologies Inc.

STANDARD ON CD-ROM

Included on the CD-ROM is the *Draft Standard for a High-Speed Memory Interface (SyncLink)*, IEEE P1596.7-199X. This is the proposed standard for the SLDRAM Bus.

NORTH-BRIDGE MEMORY CONTROLLER

The control of main memory is fundamental to the operation of any computer system. Main memory can be viewed as an array of locations having unique addresses. Instructions and data for both system software and applications are loaded into and executed from the main memory. The main memory needs to support basic data transactions. Requesters may perform transactions on specified main memory locations that read (fetch data from), write (store data to), and read-modify-write (a non-interruptible sequence of fetching data, manipulating the fetched data, and storing the manipulated data back to the original location).

The data transfer rate and latency between main memory and the cache subsystem or the CPU is crucial to system performance. In high-performance computers, the memory controller is preferably located in close physical proximity to the CPU, caches, and a high-bandwidth peripheral bus, due to its close interaction with these subsystems.

Byte Addressing: In PC platforms, objects being accessed are conventionally referenced by specifying the byte address of the least significant byte of the object. This is so, regardless of the objects' width, the data transfer width, or the width of datapaths that subsequently process the referenced object.

OVERVIEW

In PC platforms the memory controller is a major functional block within the North-Bridge. Figure 5.8 on page 445 is a simplified block diagram of an AMD-640 System Controller, an illustrative North-Bridge (note the DRAM Control block and I/O signals in the lower right corner of the figure). The memory controller receives transactions requesting data transfers between the main memory and the request source. The main memory is implemented with multiple banks of DRAM, which share a common data bus and multiplexed address bus (and other common signals), but have separate bank enables. The data, address, and control interface to the DRAM banks is a major port of the North-Bridge. Figure 5.9 on page 445 illustrates the control interface of an example configuration of the AMD-640 using six banks of SDRAM.

Articles on CD-ROM

 Throughout this section we will provide memory controller implementation examples based on a commercially available North-Bridge, the AMD-640 System Controller. The data sheet for this part is included on the companion CD-ROM. The reader is encouraged to review the data sheet for additional information not directly included in this chapter. In particular, see:

- Section 4.3, *DRAM Interface Signals*, on pp. 4-8 and 4-9, which gives a short description of each signal;

- Section 5.3, *DRAM Memory Controller*, on pp. 5-15 through 5-29, which discusses operation and provides timing diagrams. Separate subsections examine Mixing Memory, Error Correction Code, DRAM Refresh, Shadow DRAM, EDO DRAM, and Synchronous DRAM; and

- Section 7.5, *DRAM Control Registers*, on pp. 7-16 through 7-31, which provides full details for controlling all aspects of the memory controller.

DESIGN NOTE

Sources of Main Memory Traffic

Requests for main memory may come from the shared CPU/Cache-bus, the PCI-Bus, or the AGP. These are the three major ports on the North-Bridge, besides the memory controller. The cache controller on the North-Bridge additionally has a control-only port to the cache.

Traffic between the CPU and main memory results from write-through cache configurations, and from accesses to non-cacheable areas of memory. Traffic between the cache and main memory results from cache replacements brought about by cache misses. In write-back cache configurations, cache lines being replaced from the cache must be written back to main memory from the cache, if any data has been modified. The replacement lines in the instruction and data caches are subsequently filled from main memory. Traffic between AGP and main memory results from texture and other image traffic to and from the video memory and from AGP reads of control information left by the processor.

Traffic directly between the PCI Bus and main memory includes at least two types of bus masters transfers. The first type of PCI-Bus/main-memory transfers are OS initiated transfers that swap program data and code between mass storage and main memory as part of normal virtual memory management. The second type of PCI-Bus/main-memory transfers are explicitly initiated transfers by application or system software to move data items or complete files between work areas in memory and mass storage or other I/O devices.

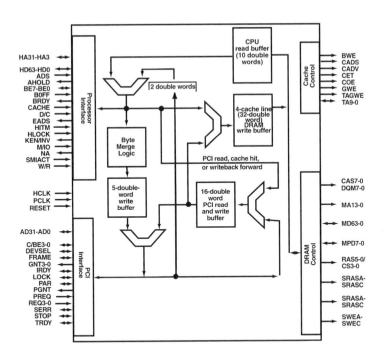

Figure 5.8 The AMD-640 System Controller (A North-Bridge)

Copyright 1997/1998, Advanced Micro Devices Inc., used with permission.

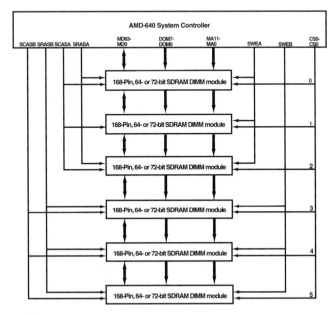

Figure 5.9 All SDRAM Bank Configuration of the AMD-640

Copyright 1997/1998, Advanced Micro Devices Inc., used with permission.

Requests are processed in a state-machine controller that controls all aspects of the memory controller's behavior, including address processing, data staging, data routing, and the activation and timing of all interfaces. The state-machine controller controls the sequencing and timing for these operations to transfer data between the requesting port and specified main memory addresses, which correspond to predetermined unique locations within the multiple banks of DRAM. Address processing logic maps the transaction addresses to bank (or bank-pair), row, column, and byte-select information, which is used to select the desired bank (or bank-pair); a particular *quartet* (for banks) or *octet* (for bank-pairs); and one or more desired bytes out of the byte-quad (for banks) or octet (for bank-pairs). Data staging is used to buffer all ports (CPU, cache, PCI, AGP and DRAM), reduce latencies via prefetching and posted writes, and enable the operation on each port to generally proceed stall-free, concurrently, and independent of each other. Data routing selectively couples data between the port buffers to accomplish the desired data transfers.

A quartet, and an octet, are a group of 4 and 8 bytes, respectively.

DESIGN NOTE

Configuration Register Access in the AMD-640

The AMD-640 has a number of configuration registers. These registers are accessed in the PCI-Bus configuration space, using configuration mechanism #1, described in the *PCI Local Bus Specification Revision 2.1*. Loosely speaking, the desired register is identified using an I/O write operation to a 4-byte wide I/O location, and the configuration data is passed using another I/O write to the next subsequent 4-byte I/O locations. This chapter abstracts this complexity and refers to writing the configuration data into a particular numbered configuration register. Each register is referred to by the prefix CR, for Configuration Register, a particular "offset" address in hex, denoted by the letter "h," and at least one bit within the register, specified in brackets. If more than one bit is involved, a bit range will be indicated within the brackets by an upper bit location, a colon, and a lower bit location. As an example, the upcoming usage "CR59h<2:0>" is a reference to the configuration register at offset 59hex, bits 2 through 0, inclusive. It is to be understood that all configuration registers must actually be accessed via the PCI configuration mechanism #1.

While the gross nature of the state-machine controller is fixed, the fine-grain behavior of the state-machine controller, and hence the memory controller as a whole, is programmable via a large number of configuration registers. These configuration registers are accessible to initialization BIOS routines via the PCI-Bus configuration address space. Figure 5.10 lists the DRAM configuration registers in the AMD-640.

Offset	Cache Control	Default	Recommended		Access
			Setting	Result	
58h	DRAM Configuration Register #1	40h	44h	10 bit Col	RW
59h	DRAM Configuration Register #2	05h	03h	banks 0-3 populated	RW
5Ah	DRAM Bank 0 Ending [HA29-22]	01h	10h	64M-02 for 8 Meg	RW
5Bh	DRAM Bank 1 Ending [HA29-22]	01h	20h	64M-04 for 8 Meg	RW
5Ch	DRAM Bank 2 Ending [HA29-22]	01h	30h	64M-06 for 8 Meg	RW
5Dh	DRAM Bank 3 Ending [HA29-22]	01h	40h	64M-08 for 8 Meg	RW
5Eh	DRAM Bank 4 Ending [HA29-22]	01h	50h	64M-08 for no RAM	RW
5Fh	DRAM Bank 5 Ending [HA29-22]	01h	60h	64M-08 for no RAM	RW
60h	DRAM Type	00h	00h 05h	Fast Page Mode banks 0-3 EDO mode	RW
61h	Shadow RAM Control Register #1	00h	CAh	Video BIOS	RW
62h	Shadow RAM Control Register #2	00h	00h	disable	RW
63h	Shadow RAM Control Register #3	00h	22h	main BIOS	RW
64h	DRAM Timing	ABh	FFh 4h 57h	slowest initially 60 nsec EDO 60 nsec FP	RW
65h	DRAM Control Register #1	00h	A4h	Page open Fast decode Latch delay	RW
66h	DRAM Control Register #2	00h	00h		RW
67h	32-bit DRAM Width Control Register	00h	00h	64 bit DRAM	RW
69h - 68h	Reserved	—	—	—	—
6Ah	DRAM Refresh Counter	00h	43h	15 μsec	RW
6Bh	DRAM Refresh Control Register	00h	80h	CBR	RW
6Ch	SDRAM Control Register	00h	00h	—	RW
6Dh	DRAM Drive Strength Control Register	00h	4Fh	24 ma drive	RW
6Eh	ECC Control Register	00h	00h	—	RW
6Fh	ECC Status Register	00h	00h	—	RO

Figure 5.10 DRAM CONTROL REGISTERS IN THE AMD-640 SYSTEM CONTROLLER

In PC platforms, the memory controller's design is heavily influenced by both technical and competitive requirements including: the use of asynchronous and synchronous DRAM, the organization of the DRAM into multiple banks, strict compatibility with the PC memory architecture, configuration flexibility, ease of system design, and aggressive performance and pricing. High performance is achieved via support for wide transfers and high clock rates and supporting system-level optimizations through improved bus transfer efficiency, reduced access latencies, and enabling system bus concurrencies. Configuration flexibility and ease of system design require that the memory controller hide most of its sophistication from the system designer, platform vendor, and especially the end user.

FPM, EDO, AND SDRAM SUPPORT

Current memory controllers must be designed to support Fast-Page-Mode DRAM, Extended-Data-Out DRAM, and Synchronous DRAM. SDRAM likely will supplant FPM and EDO DRAM in the near future, due to SDRAM's potential for superior system cost-performance. SDRAM represents a fundamentally new approach to DRAM main memory control that permits focus on system performance improvements rather than details of low-level timing. Presently, however, continued compatibility with FPM and EDO parts is important for mainstream PC platforms. Thus, the platform's memory controller must provide for the combination of the many demanding characteristics of FPM, EDO, and SDRAM. Future memory controllers will likely also support one or both of Rambus and SLDRAM.

All of these DRAM organizations multiplex row and column addresses over shared memory address pins and have multiple CPU-clock latencies for accesses to the first data item at random locations. Use of these parts requires the memory controller to carry out low-level unencoded direct control of the core.

A memory controller for asynchronous DRAM must manage and track a large number of dynamic conditions to ensure the core's proper operation. The timing parameters and their sequential relationship illustrated in the earlier simplified read-timing diagram represent but a subset of the overall DRAM timing parameters that the memory controller must comply with. The controller must implement all aspects of the timing behavior of the core's control signals and the controller's configuration must be programmed accordingly. This includes the coarse-grain inter-signal dependencies as well as the fine-grain cycle-by-cycle setup and hold-time behavior for each signal. Since the external control signals that drive the asynchronous DRAM are not captured via clocked latches, the memory controller must keep the control inputs constant while internal operations propagate through the core, optional data ouputs become valid, and the data is captured by the memory controller. The memory controller is responsible for the refresh function and tracking other time-outs affecting how accesses are implemented. To exploit page-mode timing, an on-going comparison of column addresses must be made to determine if the reduced access timing may be used. Continued CAS! signaling is then required to obtain subsequent data items within a page after the first access.

A memory controller for SDRAM must translate transaction requests for main memory into the encoded commands that the SDRAM expects. In contrast to a memory controller for asynchronous DRAM, it need only hold an encoded command valid until it is latched by the SDRAM at the end of the clock cycle. The memory controller can then transmit the next command to the SDRAM, or merely go to the idle state (by transmitting a no-operation command), while the SDRAM performs the first specified operation without further assistance from the memory controller. In conjunction with the SDRAM's internal interleaved bank organization, burst transfers, and by tracking current and past accesses, pipelining of memory accesses permits the memory controller to frequently overlap the beginning of the second access with the end of the first access. The system can thus generally hide precharge intervals caused by accesses to new random page locations. A memory controller for SDRAM must be configured to account for the access latencies (in number of cycles) of the particular SDRAM being used, but such coarse-grain timing is much more straightforward to implement than the demanding fine-grain timing required for the core control signals generated by a controller for asynchronous DRAM. A memory controller for SDRAM must also program the SDRAM upon system initialization to configure the desired behavior from the multiple available operating modes (including burst length, burst increment sequence, and read latency). As illustrated in Figure 5.11, the operating mode is programmed via address bits sent with the Mode Set Command.

CONSEQUENCES OF MULTIPLE BANKS OF DRAM

PC platform main memory is organized into multiple banks or multiple bank-pairs. This bank-focused organization permeates the memory controller's design and operation. The use of multiple banks permits increased performance through *interleaved*, or overlapping, memory access cycles to more than one bank. Also, selective mapping of row addressing bits, sequential pages in the linear memory address space maybe sequentially alternately distributed to each memory bank. Such *interleaved memory pages* increases the number of page-mode devices generally available to all execution threads. Design for the optional use of multiple banks also allows for memory expansion. To facilitate field and end user upgrades of memory, each DRAM bank is generally permitted to be of different type, density, pin configuration, and speed.

interleaved

interleaved memory pages

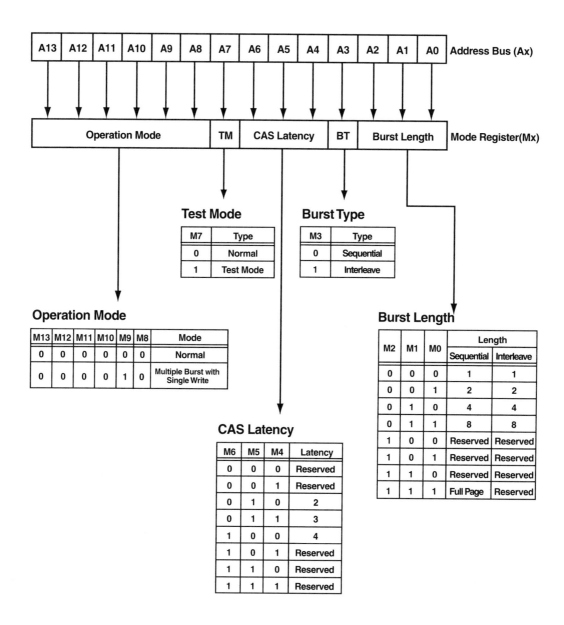

Figure 5.11 SDRAM OPERATING MODES

Reprinted by permission from *64Mb Synchronous DRAM*, copyright 1997, by International Business Machines Corporation.

The platform's memory controller must accommodate design issues that arise from the use of multiple banks in main memory. A first issue is that since it is desirable to dynamically optimize memory cycle times based on the behavior of recent access, and since the behavior of recent accesses is generally unique for each bank, the memory controller must maintain information about the state of each bank and control the timing of the DRAM memory cycles on a bank-by-bank basis.

bank-by-bank timing control

A second issue is that future memory upgrades need to be performed with little regard to matching the parameters of the original DRAM chips with those of the upgrade. It is unreasonable to require an originally installed bank of DRAM to be discarded or physically relocated. Also, since many naïve end users may perform such upgrades, such configuration flexibility greatly increases their success rate and reduces service complaints to the platform vendor. Thus, banks may be of a variety of memory capacities, having a respective variety of row/column address bit widths, and occupying various extents of the memory address space. Additionally, some platform chipsets permit further combinations.

accommodation of different bank capacities and widths

The above discussion must be revisited in view of the possible use of bank-pairs. *Bank-pairing* optionally permits two, 4-byte-wide, identical banks to function in unison as one 8-byte-wide bank-pair. This permits DRAM conforming to the older 72-pin SIMM packaging standard to provide double the bandwidth (at increased power consumption) over their use as only 4-byte-wide banks. Unless power consumption is a primary concern, such bank-pairing would normally be enabled. Figure 5.12 illustrates how six banks of 4-byte-wide FPM or EDO DRAM are configured as three, 8-byte-wide, bank-pairs in one example configuration of the AMD-640 System Controller.

Bank-pairing

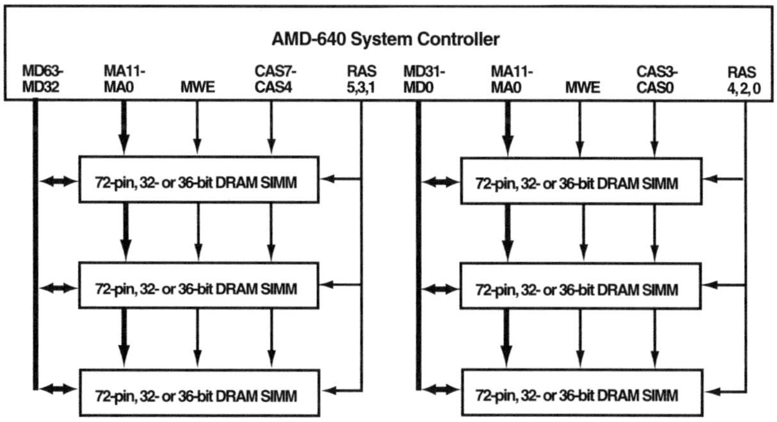

Figure 5.12 BANK-PAIRING

Copyright 1997/1998, Advanced Micro Devices Inc., used with permission.

However, when optional bank-pairing is made available, additional constraints may be imposed on bank use. For example, a unified control configuration may be used for each group of two banks, even though the banks within the group may not be operationally paired. This simplifies the logic design, but imposes the constraint that the DRAM in each bank of a bank-pair must be identical. Of course if bank-pairing is enabled, which it normally is for anything but a mobile application, the two banks should be identical anyway. The major problem of the identical bank constraint, is that while it is possible to populate only one bank of a bank-pair initially, and later correctly populate the remaining bank of the bank-pair, this presumes a level of future recollection, diligence, and care, that may in practice be difficult to achieve.

DESIGN NOTE

Memory Bank Configurations in the AMD-640

In the memory controller of the AMD-640 North-Bridge, there are six 4-byte-wide banks, which must be populated in contiguous order. The last bank populated is set in CR59h<2:0>*. Banks 0/1, 2/3, and 4/5 are considered bank-pairs. To simplify the logic design, these bank-pairs use a unified control configuration, and as a result, the DRAM in each bank of a bank-pair must be identical.

Bank-pairs consisting of 4-byte-wide FPM or EDO DRAM may be optionally configured for 8-byte-wide simultaneous accesses or separate 4-byte-wide access. Bank-pairing for SDRAM is for simplified control purposes only. The doubling of access width possible for the FPM and EDO parts is not possible for SDRAM parts. When using 8-byte-wide SDRAM, each of such banks may be optionally configured for 8-byte-wide simultaneous accesses or separate 4-byte-wide access.

While the banks within a bank-pair must be identical, different bank-pairs may still be of different data bit widths. (e.g., a first bank-pair may consist of two 4-byte-wide EDO DRAM (which may or may not be operated as a single 8-byte-wide bank-pair) while a second bank-pair may be two 8-byte-wide SDRAM.) Also, each bank-pair might be of arbitrary DRAM technology (e.g., it might be permissible to have a first bank-pair of FP and second bank-pair using EDO.)

This section refers numerous times to banks or access widths that are termed to be either 4 bytes wide or 8 bytes wide. If error checking is used, it is understood that these terms refer to widths of 36 bits and 72 bits, respectively. If error checking is not being used, it is to be understood that these terms refer to widths of 32 bits and 64 bits, respectively.

MEMORY CONTROLLER FUNCTIONS

There are a multiplicity of functions performed by the PC platform memory controller. Nevertheless, most of these functions can be conceptually partitioned into a few broad categories: the transaction reception from multiple request ports, state-machine controller, address processing logic, data routing and staging logic, I/O interface to multiple DRAM banks, and programmable configuration logic. Each of these categories will be given an initial overview, followed by more detailed discussions in select areas.

Transaction Requests from Multiple Sources

Each of the other major ports on the North-Bridge (i.e., the CPU/Cache, PCI-Buses and AGP) may be the source for a transaction with the main memory. While the exact protocols and capabilities vary among these interfaces, each somehow conveys at least an initial starting address and an indication of the transaction desired (e.g., a bus "command" control signal). Depending upon the particular bus attached, the main memory-to-bus interfaces may need to optionally support burst transfers, transfers of reduced width, and possibly other operations, such as touching, masking, and other modest manipulations (that are generally performed on the data in transit via selective transmission or routing and do not require logic that would introduce perceptible delays). Requests that involve writes will additionally include the data being written to main memory.

The transaction command information from each of the major ports is coupled to the state-machine controller. The state-machine controller is responsible for the dynamic behavior of the memory controller. It processes the transaction commands received from each of the major ports, it implements all necessary state changes to generate all required control signals and execute various types of requested DRAM accesses. The state-machine controller also performs "housekeeping" tasks, necessary for proper operation, but largely independent of the transaction commands.

processing of bus transaction commands

State-Machine Control of FPM and EDO DRAM

The portion of the state-machine controller responsible for the control of FPM and EDO DRAM is generally implemented as a multiplicity of interacting state machines, each tracking a particular aspect of operation. For example, each bank may have a dedicated state machine from which the bank's RAS! signal is derived. Likewise, there may be a similarly dedicated state machine from which the CAS! signals are derived. These and other state machines control all aspects of the activation and timing of the internal controls for row and column address multiplexing; row and column address strobes; output enables for address and data; read/write controls;

determination of timing diagram behavior

and data I/O buffering and routing. The state machines are the underlying physical mechanism that determines the timing diagram behavior of all asynchronous DRAM signals, including the interdependence between signals, and the cycle-by-cycle timing for each signal.

DESIGN NOTE

Memory Bank Selection for Asynchronous DRAM in the AMD-640

When the AMD-640 is controlling FPM and EDO DRAM, 4-byte-wide DRAM banks 0, 2, and 4 are driven by a first set of 4 CAS! lines. The 4-byte-wide banks 1, 3, and 5 are driven by a second set of 4 CAS! lines. Bank-pairs configured for 8-byte-wide simultaneous accesses effectively are driven by 8 CAS! lines. These lines double as column address strobes and byte enables (selects). Only those bytes specifically requested will have their CAS! lines brought active. The memory controller will process the starting address and access width of a request into one or more DRAM access cycles, each generating a bank select, row and column addresses, and one or more contiguous byte enables (CAS! lines). Accesses straddling 4-byte boundaries for 4-byte-wide banks, and 8-byte boundaries for 8-byte-wide bank-pairs, result in two separate cycles, with the most significant byte enables active in the first cycle and the least significant byte enables active in the second cycle.

The timing of the address, strobe, and data sequencing is a function of the type of DRAM memory being accessed in the selected bank, the address of the access to be performed, the immediate past history of accesses in the selected bank (including the address of the last access and the current state of RAS! and CAS!), the type of memory access being performed (read, write, read-modify-write, burst), and the possible need for refresh.

REPORT ON CD-ROM

To learn more about Asynchronous DRAM Timing, see the IBM Application Note, *Understanding DRAM Performance Specifications*, on the companion CD-ROM.

State-Machine Control of SDRAM

Coarse-grain timing and sequencing of the SDRAM core is carried out indirectly via digital binary-encoded commands, in direct contrast to the fine-grain analog-esque control used for FPM and EDO DRAM. A memory controller for SDRAM emits the commands for sampling on each ris-

emission of SDRAM commands

ing clock edge of the SDRAMs' clocked command interface. The SDRAM command interface maps each encoded command into the desired low-level operation and accordingly executes the fine-grain timing and sequencing of the core's control signals.

The memory controller for SDRAM generates the encoded command primarily using the CAS!, RAS! and WE! lines. These lines are commonly coupled to the command decoder of all banks, with each bank command decoder also receiving a new bank-specific CS! (chip-select) line. The four signals are captured and evaluated by the command decoder within each SDRAM. Only a select one of the bank-specific CS! lines is active, such that only one bank's SDRAM command decoder is enabled. In those banks where the CS! line is deasserted, previous commands continue execution, and the encoded command inputs are ignored.

Aspects of the interface between the memory controller and SDRAM are reminiscent of asynchronous DRAM operation, but constrained to operate within the confines of a clock period. Addresses are multiplexed as row and column address components over a dedicated address bus, shared by all banks. Data to all banks are sent over a dedicated data bus, also shared by all banks. Information on the addresses and data inputs are latched on the rising clock edge of each cycle. If a command is latched at the same time that defines meaningful processing for the contemporaneous address or data information, that information is processed during the subsequent cycle. On reads, the output data is valid for one cycle, at the end of which the memory controller must latch the data. Each address component is sent in conjunction with a separate command. The row address is transmitted over the address bus simultaneously with a Bank Activate command, which is encoded such that RAS! is asserted, but WE! and CAS! are not. The column address is transmitted over the address bus simultaneously with either a Read or Write command, which is encoded such that CAS! is asserted, RAS! is deasserted, and WE! is either deasserted or asserted, respectively.

While tracking low-level timing is greatly simplified, and the SDRAM can generally be permitted to idle between commands, the memory controller must still keep track of certain aspects of correct sequencing and certain time-outs. For example, the Bank Activate command must be given prior to either a Read or Write command. Also, a bank is not permitted to remain active without precharge beyond a critical time interval.

The memory controller also generates the DQM7! through DQM0! data mask bits, which drive the SDRAM's I/O buffers coupled to the data bus. The data masks function as per byte enables. On reads these enables select (with a two-clock latency) whether the buffers are in a high impedance mode (deasserted), or are driving the data bus with data (asserted). On writes these enables select (with zero clock latency) whether the input data from the data bus will be ignored (deasserted) or written (asserted). Finally, the memory controller for SDRAM must generate the clock enable CKE,

The command encodings chosen (and listed earlier in Table 5.1 on page 438, are clearly reminiscent of asynchronous DRAM operation. This provides designers with a level of familiarity, has mnemonic value, and likely results in some logic minimizations in the implementation of the core control signals. Nevertheless, because the clocked command interface isolates the core from the memory controller, it should be understood that the encodings are theoretically arbitrary.

which controls clock generation internal to the SDRAM. CKE may be used to initiate Power Down, Suspend, and Self-Refresh modes, depending on how the SDRAM has been configured. CAS!, RAS!, WE!, CS!, and DQMx! are all sampled on each rising clock edge.

Address Processing

The address processing functions include, in the conceptual order of processing: address relocation, address decoding, and address multiplexing. *Address relocation* acts to map certain programmable ranges of transaction-supplied addresses to different addresses. The mappings provide legacy compatibility with the PC memory architecture and functionality and performance enhancements related to reserved BIOS areas of the PC memory architecture or System Management Mode. One relocation option permits reclamation of DRAM locations that are otherwise inaccessible, because they coincide with reserved BIOS addresses. This relocation acts to extend the highest memory address available by the extent of memory relocated. A second relocation option instead makes the DRAM coinciding with the reserved BIOS addresses to be used for a private System Management address space. Shadowing is a third relocation option that permits BIOS code to be executed from the main memory DRAM, rather than slower BIOS ROM.

address relocation

Once address relocation has been performed, *address decoding* identifies the destination DRAM bank or bank-pair to the state-machine controller. The bank selects are combinational functions of the relocated address and the programmable configuration information, including the densities of the installed DRAMs, the possible use of multi-bank interleave, and the data widths of the installed banks and bank-pairs.

address decoding

Each memory cycle, the state-machine controller dynamically configures *address multiplexing* logic in the address processing logic to appropriately parse the memory address into row, column, and byte-select components and sequence the row and column address components over the common DRAM address bus. The routing of address bits to row and column address bits is a combinational function of the relocated address and the programmable configuration information, in particular the row/column address bit-width and the access byte-width of the bank or bank-pair selected by the address decode logic. Figure 5.13 illustrates a typical mapping of physical address bits to row and column address bits in the AMD-640 System Controller. The state-machine controller coordinates the address sequencing over the common DRAM address bus with the address strobes to the appropriate DRAM bank and byte selects and the data sequencing over the common DRAM data bus.

address multiplexing

EDO/FP DRAM

Reg 59h Bits 7-5		MA13	MA12	MA11	MA10	MA9	MA8	MA7	MA6	MA5	MA4	MA3	MA2	MA1	MA0	Row:Col
000	Row		23	22	21	11	20	19	18	17	16	15	14	13	12	12:8, 13:8
	Column							10	9	8	7	6	5	4	3	
001	Row		24	23	22	21	20	19	18	17	16	15	14	13	12	10:9, 12:9, 13:9
	Column						11	10	9	8	7	6	5	4	3	
010	Row		25	24	23	21	20	19	18	17	16	15	14	13	12	11:10, 12:10, 13:10
	Column					22	11	10	9	8	7	6	5	4	3	
011	Row		26	25	23	21	20	19	18	17	16	15	14	13	12	12:11, 13:11
	Column				24	22	11	10	9	8	7	6	5	4	3	
100	Row		27	25	23	21	20	19	18	17	16	15	14	13	12	13:12
	Column			26	24	22	11	10	9	8	7	6	5	4	3	

SDRAM

Reg 59h Bits 7-5		MA13	MA12	MA11	MA10	MA9	MA8	MA7	MA6	MA5	MA4	MA3	MA2	MA1	MA0	Row:Col
0xx 16 Mbit	Row			11	11	22	21	20	19	18	17	16	15	14	13	11:10, 11:9, 11:8
	Column			11	PC	24	23	10	9	8	7	6	5	4	3	
1xx 64 Mbit Rev C	Row	12	13	25	22	21	20	19	18	17	16	15	14	24	23	x4 (14:10) x8 (14:9)
	Column	12	13	11	PC	26	11	10	9	8	7	6	5	4	3	
1xx 64 Mbit Rev D	Row	25	12	13	22	21	20	19	18	17	16	15	14	24	23	x4 (14:10) x8 (14:9)
	Column	25	12	13	PC	26	11	10	9	8	7	6	5	4	3	

Figure 5.13 MAPPING OF PHYSICAL ADDRESS BITS TO ROW AND COLUMN ADDRESS BITS IN THE AMD-640 SYSTEM CONTROLLER

Copyright 1997, Advanced Micro Devices, Inc., used with permission.

DESIGN NOTE

Address Signals and Address Control in the AMD-640

In the AMD-640, up to 14 bits of multiplexed address bus signals (MA<13:0>) are shared by all banks of DRAM. DRAM banks 0, 2, and 4 share a first 4-byte-wide data bus, MD<31:0>. Banks 1, 3, and 5 share a second 4-byte-wide data bus, MD<63:32>. Banks configured as bank-pairs effectively share an 8-byte-wide data bus, MD<63:0>. MPD<7:0> is optionally used for parity and ECC error detection and correction, when DRAMs are used that support such features.

The concatenated row and column address is effectively prescaled by 2 bits for 4-byte-wide banks, due to the use of unencoded byte-selects, CAS!<3:0>. The concatenated row and column address is effectively prescaled by 3 bits for 8-byte- wide bank-pairs, due to the use of 8-bit unencoded byte-selects (CAS!<7:0> for FPM and EDO parts) or data masks (DQM!<7:0> for SDRAM parts). The same physical lines are used for CAS!<7:0> and DQM!<7:0>, the line's functionality being defined by the memory controller configuration.

For FPM and EDO parts, RAS!<5:0> is used to activate a specific bank and strobe in the row-address. For SDRAM, the same physical lines are reconfigured and renamed as CS!<5:0>, which serve solely as chip-selects, used to enable the SDRAM on-chip interface command decoders. MWE is a write-enable signal that is shared by all of the FPM and EDO DRAM.

For SDRAM, the AMD-640 provides a clock CLK and clock-enable CKE. The clock is synchronous to and running at the same rate as the CPU clock. The AMD-640 also provides additional signals SRASx!, SCASx!, and SWEx!, corresponding to the generic RAS!, CAS!, and WE! terminology used in the main text. (The x symbol represents one of three identical logic function drive signals, designated by A, B, and C, which allow parallel drive of up to three load trees.) These signals make up the encoded bit-field command that defines the SDRAM's next operation.

Programmable Configuration

A PC platform memory controller permits the system designer a wide scope of customization with respect to part types, organization, and modes of use. This flexibility in behavior is generally accomplished by using per-bank and global configuration parameters to alter the timing and sequencing of the state machines in the state-machine controller. These configuration parameters are held in the CRs detailed earlier in

Figure 5.10 on page 447. Programmable registers may be included to cover the configuration of multiple DRAM types, densities, low-level timing, error detection (including parity or ECC), drive strengths, bank access-width, and refresh.

DESIGN NOTE

System BIOS Memory Detection using the AMD-640

During platform power up and initialization, the memory detection function of the system BIOS evaluates each bank for type and size, starting with bank 0. During bank evaluation the memory controller's "last bank populated" parameter is set to the number of the bank under test. The test addresses generated are kept greater than the known size of previously evaluated banks, if any, while the last bank populated configuration ensures that no bank number greater than the one under test will be enabled. Once the type and size of a bank is determined, the last-bank-populated parameter is incremented and the type and size of the next bank is evaluated.

The type of memory is tested by a write, read, compare sequence using modified EDO timing. If the compare is correct, the bank is EDO. If the test fails, FPM timing is used, and the test repeated. If the compare is correct, the bank is FPM. If the test fails, SDRAM timing is used, and the test repeated to confirm correct operation. All tests are performed across eight consecutive bytes to confirm that both banks in a bank-pair are identical. At the end of a successful compare the memory detection routine sets the bank type in the configuration registers and then proceeds to test the size.

The size of memory is tested by starting with the maximum valid memory column address size and testing for a successful compare at all possible memory densities, starting with the largest. Upon finding a successful compare, the memory detection routine sets the bank size in the configuration registers.

The platform's system BIOS executes *Power-On-Self-Test (POST)* routines from its ROM early during system initialization. These routines will detect the type and size of DRAM installed in the memory banks attached to the memory controller and program the DRAM type and size configuration registers accordingly. The remaining configuration registers are restored from some form of nonvolatile storage, generally the CMOS Memory. The use the CMOS memory has supplanted the earlier use of switches and jumpers on the platform's motherboard to configure bank parameters. If the values in CMOS memory are not present, the POST routines will load the remaining configuration registers with default values from ROM.

Power-On-Self-Test (POST)

<u>DRAM Type and Size</u>

The particular type of FPM, EDO, or SDRAM for each bank or bank-pair must be identified, so that the state-machine controller and DRAM interface can be configured appropriately. Multiple DRAM densities are supported by indicating a starting address and size for each bank. Or alternatively, the memory controller may require population of the banks in order, contiguous population of the address space, and the specification of an ending address. This information is used by the address decoders in the address processing logic to identify the appropriate bank to be accessed for each transaction address. Because there may be more than one combination of row and column bit-widths for a given density, this information also must be provided to the memory controller. See Figure 5.13 on page 457.

DESIGN NOTE

DRAM Type and Size Support in the AMD-640

In the AMD-640, 36-bit or 32-bit FPM and EDO DRAM in 72-pin SIMMs are supported in 1-, 2-, 4-, and 16-Mbit densities. 72-bit or 64-bit SDRAM in 168-pin DIMMs is supported in 16- and 64-Mbit densities. (The greater bit widths in each type are required for the use of parity or ECC.) The type of DRAM is configured in CR60h, by bits <5:4>, <3:2>, and <1:0>, for bank-pairs 4/5, 2/3, and 0/1, respectively. (Banks within bank-pairs must be identical.)

Banks must be populated in order and contiguously populate the address space. Each bank's ending address must be specified to the memory controller. CR5A-5Fh are used for banks 0-5, respectively. The column-address size (bit-width) is specified in CR58h<7:5>, CR58h<3:1>, and CR59h<7:5>, for bank pairs 0/1, 2/3, and 4/5, respectively.

REPORTS ON CD-ROM

To learn more about Programmable Configuration, see the following reports on the companion CD-ROM:

- *Application Note AMD K86 Family BIOS Design*, Document 21329, June 1997.
- *AMD K86 Family BIOS and Software Tools Developers Guide*.

This chapter concluded our examination of component-level technologies that play important roles in PC platform architecture. We described how increased processor and I/O performance is forcing a transition from the asynchronous DRAMs common in the past to synchronous DRAMs. PM, FPM, EDO, and SDRAM operating principles were discussed. The emerging Rambus and SLDRAM memory types were briefly introduced. Finally, memory controller requirements for FPM, EDO, and SDRAM were overviewed. Chapter 6 looks at techniques to optimize the platform and the directions in which the platform is heading.

CHAPTER SUMMARY

Chapter 6
Platform Optimization Techniques and Directions

This chapter discusses how contemporary platform architectures are changing to track evolving uses of the PC platform and to continually improve system performance. The discussion relies upon and ties together the platform standards, initiatives, and technology components presented in Chapters 4 and 5.

About half of the chapter is devoted to a tutorial on platform optimization, including a survey of techniques and selected examples. Going beyond the obvious fundamentals of increasing operating rates and shifting to faster technology, the survey is a compilation of basic optimization concepts applicable to contemporary platform designs. The survey is followed by an examination of how the optimization basics are applied in contemporary 3D graphics platforms.

The second half of the chapter discusses the directions in which the PC platform is evolving and the factors presently driving the changes. Attention is especially given to the dynamic developments in platform content and connectivity. The sections on platform directions include a study of contemporary design issues, examines a planned progression of changes to the platform architecture, and looks at forecasts for the near and long-term future.

ROAD MAP OF CHAPTER 6

Section	Audience
Survey Of Platform Performance Optimizations	Students and those practitioners, managers and faculty who what to study outside their area of specialization

ROAD MAP OF CHAPTER 6

Section	Audience
Platform Directions	Students and those unfamiliar with the PC industry's vision for future platforms and connected computing
The following more detailed subsections: Performance Optimization Specifics in a Contemporary 3D Graphics Platform	All
Geometry, Rendering, and Display— The 3D Graphics Pipeline	All

SURVEY OF PLATFORM PERFORMANCE OPTIMIZATIONS

IMPROVING DATA MOVEMENT AND MANIPULATION IN THE PLATFORM

The essence of computing is data movement and manipulation. Bit patterns are moved (routed between source and destination resources) and operated on at a low level to implement functions at far-removed levels of abstraction. A universe of data movement and manipulation solutions exists for every computing problem. System performance optimization is the pursuit of those system solutions that enable getting more work done in less time for a given level of investment.

The system computing environment includes the operating system, applications, and hardware architecture. Changes in the behavior of each of these components, as well as the manner in which they interact, can have a dramatic impact on performance. Here we will emphasize how platform hardware architecture affects system performance.

Different system hardware-architecture solutions have variations in topology, system resources, and methods of operation. These system resources include the processor, a hierarchically organized memory subsystem, various I/O peripherals, buses and other interconnects, bus bridges, and resource controllers. Within each resource there are possible variations in organization and technology.

Performance optimization generally focuses on improving the speed and efficiency with which the system carries out data movements and data manipulations to accomplish high-level functions. The possible solution variations at the hardware-architecture and resource level offer different speeds and efficiencies for data movements and manipulations, leading to different levels of performance.

In the absence of radically different system-level algorithms, efficiency improvements generally require increased sophistication in the management of expensive system resources. This includes minimizing the number of required data transfers between resources and minimizing unnecessary resource use while maximizing productive resource use. Speed improvements generally involve increasing the rate of required data transfers and resource operations. Improvements to either speed or efficiency may require additional system resources. The additional resources may take the form of new types of system resources or merely augmentation (e.g., increasing bit widths) of existing resources.

Cost and other system constraints are frequently at odds with improving system speed and efficiency. In particular, the processor is often called upon to perform operations that, from strictly a performance perspective, might best be carried out by a dedicated data pump or specialized coprocessor. For a particular target market, however, the increased system cost for the additional system resources may compromise sales in an unacceptable manner.

Platform Focus Areas for Performance Optimization

Platform focus areas for optimizing performance include meeting the data requirements of applications, the appropriate use and configuration of system resources, cautious management of data movement or bus traffic between system resources, and specification of the overall system architecture and its operation. Meeting data requirements of applications primarily involves the ability to meet maximum latency delays and deliver minimum sustained throughput rates. System resources that should be examined closely for optimal operation include the CPU; buses, ports, and sideband signals; data-staging storage devices (including buffers, caches, and queues); bridges/controllers; peripherals; and memory. The specification of the system architecture and operation is done carefully to achieve performance that is well apportioned and tuned. In this section we will overview optimization issues for required data movements, for overall system design, and specific optimizations for buses, data-staging storage devices, and bridges.

Application Processing

Application processing executes data transfers among the CPU, memory arrays, and disk files, in conjunction with the maintenance and manipulation of data structures and data streams, searching, formatting, and conditional control. Application developers can minimize unnecessary data movements through good programming discipline, algorithm selection and optimization, and the use of optimizing compilers.

Data movements and Data manipulations are examined in more detail in conjunction with Figure 6.3 on page 486 & Figure 6.4 on page 487, later in this chapter.

processor recognition

CPUID instruction

Application developers should also use *processor recognition* techniques to identify particular processors. The primary tool of processor recognition is the *CPUID instruction*. This instruction returns processor information including the vendor, model number, revision, features, and name. Dynamically determined knowledge of the processor being used permits the application to exploit processor-specific optimizations without penalizing or preventing application execution on other processors. Whenever available, the use of specialty instruction sets for floating-point, multimedia, and 3D graphics delivers increased performance on corresponding specialty workloads, while reducing system bus traffic.

Reports on CD-ROM

Software Customization for Performance Optimization

If a x86 processor meets Microsoft's *Designed for Windows* certification requirements and is compatible with the physical and electrical features of a motherboard, the processor and motherboard should be functional for generic Microsoft Windows software without mandatory customization. However, customization for a specific processor is necessary to realize *any* benefits of instruction set extensions. Customization is also necessary to optimize performance for each processor's unique microarchitecture.

We have included on the CD-ROM the K6 documents listed below, which are useful to customizing BIOS, system, and application software. Comparable documents will exist for other processors. The first two provide information particular to BIOS design. The remaining documents (two on processor recognition, two on code optimization, and two on instruction set extensions) are applicable to all types of software development.

- *AMD K86 Family BIOS and Software Tools*, Developers Guide, Document 21062E/0-June 1997.
- *AMD K86 Family BIOS Design*, Document 21329, December 1997
- *AMD Processor Recognition*, Publication #20734, January 1998.
- *Processor Recognition Code Sample*, Publication #21035.
- *AMD-K6 3D Processor Code Optimization*, Publication #21924, February 1998.
- *AMD-K6 MMX Enhanced Processor x86 Code Optimization*, Publication #21828, August 1997.
- *AMD-K6 MMX Enhanced Processor Multimedia Technology*, Publication #20726C/0-June 1997.
- *AMD-3D Technology Manual*, Publication #21928, February 1998.

Overall System Architecture Performance Optimization

To optimize platform performance, attention needs to be given to the platform's hardware resources, topology, resource management policies, and performance features and management policies internal to each resource. This section presents a compilation of general and specific performance optimization guiding basics and brainstorming ideas for each of these areas. The format of the presentation is to introduce a set of performance optimization basics in a definition box. Below each box is a discussion that expands on how the particular boxed set of rules is applicable in platforms.

The rules given are for *performance* optimization. In PC platforms however, often something else is being optimized. For example, the USB and IEEE 1394 buses discussed in Chapter 4 are directly contrary to many of the performance optimization basics that we will present for platform-level buses. These buses seek to combine devices on the same bus, reduce bus widths, and increase competition for the bus, all of which negatively impact performance. What is happening is that these buses provide good performance, but are not optimized solely for performance. They are optimized for attaching large numbers of peripherals, requiring minimal system resources per peripheral, and having extreme ease of configuration.

Optimizing for performance is not always the primary goal, but it is usually an important factor in any optimization. The rules given in this chapter are thus useful for other optimizations in that you can anticipate how changes motivated by other concerns will likely affect performance.

PLATFORM PERFORMANCE OPTIMIZATION BASICS

Stipulations and Caveats

1. The rules attempt to optimize for *performance* only
2. You must use judgement, common sense, and an engaged mind to successfully apply the rules
3. You must determine when the application of a rule has reached a point of diminishing return
4. You must determine if a rule does not apply due to situational design constraints
5. You must be alert for undesirable side effects
6. Generally, you must trade off cost, power, and size against performance
7. You must weigh the impact of a change in terms of its costs and benefits
8. There will be situations in which the best choice is contrary to one or more of the rules

General Platform-Level Performance Optimization Principles

PLATFORM PERFORMANCE OPTIMIZATION BASICS[a]
General Platform Principles
1. Seek to increase operating rates.
2. Seek to increase resource operating-widths.
3. Seek to increase the efficient use of high-demand resources.
4. Seek to reduce the number of subsystems that process each task.
5. Seek to keep expensive resources continuously productive.

[a]. See Stipulations and Caveats on page 467.

The first optimization principle is fundamental. Intuitively, overall platform performance is proportional to the useful work per operating cycle times the operating rate (in cycles per second). It's obvious that work performed per unit-time goes up if you can make the platform go faster.

The second optimization principle is also fundamental, known in different form as the time-space trade-off. Loosely, this states that more bits operating in parallel will get work done faster than fewer bits operating sequentially. Thus overall platform performance, being proportional to work per unit-time, goes up if you can increase the useful work per operating cycle. For some tasks simply replicating operating resources can do this. At the lowest level this includes increasing resource bit widths.

The third general optimization principle suggests that the platform architect should, for each platform process that uses a system resource, seek solutions that decrease unnecessary use. Such solutions are instrumental in improving the performance of other processes that compete for access to the resource under consideration, and thereby generally improve the performance of the system as a whole.

As applied to buses, this means to attempt to eliminate or reduce the number of bus transactions and transfers required. Discovery of such higher efficiency bus-using processes tends to reduce process stalls and bus latencies due to the bus being busy when needed by a second process. It also reduces the need to purchase additional bus bandwidth.

Applying this principle may require the platform architect to increase widths, use data staging, divert specialty traffic to dedicated buses, use command-driven dedicated accelerators or bus-masters on isolated sub-segments, improve bus protocols, or use data compression. Such techniques are discussed throughout this section.

> ### DEFINITIONS
>
> #### Stalls and Latencies
>
> In the platform context of the present discussion, a *stall* is a platform event in which an executing task is forced to be idle unproductively, while some crucial enabling condition is unrealizable or some essential resource is unavailable to the task.
>
> At the platform level, *latency* describes the duration of a stall. In contemporary synchronous designs, platform-level tasks proceed with execution only at time intervals defined by the operating cycle of the required function-units. In turn, function-unit cycles are integral multiples of the platform's clock cycle. Depending on the platform's dynamic workload and the design of the platform, the latency of a stall may be momentary, no more than one function-unit cycle, or may be much larger. Thus, *stalls* are incidents of unproductive idling, while *latencies* are a measure of how much time is lost.
>
> *Latency* more broadly refers to the duration of any delay. At the device or device-interface level, latency describes electrical or mechanical delays that are measured in small fractions of a second, which act to limit operating rates.

The fourth general optimization principle suggests that the platform architect should, for each subsystem, seek solutions that keep task processing isolated within each subsystem and minimize the involvement of the CPU and other subsystems. Autonomous bus-masters, DMA, and special-purpose accelerators are examples of techniques to keep task processing localized and have the added benefit that they off-load the CPU. Dedicated signal paths, such as the AGP between the North-Bridge and the graphics accelerator, and a "video capture" port that couples streaming video directly into the video accelerator, are examples of techniques that keep data off of the general system buses and localized within a single subsystem. Such methods improve system bus bandwidth and processor availability, reducing the need to pay for greater bus bandwidth and processing power, and help to increase overall system concurrency and multi-tasking performance.

The fifth general optimization principle suggests that the platform architect should, for each subsystem, seek solutions that improve the utilization of expensive system resources. Ideally, the major system resources should be kept continually busy. Thus, the platform architect should look for ways to increase concurrency throughout the system, primarily by orchestrating overlapping processes in multiple independent subsystems. This is enabled by selective isolation of the various platform subsystems, explicit pipelining, and by out-of-order processing of younger short tasks that can independently overlap with, and thereby effectively hide, older long latency tasks. The platform architect should first look for solutions wherein modest additions of inexpensive resources may enable expensive resources to be more fully exploited.

Specific Performance Optimizations Made at the Platform Level

Basics for Management of Platform Interconnect Resources

PLATFORM PERFORMANCE OPTIMIZATION BASICS[b]
Bus Optimization at the Platform Level
1. Seek to reduce unnecessary bus transactions and transfers.
2. Seek to normally isolate buses capable of concurrent operation.
3. Seek to increase the number of continuously productive buses.
4. Seek to reduce simultaneous competition for each bus.
5. Seek to minimize the use of Programmed I/O (PIO).
6. Seek to command normally isolated bus-mastering accelerators.
7. Seek to transfer compressed data.
8. Seek to keep streaming data out of general-purpose subsystems.
9. Seek to maximize block sizes and minimize per-block latencies.

[b] See Stipulations and Caveats on page 467.

The above platform-level optimizations focus on how effectively expensive system resources and subsystems are interconnected with each other. Accordingly, actions taken according to these suggestions often impact the organization and operation of multiple subsystems.

Buses are the resources used to interconnect system components, either via time-share access by multiple system components, or via dedicated access between only two components. The platform architect should seek to eliminate or reduce unnecessary bus transactions and transfers for each bus throughout the platform.

Bus-bridges can be used to couple together two diverse buses or subsegments of the same bus. While frequently coupling is a necessity, it should not otherwise be done, in order to maximize the isolation of the various subsystems. Isolated subsystems can then process different tasks concurrently, maximizing overall system work.

It is also essential that contention for a bus by multiple requesters is not unduly limiting access to a crucial system resource, resulting in stalls to the processing of a task needing the resource. If necessary, the platform architect can increase the number of buses capable of concurrent operation, or decrease the number of devices that share each bus. Such measures generally mean the addition of point-to-point busing directly between devices that need coupling, and possibly the addition of physical ports to selected resources.

DEFINITION

Contention

In the present system optimization context, *contention* means the simultaneous competition for a system resource, in particular, a bus. Such competition results in stalls and increased latencies.

Arbitration is the process by which a competing process wins access to a resource that is subject to contention. Processes *request* the resource from an *Arbitrator* that will *grant* access. Arbitration algorithms must take into account factors including maximum allowable latencies, process priorities, and fairness of access.

In a bus's electrical performance context, *contention* means multiple I/O drivers fighting to drive a node to different signal levels. If not controlled this can cause unreliable operation, current spikes, high power dissipation, and premature device failure.

For many tasks, (such as compression, large block transfers, and graphics rendering), dedicated data pumps, controllers, and accelerators should be employed wherever possible. Anytime the processor can be relieved from carrying out a task by a dedicated controller, the available processing power for other tasks is increased. Generally, the system bus traffic is also reduced, increasing the available bus bandwidth for other tasks.

The transfer of compressed data clearly permits available bus bandwidth to be used more effectively, but it requires special processing by both source and destination. Such special processing needs to be integrated into the overall system operation to prevent process stalls. Compression also add latency that would not otherwise exist. The additional latency must be evaluated to determine if the use of compression is viable. Ideally, compression and decompression should be performed in peripheral subsystem dedicated hardware, and not by the processor.

Streaming data types need to be treated specially. Unless processor based DSP is required, or the streamed data is to be otherwise acted on by the processor in the near future, streaming data are preferably coupled via dedicated data paths directly into destination subsystems and kept out of caches. Large data transfers, including streaming video, must be broken into block transfers, if the data are being transferred over general-purpose buses. Otherwise, large transfer may cause excessive latencies for other devices on the bus.

System-Mediated Large Byte-Count Transfers

System software normally decomposes large data transfers into multiple smaller "block" transfers. This is necessary for a number of reasons, including maximum available main memory buffer sizes and maximum allowable latencies for other tasks that need timely access to system services and resources. However, when a file transfer is decomposed into multiple block transfers, there is invariably some time penalty incurred on each of the blocks. This *per-block latency* may be partly due to overhead delays, arising from device and interface physical limitations and interface protocol requirements, which must be incurred for each block. The per-block latency may also be due to other system events that are allowed to execute before control is returned to the ongoing transfer; or due to sloppily, carelessly, or naively written system software.

per-block latency

Three expressions useful in evaluating the effect of per-block latency are given below. *Effective Data Rate* provides the real throughput at which the large byte-count data transfer is being accomplished. *Realizable Data Rate Fraction* provides the ratio of effective data rate to raw data rate and thus makes explicit what fraction of the raw data rate is being realized. *Rate Degradation* reexpresses the Realizable Data Rate Fraction in terms of a percentage loss.

Effective Data Rate

Realizable Data Rate Fraction

Rate Degradation

The above expressions find application in the analysis of networks and wherever else large transfers must be made via smaller block transfers.[75][76]

DEFINITION
Effective Data Rate
$$\text{Effective data rate} = \frac{\text{Block size}}{\left(\dfrac{\text{Block size}}{\text{Raw data rate}}\right) + \text{Per-block latency}}$$
(sizes are in bytes, rates are in bytes per second, latency is in seconds)

[75] "The ABCs of Capacity Planning," *LAN Magazine*, Dec. 1996, Miller Freeman Inc.

[76] "Memory Technology Still Needs to 'Catch Up'," *Electronic News*, Feb. 3, 1997, Cahners Publishing Company.

DEFINITION
Realizable Data Rate Fraction

$$\text{Realizable Data Rate Fraction} = \left(\frac{\text{Effective Data Rate}}{\text{Raw Data Rate}} \right)$$

$$= \left(1 + \text{Effective raw data rate} \cdot \frac{\text{Per-block latency}}{\text{Block size}} \right)^{-1}$$

(sizes are in bytes, rates are in bytes per second, latency is in seconds)

DEFINITION
Rate Degradation

$$\text{Rate Degradation} = (1 - \text{Realizable Data Rate Fraction}) \times 100$$

$$= \frac{100}{1 + \dfrac{\text{Block size}}{\text{Realizable Data Rate} \cdot \text{Per-block latency}}}$$

(Rate Degradation is a percentage, sizes are in bytes, rates are in bytes per second, latency is in seconds)

Additional insight can be obtained by normalizing the raw data rate by the ratio of block size to per-block latency (block size / per-block latency) and plotting either the realizable data rate fraction or rate degradation as a function of the normalized raw data rate. Figure 6.1 is a plot of rate degradation. This reveals the usefulness of the (block size / per-block latency) ratio as a transfer rate performance metric.

The (block size/per-block latency) metric acts as a plot "breakpoint," in that at a normalized raw data rate equal to one, the rate degradation reaches 50%. For raw data rates an order of magnitude or less than the breakpoint, rate degradation is often negligible. For raw data rates within an order of magnitude either above or below the breakpoint, rate degradation increases rapidly with raw data rate and can be quite large. For raw data rates an order of magnitude or greater than the breakpoint, rate degradation is very large.

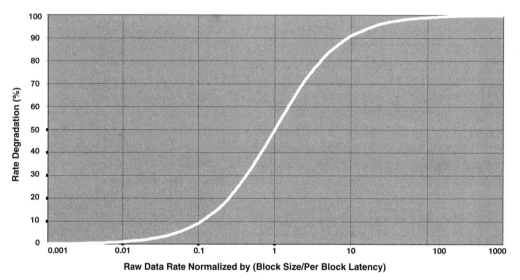

Figure 6.1 RATE DEGRADATION

Design trade-offs must be made to ensure that the effective data rate is sufficient to avoid any user-perceived discontinuities or system malfunctions, while ensuring that other system tasks are not left waiting for excessive periods during block transfers. Per-block latencies, block sizes, and the resulting rate degradation should be tracked closely for all transfers. There is little point in paying for a higher raw data rate device interface if the higher rate is not effectively realizable.

Platform Data-Staging Basics

PLATFORM PERFORMANCE OPTIMIZATION BASICS[c]
Platform Data-Staging
1. Seek to exploit spatial and temporal locality of reference.
2. Seek to avoid stalls.
3. Seek to reduce latencies.
4. Seek to reduce data traffic between subsystems.
5. Seek to smoothly couple subsystems operating at different rates.
6. Seek to identify optimal block size.

[c] See Stipulations and Caveats on page 467.

The foregoing platform-level optimization suggests that the platform architect apply data-staging techniques throughout the platform architecture, in particular within bus-bridges, and not just in the CPU or CPU-cache subsystem. Buffers and caches may be strategically located within various system resources and managed to fetch or retain data in anticipation of its future use. Such data storage devices generally exploit spatial and temporal locality of reference (for non-streaming data types) to avoid stalls, reduce latencies, and reduce data traffic between subsystems.

Data storage devices, and in particular queues (FIFOs), may also be employed to couple diverse subsystems operating at different or dynamically varying rates, while avoiding stalls in each. Queues permit a source subsystem to deliver data or commands to the queue at a rate that is faster in the short term than the destination subsystem is capable of accepting them. They also permit the destination subsystem to take data or commands from the queue at a rate that is faster in the short term than the source-subsystem is capable of delivering them.

Clearly, if we were dealing with only two subsystems, their long-term throughput is necessarily identical. Queue depth to avoid stalls to either subsystem is easily determined based on the extent to which short-term rate mismatch can occur. For the queues used in platform bridges, there are many subsystems selectively coupling with each other in a manner that is a function of the dynamic workload. Hence, the selection of queue depth is less straightforward.

Whenever data storage locations are transparent within the memory hierarchy, associative techniques are generally incorporated to ensure data coherency. This is true of the data staging techniques, whether implemented by buffers, caches, or queues.

REPORT on CD-ROM

> To learn more about Platform Data Staging Basics, see *Implementation of Write Allocate in the K86 Processors*, Document 21326, June 1997, on the companion CD-ROM.

<u>Basics for Increased Concurrency of Platform Resources</u>

PLATFORM PERFORMANCE OPTIMIZATION BASICS[d]
Concurrency Optimization

1. Seek to overlap the processing of multiple tasks.
2. Seek to explicitly pipeline task processing.
3. Seek to speculatively prefetch sequential data and command streams.
4. Seek to decompose operations into split transactions and enable increased pipelining or out-of-order processing.
5. Seek to add independent concurrently operating resources.

---

[d]. See Stipulations and Caveats on page 467.

The above listed basics are platform-level principles that suggest the platform architect should, for each subsystem, seek to increase concurrency to keep expensive or scarce resources from going idle. This can be done by seeking ways to increase opportunistic overlapped processing of independent or loosely coupled tasks, or through explicit pipelining of tightly coupled tasks. Such techniques may be applied at a variety of levels, including the application or platform-level and the device level. Later in this chapter, a 3D graphics pipeline is used to illustrate how pipelining is used at the platform level.

To further maximize concurrency and the utilization of resources, attention must be paid to minimizing stalls and latencies that interrupt processing overlap and pipelining. This requires that when a task is to be executed, the resources it needs are available, its input data is available, and its output data is accepted when generated. Methods to do this include the addition of parallel resources, data-staging techniques, and techniques that permit out-of-order processing and otherwise dynamically reschedule platform tasks.

Split transactions

Split transactions permit command and operation controllers to dynamically break operations into separate start, operation, and termination phases to increase overall system concurrency. Variations of this technique have been applied to instruction, memory, and bus controllers where multiple independent slave function units are capable of overlapped operation processing. In each of these situations, a common controller may dispatch queued nonconflicting split-transaction operations to multiple independent function-units. The controller need not wait for an older operation to finish before dispatching a younger operation to a free and available function-unit. Provided there are enough available function units, the split-transaction technique permits long duration operations to execute without stalling subsequent short duration operations.

Specific Performance Optimizations Made at the Component Level

Data Storage Optimization Basics

PLATFORM PERFORMANCE OPTIMIZATION BASICS[e]
Data Storage
1. Seek to increase the operating rate.
2. Seek to increase the hit rate.
3. Seek to improve low-level organization and management.
4. Seek to reduce the retrieval latency.

[e] See Stipulations and Caveats on page 467.

The above set of basics is directed at optimizations at the component level to data storage devices intended for data-staging applications. There are a number of storage device types that correspond to standard organization and technology forms. These standard storage device types, in increasing order of performance from a system perspective, include off-chip DRAM, multiple types of specialty off-chip DRAM, off-chip SRAM, on-chip DRAM, on-chip SRAM, and on-chip registers. Using better circuit designs and semiconductor processing technology within a storage device type can increase operating rates. When such measures do not offer sufficient improvement, then the platform architect should consider an intrinsically faster device type.

Increases in buffer hit rate are generally accomplished through larger buffer sizes, and forms of increased associatively. Better organization and management can improve one or both of operating rate and hit rate. Techniques include using a better replacement algorithm, increasing the line width, the use of sectored lines, and improving the fill method. Latencies are generally reduced at the device level by incorporating faster buffer

Chapter 5 discusses, in more detail, platform memory controller operation, including low-level memory organization and management techniques for optimized performance.

technology, and at the platform level by making sure that the buffer is managed in a way that it has the desired data when needed.

Bus Optimization Basics

PLATFORM PERFORMANCE OPTIMIZATION BASICS[f]
Bus Optimization at the Component Level

1. Seek to use a bus protocol matched to the data transfer requirements.
2. Seek to increase the speed of operation.
3. Seek to increase the effective bandwidth.
4. Seek to pipeline transfers.
5. Seek to use split-transaction transfers.
6. Seek to improve transfer efficiency.

[f.]   See Stipulations and Caveats on page 467.

The above set of basics is directed at optimizations at the component level to buses, ports, and other interconnects. There are a number of bus standards and types that correspond to established organization and technology forms. Bus optimization begins with selecting a bus protocol matched to the required data transfer characteristics. Bus operating rates can be increased by increasing the bus clock to the technology limits of a given bus standard or type. This includes improvements in bus I/O driver circuit design and processing technology. When such measures do not offer sufficient improvement, then the platform architect should consider an intrinsically faster bus type.

More generally, bus optimizations also include increases in the bus width, changes to the electrical signaling protocol beyond mere circuit and process enhancements, and increasing bus concurrency by pipeline and split-transaction methods. Bus transfer efficiencies are improved by reducing the non-data overhead associated with each bus transfer. Changes are focused on getting more data items per transfer by reducing arbitration, address, and handshake cycles relative to data cycles. A key method of accomplishing better transfer efficiency is the use of burst or block transfers.

The Chapter 5 section on Rambus technology discusses many interconnect optimization techniques in more detail.

Bridge/Controller Optimization Basics

PLATFORM PERFORMANCE OPTIMIZATION BASICS[9]
Bridge/Controller

1. Seek to isolate the various buses and ports whenever possible.
2. Seek to couple two subsystems without delay when required.
3. Seek to smoothly couple subsystems operating at different rates.
4. Seek to reduce stalls in coupled subsystems.
5. Seek to virtualize a multi-ported main memory.

[9] See Stipulations and Caveats on page 467.

The North-Bridge has a number of system optimizations that are inherent in the controller functions it performs. For example, it normally isolates the different buses and the main memory connected to it. This maximizes the opportunity for concurrent system operations to occur. As required, it performs *crossing transfers* by selectively coupling any two of the buses connected to it, or couples one of the buses with the main memory. During these coupling operations the North-Bridge acts as a bus controller, implementing the protocols of the various buses it couples. Thus, the bus transaction is translated from the protocol of the master's bus to that of the slave.

crossing transfers

Bridges may selectively couple buses for crossing transfers based on conditions established via programmable configuration. Generally a variety of different configurations can be set up for different buses, crossing directions and address regions. Some of the more common techniques for enabling crossing transfers include positive, negative, and subtractive decode.

DEFINITION
Bridge/Controller Crossing Transfer Decode Schemes

Positive Decode immediately enables a crossing transfer when the address is inside one or more predefined positive-decode address regions.

Negative Decode immediately enables crossing transfers except when the address is inside one or more predefined negative-decode address regions.

Subtractive Decode enables a crossing transfer after a predefined latency, if no slave has responded to the address.

Selective crossing transfers are discussed in more detail in U.S. Patent 5,627,976, entitled "Crossing Transfers for Maximizing the Effective Bandwidth in a Dual-bus Architecture."

These techniques were particularly useful in South-Bridges during the early ascension of the PCI Bus. Programmable configuration of crossing transfer conditions gave transparent flexibility in choice of bus type for peripheral cards. For example, during the configuration process, the bridge was programmed based on whether the graphics adapter was an ISA-Bus-based device, or whether it resided on the PCI Bus. If a program wrote to reserved video memory locations implemented on the adapter, the bridge could correctly and immediately couple or isolate the PCI and ISA Buses, entirely based on the programmed configuration.

The North-Bridge also functions as a memory controller for the main memory, implementing memory access protocols and refresh as required for the installed memory technology. In conjunction with both its memory control and bus coupling functions, the North-Bridge possesses a number of command and data buffers. These buffers are used for various data-staging techniques including posted writes, write combining, caching, and prefetching. These techniques reduce bus traffic, reduce stalls and latencies, enable different buses to operate at different rates, and support the illusion that, for much of the time, the main memory has dedicated ports for each bus.

REPORTS ON CD-ROM

To learn more about bridge operation see the following data sheets on the companion CD-ROM:

- *AMD-640 System Controller Data Sheet, 21090C/0.*
- *AMD-645 Peripheral Bus Controller, 21095B/0.*

PERFORMANCE OPTIMIZATION SPECIFICS IN A CONTEMPORARY 3D GRAPHICS PLATFORM

We will next examine more closely the operation of 3D graphics in contemporary platforms. This will give the reader better insight into overall platform operation and how the foregoing optimization rules are applied from both low-level and high-level perspectives. To do this, we start by examining Figure 6.2. This is a rearranged and abstracted representation of the "3D Graphics PC Platform" previously presented in Chapter 1. Figure 6.2 has also been annotated with each component's principal operating paradigm and functions. These characterize the role of each component from a component-localized and hardware-centric perspective. Understanding Figure 6.2 is a prerequisite to our later study of the 3D graphics pipeline from an application perspective.

Component Operating Paradigms, Functions for 3D Graphics, and Optimization Features

Microprocessor

The microprocessor's operating paradigm is that of program-controlled instruction execution of control, integer, floating-point, and other specialized instructions. For 3D graphics, the microprocessor acts to execute 3D applications and at least one Application Programming Interface (API). This execution includes geometry calculations and setup for the graphics accelerator. The geometry and setup calculations compose 3D scenes for each frame to be rendered and reduce the scenes to command and parameter data for the graphics accelerator. The composition involves floating-point calculations for object modeling, perspective translation, and lighting. High-level microprocessor-specific optimization features include a high-speed execution unit core having MMX and 3D instructions for accelerating geometry calculations, data staging between the core and the external processor bus using on-chip first- and possibly second-level caches, and an enhanced external processor bus interface running at 100 MHz.

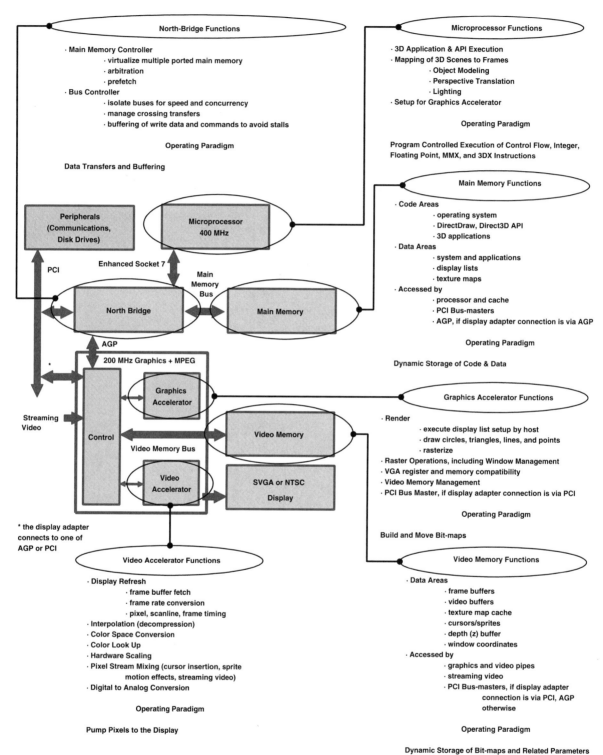

Figure 6.2 ROLES OF PLATFORM COMPONENTS IN 3D GRAPHICS

Main Memory

The main memory's operating paradigm is that of dynamic storage of code and data. For 3D graphics, main memory provides access to code and data areas by the processor and cache subsystem, PCI Bus-master peripherals, and the Advanced Graphics Port (AGP). The code areas contain the operating system, DirectDraw and Direct3D API, and 3D applications. The data areas include system and applications data, texture maps, and display lists. Optimization features for memories include larger total sizes, high-speed interfaces, high-speed core memory arrays, efficient control protocols, and multiple banks capable of concurrent operation.

Memory performance issues are discussed in more detail in Chapter 5.

North-Bridge

The North-Bridge's operating paradigm is that of selective data transfer and buffering. The North-Bridge includes bus and memory control functions. As a bus controller it manages crossing transfers between diverse bus protocols. As a memory controller it manages the DRAM main memory. Optimization features include isolating buses for speed and concurrency when not bus-crossing, buffering bus-crossing data transfers to avoid stalls, creating the illusion that the main memory is multi-ported, and implementing a dedicated port for transfers between main memory and the graphics accelerator and video memory.

Graphics Accelerator

The graphic accelerator's operating paradigm is to build and move bit maps. Its functions include managing video memory accesses by multiple requestors, rendering images into the video memory, and providing VGA compatibility. The very existence of the graphics accelerator is a platform-level optimization in that the accelerator performs rendering operations that otherwise would be executed on the processor. Other optimization features include providing acceleration specifically for 3D rendering and raster operations, performing window management, acting as a PCI Bus-master, executing display lists in memory setup by the host, and implementing AGP for transfers between main memory and the graphics accelerator and video memory.

ARTICLE ON CD-ROM

 To learn more about Graphics Accelerator, see the article "Competition Heats Up in 3D Accelerators," by Yong Yao, *Microprocessor Report*, Vol. 10, No. 3, March 5, 1996, on the companion CD-ROM.

Video Accelerator

The video accelerator's operating paradigm is to pump pixels to the display. Its functions include frame buffer fetch; establishing pixel, scanline, and frame timing; digital to analog conversion; and display refresh. Optimization features include pixel stream mixing for cursor insertion, sprite motion effects, and windowing of streaming video; interpolation; color space conversion; color lookup; and hardware scaling.

Video Memory

Front and back (dual) frame buffers effectively increase bandwidth by removing previous strict limitations on frame buffer writes.

Dual-ported video DRAM permit random access for graphics accelerator access while permitting simultaneous sequential access for the video accelerator, effectively increasing the bandwidth available to the random-access port.

The video memory's operating paradigm is the dynamic storage of bitmaps and related parameters. For 3D graphics, video memory provides access to data areas by the graphics and video accelerators, streaming video (or video capture) port, PCI Bus-master peripherals, and AGP. The data areas include front and back buffers, streaming video buffers, texture map caches, cursor/sprite definitions, depth (z) buffer, and window coordinates. General optimization features for video memories are the same as for main memories above. Specialty DRAMs are more frequently used in video memories than in main memories.

DEFINITION
Processes Accessing Video Memory Our discussion of video memory access has been greatly simplified. The following is a list, in order of decreasing priority, of processes accessing video memory for a contemporary 3D graphics accelerator.[a] • Primary stream fetch • RAM refresh • RAMDAC read/write • Secondary stream fetch • Hardware cursor fetch • Local peripheral bus (used for streaming video or video capture writes) • Read DMA • CPU accesses • Graphics accelerator accesses

[a]   *ViRGE/VX Integrated 3D Accelerator*, S3 Incorporated, June 1996, pp. 7-16.

TECHNICAL PRESENTATION ON CD-ROM

"Platform Components for 3D Graphics" is a Technical Presentation included on the CD-ROM that is a companion to the foregoing discussion of Figure 6.2 on page 482.

Stage Overlap at Frame "n"	*The Geometry Stage*
	Frame "n+2" is being composed, while . . .

Intra-Stage Data Movement	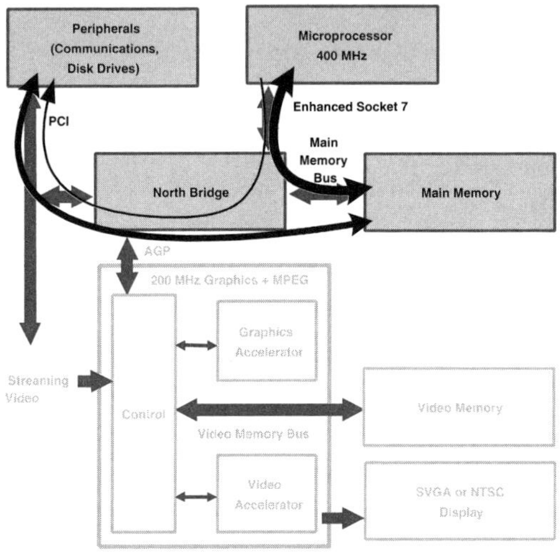 · Microprocessor controls PCI Bus Master Peripherals · Peripherals swap data and code with Main Memory · Microprocessor executes code and manipulates data in Main Memory

Intra-Stage Data Manipulation	· Build 3D Scenes and Prepare to Map to Display Frames
	   · Object Definition
	   · Modeling and Positioning
	   · World-space Definition
	      · lighting
	      · surface attributes
	   · Eye-space Translation
	      · perspective
	      · clip to eye-space
	      · back-face culling
	· Setup Display Lists for Rendering Stage
	· Define Position of Multiple Windows, Cursors, and Sprites

Figure 6.3   3D GRAPHICS PIPELINE STAGES (THE GEOMETRY STAGE)

The Rendering Stage	*The Display Stage*
frame "n+1" is being *drawn*, and while . . .	frame "n" is being *painted* to the screen.

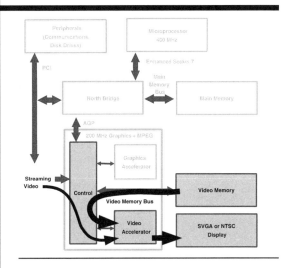

· Graphics Accelerator Reads Display Lists from Main Memory · Graphics Accelerator transfers Texture Maps · Graphics Accelerator operates directly on secondary frame buffer in Video Memory	· Video Accelerator reads primary frame buffer · Video Accelerator merges external streaming video data with frame buffer video data · Video Accelerator pumps merged stream to display

· Build Bit-Maps in Frame Buffers
· Execute Display Lists Setup in Geometry Stage
    · Draw Circles, Triangles, Lines, and Points
    · Clip to Screen Space
    · Remove Hidden Surfaces, Depth Cueing
    · Coloring, Shading, and Texture
    · Move Texture Maps from Main Memory to Video Memory as Required
	· Frame Buffer Fetch
	· Pixel, Scanline, Frame Timing
	· Color Look Up
	· Hardware Scaling
	· Display multiple windows
	· Insert moving cursors, sprites, and video
	· Format YUV 4:2:2 video for RGB
	    · interpolation (decompression)
	    · color space conversion
	    · frame rate conversion
	· Convert Digital Pixel Data to Analog Signals

Figure 6.4   3D GRAPHICS PIPELINE STAGE (THE RENDERING STAGE AND THE DISPLAY STAGE)

Geometry, Rendering, and Display—The 3D Graphics Pipeline

Elsewhere, when more abstract discussions focus purely on 3D geometry and rendering, the Display Stage may be implicitly included in the Rendering Stage. Here, our focus is on the relatively lower-level platform architecture and hardware behavior. In this context the Display Stage deserves to be treated separately.

Figure 6.3 and Figure 6.4 offer an application perspective of the 3D graphics pipeline. They apply the platform organization used in Figure 6.2 on page 482 as a template to examine the dynamic behavior of data movements and manipulations for each stage of the 3D graphics pipeline. Figure 6.3 and Figure 6.4 are intended to be viewed collectively as one large graphic that simultaneously shows the activities of three stages that make up the 3D graphics pipeline. These stages are, from left to right and in order of processing, the Geometry, Rendering, and Display Stages. We will next overview the particular data manipulations and movements that characterize each stage.

The Geometry (Modeling) Stage

setup

DEFINITION
Geometry Stage
The Geometry Stage first models, then composes descriptions, representative of a real or virtual world scene for each frame to be displayed. The descriptions take the form of sequences of commands, parameters, and other data, that can be readily processed by the Rendering Stage. The preparation of these descriptions is called *setup*.

The Geometry Stage may also compose descriptions for display control features (such as Window positions and scaling, cursors, and sprites) that are processed only by the Display Stage.

The data movements of the Geometry Stage include the execution of programs by the microprocessor and its associated manipulation of data in main memory. Peripherals swap data and code with main memory as required by the executing program. These swaps are managed by system software that also executes on the microprocessor. Ideally, the microprocessor programs the PCI Bus-master peripherals that later carry out in isolation all necessary swaps at the behest of the processor.

The Geometry Stage data manipulations build 3D scenes in preparation for mapping these scenes to display frames. This involves object definition, including modeling and positioning; definition of the world-space (the interrelationship of objects to the unseen surrounding environment) through lighting and surface attributes, and eye-space translation, including application of perspective, clipping to eye-space, and back-face culling to simplify later processing by eliminating information obviously unnecessary for rendering. Subsequent to the foregoing geometry calculations, displays lists are set up for the Rendering Stage. In the 3D architecture represented, the microprocessor builds the display lists, in memory for subsequent execution by a bus-mastering graphics accelerator that fetches and executes the stored display list. In the 3D architecture represented, the microprocessor builds the display lists in memory for subsequent execution by a bus-mastering graphics accelerator that fetches and executes the stored display list.

The Rendering Stage

DEFINITION
Rendering Stage
The Rendering Stage *draws* bit maps in the frame buffer based on the per frame descriptions set up by the Geometry Stage. The bit maps take the form of pixel data that collectively represent an image to be displayed for the current frame.

The bus-mastering graphics accelerator predominantly controls the primary data movements of the Rendering Stage. These movements include the fetching of display lists from main memory, data manipulations on the video memory as dictated by the display lists, and the transfer of any required texture maps between main memory and video memory via the AGP.

Rendering Stage data manipulations, called for by the display lists previously set up in the Geometry Stage, are executed by the graphics accelerator. These data manipulations build bit maps in the frame buffer by drawing circles, triangles, lines, and points; clipping to the screen space; using depth cueing and otherwise removing hidden surfaces; incorporating coloring, shading, and texture; and moving, manipulating, and applying texture maps to define surface features.

Rendering may be more directly controlled by the microprocessor. A more classic alternative is for the microprocessor to use PIO in the Rendering Stage to send the commands and data (functionally equivalent to the display list) directly to the graphics accelerator, which functions as a slave controller to the microprocessor.

> **DEFINITION**
>
> 3D Rendering Models
>
> *Polygonal Rendering* is the 3D rendering model underlying all the examples in this book. That is, the real world scenes are decomposed into a representation consisting of polygons (or simply triangles) and individual pixels. The polygonal model is popular in PC platforms because it offers rendering speeds supporting good user interactivity, at quality levels approaching arcade games, at relatively low cost. Other rendering techniques and algorithms exist.
>
> *Talisman* is a Microsoft rendering initiative that is a "region-based" variation on the polygonal model. It attempts to boost pixel-fill rates and reduce processing demands by limiting rendering to only those scene areas that change from frame to frame. It also attempts to reduce bus bandwidth demands by transferring compressed texture maps.
>
> *Ray tracing* is a rendering technique that offers superior quality, but has much greater computational requirements that do not support interactive use. Ray tracing techniques are usually used to render the Photorealistic images required by the motion picture industry.[a]

[a]   "3D Vendors Prepare for Rough Seas in '98," *Microprocessor Report*, MicroDesign Resources, Dec. 29, 1997.

REPORT ON CD-ROM

 To learn more about The Rendering Stage, see the article "Talisman Redefines 3D Rendering," by Peter N. Glaskowsky, *Microprocessor Report*, Vol. 10, No. 11, August 6, 1996, on the companion CD-ROM.

The Display Stage

> **DEFINITION**
>
> Display Stage
>
> The Display Stage *paints* pixels to the display generated as a function of the bit maps drawn in the frame buffer by the Rendering Stage.

The video accelerator acts as a data pump, or more specifically a pixel pump, creating and controlling pixel data streams for the continual refresh of the display. These pixel data streams define the primary data movements of the Display Stage. These movements include fetches of pixel data from selected frame buffer locations, pumping pixel data through a pixel processing pipeline (described below), merging pixel data streams from various sources, and pumping the merged pixel stream to appropriate interface circuitry for either a CRT, LCD, or other display technology.

The video accelerator manipulates the pixel data in a pixel-processing pipeline. The pipeline is programmatically configured by display control commands sent by the microprocessor. Many such commands are performed during the initialization of the display subsystem. However, others may be dynamically performed in conjunction with the rendering setup of the Geometry Stage. Common commands establish the pixel, scanline, and frame timing; perform any required frame rate conversions; and establish window boundaries and the location of cursors and sprites. Subsequent to the foregoing configuration, the video accelerator's pixel-processing pipeline performs any required interpolation, color space conversion, scaling, and color lookup; insertion of moving cursors, sprites, and streaming video; and conversion of pixel data to analog signals.

The pixels painted by the Display Stage are generally a function of display control features (discussed above) set up by the Geometry Stage.

Stage Overlap in the 3D Graphics Pipeline

The three stages reviewed above are in execution simultaneously. As annotated in Figure 6.3 on page 486 and Figure 6.4 on page 487, consider the stage processing overlap at a time when the user perceives a frame "n" being displayed. This happens when frame "n" is being read from the front frame buffer, manipulated by the pixel-processing pipeline, and painted to the screen, all in the Display Stage. Simultaneous with the painting of frame "n," the Rendering Stage is executing display lists from main memory and drawing frame "n+1" to the back frame buffer. Also simultaneous with the painting of frame "n," the Geometry Stage is composing and performing rendering setup for frame "n+2."

The overlap can also be visualized as follows. Imagine that each of the three data movement drawings (of the collective illustration formed by Figure 6.3 on page 486 and Figure 6.4 on page 487) is a separate transparency. By overlaying and aligning the transparencies of the three stages, the composite view gives the collective data movements on going simultaneously during the display of frame "n."

For the moment in time represented by Figure 6.3 on page 486 and Figure 6.4 on page 487, frame "n" previously passed through the Geometry and Rendering Stages and frame "n+1" previously passed through the Geometry Stage.

TECHNICAL PRESENTATION ON CD-ROM

 "3D Pipeline" is a Technical Presentation included on the CD-ROM that illustrates that all three stages are overlapped in each frame.

If the microprocessor is used to send rendering commands and data directly to the graphics accelerator, increased competition for the microprocessor and PCI Bus will occur between the Geometry and Rendering Stages.

Note that the main memory and North-Bridge are used in both the Geometry and Rendering Stages. Also note that the video memory is used in both the Rendering and Display Stages. Thus, though our abstract representation has ignored the possibility of the platform executing other tasks, there will be competition for these resources even between stages of the 3D graphics pipeline. Use of well-planned arbitration protocols and data staging is especially important in order to effectively manage stalls and reduce latencies that occur due to such resource competition.

ARTICLE ON CD-ROM

 To learn more about Stage Overlap in the 3D Graphics Pipeline, see the article "PC Graphics Reach New Level: 3D," by Yong Yao, *Microprocessor Report*, Vol. 10, No. 1, January 22, 1996, on the companion CD-ROM.

SUMMARY OF CONTEMPORARY PLATFORM OPTIMIZATIONS

Included below is the combined list of the optimizations discussed in this major section. These basic principles can be seen in contemporary platform designs, which have gone beyond merely increasing operating rates and shifting to faster technology.

PLATFORM PERFORMANCE OPTIMIZATION BASICS[h]

Compilation of all Optimization Basics

1. Seek to increase operating rates.
2. Seek to increase resource operating-widths.
3. Seek to increase the efficient use of high-demand resources.
4. Seek to reduce the number of subsystems that process each task.
5. Seek to keep expensive resources continuously productive.
6. Seek to reduce unnecessary bus transactions and transfers.
7. Seek to normally isolate concurrent operation buses capable of.
8. Seek to increase the number of continuously productive buses.
9. Seek to reduce simultaneous competition for each bus.
10. Seek to minimize the use of Programmed I/O (PIO).
11. Seek to command normally isolated bus-mastering accelerators.
12. Seek to transfer compressed data.
13. Seek to keep streaming data out of general-purpose subsystems.
14. Seek to maximize block sizes and minimize per-block latencies.
15. Seek to exploit spatial and temporal locality of reference.
16. Seek to avoid stalls.
17. Seek to reduce latencies.
18. Seek to reduce data traffic between subsystems.
19. Seek to smoothly couple subsystems operating at different rates.
20. Seek to identify the optimal block size.
21. Seek to overlap the processing of multiple tasks.
22. Seek to explicitly pipeline task processing.
23. Seek to speculatively prefetch sequential data streams.
24. Seek to decompose operations into split transactions and enable increased pipelining or out-of-order processing.
25. Seek to add independent concurrently operating resources.
26. Seek to optimize data storage devices
    a. Seek to increase the operating rate.
    b. Seek to increase the hit rate.
    c. Seek to improve low-level organization and management.
    d. Seek to reduce the retrieval latency.

[h.] See Stipulations and Caveats on page 467.

PLATFORM PERFORMANCE OPTIMIZATION BASICS[i] (CONT.)

Compilation of all Optimization Basics

27. Seek to optimize buses.

    a. Seek to increase the speed of operation.

    b. Seek to increase the effective bandwidth.

    c. Seek to pipeline transfers.

    d. Seek to use split-transaction transfers.

    e. Seek to improve transfer efficiency.

28. Seek to use a bus protocol matched to the data transfer requirements.

29. Seek to optimize Bus-bridges and Controllers

    a. seek to isolate the various buses and ports whenever possible.

    b. Seek to couple two subsystems without delay when required.

    c. Seek to smoothly couple subsystems operating at different rates.

    d. Seek to reduce stalls in coupled subsystems.

    e. Seek to virtualize a multi-ported main memory.

[i] See Stipulations and Caveats on page 467.

Contemporary platforms use sophisticated organization and management of multiple autonomous subsystems that operate concurrently, but at independent rates, coupled loosely via bridges that perform data staging to avoid stalls, reduce latencies, and virtualize ports to high-demand resources. The autonomous subsystems make use of bus-mastering data pumps, dedicated accelerators, and peripherals; data staging; efficient protocols; and explicit pipelining. Performance has been increased and costs reduced by keeping platform resources continuously and efficiently productive.

Platform optimization is a dynamic problem. Platform architecture is a moving target. Designs must be continually adapted to changes in application requirements and new uses of the platform. The next section examines the directions the PC platform is taking to track these changes.

ARTICLES ON CD-ROM

To learn more about Platform Optimizations, see the following articles on the companion CD-ROM:

- "A Performance Analysis of Pentium Processor Systems," by Michael Bekerman and Avi Mendelson, *IEEE Micro*, Vol. 15, No. 5, October 1995.
- "Limited Bandwidth to Affect Processor Design," by Doug Burger, James R. Goodman and Alain Kägi, *IEEE Micro*, November/December 1997.

OVERVIEW OF CONTEMPORARY ISSUES IMPACTING PC PLATFORMS

PLATFORM DIRECTIONS

The most important aspects of contemporary platform development pertains to *connectivity* and *content*. These are associated with new uses of the PC, changes in the base of PC users, and new views of PC platforms.

VIDEO ON CD-ROM

Atiq Raza, AMD CTO and Executive VP, replies to the question: "How are the changes in connectivity and content impacting PC systems?"

DEFINITION
Connectivity

Connectivity the connection of a PC platform to computing, storage, or I/O resources. The resources may be local or remote. The resources may be accessed via connection with workgroup servers, the corporate data center, a personal satellite link, the TelCo (Telephone Company) central office, the Internet or an intranet. The connection may be via modem or network and may be wired or wireless.

Connectivity in new platform installations is changing rapidly, becoming more commonplace and more diverse. Connectivity is predominantly via network for businesses of all sizes and via modem for consumers and small businesses. Connections are predominantly wired, with emerging use of wireless. Figure 6.5 illustrates some of the many methods of connectivity available today.

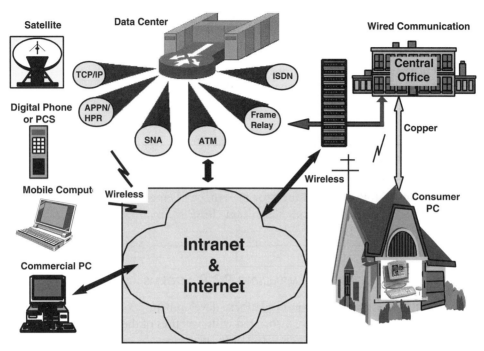

Figure 6.5 METHODS OF CONNECTIVITY

Adapted with permission of Advanced Micro Devices Inc., from *Competing with Intel,* Copyright 1997.

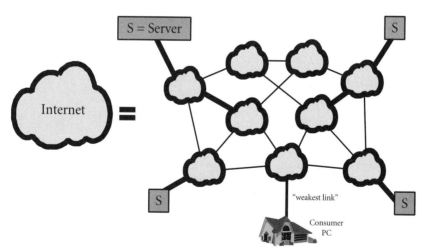

Figure 6.6 VARIATIONS IN INTERNET BANDWIDTH

Adapted with permission of Advanced Micro Devices Inc., from *Corporate Strategy,* Copyright 1997.

> **DEFINITION**
>
> Data Concentration
>
> Data Concentration is the implementation of multi-user access to (hard disk) storage servers via workgroup, intranet, and Internet networking technologies, with an emphasis on reducing client storage. Data concentration can reduce overall system storage requirements by reducing unnecessary multiple copies, facilitates on-demand access of critical information to anyone with the appropriate access permissions, and enables project data to be backed up more easily by data-center personnel.
>
> Ideally, data concentration could manage hard disk storage on all machines coupled to the network from an overall system perspective. Such an ideal is similar to recent proposals for *thin clients*, *Network Computers*, and *NetPCs*, all of which shift storage requirements, in various degrees, to networked storage servers. In conventional practice, data is kept on servers rather than on users' machines whenever applicable and practical, by management initiative and on an ad hoc basis decided by content creators and users, under permissions decided by server administrators and management.

Commercial data concentration is the most significant factor driving connectivity growth. Large entities are rapidly building and expanding private intranets to provide better organization, control, and increased utilization of geographically distributed computing resources. In conjunction with this activity, commercial bandwidth is growing an order of magnitude at a time and faster than PC processing growth. This increase in connectivity, and the disparity in growth between bandwidth and processing power, are evolving the PC platform and are redefining PC platform market segments.

The Internet also provides data concentration, but in the public infrastructure. It does so, in that publicly accessible databases and archives reduce the need for users to acquire and maintain individual copies of popular information. This public infrastructure is built upon the storage servers of Internet Service Providers (ISPs) providing subscribers with Web site hosting services, Usenet and other news services, and storage and forwarding of e-mail.

However, unlike the order-of-magnitude growth in the commercial sector, the growth in Internet access bandwidth for consumers is slower. This growth is being paced by the connection between the Internet Service Provider and the end user, which typically is the slowest part of the link. High-speed links to the Internet are presently beyond the reach of most households' budget. Figure 6.6 on page 496 graphically depicts the variations in bandwidth that exist between the nodes that comprise the Internet.

DEFINITION
Content
In the same way that the program *content* on a television channel describes the nature of the program being broadcast, in the PC world *content* connotes the type of subject matter that the user chooses to access or manipulate on the platform. In the broadest sense, content is whatever subject matter the user chooses to have delivered, or to interact with, using the PC platform. More narrowly, the term is most often applied to professional-quality entertainment, news, education, games, or an information/database retrieval facility or service.

PC platforms for users are coming to be thought of, not as computing devices, but as user-operated tools (or information appliances) for *content access*. For example, many consumers view PCs as Internet-access devices. In this emerging paradigm, enabled by evolving sophistication that better hides underlying complexity, applications are now often described in terms of the *content* they provide, generate, or manipulate for the user.

PC content is continuing to change rapidly. New multimedia-based content forms are relying on intensive use of 2D and 3D graphics, 3D-quality audio, quality video, and voice recognition and voice synthesis. The source of multimedia data today is now expanded beyond the CD-ROM to include DVD-ROMs and the Internet. These multimedia technologies are being used commercially for the visualization and presentation of business data. In games they are providing consumers with realism for simulated worlds previously available only in arcades or in expensive commercial applications. The new multimedia-based content is providing significantly enhanced user interfaces and experiences for all applications compared to earlier PCs.

Internet and intranet content is characterized primarily by the Web-browser navigation paradigm. The use of the Internet for data centralization and its complement—information retrieval (including searching, browsing, and surfing)—is now well established among computer-literate consumers. In the commercial PC market Internet technology is also increasingly used for the dissemination of both internal and external information.

The emergence of these new content types is driving a relentless and rapid flow of enhancements at both the processor and the platform level. Rich graphical content is particularly demanding on all aspects of platform performance and is driving new standards and designs for all PC platform components and interconnects. Microprocessor enhancements include higher frequencies, increased instruction-level parallelism, and superscalar units for emerging specific content. Platform enhancements include new means to access, process, and display content and infrastructure support for processor enhancements.

The rapid growth of Internet and intranet content and the requisite connectivity has led to fast growth in the storage server platform segment. While the bulk of servers have historically come from non-PC platforms, Internet Service Providers and data centers are viewing PC platforms from a new perspective as high-performance/low-cost Windows NT-based multi-processor PCs increasingly penetrate into the Internet and intranet server market.

Recent changes in content and connectivity have led to fast growth in storage servers.

Server growth is particularly strong in the commercial segment. In particular, intranet-connected servers are being used to accomplish data (storage) concentration. While growth in the Internet also clearly impacts server sales, the effect is somewhat muted by the tendency of ISPs to concentrate a greater number of user ports per server, increasing latencies and throughput, than would generally be acceptable in a commercial intranet environment. Internet growth is also occurring at a slower rate than intranet growth, being limited by the lack of cheap high-speed connectivity. The most likely candidates for providing Internet connectivity, the Telephone Companies, have been slow in adapting to the rapidly developing needs of Internet users. Inexpensive Internet connections are tediously slow. High-speed Internet connections have high setup costs and metered access with significant usage rates. In either case, the user's finite on line budget—of time or money—significantly limits their Internet activity.

CONTEMPORARY PLATFORM STRATEGIC ISSUES

A number of key issues have a significant influence on PC platform design. Today, platform features and techniques are of necessity being enhanced in order to realize the performance potential of present and forthcoming high-performance microprocessors. Due to the rapid pace of increasing performance, these changes can no longer be done in isolation. As a result, co-design of processors and PC platforms has become standard. Internet, multimedia, networking, and communications technologies are continuing their ascension. The perception that PC users are rapidly adopting and demanding these technologies is further redefining the PC platform as features are added to track shifts in how PCs are being used. This section examines these issues and their impact on the PC platform.

This section overviews the contemporary platform environment and the design and business issues that exist for processor and platform design. Future Platforms are discussed at the end of this chapter.

Directions in Optimization of Contemporary Systems

A number of features and techniques are being applied at the processor and platform level to optimize systems performance in the near term. These optimizations, driven primarily by the new connectivity and content, are rapidly continuing, at the microprocessor, chipset, and motherboard levels.

At the processor level, optimizations include faster clock rates, faster bus rates, improved architectural performance, and changes to the platform memory hierarchy. In addition to its traditional computation and control roles, the processor in contemporary platforms is called upon for signal processing for playback decoding of digital multimedia; local encoding for authoring of digital multimedia and imaging; and for geometry computations and rendering setup to support the 3D graphics display subsystem.

At the chipset and motherboard levels, there is a seemingly insatiable demand for bus and memory bandwidth. The memory and I/O subsystems must be optimized to sustain the higher processor performance and higher bandwidth data transfers required for access, processing, and display of rich 3D graphics. Support must also be included for emerging networking, communications, multimedia, graphics, and I/O standards and associated newer infrastructure chips. The platform must also reflect associated changes that are occurring in the interface between hardware and software. Platforms must support these new standards and interfaces in order for them to be successful.

General platform optimizations are being performed within the Socket 7 infrastructure. These changes will extend Socket 7's viability by providing increased performance and new standards and features. AMD refers to the enhanced Socket 7 as "Super 7." For uniprocessor systems, Super 7 promises to be highly competitive on a performance-to-cost basis with platforms based on the P6 processor bus.

Platforms based on the new Super 7 chipsets will extend frequency and bus bandwidths, permit larger main memory and caches, and allow for a backside cache. They also will offer I/O system improvements to display, disk, and communications subsystems. These platforms will support the most important new standards such as ACPI, AGP, 1394, USB, and DVD-ROM. Super 7 chipsets will offer improved PCI system bus efficiency by incorporating the latest interleaved system bus-mastering and faster arbitration protocols. Sophisticated internal bridge architectures, including such techniques as bus transaction buffering, posted write buffers, and bus prefetch, will allow for multiple internal concurrent subsystems.

3D content requires Socket 7 infrastructure enhancements in the buses coupling the processor, North-Bridge, the memory subsystem, and the graphics subsystem. The processor bus for Super 7 is 100 MHz, compared to 66 MHz for the earlier Socket 7 processor bus. This increase is planned in conjunction with increasing the main memory bus bandwidth to 100 MHz. These optimizations are needed to reduce the penalty for off-chip accesses, which occur on cache-line write-backs to main memory, cache-line fills from main memory, and all non-cacheable accesses to main memory and other addressable platform components. Slow off-chip accesses, while relatively infrequent, act to limit the benefit realizable from processor core-frequency speedups.

The increase in the processor bus speed happens to be closely interrelated to many other system issues, and requires consideration and management of a host of complex factors. See "Co-Design of Processors and Platforms" later in this chapter.

In addition to extending the main memory bus bandwidth to 100 MHz, the new Super 7 platforms will support larger and faster caches, ultimately including an on-chip backside cache. In each memory subsystem within the platform, a variety of competing memory technologies and organizations are being considered. These include EDO, SDRAM, Rambus, and SLDRAM. These memory technologies all differ in terms of their costs, ease of system design, latency and bandwidth of their interface, and the efficiency of their transfer protocols.

Advanced memory technologies and organizations are discussed in Chapter 5. The last section in Chapter 5 is devoted to a detailed discussion of Rambus.

Super 7 platforms are also making specific optimizations in their graphic subsystems to support the display of contemporary 3D graphic applications. Primary among these optimizations is the inclusion of AGP. Motivated by the demands of 3D content, this new point-to-point bus directly couples the graphics accelerator to the North-Bridge. Contemporary Super 7 3D graphics accelerators will be AGP compatible, have texture mapping hardware assist, and also incorporate other hardware acceleration for 3D rendering.

Video on CD-ROM

 Atiq Raza, AMD CTO and Executive VP, replies to the question: "What are the difficulties in achieving optimal graphics performance?"

Advances in a PC platform's processor performance, 3D graphics performance, and supporting architecture must be concurrent and well coordinated. Increased speed processors need platform architectures that can sustain the processor's performance capabilities. The performance and capabilities of the entire system are readily discernible when using new content having rich 3D graphics. In the negative, rich 3D content will visually highlight the inadequacy of older platforms and slower processors. Frames may be noticeably dropped, audio synchronization with the display may be lost, and interactivity may be sporadic. In the positive, rich

3D content enables the user to visually appreciate the benefits of having a well-proportioned and-tuned advanced architecture platform with a fast processor. The presence of textures and other advanced 3D attributes, enabled by high-performance 3D graphics accelerators, are clearly visible and are impressive.

Illustrative Progression of Platform Architecture

We next survey a succession of platform developments planned to occur over 1998. Compared to earlier systems, these contemporary systems offer improvements in microarchitectural performance and memory hierarchy efficiencies. Another important aspect, notable in each platform shown, is the constant upward march of core frequencies.

Figures 6.7-6.9 illustrate the rapid evolution that is occurring in platform architecture. Figure 6.7 shows a highly abstract view of a typical high-performance system in early '97. This system uses a frontside cache operating at the processor bus rate of 66 MHz. All bus traffic between the graphics accelerator and main memory makes use of the 33-MHz PCI system bus.

A Super 7 system planned for mid '98 is shown in Figure 6.8. This system also features 100-MHz processor and memory buses and the addition of instruction set extensions for 3D graphics. This system also augments the earlier Socket 7 system by the addition of a 133-MHz Advanced Graphics Port (AGP). The increased memory bus speed decreases latencies and improves throughputs for transfers via AGP to the graphics accelerator, or via the processor bus to the frontside secondary cache and to the processor core, including the on-chip primary cache. The increased processor bus reduces penalties for all off-chip accesses (cacheable and noncacheable), reduces the latencies for primary and secondary cache-line fills, and increases the effective throughput of the entire memory system.

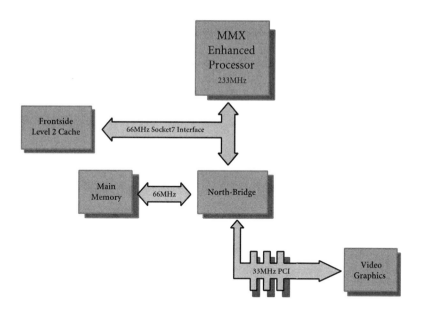

Figure 6.7 66MHz Socket 7 Bus Platform

Adapted with permission of Advanced Micro Devices Inc., from *A New World Order—Alternative, Microsoft Windows Platforms,* Copyright 1997.

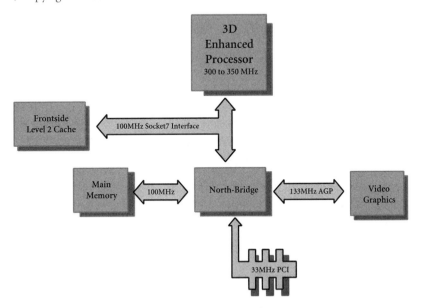

Figure 6.8 A 100MHz Super 7 Bus Platform

Adapted with permission of Advanced Micro Devices Inc., from *A New World Order—Alternative, Microsoft Windows Platforms,* Copyright 1997.

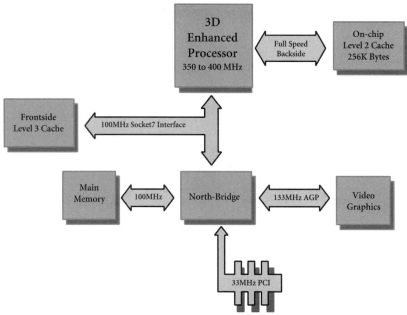

Figure 6.9 A 100MHz Super 7 Bus Platform with Backside Cache

Adapted with permission of Advanced Micro Devices Inc., from *A New World Order—Alternative, Microsoft Windows Platforms,* Copyright 1997.

Figure 6.9 illustrates a Super 7 platform with backside cache, planned for the second half of '98. This platform augments the frontside cache with an on-chip 256KB backside cache that runs at the processor's core frequency. This significantly reduces latencies for primary cache-line fills and improves the apparent main memory performance perceived by the processor for cacheable accesses. The backside cache filters out many accesses that would otherwise result in traffic on the processor bus port to the North-Bridge, increasing the available bandwidth to main memory for other system components.

Co-Design of Processors and Platforms

The relation between processor design and PC platform development is drawing closer. Platforms define the system context (or environment) in which the processor functions. Faster processors require greater care and sophistication in the design and implementation of the platform. This is requiring a closer coupling between processor and platform development in each succeeding generation of the PC platform.

Both processor and systems technology are currently undergoing rapid evolution. Each technology is being buffeted by fast ongoing changes in speed, density, performance, level of integration, new features, and new industry standards. To avoid being caught with a new product design that is obsolete at introduction, product cycles are shortening in the face of this rapid technology march. Since higher profits are generally realized in the early stages of the product cycle than later, it is very important to orchestrate an early stage offering.

Early stage offerings are major feats to accomplish. In order to succeed, processor vendors must ensure that there will be an available supply of chipsets and motherboard reference designs with performance and features that enable and complement each new processor model. The design of the chipsets and motherboards must be carried out to ensure that the combination of processor and platform delivers a competitive offering that addresses platform vendors' wants and needs with respect to performance, features cost, constraints, volume, ease of design, and infrastructure support for new processor features.

Processor and platform co-design describes the close working relationship that has of necessity developed between processor design and the design of the surrounding parts of the system, especially the motherboard and its associated chipset. Co-design includes extensive technical and business exchanges between processor and platform designers.

Through co-design exchanges, complex hardware and software interactions between the processor and the surrounding system are cooperatively understood and mastered. As a result, the risk of latent compatibility problems is greatly reduced and better ease of system design generally results. Also, processor and platform designers have better knowledge of both parties' design constraints, capabilities, and volume expectations, and can act accordingly. Co-design also enables coordination of infrastructure support for new advanced technology features and standards, permitting their rapid introduction.

Both the processor and platform vendors benefit from co-design. They both share in the timely delivery of aggressively competitive systems with improved profitability. End users enjoy increased application performance and value, and thereby benefit from co-design as well.

Video on CD-ROM

 Atiq Raza, AMD CTO and Executive VP, replies to the question: "Why is co-design so critical to PC systems development?"

Continual Redefinition of the PC Platform

There is a reinforcing circle of interaction that includes advances in processor and platform technology, development of new applications, and

The market segments are used as an abstraction of buyer needs and behavior. Illustrated by the evolution of the PC platform, the original PC platform was redefined over the course of a decade into the now familiar desktop, laptop, and workstation segments. In the last several years these segments have been further redefined by distinctions between enterprise/ workgroup/home-office, server/ client, modem/networked/isolated, Internet/intranet access, and others.

user demand for new applications and hardware. New applications are enabled by and exploit advanced technology that is introduced into limited editions of platform models within a chosen market segment. Further, new types of applications will likely emerge that make novel eclectic use of these redefined platforms with their enhanced technologies. If successful, the new types of applications generate significant end-user enthusiasm and demand. As more users purchase these applications, platform purchases indirectly result. The purchases come from users new to the platform and from existing platform users that need to upgrade in order to meet the advanced technology requirements of the new applications in an acceptable fashion.

If the new type of application develops a sufficient user base, the user base may come to be viewed as its own emerging platform segment. In this manner, PC platform market segments are being continually redefined, as processor and platform designers attempt to track shifts in the way PCs are being used. The redefinition takes the form of additional novel platform segments and growth-motivated division of previously existing segments. Each new segment has optimized platform architectures tailored to its specific needs.

Supported by demand as well as driven by aggressive competition, successful advanced technology is cost-reduced and made more widely available, while new advanced technology is designed into future platform releases. This again encourages new applications, and the process runs full circle. Thus we can expect further expansions in new technology, new types of applications, and new platform segments, as the process continues in a positive growth spiral.

A major thrust of platform redefinition ongoing today is driven by diverse new applications exploiting the convergence of connectivity and content technologies. Applications are using the Internet, Web, and networking and other communications technologies to enable and enhance aspects of productivity, message passing, socialization, and access to remote and distributed databases. Applications rely on multimedia technologies to enhance their ease of use and to create positive memorable experiences that meet or exceed those from other competitive media technologies. Applications intended to entertain are attempting to turn the PC into a game platform, or a home entertainment center with hybrid TV and PC capabilities.

NEXT-GENERATION PLATFORMS

Bridging the gap between the previously discussed K6 platforms and the platforms beyond the millennium, lies K7-based platforms. K7 processors will continue to make microarchitectural enhancements and increase clock rates. Expected core clock rates for the initial shipments of K7 are at 500 MHz. In addition, K7 will require some significant changes in PC platform designs. In particular, K7 platforms will use a variant of Digital's EV6 multiprocessor bus and the platform's processor and cache will be integrated into a processor module.

Figure 6.10 shows what the K7 Processor Module is expected to look like. This module integrates the highest-level cache on a common module card with the processor. Careful card design and component selection permits the highest-level cache to run at frequencies much higher than the 100-MHz Super 7 bus. The module is designed and manufactured by the processor vendor (AMD in this case) to ensure that the cache and processor combination is reliable. AMD plans for the K7 Processor Module to be mechanically compatible with the physical infrastructure for Intel's Slot 1.

Other logic can be added to the module beside the cache. By integrating any logic that is processor specific, it becomes much easier for a system manufacturer to incorporate subsequent processor module generations.

AMD-K7™ Processor

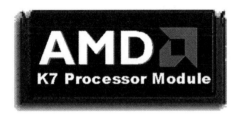

- **Driven by customer requirements**
- **Clock speeds in excess of 500 MHz**
- **Advanced bus interface, "Alpha" EV6 bus protocol**
- **Plan of record: slot "A" mechanically identical to Intel's slot 1**
- **Enabling alternative platforms for 1999 and Beyond**

Figure 6.10 AMD-K7 PROCESSOR

Copyright 1997/1998, Advanced Micro Devices Inc., used with permission.

The K7 processor module bus is expected to have a 64-bit data bus and a packetized command bus. The bus will likely use high-performance signaling techniques including clock forwarding, double-data rate transfers, and point-to-point connections. It is expected that the K7 bus will be designed for coupling to either a memory controller or a multiprocessor controller. At a presumed initial "fractional" speed of 250 MHz, the K7 bus will support a bandwidth to main memory of 2 GB/s.

In the near term, K6- and K7-based processor and platform research and development objectives will be centered on further growing the user base of PC platforms and to track perceived shifts in use among existing users. Key focus areas of these efforts are to reduce user frustration and customer support costs associated with platform configuration and system crashes, enable new applications that deliver an "enhanced user experience," and to further the transition of the consumer PC platform into a simple-to-use entertainment appliance for "content access."

As new technology puts otherwise perfect digital "masters" of films in the hands of the public, expect the entertainment industry to ensure that embedded copyrighted content protection becomes standard.

K6- and K7-based entertainment-oriented PCs will attempt to increasingly shield the user from PC internal complexities. These devices will support rich graphical content through improved multimedia features, including 3D graphics, 3D audio, and streaming video. The graphics subsystem and a requisite DVD-ROM will support the display of "Hollywood" content at somewhat better than VCR quality. Such PCs will be equipped with improved communications, presently based on 56K modems or ISDN adapters, but shifting in the next few years to XDSL schemes. The communications functions of the platform will support voice, telephony, and conferencing. These technologies and Internet connectivity will enable the significant (but still limited) use of on-demand broadcast services and secure commerce.

Figure 6.5 on page 496 and Figure 6.6 on page 496, earlier in the chapter, illustrated the link to the home and its relationship to the Internet connectivity cloud.

The likely eventual pervasiveness of DVD-ROM will significantly raise users' standard for multimedia quality on the PC with its use of MPEG-2 quality video and AC-3 audio. Internet entertainment content will be competing against these raised expectations. The delivery of competitive quality Internet multimedia content, and its ability to supplant TV and other entertainment forms, will be paced by the availability of affordable high-speed user access rates. User access communications rates are determined by the link between the user's Internet Service Provider and the user's home. This is the slowest link in the Internet connectivity "cloud."

A Vision of Platforms Beyond the Millennium

The remainder of this section examines how current trends and predictions may impact the PC platform and society, once the underlying technologies are mainstream and well beyond today's demonstrations, field trials, and hobbyist experimentation. We have organized the following discussion loosely along the lines of Future Content, Connectivity, Hybrid Content/Connectivity, Platforms, and Platform Industry Directions.

Future Content

Enabled by the authoring capability of future platforms, there will be an explosion in content for entertainment, productivity, and education. Much of the new content will make intensive use of multimedia, visualization techniques, and simulated environments. PC entertainment applications will be overwhelming competition for other free-time activities including TV, as we now know it. The trend to suppress the underlying technology will continue. Many applications will become invisible to the user, being indirectly selected based on what the user will perceive as a selection from different variations in content.

Future Connectivity

A hope and promise of the computer industry is that in the next five to ten years, communications bandwidth will be dramatically more available than it is presently. In particular, it is expected that "fast" (1-10 Mbit/s) communications rates will be available at affordable rates to the masses. Figure 6.11 graphically depicts the relative growth of network bandwidth versus the growth of PC processing power. Industry visionary George Gilder has suggested that this shift in dominance, as represented by the crossover point shown in the figure, calls for completely rethinking systems architectures. In particular, he suggests that the focus of networked platforms be placed on what can be achieved via fast connectivity over what can be achieved via local processing.

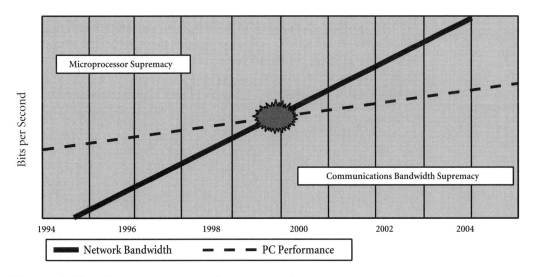

Figure 6.11 COMMUNICATIONS BANDWIDTH ASCENSION

Adapted with permission of Advanced Micro Devices Inc., from *Competing with Intel,* Copyright 1997, based on George Gilder's Telecosm articles as published in Forbes ASAP and available on the George Gilder Web Site.

Connectivity for the last mile to the user in today's undeveloped countries will come about predominantly via Wireless Local Loop (WLL). WLL encompasses various forms of land-based wireless repeater technology.

Another industry visionary, Nicholas Negroponte, has emphasized the ramifications of worldwide connectivity even at slow communications rates, see "The Third Shall Be First," by Nicholas Negroponte, *Wired*, January 1998, p. 96. Negroponte predicts that worldwide school connectivity for education purposes will occur in the next few years, enabled by $2,700 Geostationary-Earth-Orbiting satellites' (GEOs) satellite links, and eagerly underwritten by loans from the World Bank. Longer term, Negroponte implies Low-Earth-Orbiting satellites (LEOs) will provide more pervasive connectivity until the eventual time when unlimited local telephony will eventually be available "in every civilized place" at low fixed rates.

Negroponte suggests that even at slow rates by U.S. standards, per-school access to Internet-connected world libraries would significantly impact the education programs of the poorest third-world countries. Negroponte implies that developing countries appreciate the significance of Internet connectivity better than in some developed nations, are therefore better poised for the digital world, and that "the 'Third World' five years from now may not be where you think it is."

Future Hybrids of Content and Connectivity

This wide availability of fast networking will encourage pervasive use of a number of Internet/intranet web-oriented applications that have developed a following, but are likely considered as presently at the field-trial-stage or as hobbyist by society at large. These applications include Web access for broadcasting of information and entertainment, secure commerce, socialization, video conferencing, collaborative computing, interactive gaming, casting of votes, and remote security monitoring and facility management. Figure 6.12 and Figure 6.13 illustrate this future view of fast-network-enabled Internet and intranet-connected computation.

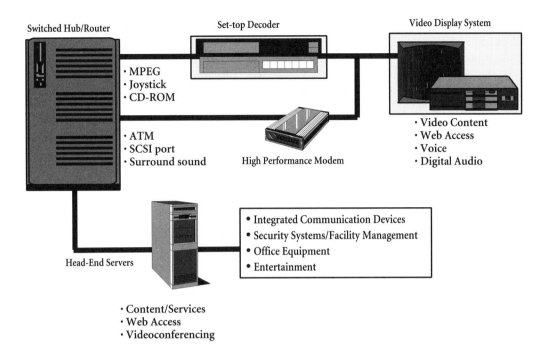

Figure 6.12 INTERNET-CONNECTED COMPUTATION

Adapted with permission of Advanced Micro Devices Inc., from *Competing with Intel*, Copyright 1997.

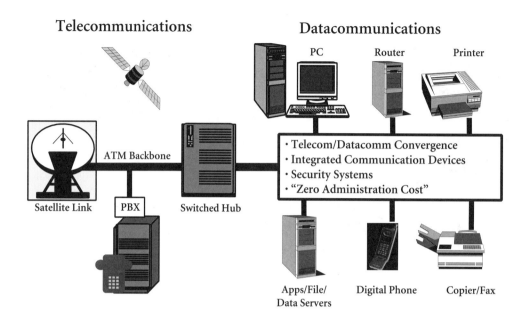

Figure 6.13 INTRANET-CONNECTED COMPUTATION

Adapted with permission of Advanced Micro Devices Inc., from *Competing with Intel,* Copyright 1997.

Ubiquitous fast networking will also finally make practical several Internet-centric visions based on the pervasive integration or coordination of remote platforms and facilities over arbitrary geographic domains. This covers a broad spectrum of applications. On the simple side, minimalist network platforms (thin clients, Network Computers, information appliances, and NetPCs) can exploit storage and processor concentration on intranets to reduce the hardware, software, setup, and maintenance costs of the overall network. On the elaborate side, worldwide-connected computation could regularly treat remote platforms, facilities, and workgroups as real-time subsystems of a single geographically distributed multiprocessing platform.

Future Platforms

Content and connectivity will continue to strongly influence the definition of PC platforms. Continued expansion, redefinition, and blurring of market segments will occur as PC platforms are evolved to track changes in use. The Internet, networking, multimedia, Personal Communications Services (PCS), and Personal Digital Assistant (PDA) technologies will fuel continued new applications and uses. The complexity underlying PC platforms will be buried as they infiltrate and replace the hardware, infra-structure, and business models behind present-day TV, telephones, and fax machines.

Accompanying the growth of widely available fast communications rates will be increased growth in the infrastructure of the Internet and of institutional intranets. This infrastructure will be in the form of switches, routers, and new classes of powerful remote compute and storage *head-end* servers for specialized services and content. Servers will integrate por-tions of the net-fabric by coming standard with integral gigabit-Ethernet routers and switches.

VIDEO ON CD-ROM

 Atiq Raza, AMD CTO and Executive VP, replies to the question: "How will the use of servers grow in the future?"

ARTICLE ON CD-ROM

 To learn more about Future Platforms, see the article "Multimedia Storage Servers: A Tutorial," by D. James Gemmell, Harrick M. Vin, Dilip D. Kandlur, P. Venkat Rangan and Lawrence A. Rowe, *IEEE Computer*, Vol. 28, No. 5, May 1995, on the companion CD-ROM.

Upon the achievement of affordable high-speed access to the Internet, the Entertainment PC will require further improvements in bus and interface bandwidths and system partitioning. As an example, Internet broadcast content will ultimately consist of multiple sub-streams including video, audio, control, and secondary content. Secondary content sub-streams include captioning, alternate languages, supplementary information and URL links. Platform architectures will be optimized for coupling each sub-stream directly to the appropriate platform subsystems, bypassing the pro-cessor and main memory whenever possible.

Platform Industry Directions for the Future

Many aspects of contemporary industry direction will continue. Users will continue to buy content and connectivity first, software second, and hard-ware last. Accordingly, new platform technology will be continually intro-duced or made more widely available to raise platform baseline features, facilitating application development, and thereby enabling new applica-tions. The success of compelling new applications requiring the new plat-form technology will in turn drive platform sales and market growth.

The PC industry as a whole will expand its market by capturing market share from other forms of content delivery. PC platforms will be refined until collectively the PC platform is the preferred content delivery instrument for all forms of consumer content. This will result in nothing less than the eventual assimilation of all but the most basic consumer electronics.

While many PC platforms will be capable of functioning as a unified consumer content delivery device, the more likely scenario is that specialty market segments and platforms will be developed for the various device classes. Specialty platforms of the new diverse PC market segments will capture the new installation and replacement market for "single function" devices such as TVs, VCRs, video games, high-fidelity sound systems, and telephones. These devices (as we know them today) will be absorbed into PCs in the same way that the typewriter, adding machine, and data terminal already have been absorbed. They will otherwise exist only as antiques, or will be produced in a format where they will be considered and priced like an incidental tool, gadget, or toy.

The PC industry (including processor, chipset, motherboard, and system vendors) has transcended its namesake role and is poised to begin the new millennium in the business of providing Platforms for Content and Connectivity. This new class of electronics devices will be appliances for content access and tools for content authoring that are implicitly connected to the intranet or an intranet. As the PC industry has evolved in an environment of rapid-pace product development and rollout, it is poised to rapidly take over the markets of today's major consumer electronics.

CHAPTER SUMMARY

In this final chapter, we examined the nature of platform evolution. First we surveyed a number of basic guidelines for optimizing platforms. We next illustrated how many of these optimization basics are used within a contemporary 3D-graphics platform. The 3D graphics study was made from both component and application perspectives. The component perspective characterized the role of each component, describing its principal operating paradigm and functions in the platform. The application perspective gave insight into how the components are orchestrated and optimized at the platform level. This was done through a study of how the individual platform components are collectively and dynamically managed to implement a high-performance multi-stage 3D Graphics Pipeline.

We also presented how the changes in content and connectivity are rapidly evolving the platform, as optimizations are continually being required to track the changes in application requirements and new uses of the platform. New standards are emerging for networking, communications, multimedia, graphics, as well as for processors, memory, and peripheral interconnect. Platform designs and infrastructure are being optimized and redefined in a continual effort to support the new standards, enable higher speed connectivity, sustain higher processor performance, provide higher bandwidth data transfers, and display rich graphical content.

References to Authors and Other Individuals

References to Suggested Readings

Copyright and Legal Notices

A number of organizations and firms have given us permission to include in the book and/or on the companion CD-ROM copies of various articles from periodicals and conference proceedings, reports, white papers, specifications, standards, and other documents, as well as figures, tables, and graphs. The organizations and firms involved retain the copyrights to this material. None of the contents of the book (in either its hard copy or CD-ROM format) and none of the materials reprinted in the book or CD-ROM, should be copied or distributed, in whole or in part, in any form whatsoever except for a bona fide *fair use* copy by a reader who has purchased the book. To copy, republish, post on servers, or redistribute any of the material identified above, in any form whatsoever, requires the person wishing to do so to obtain prior written permission from the holder of the associated copyrighted material. Such permission is not automatically granted to the purchasers or other readers of this book and the companion CD-ROM. The IEEE Computer Society Press holds the copyright for this book, both in its hard copy and CD-ROM format.

"What is a fair use copy?" Loosely, a fair use copy is a limited copy that Congress expressly permits without the permission of the copyright holder, provided that the copy is made in a socially desirable manner that is not unfair to the copyright holder. Unfortunately, deciding whether a given instance of copying is a fair use is quite complicated. The issue is often viewed from very different perspectives by the copyist and the copyright holder. When disputes arise, the courts evaluate whether Congress's fair use intent is being met by weighing the totality of the circumstances as determined from such questions as: Is the copying being done merely to positively impact the business income or expenses of the copyist? Is the copying being done principally for the benefit of the copyist? What is the potential for society to benefit from the copying? Is the extent of copying justifiable or excessive in light of the other considerations? How is the copyright holder adversely impacted by the copying?

While not relieving the reader of the burden of evaluating whether copying is fair use or not, and not speaking for the copyright holders, we offer the following observations. For material that is normally charged for but provided under restricted conditions here solely for the educational purposes of this book, we expect that the copyright holder may strongly

COPYING OR DISTRIBUTING MATERIAL FROM THE BOOK OR COMPANION CD-ROM

521

object to copies being made in most circumstances. In this category, the articles from Computer Society periodicals and conference proceedings, the IEEE Standards, and the Microprocessor Report articles come particularly to mind. Conversely, for material that is normally freely distributed to individuals via the Web or other means, such as a number of the white papers and data sheets, we expect that the copyright holder will not likely object to copies being made solely for individual convenience. Unauthorized copying for other than personal use and individual convenience will undoubtedly be strongly objected to by all copyright holders.

DISCLAIMER This publication consists of the book and its companion CD-ROM and is designed to provide information in regard to the subject matter covered. The statements and opinions expressed in this publication are those of the authors and not of any third-party. For purposes of education, certain details of described products may have been simplified or omitted. Therefore, product descriptions may depart from actual products being marketed or sold. Neither this publication, nor its sale and distribution, constitutes any consulting or professional service on the part of the publishers or the authors. If further advice or expert assistance is required, the services of a competent professional person should be sought. This publication includes a large number of documents, computer programs, and other material generated by and included with the permission of third parties, for which the publishers and authors cannot completely certify with respect to reliability and safety. A reasonable attempt has been made to scan the entire publication to guard against the inclusion of malicious programs and other objectionable material and no such matter is known to exist. However, due to practical limitations on what can be readily detected, neither the publishers nor the authors guarantee that malicious or objectionable material is totally absent from the publication. There is thus some risk that the reader incurs in using the included third party materials. We recommend that prior to using these materials, the prudent reader should diligently follow the usual and customary cautionary practices of: (1) maintaining multiple frequent backups of mission critical files and programs; and (2) running periodically updated virus-checking software to continually scan for potential viruses. Any malicious or objectionable material that is brought to the authors' attention will be removed in subsequent revisions. Neither the publisher, the authors, nor any third-party provide any opinion, make any warranty, extend any license, or assume any liability with respect to claims of infringement of any intellectual property in conjunction with the use of the information contained in the book or on the companion CD-ROM. Although every precaution has been taken in the preparation of this publication, the publisher and authors assume no responsibility for errors or omissions nor is any liability assumed for damages resulting from the use of the information contained herein.

Product names used in this publication—e.g., Intel's Pentium processor, Microsoft's Windows NT, or Adobe's Acrobat Reader—are for identification purposes only and may be trademarks of their respective companies. The following list is meant to be illustrative of such marks and is not intended to be an exhaustive or comprehensive list of all marks. It is included due to the marks' high frequency of occurrence. AMD, the AMD logo, AMD-K6, and RISC86 are registered trademarks, and AMD 3D and K6 are trademarks of Advanced Micro Devices Inc. Microsoft, the Microsoft logo, Windows, Windows 95, and Windows NT are trademarks of Microsoft Corporation. Intel, the Intel logo, MMX, i386, i486, Pentium, PentiumPro and Pentium II are trademarks of Intel Corporation. Verilog is a registered trademark of Cadence Design systems Inc. Unix is a trademark of AT&T.

Glossary/Index

Numerics

E

point-and-click activated text or graphics objects. The reader activates these objects to move within the same document, to go to a new machine-readable document; 332

I

I/O address space is the address space nominally used for I/O peripherals; 381

I/O window refers to decoded address regions for I/O; 401

IAB (Internet Architecture Board); 367

I-Cache TLB; 180

IEEE 1394; 324, 330, 342, 344, 346, 372, 375, 402

IEEE 1394 is a new standard for high-speed serial peripherals designed for hot plug and play connectivity; 43

IEEE 1394 Trade Association; 377

IEEE 802-1990; 361

IEEE 8802-2

1994; 361

IEEE 8802-3

1996; 361

IESG (Internet Engineering Steering Group); 367

IETF (Internet Engineering Task Force); 367

IHV; 342

IHV (independent hardware vendor); 322

ILP (instruction level parallelism); 369

Immediate values forwarding; 242

Implicit register renaming; 307

Implicit renaming scheme; 93

Incident-Wave Switching is a propagation technique, in which bus drivers drive the signal traces to the final switching voltage and the traces are terminated and laid out to minimize reflected waves; 395

Independent commitments; 275

Independent Hardware Vendors; 322

Indirect register names; 140

Initial vector OpQuad generation logic; 142

Initiator refers to the master device in a bus transfer; 396

Instruction boundary; 113, 117

Instruction buffer; 113

Instruction decode control register; 100

Instruction fetch; 113

Instruction length; 117, 121

Instruction Level Parallelism (ILP); 181

Instruction register; 98, 113

Instruction register 1; 113

Instruction register 2; 113

Instruction Set Architecture; 368

Instruction set architecture (see architecture); xi, 4

Instruction window; 76

Instruction-TLB (also called I-TLB); 112

Integer architectural register set; 89

Integer microarchitecture register set; 90

Integer register; 89

Integrated Services Digital Network; 352

Intel 80286; 381

Intel 8086; 381

Intel 8088; 381

Intel Pentium processor; 390

Interleaved memory pages increase the number of page-mode devices generally available to all execution threads; 449

Interleaved refers to overlapped memory cycles in multiple memory banks; 449

Internet; 362, 365

Internet Official Protocol Standards; 367

Internet refers to an interconnected conforming system of networks used for global file transfer and data communications; 365

Interpolation is the inverse of subsampling; 49

Interpolation is the recreation of chroma information from a subsampled YUV data stream; 51

Interrupts; 83

Interstitial grid PGAs have alternating pin rows/columns that are collinear, while adjacent pin rows/columns are offset by half the pin-spacing; 411

Intranet refers to an Enterprise Network that uses the Internet standard Transmission Control Protocol / Internet Protocol and related HTTP addressing standard; 362

Invalid cache coherency states; 109

Invalid cache line; 110, 111

Invalid cache subblock; 110

Invalid Op; 86, 208, 256

Invalid operand value; 223

Invalid OpQuad; 184, 192, 194, 216

IPC (instructions per clock cycle); 369

IRQ refers to interrupt request; 381

ISA; 389, 391, 402

ISA Bus; 324, 381, 382, 384, 385, 386, 389, 390, 391, 393, 395

ISA Bus, or Industry Standard Architecture Bus, was the peripheral bus used in the PC/AT, and is the most important legacy bus in PC platforms. Its use in PC platforms is being phased out; 41

N

S

U

V

W

IEEE
COMPUTER
SOCIETY

Press Activities Board

IEEE Computer Society Publications

The world-renowned Computer Society publishes, promotes, and distributes a wide variety of authoritative computer science and engineering texts. These books are available in two formats: 100 percent original material by authors preeminent in their field who focus on relevant topics and cutting-edge research, and reprint collections consisting of carefully selected groups of previously published papers with accompanying original introductory and explanatory text.

Submission of proposals: For guidelines and information on Computer Society books, send e-mail to cs.books@computer.org or write to the Project Editor, IEEE Computer Society, P.O. Box 3014, 10662 Los Vaqueros Circle, Los Alamitos, CA 90720-1314. Telephone +1 714-821-8380. FAX +1 714-761-1784.

IEEE Computer Society Proceedings

The Computer Society also produces and actively promotes the proceedings of more than 130 acclaimed international conferences each year in multimedia formats that include hard and softcover books, CD-ROMs, videos, and on-line publications.

For information on Computer Society proceedings, send e-mail to cs.books@computer.org or write to Proceedings, IEEE Computer Society, P.O. Box 3014, 10662 Los Vaqueros Circle, Los Alamitos, CA 90720-1314. Telephone +1 714-821-8380. FAX +1 714-761-1784.

Additional information regarding the Computer Society, conferences and proceedings, CD-ROMs, videos, and books can also be accessed from our web site at http://computer.org/cspress